lonely planet

Korea

Robert Storey
Alex English

LONELY PLANET PUBLICATIONS
Melbourne • Oakland • London • Paris

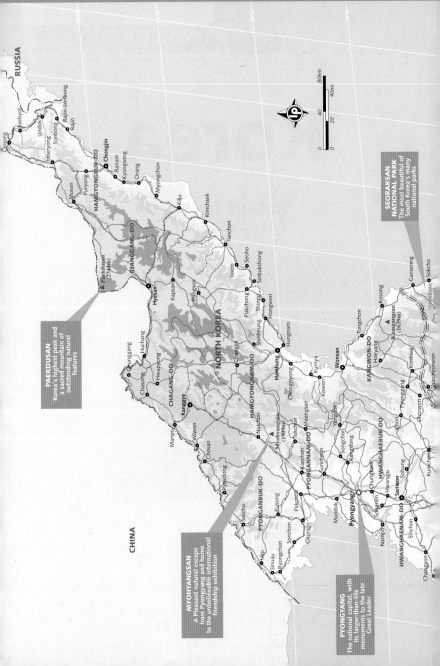

KOREA

RUSSIA

Onsong
Saebyol
Undok
Hoeryong
Songbong
Rajin-Sonbong
Sonbong
Rajin

HAMGYONGBUK-DO
Musan
Puryong
Chongjin
Ranam
Kyongsong
Orang
Myongchon

YANGGANG-DO
Kilju
Kimchaek

▲ Paekdusan
(2744m)

Hyesan
Kapsan
Pungsan
Tanchon

Hiwon
Seoho
Sintukchong

Pukchong
Hongwon

CHAGANG-DO
Chunggang
Huchang
Hwaplyong
Chasong
Manpo
Kanggye
Wiwon
Chosan

NORTH KOREA

Shinheung
Hungnam
Hamhung
Chongpyong

Changjin

HAMGYONGNAM-DO

Nujdm
Myohyangsan
(1909m)
Tokchon

Pyokdong
Kaechon
Kujang

Sakchu

PYONGANBUK-DO
Kusong
Pakchon

Sonchon

Uiju
Sinuiju
Ryongchon

Chongju

Yangdok
Yunhya
Kowon

Wonsan

KANGWON-DO
Kosong
Hoeyang
Pyonggang

Changyon

Mundok

Yangchon
Songdong
Kangdong

Songchon

Pyongyang

PYONGNAMNAM-DO

Maengsan

Chungwhe

Sariwon
HWANGHAEBUK-DO
Hwangju
Suhung
Ichon
Kumhwa

DMZ

Sepho
Chorwon
Pyonggang

Tongchon

Kumgangsan
(1639m)

Kimhwa

Ichon

Namp'o

HWANGHAENAM-DO
Sinchon

Sohung

Haeju
Kuristong

Ganseong
Sokcho

Seoraksan
(1708m)

CHINA

PAEKDUSAN
Korea's highest peak and
a sacred mountain of
outstanding natural
features

MYOHYANGSAN
A Pleasant natural escape
from Pyongyang and home
to the unbelievable international
friendship exhibition

PYONGYANG
The national capital, with
its larger-than-life
monuments to the late
Great Leader

**SEORAKSAN
NATIONAL PARK**
The most beautiful of
South Korea's many
national parks

80km
40
40mi
20
0
0

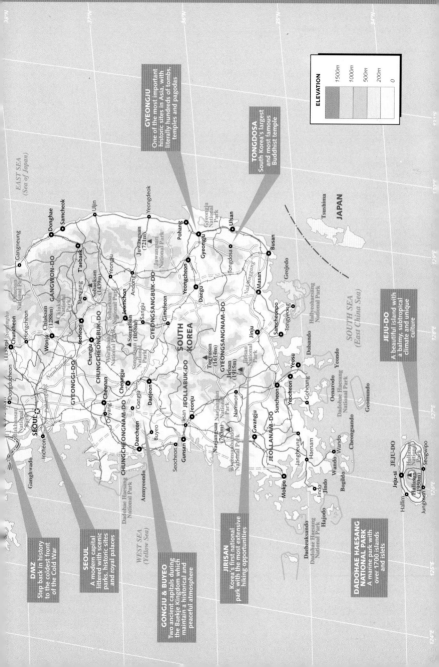

KOREA

ELEVATION
1500m
1000m
500m
200m
0

EAST SEA
(Sea of Japan)

SOUTH SEA
(East China Sea)

WEST SEA
(Yellow Sea)

JAPAN

Tsushima

GYEONGJU
One of the most important historic sites in Asia, with literally hundreds of tombs, temples and pagodas

TONGDOSA
South Korea's largest and most famous Buddhist temple

JEJU-DO
A beautiful island with a balmy, subtropical climate and unique culture

DMZ
Step back in history to the coldest front of the Cold War

SEOUL
A modern capital littered with scenic parks, historic sites and royal palaces

GONGJU & BUYEO
Two ancient capitals during the Baekje Kingdom which maintain a historical and peaceful atmosphere

JIRISAN
Korea's first national park with the most extensive hiking opportunities

DADOHAE HAESANG NATIONAL PARK
A marine park with over 1700 islands and islets

SOUTH KOREA

SEOUL

GANGWON-DO

GYEONGGI-DO

CHUNGCHEONGBUK-DO

CHUNGCHEONGNAM-DO

GYEONGSANGBUK-DO

GYEONGSANGNAM-DO

JEOLLABUK-DO

JEOLLANAM-DO

JEJU-DO

Korea
5th edition – April 2001
First published – April 1988

Published by
Lonely Planet Publications Pty Ltd ABN 36 005 607 983
90 Maribyrnong St, Footscray, Victoria 3011, Australia

Lonely Planet Offices
Australia Locked Bag 1, Footscray, Victoria 3011
USA 150 Linden St, Oakland, CA 94607
UK 10a Spring Place, London NW5 3BH
France 1 rue du Dahomey, 75011 Paris

Photographs
All of the images in this guide are available for licensing from
Lonely Planet Images.
email: lpi@lonelyplanet.com.au

Front cover photograph
Seoul, a myriad of paper lanterns lights the Buddhist temple Jogyesa
(Craig Brown, Stone)

ISBN 0 86442 697 6

text & maps © Lonely Planet 2001
photos © photographers as indicated 2001

Printed by SNP Offset Sdn Bhd
Printed in Malaysia

**Although the authors
and Lonely Planet try
to make the informa-
tion as accurate as
possible, we accept
no responsibility for
any loss, injury or
inconvenience sus-
tained by anyone
using this book.**

Contents – Text

THE AUTHORS   7

THIS BOOK   8

FOREWORD   10

INTRODUCTION   13

FACTS ABOUT KOREA   15

History 15
Geography 24
Climate 24
Ecology & Environment 24
Flora & Fauna 25

Government & Politics 26
Economy 27
Population & People 28
Education 28
Arts 28

Society & Conduct 31
Religion 36
Language 38

FACTS FOR THE VISITOR   40

Highlights 40
Suggested Itineraries 40
Planning 40
Responsible Tourism 41
Tourist Offices 41
Visas & Documents 42
Embassies & Consulates 45
Customs 46
Money 46
Post & Communications 49
Internet Resources 53
Books 54
Newspapers & Magazines 56
Radio & TV 56

Video Systems 57
Photography & Video 57
Time 57
Electricity 57
Weights & Measures 57
Laundry 57
Toilets 57
Health 58
Gay & Lesbian Travellers 62
Disabled Travellers 63
Senior Travellers 63
Travel With Children 63
Useful Organisations 63
Dangers & Annoyances 63

Emergencies 64
Legal Matters 64
Business Hours 65
Public Holidays & Special
Events 65
Activities 66
Courses 69
Work 70
Accommodation 71
Food 74
Drinks 77
Entertainment 78
Spectator Sports 80
Shopping 80

GETTING THERE & AWAY   83

Air 83
Overland 88

Sea 88
Organised Tours 91

GETTING AROUND   92

Bus 93
Train 95
Bullet Taxi 96

Car & Motorcycle 97
Bicycle 98
Hitching 98

Boat 98
Local Transport 98
Organised Tours 99

SEOUL   100

History 104
Orientation 104
Information 105
Gyeongbokgung 109
National Folk Museum 109
The Blue House 112
Jongmyo 113

Changgyeonggung 113
Changdeokgung 113
Tapgol Park 113
Jogyesa 113
Unhyeongung 113
Bosingak 114
Gwanghwamun Intersection ..114

Deoksugung 115
Namdaemun 116
Postal Museum 116
Namsan Park 116
Jangchung Park 117
Dongdaemun 117
Agricultural Museum 117

2 Contents – Text

Railway Museum 117
Yeouido 117
War Memorial 118
Yongsan Family Park 118
Seodaemun Prison
History Hall 119
Bong-Eunsa 120

Olympic Stadium 120
Olympic Park 120
Lotte World 120
World Cup Stadium 120
Seoul Dream Land 123
Children's Grand Park 123
Activities 123

Places To Stay 125
Places To Eat 130
Entertainment 136
Things To Buy 142
Getting There & Away 144
Getting Around 146

GYEONGGI-DO 150

Bukhansan National Park ..150
Suraksan 153
Seoul Equestrian Park 154
Namhansanseong
Provincial Park 155
Suwon 155

Korean Folk Village 157
Everland 158
Icheon 158
Yeoju 159
Incheon 159
Yellow Sea Islands 164

Panmunjeom 166
Odusan Unification 168
Observatory 168
Ganghwado 169
Songtan 171
Ski Resorts 172

GANGWON-DO 173

Chuncheon 173
Around Chuncheon 175
Bangtaesan Nature Forest ..178
Misan Valley 178
Sokcho 179
North Of Sokcho 183
Seoraksan National Park 183

Naksan Provincial Park 187
Gangneung 187
Around Gangneung 189
Odaesan National Park 190
Yongpyeong Ski Resort 192
Donghae 193
Mureung Valley 194

Samcheok 195
Around Samcheok 196
Taebaeksan Provincial Park 197
Wonju 198
Chiaksan National Park 199

GYEONGSANGBUK-DO 200

Daegu 200
Palgongsan Provincial Park ..206
Gyeongju 207
Around Gyeongju 218
Gayasan National Park 224
Gimcheon 226

Jikjisa 226
Andong 227
Hahoe Folk Village 229
Dosan Seowon 230
Cheongnyangsan Provincial
Park 231

Buseoksa 231
Juwangsan National Park ..231
Uljin 232
Around Uljin 233
Pohang 234
Ulleungdo 237

GYEONGSANGNAM-DO 243

Busan 243
Gajisan Provincial Park 256
Junamho Bird Sanctuary 258

Bugok Hot Springs 258
Jinju 258
Tongyeong 261

Geojedo 263
Namhaedo 263
Jirisan National Park 265

JEOLLANAM-DO 268

Gwangju 269
Around Gwangju 273
Gurye 274
Hwaeomsa 274
Suncheon 275

Jogyesan Provincial Park 276
Nagan Folk Village 277
Yeosu 277
Around Yeosu 280
Mokpo 280

Dadohae Haesang National
Park 283
Wolchulsan National Park ..284
Duryunsan Provincial Park 285
Bogildo 287

JEJU-DO 288

Jeju-Si 290
Getting There & Away 296
Getting Around 297
Around The Island 299

Beaches 299
Sangumburi Crater 299
Manjanggul 300
Gimnyeong Maze 300

Seongsan Ilchulbong 300
Sinyang Beach 301
Udo 301
Seong-Eup Folk Village 302

Jeju Folk Village 302
Seogwipo 303
Yakcheonsa 306
Jusangjolli Rocks 306
Jungmun Resort 306
Sanbanggulsa 307

Yongmeori Coastline 307
Jeju Art Park 307
Gapado & Marado 308
Anti-Mongol Monument 308
Shincheonji Art Museum 308
Horse Racetrack 308

Hallim 308
Hyeopjaegul 308
Mystery & Ghost Roads 309
Hallasan National Park 309

JEOLLABUK-DO   312

Jeonju 312
Around Jeonju 316
Daedunsan Provincial Park ..316
Maisan Provincial Park 317
Deogyusan National Park ..317

Jeongeup 319
Gangcheonsan County
Park 319
Naejangsan National Park ..319

Byeonsanbando National
Park 323
Gunsan 323
Around Gunsan 323

CHUNGCHEONGNAM-DO   326

Daejeon 326
Gyeryongsan National Park ..330
Gongju 332
Magoksa 335

Buyeo 335
Boryeong 338
Taean Haean National Park ..340
Haemi 340

Around Haemi 341
Deoksan Provincial Park 341
Cheonan 341

CHUNGCHEONGBUK-DO   344

Cheongju 344
Songnisan National Park 347
Chungju 349

Suanbo Hot Springs 350
Woraksan National Park 351
Jecheon 351

Around Danyang 353
Sobaeksan National Park 355

NORTH KOREA   357

Facts about North
Korea 359
History 359
Geography 368
Climate 368
Ecology & Environment 368
Flora & Fauna 369
Government & Politics 370
Economy 371
Population & People 373
Arts 373
Religion 373
Language 375
Facts For The Visitor 376
Planning 376
Tourist Offices 376
Visas & Documents 376
Embassies 378
Customs 379

Money 379
Post & Communications 380
Internet Resources 381
Books & Maps 382
Media 383
Photography & Video 384
Time 384
Electricity 384
Health 384
Women Travellers 384
Senior Travellers 385
Dangers & Annoyances 385
Business Hours 386
Public Holidays & Special
Events 386
Work 386
Accommodation 386
Food 386
Drinks 386

Getting There & Away 386
Air 386
Train 388
Departure 389
Organised Tours 389
Getting Around 391
Organised Tours 391
Non Tour-Group
Transport 391
Pyongyang 392
Around The Country 401
Myohyangsan 401
Kaesong 402
Panmunjeom 403
Kumgangsan 403
Paekdusan 404
Rajin-Sonbong Zone 405

LANGUAGE   407

GLOSSARY   416

INDEX   424

Text 424   Boxed Text..........................431

MAP LEGEND   back page

METRIC CONVERSION   inside back cover

Contents – Maps

GETTING AROUND

Domestic Air Fares - South
Korea.......................................92

SEOUL

Greater Seoul 102-3	Gwanghwamun Area 116	Daehangno 132
Central Seoul 110-11	Gangnam-gu 121	Hong-Ik University 137
Tapgol Park Area 114	Sinchon 130	Itaewon 139

GYEONGGI-DO

Gyeonggi-do 151	Suwon 156
Bukhansan National Park ..152	Incheon 160

GANGWON-DO

Gangwon-do 174	Gangneung 188	Chiaksan National Park 198
Chuncheon 176	Odaesan National Park 190	
Sokcho & Seoraksan National	Donghae 193	
Park 180-1	Samcheok 195	

GYEONGSANGBUK-DO

Gyeongsangbuk-do 201	Central Gyeongju 209	Pohang 235
Daegu 202	Gyeongju 216-17	Ulleungdo 238
Central Daegu 204	Andong 228	Dodong-ri 240
Palgonsan Provincial Park ..207	Juwangsan National Park ..232	

GYEONGSANGNAM-DO

Gyeongsangnam-do 244	Dongnae &	Jinju 259
Busan 246	Geumjeongsanseong 250	Tongyeong 262
Central Busan 248	Haeundae 252	Jirisan National Park 264
	Busan Subway 257	

JEOLLANAM-DO

Jeollanam-do 269	Jogyesan Provincial Park ...276	Mokpo 281
Gwangju 270	Yeosu 278	Wando 286

JEJU-DO

Jeju-do 289	Sinjeju 294	Hallasan National Park 310
Jeju-si 291	Seogwipo 304	

JEOLLABUK-DO

Jeollabuk-do 313
Jeonju 314
Deogyusan National Park ..318
Gangcheonsan County
Park 320
Naejangsan National Park ..321
Seonunsan Provincial Park ..322
Byeonsanbando National
Park 324

CHUNGCHEONGNAM-DO

Chungcheongnam-do 327
Daejeon 328
Gyeryongsan National Park ..331
Gongju 333
Buyeo 336
Sapsido 339

CHUNGCHEONGBUK-DO

Chungcheongbuk-do 345
Cheongju 346
Songnisan National Park 348
Woraksan National Park 352
Danyang Resort & Sobaeksan
National Park 354

NORTH KOREA

North Korea 358
Pyongyang 394-5

MAP INDEX

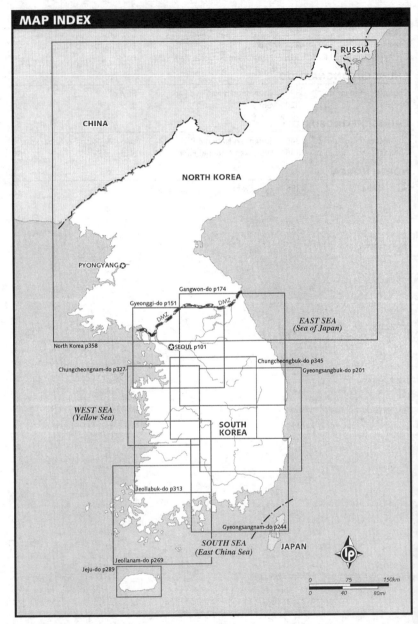

RUSSIA

CHINA

NORTH KOREA

PYONGYANG

Gangwon-do p174

Gyeonggi-do p151

DMZ   DMZ

EAST SEA
(Sea of Japan)

North Korea p358

SEOUL p101

Chungcheongbuk-do p345

Chungcheongnam-do p327

Gyeongsangbuk-do p201

WEST SEA
(Yellow Sea)

SOUTH
KOREA

Jeollabuk-do p313

Gyeongsangnam-do p244

SOUTH SEA
(East China Sea)

JAPAN

Jeollanam-do p269

Jeju-do p289

| 0 | 75 | 150km |
| 0 | 40 | 80mi |

The Authors

Robert Storey

Robert has had a chequered past, starting with his first job (a monkey-keeper at a zoo) and continuing with a stint as a slot machine repairman in a Las Vegas casino. It was during this era that he produced his first amazing book, *How to Do Your Own Divorce in Nevada,* which sold nearly 200 copies. Since this wasn't enough to cover costs, Robert decided to skip the country and sought refuge in Asia.

But you can't keep a good writer down. Robert's first guidebook, *Taiwan On Your Own,* attracted the attention of Lonely Planet. Since then, he has been involved in over a dozen LP projects. Robert is still on the Asian trail and is contemplating a move to India. He is currently working to complete first novel, *Life in the Fast Lane.*

Eunkyong

Eunkyong was born and bred in Seoul, South Korea. After completing some useless tertiary studies in Asian history and education, she discovered the joys of working in a trading company. Shortly afterwards she escaped to Shanghai, China. In China she undertook some intensive Chinese studies and embarked on her Masters in Chinese history.

Her studies were cut short once again when she married her Australian husband Alex and decided that travelling with him was more stimulating than studying in Shanghai. For five years, Eunkyong and family – Alex and Oscar, born in 1998 – lived, studied, worked, travelled and played on the swings throughout East Asia.

Eunkyong has finally returned to school, this time studying textile design in Melbourne, Australia. This is her first book for Lonely Planet.

FROM THE AUTHORS

Robert Several local Koreans, expats and foreign visitors to Korea generously donated time and useful information to this project. Special thanks go to Brandon Miller, Jonathan Fulton, Robyn Albers, Paul Goldberg, Fred Dustin, James May, Mike Spavar, Mark Tuttle, Jad Michaelson, Gary Rector, Eugene Campbell, James Russell, Lee Hyeyoung and Jeong Hyewook.

Eunkyong I would firstly like to thank Oma and Appa for looking after the gypsies every time we turned up on their doorstep in Seoul. Special thanks to Appa for the loan of the blue truck. I would also like to thank Miyoung and family in Busan; Jintae and his crook knee; Caroline and co. for looking after Alex in Beijing; and the countless friendly and helpful Koreans who kept us on the road. Finally, a big thanks to my two porters, Oscar and Alex.

This Book

From the Publisher

The production of this book would at times have tested the staunch-es of comrades. With this new edition there were new people, and very different ways of dealing with spellings, with place names, with Korean script, and with maps. The crack team at Lonely Planet who pulled off this 'third great arduous march' were: Chris Tsismetzis, co-ordinating designer, Corie Waddell, Sophie Reed and Nicholas Stebbing, who assisted on script and maps, Jakov Gavran and Tim Fitzgerald, supervising designers, Michael Day, coordinating editor, Kate Daly and Nicole Buckler, editors, Jocelyn Harewood, supervising editor, Quentin Frayne, Master of Babel, Glenn Beanland, Lonely Planet Images, Matt King, illustrations, Lisa Borg and Andrew Tudor, Quark Lords, Leonie Mugavin, transport guru, Cathy Viero, woman of letters. To all concerned, *Jongmal Chollima soktoimnida* (It is really Chollima speed).

Thanks

Many thanks to the travellers who used the last edition and wrote to us with helpful hints, useful advice and interesting anecdotes.

George Acosta, N Adler, R Allen, Tom Anderson, T Archer, Alan Arthur, Someya Asako, Rick Attenburg, Dionne Avard, Tamara J Bahr, Justin P Barrass, T Barron, Jacqui Bauer, Dale Baxter, Penny Bayfield, Qani Belul, Shane Berg, Joachim Bergmann, Patrice Beriault, Nadine Bertal-li, Bentley Boren, John Brandt, Kimberly Bristol, Michael Bujold, David Burns, Juan Bustamante, Aaron Butt, Irene Calder, Tess Camagna, Jen-nifer Cameron, Peter Caruana, Eugene Chang, Jung Chang Hoon, Rose Chessman, Jan Christoffersen, Sebastien Cormier, Dan Costello, Elizabeth Csanitz, Kelly Dawson, Annemarie & Hans de Graaf, Tom Delaney, Jamie Demas, Christine DeMerchant, Jennifer Depto, Nicol DeVocht, Audra Dewhurst, Karl Diedrich, Kevin Divine, Keri Downs, Joanne Effa, David Ellis, Viola en Tanja, M Errico, Richard Ewen, Lisa Fairbrother, Darina Farrell, Anthiny Ferrantte Jr, William Fink, R Fitz-carl, Hans Fix, Alexander Flirt, M Folkesson, Elizabeth & Martin Forbes, Nigel Foster, Otmar Franz, Dan Free, Doug French, Regina Fritsche, Johann Fuerstner, Max Gadot, Robert Gardner, Dan Gedacht, Laurent Gerard, Greg Giaccio, Jane Gindin, Eugene Gleser, J Glover, Diane Grayson, Leon Greer, Hilary & Mark Griffiths, Xavier Gros, Michelle Grott, Svend Haakon Kristensen, Mizushi Hajime, Tanja Haller, Roger Hannaker, Fumiko Hattori, Katya Hayes, Di Head, Jack Hedges, Jeffrey Hermanoff, Pierre Van Den Heuvel, Jan Hiurhedi, David Hogarth, Chuck Hohenstein, Stephen Hope, Damien Horigan, Shane Howard, Kim Hoyle, Jaromir Hudos, Sophie Huit, Martin Hurley, Vanessa Huth, Kim Hyung-Uk, Bob James, Mary Jean Chan, Gary Jennings, Mike Johnson, Lee Junmo, Andrew Karkus, Ari Katz, Russell Kenny, Gil Kezwer, Munindra Khaund, Charles Kim, Hyung-Uk Kim, Nerida Kim Dowling, Laura Kluthe, Leslie Kodish, Eddie Koh, Michael Kohn,

THANKS
Many thanks to the travellers who used the last edition and wrote to us with helpful hints, advice and interesting anec-dotes. Your names appear in the back of this book.

Lee Kok Piew, Chris Kooijman, Britta & Michael Koss, Jenny Kotauskos, Catherine Lamb, JoAnn Landingham, Terence Langdon, Deryk Langlais, Robert Langridge, Julie Larson, Yann Le Bail, Keith A Leitich, Julia Leslie, Katie Lewis, Ernestine Lobb, Stephen Lodziak, Stephen Lowe, Amanda Lugton, Noel Machat, Shawn MacWha, Micheal Magercord, A Manuel, Rick Marusyk, Ben Masters, Alexander Matskevich, Ichiro Matsuo, Caspar Mays, Thomas McBride Jr, Dr John McCorquodale, Robert McCoy, Mary McEwan, Turi McKinley, Craig McLeman, John McNeil, Bev McPhail, Brett Meyer, Richard Middleton, Carol Miller, Ron Miller, Michael Moeller, Wolfgang Mohl, Derrick Moore, Ian Morgan, Travis B Mostoller, Dr Joseph Muhlberger, Rosemary & Michael Murray, Kyung Nam Masan, Jeff Nelson, Brian Nomi, Daniel Noudin, Mara O'Brien, Dong-yoon Oh, Sven-Olof Ohlsson, Peter Oram, Shane O'Rourke, Steve Oszewski, Ruth Owada, Soonok Park, James Parsons, Alex Pasquali, Stan Paulic, Chuck Pense, Charlene & Gary Peterson, Cory Pettit, Rainbow Pettorello, Mark Phillips, Monica Piecha, Shawn Plummer, Brittany Podolak, Elliot Podwill, Yves Prescott, E C Pukpundang, Michael Ray, Lance Reeher, Julie A Reid, Carly Reiter, David Ritchie, Martin Robinson, John Robinson Jr, Andrew Rodgers, Carrie A Rogers, C A Rohn, Daphne Rosenzweig, Bill Roth, Richard Royston, Rick Ruffin, Michelle Sale, Kampbell Salehi, Roger Satterthwaite, Marilyn Schick, Nick Schilov, Byron Schmuland, Duncan Schofield, David Seguin, Eric Tan Wee Shan, Tammy Sheehan, Kenny Shin, Lizz Singh, Preston Smith, Shannon Smith, Leif Soderlund, Hyuinil Sohn, Brian Stanley, Jason Strauss, Martin Sulev, Amanda Suutari, Ann Swallow, Naomi Tanner, A Taoist, Lars Terje Holmaas, Dan Thompson, Richard Treleaven, Erik Tschopp, Michael E Turner, Steve Vantorre, Monty Vierra, Peter Viggo Jakobsen, Vinod Vijayakumar, Brenda Walker, J Watson, Richard Watson, Tori Watson, Cy West, John Westbrook, Stephen J Whelan, Madeline Wilks, Jane Willdigg, Andrew Wind, Bradley Windsor, William S Wise, Jeanne Witsken, Clayton Wood, Barrie Wraith, Heike & Bruce Wrenn, Rachel Wright, Armagan Yamaner, Pazu Yau, Jay Yoo, Se-Joon You, Alan Young, David Young, Graham Young, Oliver Zoellner.

Foreword

ABOUT LONELY PLANET GUIDEBOOKS

The story begins with a classic travel adventure: Tony and Maureen Wheeler's 1972 journey across Europe and Asia to Australia. Useful information about the overland trail did not exist at that time, so Tony and Maureen published the first Lonely Planet guidebook to meet a growing need.

From a kitchen table, then from a tiny office in Melbourne (Australia), Lonely Planet has become the largest independent travel publisher in the world, an international company with offices in Melbourne, Oakland (USA), London (UK) and Paris (France).

Today Lonely Planet guidebooks cover the globe. There is an ever-growing list of books and there's information in a variety of forms and media. Some things haven't changed. The main aim is still to help make it possible for adventurous travellers to get out there – to explore and better understand the world.

At Lonely Planet we believe travellers can make a positive contribution to the countries they visit – if they respect their host communities and spend their money wisely. Since 1986 a percentage of the income from each book has been donated to aid projects and human rights campaigns.

Updates Lonely Planet thoroughly updates each guidebook as often as possible. This usually means there are around two years between editions, although for more unusual or more stable destinations the gap can be longer. Check the imprint page (following the colour map at the beginning of the book) for publication dates.

Between editions up-to-date information is available in two free newsletters – the paper *Planet Talk* and email *Comet* (to subscribe, contact any Lonely Planet office) – and on our Web site at www.lonelyplanet.com. The *Upgrades* section of the Web site covers a number of important and volatile destinations and is regularly updated by Lonely Planet authors. *Scoop* covers news and current affairs relevant to travellers. And, lastly, the *Thorn Tree* bulletin board and *Postcards* section of the site carry unverified, but fascinating, reports from travellers.

Correspondence The process of creating new editions begins with the letters, postcards and emails received from travellers. This correspondence often includes suggestions, criticisms and comments about the current editions. Interesting excerpts are immediately passed on via newsletters and the Web site, and everything goes to our authors to be verified when they're researching on the road. We're keen to get more feedback from organisations or individuals who represent communities visited by travellers.

> Lonely Planet gathers information for everyone who's curious about the planet – and especially for those who explore it first-hand. Through guidebooks, phrasebooks, activity guides, maps, literature, newsletters, image library, TV series and Web site we act as an information exchange for a worldwide community of travellers.

Research Authors aim to gather sufficient practical information to enable travellers to make informed choices and to make the mechanics of a journey run smoothly. They also research historical and cultural background to help enrich the travel experience and allow travellers to understand and respond appropriately to cultural and environmental issues.

Authors don't stay in every hotel because that would mean spending a couple of months in each medium-sized city and, no, they don't eat at every restaurant because that would mean stretching belts beyond capacity. They do visit hotels and restaurants to check standards and prices, but feedback based on readers' direct experiences can be very helpful.

Many of our authors work undercover, others aren't so secretive. None of them accept freebies in exchange for positive write-ups. And none of our guidebooks contain any advertising.

Production Authors submit their raw manuscripts and maps to offices in Australia, USA, UK or France. Editors and cartographers – all experienced travellers themselves – then begin the process of assembling the pieces. When the book finally hits the shops, some things are already out of date, we start getting feedback from readers and the process begins again ...

WARNING & REQUEST

Things change – prices go up, schedules change, good places go bad and bad places go bankrupt – nothing stays the same. So, if you find things better or worse, recently opened or long since closed, please tell us and help make the next edition even more accurate and useful. We genuinely value all the feedback we receive. Julie Young coordinates a well travelled team that reads and acknowledges every letter, postcard and email and ensures that every morsel of information finds its way to the appropriate authors, editors and cartographers for verification.

Everyone who writes to us will find their name in the next edition of the appropriate guidebook. They will also receive the latest issue of *Planet Talk*, our quarterly printed newsletter, or *Comet*, our monthly email newsletter. Subscriptions to both newsletters are free. The very best contributions will be rewarded with a free guidebook.

Excerpts from your correspondence may appear in new editions of Lonely Planet guidebooks, the Lonely Planet Web site, *Planet Talk* or *Comet*, so please let us know if you *don't* want your letter published or your name acknowledged.

Send all correspondence to the Lonely Planet office closest to you:

Australia: Locked Bag 1, Footscray, Victoria 3011
USA: 150 Linden St, Oakland, CA 94607
UK: 10A Spring Place, London NW5 3BH
France: 1 rue du Dahomey, 75011 Paris

Or email us at: talk2us@lonelyplanet.com.au

For news, views and updates see our Web site: www.lonelyplanet.com

HOW TO USE A LONELY PLANET GUIDEBOOK

The best way to use a Lonely Planet guidebook is any way you choose. At Lonely Planet we believe the most memorable travel experiences are often those that are unexpected, and the finest discoveries are those you make yourself. Guidebooks are not intended to be used as if they provide a detailed set of infallible instructions!

Contents All Lonely Planet guidebooks follow roughly the same format. The Facts about the Destination chapters or sections give background information ranging from history to weather. Facts for the Visitor gives practical information on issues like visas and health. Getting There & Away gives a brief starting point for re-searching travel to and from the destination. Getting Around gives an overview of the transport options when you arrive.

The peculiar demands of each destination determine how sub-sequent chapters are broken up, but some things remain constant. We always start with background, then proceed to sights, places to stay, places to eat, entertainment, getting there and away, and getting around information – in that order.

Heading Hierarchy Lonely Planet headings are used in a strict hierarchical structure that can be visualised as a set of Russian dolls. Each heading (and its following text) is encompassed by any preceding heading that is higher on the hierarchical ladder.

Entry Points We do not assume guidebooks will be read from beginning to end, but that people will dip into them. The tradi-tional entry points are the list of contents and the index. In addition, however, some books have a complete list of maps and an index map illustrating map coverage.

There may also be a colour map that shows highlights. These highlights are dealt with in greater detail in the Facts for the Visitor chapter, along with planning questions and suggested itin-eraries. Each chapter covering a geographical region usually begins with a locator map and another list of highlights. Once you find something of interest in a list of highlights, turn to the index.

Maps Maps play a crucial role in Lonely Planet guidebooks and include a huge amount of information. A legend is printed on the back page. We seek to have complete consistency between maps and text, and to have every important place in the text captured on a map. Map key numbers usually start in the top left corner.

Although inclusion in a guidebook usually implies a recommen-dation we cannot list every good place. Exclusion does not necessarily imply criticism. In fact there are a number of reasons why we might exclude a place – sometimes it is simply inappropriate to encourage an influx of travellers.

Introduction

On a busy city street in Seoul, the peak hour traffic fumes and rumbles. Metres below the ground, sleek subway trains move commuters at lightning speed. In art deco coffee shops, fashionably dressed teenagers chat on mobile phones. Outside, workmen with jackhammers pound one-storey buildings into dust to make way for 30-storey skyscrapers. And in manufacturing plants across the country, workers churn out cars, container ships and computers.

This is one face of South Korea, a country which – in the span of one generation – rose from the ashes of war to become a modern industrial giant. Yet, behind the facade of well-stocked department stores and museums of modern art, you will find another Korea.

Even in the booming metropolis of Seoul, the capital of South Korea, you can still see stately and sublimely crafted palaces from the Yi Dynasty. Move into the city's back alleys and you will discover serene temple complexes where monks pray amid plumes of incense smoke. In the city's parks, you may be treated to a traditional drum dance, or folk music played on venerable wind and string instruments. Maybe you will encounter a fortune teller who, for a small fee, will foretell your destiny.

If you head to the outskirts of Seoul, you can visit specially preserved 'cultural villages', where silk, paper, porcelain, wood carvings and calligraphic scrolls are hand made by skilled craftspeople. Once out of the city, the countryside is dotted with still-functioning Buddhist monasteries. Curious travellers will find the monks responsive and hospitable.

Korea's beautiful, forested mountains offer endless trekking possibilities and, during the famously cold winters, the opportunity for skiing. Even at the summit of a remote peak, you may be in for another encounter, as you stumble spellbound upon a small group performing a shamanistic ritual.

Then there are Korea's innumerable islands scattered like confetti off its southern and eastern shores, many of them intriguing variations of the mainland culture. A visit to any one of these places will leave an indelible impression.

The people of South Korea are spontaneous, friendly, patriotic, a little romantic, and interested in foreigners and the outside world. Wherever you go, even in cosmopolitan Seoul, you will be regarded with curiosity. You will be constantly approached by people who will want to strike up a conversation, whether they be soldiers, hotel proprietors, students, businesspeople or street vendors. They will try their best, regardless of language or cultural differences, to establish a rapport with you – always with humour and without being overbearing. If you respond with friendship and a little imagination you will often find yourself the recipient of the most unexpected and disarming hospitality. Any foreigner who shows a sincere interest and amiability towards the Korean people is likely to be invited out for the evening, or into people's homes.

Sadly, the situation in North Korea is much different. Though the country claims to be a 'paradise on earth' and foreign guests are met with warm hospitality, there are few chances to establish the sort of sincere friendships that are so common in the South. Your opportunity to get to know the North Koreans on a personal level will be very limited, if indeed you are permitted to speak to anyone but your tour guide. North Korea is a totally closed society, and at the present time outsiders are only permitted a quick, superficial glance.

Not surprisingly, history weighs heavily on all Koreans. The cost of their survival as a nation has, at times, been devastating. The most recent example of this was the Korean War in the early 1950s, but even before this the Koreans had to suffer repeated incursions by belligerent neighbours. Continually on the alert and prepared for invasion, the armed forces have always been an important element of Korean society. This is no less true today than in the past. It would be fatuous to try to ignore the ubiquitous presence of the army in both North and South Korea, but it would also be a grave mistake to allow these realities to prejudice your view of this country and its people. Koreans have felt the hot breath of contesting powers for centuries.

Besides its people, there's one last plus which ought to put Korea firmly on the traveller's route: its safety and cleanliness. This is true even in the North which, if nothing else, is a place of great orderliness.

In the North, your visit will be totally arranged for you and a guide will accompany you at all times. In the South, you will have freedom to roam, and you will appreciate the fact that the crime rate is low, the public transport is well organised, the food is good, the hotels are comfortable and all but the most rustic of roads are paved.

You might think that the finest examples of oriental culture are to be found either in Japan or China, and that Korea merely offers a pale reflection of these. But you would be wrong. Korea is one of the unexplored gems of Asia. It once acquired the nickname of the 'Hermit Kingdom', after it closed its borders to the outside world in the late-19th century as a result of what seemed to it unbearable pressures from the outside. That name still fits North Korea, but South Korea is certainly one of the most open and rapidly changing societies in Asia.

Facts about Korea

HISTORY
In the Beginning
Korean folklore fixes the date of the nation's birth to a semi-deity named Tan'gun at around 2333 BC. But according to the latest research its origins go back even further to 30,000 BC, when migrating tribes from central and northern Asia first arrived on the peninsula.

The earliest outside influences assimilated by these nomadic tribes came from the Chinese, who had established an outpost near present-day Pyongyang during the Han dynasty. Constant wars with the Chinese dictated the necessity for an early alliance between the besieged tribes of the north. Four centuries later, following the demise of Han, the remaining tribes of the northern half of the peninsula united, which eventually led to the formation of the first Korean kingdom – Goguryeo – around the 1st century AD.

Not being subject to the same immediate pressures, the tribes of the south were slower to coalesce. However, by the 3rd century AD two powerful kingdoms – Silla and Baekje – had emerged to dominate the south. Sandwiched between them for a while was the loose confederacy of Gaya, but this had a relatively brief existence, since the leaders of its constituent tribes were rarely able to present a common front when threatened with invasion.

Three Kingdoms Period
The next four centuries – known as the Three Kingdoms Period (Goguryeo, Baekje and Silla) – witnessed a remarkable flowering of the arts, architecture, literature and statecraft. Chinese influences were absorbed, reinterpreted and alloyed with traditional Korean beliefs. Probably the single most formative influence was Buddhism, which in time, became the state religion of all three kingdoms.

The Three Kingdoms Period was also the time when the developments which first took place in Korea began to be exported to Japan. Architects and builders from Baekje, for instance, were primarily responsible for the great burst of temple construction which occurred in Japan during the 6th century. There were times in Japan's early history when there were more Koreans involved in influential secular and religious positions than there were Japanese. This transmission of cultural developments accelerated during periods of conflict between the three kingdoms.

There was, of course, much rivalry between the kingdoms and wars were fought constantly in attempts to gain supremacy, but it was not until the 7th century that a major shift in power occurred.

Silla Dominance
The rise of the Tang dynasty in China during the 7th century provided Silla with the opportunity to expand its control over the whole peninsula. An alliance of the two was formed, and the combined armies first attacked Baekje (which quickly fell), followed by Goguryeo in AD 668.

The alliance, however, was short-lived, since it turned out to have been a convenient ruse by the Tang ruler to establish hegemony over Korea. The Silla aristocracy had no intention of subscribing to such a plan and so, in order to thwart Tang designs, switched allegiance to what was left of the Goguryeo forces. Together, the two Korean forces were able eventually to drive out the Chinese. Silla thus united the peninsula for the first time and this unification was to last through various changes of regime right up until partition after WWII. Yet Silla was to learn, as all other Korean dynasties have had to, that the price of this often precarious independence depended on the recognition of the vastly superior forces of China and payment of a tribute.

Unified, Silla presided over one of Korea's greatest eras of cultural development. Nowhere is this more apparent than in the countless tombs, temples, pagodas, palaces, pleasure gardens and other relics which dot the countryside in and around present-day Gyeongju, the former Silla capital. Buddhism flourished, with state funds being lavished on the construction of temples and images, while monks were dispatched to China and India for study.

The cohesiveness of Silla society was based on the twin pillars of *golbun* – a rigid hierarchy of rank based on ancestry and the *hwarang* – a kind of paramilitary youth organisation for the training and educating of the sons of the Silla elite. Yet it was the rigidity of this system which also brought about its eventual downfall.

By the beginning of the 9th century, discontent among those who were excluded from power had reached such a pitch that the kingdom began to crumble. Threatened by rival warlords to the north and west, the end came surprisingly bloodlessly when the last Silla king, unwilling to contemplate further destruction, offered his kingdom to the ruler of Later Goguryeo, set up in the northern half of the peninsula. As a result, the capital was moved to Gaeseong, north of Seoul, and the peninsula was reunited.

The last Silla king was allowed to live out the rest of his days as an honoured guest in his rival's capital. Gyeongju sank into obscurity and remained that way until 're-discovered' in the 20th century – a blessing in disguise. Had its value been recognised earlier, it would have caused the city's priceless artefacts to have been looted and perhaps lost forever.

Goryeo Dynasty

The new dynasty, which took the name of Goryeo, abolished the hierarchy golbun and restructured the government. Emphasis was placed on a Confucian examination system for state officials, similar to China's except that eligibility for the examination was limited to the sons of the ruling oligarchy. With stability restored, the new dynasty prospered. It was during this time that Buddhism, through royal patronage, reached the height of its development and acquired considerable secular power through the acquisition of land and wealth.

In time, however, the Goryeo government became as despotic and arrogant as that of Silla, except that in this case it was the literati who monopolised the top positions, rather than warrior-aristocrats. Disaffected military officers eventually reduced the power of these bureaucrats by assassinating one of the Goryeo kings and installing his son as a puppet ruler. Yet, at the same time, events were taking place on Korea's northern borders which would radically impinge upon the nation's ability to survive as an independent kingdom.

Throughout the later years of the Goryeo dynasty, marauding Khitan tribes began making life difficult for the kingdom; they were only kept in check by an alliance with the Mongols of China. The alliance was a reluctant one on the part of Goryeo, since it involved the payment of a large annual tribute, and eventually it was broken off.

The reckoning didn't come until 1231 – because the Mongols were preoccupied with their own internal problems – but when it did the decision to rescind the treaty proved disastrous. The Mongols invaded with vastly superior forces, quickly took Gaeseong, and forced the king to take refuge on Ganghwado. There he remained relatively safe but was totally powerless to stop the Mongols laying waste to the peninsula for the next 25 years. A bitter truce was arranged in 1259. The Goryeo monarch was restored to his kingdom (minus Jejudo, which the Mongols used for rearing horses). This was on the condition that Goryeo crown princes would be held hostage at Beijing until the deaths of their fathers; that they would be forced to marry Mongol princesses; and that the tribute would be restored.

The tribute was a heavy one for Korea to shoulder. It included gold, silver, horses, ginseng, hawks, artisans, women and eunuchs – but that was not all that Goryeo was compelled to provide. There were also demands to provide soldiers and ships for the ill-fated Mongol attempt to invade Japan between 1274 and 1281. These demands led to intolerable strains being placed on the fabric of Korean society and were the root cause of the eventual downfall of the Goryeo kingdom.

Still, Goryeo survived for a little while longer, and reasserted its independence when rebellions in China led to the ousting of the Mongols and their replacement by the Ming dynasty. There were reforms and wholesale purges of pro-Mongol aristocrats, but the rot had spread too far, and rebellions broke out. This climaxed in the overthrow of the Goryeo monarch, and the foundation of a new dynasty being built by one of the king's former generals, Yi Seonggye.

Yi (Joseon) Dynasty

The new regime staked its future on the ideals and practices of Neo-Confucianism. These combined the sage's original ethical and political ideas with a quasi-religious practice of ancestor worship and the idea of the eldest male as spiritual head of the family. Buddhism, regarded as an enemy and rival, was suppressed. The monasteries' estates were confiscated, their wealth sequestered and the building of monasteries limited to rural areas. As a result of these events, Buddhism has never recovered its former dominance (though there has been a resurgence in recent years).

The next 150 years were a time of relative peace and prosperity, during which great strides were made under a succession of enlightened kings. The most beloved of these was Sejong (1418–50) who presided over the invention of a phonetic script, *hangeul*, for the Korean language. The new script was an outstanding achievement and, since it was infinitely simpler than Chinese, led to a vast increase in literacy. However it was not introduced without considerable opposition among the intelligentsia, many of whom regarded it as subversive and worried about the reaction of the Ming court.

Japanese Invasion of 1592

The period of peace came to a dramatic end in 1592 when the country was invaded by a newly united Japan under Toyotomi Hideyoshi, following Korea's refusal to join with them in an invasion of China. Exploiting to the full their superior weaponry – including muskets supplied by the Portuguese – the Japanese overran the peninsula in just

Korea's greatest military hero,
Admiral Yi Sun-shin (AD 1545–98)

one month. At sea, however, they were soundly defeated by Korea's most admired military hero, Yi Sun-shin, the famed inventor of the world's first ironclad ships (known as turtle ships, or *geobukseon*). In their naval encounters with Admiral Yi Sun-shin, the Japanese lost more than 500 ships in less than six months. Unfortunately, the admiral fell foul of the Yi court and was dismissed (not the last time the Korean bureaucracy has bungled). It was only when his successor failed to match up that Yi was belatedly recalled.

The war dragged on for four years, until Korean guerrilla resistance and Chinese intervention forced it to a conclusion. Nevertheless, the Japanese invaded again the following year, though this time the war was confined to the southern provinces, and came to an end when Hideyoshi died and the invaders withdrew.

The Japanese invasion was an unprecedented disaster for Korea. Many craftspeople and intellectuals were taken prisoner and transported to Japan so that their skills could be exploited. Almost all of Korea's temples and palaces were burnt to the ground during this period.

The Manchu Invasion

The early-17th century was a time of conflict in China. The Manchus there were in the process of overthrowing the Ming court, with whom the Koreans had treaty obligations. Though unsure which side to declare for, the Korean court decided to side with the Ming, incurring the wrath of the Manchus who, as soon as they had consolidated their hold over China, turned to invade Korea. The Korean forces were routed and severe restrictions placed on the country's sovereignty.

Korea – the Hermit Kingdom

Profoundly shocked and exhausted by this series of events, Korea folded its wings and withdrew into itself over the next century while the pace of change around it continued to accelerate – largely due to the spread of Western ideas and contacts. Nowhere was this more apparent than in the number of converts to Catholicism and, later, to various sects of Protestantism. Frightened by the growing influence of these groups, the Yi court panicked and in the repression which followed, hundreds of people were executed. But the event which most shook their confidence was the occupation of Beijing by the French and British in 1860. In a vain attempt to shut off these dawning realities, the country was closed to all foreigners. It was as a result of this period that Korea acquired the name of the 'Hermit Kingdom'.

It was a policy doomed to failure. The late-19th century was no time to turn a blind eye to the increasing industrial and military might of the USA, Japan, and the European maritime nations. Sooner or later, one or more of these nations would force the Koreans to open their doors. This happened some 25 years later, as a result of independent occupations of the island of Ganghwado by the French and Americans, and a naval skirmish, engineered by the Japanese, which led to a so-called 'treaty of friendship'. The treaty was naturally biased in favour of the Japanese. Korean ports were opened to Japanese traders and the policy of excluding foreigners was abandoned. Suddenly, a very ill-prepared Korea found itself blown like a leaf in the winds of imperial rivalries.

Japanese Control

The Donghak uprising of 1894, by followers of a new religious sect founded in 1860 by Choe Che-u (which combined elements of Confucianism, Buddhism, Taoism and shamanism), set off a chain of events. This led to the Sino-Japanese War and the defeat of China, and, ultimately, the installation of a Japanese-controlled government in Seoul. With China out of the picture, the Russians quickly jumped into the political arena, and the Koreans became pawns in yet another struggle between giants.

During this time, pro-Japanese and pro-Russian Korean governments followed each other in rapid succession. Queen Min – the real power behind the Yi throne – was assassinated by Japanese agents, and for a year and a half King Gojong took refuge inside the Russian legation. In the end the struggle for supremacy was settled by the Russo-Japanese War of 1904, which Japan won. Subsequently, Korea was occupied by the Japanese. Finally, in 1910, following public riots and serious guerrilla activity by elements of the disbanded Korean army, the Japanese annexed the country and abolished the monarchy.

Annexation by Japan was not something the Koreans took to well. After the failure of a Korean delegation to gain the right of self-determination at the Versailles Conference (at the close of WWI), an independence movement was formed by a group of patriots. They leafleted in Seoul and provoked public demonstrations against the Japanese occupation. The unrest quickly spread to the rest of the country. The Japanese troops and police panicked, and in the brutal repression which followed over 7000 Koreans were shot and many thousands more seriously injured. Cosmetic reforms were brought in to try and contain the uprising, but at the same time the ranks of the secret police were rapidly expanded and censorship tightened.

As WWII drew near, Japan's grip on Korea was tightened even further. The Japanese language was made mandatory as the medium of instruction in schools, all

Japan's Discomfort

In 1996, the Korean and Japanese governments nearly came to blows over the sovereignty of a couple of rocks (called Dokdo in Korean, Takeshima in Japanese) in the Sea of Japan in early 1996. Even the sea itself is a source of Korean grumbling; Korean scholars have revealed early Western maps that show the sea was originally known as the 'Sea of Korea'. Maps produced in Korea currently label it as the 'East Sea'.

In fact, the sea issue is just one of a host of grievances which the Koreans have against Japan. Repeated invasions by the Japanese and the more recent occupation of Korea from 1910 to 1945 have left the Koreans with an almost obsessive enmity towards their neighbour across the Sea of Japan (or 'East Sea', if you will).

Perhaps no issue burns as brightly as that of the 'comfort women'. During WWII, an estimated 200,000 women were used as sex slaves by the Japanese military, servicing 10 to 30 men a day. More than half of these women were Korean. In December 1991, 35 (now elderly) Korean women sued the Japanese government for W700 million in compensation. The Japanese government finally issued a blanket apology in August 1993 and set up a private charitable fund for voluntary contributions, the Asian National Fund for Women. But the Japanese government continues to refuse to pay the women directly claiming that the US$500 million paid to South Korea in 1965 settled all war claims. The former comfort women are outraged, seeing the private 'charitable fund' as a smokescreen to absolve the Japanese government from legal liability. For an update on the issue, see the Web site of the Korean Council for the Women Drafted for Military Sexual Slavery by Japan (http://witness.peacenet.or.kr).

Japan's reluctance to admit legal liability is because the comfort women issue is just the tip of the iceberg. During WWII, over one million Koreans were sent abroad (mostly to Japan and China) by the Japanese government. Some were in Japan merely to get an education, but the majority were pressed into military service or forced labour. Some of these now-elderly survivors are pressing lawsuits against big Japanese companies which, they say, used them as little more than slave labour. One successful lawsuit has been won by Kim Kyong-sok, a South Korean who sued NKK (a Japanese steel company) for US$38,000 in back wages. Encouraged by this, more lawsuits are being filed. It's a nightmare that keeps Japanese politicians and business executives awake at night.

For their part, Japanese visitors to Korea are routinely astonished to discover that their country is so vilified. Japan's educational system presents students with such a sanitised version of the nation's military past that young Japanese have to go abroad to find out what really happened during WWII. The issue of Japan's whitewashed history textbooks is yet another bone of contention between Korea and Japan.

The Japanese government has tried to make amends. During a summit meeting in Tokyo in October, 1998, Japanese Prime Minister Keizo Obuchi issued a formal apology to Korea's President Kim Dae-jung for Japan's wartime behaviour. And in a more bizarre turn of events, the Korean and Japanese governments negotiated the return of 20,000 Korean noses which were removed and taken back to Japan as trophies in the Hideyoshi invasion of the late 16th century. The noses, safely resting in 'nose tombs', were returned to South Korea where a burial ceremony was performed. Unfortunately, it is unlikely that these recent goodwill gestures will greatly improve relations between Japan and its resentful neighbour across the 'East Sea'.

public signs had to be in Japanese, the teaching of Korean history was banned and hundreds of thousands of Korean labourers were conscripted to assist the Japanese army both in Korea and in China. It was a time which the Koreans regard as attempted cultural genocide, and the scars are a long way from being healed even today.

Post WWII

As much as the Koreans rejoiced at being freed of Japanese rule, the country's hopes for a new era of peace and independence were soon dashed. A deal had been struck between the USSR, the USA and Britain over the fate of postwar Korea. The USSR was to occupy the peninsula north of the 38th parallel and the USA was to occupy the country south of that. Though never intended as a permanent division, it turned out that way once the occupying troops were in position. Negotiations for a provisional government floundered because neither side was willing to make concessions which would result in the loss of its influence over the proposed new government. A UN commission was set up to try and resolve the problem and to oversee elections for a united government, but it was denied entry to the North and was forced to confine its activities to the South. The new government which was elected in the South declared its independence. The stage was set for the Korean War.

The Korean War

By 1948, Soviet and American troops had been withdrawn, but while the Americans supplied only arms considered necessary for self-defence to the South, the USSR provided the North with a vast array of weaponry with which to create a powerful army. On 25 June 1950, the North Korean army invaded. The Americans responded by sending in troops who were soon joined by contingents from 16 other countries, following a UN resolution supporting the American action. The USSR absented herself from the Security Council deliberations.

The war went badly for the UN at first and its troops were soon pushed into a small pocket around Busan. But following a daring landing at Incheon under the command of General MacArthur, its fortunes changed. Within a month, the North Korean army had been thrown back to the borders of Manchuria.

Having lost the war, the North Koreans decided to outsource the job to the Chinese. In November 1950, over one million communist Chinese troops poured into Korea and the UN forces were pushed back below the 38th parallel. The conflict continued for the next six months with both sides alternately advancing and retreating until a stalemate was reached just north of the 38th parallel.

Negotiations for a truce were started but dragged on for two years, eventually leading to the creation of the De-Militarised Zone (DMZ) and the truce village of Panmunjeom where both sides have met periodically ever since to exchange heated rhetoric.

At the end of the war, Korea lay in ruins. Seoul had changed hands no less than four times and was flattened. Millions of people were left homeless, industry destroyed and the countryside devastated. In the South, 47,000 Koreans had lost their lives and around 200,000 were wounded. Of the UN troops, 37,000 were killed (mostly Americans) and 120,000 wounded. Combined military and civilian casualties in the North were estimated at up to two million.

Post Korean War

North Korea went on to become one of the most closed countries in the world, ruled by the eccentric and uncompromising Kim Il Sung, and later by his son Kim Jong Il. (See the North Korea chapter for more details.)

In South Korea, economic recovery was slow and the civilian government of President Syngman Rhee was weak and corrupt. In 1961, following blatantly fraudulent elections, massive student demonstrations and the resignation of Rhee, a military dictatorship was established with General Park Chung-hee emerging as its strongman. Pressures soon mounted for the return of a civilian government and so, in 1963, Park retired from the army and stood as a candidate for the Democratic Republican Party. The party won the elections and Park was named president. Park was re-elected as president in 1967 and again in 1971, though he only very narrowly missed defeat in 1971 at the hands of his rival, Kim Dae-jung.

To his credit, Park created an efficient administration and was the architect of

The Philosophical Flag

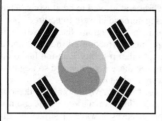

The South Koreans may well have the most philosophical flag in the world. The white background represents both Confucian 'purity' and the Buddhist concept of 'emptiness'. In the centre lies a *taegeuk*, the Taoist symbol of balance or harmony between opposites. It was adapted from the Chinese, who usually depicted it in black and white, divided vertically. The Korean version is more colourful and divided horizontally, with the top, red half representing *yang* (heaven, day, male, heat, active, construction etc). The blue lower half represents *eum* (earth, night, female, cold, passive, destruction etc). These twin cosmic forces are cycled perpetually, in perfectly balanced harmony, despite their superficial opposition; wisdom doesn't see them as fighting each other, but rather as two sides of the same coin.

The three lines at each corner, known as trigrams, were borrowed from the most important ancient book of Chinese thought, the *Classic of Changes* (Korean: the *Ju Yeok*; Chinese: the *I Ching*). The three unbroken bars symbolise heaven-creative, while the opposite three broken bars symbolise earth-receptive. The trigram in the upper right corner is water-treacherous danger, and in the opposite corner lies fire-loyal love.

Something similar to this flag was created in 1882 by a team of reformist envoys to Japan, as they realised they had no modern standard to represent Korea as an equal among nations. The current design was adopted by the Shanghai-based government-in-exile during the Japanese occupation of 1910–1945 and became standardised as the national flag of the Republic of Korea in 1948. It is called the Taegeukgi. One may well wonder whether the top half of the horizontally-divided taegeuk, being red, was some sort of omen – the northern half of Korea later becoming communist.

South Korea's 'economic miracle'. But in October 1972, in an attempt to secure his position, he declared martial law and clamped down on political opponents. Like Kim Il-sung, he created his own personality cult and his record on human rights grew progressively worse. A botched assassination attempt in 1975 killed his wife. A rigged poll in 1978 resulted in Park's 're-election'. On 26 October 1979, he was assassinated by Kim Chae-kyu, chief of the Korean Central Intelligence Agency.

The 1980s

After 18 years of Park's tyrannical rule, Koreans were ready for a change. The brief period of political freedom which followed Park's death aroused popular sentiment for free elections.

Unfortunately, such hopes were soon dashed. On 17 May 1980, General Chun Doo-hwan re-established martial law and arrested leading opposition politicians, including Kim Dae-jung. Student protests erupted the next day in Kim's home town of Gwangju and were brutally suppressed – about 200 civilians were killed, over 1000 injured and thousands more arrested. The 'Gwangju Massacre' has haunted the nation's conscience ever since.

In the rigged elections which were staged shortly after this, Chun secured his position as president. Kim Dae-jung was tried for treason and sentenced to death, but so transparent were the charges against him that Chun was reluctantly forced to commute the sentence to life imprisonment following worldwide protests. Probably the single most important factor which saved Kim was Chun's need for a continued and substantial American military presence in South Korea. Kim Dae-jung was released some time later in order to allow him to go to the USA for medical treatment. He stayed on there as a lecturer at Harvard University until his return to Korea in 1987.

Having consolidated his power, Chun, surprisingly, lifted martial law, granted amnesty to quite a few detainees, and allowed the National Assembly to debate issues somewhat more freely than was ever possible during Park's regime. Press censorship, nevertheless, remained tight under a 'voluntary restraint' system.

During an official visit to Burma in late 1983, Chun miraculously escaped assassination at the hands of North Korean agents. In 1987, two North Koreans posing as Japanese tourists bombed a Korean Air flight, causing 115 deaths. Hopes of reunification of the two Koreas remained remote as ever.

Because of continued opposition to his rule, Chun announced his intention to step down from the presidency in February 1988. Shortly afterwards, Roh Tae-woo, a classmate and confidant of Chun's, was nominated by the ruling party to succeed him. For a while it seemed that real democracy was still just a distant dream.

What happened next took the world by storm. Thousands of students in every city across the nation took to the streets to demonstrate. They were met by riot police, tear gas and mass arrests. Within a matter of days the country was at flash point. The students were quickly joined by tens of thousands of industrial and office workers, and even Buddhist monks. Though threatening draconian measures to quell the disturbances, Chun largely took a back seat and left Roh to negotiate.

Under intense American pressure to compromise, and well aware of the obvious fact that the government wasn't just confronted with a bunch of radical students, Roh invited the opposition Reunification Democratic Party to talks. The two leaders of the opposition were Kim Young-sam and Kim Dae-jung.

Kim Dae-jung had returned from exile in the USA the year before but had been kept under virtual house arrest since then. The two opposition leaders suddenly found themselves on centre stage, but a deal with the government proved to be elusive. What was being demanded were free, direct, popular presidential elections, the release of political prisoners, freedom of the press and a number of other reforms. Roh felt he could not concede these demands and so negotiations were broken off.

But not for long. While massive demonstrations continued on the streets, the country was convulsed by a wave of strikes by industrial workers. Civil war and a military coup were getting dangerously close. Realising this, Chun gave Roh the go-ahead to concede all of the opposition's demands.

The deal set in motion campaigns for the presidential elections by both the ruling Democratic Justice Party and the opposition Reunification Democratic Party. At first, it seemed that the two Kims of the opposition party would form an alliance and agree to one of them running for president in order not to split the opposition vote. A lot of pledges were made in this respect early on in the campaign but, in the end, they both announced their candidacy. In terms of gaining the presidency, this proved to be a fatal mistake.

In the elections which followed, neither of the Kims were able to match Roh's share of the vote (37%) though their combined total (55%) was considerably more than Roh's. Roh therefore became the next president. There was a good deal of sabre-rattling during the election campaign, with various army officers threatening a coup should Kim Dae-jung win the election, but the one thing which probably restrained them most was the thought that the 1988 Olympics scheduled for Seoul might have to be cancelled if such an event occurred. As a matter of national pride, few people in South Korea wanted that to happen.

With Roh in power but restrained by two powerful opposition parties, some of the heat went out of South Korean politics. The students continued violent demonstrations every spring (coinciding with mid-term exams, which were cancelled as a result), but the radicals began to look increasingly out of touch.

Across the Divide

During the three-day meeting that took place in Pyongyang (13–15 June 2000) between South Korea's President Kim Dae-jung and North Korean leader Kim Jong-il, everything from foreign investment to reunification was discussed. It was quite a spectacle. The two sides promised to soon arrange visas so that families separated by the war could visit one another, and Kim Jong Il said he would make a reciprocal visit to Seoul. The foreign news media was dazzled. Photos of the two Kims clinking champagne glasses dominated the front pages of newspapers around the world.

That the meeting took place at all was perhaps even more amazing than what was negotiated. Doomsayers had predicted that the announced meeting would never occur and, even if it did, nothing useful would be negotiated and Kim Dae-jung might even be kidnapped.

The meeting, in fact, went better than anybody had dared hoped. However, it raised almost as many questions as it answered. Chief among these was the fate of the 37,000 US troops in South Korea – it has been a relentless demand of North Korea that these troops must go before the Cold War can end. Another disturbing issue is the North's suspected secret weapons programs (nuclear, chemical and biological). South Koreans have also been wondering just how much reunification (if that is indeed the goal) is going to cost them – North Korea is believed to need more than US$1 trillion in aid and investment to bring its economy into the 21st century. Pessimists have also voiced concern that some of this investment will simply be funnelled into the North's secret weapons program, increasing the possibility of a future war. And questions about democratic political reforms in the North are simply too delicate to raise at this time.

Such discomforting issues have, for the moment, been sidelined. The summit meeting had been deemed a great success. Indeed, one would have to be a spoilsport to simply say that nothing has changed. The possibility of a second Korean War has been greatly diminished. There is even talk of nominating the two Kims for a Nobel Peace Prize. The Koreans are euphoric. The rest of the world can only hope that the euphoria is justified.

Roh's government brought forward numerous democratic reforms, giving South Koreans an unprecedented level of freedom to voice their opinions without fear of imprisonment. Restrictions on South Koreans travelling abroad were also lifted.

While the students achieved widespread support for their courageous opposition to the repressive Chun regime, renewed violent protests quickly squandered this goodwill and even produced a strange nostalgia for Chun's military dictatorship. Public disgust with the students sharply increased in 1989, after students set a fire trap which killed seven policemen and injured 30 others at Dongui University in Busan. The police were on campus at the time to rescue another policeman who had been kidnapped by the students.

Seoul made considerable progress on the diplomatic front by establishing relations with the Soviet Union in 1990 and with China in 1992. However, both acts greatly angered North Korea.

On 18 December 1992, the DLP (Democratic Liberal Party) candidate Kim Young-sam (who had merged his opposition party with the DLP in 1990) won the general election, soundly defeating his old opposition rival, Kim Dae-jung, and the billionaire head of the Hyundai company, Chung Ju-yung.

Immediately after his election, the new president embarked on his promised anti-corruption campaign. Kim publicly stated his own net worth at US$2.1 million (almost poverty level for a South Korean president) and then pushed through legislation to force other government officials to reveal their assets.

After evidence surfaced in 1995 that former presidents Chun and Roh had pocketed

millions of dollars in elicit 'campaign contributions', there was a massive public out-
cry to prosecute both men for bribery, as
well as their role in the Gwangju Massacre.
Although he resisted at first, President Kim
finally supported the necessary legislation
to extend the statute of limitations. In August 1996, Chun was given the death sentence and Roh was sentenced to 22 years in
prison. But in December 1997, President
Kim Young-sam granted a presidential par-
don to Chun and Roh, and the two were released from prison.

On 18 December 1997, a presidential
election swept Kim Dae-jung into office,
the first time in Korea's history that an opposition candidate had won the presidency.
He then began his 'sunshine policy' to
mend relations with North Korea, for
which he was awarded the Nobel Peace
Prize in 2000.

GEOGRAPHY

The Korean peninsula borders China and
Russia in the north, faces China in the west
across the Yellow Sea (which the Koreans
call the West Sea) and Japan to the east
and south across the Sea of Japan (which
Koreans label the East Sea). The peninsula
is divided roughly in half, just north of the
38th parallel between the two countries,
North and South Korea.

South Korea's land area is 99,373 sq
km, making it slightly larger than Portugal. Its overall length from north to south
is approximately 500km, while at its nar-
rowest point it's 216km wide. While 70%
of the country is mountainous, few of the
mountains are very high. South Korea's
tallest peak is Hallasan (1950m) on the island of Jejudo.

CLIMATE

Korea has four distinct seasons. Autumn is
delightfully cool and dry. April, May and
June are generally pleasant months, before
the summer monsoon rains. Winter, from
November to March, sees temperatures
hovering either side of 0°C, but it can be
bitter in the mountains, with temperatures
down to –15°C.

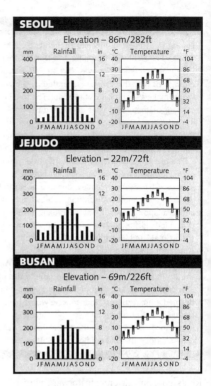

Jejudo, off the south coast (and therefore the nearest part of Korea to the equator) is the warmest place in South Korea.
It is also the wettest. Winter is particularly
dreary – it rains and rains – and will leave
you wondering why the whole island
doesn't wash away.

ECOLOGY & ENVIRONMENT

War has taken a serious toll on Korea's
environment. In addition, South Korea has
10 nuclear power plants. However, South
Korea is one of the world's leading nations in reafforestation.

Since 1995, the government has ruled that
only officially-designated rubbish bags can
be used for trash collection. Not using them
can result in a fine. Profits from the high-
priced bags are earmarked for government-
sponsored environmental projects.

FLORA & FAUNA
Flora
The northern part of South Korea is the coldest region, and the flora tends to be alpine. Trees typically found here are beech, birch, fir, larch, oak and pine. Further south deciduous trees dominate. The south coast and Jejudo are the warmest and wettest parts of the country, and the vegetation tends to be lush. Some common species include aralias, azaleas, camellias, gingko trees and heathers. The south is also Korea's ginseng-growing region.

Fauna
Given Korea's history of war and recent industrialisation, it's not surprising that the local wildlife has taken a beating. Nevertheless, some hardy species manage to survive in the remote mountain regions. The largest wild creature in the country is the Korean black bear. Deer are reasonably common in the national parks.

Birds do a reasonably good job of surviving alongside human society. Biologists have identified 379 species of birds in Korea, of which 266 are migratory.

Endangered Species
Siberian tigers are no longer found in Korea, and it's possible that they will even become extinct in Siberia as well.

National & Provincial Parks
The South Koreans have done a first-rate job of protecting scenic areas, and the whole country is dotted with beautiful parks. A lot of travellers have commented that the parks are perhaps the best of Korea's many fine attractions.

Korea has two grades of parks: national and provincial. The national parks tend to be more popular than the provincial parks, if only because they are better known. The three most popular national parks are Seoraksan, Hallasan and Jirisan. In fact, they are so popular that you probably should avoid them during holiday times.

In a number of parks, the government periodically closes a number of walking trails for up to three years in order to give the wilderness some time to recover from the crush of hikers.

Fires and cooking are prohibited in most national parks, except in designated campsites. Smoking is prohibited on mountain trails, and amazingly this is enforced (the fine is W300,000).

National Parks At the present time, there are 20 national parks in South Korea:

Bukhansan is in the northern suburbs of Seoul and is therefore very accessible.

Byeonsanbando, on a peninsula in the western part of Jeollabuk-do, is dotted with temples such as Naesosa and Daeamsa.

Chiaksan is in Gangwon-do, east of Wonju, and the temple of Guryongsa. The summit of Chiaksan reaches 1288m.

Dadohae Haesang is a huge marine park which consists of hundreds of islands strung along the south-western tip of Korea. The westernmost part of the park is the spectacular island of Hongdo.

Deogyusan is located in Jeollabuk-do, south-east of Daejeon.

Gayasan lies in both Gyeongsangbuk-do and Gyeongsangnam-do, and is 64km west of Daegu. The highest peak in the park is 1430m and the temple of Haeinsa is located here.

Gyeongju is near Gyeongju in Gyeongsangbuk-do. Unlike the previously mentioned parks, the attractions here are mainly cultural. Gyeongju was the capital of the ancient Silla kingdom and there are many historical relics and temples from that era spread throughout the park.

Gyeryongsan is in Chungcheongnam-do, just west of Daejeon.

Hallasan, on Jejudo, is dominated by an extinct volcano: South Korea's highest peak.

Hallyeo Haesang is off the southern coast near Busan. There are approximately 400 small islands within the park's boundaries.

Jirisan straddles the border of three provinces: Jeollanam-do, Jeollabuk-do and Gyeongsangnam-do. The summit of Jirisan reaches 1751m, making it South Korea's second highest peak. The beautiful Hwaeomsa is the most important temple in this park.

Juwangsan is in Gyeongsangbuk-do, near Cheongsong.

Naejangsan is located just north of Gwangju. It straddles the borders of Jeollanam-do and Jeollabuk-do.

Odaesan is in the province of Gangwon-do, south of Seoraksan.

Seoraksan is located in Gangwon-do, near the city of Sokcho, this is perhaps South Korea's most beautiful and popular park.

Sobaeksan straddles the border between Gyeongsangbuk-do and Chungcheongbuk-do to the north of Gyeongju.

Songnisan is 15km east of Po-eun in Chungcheongbuk-do Province. Within the park is Beojusa, a famous temple.

Taean Haean, a coastal park, is at the western end of Chungcheongnam-do.

Wolchulsan, located in the south-west corner of Jeollanam-do, is known for its fantastically shaped rock formations.

Woraksan, in Chungcheongbuk-do, is near the very popular Suanbo Ski Resort and Suanbo Hot Springs.

Provincial Parks There are 19 provincial parks in South Korea and some of them are easily as spectacular as the national parks. Furthermore, provincial parks tend to be relatively uncrowded simply because they are less well known. The following parks are listed by province.

Chungcheongnam-do

Chilgapsan (561m) is a small but very steep mountain. Temples in this thickly-forested park include Janggoksa and Gangneung.

Deoksan is known for its waterfalls, valleys and hot springs. The largest temple here is Suedoksa. The park is to the west of Cheonan.

Gangwon-do

Donghae is also known as Naksan Provincial Park, this beachside park has fine facilities for swimming. Other major sights in the park include Naksansa and Uisangdaesa.

Gyeongpo is another beachside park, but it's very developed and touristy. It's 6km north of Gangneung.

Taebaeksan (1568m) is the sixth highest peak in South Korea and one of the country's three sacred mountains.

Gyeonggi-do

Namhansanseong is an old mountain fortress (sanseong) about 26km south-east of central Seoul and makes a good day trip from the city.

Gyeongsangbuk-do

Cheongnyangsan (870m) besides the eponymous main peak, has 11 other scenic peaks, eight caves and a small, pretty temple, Cheongnyangsa.

Geumosan is just outside the city of Gumi, a major industrial area, and the park is mostly a recreational area for the local workers.

Mungyeongsaejae straddles the mountain pass that connects Chungcheongbuk-do and Gyeongsangbuk-do. It's not spectacular but does offer pleasant scenery.

Palgongsan is north of Daegu and has a big temple called Donghwasa. There is also a big standing Buddha on the peak of a mountain.

Gyeongsangnam-do

Gajisan has a collection of major temples including Seongnamsa (right at the mountain), Unmunsa (to the north of the mountain), Pyochungsa (south of the mountain and just outside the park boundary). Nearby (but outside the park) is Tongdosa, one of the five big temples of Korea.

Yeonhwasan (477m) is home to one moderate-sized temple, Okcheonsa, and several hermitages.

Jeollabuk-do

Daedunsan (878m) is a very small and compact place and spectacularly beautiful. It's notable for granite spires, cliffs, great views and hiking trails.

Maisan (685m) means 'horse ears mountain', which roughly describes the shape of the two rocky outcrops which make up its twin peaks. The temple Tapsa is stuck right between the two 'horse ears'.

Moaksan (794m), south-west of Cheongju, is where you'll find Geumsansa, a temple famous for shamanism.

Seonunsan is a beautiful place with Seonunsa and small sub-temples perched all around a gorge near the sea.

Jeollanam-do

Duryunsan (703m) is the most south-western peak in Korea and the location of Taehungsa, a major Zen meditation temple.

Jogyesan (884m) is the home of Songgwangsa, the main temple of the Jogye sect of Korean Buddhism.

Mudeungsan (1187m) is just east of Gwangju. There are numerous hiking trails and it's a popular walking area for residents of Gwangju. However, it's not otherwise spectacular.

GOVERNMENT & POLITICS

Power emanates from the Blue House (the president's residence and office), which is located behind the former royal palace complex, the Gyeongbokgung, in Seoul. The government is democratic, based on the separation of power among three branches: executive, legislative and judicial. The president is elected to a five-year term, and nominates cabinet. Current president, Kim Dae-jung, elected in 1997, was awarded the Nobel peace prize in 2000. The legislative is a 273-member National Assembly. Representatives are elected to serve four years. There has been no vice-president since the 1960s. The prime-minister, head of cabinet, acts as a conciliator between the branches. The judiciary is completely independent.

At the time of writing, President Kim Dae-jung's Millennium Democratic Party (MLD) holds only 115 seats out of the 273 total in the National Assembly. The conservative (and staunchly anti-communist) United Liberal Democrats (ULD) hold only 17 seats. The MLD and ULD have formed a coalition along with a few independents and have a parliamentary majority with just one vote to spare. The largest party is, ironically, in opposition – the Grand National Party (GNP), led by Lee Hoi chang.

ECONOMY

South Korea has witnessed an amazing rags-to-riches story over the past four decades. Rising from the debris of the Korean War, South Korea has gone on to achieve a standard of living which rivals the nations of Western Europe.

If any one person could be called the 'father' of this economic miracle, it would have to be former dictator Park Chung-hee who ruled the country from 1961 until his assassination in 1979 (see History, earlier). As strict as Park was on matters of national security (some would say paranoid), he did give his eager young technocrats a free hand to plan the economy.

The development model chosen was, ironically, much like that of Korea's former colonial master, Japan. 'Government-guided management' and 'export or die' became the twin slogans for economic progress. Features of the new order included ambitious five-year plans, borrow-ing billions of US dollars in cash (mostly from the USA), paying low salaries at home to sell abroad and restricting imports. Within a decade, South Korea's economic indicators went through the roof and the country joined Hong Kong, Taiwan and Singapore as one of Asia's 'economic tigers' (also called 'little dragons').

Unfortunately, 'government-guided management' was a two-edged sword. Unlike the other tigers, the South Korean economy was directed by a civil service which soon grew to mammoth proportions. In time, the bloated bureaucracy came to control everything from the flavour of ice cream to the price of ginseng. In recent years there has been a sincere effort to slay the red-tape dragon, but the bureaucrats are being wrenched from their desks kicking and screaming all the way.

A key feature of Korea's economy are the *jaebeol*, huge family-run conglomerates that owe their survival to government-subsidised bank loans. The tight-knit relationship between the jaebeol and government officials has led to more than a few indictments for corruption, and has made the phrase 'Korea, Inc' more of a truism than the more commonly known 'Japan, Inc'. Officially there are 30 jaebeol. The top five, Hyundai, Samsung, Daewoo, LG (Lucky Goldstar) and SK (Sunkyong), account for more than a third of the total sales of all South Korean companies and 50% of the country's exports.

In 1997, Asia lurched into an economic crisis, and South Korea was badly affected. As a direct result, President Kim Dae-jung has launched a number of bold reforms aimed at reducing the power and influence of the jaebeol. The reform process – still not complete – promises to restructure South Korea's economy considerably.

Sharply increasing wages is another big change of recent years. From the late 1980s onward, the country has often been rocked by large and occasionally violent strikes. Nowadays, South Korea is no longer considered a low-wage country. Many companies have responded by moving factories to China, or by hiring illegal immigrants to do the drudge work. It's a scene not unlike that found in many developed Western economies.

POPULATION & PEOPLE

The population of South Korea stands at 47 million, with an annual increase of 0.7% (one of the lowest rates of population growth in Asia). Population density is 483 people/sq km – in other words, it's crowded. However, the population is very unevenly distributed – over 70% live in urban areas, while some mountainous regions remain nearly pristine. About 25% of South Koreans live in Seoul, but the figure rises to 35% when you include its suburbs.

The Koreans are a nation of people with remarkably little cultural or racial variation. Modern Korean origins probably lie in the assimilation of local aboriginal tribes with newcomers of central Asian origin, who migrated into the peninsula from around 5000 to 1000 BC.

Korean creation myths suggest that the Koreans are of divine origin: life was brought forward by the creation and subsequent union of a heavenly king and a woman who started life as a bear. The bear became human by living on 20 cloves of garlic in a cave for 100 days. (The Korean obsession with the pungent garlic clove apparently started early.) The bear element in the myth is shared by Siberian creation myths, supporting the hypothesis of the central-Asian origins of the Koreans.

There are almost no ethnic minorities in Korea. There are perhaps 10,000 persons of Chinese origin, but even they have been largely assimilated.

EDUCATION

The *hangeul* phonetic alphabet, which replaced the mindboggling array of Chinese characters in the 15th century, was a boon to literacy in Korea. South Korea's literacy rate now stands at 97%. For most Koreans, 12 years of education is the norm (from age 6 through to 18).

Gaining entrance to a university is a formidable task and students are pushed, pulled and badgered for years by their parents to prepare for the much-feared entrance exams. Preparation begins at an early age, so getting into a good elementary school is important. One reason why virtually all Koreans want to live in Seoul is because the best schools are there.

Fortunately, this much-criticised system is being reformed; the new system emphasises student work and also includes teacher evaluations. This is a recent conversion and many kinks in the system still need to be ironed out.

ARTS
Dance

Traditional Korean folk dances take a wide variety of forms. The most popular ones include drum dances (*seungmu*), mask dances (*talchum*) and solo improvisational, or shamanistic dances (*salpuri*).

Of the three, the drum dances are by far the most exciting, and require a great deal of skill to execute. The dancers perform in brightly-coloured traditional clothing, twirling a very long tassel from a cap placed on their heads. Making it all the more difficult is the fact that the drums are not set on the ground, but are instead suspended from a cloth strap draped around the dancer's neck and shoulder. Tremendous coordination is required to dance, twirl and play the drums at the same time.

Music

Korean traditional music (*gugak*) places much emphasis on stringed instruments, most notably the *gayageum*. Other popular instruments include chimes, cymbals, drums, horns and flutes.

Since Goguryeo times the *geomun-go* (six-string zither) has been one of the principal instruments of Korean traditional music.

Traditional music can be further subdivided into two categories: court music (*jeongak*) and folk music (*minsogak*). Court music was the favourite of the upper crust, much as opera and classical orchestra was favoured by Europe's aristocrats. The melody tends to be slow and serious.

Folk music, or 'traditional pop music', was for the people. It is faster than court music, and more lively. In times past it was a favourite of farmers, and today is still played to accompany shamanistic rituals.

Rock'n'roll has pretty much come and gone, though old-timers (people over 30) still seem to like it. For the current 20-something crowd, techno and techno-rap are all the rage.

Literature

The monk Illyeon wrote *Samgukyusa* ('Myths & Legends of the Three Kingdoms') in the 12th century, which remains the most important work of early Korean literature. It's also a good read in English.

Beginning with the Joseon dynasty, Korean literature gets more interesting. There were many forms of poetry based on Chinese models (and still written in Chinese characters). The first real Korean novel, *The Legend of Mr Hong Gil-dong*, dates from this time.

The hangeul writing system (introduced in the 15th century) gave a major boost to Korean literature, though outside of courtly circles most of the nation remained illiterate until the late-19th century.

The Japanese takeover (1910 to 1945) had a huge impact on Korean literature. After the occupation ended, there was a sharp turn away from Chinese and Japanese influence of any kind. Conversely, Western influence, especially after the Korean War, increased dramatically.

The best known Korean novelist of the 20th century is Ahn Cheong-hyo. Ahn is notable because he writes the same novel in both Korean and English! Two famous ones are *Silver Stallion* (about the Korean War) and *White Badge* (about Koreans fighting in the Vietnam War). Both have been made into Korean movies.

The Shadow of Arms by Hwang Suk-young is a powerful novel that explores Korean culture as it is experienced by a young boy living in the Korean countryside.

The 1970s and '80s saw much dissident literature, popular with youth. The 1990s has seen a Taoist-style ecological consciousness literary movement. Cho Chong-nae's 10-volume novel *The Taebaek Mountains* covers the period from 1945 to 1955 and has been popular in this decade. It was also made into a movie.

Architecture

Examples of Korean traditional architecture are to be found in temples, shrines, palaces and gates. This style is characterised by massive wooden beams set on stone foundations, often built with notches instead of nails and thus easily dismantled and moved. Roofs are usually made from heavy clay tiles.

Seoul boasts the nation's best architecture, both traditional and modern. The best Joseon dynasty remains (see History, earlier) would have to be Korea's former seat

---

Ondol

Korea's architectural gift to the world is the unique underfloor heating system known as ondol. In winter, the entire floor is turned into a giant radiator. Traditionally, coal was burned in an oven under a clay floor. The problem with this was the danger of carbon monoxide poisoning if the floor developed any cracks. The introduction of concrete floors more or less solved the problem. Modern houses now use hot water pumped through pipes in the floor. The older style ondol is very rare now and there is little likelihood that you'll encounter the carbon monoxide problem. Not surprisingly, many Koreans (and foreigners too) abandon their bed for the floor during the winter months. There's nothing quite so cosy, nor quite so Korean, as sleeping on a hot floor in the dead of winter!

of power, the Gyeongbokgung. Of course, the great gates of the city, such as Namdaemun and Dongdaemun, are worth a mention. The Korean Folk Village in Suwon gives a good idea of what was traditional village architecture. The Japanese created some large and beautiful structures (ie, Seoul City Hall, Seoul Central Post Office, Seoul Station) which many Koreans want to tear down, because they are reminders of a colonial past.

Painting

Chinese influence is visible in traditional Korean paintings. The basic tools (brush and water-based ink) are those of calligraphy, which influenced painting in both technique and theory. The brush line, which varies in thickness and tone, is the important feature of Korean painting.

The first westerners to visit both China and Korea criticised the local watercolour painting, finding them flat and lacking in depth, shading and realism. The Koreans in turn were astonished by the oil paintings brought in from the West, which to them resembled mirror images. But in the end, they were rejected as art because they were devoid of expressive brushwork and imagination.

The function of traditional landscape painting was as a substitute for nature, the intent to allow the viewer to wander the painting imaginatively. The painting is meant to surround the viewer, and there is no 'viewing point' as there is in Western painting.

Of course times will change, and modern Korean artists study both traditional and Western techniques.

Sculpture

Examples of traditional sculpture are mainly stone Buddhist statues and pagodas. The best free-standing Buddha is Seokguram (see the Gyeongju section in the Kyeongsangbuk-do chapter).

Gyeongju also chips in with excellent Silla-period (see History, earlier) pagodas, such as the ones at Bulguksa. Silla pagodas are three storeys high, simple and elegant. Goryeo temples have a different style. Those from the Joseon dynasty are in a variety of styles, and comparatively ornate.

The best stone sculptures are at mountain temples and hermitages. Cast bronze was more common for Buddhas and bells in urban temples.

Shamanist wood carvings (used as spirit guardian posts in villages) are found all over. Some stone versions of spirit-guardians also exist. The 'grandfather stones' of Jejudo are a variation on the theme.

Confucianists didn't do sculpture – it was considered too 'Buddhist'.

Modern sculpture is burgeoning – the Seoul area is rich in newly-developed 'art sculpture parks', so be sure to visit Daehangno (University St) and Olympic Park. In Kyeonggi-do try the National Museum of Modern Art (in Seoul Grand Park) or the Hoam Art Museum inside Yong-in Everland. In Jejudo there's the Jeju Art Park.

Pottery

Archaeologists have unearthed bits and pieces of Korean pottery dating back 10,000 years. Glazing is a skill the Koreans seem to have learned from the Chinese between AD 200–600, but the Koreans soon made their own innovations. During the Goryeo dynasty (AD 918–1392), Korea turned out celadon pottery with a blue-green tinge, which was highly sought after by the Chinese.

The pottery business took a turn for the worse during the Mongol invasion of the 13th century, and the Koreans mostly produced *buncheong* ware – greyish pieces with simple folk designs. But now it was the turn of the Japanese to admire Korean pottery, and their lust for buncheong led to the Imjin War (sometimes called the 'Pottery War') – where whole families and villages of Korean potters were abducted and resettled in Japan to produce buncheong for their new masters. This is one more cause for Korean resentment towards the Japanese.

Perhaps the perfection of Korean pottery came during the Joseon period (1392–1910), when the country started turning out stunning white porcelain.

Cinema

After years of languishing in the doldrums, the Korean film industry is finally starting to make a splash. For years, the jaebeol (who have all the cash) were prohibited from financing film studios for fear of 'cultural hegemony'. Government forced cinemas to limit foreign films to 60% of the total shown, and directors were hobbled by censorship. The result was that the cinemas simply financed some very low-budget films just to meet the government's quota, while concentrating on making money from imported films.

Things have changed for the better. The quota system has been relaxed, though subsidies for Korean film makers still continue. The last few years have seen directors dealing with a whole range of topics, from serious social issues to light entertainment. The spy thriller *Swiri* became Korea's all-time top box office draw in 1999 (and opened at No 1 in Japan in February 2000). Also released in 1999 was the black comedy *Attack the Gas Station!* another very popular film with good export potential. Year 2000 brought another big hit, *Nanta* ('Wild Beating'), a fantastic musical where kitchen utensils are used as musical instruments.

Korea currently hosts three international film festivals a year. The largest is the Busan International Film Festival, usually held in October. There is also a 'Fantastic Film Festival' (www.pifan.com) held during July in the city of Bucheon, close to Incheon (less than one hour from Seoul). Another film festival is staged in Jeonju, in the province of Jeollabuk-do, during late April and early May.

Theatre

Performance art and modern theatre are areas in which Koreans excel, be it adaptations of Western drama or locally written and produced plays. Comedies – sometimes livened up with song and dance – seem to be particularly popular, and audience participation is occasionally encouraged.

Seoul has a large number of theatres, mostly concentrated in the area known as Daehangno (University St). If you go to Daehangno, it's easy enough to find out what's on, as posters pasted on ubiquitous noticeboards advertise the current offerings. Unfortunately, virtually no plays are performed in any language other than Korean.

Opera

Traditional operas take different forms. A style featuring a solo storyteller singing to the beat of a drum while telling a story (and sometimes waving a paper fan) is called *pansori*. Somewhat more similar to Western opera is *changgeuk*, which can involve a large cast of characters.

Calligraphy

The art of writing with brush pens and ink originated in China, but the Koreans have adopted this skill to suit their own needs. Calligraphy can be done in both traditional Chinese characters (*hanja*; see boxed text, later in this chapter) or in the Korean phonetic alphabet, hangeul.

SOCIETY & CONDUCT
Traditional Culture

Meeting the Koreans A short nod or bow is considered respectful when greeting somebody or when departing, but don't overdo it.

Korea is probably the most Confucian nation in Asia. At the heart of Confucian doctrine are the so-called Five Relationships. These prescribe behaviour between ruler and subject, father and son, husband and wife, old and young, and between friends. This structuring of relationships is very important in making sense of Korean society.

All relationships require a placement in some sort of hierarchy for one party to determine how to behave with respect towards the other. The middle-aged male office worker thrusting ahead of you to pay for a Coke at 7-Eleven does not even register your presence. You have not been introduced and he has nowhere to place you on the scale of relationships. An introduction and an exchange of business cards would immediately place you into a category that would demand certain behaviour from him.

Once contact has been established everything changes. Courtesy is highly valued.

Where Have All the Young Girls Gone?

By the early 21st century, many young Korean men won't be able to get married – at least not to Korean brides. A dire shortage of marriageable women is now looming over South Korea's social future. By the year 2010 it is estimated that there will be 128 single men at 'peak marriage age' (27 to 30 years old) for every 100 single women at peak eligibility (age 24 to 27). And those numbers get worse every year.

What's going wrong? Most young families these days want only two children, and one of each gender is seen as ideal. Two sons are acceptable but two daughters are not. Ultra-sound scans are used to discover the sex of a foetus, and if female she will often be aborted. It is illegal in South Korea for doctors to inform prospective parents of the sex of their foetus, but this has been widely ignored; the first arrest of a doctor for violating the law was in September 1996. Intriguingly, the busted doc was a woman.

So why don't Koreans want daughters? The answers mostly stem from the strong residual neo-Confucianism in their social mores. It remains all important that a man's family name be passed on to future generations. Only males can properly perform the ancestor worship ritual ceremonies that are still widely practiced. Economic security in the golden years is a further concern. Another factor in this is the expense of marrying a daughter off, which was traditionally minor but has grown exponentially since the Korean War.

That is expected to change radically. It may start costing a lot of money to marry your son to an attractive, well-educated Korean woman, presuming he can find one. Many other worrisome social trends now predicted by the Korean media include rises in involuntary bachelorhood, rapes, prostitution, kidnapping and harassment of young women and a sharp population drop (baby bust) in the next century.

Making the trend worse is the continuing gender imbalance of marriage to foreigners. Around three Korean-alien weddings are registered with the government every day; over 80% of them are Korean-woman foreign-male. No one has yet seriously proposed legally banning Korean girls from marrying non-Korean men, but it would be no surprise if a 'social movement' discouraging those unions suddenly materialised.

Theoretically, South Korea could 'import' young women from other countries. North Korea may prove to be a treasure-trove of eligible (and willing) girls, since genders seem to be in fair balance there, but it cannot be tapped under the current regime. Furthermore, most of Korea's north-east Asian neighbours such as Japan, China and Taiwan have similar problems of bride-shortage. The final factor against an import solution is that few non-Korean women can endure the behaviour typical of Korean men.

This points to what may be the biggest social change to come: Korean men may start treating 'their' women better than before. Look for gentlemanly behaviour to increase while physical, emotional and mental abuse declines, as South Korean men have to compete fiercely to gain and keep their brides. The social status of Korean women may make a historic leap forward!

Most Koreans will go out of their way to be pleasant and accommodating. And you should return the favour – be polite and smiling even when bargaining over prices.

You are likely to encounter peculiar kinds of strongly held opinions from Koreans. Examples might be that the hangeul script is the world's most perfect writing system, that

there are no homosexuals in Korea, that the Sea of Japan must be called the East Sea and that acid rain causes baldness. There is probably not much point arguing about these kinds of issues.

Social Hierarchy Korean relationships are much complicated by the social hierarchy

Persons with higher status may well act arrogant and demeaning towards persons with lower status. High status is governed by many factors – for example, who is the older of the two? Who has the more prestigious job? Who attended the better university or elementary school?

This notion of social status is one aspect of Korean culture that many foreigners (or those who prefer equality) find unpleasant. If you are working in Korea, your employer might make it all too clear that he or she is on the top of the social totem pole, and you are at the bottom. But for short-term tourists, this is seldom a problem – indeed, the Koreans are most anxious to make a good impression and therefore visitors are accorded considerable respect. But even this depends on which country you're from – people from rich countries have a higher position in the social hierarchy than those from the third world. The Koreans even have a grudging respect for the Japanese (whom they profess to loathe) because Japan is a wealthy country.

Geomancy Derived from the Chinese characters meaning 'wind and water', geomancy (*pungsu*) is the art of remaining in proper physical harmony with the universe. If a Korean person finds that their business is failing, a geomancer might be consulted.

Sometimes the solution will be to move the door of the business establishment, at other times the solution may be to relocate an ancestor's grave.

Korea's former and present rulers have all understood the importance of geomancy. When one empress died, 16 hours were spent arranging the feet of her corpse to get them into the auspicious position before the funeral could commence. The palaces and temples of Seoul have all been correctly arranged according to the laws of geomancy. When the Japanese came to conquer Korea, they deliberately constructed their Capitol building to obstruct the geomantic 'axis of power' on which the nation's fate was hinged.

In this day of modern high-rises and housing estates, most Koreans have had to push aside concerns about which direction their home or business is oriented toward. However, the position of an ancestor's grave is still taken very seriously.

The Zodiac The Korean zodiac (*sibijigan*) is the same as that used by the Chinese. As in the Western system of astrology, there are 12 signs. Unlike the Western system, your sign is based on which year, rather than which month, you were born; though the day and time of your birth are also carefully considered in charting your astrological path.

Korean Zodiac

Rat	1924	1936	1948	1960	1972	1984	1996
Ox/Cow	1925	1937	1949	1961	1973	1985	1997
Tiger	1926	1938	1950	1962	1974	1986	1998
Rabbit	1927	1939	1951	1963	1975	1987	1999
Dragon	1928	1940	1952	1964	1976	1988	2000
Snake	1929	1941	1953	1965	1977	1989	2001
Horse	1930	1942	1954	1966	1978	1990	2002
Goat	1931	1943	1955	1967	1979	1991	2003
Monkey	1932	1944	1956	1968	1980	1992	2004
Rooster	1933	1945	1957	1969	1981	1993	2005
Dog	1934	1946	1958	1970	1982	1994	2006
Pig	1935	1947	1959	1971	1983	1995	2007

An additional consideration: Korean babies are already one year old when they are born, and gain another year by the next lunar new year. So a Korean baby born in January may be two years old by February!

Fortune tellers are common in Korea. Making use of astrology, palm reading and face reading, fortune tellers claim they can accurately predict the future. If you are so inclined, you can try out this service, though you are almost certain to need an interpreter since few fortune tellers in Korea can speak English.

If you want to know your sign, or those of coming years, look up this chart. Bear in mind, though, that it's complicated by the fact that Korean astrology goes by the lunar calendar. The lunar new year usually falls in late January or early February.

It's said that the animal year chart originated when Buddha commanded all the beasts of the earth to assemble before him. Only 12 animals came and they were rewarded by having their names given to a specific year. Buddha also decided to name each year in the order in which the animals arrived – the first was the rat, then the ox, tiger, rabbit and so on.

Lunar Calendar Koreans use both the international Gregorian (solar) calendar and the lunar calendar, which was adopted from China.

Lunar dates do not correspond exactly with solar dates because a lunar month is slightly shorter than a solar month. The Koreans add an extra month every 30 months to the lunar calendar, essentially creating a lunar leap year. Thus, the lunar New Year can fall anywhere between 21 January and 28 February on the Gregorian calendar.

The Koreans believe that their race was born precisely in the year 2333 BC (see History, earlier). Therefore, the year 2000 is 4333 in the traditional calendar, and you'll find this date printed on Korean-made calendars even now.

Dos & Don'ts

Shoes Off In most people's homes, and at all yeogwan (a small family-run hotel),

never wear your shoes into the room. Take them off and leave them outside or place them on a sheet of paper so they don't touch the floor.

Losing Face The one thing to bear in mind is the Korean concept of *gibun*. Great efforts are made to smooth over potential problems, such as remarks that could lead to political disagreements. If you say something silly, there will be, at the most, an embarrassed laugh before someone steers the topic on to safer ground.

Arguments, or any situation that is going to lead to one party having to back down, will involve a loss of face, and this is a big no-no.

The concept of face extends to the nation as well. Patriotic Koreans (which basically means all Koreans) consider it vitally important that foreigners have a good impression of their country.

I came across two Korean men fighting in an alley and a few other Koreans were watching. But when the brawling duo saw me, the foreigner, they immediately stopped fighting. First there was embarrassed silence, then friendly smiles and I was escorted out of the alley. I was really tempted to sneak back to see if the fighting had resumed, but I didn't dare.

Marie Scott

Don't Blow It Blowing your nose in a public place is considered rude behaviour, which can be a real problem in restaurants after you've just eaten a plate full of spicy hot Korean food. The solution is to retreat to a public restroom or some other private place to carry out this vital function.

Unlucky Numbers When the Koreans borrowed the Chinese counting system, they also borrowed the 'unlucky' number four. It's unlucky because it also sounds just like the Korean word for death (*sa*) which was also borrowed from Chinese. If you have any Korean friends coming to visit you in your own country, you probably should not check them into a fourth floor hotel room. This will not be a problem in

Korea itself, because most hotels don't have a fourth floor and hospitals *never* do.

Body Language Beckoning someone is done with the palm down and fluttering fingers – avoid pointing or gesturing with one finger at somebody as this is considered impolite.

Polite Bow When greeting someone important, and saying goodbye or thanks, it's polite to bow. Just how far down you bow depends on the status of the person in question – you needn't get down on your hands and knees, but a slight nod of the head is generally appropriate. Ask a Korean person to instruct you how to perform this subtle gesture.

Deadly Chopsticks When not eating, never leave your chopsticks pointing down into the bowl. Always place them across the top of the bowl or on the table. To the Koreans, leaving chopsticks sticking vertically into the bowl looks like sticks of incense in a bowl of ashes – a clear death sign.

Red Ink Don't write a note in red ink. If you want to give someone your address or telephone number, write in any colour but red. Red ink conveys a message of unfriendliness.

Keep It Neat In Korea, you are judged by your appearance, more so than in the West. Travellers who dress like slobs will lose considerable face.

In general, Koreans are very fashion conscious – they dress very neatly, especially in trendy Seoul and Pusan (less so in the countryside). Shorts can be worn, but again the emphasis is on high-fashion shorts – most women wear pantyhose with shorts. Stylish high-tech 'sports sandals' are acceptable outdoor wear, but thongs and slippers are for indoor use only. Long hair and beards on men is rare, though these days young people dye their hair a variety of colours.

Embarrassed Smiles A driver almost runs over you, then stops and gives you a big grin. Foreigners often get enraged by this, but in fact the driver is not laughing at

Desperately Seeking Kim

There are only a few hundred surnames in Korea. However, over 20% of the population uses the surname 'Kim', and 15% 'Lee', though there are some variations in the romanised spellings. In traditional Confucian culture, it is considered incest to marry someone with the same surname (thus, the same clan), which certainly limits marriage prospects among Koreans! Some Koreans have ignored the law and have lived together for years (and even had children) despite a legal ban. A temporary law was passed in 1988 (and expired at the end of 1996) permitting these cohabiting couples to legalise their union. Of course, there is talk of repealing the law altogether that bans people of the same clan from marrying, but this legal change is bitterly opposed by the Confucianists (who seem to wield considerable political power).

The vast majority of Korean surnames are only one syllable in length, while the given name is usually (but not always) a two-syllable word separated by a hyphen in romanised form. Thus, a name like Kim Chung-hi would be typical. However, for the 'benefit of foreigners', some Koreans will reverse the order on their namecards so the preceding example becomes Chung-hi Kim. Just look for the hyphen to figure out which is the given name. However, most Koreans will insist that you call them by their family name until you get to know them very well, so it's just 'Kim' or 'Lee'. This means that if you stay in the country for any length of time, you will soon have dozens of friends with the same name – it's quite a drag when your roommate leaves a written message saying 'Kim called at 4 pm and wants you to call back'.

you – it's a sign of embarrassment, and a silent form of apology.

Treatment of Animals

For the most part, Koreans treat animals as well as westerners do. Unlike in many other Asian countries, you will almost never find half-starved, diseased dogs wandering the streets of Seoul. Nor is there any evidence that Korean farm animals are treated any worse than their Western counterparts.

The Korean government cracked down some time ago on the practice of eating endangered species – restaurants no longer dish up bear paws and tiger meat. However, some Koreans travelling abroad (especially in China) have been known to partake in an endangered-species barbecue.

Two creatures which do not get protection are the lowly octopus and the giant prawn. The problem isn't that the world faces an octopus or a shrimp shortage, it's that at least some Koreans like to eat these creatures before they're dead! The prawns squiggle, but live octopus tentacles make a meal that literally fights back. Diners need to be skilled with chopsticks to pry their squiggling delicacies off the plate, plus they need to chew fast to prevent the suckers from sticking to their teeth. While there can be no doubt about the freshness, this is a meal that might haunt you in your sleep.

Dogs are, blessedly, executed before being eaten. Like the Chinese, the Koreans believe that eating dog meat has various medicinal properties and is good for ones health. Unlike the Chinese (who eat dog in winter to ward off colds and flu), the Koreans eat dog in summer. It's believed that *bosintang* (dog soup) makes you hot (certainly true with all those spices) and many Koreans think that sweating is healthy.

Ever since the 1988 Olympic Games in Seoul, the Korean government has been sensitive to Western criticism about eating dog. Therefore, dog restaurants are no longer allowed to display signs in English, and are restricted to back-alley locations rather than main thoroughfares. Many Koreans do not admit to eating dog (in the presence of westerners at least) and profess

disdain at this practice. They will also respect the hell out of you if you do it. This is largely a male activity – Korean men consider it one way to demonstrate their macho prowess. However, before ordering a plate of Fido fricassee, bear in mind that dog meat is expensive. Figure W15,000 to W20,000 a bowl, though the portions are large. Like elsewhere in the world, you always pay a bundle for health food.

RELIGION

There are four broad streams of influence in the Korean spiritual and ethical outlook, they are: shamanism, which originated in central Asia; Buddhism, which entered Korea from China around the 4th century AD; Confucianism, a system of ethics of Chinese origin; and Christianity, which first made inroads into Korea in the 18th century.

Shamanism

Shamanism is not an organised religion. It has no temples, no body of scriptures or written texts, and has been subject to persecution since early in the Yi dynasty. Also, it is not exclusive to Korea. Nevertheless, it is an important part of Korean religious experience. Central to shamanism is the *mudang*, or shaman (almost always female), whose role is to serve as an intermediary between the living and the spirit worlds. The mediating is carried out through a *kut*, a ceremony that includes dance, song and even dramatic narrative.

Shamanist ceremonies are held for a variety of reasons: during minor illness; before setting out on a journey; during deep financial problems; to send a deceased family member safely into the spirit world; or it might be held by a village on a regular basis to ensure the safety and harmony of its members.

To a certain extent, shamanism has been stigmatised by modern education as a form of superstition, and about half of all Koreans nowadays profess to be religious sceptics. But shamanism continues to be an active cultural force, and official records claim that there are 40,000 registered mudang in South

Korea. Anthropologists maintain that the actual figure is perhaps closer to 100,000, as many mudang do not register.

Shamans are typically female and uneducated, and for this reason it is scorned most by educated urban males. Yet many Koreans continue to turn to mudang for solace and assistance.

Buddhism

The founder of Buddhism – Buddha (or one of the incarnations of Buddha) – was Siddhartha Gautama. He was born around 563 BC at Lumbini on the border of present-day Nepal and India. Born of a noble family, he questioned the comforts of his existence and for many years led the life of an ascetic. He was to turn his back on this life too. After a period of intense meditation, he achieved 'enlightenment', which is the essence of Buddhahood.

Buddhism has been greatly complicated by the fact that it has fractured into a vast number of schools of thought. Basically these can be divided into the Hinayana (Lesser Vehicle) and the Mahayana (Greater Vehicle) schools, the former emphasising personal enlightenment and the latter seeking the salvation of all beings. Nevertheless, at the heart of all Buddhism are the teachings of Gautama.

Buddhism in Korea belongs to the Mahayana school and, since its arrival, has split into a great number of smaller schools of thought, the most famous of which is *Seon*, better known to the outside world by its Japanese name Zen.

There are 18 Buddhist sects in Korea, but the largest by far is the Jogye sect, with its temple headquarters in Seoul's Jogyesa. It is an amalgamation of two Korean schools of Buddhism: the Seon sect, which relies on meditation and the contemplation of paradoxes, among other things, to achieve sudden enlightenment; and the Gyo school, which relies more heavily on extensive scriptural study. The major temples of the Jogye sect are located as follows (by province):

Seoul Jogyesa, Hwagyesa, Bong-eunsa, Doseonsa
Chungcheongbuk-do Deokjusa, Gosansa, Mireuksaji, Beopjusa, Dodeoksa

Chungcheongnam-do Gapsa, Gwanchoksa, Magoksa, Sinwonsa, Sudeoksa, Donghaksa
Jeju-do Gimnyeongsa, Gwaneumsa
Jeollabuk-do Anguksa, Geumsansa, Mireuksaji, Naejangsa, Naesosa, Silsangsa, Songgwangsa, Seonunsa, Tapsa (Unsusa)
Jeollanam-do Jeungsimsa, Hwaeomsa, Mihwangsa, Baegyangsa, Seonamsa, Songgwangsa, Daeamsa, Daeheungsa, Unjusa
Gangwon-do Cheongpyeongsa, Gukhyangsa, Guryongsa, Naksansa, Beopeungsa, Sangwonsa, Sinheungsa, Sutasa, Woljeongsa
Gyeonggi-do Jeondeungsa, Bongseonsa, Sileuksa, Yongjusa
Gyeongsangbuk-do Jikjisa, Huibangsa, Heungyeongsa, Gounsa, Mt Namsan (five temples), Baekryeonsa, Bulguksa, Bunhwangsa, Buseoksa, Sinseonsa, Donghwasa, Eunhaesa, Unmunsa
Gyeongsangnam-do Haeinsa, Guwolsa, Beomeosa, Pyochungsa, Seoknamsa, Ssanggyesa, Tongdosa

The Jogye sect represents around 90% of Korean Buddhists. Next in size is the Taego sect, representing about 7% of the total. The Taego sect distinguishes itself by permitting its monks to marry. The Japanese installed this system of married monks during their occupation of Korea. Headquarters for the Taego sect is in Seoul, at Bongwonsa, a magnificent temple close to Ehwa Women's University.

Buddhism, a remarkably adaptable faith, has coexisted closely with shamanism in Korea. Almost all Buddhist temples have a *samseonggak* ('three spirit hall') on their grounds, which house shamanist deities. Buddhist priests also often carry out activities associated with shamanism, such as fortune telling and the sale of good-luck charms.

Buddhism suffered a sharp decline after WWII. Part of the reason had to do with the Japanese colonisation of Korea – Buddhist monks were coerced to support unity with Japan. Those monks who proved uncooperative simply disappeared. Furthermore, as South Korea's postwar economic boom got underway, Buddhism seemed to have little to offer – Koreans were not about to cast off their pursuit of worldly desires to become a nation of fasting monks and nuns.

Ironically, South Korea's success in acheiving developed-nation status may have also caused a revival of Buddhism. Western-isation has gone so far in South Korea that the country is suffering from an identity cri-sis – the last thing Koreans want to be called is Westernised Asians. As national pride re-asserts itself, more and more South Koreans are seeking their cultural roots, including Buddhism. Pilgrimages to temples have in-creased, and a huge amount of money is flowing into temple reconstruction. It is es-timated that approximately 25% of South Koreans are now Buddhists, about equal to the number of practising Christians.

Maps produced in Korea mark temple sites with what appears to be a swastika. You will also see this symbol on the temples themselves.

If you look closely, you'll see it's actually the reverse image of a swastika. This is, in fact, an ancient Buddhist religious symbol.

Confucianism

Confucianism, properly speaking, is a sys-tem of ethics rather than a religion. Confu-cius (555–479 BC) lived in China during a time of great chaos and feudal rivalry known as the Warring States Period. He emphasised devotion to parents and family, loyalty to friends, justice, peace, education, reform, and humanitarianism. He also emphasised respect and deference to those in positions of authority, a philosophy later heavily ex-ploited by emperors and warlords. However, not everything said by Confucius has been universally praised – it seems he firmly be-lieved that men are superior to women.

Confucius' philosophy was misused to justify China's overweening bureaucracy, a problem which exists to this day. On the other hand, his ideas led to the system of civil service and university entrance exami-nations, where one gained position through ability and merit, rather than from noble birth and connections. Confucius preached against corruption, war, torture and excessive taxa-tion. He was the first teacher to open his school to all students on the basis of their willingness to learn rather than their noble birth and ability to pay for tuition.

As Confucianism trickled into Korea, it evolved. Religious evolution produced Neo-Confucianism, which combined the sage's original ethical and political ideas with a quasi-religious practice of ancestor worship and the idea of the eldest male as spiritual head of the family.

Confucianism was viewed as being en-lightened and radical when it first gained popularity. However, over the years it has become paternalistic and conservative. In fact, many younger Koreans regard Confu-cianism as something of an embarrassment, which explains why so many have defected to Christianity. Yet Confucianism lives on as a kind of ethical bedrock (at least sub-consciously) in the minds of most Koreans.

Christianity

Korea's first exposure to Christianity was via the Jesuits from the Chinese imperial court of the late-18th century. A Korean aristocrat was baptised in Beijing in 1784. When it was introduced to Korea, the Catholic faith took hold and spread quickly; so quickly, in fact, that it was per-ceived as a threat by the royal family and vigorously suppressed, creating Korea's first Christian martyrs.

Christianity got a second chance in the 1880s, with the arrival of American Protes-tant missionaries. The founding of schools and hospitals won them many followers.

Nowhere else in Asia, with the exception of the Philippines, have the efforts of pros-elytising missionaries been so successful. About 25% of all Koreans are Christian.

Church Services For those people who wish to attend English-language church services while in Korea, there is a listing every week in the Saturday edition of the *Korea Times*.

LANGUAGE

The language of Korea is Korean – there are no minority languages of any significance.

See the language chapter at the back of this book for details.

Hanja

Around 70% of all Korean dictionary entries are of Chinese origin, although the roots of the two languages are unrelated. The loaned words from Chinese are apparent to anyone who has studied both languages. For example, 'mountain' is *shan* in Chinese and *san* in Korean; 'south' is *nan* in Chinese and *nam* in Korean. Before the invention of the hangeul alphabet, Korean was written exclusively in Chinese characters known as *hanja*.

In 1970, President Park Chung-hee banned hanja because hangeul was so much easier to learn and was seen as the key to increasing literacy. Furthermore, the hangeul alphabet is Korea's own invention, while Chinese characters are an exotic import and thus an insult to national pride. The Koreans were further put off hanja by the fact that the Japanese (who also use Chinese characters) tried to force Korea to abandon hangeul and adopt hanja during the Japanese occupation.

The South Koreans had a sudden change of heart in 1975. Hanja was restored to high school textbooks, but placed in parentheses after the hangeul words. The Ministry of Education drew up an official list of 1800 hanja characters which Korean students had to learn. Korean dictionaries identify 4888 characters, but very few Koreans know even half of these. Ironically, the ban on hanja remains in elementary schools, though it is not enforced and private elementary schools often teach hanja.

Interest in learning Chinese characters was given a big boost in 1993 when Korea established diplomatic relations with China. Unfortunately, the issue has been complicated by the fact that communist China simplified 2238 characters in the 1950s, thus making them look very different from hanja (which is based on traditional Chinese). However, the traditional characters are used in Hong Kong and Taiwan, and now there is a serious movement afoot in mainland China to return the characters to their original complex form.

Nowadays, very few South Koreans could be described as being functionally literate in hanja. In Korea, Chinese characters are usually restricted to maps, limited use in newspapers, restaurant signs and occasionally for writing names (as in name cards).

From its founding, North Korea banned the use of Chinese characters. However, this was rescinded in 1964. Officially, North Korean students are expected to learn around 2000 Chinese characters, though it's questionable how many of them really do. Certainly the shortage of reading material in the North would mean that few have the opportunity to practise hanja.

Facts for the Visitor

HIGHLIGHTS

The royal palaces and museums of Seoul will give you an excellent introduction to Korea's complex culture and history. Gyeongju, in south-east Korea, has an overwhelming collection of historical sights. The Korean Folk Village at Suwon is a tasteful re-creation of Korea's traditional culture.

Outstanding mountainous beauty spots include the national parks at Seoraksan, Bukhansan and Naejangsan. Temple enthusiasts should visit Songnisan and Gayasan national parks. Spectacularly beautiful islands include Jejudo, Ulleungdo and the hundreds of islands that make up Dadohae Haesang National Park.

SUGGESTED ITINERARIES

A traveller devoting just one week to South Korea will probably only have time for a few days in the Seoul area and a mad-dash excursion (perhaps down to Gyeongju).

With two weeks, you could easily include a stop-off at one of the national parks on the way to Gyeongju, plus an excursion down to Jejudo.

With three weeks, you'll have time to explore several national parks. Some of the best include Bukhansan, Seoraksan, Jirisan and Songnisan.

With one month to travel in Korea, you can do all of the above plus make some excursions to outlying islands (such as Ulleungdo and the islands of Dadohae Haesang National Park). If the weather is cool, consider checking out the hot springs resorts. During winter, add skiing to your agenda. A day trip to Panmunjeom, the 'truce village' on the North Korea border, is another worthwhile trip.

A two-month journey could encompass nearly all the important tourist sites mentioned in this book. With 20 beautiful national parks and 19 provincial parks, numerous temples and museums, there is plenty to keep you busy.

PLANNING
When to Go

The best time of year for a visit is autumn, from September through November. The weather is fine and the forests are riotously colourful and at their best in late October and early November. Winter is dry and cold, but some travellers enjoy the snow. April and May is a beautiful time, with mild temperatures and flowers blooming everywhere. Summer is not a particularly good time to be in Korea. While it's the only time for the beach, you will have to deal with hot and muggy weather plus jumbo crowds of people in all scenic areas. This is also the wet season, during which Korea gets some 70% of its annual rainfall.

Maps

The various tourist offices have a number of free maps, and these are certainly worth picking up. Definitely do this in Seoul because these maps are not readily available elsewhere.

Big tourist hotels also have giveaway maps – just look in the brochure stand in the hotel lobby.

Korea's largest retail outlet for topographic maps is Jung-ang Atlas Map Service in Seoul (☎ 02-730 9191). If you are planning on doing any serious hiking this is certainly the place to stock up.

Excellent road atlases are available from large bookshops in Seoul and elsewhere. Look for one which uses *hangeul* (Korean phonetic alphabet) script exclusively – a few use Chinese characters intermittently.

Most tourist information desks in city halls have free, quite detailed maps, however, most are in Korean though some are in English. Seoul City Hall has maps available in both English and Korean.

The Koreans have a hard time dealing with their nation's division. Consequently, very few maps produced in Korea (both North and South) show the heavily fortified DMZ (Demilitarized Zone). The idea is to maintain the illusion that Korea is an undivided nation. Unaware of Korea's politics, a few travellers have been misled by the maps to such an extent that they thought they could travel north all the way to China!

What to Bring

In most cases, anything you forget to bring along can be purchased inexpensively in Korea. Two things that are difficult to find are deodorant and tampons (*tempo*). The Lotte Hotel pharmacy in Seoul is one possible source. Otherwise, you may have to explore the black market near US military bases (local expats can guide you to the exact locations). Black market items are expensive, but sometimes they are your only option.

RESPONSIBLE TOURISM

You'll make life easier for those who come after you if you try to be an ambassador of goodwill (see the Society & Conduct section in the Facts about Korea chapter).

TOURIST OFFICES
Local Tourist Offices

The Korean National Tourism Office (KNTO) deserves a plug for being one of the most helpful and best organised tourist offices in Asia, if not the world. KNTO produces an extensive range of well-illustrated booklets and maps, some of which you can pick up at Korea's three international airports (Seoul's Gimpo, and Busan and Jejudo). KNTO has an excellent information centre in Seoul – see the Seoul chapter for details. You can ring their main office in Seoul (☎ 02-757 0086) or write to them at KPO Box 1879, Seoul 110-618.

Almost every city has a tourist information office located in the city hall, which exists to assist visitors. In Seoul, this office is well equipped with maps and staffed with English speakers, but in more remote parts of the Korea, the staff will be non-English speakers and have scant literature to offer you. In every large city, you should be able to call the tourist information help line (☎ 1330). If this number doesn't work for the city you are in, there is a nationwide toll-free number (☎ 080-757 2000).

In some large cities, there are also tourist information booths with English-speaking staff located in crucial spots such as tourist sites and some railway or bus stations.

KNTO Tourist Offices Abroad

Australia
(☎ 02-9252 4147, **e** knto@yesnet.com.au) 17th floor, Tower Bldg, Australia Square, George St, Sydney, NSW 2000
Canada
(☎ 416-348 9056, **e** knto.tt@sympatico.ca) Suite 1903, 700 Bay St, Toronto, Ontario M5G 1Z6
China
(☎ 10-6526 0837, **e** bjknto@a-1.net.cn) room 408–410 B Tower, COFCO Plaza No 8, Jianguomen Neidajie, Beijing
France
(☎ 01 45 38 71 23, **e** knto@club-internet.fr) Tour Maine Montparnesse, 33 Avenue du Maine, Paris
Germany
(☎ 069-233 226, **e** kntoff@euko.de) Baseler Strasse 48, 60329 Frankfurt
Hong Kong
(☎ 2523 8065, **e** kntohk@netvigator.com) suite 3203, 42nd floor, Tower I, Lippo Centre, 89 Queensway, Admiralty
Japan
Tokyo (☎ 03-3597 1717, **e** tokyo@knto.or.jp) Room 124, Sanshin Bldg, 4-1-1, Yuraku-cho, Chiyoda-ku, 100
Fukuoka (☎ 092-471-7174, fax 474-8015) 6th floor, Assahi Bldg, 1-1, 2-chome, Hakata-ekimae, Hakata-ku
Osaka (☎ 06-6266-0847, fax 6266-0803) 8th floor, KAL Bldg., 1-9, 3-chome, Hon-machi, Chuo-ku
Sendai (☎ 022-711-5991, fax 711-5993) 1st floor, Nihonseimei-Sendaikotodai-Minami Bldg, 1-5-15 Kamisugi, Aoba-ku
Nagoya (☎ 052-933-6550, fax 933-9553) 2nd floor, Toyopet-Nissei Bldg, 13-30 Higashisakura, Higashi-ku
Singapore
(☎ 533 0441, fax 534 3427, **e** kntosp@ singnet.com.sg) 20-01 Clifford Centre, 24 Raffles Place 7, Singapore 048621
Taiwan
(☎ 02-2720 8049, **e** kntotp@ms5.hinet.net) Room 2005, International Trade Centre, 333 Keelung Rd, Section 1, Taipei
Thailand
(☎ 02-231 3895, **e** kntobk@asiaaccess.net.th) 15th floor, Silom Complex Bldg, 191 Silom Rd, Bangkok 10500

UK
(☎ 020-7321 2535, e koreatb@dircon.co.uk)
3rd floor, New Zealand House, Haymarket,
London SW1Y 4TE
USA
California (☎ 213-382 3435) Suite 1110, 3435
Wilshire Blvd, Los Angeles, CA 90010
Illinois (☎ 312-981 1717), Suite 910, 737
North Michigan Ave, Chicago, IL 60601
New Jersey (☎ 201-585 0909), Suite 100, 1
Executive Drive, Fort Lee, NJ 07024

VISAS & DOCUMENTS
Passport
A passport is essential, and if yours is
within a few months of expiration, get a
new one now – Korea and many other countries will not issue a visa if your passport
has less than six months of validity remaining. Also, be sure it has plenty of space for
visas and entry and exit stamps – you can
have extra pages added at your country's
embassy.

Losing your passport is very bad news –
getting a new one means a trip to your embassy and much paperwork. This matter
will be expedited considerably if you have
an old, expired passport. Alternatively, an
original birth certificate plus picture ID
should do. If you have none of the above,
expect to wait several weeks while the embassy staff confirms that you exist. If you're
going to be in Korea for a long period of
time, it's wise to register your passport at
your country's embassy in Seoul, in case
you ever need a replacement.

Visas
Transit Visa With an onward ticket, visi-
tors from almost anywhere will be granted
a transit stay of up to 30 days without a visa.
Countries which don't qualify include
Cuba, China, the Philippines, Mongolia,
Nepal, India, Iran, Sri Lanka, Vietnam,
Laos, Cambodia, Nigeria, Ghana, Albania,
Macedonia and the 12 CIS republics. How-
ever, even nationalities on this list will be
granted a 30-day stay if they have already
been issued with a visa to the USA, Canada,
Australia, New Zealand or Japan.

The 30-day stay is not extendible and
there are steep fines for overstaying the visa.

Visa Exemptions South Korea has reciprocal visa-exemption agreements with numerous countries. There are visa exemptions
for nationals of all West European nations.
If you fall into this category you'll be given
a 90-day permit, or 60 days in the cases of
Italy and Portugal. New Zealanders, Israelis,
Singaporeans, Thais and Mexicans also
qualify for the 90-day deal.

Tourist & Business Visas Nationals of all
other countries – including Australia, the
USA and Canada – require visas for stays
over 30 days. If your nationality does not
qualify you for a visa exemption and you
need more than 30 days, apply for a visa before you go to South Korea.

South Korean embassies and consulates
are notoriously fickle. Many of them require that your visa photos be oddball sizes
(6x6cm, for example). And they can be
slow in issuing visas – allow at least three
working days no matter what they tell you.
On the other hand, some of the consulates
will accept standard 3x5cm passport photos
and issue the visa the same day you apply.

Visas are usually issued for a stay of 90
days. Onward tickets and/or proof of 'adequate funds' are not normally required. If you
apply for a visa in your own country, you
might get a multiple-entry visa – you usually
cannot get this if you apply at a South Korean
embassy in a nearby Asian country.

If you're coming to South Korea on business, then say so on the application. Most
countries do not care if you do business on
a tourist visa, but the South Koreans do.
The immigration authorities seem to enjoy
imposing stiff fines on individuals who 'violate' the terms of their visa.

Work Visas Applications can be made inside the country and are processed in as little as one week, but you must exit the
country to pick up the visa (the legislature is
considering a proposal to allow you to complete the process without leaving the country). You can also apply for a work visa
before entering Korea, though in this case it
may take two to four weeks for the visa to be
issued. You do not need to exit the country

to renew your work visa provided that you continue working for the same employer.

Your contract has to be turned in to the Korean authorities by your prospective employer. The employer does all the bureaucratic processing, then just mails you a visa-confirmation paper. The contract is unsigned by you, the employee, at that point (and there might be a penalty if it was!). After getting the visa and entering Korea, you sign the contract and take it with your passport to the immigration office to get a residence permit. There are penalties for starting to work *before* getting the visa, or if the starting date on the contract is prior to your visa-commencement date.

Working visas are valid for one year and are extendible for at least a further year.

Visa Extensions As a general rule, tourist visas cannot be extended. About the only exceptions are for emergencies, such as accidents or illness, cancelled flights, or loss of a passport. You are supposed to apply for this extension at the local immigration office at least one day before the visa expires. Overstaying your visa can result in a stiff fine.

Resident Certificate If you are working or studying in South Korea on a long-term visa it is necessary to apply for an alien registration certificate within 90 days of arrival. This must be done at the immigration office of your province of residence, which is not necessarily the closest immigration office to where you live.

Re-Entry Visas If you don't want to forfeit your working visa, you should apply for a multiple re-entry visa before making any trips out of the country. This must be done at the immigration office of whichever province you happen to be living in. The fee is W50,000 for multiple entry, W30,000 for single entry. Serious proposals have been floated to eliminate re-entry visas, but it hasn't happened yet.

Travel Insurance

Whatever insurance you have at home is probably not valid in Korea. There are vari-

ous types of travel insurance policies. Some will cover losses due to theft, accident, illness and death (at least your relatives benefit).

Travel insurance is something you should arrange before you venture abroad. You can, of course, purchase an insurance policy after arrival in Korea, though finding a policy written in English may be tricky. Rates vary, so shop around. Travel agents and insurance sales people should be able to give you the inside scoop on these policies. The international student travel policies handled by various student travel organisations are usually good value. Carefully read over any policy before you sign on the dotted line, and check the small print.

Some policies specifically exclude 'dangerous activities', which can include scuba diving, motorcycling, even trekking. If such activities are on your agenda you don't want that sort of policy. A policy might even specify that you need a licence for a certain activity (such as driving a motorcycle) and a locally acquired motor cycle licence may not be valid under your policy!

You may prefer a policy which pays doctors or hospitals directly, rather than you having to pay on the spot and claim later. If you have to claim later make sure you keep all documentation. Some policies ask you to call back (reverse charges) to a centre in your home country, where an immediate assessment of your problem is made.

Check if the policy covers ambulances or an emergency flight home. If you have to stretch out you will need two seats – and somebody has to pay for them!

Driving Licence & Permits

Driving Licence To drive in Korea, you must be at least 21 years old, have 12 months driving experience, have a passport and an international driving permit. A national licence from your own country is not acceptable.

Short-term visitors can use an international driving licence, but if you stay over three months, you're expected to obtain a Korean licence. If you already have a driving licence from your home country, you can exchange it for a Korean licence. This saves you from taking the written exam (in Korean!) and the driving test. The procedure for doing this follows.

You will need your passport, alien registration certificate, driving licence and three 3x4cm photos. If you are *not* from the USA, Canada, UK, France, Germany or Japan, you will also need a certificate from your embassy (with Korean translation) stating that you are licensed to drive in your home country.

Bring cash for fees and some change (needed for making photocopies). You must take a physical examination, including an eye test.

If you are from one of the lucky countries mentioned above, you should be able to pick up your new Korean licence one week later. If you are not from one of these favoured countries, you might have to wait three months or more while the Koreans check to make sure that you really are licensed to drive at home! (In that case, it might just be quicker to learn Korean and take the Korean driving test.)

International Driving Permit If you plan to be driving abroad, get an International Driving Permit. These *cannot* be issued in Korea unless you've first obtained a Korean licence – in other words, get it before you leave home.

In some countries these permits are issued by the local motor vehicle department but in other places you have to get it from your local automobile association. The validity varies from country to country – in some places you only get one year, while other countries will give you three years. If you can only get a one-year permit, then obviously there's no sense getting one far in advance of departure.

Make sure that your permit states that it is valid for motorcycles if you plan to drive one.

Vehicle Documents If you intend to drive, bring copies (or preferably originals) of your vehicle insurance documents from your home country. Being able to prove that you have a good insurance history will net a substantial discount (over 50%) when you purchase liability insurance in Korea.

Hostel Card

An International Youth Hostel (IYH) card can be of some limited use in South Korea, and considerably more use in nearby Japan. However, the vast majority of travellers will not need one in Korea because they will be staying in private hotels or guesthouses. (For information on Korea's hostels, see the Accommodation section later in this chapter.)

Student Cards

Full-time students can often get some good discounts on tickets with the help of an International Student Identity Card (ISIC). This card entitles the holder to a number of discounts on air fares, train fares, museums etc. To get this card, inquire at your campus. These can also be issued in Korea at the Korean International Student Exchange Society (KISES; ☎ 02-733 9494), Room 505, YMCA Bldg, Jongno 2-ga (next to Jonggak subway station) in Seoul. A student ID card or a university letter of acceptance is required.

Student Travel Australia (STA) issues STA Youth Cards to persons aged 13 to 26 years.

Educational Qualifications

If you are going to teach in Korea, the Korean government wants to see *originals* (not copies) of your diploma, transcripts and other teaching credentials.

Vaccination Certificate

Useful (though not essential) is an International Health Certificate to record any vaccinations you've had. These are normally issued by hospitals, vaccination clinics or public health departments. They can also be issued in Korea.

Photos

A collection of small photos (3x5cm, *not* 3x5 inches!) for visas will be useful if you're planning on visiting several countries, but will also come in handy if you apply for work. Of course, these can be obtained in Korea and most other countries, but you'll save yourself some time by having a few in reserve (10 should be sufficient). Visa photos must have a neutral background, so forget about using snapshots from your last birthday party.

Copies

Important documents (passport data page and visa page, credit cards, travel insurance policy, tickets, driving licence etc) should be photocopied before you leave. Leave a copy with someone at home and keep another with you, separate from the originals.

Useful things to photocopy include your passport (data pages only), credit cards, airline tickets, educational and employment qualifications and driving licence. If you're travelling with your spouse, a copy of your marriage certificate could come in handy.

Keep a list of your travellers cheques serial numbers separate from the cheques themselves and, while you're at it, throw in an emergency stash of about US$200.

Travellers can also take advantage of Lonely Planet's free online Travel Vault. Your password-protected Travel Vault is accessible online anywhere in the world – create it at www.ekno.lonelyplanet.com.

EMBASSIES & CONSULATES
South Korean Embassies

South Korean embassies abroad include:

Australia (☎ 06-273 3044) 113 Empire Circuit, Yarralumla, ACT 2600

Austria (☎ 01-478 1991) Gregor-Mendel Strasse 25, A-1180, Vienna

Belgium (☎ 02-375 3980) Avenue Hamoir 3, 1180 Bruxelles

Canada (☎ 613-244 5010) 150 Boteler St, Ottawa, Ontario K1N 5A6

China (☎ 10-6532 0290) No 3, 4th Ave East, Sanlitun, Chaoyang District, Beijing 100600

Denmark (☎ 3946 0400) Svanemollevej 104, 2900 Hellerup

France (☎ 01 47 53 01 01) 125 Rue de Grenelle, 75007 Paris

Germany (☎ 30-260 650) Schoeneberger Ufer 89–91, 10785, Berlin

Hong Kong (☎ 2529 4141) 5th floor, Far East Finance Centre, 16 Harcourt Rd, Central

Ireland (☎ 01-608 800) 20 Clyde Rd, Ballsbridge, Dublin 4

Israel (☎ 03-527 0185) Room 471–3, Dan Hotel, 99 Hayarkon St, Tel Aviv, 63903

Italy (☎ 06-808 8769) Via Barnaba Oriani, 30, 00197, Rome

Japan (☎ 03-3452 7611) 1-2-5 Minami-Azabu, 1-chome, Minato-ku, Tokyo 106

Netherlands (☎ 070-358 6076) Verlengde Tolweg 8, 2517 JV, The Hague

New Zealand (☎ 04-473 9073) 11th floor, ASB Bank Tower Bldg, 2 Hunter St, Wellington

Norway (☎ 2255 2018) Inkognitogaten 3, 0224, Oslo 2

Philippines (☎ 2-811 6139) 10th floor, The Pacific Star, Makati Ave, Makati, Metro Manila

Russia (☎ 095-956 1474) Ul Spiridonobka Dom 14, Moscow

Singapore (☎ 256 1188) 101 Thomson Rd, United Square, 10-03, Singapore 307591

Your Own Embassy

It's important to realise what your own embassy – the embassy of the country of which you are a citizen – can and can't do to help you if you get into trouble. Generally speaking, it won't be much help in emergencies if the trouble you're in is remotely your own fault. Remember that you are bound by the laws of the country you are in. Your embassy will not be sympathetic if you end up in jail after committing a crime locally, even if such actions are legal in your own country.

In genuine emergencies you might get some assistance, but only if other channels have been exhausted. For example, if you need to get home urgently, a free ticket home is exceedingly unlikely – the embassy would expect you to have insurance. If you have all your money and documents stolen, it might assist with getting a new passport, but a loan for onward travel is out of the question.

Some embassies used to keep letters for travellers or have a small reading room with home newspapers, but these days the mail holding service has usually been stopped and even newspapers tend to be out of date.

Sweden (☎ 08-660 0330) Laboratoriegatan 10, 115 27, Stockholm

Switzerland (☎ 031-351 1081) Kacheggweg 38, 3000 Bern 15

Taiwan (Visa Office; ☎ 02-2758 8320) Korea Trade Centre, room 2214, 333 Keelung Rd, Section 1

Thailand (☎ 02-247 7537) 23 Thirmruammit Rd, Ratchadpisek, Huay Kwang, Bangkok 10320

UK (☎ 020-7227 5500) 60 Buckingham Gate, London SW1E 6AJ

USA (☎ 202-939 5600) 2450 Massachusetts Ave NW, Washington DC 20008

Embassies in South Korea

About 75% of Seoul's foreign embassies are in an area south-east of Itaewon known as 'UN Village'. However, some of the most visited embassies (Canada, the USA, Australia, New Zealand, the UK, Japan, China etc) are in central Seoul.

Some useful embassies include:

Australia (☎ 730 6490) 11th floor, Kyobo bldg, 1-1 Jongno1-ga, Jongno-gu

Canada (☎ 3455 6000) 10th floor, Kolon bldg, 45 Mugyo-dong, Jung-gu

China (☎ 319 5101) 83 Myeong-dong 2-ga, Jung-gu

France (☎ 312 3272) 30 Hap-dong, Seodae-mun-gu

Germany (☎ 748 4114) 308-5, Dongbinggo-dong, Yongsan-gu

Ireland (☎ 774 6455) Daehan Fire & Marine Insurance bldg, 51-1 Namchang-dong, Jung-gu

Israel (☎ 564 3448) 823-21 Yeoksam-dong, Gangnam-gu

Italy (☎ 796 0491) 1-398 Hannam-dong, Yongsan-gu

Japan (☎ 733 5626) 18-11 Junghak-dong, Jongno-gu

Netherlands (☎ 737 9514) 14th floor, Kyobo bldg, Jongno1-ga, Jongno-gu

New Zealand (☎ 730 7794) 18th floor, Kyobo bldg, Jongno1-ga, Jongno-gu

Philippines (☎ 577 6147) 9th floor, Diplomatic Centre, 1376-1, Seocho 2-dong, Seocho-gu

Russia (☎ 552 7096) 1001-13 Daechi-dong, Gangnam-gu

Singapore (☎ 774 2464) 19th floor, Samsung Taepyeongno bldg, 310 Taepyeongno 2-ga, Jung-gu

Taiwan (Visa Office; ☎ 399 2767) 6th floor, Gwanghwamun Bldg

UK (☎ 735 7341) 4 Jeong-dong, Jung-gu

USA (☎ 397 4114)82 Sejongno, Jongno-g

CUSTOMS

Korean customs officials are generally easygoing, though officially you should declare any goods you acquired outside Korea that have a total value exceeding US$400.

More seriously, it is required that you declare amounts of over US$10,000, and this *includes* travellers cheques. By not doing so you could risk having the balance confiscated when you try to leave with it. Upon departure, travellers are *often* asked how much money they are taking out – if you declare a figure over US$10,000 you will have some explaining to do.

There is a duty-free allowance of 200 cigarettes (or 50 cigars or 250g of tobacco), two ounces (59mLs) of perfume and one bottle of spirits (not exceeding one litre).

For those leaving the country with antiques (even fake antiques) purchased in South Korea, take note of the Cultural Properties Preservation Law. The law forbids the export of items deemed as 'important cultural properties'. If you've bought something which you think might qualify, save the receipt and contact a Cultural Properties Appraisal Office at Gimpo airport (☎ 02-662 0106), Gimhae airport (☎ 051-973 1972), Busan boat terminal (☎ 051-441 7265), Jejudo airport (☎ 064-742 4276) or Incheon boat terminal (☎ 032-885 4420).

Needless to say, customs will not be amused if you try to import explosives, guns or narcotics. While most budget travellers leave their dynamite and AK-47s at home, more than a few foreigners have run into trouble with drugs. Unless you wish to research living conditions inside Korean prisons, it would be wise to leave any recreational chemicals at home.

MONEY
Currency

The South Korean unit of currency is the *won* (W), with coins of W1, W5, W10, W50, W100 and W500. The W1 and W5 coins are rarely seen outside of banks, and if it should get your hands on one you'll have a hard time spending it. Notes come in denominations of W1000, W5000 and W10,000.

Exchange Rates

At the time of going to print, exchange rates for Korean won were as follows:

country	unit		won (W)
Australia	A$1	=	597
Canada	C$1	=	742
China	RMB1	=	138
Euro	€1	=	980
France	FF10	=	1495
Germany	DM10	=	5014
Hong Kong	HK$1	=	146
Japan	¥100	=	1053
New Zealand	NZ$1	=	453
Taiwan	NT$1	=	35
UK	UK£1	=	1944
USA	US$1	=	1338

Exchanging Money

Large cities are thick with banks offering foreign exchange services, and in smaller cities there should be at least one bank which can do this. There are also a small but growing number of licensed moneychangers which keep longer hours than banks. Hotels can also change money during weekends and holidays, though at a poorer exchange rate. In the outlying islands (except Jejudo) there are no reliable places to change money. Foreign exchange services are also offered at South Korea's three international airports. There is typically a 1½% commission on foreign exchange.

Theoretically, you should have your exchange receipts when reconverting won back to foreign currency. In practice, you can usually change up to US$2000 worth of won at the airport exchange services without showing receipts. If you change large amounts, your passport may be stamped to make sure you don't go over the limit. You will always need to show your passport to change money.

Banking hours are from 9.30 am to 4 pm on weekdays and until 1.30 pm on Saturday.

To open up a bank account, you must have an alien registration certificate.

Cash Within all US military bases, including the United Service Organization (USO; an information, entertainment and cultural centre that services the US military) and DMZ, you can use US currency (notes and coins). Occasionally you'll find shops near the bases, particularly in Itaewon, that will accept US currency. Otherwise, you'll have to use Korean money for all transactions.

US dollars are easiest to exchange, but other major currencies, especially Japanese yen, can be changed in Seoul (it's more difficult in the hinterlands). Bills which are dirty, tattered and torn could be difficult to dispose of.

South Korea is unusual in that many (though not all) banks and moneychangers can exchange US coins (in most Asian countries, only notes can be exchanged).

Travellers Cheques The exchange rate for travellers cheques is slightly more favourable than for cash. Travellers cheques in US dollar denominations will be easiest to change.

If you are not a resident of Korea but want to buy travellers cheques in Seoul, this can be done at some banks if you use a credit card to purchase the cheques. You could also buy travellers cheques if you have money wired to a bank in Korea. The main advantage of doing this is if you are going further into the hinterlands of Asia where credit cards are not easily used. Korea Exchange Bank and Korea First Bank are two places that sell travellers cheques, though there are others.

ATMs You'll find 'cash advance' machines in all cities. The ones next to banks and shopping centres tend only to accept Korean cards. The ones that work on foreign ATM and credit cards are most common in large subway stations and in convenience stores. Look for machines marked 'HanNet' or 'Samsung' (there should also be a listing of cards they accept such as Cirrus, Plus, Visa or MasterCard). Be careful of inserting your card into a machine where the display is in Korean only – you may have a hard time figuring out how to get it back!

Credit Cards You will have no problem finding opportunities to put any of your credit cards to use in Seoul or Busan, but paying with plastic is much less common out in the hinterland. International credit cards such as American Express, Diners Club, Visa, MasterCard and JCB are the most readily accepted. The main offices of credit card companies are:

American Express (☎ 02-399 2929, 552 7600) 17th floor, Gwanghwamun Bldg, Seoul
Diners Club (☎ 02-222 6100) 949-1 Dogok-dong, Gangnam-gu, Seoul
MasterCard (☎ 02-730 1221, toll-free 00798 11 887 0823) 11th floor, Royal Bldg, 5 Dangju-dong, Jongno-gu, Seoul
Visa (☎ 02-524 8000, 752 6523, toll-free 080-023 4031) 50 Sogong-dong, Jung-gu, Seoul

International Transfers Getting money wired to you in Korea poses no special difficulty – inquire at any foreign exchange bank for the exact procedure.

Sending money out of Korea is somewhat more complicated and nonresident foreigners will encounter difficulties. However, obtaining a bank draft for an amount under US$1000 is usually not questioned. Telegraphic transfers are also possible, but cost considerably more than bank drafts and you will be scrutinised more closely. Legal foreign residents are permitted to send out two-thirds of their salary – for all others, there is a maximum limit of US$10,000.

You need to have your passport available when you wire money out of Korea – the amount you send is stamped into the passport to make sure that you don't exceed the US$10,000 limit.

Black Market There is no real black market for currency (though there is a black market for imported goods smuggled out of US military bases). Travellers should be aware that people who have changed money informally in shops (mostly in Seoul's Itaewon district and Namdaemun market) have often wound up with counterfeit bills. If you need to change currency, do it at a bank or the airport.

Security

Korea does not have serious problems with muggings or pickpocketing, but theft does exist and prudence is advised.

Rather than lose your precious cash and travellers cheques (not to mention passport), large amounts of money and other valuables should be kept safe and secure from prying fingers. Various devices that can usually thwart pickpockets include pockets sewn on the inside of your jeans, Velcro tabs to seal pocket openings, a money belt under your clothes or a pouch under your shirt or top.

A vest worn under your outer jacket will do very nicely, but only during the colder months. Beltpacks are a fairly easy target for pickpockets, though you may be able to close the zippers securely with clips.

A secret stash of perhaps US$200 (maybe inside your backpack frame?) is a good idea for those special emergencies.

Costs

South Korea is a developed country, and most prices are comparable to what you'd pay in the West.

There are ways to minimise expenses. For the budget traveller, dormitory accommodation could cost as little as US$7 a night and food perhaps another US$7 a day. So if you do nothing but eat and sleep, you could theoretically survive on US$14 a day. In practice, you'd probably better figure on US$25 a day as a more realistic starting figure, but that allows for very few souvenirs or luxuries. More typically, a mid-level traveller can get by comfortably on US$35 to US$50 a day, not counting shopping sprees.

For those for whom money is no object, Seoul, like any major city, is of course very accommodating. Top-of-the-range hotels provide international standards of service at international prices.

Some typical costs include:

• local phone call W50, major newspaper W500, loaf of bread W1300–W2400, glass of beer W1500–W5000, Big Mac W3000
• budget hotel W25,000, mid-range hotel W50,000, main course at a good restaurant W15,000–W30,000

• one litre of petrol W1200, around 100km by train W2500–W6000, around 100km by bus W3500–W5500

Tipping & Bargaining

Tipping is generally not necessary or expected in Korea. A 10% service charge is added to the bill at higher end tourist hotels, which might be thought of as a mandatory tip (except that there's no certainty it will go to staff). In the international hotels, international standards apply with regard to tipping. At airports, there is a standard mandatory 'tip' of W2000 for porter service.

Big department stores have fixed prices, just like in the West, and their low-paid employees are in no position to offer you a discount. However, some department stores are divided into small sections which are rented to individual shopkeepers – asking for a discount in such places sometimes works. The same goes for small street markets and shops.

The Koreans don't take well to nastiness in bargaining sessions – always remember to be polite and smile. If your bargaining gets too shrill or persistent and the shopkeeper starts to get angry, that is a sign to end the negotiations swiftly – either pay up and take the goods, or graciously depart from the scene. At the end of any transaction, always smile and say *'kamsa hamnida'* (thank you).

Taxes & Refunds

Most items purchased in South Korea are subject to a 10% value-added tax (VAT), which is included in the selling price. At upmarket hotels, it is usual to add a 10% VAT on top of the 10% service charge, making for a steep 20% surprise surcharge when you go to pay your bill. VAT is not normally charged at homestays or bottom-end hotels.

The 10% VAT applies to all goods sold in Korea. It is possible to get a VAT refund if you are a nonresident of Korea, though it's almost more trouble than it's worth. Basically, you have to shop at one of the upmarket department stores or boutiques which display a 'Tax-free Shopping' sign or 'Global Refund' logo somewhere within

the store. If you purchase a minimum of W50,000 at one of these places, ask for a 'VAT refund cheque', which you must present to the customs office in the airport on your day of departure from Korea. You'll be given a voucher that can be redeemed at the 'cash refund counter' – conveniently located in front of the airport duty-free shop.

If you work (legally) in Korea, income tax will be withheld from your salary by your employer. You are expected to file an income tax return during the month of May, and it is possible that you will be refunded some of those monies.

POST & COMMUNICATIONS
Postal Rates

Domestic postal rates are W170 for up to 25g, W190 for up to 50g and postcards cost W140. Domestic parcels are also cheap at W1500 for up to 2kg, W2500 for registered and W3000 for express.

International rates vary according to region. The Korean postal service divides the world into four zones:

Zone 1 North-East Asia
Zone 2 South-East Asia
Zone 3 Australia, New Zealand, the USA, Canada, Middle East, Western Europe and Oceania
Zone 4 Eastern Europe, Africa and Latin America

The rates in won are as follows:

item	zone 1	2	3	4
postcards	350	350	350	350
aerograms	400	400	400	400
letters				
(10g)	480	500	420	450
(20g)	580	630	450	510
registered letter				
(10g)	1780	1800	1720	1750
printed matter				
(20g)	300	350	250	250

Receiving Mail

Post offices are open from 9 am to 6 pm Monday to Friday (until 5 pm during winter) and until noon on alternate Saturdays.

You'll find the poste restante counter on the 3rd floor of the Seoul Central Post Office (CPO). All incoming mail is entered into a logbook, which you have to sign when you pick up mail – check carefully for your name as letters are often misfiled. Normally, hotels will hold mail for a limited period, or a longer period if you let them know you are expecting mail.

Sending Mail

Public mail boxes are always coloured red. Domestic mail can be delivered in about two days if it bears an address in Korean characters – if written in English, figure on a week.

If you're sending parcels or printed matter, don't worry about chasing around for cardboard boxes and the like. Major post offices like the Seoul CPO have excellent, inexpensive packing services.

Sending printed matter is much cheaper than letters, but to get this discount you must seal the envelope with string rather than with tape or glue. The postal packing services know just how to prepare printed matter so that you can get this discount, so it's worth your while to let them do it.

If speed is of the utmost importance, you can send documents and small packets by Express Mail Service (EMS) Speedpost (*gukjeteukgeup-upyeon*).

Private Couriers If you need to send things too large or valuable to trust to the post office, or simply need more speed, there are a number of foreign private courier services available. The main courier services all offer pick-up service. In Seoul, they are:

Airborne Express (☎ 02-334 8200)
DHL (☎ 02-716 0001)
Fed Ex (☎ 02-661 8800, toll-free 080 023 8000)
Skypacks (☎ 02-553 3773)
United Parcel Service (☎ 02-3665 3651)

Telephone

There is a 30% discount on long-distance calls (domestic and international) made from 9 pm to 8 am Monday through Saturday, and for 24 hours on Sunday and public holidays.

Pay phones accept three types of coins, W10, W50 and W100 (but *not* W500). Pay phones can be used for local and long-distance calls, and there is no time limit as long as you keep feeding money into the machine. The cost for local calls is W50 for three minutes.

When using local-call phones you often find that the phone is off the hook and there is still a credit on the phone. The reason for this is that it is not possible to get change from a W100 coin, but you can use the credit from a W50 call to make further calls as long as you don't hang up. To make another call, simply press the green button on the phone (it doesn't always work).

When calling from your hotel room, dial ☎ 9 to get an outside line. There is usually no charge at all for making local calls.

To make an IDD call, first dial ☎ 001, then the country code, area code (minus the initial zero if it has one) and the number you want to reach.

Phone Cards Korea abounds with card phones and these can be used for local, long-distance and international calls. The magnetic telephone cards come in denominations of W2000, W3000, W5000 and W10,000, but you get a 10% bonus (for example, a W5000 card is really worth W5500). The phone cards (*jeonhwa kadeu*) can be bought from banks, shops nearby the card phones and 24-hour convenience stores. The cards are not superb quality. If your card's magnetic strip gets damaged, take the card to any Korea Telecom office and it will be exchanged for free.

There are also credit card phones, but these are a pain to use – few bother.

Lonely Planet eKno Communication Card is another option. Besides offering a means to make international calls, it can be used for messaging services, free email and travel information. You can join online at www.ekno.lonelyplanet.com, or by phone from Korea by dialling ☎ 00798-14-800-4442. Of course, for domestic calls, you'd be better off using a local phone card.

It is possible to place International Direct Dialling (IDD) calls at Korea Telecom's

Capital City & Provincial Area Codes

In recent times, the government has rationalised area codes, doing away with separate area codes for counties and towns and replacing them with provincial area codes. The larger cities, such as Seoul and Busan, also have their own area codes.

Busan	☎ 051
Chungcheongbuk-do	☎ 043
Chungcheongnam-do	☎ 041
Daegu	☎ 053
Daejeon	☎ 042
Gangwon-do	☎ 033
Gwangju	☎ 062
Gyeongsangbuk-do	☎ 054
Gyeongsangnam-do	☎ 055
Gyeonggi-do	☎ 031
Incheon	☎ 032
Jeju-do	☎ 064
Jeollabuk-do	☎ 063
Jeollanam-do	☎ 061
Seoul	☎ 02
Ulsan	☎ 052

public card phones, but this is the most expensive option.

You'll save a bundle if you can use an international phone card. The average Korean knows nothing about these cards, so only a few places sell them. In Seoul, you can buy them at the Net Cyber Cafe (☎ 02-733 7973) and USO (☎ 02-795 3028). These phone cards are produced by a number of competing companies – which card you should buy depends on where you are calling to. The American Access phone card costs W10,000, and if you call the USA or Canada, you can talk for 100 minutes; for Japan and Australia 71 minutes; for the UK 95 minutes. The Hanhwa card also costs W10,000 – you can call the USA for 90 minutes; Japan 60 minutes; the UK, Germany and Canada 40 minutes; Hong Kong 33 minutes; Taiwan 25 minutes; Australia and New Zealand 29 minutes. The Naray

card is the best deal for the USA – W10,000 gets you 120 minutes. The best card for Asia is probably the Onse card – W10,000 delivers 75 minutes to Japan. The card from SK Telecom is a relatively poor deal – for W10,000 you only get 30 minutes to talk to the USA. Korea Telecom plugs its Worldphone Card, which offers 'up to' a 51% discount off regular rates – not a big bargain.

Phone Companies Korea Telecom is not the only long-distance phone company in the country. Competition is offered by Dacom and Onse. To use Dacom or Onse, you have to first set up an account, then get a user ID number and personal identification number. Almost all expats have an account with Onse, but for short-term visitors this is not an option.

To place an international call through Korea Telecom's English-speaking operator, dial ☎ 0077. For information about international dialling (country codes, rates, time differences etc), dial ☎ 00794. Placing a call through an international operator means that you must pay for a three-minute minimum call. There are four types of operator assisted calls: station to station, person to person, reverse charges and credit card calls.

Home Country Direct Another dialling option is called 'home country direct', which allows you to talk directly to an operator in the country you are calling. This system is useful only for collect calls or if you want to charge the call to a credit card, and the service is not available for every country. There are special home country direct telephones at Gimpo airport and at the KNTO in Central Seoul. You can also access home country direct at any card phone – insert the card or push the red button, dial ☎ 00722 (or ☎ 007291 for the USA, excluding Hawaii and Guam) followed by the country direct code.

Internet Calls Yet another option is to make calls through the Internet. This can be arranged through companies such as Net2phone (www.onlinecalls.net/econ) and New World (www.newworldtele.com). Rates as low as US$0.10 per minute are

International Dialling Codes

Australia	
Optus	☎ 611
Telstra	☎ 610
Austria	☎ 430
Canada	☎ 015
China	☎ 860
France	☎ 330
Germany	☎ 049
Hong Kong	☎ 852
Indonesia	☎ 620
Italy	☎ 390
Japan	
(IDC)	☎ 813
(ITJ)	☎ 812
(KDD)	☎ 081
Malaysia	☎ 060
New Zealand	
(TNZI)	☎ 640
(CLEAR/NEW)	☎ 641
Singapore	☎ 650
Taiwan	☎ 886
Thailand	☎ 660
Turkey	☎ 900
UK	
(BT)	☎ 440
(Mercury)	☎ 441
USA	
(AT&T)	☎ 1
(IDB)	☎ 8
(MCI)	☎ 4
(PGE)	☎ 9
(Sprint)	☎ 6

IDD (Dacom)	☎ 002
IDD (Onse)	☎ 008
International operator	☎ 00799
International dialling assistance	☎ 00794
Korea's country code	☎ 82
Local directory assistance	☎ 114
Long-distance directory assistance	☎ area code + 114
Phone repairs	☎ 110
Report a spy	☎ 113
Toll-free prefix	☎ 080
Telegram (domestic)	☎ 115
Telegram (international)	☎ 005
Time	☎ 116
Weather (local)	☎ 131
Weather (long-distance)	☎ area code + 131

Mobile Phones Korea uses CDMA technology, which is (sort of) compatible with the USA but incompatible with the GSM system that is common in Europe and Asia. So if you have a GSM phone, you won't be able to use it in Korea.

Not that this is a big problem. Short-term visitors can rent mobile phones for about W8000 per day at any of Korea's international airports. Making international calls on these phones using special pre-paid phone cards can be quite economical.

For long-term residents, the news is good. There are currently five competitors in the Korean mobile market, and some companies will give you incentives such as a free mobile phone if you sign up for two years of service. The downside is that there have been many complaints about the quality of mobile service and the charges for airtime, so be careful about signing a contract.

At the present time, the players in this market are: SK Telecom (☎ 011), Hansol (☎ 018), KT Freetel (☎ 016), Shinsegi (☎ 017), and LG Telecom (☎ 019). SK Telecom is most expensive but has the best service, while the cheapest is Shinsegi. The others fall somewhere in between. KT Freetel is very popular with expats. Of course, technology is advancing rapidly and the situation could change tomorrow.

possible. For this to work, you need a reasonably fast Internet connection.

Useful Phone Numbers The Korean Yellow Pages is published annually in English, and is available from major bookshops in Seoul. If you can't find a copy, contact the publisher directly (☎ 02-725 0411). There are no White Pages available in English, so you'll have to manage with hangeul.

Directory assistance	
(toll-free)	☎ 080-211 0114
English Operator	☎ 080-211 0114
IDD (Korea Telecom)	☎ 001

Pagers As everybody switches to mobile phones, pagers are dying away. Nevertheless, some people still use them. The cheaper pagers can only be used in the Seoul metro-politan area, while the pricier models work throughout South Korea.

Even if you don't have your own pager, it's still useful to know how to contact somebody by this method. The system is fully automated – you don't speak to an operator at all. All Korean pager numbers start with 012 or 015 followed by at least seven digits. Simply dial this number (no area code necessary) and you will hear either a beep or a recorded voice message followed by a beep. At this point you have two options – you can punch in your phone number or leave a voice message. For the first option, after the beep press '1', dial your phone number, finish by pressing the asterisk (or pound sign) and wait a couple of seconds before hanging up. To leave a voice message, after the beep press '2', start talking (maximum 25 seconds), and again press an asterisk or pound sign before hanging up. If you forget to press the asterisk or pound sign, it still seems to work (despite the fact that the paging companies say it won't)!

Fax

Korea Telecom's major offices all offer a fax service. Aside from business centres in tourist hotels, there are also many small shops offering photocopying and fax service – these are most numerous around university areas.

Email & Internet Access

If you're one of those people who can't keep your fingers off a keyboard for more than 24 hours, then you've come to the right country – South Korea is a mecca for Internet and email addicts. There are several ways to get online – which one you choose probably depends on whether you are a permanent resident or just a short-term visitor to Korea.

If you don't happen to have your own computer, you can still go online by visiting a cyber cafe. Cyber cafes in Korea are cheap, typically charging W3000 for 30 minutes of use, and serve coffee plus various simple foods. Failing that, Internet gaming rooms (*PC-bang* in Korean) exist in plague proportions, though it's hard to get any serious work done with all the cigarette smoke and digital

warfare going on. If you'd rather go somewhere more respectable, a few super-deluxe hotels have business centres equipped with computers and modems, but fees are high.

IBM.net has a phone number in Seoul (☎ 02-761 3003) for connecting to its network. America Online Members can gain access by dialling one of the AolGlobalnet Access numbers (Seoul ☎ 02-2775 6647; Busan 051-462 5408). Compuserve's access number in Seoul is via Equant (☎ 02-775 6647) or World Connect (☎ 02-725 1003).

If you take up residence in Korea, you can establish a local Internet account (about W15,000 a month for unlimited usage). Phone numbers (in Seoul) for Korea's more popular Internet service providers are as follows: Nextel, on (☎ 02-2202-9300, www.uriel.net); Chollian (☎ 02-709 3700, www.chollian.net); Kornet, on (☎ 080-014 1414, www.kornet.net); Unitel, on (☎ 02-528 0114, www.unitel.co.kr); Hitel, on (www.hitel.net); Nownuri (☎ 02-590 3800, www.nownuri.co.kr); and ELIMnet (☎ 02-3149 4800, www.elim.co.kr). Unitel and Chollian have captured most of the expat market because they offer content in English (the others are almost strictly hangeul). PSINet (☎ 02-531 7700), also known as INet, specialises in Web hosting.

A number of companies (only in major cities) are starting to offer broadband (most ADSL) services, but this is not very developed yet. The cost is reasonable.

INTERNET RESOURCES

The World Wide Web is a rich resource for travellers. You can research your trip, hunt down bargain air fares, book hotels, check on weather conditions or chat with locals and other travellers about the best places to visit (or avoid!).

There's no better place to start your Web explorations than the Lonely Planet Web site (www.lonelyplanet.com). Here you'll find succinct summaries on travelling to most places on earth, postcards from other travellers and the Thorn Tree bulletin board, where you can ask questions before you go or dispense advice when you get back. You can also find travel news and updates to many of our most popular guidebooks, and the sub-WWWay section links you to the most useful travel resources elsewhere on the Web.

The Koreans themselves have set up a number of good Web sites that travellers find useful. However, you may need a very fast Internet connection – the Korean sites tend to be highly graphics intensive and Web pages load very slowly.

Of course, the Internet changes so fast that almost anything one can say about it is liable to be out of date tomorrow. With that thought in mind, some sites to be seen include the following:

Korean National Tourism Organization
(KNTO) This enterprise runs a site with plenty of useful data of interest to travellers.
www.knto.or.kr or www.visitkorea.or.kr

1stopKorea.Com A useful Web site for expats.
www.1stopkorea.com

Life in Korea This is yet another expat-oriented Web site. Good information on clubs, activities and events.
www.lifeinkorea.com

KoreaLore This site deals with a little bit of everything – culture, language, arts, religion, places and technology. It's run by an expat who has become a Korean citizen.
www.korealore.com

Korean Yellow Pages More than a phone directory – you can make hotel reservations, rent a mobile phone, find out what's showing at the local cinemas and much more.
www.yellowpages.co.kr

Inside Korea Run by the Ministry of Culture & Tourism, this site has some interesting cultural information.
www.insidekorea.com

The Korea Herald One of the two daily English newspapers in Seoul. Their site is worth a look.
www.koreaherald.co.kr

The Korea Times The other daily English-language newspaper in Seoul. Their news site is brilliant (better than the printed edition even).
www.koreatimes.co.kr

Korea Web Weekly Published by the Korean Nationalists Association, its' a US-based site for flag-waving Korean nationals and other Koreaphiles. Some of the stuff posted here is decidedly xenophobic and occasionally pro-North Korean.
www.kimsoft.com

Korea Central News Agency The official mouthpiece for North Korea. You'll find plenty of laughable (but deadly serious) propaganda posted here. This Web site might be best accessed from outside South Korea, as until very recently it was prohibited for South Koreans (foreigners are a shady area!) to visit or have any contact with North Koreans, via the Internet or otherwise.
www.kcna.co.jp

American Chamber of Commerce in Korea
ww.amchamkorea.org

European Union Chamber of Commerce
www.eucck.org

Dave's ESL Cafe The Web site to visit for aspiring ESL teachers and students.
www.eslcafe.com

Aside from Web sites, there are mailing lists, which are basically electronic bulletin boards that anyone can participate in. One of the most popular with foreign residents of Korea is Kexpat ('Korean expats'). To subscribe, send a message to e kexpat-d-request@uriel.net. Type 'subscribe kexpat' in the subject line. To post a message, email it to e kexpat@uriel.net.

Take a look at Liszt, the mailing list directory, at www.liszt.com to find out about other mailing lists (not only Korean ones).

The soc.culture.korean newsgroup is also an excellent resource.

BOOKS

Most books are published in different editions by different publishers in different countries. As a result, a book might be a hardcover rarity in one country while it's readily available in paperback in another. Fortunately, bookshops and libraries search by title or author, so your local bookshop or library is best placed to advise you on the availability of the following recommendations.

Lonely Planet

For those with more time to explore Korea's capital, Lonely Planet publishes the *Seoul* city guide.

This guidebook only covers the basics of the Korean language. For a more in-depth look, see Lonely Planet's *Korean Phrasebook*.

Guidebooks

The Berlitz *Korean For Travellers* has extensive vocabulary lists but it doesn't offer much help with grammar. To delve even further into the language, *An Introductory Course in Korean* by Fred Lukoff (Yonsei University Press) is a popular textbook available in Korea.

Korea Guide: A Glimpse of Korea's Cultural Legacy by Edward B Adams (Seoul International Publishing House) is highly informative and colourful. If you want to appreciate the splendour of Gyeongju, the historic ancient capital of the Silla kingdom, the same author has done a magnificent job in *Korea's Golden Age*.

For illuminating background reading and good photographs, turn to the *Korea* Insight Guide (1983).

Travel

To Dream of Pigs by Clive Leatherdale (Desert Island Books) is an excellent travelogue of both North and South Korea.

Korea and Her Neighbours by Isabella Lucy Bird Bishop is the delightful narrative of a well-heeled British woman travelling through Korea at the end of the 19th century.

History & Politics

One of the most up-to-date histories available is *Korean Old and New: A History* (Korea Institute, Harvard University). Also very current is *Korea: Tradition & Transformation* by Andrew C Nahm (Hollym Publications, Seoul).

The Comfort Women (1995) deals with the explosive topic of how Korean (and other women) were used as sex slaves by Japanese soldiers during WWII. An even more graphic book on the same topic is *True Stories of the Korean Comfort Women*, edited by Keith Howard.

The Two Koreas: A Contemporary History by Don Oberdorfer will quickly bring you up to speed on how both North and South Korea are what they are today.

Korea's Place in the Sun: A Modern History by Bruce Cumings offers a somewhat alternative view of the nation's history.

The Abacus and the Sword: The Japanese Penetration of Korea by Peter Duus offers a view of the Japanese occupation that will not necessarily please the average Korean.

The entire Joseon dynasty is well-covered by *The Confucian Transformation of Korea* by Martina Deuchler. The same author also did a fine earlier work, *Confucian Gentlemen and Barbarian Envoys*, which covers the opening of Korea between 1875 and 1885.

Korea's Golden Age, by Edward B Adams, is a beautifully illustrated guide to Silla culture written by a man who was born in Korea and who has spent most of his life there. Worth purchasing for anyone considering a trip to Korea's 'living museum', Gyeongju.

Business & Economics

Troubled Tiger: Businessmen, Bureaucrats and Generals in South Korea (ME Sharpe, 1984) by Mark Clifford is a highly recommended 'unauthorised biography' of Korea Inc.

An unusual blockbuster is *The Chaebol* by Steers, Shin & Ungson (Harper & Row, New York, 1989). Its look into the workings of Korea's big corporate conglomerates is not too flattering.

Korean Dynasty: Hyundai and Chung Ju Yung (ME Sharpe, 1994) by Donald Kirk is the story of Korea's largest jaebeol.

Asia for Women on Business by Tracey and Patricia Wilen doesn't deal with Korea exclusively, but the Korea chapter is relevant and useful.

Doing Business With Korea by Paul A Leppert has a title which says it all. Ditto for *Practical Guide to Understanding South Korean Business Culture* by Peggy Kenna and Sondra Lacy.

General

In the Shadow of the Moons (1998) by Hong Nan-sook is the most recent bestseller about Korea. The author is the ex-wife of Moon Sun-myung's oldest son (Moon Sun-myung, best known as the leader of the 'Moonies', is the founder of the Unification Church). Ms Hong was married to Moon's son for 14 years before divorcing him, and the book portrays a harrowing tale of abuse.

Ten Thousand Sorrows by Elizabeth Kim is a moving (and not for the squeamish) account of a Korean war orphan.

A good primer in Korean culture is *Korea's Cultural Roots* by Jon Carter Covell, which covers shamanism, Confucianism and Buddhism. Sequels by the same author include *Korea's Colorful Heritage* and *The World of Korean Ceramics*. Teaming up with her son Alan, the Covell's produced *Korean Impact On Japanese Culture: Japan's Hidden History*. Alan Covell went on to write *Folk Art and Magic: Shamanism in Korea*. All these books are published by Hollym Publications.

NEWSPAPERS & MAGAZINES

Korea has two locally published English-language newspapers: *The Korea Times* and *The Korea Herald*. These papers are published Monday through Saturday – Sunday is their day off. Both seem to glean their stories from Korea's official Yonhap news agency, which is why both papers report identical news. The *Herald* has a better TV listing and seems to be more popular than the *Times*, but the difference is not huge.

Backpackers Korea is a useful, free bilingual newspaper that is published periodically. Look for copies around airports and at the KNTO office in Seoul.

Look for the free magazine *Seoul Classified* (www.seoulclassified.co.kr), which contains some useful practical information.

Seoul Scope is a monthly magazine in English, which ostensibly costs W2000 per issue but is in fact found free at the KNTO tourist office. You can order a subscription for W20,000 per year by ringing up the office in Seoul (☎ 02-743 7784). It isn't really that good, but does serve as a useful introduction to Korea.

Koreana magazine is the best source on arts and culture. It's published quarterly by the Korea Foundation and costs W4500 per issue or W18,000 per yearly subscription.

The *Korea Economic Report*, *Korea Post* and *Business Korea* are locally published monthly magazines, which are mostly of interest to Koreans learning to speak English.

If you want to check up on your horoscope, *USA Today* is on sale at various venues around town.

RADIO & TV

There are five Korean-language TV networks: KBS1, KBS2, MBC, SBS and EBS. Many foreign movies are shown with Korean dubbing, but the original language can be heard by switching to the second audio channel.

AFKN is an English-language TV station run by the US military and features typical US shows, but in most areas you can only get it on cable. On AFKN, commercial advertising is axed, but this is replaced with military advice and safety tips like 'wear your uniform proudly' and 'driving and alcohol don't mix'. Broadcasting is 24 hours a day, though it's mostly trash between midnight and 6 am.

AFKN radio broadcasts in English at different frequencies depending on location, as follows: Seoul, AM 1530, FM 102.7; Daejeon, AM 96.1, FM 12; Daegu, AM 585, FM 99.3; Pohang, AM 1512; Busan AM 1260, FM 88.1; Jejudo, AM 1512. For find the frequencies of other cities, call ☎ 02-7914 8095.

Arirang is a government subsidised TV station that broadcasts programs on Korean culture, fine arts, politics, economics and history. Programs are in both Korean and English. Arirang is only available on cable. Visit the Arirang Web site for the latest program listings (www.arirang.co.kr).

Korea has numerous cable TV companies, but most only operate in a specified district. You need to find out which company serves your area, and also what stations they carry – just ask your Korean neighbours, somebody should know. Typically, there are installation costs running from W50,000 to W100,000, plus a monthly charge of W20,000 to W30,000, depending on your neighbourhood. At this price, you should receive all the local stations (including AFKN) plus all the freebie services from satellite (EBS-wiseong, KBS-wiseong, CNN, Star World, Star Sports and some Japanese programs) plus all the local pay cable stations (eg Arirang, K-MTV, Channel V, Doosan Super Network etc). For an extra fee there is the Catch One movie channel. If you don't need Arirang and the movie channels, you can get a cheap cable service that runs only W4000 per month and supplies everything except the pay cable stations (you still get CNN-I, Star and AFKN).

Satellite TV is also available, if you are willing to purchase your own dish antenna. There are a number of companies that can sell these systems.

A complete TV and radio program schedule is listed in the daily English-language newspapers. The Korean Yellow Pages Web site (www.yellowpages.co.kr) also has program listings (click the 'Entertainment' link).

VIDEO SYSTEMS
South Korea has adopted the NTSC video standard. This is the same standard used in the USA, Canada and Japan, but is incompatible with the PAL standard (used in Australia, Hong Kong, New Zealand, the UK and most of Europe) and SECAM (France, Germany, Luxembourg). Video rental shops are abundant and many foreign movies are in English with Korean subtitles.

PHOTOGRAPHY & VIDEO
All the big-name brands of print film are readily available in Korea at reasonable prices. Processing facilities are of an international standard and are not expensive. Slide film is a little more difficult to come by, and is most readily available in Seoul. Blank video cassettes are readily available.

For processing slide film, prices seem to vary depending on where you ask. Professional processing shops are usually cheapest and fastest – most offer one-day service. Ordinary camera shops can take three days and charge double.

Korea is not a particularly good place to buy photographic or video equipment, due to prohibitive import taxes. It's better to purchase it in Hong Kong, Singapore, Taipei or even Tokyo.

The traditional Korean *ondol,* or underfloor heating system, can slowly cook your film if you leave it or your camera on the floor.

Aspiring paparazzi should be aware that monks generally do not want their photograph taken. Student rioters are also not particularly fond of being photographed, and

it's best not to argue with somebody holding an iron bar or a firebomb.

Photography of military facilities can be a sensitive matter – it's best not to risk having your film confiscated. Photographs can be taken around airports, but do not even think about photographing airport security procedures!

TIME
The time in South Korea is Greenwich Mean Time plus nine hours. When it is noon in South Korea it is 1 pm in Sydney, 3 am in London, 10 pm the previous day in New York and 7 pm the previous day in San Francisco. Daylight savings time is *not* observed.

ELECTRICITY
Korea has converted to 220 V, though you might still find 110 V in some older buildings. Both 110 and 220 V are 60 Hertz (60 cycles per second). The way to tell the difference in voltage is from the design of the electrical outlets – two flat pins is 110 V and two round pins is 220 V. There is no third wire for ground (earth).

WEIGHTS & MEASURES
The international metric system is the standard measure for everything except the size of real estate, which uses the traditional Chinese system. In the case of buying or renting a flat, area is measured in *pyeong*, with one pyeong being equal to 3.3058 sq metres.

LAUNDRY
Most hotels, including budget *yeogwan*, do laundry if you prefer not to do it yourself. Charges for this service are usually reasonable, but ask first.

Laundrettes do exist in large cities (especially Seoul), and are most common around university areas. Charges are typically W4000 for a large load.

TOILETS
Kudos to the Koreans for their public toilets. You'll find these facilities everywhere – in parks, railway stations, bus stations, department stores, museums and all petrol stations. Korea's public toilets are free of charge and

Pit Stops

One of the most obvious changes to Korea's expressways in recent years has been the dramatic improvement in roadside rest areas. The days of greasy and salty salmonella take-away food and toilets that you could smell even before you saw the first turn-off sign have long gone. Since mid-1999, the Korean Highway Corporation (KHC) has been reforming the management of roadside rest areas. The result: the toilets are now filled with fresh flowers, and graced with classical music, air-fresheners and framed scenic prints. The ladies toilets even have powder tables and baby-changing areas. To top things off, the quality of food and service has improved immensely.

Today, you will notice a queuing scenario as you pull up for a pit stop: buses humming in a line, a steady bustle of people going in and out of the toilets and restaurants and men in uniform blowing whistles to keep order.

Now that the rest areas are spic and span, you can head back calmed and refreshed into the chaos and traffic of the expressways. But don't despair, according to KHC, 'intelligent expressways', offering a pleasant and safe road experience, are just around the corner.

– in most cases – clean. The Seoul city council decreed that every building higher than five stories must open their toilets on the ground floor to public use free of charge. Even in the congested subways you can find clean and uncrowded restrooms. It's a sharp contrast to other cities in the region (shame on you, Hong Kong).

Public toilets come in two flavours – typical Asian squat-style and Western throne-style. Most public toilets are of the squat variety, which, for the uninitiated, take some getting used to. Using one of these while standing up can take considerable skill – one male traveller compared it to those water-pistol games at the amusement park. Remember to face towards the hooded end of the toilet when you squat.

What to do with used toilet paper is an important issue. In general, if you see a wastebasket next to the toilet, that is where you should throw used tissue. The plumbing systems in Korea cannot cope with toilet paper.

Another toilet tip – you will seldom find free tissue paper available in the toilet stalls themselves, so keep a small stash with you at all times. Fortunately, it is very easy to buy almost everywhere (from both shops and machines) – the price is W200 to W300 a pack.

HEALTH

No vaccinations are required to enter South Korea, though this doesn't mean you shouldn't get any. Hepatitis B is endemic in South Korea and malaria is also present, although not widespread. Also, if you will be travelling to less developed countries on your journey, it certainly isn't a bad idea to get a few prophylactic jabs in the arm. Vaccinations you should consider include the following: cholera, rabies, hepatitis B, BCG (tuberculosis), polio, and TABT (protects against typhoid, paratyphoid A and B, and tetanus) and diphtheria.

That having been said, South Korea is a very healthy country. Opinions are divided as to whether you can drink the tap water – some South Koreans do, some don't. If you do drink unboiled water, it's unlikely you'll suffer any illness more serious than diarrhoea.

Emergency medical care in hospitals is excellent and reasonably priced. However, westerners are liable to become very frustrated with most Korean doctors because they will not answer questions from patients regarding illness, laboratory tests or the treatment being given. Questions are regarded as insults to the doctor's competence, thus causing a loss of face. You might not even be informed that you are dying, since this would imply that the doctor is too incompetent to cure you. Doctors who have studied and worked abroad are more accustomed to Western ways.

Self-treatment poses risks, but Korean pharmacists are willing to sell you all sorts of dangerous drugs over the counter without a prescription. Be careful about abusing over-the-counter antibiotics and steroids – many people do, sometimes with serious consequences (steroids can cause blindness, for example). Korean pharmacists know the English names of most drugs but can't pronounce them. However, they can generally read English well, so try writing down what you want. To find a Korean pharmacy, simply look for the character:

약

Predeparture Planning

Immunisations Plan ahead for getting your vaccinations: some of them require more than one injection, while some vaccinations should not be given together. Note that some vaccinations should not be given during pregnancy or in people with allergies – discuss with your doctor.

It is recommended you seek medical advice at least six weeks before travel.

Discuss your requirements with your doctor, but vaccinations you should consider for

Medical Kit Check List

Following is a list of items you should consider including in your medical kit – consult your pharmacist for brands available in your country.

☐ **Aspirin or paracetamol (acetaminophen in the USA)** – for pain or fever
☐ **Antihistamine** – for allergies, eg, hay fever; to ease the itch from insect bites or stings; and to prevent motion sickness
☐ **Cold and flu tablets, throat lozenges and nasal decongestant**
☐ **Multivitamins** – consider for long trips, when dietary vitamin intake may be inadequate
☐ **Antibiotics** – consider including these if you're travelling well off the beaten track; see your doctor, as they must be prescribed, and carry the prescription with you
☐ **Loperamide or diphenoxylate** –'blockers' for diarrhoea
☐ **Prochlorperazine or metaclopramide** – for nausea and vomiting
☐ **Rehydration mixture** – to prevent dehydration, which may occur, for example, during bouts of diarrhoea; particularly important when travelling with children
☐ **Insect repellent, sunscreen, lip balm and eye drops**
☐ **Calamine lotion, sting relief spray or aloe vera** – to ease irritation from sunburn and insect bites or stings
☐ **Antifungal cream or powder** – for fungal skin infections and thrush
☐ **Antiseptic (such as povidone-iodine)** – for cuts and grazes
☐ **Bandages, Band-Aids (plasters) and other wound dressings**
☐ **Water purification tablets or iodine**
☐ **Scissors, tweezers and a thermometer** – note that mercury thermometers are prohibited by airlines

this trip include the following (for more details about diseases, see the individual disease entries later in this section).

Diphtheria & Tetanus Vaccinations for these two diseases are usually combined and are recommended for everyone. After an initial course of three injections (usually given in childhood), boosters are necessary every 10 years.

Hepatitis B Travellers who should consider vaccination against hepatitis B include those on a long trip, and those visiting countries where there are high levels of hepatitis B infection, where blood transfusions may not be adequately screened or where sexual contact or needle sharing is a possibility. Vaccination involves three injections, with a booster at 12 months. More rapid courses are available if necessary.

Malaria Medication Antimalarial drugs do not prevent you from being infected but kill the malaria parasites during a stage in their development and significantly reduce the risk of becoming very ill or dying. Expert advice on medication should be sought, as there are many factors to consider, including the area to be visited, the risk of exposure to malaria-carrying mosquitoes, the side effects of medication, your medical history and whether you are a child or an adult or pregnant. Travellers to isolated area in high risk countries may like to carry a treatment dose of medication for use if symptoms occur.

Health Insurance Make sure that you have adequate health insurance. See Travel Insurance under Visas & Documents for details.

Travel Health Guides Lonely Planet's *Healthy Travel Asia & India* is a handy pocket size and packed with useful information including predeparture planning, emergency first aid, immunisation and disease information and what to do if you get sick on the road. Travel with Children from Lonely Planet also includes advice on travel health for younger children.

There are also a number of excellent travel health sites on the Internet. From the Lonely Planet home page there are links at www.lonelyplanet.com/weblinks/wlheal.htm to the World Health Organization and the US Centers for Disease Control & Prevention.

Infectious Diseases

Hepatitis is a general term for inflammation of the liver. It is a common disease worldwide. There are several different viruses that cause hepatitis, and they differ in the way that they are transmitted. The symptoms are similar in all forms of the illness, and include fever, chills, headache, fatigue, feelings of weakness and aches and pains, followed by loss of appetite, nausea, vomiting, abdominal pain, dark urine, light-coloured faeces, jaundiced (yellow) skin and yellowing of the whites of the eyes. People who have had hepatitis should avoid alcohol for some time after the illness, as the liver needs time to recover.

Nutrition

If your diet is poor or limited in variety, if you're travelling hard and fast and therefore missing meals or if you simply lose your appetite, you can soon start to lose weight and place your health at risk.

Make sure your diet is well balanced. Cooked eggs, tofu, beans, lentils (dhal in India) and nuts are all safe ways to get protein. Fruit you can peel (bananas, oranges or mandarins, for example) is usually safe and a good source of vitamins. Melons can harbour bacteria in their flesh and are best avoided. Try to eat plenty of grains (including rice) and bread. Remember that although food is generally safer if it is cooked well, overcooked food loses much of its nutritional value. If your diet isn't well balanced or if your food intake is insufficient, it's a good idea to take vitamin and iron pills.

In hot climates make sure you drink enough – don't rely on feeling thirsty to indicate when you should drink. Not needing to urinate or voiding small amounts of very dark yellow urine is a danger sign. Always carry a water bottle with you on long trips. Excessive sweating can lead to loss of salt and therefore muscle cramping. Salt tablets are not a good idea as a preventative, but in places where salt is not used much, adding salt to food can help.

Herbal Medicine (Hanyak)

Korea has two systems of medicine – Western and traditional. Korea's traditional medicine has been influenced by the Chinese variety, though the Korean's have added their own ingredients to the herbal brew.

If any herb is associated with Korea, it's ginseng (*insam*). There are two kinds of ginseng: red and white, and the red ginseng is by far the more expensive. It is possible to buy ginseng in a number of forms: in its raw state at markets; in capsules; in tea; as a powder; and as a liquid extract.

The second most popular herb in Korea is a mushroom called *yeongji beoseot*, known to westerners as *Ganoderma lucidium karst*. It's expensive stuff, but claimed to be effective against everything from stomach ulcers to ageing. Considerably less expensive is another mushroom called *unji beoseot*, which could be translated into English as 'cloud fungus'. This one has recently been touted as a possible cure for cancer.

There are many other types of medicines. Possible ingredients – to name a few – include ginger, cinnamon, anise, nutmeg, the dried skins of fruits, powdered deer antlers, rhinoceros horn, cockroach droppings, dead bees and snake bile.

Adherents of herbal medicine claim that you don't use a single herb but rather a combination of herbs to produce the desired result. The herbs, when properly mixed, are believed to have a synergistic effect. That is, the whole is greater than the sum of its parts.

Another important property of herbal medicine is that the effects are supposed to be gradual, not sudden or dramatic. That is, you start taking herbs at the first sign of illness, such as a scratchy throat, or even before you get sick, as a preventive measure. So in the cold and flu season you might start taking herbs before you even have your first cough or sniffle, so that you can build up resistance.

When reading about the theory behind herbal medicine, the word 'holistic' appears often. Basically, this means that herbal medicine seeks to treat the whole body rather than focusing on a particular organ or disease. Using appendicitis as an example, a doctor may try to fight the infection using the body's whole defences, whereas a Western doctor would simply cut out the appendix. In the case of appendicitis, the Western method might be more effective, but herbal medicine has sometimes proven better in treating chronic illnesses such as migraine headaches and asthma.

There are almost 300 million chronic carriers of **hepatitis B** in the world. It is spread through contact with infected blood, blood products or body fluids, for example through sexual contact, unsterilised needles and blood transfusions, or contact with blood via small breaks in the skin. Other risk situations include having a shave, tattoo or body piercing with contaminated equipment. The symptoms of hepatitis B may be more severe than type A and the disease can lead to long term problems such as chronic liver damage, liver cancer or a long term carrier state. Hepatitis C and D are spread in the same way as hepatitis B and can also lead to long term complications.

There are vaccines against hepatitis A and B, but there are currently no vaccines against the other types of hepatitis. Following the basic rules about food and water (hepatitis A and E) and avoiding risk situations (hepatitis B, C and D) are important preventative measures.

Sexually Transmitted Diseases

HIV/AIDS and hepatitis B can be transmitted through sexual contact – see the relevant sections earlier for more details. Other STDs include gonorrhoea, herpes and syphilis; sores, blisters or rashes around the genitals and discharges or pain when urinating are common symptoms. In some STDs, such as wart virus or chlamydia, symptoms may be less marked or not observed at all, especially in women. Chlamydia infection can cause infertility in men and women before any

Everyday Health

Normal body temperature is up to 37°C (98.6°F); more than 2°C (4°F) higher indicates a high fever. The normal adult pulse rate is 60 to 100 per minute (children 80 to 100, babies 100 to 140). As a general rule the pulse increases about 20 beats per minute for each 1°C (2°F) rise in fever.

Respiration (breathing) rate is also an indicator of illness. Count the number of breaths per minute: Between 12 and 20 is normal for adults and older children (up to 30 for younger children, 40 for babies). People with a high fever or serious respiratory illness breathe more quickly than normal. More than 40 shallow breaths a minute may indicate pneumonia.

symptoms have been noticed. Syphilis symptoms eventually disappear completely but the disease continues and can cause severe problems in later years. While abstinence from sexual contact is the only 100% effective prevention, using condoms is also effective. The treatment of gonorrhoea and syphilis is with antibiotics. The different sexually transmitted diseases each require specific antibiotics.

It's easy enough to buy condoms (same word in Korean) at any pharmacy or convenience store. In some hotels you may well find a condom machine in your room (so if you forgot to bring the condoms, then at least bring two W500 coins).

Insect Bites & Stings

Thanks to Korea's cold climate, insects are not a major threat to your health, as they can be in tropical countries. Nevertheless, insect bites can be a nuisance if you do much summer hiking. For those with allergies, certain types of insect bites can even be life-threatening.

Mosquitos are an annoyance during summer. Mosquito incense coils are effective, but a more modern solution is 'electric mosquito incense' (jeonjamogihyang), which consists of a small plastic bottle of insecticide which is slowly vaporised by an elec-

tric heater. The entire unit (bottle and electric heater) only weighs a few grams and is easy to travel with. You can purchase both the heater and insecticide in Korean pharmacies. A variation on the theme is a cardboard pad (soaked in insecticide) and an electric heater – this design is perhaps superior since there is no possibility of a leaky bottle making a mess out of your backpack. Breathing the vaporised insecticide over the long-term can lead to sinusitis.

If you are allergic to red ant bites or bee and wasp stings, it might be prudent to carry some epinephrine in your first-aid kit.

WOMEN TRAVELLERS

Korea is still very much a male-oriented society, and women's rights have been slow in becoming an issue.

In general, Korea is a safe place for women travellers. Of course, sexual assaults are not unknown. Korean men tend to be big drinkers, and you may meet some fairly aggressive drunks late at night. Nevertheless, there's no need to take excessive safety measures.

The Australian government has a useful Web site with travel tips for women that are relevant to any nationality or destination. Check it out at www.dfat.gov.au/consular/womtrav.html.

GAY & LESBIAN TRAVELLERS

Koreans are somewhat schizophrenic when it comes to gay and lesbian issues. On the one hand, the country has never passed any laws that overtly discriminate against homosexuals. On the other hand, one should not mistake this superficially non-hostile legal environment as being a sign of tolerance.

Korean law does not mention homosexuality simply because it's considered so bizarre that it's unmentionable in public. When uncomfortably confronted with the issue, most Koreans will insist that there are no gays and lesbians in Korea – it's a 'foreign problem'.

As long as the 'problem' remains invisible, Koreans will ignore it. Recent attempts by gays and lesbians to come out of the closet have met with moderate success.

Bars, discos and saunas catering to a gay clientele now exist, but they keep a low profile. They also are not very profitable – at the present time, the number of Koreans willing to openly patronise these places is still very small.

In Seoul, an organisation called Sappho (e sapphorok@yahoo.com) arranges get-togethers in Seoul every month, and welcomes foreign women.

Take a look at Utopia, Asian Gay & Lesbian Resources (www.utopia-asia.com) for up-to-date information on gay and lesbian issues, bars and happenings in Korea.

DISABLED TRAVELLERS
Unfortunately, Korean cities are geared heavily towards the physically able. A particular nightmare exists for those who have difficulty ascending and descending stairs. Many intersections can only be crossed by descending into the subway system, a particular problem in Seoul, Busan, Dae-gu and other cities. To make matters worse, it's easy to get confused in this underground labyrinth and emerge from the subway at the wrong exit, which forces you to descend again and seek another route.

A minor compensation is that the pedestrian footpaths in Korea are generally wide and unobstructed, at least along the major boulevards. Unfortunately, there are no wheelchair cutouts – the high kerbs can be a serious obstacle. Also, the back alleys have no footpaths and are often blocked by illegally parked cars.

SENIOR TRAVELLERS
Some of the palaces and museums offer discounts or even free admission to seniors aged 65 and over. You'll need to show identification, such as your passport, to take advantage of this. Discounts on the subway and bus system are more problematic – a special senior citizen's ID card is required, and you can only obtain this if you are a resident of the city in question.

TRAVEL WITH CHILDREN
Toddlers under two years can generally travel for free. Kids aged between two and 12 typically get 50% discounts on tickets and admission fees.

USEFUL ORGANISATIONS
In Seoul, the Foreign Community Service (FOCUS; ☎ 02-798 7592, 797 8212) provides referrals to hospitals, doctors, lawyers, schools and other services in South Korea. This place could be good for advice on activities, renting apartments etc, but it's mostly oriented to long-term foreign residents rather than short-term travellers. The office is open from 9 am to 5 pm Monday to Friday, and there's a 24-hour answer phone for emergencies.

If you have trouble with transport, food, shopping or accommodation, there is a KNTO Tourist Complaint Center (☎ 02-735 0101, e tourcom@knto.or.kr), KPO Box 1879, Seoul 110-618. For complaints about taxis or local transport, you can also try the Transportation Complaint Center (☎ 02-392 4745).

Business travellers might find it useful to contact the following organisations:

Convention & Exhibition Center (COEX; ☎ 02-551 0114), 159-1 Samseong-dong, Gangnam-gu, Seoul.
Federation of Korean Industries (FKI; ☎ 02-780 0821), 28-1 Yeouiddo-dong, Yeongdeungpo-gu, Seoul
Foreign Investment & Trade Service Center (FITS; ☎ 02-731 6800; e fits@www.metro.seoul.kr)
Korea Chamber of Commerce & Industry (KCCI; ☎ 02-316 3114), 45 Namdaemunno 4-ga, Jung-gu, Seoul
Korea Foreign Trade Association (KFTA; ☎ 02-551 5114), 159-1 Samseong-dong, Gangnam-gu, Seoul
Korea Trade Promotion Corporation (KOTRA), 300-9, Yeomgok-dong, Seocho-gu, Seoul (☎ 02-3640 7114)
World Trade Center Seoul (WTCS; ☎ 02-551 5114), 159-1 Samseong-dong, Gangnam-gu, Seoul

DANGERS & ANNOYANCES
Crime
Korea is one of the safest countries in Asia, and the crime rate is lower than in many, and probably most, Western countries.

However, there is no guarantee that you'll never encounter trouble. Korea does have strict gun control and relatively few drug addicts – both factors help to keep the lid on crime.

Unfortunately, burglaries, rapes and muggings do occur, and foreigners have occasionally been the victims. Pickpocketing can occur in crowded areas, but it is easy to thwart this with a moneybelt or zippered pockets.

Probably the biggest danger to your safety is being lulled into a false sense of security. Korea really is much safer than many other places, and foreigners will do things they wouldn't consider doing at home – such as leaving their door unlocked, leaving their luggage unattended while they use the public toilets, carrying large quantities of cash in public and walking alone down dark alleys of major cities at 3 am.

Finally, it's a harsh truth that your fellow travellers may not be totally honest. If your camera disappears from your backpack while you were taking a shower at the youth hostel, the thief will quite probably be a foreigner rather than a Korean.

Student Riots

Student rioting is a seasonal sport most common in late spring or early summer. Although fatalities are rare, injuries are common. It's pretty easy to avoid riots, but some foreigners get themselves hurt because they want to 'see the action' up close.

Macho Posturing

Korean men seem to be under quite a lot of social pressure to drink, and more than a few do so to excess. Most drinkers are 'friendly drunks' whose worst habit is vomiting in the gutter. However, some men can become quite hostile after they've drunk enough to lose their inhibitions.

Foreign males who head out for a night on the town should watch out for aggressive locals (and this particularly applies in Seoul's Itaewon neighbourhood). Some of the bumps you get on the street late at night may not be accidental. The thing to do is to stay cool and

keep walking. It's no use arguing with a drunk, and if you try to fight your way out of a situation there's a chance that you'll get pounced upon by incensed passers-by.

'Stealing' Korean Women Many Korean men seem to believe that Western men are out to 'steal their women'. Especially when greased with alcohol, Korean men are liable to get aggressive towards a foreign man who is accompanied by Korean woman (or a woman who looks Korean). The woman may also be given a hard time.

If you are Western male out with an Asian female friend, at least take the precaution of not holding hands or showing any other intimacy in public. In an actual confrontation, the woman should shout some abuse at the antagonist in any language *other* than Korean – this might convince the aggressor that the woman is Chinese, Japanese, or some other nationality besides Korean. If this revelation sinks in, he might suddenly apologise!

In the opposite scenario (where a Korean male is being accompanied by a Western woman), there is never a problem. Korean females are apparently not worried about Western women stealing their men.

EMERGENCIES

If no English is spoken when you dial the police or fire department, keep trying. On a public phone just push the red button before dialling emergency numbers – you won't need a phone card or coins. Useful emergency telephone numbers follow:

Ambulance	☎ 119
English Operator	☎ 080-211 0114
Fire	☎ 119
Police	☎ 112

Foreign Community Service (FOCUS; ☎ 02-798 7592, 797 8212) has a 24-hour emergency help line.

LEGAL MATTERS

The way most foreigners wind up in the clutches of the legal system is by getting busted for drugs, for working illegally or for having a traffic accident. Also, a popular hobby for English teachers is suing their employer after being cheated on wages.

In Seoul, you can call Volunteer Lawyers (☎ 02-522 9100) or the Association for Foreign Worker's Human Rights (☎ 02-795 5504). Otherwise, contact your embassy.

BUSINESS HOURS

For most government and private offices, business hours are from 9 am to 6 pm Monday to Friday, and from 9 am to 1 pm on alternate Saturdays. Offices close at 5 pm from November to February.

Department stores open from 10.30 am to 7.30 pm daily, while small shops may stay open from dawn until late at night.

PUBLIC HOLIDAYS & SPECIAL EVENTS

There are two types of public holidays: those that are set according to the solar calendar and those that follow the lunar calendar. Solar holidays include:

New Year's Day 1-2 January
Independence Movement Day (Samil-jeol) 1 March. Anniversary of the 1919 Independence Movement against the Japanese.
Arbour Day 5 April. Trees are planted across the nation as part of South Korea's ongoing reafforestation program.
Children's Day 5 May. A day to take the kids to the amusement park or zoo.
Memorial Day 6 June. To honour those who died in war.
Constitution Day 17 July. To commemorate the founding of the Republic of Korea, 17 July 1948.
Liberation Day 15 August. In memory of the Japanese acceptance of the Allied terms of surrender in 1945.
National Foundation Day 3 October. In memory of Tan-gun, the legendary first Korean, who was born in 2333 BC.
Christmas Day 25 December

Lunar holidays, of course, fall on different dates in different years (see the Lunar Calendar section in the Facts about Korea chapter). There are three lunar festivals which have been designated public holidays. They are:

Lunar New Year (Seollal) – first day of the first moon. You can expect Korea to grind to a halt

Buddha's Birthday, or the Feast of the Lanterns, is celebrated by the lighting of countless candles and paper lanterns.

at this time. The schedule for the next five years is as follows: 24 January 2001; 12 February 2002; 1 February 2003; 22 January 2004; and 9 February 2005.
Buddha's Birthday or **Feast of the Lanterns** (Bucheonim Osinnal) – eighth day of the fourth moon. In Seoul, there is an evening lantern parade from Yeo-eui-do Plaza to Jogyesa on the Sunday prior to the actual holiday. Buddha's Birthday will fall on the following dates: 30 April 2001; 19 May 2002; 8 May 2003; 26 May 2004; and 15 May 2005.
Chuseok ('Korean Thanksgiving') – 15th day of the eighth moon (the same day as the Chinese Mid-Autumn Festival). Everyone, even expats, call this holiday by its Korean name. This is South Korea's biggest holiday, with virtually everybody returns to their family homes, to prepare offerings to their ancestors. If the weather is favourable the evening is spent moon-gazing. This holiday will fall on the following dates: 1 October 2001; 21 September 2002; 11 September 2003; 28 September 2004; and 18 September 2005.

Festivals of all kinds have proliferated in recent years. There are events celebrating pottery, *gimchi* (the national dish, made of pickled vegetables, garlic and chilli), ginseng, taegwondo, historic milestones and mud(!) – you name it, the Koreans have an event for it. Some of the more notable events include:

International Labour Day 1 May. This is *not* an official public holiday, in part because of its Marxist connotations (all Communist countries celebrate 1 May as a major public holiday). Despite the official frown, banks and many other businesses close at this time.

Dano Festival This is held throughout South Korea on the fifth day of the fifth lunar month. It features processions of shamans and mask dance dramas. The schedule for the next five years is: 25 June 2001; 15 June 2002; 4 June 2003; 22 June 2004; and 11 June 2005.

National Folk Arts Festival The date and the venue for this festival changes from year to year, but it generally falls in September. It is an excellent opportunity to see traditional festival activities, and includes real crowd-pullers, like the wagon battle and torch-hurling events. Check with KNTO to find out when it's scheduled.

Cherry Blossom Festival This week-long event is held in the southern city of Jinhae in the province, Gyeongsangnam-do, and usually falls in the first half of April. An exact date is hard to give because the weather (and thus, the cherry blossoms) won't always cooperate.

Hangeul Day 9 October. This day commemorates the establishment of the Korean hangeul writing system in the 15th century.

ACTIVITIES
Baduk (Korean Chess)
This game originated in China (where it was called *wei chi*) and was further refined in Japan (where the game is known as *go*). It consists of a playing board with flat black and white stones. Players take turns placing stones on the board, trying to capture both territory and each other's stones. As with Western chess, the rules are simple but the techniques can be very complex.

It's easy to find partners who can teach you the art of Korean chess – try the local pubs. Frequently, a fair bit of alcohol is consumed during these games and money often changes hands. As with Western chess, major championships are followed in the news media.

Canoeing & Rafting
Korea only has three rivers that attract white water enthusiasts. The Naerincheon, near Inje in Gangwon-do is considered the best. In the southern part of Gangwon-do, near Yeong-

wol, is the Donggang. About 50km north of Seoul is the Hantangang Resort, which also has some rafting (*keumnyutagi*) activities.

For further information, contact the Pine River Canoe School in Seoul (☎ 02-3473 1659) or Inje (☎ 0365-461 4586).

Cycling
Cycling (*ssaikeulling*) is almost suicidal in cities, but is a reasonable form of recreation in the countryside. Bicycles are usually only available for rent in tourist areas like Gyeongju and Jejudo. There are mountain-biking clubs in major cities that arrange group outings.

Golf
In Korea, golf (*golpeu*) is a prestigious sport – for business executives and politicians it's almost mandatory. Country clubs tend to charge outrageous membership fees, but nonmembers are grudgingly allowed to play. Nonmembers can expect to pay W80,000 on weekdays and W85,000 on weekends, which should include caddie fees. When you enter the country, golf clubs should be declared at customs.

There are over 80 golf courses in Korea. KNTO puts out a few publications that lists all the golf courses (or check the KNTO Web site).

In urban areas, golf putting ranges are popular. Fees are typically from W15,000 to W20,000 per hour.

Hash House Harriers
The Hash is an informal, loosely-strung international club with branches all over the world. It appeals mainly to young people or the young at heart. Weekend activities typically include an afternoon easy jogging session followed by a dinner and beer party, which can extend until the wee hours of the morning.

There is no club headquarters, but every branch of the Hash is supposed to have a 'Grandmaster' who can be contacted for information. It would be useless to publish the Grandmasters' phone numbers as this changes quickly. Commonwealth embassy staffers often know about it, and sometimes notices are posted at local expat pubs. The Web site, called Guide to Hashing in Korea (homepages.go.com/~sngmstr/korea.html) can fill you in on club locations and contact details.

Health Clubs

In these days of cappuccino and 'fusion food' restaurants, joining a health club is almost *de rigueur* for the young executive on the go. The fitness craze has most definitely caught on in Korea, and it's fairly easy to find clubs offering all sorts of punishing exercise equipment, tennis courts, swimming pools, hot tubs and various other accoutrements. Major hotels offer these facilities for guests and members, but there are plenty of private clubs that allow short-term visitors for around W10,000 per day. Monthly memberships at a health club should cost about W250,000.

Hiking

Every province of Korea offers outstanding opportunities for hiking *(deungsan)*. Indeed, you'll find many challenging walking and climbing areas as close as the suburbs of Seoul.

Perhaps the biggest problem with hiking in Korea is escaping the crowds – at times it feels as if you're riding the Seoul subway rather than visiting the wilderness. Some areas are so popular that you sometimes have to stand in line to reach the summit of a peak. Fortunately, this predicament can be bypassed if you simply avoid the most popular spots during weekends and holidays.

If you want to travel with a group, Korean friends can help you join a mountaineering club *(san ak hoi)*, although don't expect hikers at the Korean clubs to be able to speak much English.

Koreans are serious about the great outdoors; any excursion away from the concrete of Seoul is prepared for with a thoroughness worthy of an assault on Everest. This includes ice axes (in summer) and ropes (for walking up a gentle slope). Koreans also must be the best-dressed hikers in the world – check out the red vests, yellow caps and multi-coloured knee-high socks. All the equipment and fancy clothing makes for heroic photos – a camera is *de rigueur*.

While the Koreans no doubt overdo it, there are a few things which you should bring. Useful if not fashionable items include sun protection (sunglasses, sunscreen lotion and sunhat), rain gear, food, maps, compass, mosquito repellent and warm clothing. The most important item you can bring is water – no less than 2L per person per day in summer.

Mountain areas have notoriously fickle weather, and this problem should not be taken lightly. At high altitudes, it can go from sunny and mild to dangerously cold and wet in remarkably little time. It's best to dress in layers – shirts, sweaters and nylon wind-jackets can be peeled off and put on as needed. Bring proper rain gear or you may live (or may not live) to regret it.

A serious issue for hikers is something called 'declination' – the angle between true north and magnetic north. The problem gets more severe the farther you are from the equator, and South Korea lies very far to the north. Declination in Korea is about 20° north-east – that is, when you look at your compass dial, true north is about 20° to the north-east of where the compass needle is pointing.

Horse Riding

Jejudo (where the Mongol invaders once reared their horses) is without a doubt the prime location for this hobby, though there are commercial stables at membership resorts around Seoul.

Hot Springs

Korea has plenty of health spas where you can soak away your aches and pains. The drawback is that every single useable hot spring *(oncheon)* has been developed – forget about frolicking nude in a large outdoor pool surrounded by trees and boulders. In Korea, the hot water is simply piped into hotels and guests are expected to do their frolicking in private pools usually located in the hotel's basement. Nudity is acceptable, but the pools are segregated by sex. For those too shy to be naked in front of 100 Koreans (or if you want to bathe with a member of the opposite sex), hotel rooms can usually be rented with hot spring water piped directly to the bathtubs (but check that out before you pay!). Even if you are not staying at the hotel, you can usually use the baths for between W1000 to W8000 – a private room will easily cost 10 times more.

Despite the lack of a natural outdoor setting, soaking in a steaming hotel public bath isn't the worst way to spend a cold winter evening. All sorts of health benefits are claimed due to the mineral content of the water. Since mineral content varies from one spring to the next, each one has its own reputation for curing a particular ailment.

Perhaps the most enjoyable hot springs are the ones found at ski resorts. You can get in a full day of skiing and soak those tired muscles in the evening. Even when there's a lack of snow, a good day of hiking followed by a hot water soak is one way to reach nirvana. All hot spring resorts can be extremely crowded on holidays.

Paragliding

Paragliding (and to a lesser extent, hanggliding) has taken off in South Korea. The most popular venue seems to be around the base of the mountain, Hallasan, on the island of Jejudo. The KNTO has the scoop on local paragliding clubs.

Skating

Both roller blades and ice skating (seukeiteu) are popular pastimes. A few large cities have good indoor ice-skating rinks, but in most other areas it's outdoors and therefore strictly a winter sport.

Skiing

Although Korea's mountains don't compare with the Swiss Alps, there are some good places where you can practise the art of sliding downhill (seuki). The ski season runs from early December to mid-March. Facilities include artificial snow and equipment hire. These places can be crowded at weekends – get there early if you need to hire equipment. Since ski resorts are on remote mountaintops, some of them don't have a regular bus service, but numerous travel agencies run tour buses as part of a package tour. Otherwise, hire a taxi for the last leg of the journey.

See the index of this book for a listing of ski areas.

Swimming

In crowded South Korea, most urban residents do their swimming (suyeong) in shallow pools in which there is no chance of drowning. There are a number of inexpensive public pools that get very crowded, and private ones that cost quite a bit more but offer special monthly membership deals.

Most of South Korea's lakes are in fact reservoirs. Swimming is not permitted at such places since this is drinking water. Also, the lake levels drop during dry weather, leaving a rather ugly 'bathtub ring' around the reservoirs which makes swimming unappealing.

It's a different story at the seashore. The beach season is basically July and August, and during the rest of the year most beaches are not even open to the public. As you will soon discover, South Korea's beaches are lined with barbed-wire fences. These are partially removed during the summer months to give the public access, but all coastal areas are heavily guarded and that particularly applies to areas close to North Korea. You are not supposed to be on the beach at night, and soldiers enforce this rule. In case you're wondering, North Korea has fences along the beach too (though in the North the fences are electrified).

Tennis

For fans of this pastime (teniseu), there are public tennis courts in city parks. These tend to be very crowded, but you can sometimes get on if you go during normal working hours. Forget it on weekends and holidays.

Not surprisingly, deluxe tourist hotels and private health clubs offer better facilities.

Windsurfing

The sport of windsurfing *(windeusseoping)* has gained a following in southern areas, such as Busan and Jejudo. Windsurfing championships are sometimes held at Haeundae Beach in Busan.

COURSES

Korean law requires that foreigners studying at a university have a sponsor and have either a student visa or a working visa. Universities do check, and you can be heavily fined if you sign up for a course before you have the necessary visa. The universities can sponsor you for a student visa if you are a full-time student. Obtaining the visa takes about eight to 10 weeks.

Private institutes, on the other hand, usually don't ask and don't want to know about your visa status. Technically they are supposed to check on this, but most are more than happy to take your money. However, you *could* possibly run into problems with the authorities, so if you pursue this route at least be discreet.

Language

By far the most popular courses for foreigners are language courses. Seoul is the main venue for this activity, though you can certainly study at schools elsewhere.

Yonsei University (www.yonsei.ac.kr) has an intensive course (20 hours per week). It's said to be the largest Korean language program in the country. The cost is W1.3 million for 10 weeks. The school can sponsor you for a visa, and there is dorm accommodation available (not comfortable, but cheap). There is also a part-time evening program (three hours per night, three nights per week) which costs W560,000 for 10 weeks, but it does not offer visa sponsorship (you must have a resident visa).

Sogang University is reputed to have the best of the university programs. There is a choice of 15 or 20 hours per week for 10 weeks.

Ewha Women's University has a full-time course of 20 hours per week for 10 weeks, or a part-time course of 6.5 hours per week

(cost is W400,000). The language courses are open to men as well as to women.

There are several private language institutes offering tuition for foreigners – everything from one-on-one tutoring to large classes. Tuition costs at these places can range from W4000 to W28,000 per hour, depending on how many students are in the class.

Several satisfied customers have recommended the privately run Seoul Korean Language Academy (☎ 563 3226) in Gangnam-gu. The Language Teaching Research Centre (LTRC; ☎ 737 4641) in central Seoul is another option.

Sisayeongeosa (☎ 276 0509) is a major educational publishing company, which also has language classes for foreigners – there is a branch in central Seoul and in the Sinchon area.

A few other institutes that might be worth trying include Pagoda (☎ 274 4000), ELS International (☎ 278 0509) and BCM Publishers (☎ 567 0644). Other language schools advertise in the *Korea Times* and *Korea Herald*.

Taegwondo

This traditional Korean form of self-defence, or martial art, evolved from an earlier

A Silla-period temple guardian stands at the ready, *taegyeon* fashion.

The flying kick is a feature of *taegwondo*,
Korea's indigenous martial art.

form called *taegyeon*. Nowadays, almost all
South Korean males are inducted into the
army to do their stint of national service and
are taught taegwondo as part of their training – as a result, bar room brawls in Korea
can get pretty nasty.

Taegwondo has a large following in the
West, and serious students make the long
journey to South Korea to study it. Classes
for men, women and children are conducted
at private institutes in every Korean city.

Cooking

Although there are plenty of do-it-yourself
books that try to explain the fine art of Korean cooking, there's nothing like getting
hands-on gimchi-making experience under
the skilled guidance of a teacher. In all large
Korean cities, plenty of private institutes
cater to this need, but only a few are staffed
with English-speaking instructors. Without
a doubt, Seoul is the easiest place to find a
cooking course taught in English, but it
should be possible in other communities
where there is a large expat population (especially around US military bases).

WORK

One unusual method of fund-raising is to
turn in a North Korean spy – the government pays from W1,000,000 to W5,000,000
for each one you report.

Failing that, you just might need to get a
job. Korea has long been a popular place to
look for work – mainly English teaching at

private language schools (*hagwon*). Some
foreigners do find other jobs (usually at
lower pay), such as proof-reading translated
documents. However, these jobs tend to
metamorphose into English teaching anyway, so you might as well start as an English teacher and get paid accordingly.

It is illegal to work on a tourist visa, but
many people still do (and some get deported
for doing so). However, if you are suitably
qualified (have graduated with a bachelors
degree in *something*), and are prepared to
spend a bit of time in Korea, there is no
need to run the risks of working illegally.
Many schools in Korea are willing to sponsor English teachers on one-year contracts.
Remuneration for English teaching on this
basis can be quite lucrative, but there are
several drawbacks.

The first problem is that many written
agreements include ways to keep you to the
end of your contract (a fine of two month's
wages for early resignation is common, and
schools usually only pay once monthly so
this is easily enforced). The second is that
your employer may promise you the moon,
the stars and a bucket of chicken wings, but
many schools simply cheat on wages. If you
are being paid less than your contract stip-
ulates or being forced to work overtime
without pay, there isn't a whole lot you can
do other than quit. Unfortunately, you will
lose your work visa within just a few days
of quitting, which means you must leave the
country. A work visa is valid for one job
only – if you quit and want to seek other
employment, you must apply for a new
work visa. In theory, if you've been cheated
by an employer, you can take the case to
court – in practice, this seldom works.

If you are working illegally, you have no
legal rights and are more likely to be
cheated. At the end of the month your employer may tell you that he's short on cash,
but will promise to pay you next month.
Come next month, and it's the same story,
ad infinitum, ad nauseam, ad fraudulentium.

Despite these drawbacks, working can
pay off. Korea is filled with foreign workers – legal and illegal – and the jobs are not
only in Seoul. If at all possible, try to do

things legally. If you feel that you can guarantee your employer a year of your time and are willing to run the risk of working for someone who might cheat you, then it would be worth your while scouting around for a school in Korea that is willing to offer you sponsorship.

The obvious place to look is the classifieds section of the daily English-language newspapers. Some people maintain that the best jobs are never advertised here, and that it is only the schools that consistently lose staff that need to advertise. On the other hand, it is not uncommon to meet teachers who found their jobs through the newspaper and are happy with their work.

Some schools can be found through the Internet. Dave's ESL Cafe (www.eslcafe.com) is *the* Web site to visit for aspiring ESL teachers and students.

The TESLJB-L mailing list is also helpful – subscribe by sending a one-line message to listserv@cunyvm.cuny.edu. Leave the subject line blank, and in the body of the message type 'subscribe TESLJB-L John Smith' (substitute your name for 'John Smith').

Or you could simply walk door to door and talk to the schools.

One other way to find work is to book yourself in to the Inn Daewon in Seoul (see the Places to Stay – Budget section of the Seoul chapter). This is where many destitute backpackers end up, and it's a standby for English-language schools that need to find a substitute teacher in a hurry.

ACCOMMODATION
Camping
Korea is a paradise for campers – at least when the weather cooperates. Every national park has camping grounds and most are free. When a fee is charged, it's usually no more than W4000 and this buys you access to fine facilities like hot showers and flush toilets. Most camping grounds are government-run, though a few private ones exist.

Because Korea is a crowded place, the wilderness really takes a beating. Therefore, campers should be extra diligent in the matter of protecting the environment. If you intend to cook, you should carry a portable gas stove. Building wood fires in the forest is not recommended – it's environmentally ruinous, not to mention hazardous when the weather is dry. Human waste and used toilet paper should be buried at least 50m from surface water. However, other paper and plastic rubbish should not be buried – if you backpacked it in, you can backpack it out.

The national park service has closed a number of backcountry areas to camping and cooking in order to give the wilderness a badly needed rest. If you have any questions about locations where camping is prohibited, make local inquiries.

Mountain Huts & Shelters
Along the hiking trails in many national parks are strategically-located shelters *(daepiso)* or huts *(sanjang)*. Don't expect much more than a wooden floor on which to roll out a sleeping bag. Toilets tend to be the smelly latrine variety. Drinking water is almost always available and some huts have basic items for sale like food and drinks, though you should not count on this.

The huts and shelters are almost certain to be open during the busy summer hiking season, and often in autumn when Koreans head for the hills to watch the leaves turn colours. A few (but not many) huts and shelters are open in the springtime, but you can forget it in winter.

The better-appointed places charge a basic fee of W1000 to W3000 for use of the facilities.

Hostels
There are 45 youth hostels scattered around the country. Unlike their counterparts in Europe, America and Australia, South Korean hostels are generally huge, luxurious places with incredible facilities and some private rooms. All the hostels have their own restaurants with meals at W3000 to W5000. The main drawback is that hostels are not always conveniently located.

Dorm beds vary between W7000 and W11,000 – non-members add W2000 – but the private rooms cost as much as W85,000 (or W120,000 for non-members). You can become a member by paying a W30,000 annual fee. A membership card can also net you some discounts at various amusement parks and on some boat cruises.

For more information and reservations contact the Korea Youth Hostel Association (☎ 02-725 3031), Room 408, Jeokseon Hyundae Bldg, Jeokseon-dong, Jongno-gu, Seoul, 110-052.

Guesthouses

Western-style accommodation in the major centres is generally very expensive, so budget travellers usually head for the traditional Korean inns known as *yeoinsuk* or *yeogwan*. The more upmarket yeogwan are called *jang yeogwan* (sometimes just abbreviated to *jang*).

The difference in name gives an indication of what kind of facilities you can expect and the price you'll pay. Yeogwan usually have at least some rooms with private bath, while yeoinsuk almost never do. Rooms in jang yeogwan all have private bath. Basic yeoinsuk rooms generally cost from W15,000 to W20,000. Prices in yeogwan cost around W25,000, but in smaller towns (especially resort areas) you will get charged more than in major cities, at least during the summer tourist season – figure on about W35,000. Many yeogwan and budget hotels typically put up the price another W5000 on Saturday night.

Yeoinsuk are becoming an endangered species, while relatively pricey jang yeogwan are rapidly multiplying. To judge from some of the sounds coming through the paper-thin walls, many of the cheaper yeoinsuk are surviving primarily as pay-by-the-hour love hotels (or many Koreans are afflicted with severe breathing problems).

Probably the easiest way to save money on accommodation is to double up. Doubles and singles are usually the same price, though a third person might be charged extra.

The proprietors are highly unlikely to speak English but they'll expect you to want to see the room and bathroom facilities before you decide to stay. If they don't offer to show you the room, then ask to see it (*'bang-eul bolsu isseoyo'*).

Yeoinsuk and yeogwan are usually clustered around bus and railway stations. You should learn to recognise the Korean characters for yeoinsuk and yeogwan, as well as the symbol for bath, which you'll find on the signs of all jang yeogwan. The bath symbol indicates that all rooms have private bath. Unfortunately, the same symbol is used on public bathhouses (*mogyoktang*).

Homestays

A place where you pay a fee to stay in a private home is known as a *minbak*. In many rural parts of Korea, elderly women congregate at bus stations and encourage tourists to stay in their homes. You would stay at a minbak either because it's cheaper than a hotel, or (at least in resort areas) the only thing available at short notice during peak holiday times. Minbak rates are usually slightly lower than yeogwan, and long-term discounts can be negotiated.

A home stay in Seoul is not necessarily cheap (minimum W35,000), nor will you find elderly women standing in bus terminals drumming up business. In Seoul, home stays are organised by the Ministry of Culture & Tourism as a sort of cultural exchange program.

There are several organisations in Seoul that can arrange homestays. As follows:

Korean Homestay (www.homestay.andyou.com)
Homestay Korea (☎ 02-722 7360),
    www.homestaykorea.com
Labo International Exchange Center
(☎ 02-817 4625, **e** klabo@chollian.co.kr)
    www.labostay.or.kr
Korea Youth Exchange Promotion Association ☎ (02-817 6325, **e** kyepa2@kyepa.or.kr)
    www.kyepa.or.kr
WAWO (☎ 02-254 2916)
    www.wawo.co.kr

Hotels

In all price levels, you may have a choice between a 'Korean-style room' (also called 'ondol') and a 'Western-style' room. In a Korean-style room, you sleep on the floor. This is true even in five-star hotels – don't associate the notion of 'Korean-style' with 'cheap' – some of these rooms are fit for a king (and note that none of Korea's kings ever had cable TV).

The KNTO divides Korea's hotels into rating categories: super deluxe (equivalent to five-star), deluxe (four-star), 1st class (three-star), 2nd class (two-star), 3rd class (one-star). Yeoinsuk, yeogwan and youth hostels are excluded from the ratings, though jang yeogwan should at least be considered one-star hotels (and the plush ones could be considered two-star). In many respects, the lower end of the mid-range hotels represents less of a bargain than jang yeogwan, but they often do have English-speaking staff and business facilities.

Exactly how much you'll pay varies by location and season. As a general guideline, the least expensive double rooms would typically cost W40,000 in a 3rd class hotel, W50,000 in 2nd class, W80,000 in 1st class, W140,000 in deluxe class and W200,000 in super deluxe. The most expensive suites cost so much that for about the same price you could almost buy your own house. In addition to the room rates, many mid-range places and all top-end ones will charge an extra 10% tax, plus another 10% service charge.

Many upmarket hotels offer substantial discounts during the winter season (December through February).

Motels

The word 'motel' doesn't have quite the same meaning in Korea as it does in the West. Generally, these are upmarket yeogwan. Prices are still very reasonable, perhaps W25,000 to W35,000 per night. They tend to be a little more spacious than yeogwan, and many double as love hotels. But if you don't mind frilly pink beds with strategically placed mirrors and a condom machine on the wall, motels are acceptable accommodation. You should learn to recognise the Korean characters for 'motel'.

Rental Accommodation

In many cases you can come to an agreement with the owners of a yeogwan for a better monthly deal on a room. However, it's advisable to spend at least one night in the yeogwan first before handing over a

month's rent – you may discover that the place is unsuitable for your needs.

Yeogwan living has drawbacks, like not being able to cook for yourself, or having to be home by midnight when the yeogwan closes. It also makes it impractical to have your own telephone installed, though you can bypass the problem with a pager or mobile phone.

Renting houses and apartments in Korea works very differently than in most Western countries. The problem is the requirement for astronomical deposits. The deposits are known as 'key money' (*jeonse*), and a figure of W50 million is not unusual in the better parts of Seoul. The way it works is that if you pay key money, you do not have to pay any monthly rent at all, and when you move out your entire deposit will be refunded. This sounds like a good deal, but as the locals point out, the tenant takes all the risks. Although the landlord is required to refund the deposit when you leave, in some cases your money will be channelled into dodgy investments (or outright gambling) and may be lost. Theoretically, you would have an excellent legal case against a landlord who loses your deposit, but in practice you could spend months or years pursuing the matter in a Korean court without good results.

The Western system of paying a small deposit and then a monthly fee (*wolse* in Korean) does exist in Seoul, and has become more common in recent years thanks to an oversupply in the housing and business rental market. A variation on the theme is that you pay the rent in advance for one or two years in a lump sum, from which a certain amount of money is deducted every month.

Be sure to inquire about the monthly maintenance fee (*gwallibi*). In fact, little or no free maintenance is likely to be done and is often just another way to extract some extra rent.

Finding an apartment is a matter of deciding on an area that you want to live in and then seeking out real estate agents. It helps considerably to bring a Korean-speaking friend along. In Seoul, check out the bulletin board in the USO.

The ideal solution is to find an apartment or to rent a room in a boarding house, known locally as a *hasukjip*. Boarding houses are probably a better alternative to the expense of renting an apartment, but conditions in these houses are not always ideal. Before committing to anything, check to see whether there are cooking facilities and if a curfew is in effect.

Best of all, if you're working in Korea, inquire as to whether a provision of accommodation can be built into your employment contract. Many employers provide accommodation for their foreign staff, and there's no reason why *your* employer shouldn't make some effort towards helping you get set up in Korea too.

Since 1997 foreigners have been permitted to purchase their own homes in South Korea.

FOOD

The generic cuisines available in South Korea are Korean, Chinese, Japanese, a smattering of other Asian flavours, and a growing Western-food scene.

Korean Food

The one element of Korean cooking which receives the most comments, both positive and negative, is that staple of the Korean diet, gimchi. Gimchi is basically grated or chopped vegetables mixed with various other ingredients – notably chilli, garlic and ginger – and left to ferment in an earthenware pot. The result is served up as a side dish or as the principle component of any Korean meal, even breakfast. It has a raw, tangy taste and is very spicy.

Most foreigners can't face gimchi at 7 am, but it does make a tasty addition to lunch or dinner. Many foreigners describe their first encounter with gimchi as a 'near death experience', but then they get used to it, and finally become thoroughly addicted.

At the basic end, an omelette with rice (*omu raiseu*) is a cheap dish which has sustained many a backpacker. Another budget travellers' special is *gimbap*, the Korean version of Japanese sushi wrapped in dried seaweed (actually 'laver' rather than common seaweed). Sushi not wrapped in laver is called *chobap* (it can be unwrapped, or wrapped in fried egg). Thanks to the liberal use of spices, Korean sushi is usually tastier than the Japanese variety. Gimbap is always served with some yellow-coloured pickled *daikon* (radishes). If you ask, you can eat it without meat – salvation for vegetarians.

Another inexpensive dish is *mandu* – delicious Korean-style dumplings. If you like spices, try the gimchi dumplings *(gimchi mandu)*.

Unless you're vegetarian, you should definitely try *bulgogi*, probably the favourite dish of foreign visitors. Bulgogi, which literally means 'fire beef', is often translated as 'Korean barbecue'. Strips of beef marinated in soy sauce, sesame oil, garlic and chilli are grilled on a hot plate right on the dining table. Basically, you do your own table-top cooking. Eating this

How to Make Gimchi

Mastering the ins and outs of gimchi-making is a fine art, something only acquired through experience. Virtually every woman in Korea is taught that this an essential skill that must be learned if she hopes to find a good husband. But even if you're male and not in the market for marriage, producing your own gimchi can be a reward in itself, once you've acquired a taste for this spiciest of spicy vegetables.

You'd be wise to find a Korean (probably female) to teach you, but if you'd like to take a stab at it yourself, here is a basic recipe:

Step 1: Mix sea salt and Chinese cabbage. Set aside for one to three hours and then rinse thoroughly.

Step 2: Prepare flour paste (this is optional). Mix flour and water, boil it for two or three minutes, then cool it down.

Step 3: Mix the cabbage with the flour paste and the following ingredients: chopped radish, carrot, garlic, ginger, onion, green onion and brown sugar (just a pinch). Then knead it.

Step 4: Add hot pepper and a little extra salt. Leave it to mature for two days, preferably in a special ceramic gimchi pot.

way is a leisurely social affair, and it makes sense to share it with at least one other person, rather than to do it solo. Prices vary, but they should be in the W10,000 to W15,000 range.

Similar to bulgogi is *galbi*, which uses short ribs instead of strips of beef. Most bulgogi restaurants also serve galbi.

A popular dish that uses gimchi as a primary ingredient is *bibimbap*. Basically it consists of a bed of rice with gimchi, vegetables, meat and a dollop of hot chilli on top. There are variations on the theme which exclude meat – a boon to vegetarians. Bibimbap is usually served in a thick, heated iron bowl, so that the dish is still cooking when it is placed in front of you. The whole thing should be stirred up with a spoon before eating.

Sinseollo is similar to Japanese *shabu-shabu*. Meat, fish, vegetables and tofu are simmered together in a broth right at your table. This is another dish that most foreigners enjoy.

A notable Korean speciality is *naeng myeon*, or cold noodles. The noodles are made of buckwheat and are very healthy. *Kong guksu* is a noodle dish made in a soy milk broth. More appealing to Western tastes is *mak guksu*, a combination of vegetables and meat slices with noodles in chicken broth.

Korean gourmet cuisine is best represented by *hanjeongsik*, a banquet meal with a vast array of dishes. Again, there are vegetarian versions if you ask.

Stews Korean stews *(jjigae)* are very tasty and inexpensive. There seems to be an almost endless variety of stews, but one of the most delicious is *dubu jjigae* or bean curd stew. Another variation of it is bean paste stew *(doenjang jjigae)*, which resembles Japanese *miso*.

Another excellent, though more expensive, stew is *galbi jjim*, in which the main ingredient is beef short ribs. These dishes come with rice and a serving of gimchi. There is also fiery hot gimchi stew *(gimchi jjigae)*, for those who can't get enough of the stuff in the side dishes provided.

Cow intestine stew *(gopchang jeongol)* generally gets mixed reactions – definitely an acquired taste.

Soups Probably the most famous Korean soup is *samgye tang*, or ginseng chicken soup. A small, whole chicken stuffed with ginseng and glutinous rice is served with soup in a claypot.

Galbitang is beef short-rib soup served with rice and gimchi. *Seolleongtang* is a hearty beef stock soup mixed with rice. *Gomtang* (beef soup) is simple beef with bones cooked in broth. *Kkorigomtang* (ox tail soup) is self-explanatory. *Yukgaejang* (spicy beef soup) often contains cows entrails, which doesn't always cheer Western diners. *Maeuntang* (pepper pot soup) is excellent but *very* spicy.

Street-Stall Food Street stalls are worth exploring, both for the traveller on a tight budget and for others interested in sampling the full gamut of Korean cuisine. A very palatable example is *twigim*, a Koreanised version of Japanese tempura – vegetables, seafood and dumplings deep fried in batter. Also common are stalls specialising in Korean pancakes. The most basic is *pajeon*, or green onion pancakes. Mung bean pancakes *(bindaetteok)* contain bean sprouts and pork.

Spicy rice rolls *(tteokbokgi)* are a popular snack, consisting of rice dough rolls simmered in a hot sauce.

Desserts Korean junk food is prime stuff and has become a major export item. Read the small print and you'll find the 'made in Korea' label on packages of cakes, cream puffs and frozen ice cream bars in such disparate locations as Hong Kong, Vietnam, Taiwan and even in the ethnic grocery stores of San Francisco and Melbourne. However, Koreans seldom eat dessert after a meal, as is the common practice in the West. Junk food is usually for snacks.

Of course, there's all the usual stuff – ice cream, chocolate, pies – but you might want to try something distinctly Korean. A popular dessert that seems to be a Korean-Chinese-Western hybrid is known as red bean parfait *(patbingsu)*. It's made with sweetened red beans mixed with crushed ice, fruit cocktail, milk and ice cream. It can be bought all over the place, but is usually only sold during summer.

Pushcarts all over the country sell *hotteok*, a fried sweet roll that resembles a doughnut without the hole. It usually has a cinnamon and honey paste in the centre and is delicious.

Chinese Food

Chinese restaurants have definitely caught on with the Koreans. However, the food has been heavily 'Koreanised', and connoisseurs of Chinese cuisine consider the Korean version a travesty of the real thing.

Connoisseurs aside, if you want some grease in your diet, you may want to give fried rice *(bokgeumbap)* a try – it typically costs W5000 or less. A less greasy and popular dish is *(jjajang myeon)*, a northern Chinese speciality that is a little similar to spaghetti bolognaise. Moving up in price and quality, you might want to try sweet and sour pork *(tangsuyuk)* or a rice, vegetable and meat dish *(japtangbap)*.

Japanese Food

Intriguingly, though most Koreans claim to hate Japanese food, there is no shortage of clientele in the Japanese restaurants.

The Koreans have adopted sushi *(gimbap)* as their own, but you'll find it in all Japanese restaurants. A variation on the theme is *yubu chobap*, which is prepared in a similar way to sushi except that bean curd and rice is mixed with vinegar and wrapped up into a thin omelette egg roll.

Another famous Japanese cold dish is *saengseon hoe*, (the equivalent to Japanese sashimi, or raw fish. In Japan it gets served with hot green horseradish *(wasabi)*, but the Koreans prefer to it with either soy or hot chilli sauce and rice.

The cheaper Japanese hot dishes include tempura, known locally as *twigim*. The most common are shrimp tempura with vegetables *(saeu twigim)*, fish tempura *(saengseon twigim)* and vegetable tempura *(yachae twigim)*.

Other Asian Food

Although not common, in big cities you can find a few Indian, Pakistani, Thai and Vietnamese restaurants. Prices tend to be mid range. Indian restaurants in particular offer some hope for vegetarian diners.

Western

Your first Western meal in Korea is likely to be breakfast. And, as you'll soon discover, your fellow diners are likely to be Koreans. The truth is that many young Koreans tend to shun traditional breakfasts, which are based on gimchi, rice, seaweed and fish. The past few years have seen an outbreak of Western-style bakeries and coffee shops *(keopisyop)*. Some of these are big chain stores – *Dunkin Donuts* and *Paris Baguette* are the most widespread, and the Japanese chain *Doutor* has a significance presence. It's interesting that the big chains tend to charge much less for their coffee (and offer free refills) than the Korean coffee houses.

Donuts and coffee are readily available, but big 'American-style' breakfasts (eggs, bacon, toast with jam) are much harder to come by. The Koreans have not taken to this, and if this is what you need, you may have to explore the expensive coffee shops in the big hotels.

When it comes to lunch and dinner, you'll have considerably more choice. There has been a recent explosion of mid-priced Western-style restaurants dishing up Italian, French, German and American food. Spaghetti, steak, salad and even the occasional burrito can be obtained without much difficulty.

The news is good at the lower end of the food chain – Seoul, Busan and other large cities have yielded to the razzle-dazzle of the fast-food industry with abandon. It probably won't be long before an assiduous Korean archaeologist unearths a Neolithic McDonald's and proves that the Big Mac was actually a Korean invention. Hot dogs *(hatdogeu)*, hamburgers *(haembeogeu)*, French fries, pizza and other staples of Western fast-food culture are very much in evidence. Prices at the familiar chain stores are in line with what you'd pay in the West.

It can be debated whether or not fried or roasted chicken is really a Western food, but this is one thing the Koreans do very well. Nor do you need to seek out a foreign chain like KFC – small Korean pubs called 'hofs' *(hopeu)*, dish up this delicious stuff throughout the country, usually at very reasonable prices. Just look for the roasted chickens in the display window.

Self-Catering

Aside from saving money, self-catering gives you a little more control over what you eat, and is a particularly good idea for vegetarians. One great feature of Korea is the existence of little hole-in-the-wall grocery stores open from early morning to late at night. These are found everywhere, so you'll never have to walk far to pick up that package of noodles, ham, bread, tuna or chocolate.

By contrast, large Western-style supermarkets are a rarity, though they are increasing in number. Mostly these are found in the basements of large department stores. Also, any city or town of significant size has an Agricultural Cooperative Supermarket, a government-sponsored scheme that offers good prices and variety.

The biggest problem with self-catering is simply finding cooking facilities. Some yeogwan have boiling hot water available from an electric thermos, but this is the exception rather than the rule. If you ask politely, the *ajumma* (a term of respect for a woman who runs a restaurant or hotel) might boil some water for you, but don't count on it – most yeogwan try to discourage travellers from eating in their rooms because they don't want to clean up the mess.

In many cities, the 24-hour convenience stores are a possibility for a cheap lunch or snack. These places invariably sell instant noodles packaged in a styrofoam bowl, but also sandwiches and hot dogs. Most (but not all) convenience stores have hot water, microwave ovens, disposable chopsticks and a table (no chairs though), so you can consume your instant banquet on the premises. You can easily fill your stomach for W1000 to W2500.

DRINKS
Non-Alcoholic

Korea produces what are arguably the best herbal teas in the world. Ginseng tea is the most famous, but also check out *ssanghwa* tea, made from three different roots and often served with an egg yolk or pine nuts floating in it. Ginger tea *(saenggangcha)* is also excellent. Citron tea *(yujacha)* and five flavours tea *(omijacha)* are positively yummy.

Tea or coffee rooms *(dabang)* are great social centres. Little food is served, though they might come up with some rice crackers. The coffee tends to be expensive. A few dabang are fronts for prostitution – they offer 'home delivery'. A good way to distinguish the legitimate from the illegitimate is that the places offering a call-girl service have a lineup of motorscooters out the front.

Alcoholic

Koreans love their brew and there is no shortage of drinking establishments. Boozing it up is mostly a male group activity in Korea. Visit a typical pub in Seoul and you'll see plenty of Koreans (mostly men) getting drunk, often with a great deal of boisterous toasting and, as time passes, collective singing. Anyone with an aversion to mixing drinks will be made to suffer sorely by these gatherings. Korean drinkers frequently switch from beer to whisky to the local brew, *soju*, and from there to anything they can get their hands on, short of paint thinner.

A traditional drink is *makgeolli*, a kind of caustic milky white rice brew, which is cheap but potent enough to embalm a frog. It's sold in raucous beverage halls known as *makgeolli jip*. Soju is the local firewater: a robust drink distilled from rice, yams or tapioca, and potent as toilet bowl cleanser.

Korea's best wine is Gyeongju Beobjoo. There are also inexpensive wines that are not bad, such as Majuang Red and Majuang White. Some drinkers try to mitigate the effects of indulgence by slaking their thirst with ginseng wine *(insamju)*. Beer *(maekju)* comes in several brands: OB, Crown and Red Rock are the most popular.

For real men, Korea has a type of aphrodisiac moonshine with a dead snake floating in it (*baem sul*).

All types of Korean booze can be bought in the 24-hour convenience stores, at a fraction of the price you'd pay in a club.

ENTERTAINMENT
Pubs
Pubs are known as 'hofs' (*hopeu*) or soju parlours (*sojubang*), but these places can be expensive. Generally hofs double as restaurants, and it is expected that patrons buy something to eat, even if it is just some nibbles. These small dishes of finger food, which can include fresh oysters, dried squid, salted peanuts and seaweed (*gim*), are known as *anju*, and this is where the hofs make a lot of their money. Just going in for a couple of beers is usually frowned upon. On the other hand, very few of these places have a cover charge. A few of the more hip places have a good CD collection.

One Korean innovation with a long history are soju tents (*daepotjip*). These are usually set up in the evening alongside the bank of a river, and feature inexpensive drinks and snacks. The government frowns on these places, believing that they are a relic from the poverty-stricken past and have no place in modern Korea. Problem is, they're extremely popular! Soju tents are restricted to certain areas – their legal status is shaky and you'll have to look for them. If the government ever gets really serious about 'cracking down', soju tents will, unfortunately, become a thing of the past.

Billiards & Bowling
The Koreans are keen on bowling (*bolling*) and even keener on billiards (*danggu*). Billiard halls are to be found everywhere – an unmistakable sign identifies these places.

Cinemas
Young Koreans are certainly fond of movies, and the cinemas (*yeonghwagwan* or *geukjang*) tend to pack out on weekends and holidays. Indeed, for some major film releases you might even have to buy a 'black market' ticket from scalpers who hang around the cinemas on Sundays. However, for most films this won't be a problem, especially on weekdays. Admission typically costs W6000.

Foreign movies retain the dialogue in English, French or whatever, with Korean subtitles. Imported Western films are exceedingly popular.

Although drive-in movie theatres are a 1950s phenomena that has been slowly dying out in the West, in Korea's it's suddenly all the rage. For better or worse, it's a tribute to the country's growing car culture. Of course, drive-ins do brisk business in summer and pretty much close down during the long, bitter winters. Unlike walk-in cinemas, drive-in theatres are widely disbursed to the suburban fringe of the big cities, and you'll pretty much have to ask your Korean friends to find these places. Admission typically costs W15,000 per car, with no restriction on the number of passengers inside the vehicle. And yes, a car *is* required.

Dance Dance Revolution (DDR)
Until you've seen this, it's hard to describe. DDR machines, which originated in Japan, have taken South Korea by storm. Put your money into the slot and try to dance to the (very loud) techno music by putting your feet wherever the floor lights up. Watch the Koreans do it and you'll get the idea.

You won't have any trouble finding a DDR machine – indeed, you'll have trouble avoiding them. Just how long the craze will last is anybody's guess.

Drama Theatres
Most of Korea's drama theatres (*sogeukjang*) are concentrated in Seoul, especially in the Daehangno entertainment district (see the Entertainment section of the Seoul chapter). Unfortunately, performances are almost entirely in Korean.

Gambling
The only forms of gambling (*noreum*) legally available to the average Korean are the national lottery (tickets can be bought everywhere) and horse racing (see the Seoul

Equestrian Park section in the Gyeonggi-do chapter).

It's a different story for foreigners. If you're a compulsive gambler and can't wait to get to Las Vegas, then you can lose your fortune in South Korea at one of the special casinos *(kajino)* designed to milk foreign tourists (Koreans are not allowed).

There are 13 casinos in Korea – all located within tourist hotels as follows:

Seoul Sheraton Walker Hill Hotel
Incheon Olympos Hotel
Busan Seorak Park Hotel, Seoraksan, Paradise Beach Hotel
Gyeongju Hilton Hotel
Jeju-do Grand, Oriental, KAL, Holiday Inn
Seogwipo Jeju-si Hyatt Regency, Shilla, KAL and Lotte

Karaoke

As most people would be aware, karaoke *(norae bang* or *KTV)* is a Japanese invention. For the uninitiated, it's basically one big amateur singing contest to the accompaniment of a video tape (or laser disk). The idea is to give you the chance to be a star, even if nobody but you gets to hear the performance.

In Korea, there are two variations on the theme. A 'type 1' karaoke is a bar or lounge in which you sing in front of others. In this type of place there will usually be no cover charge, though you are expected to buy drinks and snacks. A 'type 2' karaoke is a little booth (around W12,000 per hour) in which you sit by yourself (or with a friend) and sing along with a video tape and record your performance. You can take home your recorded tape to enjoy at your leisure.

Korea is unusual in that the karaoke business is organised on an industry-wide level. Songs (some of which are in English) are numbered and all the clubs use the same numbering system – if you ask for song No 112, it will be the same at every karaoke in Korea.

If checking into a hotel for the evening, it's worth looking next door to make sure you *aren't* next to a karaoke club – the music and yodelling typically goes on until midnight.

Discos

Discos *(diseukojang)* certainly exist in Korea, but they have declined somewhat. Apparently, the karaoke business has offered formidable competition.

A pretty steep 'table charge' gets you your first beer and snack at the Korean-style places. The system may differ in places that cater to foreigners, such as in Seoul's Itaewon neighbourhood.

The discos at the big tourist hotels are flashy and very good for meeting people, but these places often come with a steep cover charge and expensive drinks. If it helps any, they accept credit cards.

Saunas

In Western countries, saunas *(sa-u-na)* are most popular during winter. However, Koreans believe that sweating is good for you – therefore saunas are most crowded in summer. No matter what time of year you go, it can be a relaxing experience.

Some saunas are segregated by sex, and nudity is the norm. Others actually allow both sexes, and even children are permitted – you are expected to wear a swimsuit in such places.

Prices vary, but W10,000 to W15,000 is typical. Many saunas are open all night, and you can nap in a lounge chair wearing a bathrobe (supplied by the sauna). If you're a diehard budget traveller, this is one way to save a night's accommodation but still live in style!

Saunas typically provide massage services for an additional fee. In Korea (and many other Asian countries) blind people are frequently employed in this job because they are believed to have better touch.

Women's saunas usually offer mudpacks and facial beauty treatments.

Video Parlours

Video parlours *(bidiobang)* are supposedly illegal, which explains why they try to maintain a low profile. They are basically no different from video rental shops, except that you watch the movies on their equipment. There is no reason why they should be illegal, except that Hollywood fears that these places compete against box office cinemas. The dispute over video parlours has boiled over into trade negotiations between South Korea and the USA, thus the need for the Koreans to at least maintain the appearance of illegality. Legal or not, you can find these places easily enough if you ask a local to assist you.

SPECTATOR SPORTS
The traditional Korean sports have a heavy tendency to be based on martial arts and hunting. These days, Korea's mass media focuses on Western-style sports.

Archery
The traditional Korean wooden bow has gradually given way to more modern fibreglass models. Competitions are most common during festivals, and this is one of the few traditional sports in which women can participate.

Baseball
Baseball (yagu) is big in South Korea and teams are sponsored by the leading jaebeol (huge family-run conglomerates). Seoul's two teams are the OB Bears and the LG Twins. Other notable teams include the Samsung Lions and the Lotte Giants.

Baseball season is roughly from April through October. In Seoul, games are held in the Olympic Stadium (in the Seoul Sports Complex) and in Dongdaemun Stadium. Tickets cost between W2000 and W4000, depending on the seat.

Basketball
Basketball (nonggu) also has a devoted following, and is one of the few spectator sports that can be played in winter. The Korea Basketball League permits each team to have two foreign players, most of whom are Americans. Again, the jaebeol are big sponsors, with teams like the LG Sakers and SK Knights.

During the season, games are broadcast live on TV. If you're interested, you can go to see the real thing at the Olympic Stadium in Jamsil, in the Seoul Sports Complex and in Jangchung Stadium.

Soccer
Soccer (chukgu) is big in South Korea. Indeed, the country will be hosting the FIFA World Cup in the year 2002, though part of the competition will also be hosted in Japan. As with baseball, the jaebeol sponsor the major soccer teams, such as the Hyundai Horang-e, the LG Cheetahs, the Daewoo Royals and the Yukong Elephants.

Soccer season is from April through November. Matches are mostly held at the Olympic Stadium in Chamshil.

Ssireum
Ssireum is a traditional form of Korean wrestling. Two opponents face off each other, and one loses if any part of the body other than the feet touches the ground. Ssireum bears some resemblance to the better-known Japanese sumo.

SHOPPING
Antiques
There are heaps of antiques on sale, most of them fake. Of course, there's nothing wrong with buying a reproduction, provided you aren't paying 'genuine antique' prices. Theoretically, it's illegal to take rare antiques and other 'cultural treasures' out of Korea. In practice this is seldom a problem because you aren't likely to find many cultural treasures on sale in the marketplace. However, it would be useful to get a receipt when buying anything that looks antique just in case customs wants to give you a bad time when you depart. See the Customs section earlier in this chapter for more information.

Ceramics
Ceramics are a Korean craft with a long pedigree – going back to the days of the Goryeo dynasty, when the crackle-glazed celadon pottery was regarded as perfection itself.

Clothes
In Korea, you can find all manner of clothes, from high-fashion to blue jeans. If you've got a taste for the exotic, consider buying a Korean hanbok. Until Western-style clothing arrived in the 19th century,

PATRICK HORTON

Two women paint watercolours. Seoul's parks are centres of social activity and creativity.

PATRICK HORTON

apgol Park: An elderly man practises caligraphy.

PATRICK HORTON

A freelance masseur plies his trade.

SIMON ROWE

Changdeokgung, Seoul: Food stalls can be the best places to sample authentic Korean cuisine.

JULIET COOMBE

'Mandu', Korean steamed dumplings, on sale at a street stall

PATRICK HORTON

Savouries, Namdaemun Market

PATRICK HORTON

Inexpensive, authentic and you know it's fresh

Soccer Wars

'Football is not a matter of life and death – it is far more important than that.'

Bill Shankly, Liverpool Football Club

Once every four years, FIFA (Federation of International Football Associations) stages the greatest soccer competition on earth, the World Cup finals. But competition on the playing fields is only half the battle. Just as important – if not more so – is deciding which nation gets the honour of hosting the games.

Throughout the 20th century, the World Cup had never been staged in Asia. In 1996, FIFA decided to correct this oversight, and announced that the 2002 games would be held in Asia. Both Japan and South Korea put in a bid to host the games. And then all hell broke loose.

Joao Havelange, FIFA's autocratic president, seemed sure that Japan was the best venue. But the Koreans soon made it clear that they weren't going to take 'no' for an answer. At Seoul's Gimpo international airport, the Koreans put up a banner reading, 'Dream For All: 2002 World Cup Korea'. President Kim Young-sam made frequent appearances in public sporting a World Cup 2002 T-shirt and cap. Even Buddhist monks were enlisted in the cause, praying three times daily in front of the TV cameras to bring the world's biggest football event to Korea. And behind the scenes, Korea launched a fierce lobbying campaign. The Korean news media added a few anti-Japanese rumblings, associating Japan's World Cup bid with Hideyoshi's 1592 invasion of Korea and the WWII comfort women issue.

In the end, FIFA's governing body was so divided by the intense rivalry that a compromise had to be reached. In an unprecedented (and controversial) move, it was decided to split the games between two countries. Of the 64 games to be played, half would be staged in Korea, half in Japan.

For their part, the Koreans seemed to be elated with the decision. They soon announced that the games would be staged in 10 Korean cities: Seoul, Incheon, Suwon, Busan, Daegu, Daejeon, Ulsan, Cheongju, Gwangju and Seogwipo. The Koreans then began work on the multi-billion dollar infrastructure that would be needed to make the games a success.

In August 1997 the great Asian economic crisis struck. Teetering on the brink of financial default, Korea had to go cap in hand to the IMF for a huge loan. Despite this, the nation was unwilling to back out of hosting the games.

Fortunately, the Korean economy has recovered nicely. Construction is now proceeding at a feverish pace to complete the 10 new stadiums, roads, railroads and airports that will be needed to accommodate millions of visitors in June 2002. The Koreans may be getting only half the games, but they certainly don't believe in half measures.

---

the brightly coloured hanbok was worn by both men and women.

Today, only women wear the traditional hanbok, and only for formal occasions. The traditional hanbok is a very conservative garment – it's floor length and very baggy, deliberately designed to hide the woman's figure. On seeing a woman dressed in a hanbok for the first time, many westerners assume that she is pregnant! Be assured that this is not generally the case, and it would be a major *faux pas* on your part to 'congratulate' her (she might not even be married!).

Traditional hanbok are generally custom-made and rather expensive. A more practical alternative is the 'reformed hanbok', which is less brightly coloured, and less expensive.

Embroidery & Macramé

Visit any Korean home and you'll see scores of examples of embroidery. It's a national hobby among the women and highly

Korea's traditional garment the *hanbok:* worn today only by woman during ceremonial occasions

regarded as a decorative art. Many fabric shops specialise in it, along with incredibly ornate brocades, and will sell everything from handkerchiefs and pillow cases to room-size screens.

Another national hobby is macramé. Common items are colourful wall hangings and the long *norigae* tassels which adorn the front of every hanbok. The latter always hang from a painted brass headpiece, which itself is often very colourful.

Ginseng
Korea is the ginseng capital of the world, and for many Asians it is a magical cure-all. Japanese and Chinese tourists buy as much of the stuff as they can get their hands on and, as result, the government has restrictions on how much an individual can take out of the country (3kg in its raw state).

Lacquerware & Brassware
Lacquerware is one of Korea's ancient arts and lacquered boxes are just one example of this tradition. The art also encompasses furniture, from tables and chairs to wardrobes and storage chests. The latter can be particularly stunning. A great deal of attention is also given to the brass fittings. Naturally, these larger items are bulky – and more expensive – so, if you were to buy them, you'd have to arrange for them to be shipped to your home country. Most retailers can make these arrangements for you.

Precious Stones
Korea produces a wide range of precious and semiprecious stones. These include amethysts, smoky topaz, rubies, sapphires, emeralds and, of course, jade. Korean jade is lighter in colour, as well as being cheaper than Chinese green jade and is often almost white.

Sporting Equipment
One of Korea's main exports is sporting equipment. There are good deals to be had on tents, sleeping bags, hiking boots, backpacks, rock-climbing equipment, tennis rackets and other such items. Indoor sports enthusiasts will find various sorts of springs, weights, trampolines and various other devices.

Wooden Masks
The carved wooden masks which you'll come across in many souvenir shops are a big hit with foreigners. Only rarely do these resemble the shamanistic spirit posts found all over Korea. These souvenir masks concentrate on exaggerated facial expressions, which range from the grotesque to the humorous. They usually cost around W20,000, though the size determines the price.

Getting There & Away

AIR
Airports & Airlines

Most major international airlines fly into South Korea. The Koreans also operate two airlines of their own, Asiana Airlines (*Asiana Hanggong*) and Korean Air (KAL; *Daehan Hanggong*).

Seoul's Gimpo Airport is the principal gateway to South Korea, but there are international airports at Busan and Jeju, mostly serving the Japanese market. Gimpo Airport is due to become a domestic airport when the new Incheon International Airport opens.

Buying Tickets

World aviation has never been so competitive, making air travel better value than ever. But you have to research the options carefully to make sure you get the best deal. The Internet is an increasingly useful resource for checking air fares.

Full-time students and people under 26 years (under 30 in some countries) have access to better deals than other travellers. You have to show a document proving your date of birth or a valid International Student Identity Card (ISIC) when buying your ticket and boarding the plane.

Generally, there is nothing to be gained by buying a ticket direct from the airline. Discounted tickets are released to selected travel agents and specialist discount agencies, and these are usually the cheapest deals going.

Many airlines offer some excellent fares to Web surfers. They may sell seats by auction or simply cut prices to reflect the reduced cost of electronic selling.

Many travel agencies around the world have Web sites, which can make the Internet a quick and easy way to compare prices. There is also an increasing number of on-line agents which operate only on the Internet. On-line ticket sales work well if you are doing a simple one-way or return trip on specified dates. However, on-line superfast fare generators are no substitute for a travel agent who knows all about special deals, has strategies for avoiding layovers and can offer advice on everything from which airline has the best vegetarian food to the best travel insurance to bundle with your ticket.

You may find the cheapest flights are advertised by obscure agencies. Most such firms are honest and solvent, but there are some rogue fly-by-night outfits around. Paying by credit card generally offers protection, as most card issuers provide refunds if you can prove you didn't get what you paid for. Similar protection can be obtained by buying a ticket from a bonded agent, such as one covered by the Air Travel Organiser's Licence (ATOL) scheme in the UK. Agents who only accept cash should hand over the tickets straight away and not tell you to 'come back tomorrow'. After you've made a booking or paid your deposit, call the airline and confirm that the booking was made. It's generally not advisable to send money (even cheques) through the post unless the agent is very well established – some travellers have reported being ripped off by fly-by-night mail-order ticket agents.

If you purchase a ticket and later want to make changes to your route or get a refund, you need to contact the original travel agent. Airlines only issue refunds to the purchaser of a ticket – usually the travel agent who bought the ticket on your behalf. Many travellers change their routes halfway through their trips, so think carefully before you buy a ticket which is not easily refundable.

Travellers with Specific Needs

If they're warned early enough, airlines can often make special arrangements for travellers such as wheelchair assistance at airports or vegetarian meals on the flight. Children under two years travel for 10% of the standard fare (or free on some airlines) as long as they don't occupy a seat. They don't get a baggage allowance. 'Skycots', baby food and nappies should be provided

Air Travel Glossary

Cancellation Penalties If you have to cancel or change a discounted ticket, there are often heavy penalties involved; insurance can sometimes be taken out against these penalties. Some airlines impose penalties on regular tickets as well, particularly against 'no-show' passengers.

Courier Fares Businesses often need to send urgent documents or freight securely and quickly. Courier companies hire people to accompany the package through customs and, in return, offer a discount ticket which is sometimes a phenomenal bargain. However, you may have to surrender all your baggage allowance and take only carry-on luggage.

Full Fares Airlines traditionally offer 1st class (coded F), business class (coded J) and economy class (coded Y) tickets. These days there are so many promotional and discounted fares available that few passengers pay full economy fare.

Lost Tickets If you lose your airline ticket an airline will usually treat it like a travellers cheque and, after inquiries, issue you with another one. Legally, however, an airline is entitled to treat it like cash and if you lose it then it's gone forever. Take good care of your tickets.

Onward Tickets An entry requirement for many countries is that you have a ticket out of the country. If you're unsure of your next move, the easiest solution is to buy the cheapest onward ticket to a neighbouring country or a ticket from a reliable airline which can later be refunded if you do not use it.

Open-Jaw Tickets These are return tickets where you fly out to one place but return from another. If available, this can save you backtracking to your arrival point.

Overbooking Since every flight has some passengers who fail to show up, airlines often book more passengers than they have seats. Usually excess passengers make up for the no-shows, but occasionally somebody gets 'bumped' onto the next available flight. Guess who it is most likely to be? The passengers who check in late.

Promotional Fares These are officially discounted fares, available from travel agencies or direct from the airline.

Reconfirmation If you don't reconfirm your flight at least 72 hours prior to departure, the airline may delete your name from the passenger list. Ring to find out if your airline requires reconfirmation.

Restrictions Discounted tickets often have various restrictions on them – such as needing to be paid for in advance and incurring a penalty to be altered. Others are restrictions on the minimum and maximum period you must be away.

Round-the-World Tickets RTW tickets give you a limited period (usually a year) in which to circumnavigate the globe. You can go anywhere the carrying airlines go, as long as you don't backtrack. The number of stopovers or total number of separate flights is decided before you set off and they usually cost a bit more than a basic return flight.

Transferred Tickets Airline tickets cannot be transferred from one person to another. Travellers sometimes try to sell the return half of their ticket, but officials can ask you to prove that you are the person named on the ticket. On an international flight tickets are compared with passports.

Travel Periods Ticket prices vary with the time of year. There is a low (off-peak) season and a high (peak) season, and often a low-shoulder season and a high-shoulder season as well. Usually the fare depends on your outward flight – if you depart in the high season and return in the low season, you pay the high-season fare.

Warning

The information in this chapter is particularly vulnerable to change: Prices for international travel are volatile, routes are introduced and cancelled, schedules change, special deals come and go, and rules and visa requirements are amended. Airlines and governments seem to take a perverse pleasure in making price structures and regulations as complicated as possible. You should check directly with the airline or a travel agent to make sure you understand how a fare (and ticket you may buy) works. In addition, the travel industry is highly competitive and there are many lurks and perks.

The upshot of this is that you should get opinions, quotes and advice from as many airlines and travel agents as possible before you part with your hard-earned cash. The details given in this chapter should be regarded as pointers and are not a substitute for your own careful, up-to-date research.

by the airline if requested in advance. Children aged between two and 12 can usually occupy a seat for half to two-thirds of the full fare, and do get a baggage allowance.

Departure Tax

In Korea, all airport departure taxes (called 'PSC' for 'passenger service charge') must be paid in Korean *won*. On international flights, the fee is W9000. Children under age two are exempted. Ditto for military personnel stationed in Korea if travelling on official orders.

There is a W3000 airport tax on domestic flights but this is included in the ticket price.

USA

The USA sells some of the least expensive air tickets around, thanks to cut-throat competition and government regulations against price fixing. But it's hard to get the best deals on short notice – if you need a bargain price, plan to buy your ticket weeks or even months before departure.

Currently, there are direct nonstop flights connecting Seoul to Anchorage, Boston, Chicago, Honolulu, Los Angeles, Dallas, New York, Seattle or San Francisco. A few flights have a transit stop at Narita Airport in Japan.

Discounters in the USA are known as 'consolidators' (though you won't see a sign on the door saying 'Consolidator').

Council Travel (☎ 800-226 8624) is America's largest student travel organisation, but you don't have to be a student to use it. Their Web site is at www.ciee.org. Council Travel has an extensive network in all major US cities – look in the phone book or check out their Web site.

One of the cheapest and most reliable travel agents on the West Coast is Overseas Tours (☎ 415-692 4892) in Millbrae, California. Their Web site is at www.overseas tours.com.

Another good agent is Gateway Travel (☎ 2000,800-441 1183), with headquarters in Dallas, Texas, but with branches in many major US cities.

Some quotations for one-way/return tickets are:

destination	one-way (US$)	return US$)
Honolulu-Seoul	450	609
Los Angeles–Seoul	435	582
San Francisco–Seoul	450	550
New York–Seoul	670	780

Canada

As in the USA, Canadian discount air ticket sellers are known as 'consolidators'. Air fares in Canada tend to be at least 10% higher than in the USA.

Travel Cuts is Canada's national student travel agency and has offices in all major cities. You can find them in the phone directory, or call the Toronto office (☎ 416-977 5228), or visit their Web site at www.travelcuts.com.

Other agencies that have received good reviews are Avia (☎ 514-284 5040) in Montreal and Mar Tours (☎ 416-536 5458) in Toronto.

Return Vancouver-Seoul discount tickets are available for C$1617. From Toronto, return fares start from C$1338.

Australia

Two well-known travel agencies are STA Travel and Flight Centre. STA Travel (www.sta.travel.com.au) has offices in all major cities and on many university campuses, but you don't have to be a student to use its services. Flight Centre has dozens of offices throughout Australia and New Zealand. Their Web site is at www.flight centre.com.au.

The high season for most flights from Australia to Asia from December to January; if you fly out during this period expect to pay more for your ticket.

Low season return tickets between Seoul and Sydney or Brisbane start from A$1200 and from A$1450 during the high season.

New Zealand

Only KAL flies the Auckland-Seoul route direct, though Air New Zealand and other airlines will get you there with a stopover. Low season return fares start at around NZ$1440, a high season return from NZ$1680. Flight Centre has a large central office (☎ 309 6171) at 3A National Bank Tower, 205–225 Queen St, Auckland.

UK

At the time of writing, KAL was the only airline flying London-Seoul direct, though some other carriers let you make the journey via Hong Kong or Singapore.

Discount air travel is big business in London. Advertisements for many travel agencies appear in the travel pages of the weekend broadsheet newspapers, in *Time Out*, the *Evening Standard* and in the free magazine *TNT*.

For students or travellers under 26 years of age, popular travel agencies in the UK include:STA Travel (☎ 020-7361 6262), www.statravel.co.uk, which has an office at 86 Old Brompton Rd, London SW7, and branches across the country. Usit Campus (☎ 0870 240 1010), www.usitcam pus.co.uk, which has an office at 52 Grosvenor Gardens, London SW1, and branches throughout the UK. Both of these agencies sell tickets to all travellers but cater especially to young people and students.

Other recommended travel agencies are:

Trailfinders (☎ 020-7938 3939), 194 Kensington High St, London W8.
www.trailfinders.co.uk,
Bridge the World (☎ 020-7734 7447),
4 Regent Place, London W1.
www.b-t-w.co.uk,
Flightbookers (☎ 020-7757 2000),
177–178 Tottenham Court Rd, London W1
www.ebookers.com1.
Quest Travel (☎ 020-8547 3123), 10 Richmond Rd, Kingston-upon-Thames, Surrey KT2 5HL. www.questtravel.co.uk
North-South Travel (☎ 01245 608 291), Moulsham Mill, Parkway, Chelmsford, Essex CM2 7PX. North-South Travel donate part of their profit to projects in the developing world. www.nstravel.demon.co.uk,
Flight Centre (☎ 020-8543 9070), 112-134 The Broadway, London SW19 1RL.

British Airways and KAL offer London-Seoul services at competitive prices. The lower end of the market for London-Seoul one-way/return tickets is £261/435.

Continental Europe

Aside from London, there are direct flights between Seoul and five European cities: Frankfurt, Amsterdam, Paris, Zurich and Rome.

In The Netherlands recommended agencies include NBBS Reizen (☎ 020 620 5071), www.nbbs.nl, 66 Rokin, Amsterdam, plus branches in most cities and Budget Air (☎ 020 627 1251), www.nbbs.nl, 34 Rokin, Amsterdam. Return fares from Amsterdam start from €1513.

In Germany usitCampus (Call Centre ☎ 01805 788336, Cologne ☎ 0221 923990), www.usitcampus.de, has several offices in Germany (you'll find the details on the Web site). From Frankfurt, return fares to Seoul start from €919.

Usit Connect Voyages (☎ 01 42 44 14 00), 14 rue de Vaugirard, 75006 Paris are a good travel agency with branches across France. Also recommended are OTU Voyages (☎ 01 40 29 12 12), www.otu.fr, 39 ave Georges-Bernanos, 75005 Paris. Expect to pay around €919 for a return fare from Paris.

Recommended travel agents in Italy include CTS Viaggi (06 462 0431), 16 Via Genova, Rome. And Passagi (☎ 06 474 0923) Stazione Termini FS. Return fares from Rome are around €588.

In Switzerland, try SSR (☎ 022 818 02 02), www.ssr.ch, 8 rue de la Rive, Geneva, plus branches throughout the country or Nouvelles Frontières (☎ 022 906 80 80), 10 rue Chante Poulet, Geneva. Return fares from Zurich start from €1096.

The CIS

The Commonwealth of Independent States – better known as the 'former Soviet Union' – actually borders (North) Korea. A large number of Russian tourists may be found in Seoul and Busan. Direct flights connect Seoul with such destinations as Moscow (US$700/1200), Vladivostok, Yuzhno Sakhalink, Krasnoyarsk, Almaty, Tashkent and Bishkek.

There are once-weekly flights linking Busan to Vladivostok and Yuzhno Sakhalink, in Siberia.

China

In contrast to other fares, travel agents cannot give discounts on China-Korea air tickets, and return tickets cost exactly double the one-way fare. The Chinese government owns the airlines and sets the prices – air tickets to and from China are mostly expensive, though some routes are surprisingly reasonable. Airlines flying China-Korea include Asiana, KAL, Air China, China Eastern, China Southern and China Northern.

There are direct flights connecting Seoul to Beijing (US$290/315), Shanghai (US$250/335), Tianjin, Guangzhou (US$613/1226), Qingdao, Yantai, Dalian (US$217/434), Shenyang (US$248/497), Changchun, Harbin and Sanya.

There are also flights from Busan to both Beijing and Shanghai.

Hong Kong

Look for a deal in Hong Kong where you can get Seoul as a free stopover, especially if you're flying to the US West Coast.

Beware, some travel agents in Hong Kong are little more than crooks. Some reliable agents in Hong Kong include the following:

Phoenix Services
(☎ 2722 7378, fax 2369 8884) Room B, 6th floor, Milton Mansion, 96 Nathan Rd, Tsimshatsui. They are scrupulously honest and get good reviews from travellers.

Shoestring Travel
(☎ 2723 2306, fax 2721 2085) Flat A, 4th floor, Alpha House, 27-33 Nathan Rd, Tsimshatsui

Traveller Services
(☎ 2375 2222, fax 2375 2233) Room 1012, Silvercord Tower 1, 30 Canton Rd, Tsimshatsui

There are at least 10 direct Hong Kong–Seoul flights daily; more when you count flights that stop off elsewhere (eg, Taipei) en route. The lowest priced tickets on offer cost US$380/420 for one-way/return.

There is also a twice-weekly flight between the city of Jeju and Hong Kong.

Guam & Saipan

For the Koreans, Guam and the nearby island of Saipan have emerged as fashionable honeymoon and vacation spots. Guam is just 4½ hours from Seoul by air. Asiana flies to both destinations (KAL dropped the route after a bad air crash at Guam Airport). One-way/return fares begin at US$300/340.

Japan

In Japan, you could be forgiven for thinking that a 'cheap air ticket' is an oxymoron. Most flights between Korea and Japan are outrageously priced, though with some effort it is possible to get something reasonably priced on the busiest routes (Tokyo-Seoul, for example) where foreign carriers offer heavy competition.

Tokyo is the best place in Japan to shop around for air ticket discounts. You should start your search by checking the travel ad section of the *Tokyo Journal*. Three longstanding travel agencies where English is spoken and discounted tickets are available are: Across Traveller's Bureau (Shinjuku: ☎ 03-3374 8721; Ikebukuro: 03-5391

2871); STA Travel (Yotsuya: ☎ 03-5269 0751; Shibuya: 03-5485 8380; Ikebukuro: 03-5391 2922); and Just Travel (Taka-danobaba: ☎ 03-3207 8311). There is also an STA in Osaka (☎ 06-262 7066).

Direct nonstop flights connect Seoul to 19 Japanese cities, as follows (with cheapest one-way/return fares shown):

destination	one way (US$)	return (US$)
Aomori	332	475
Fukuoka	210	301
Fukushima	320	457
Hiroshima	275	393
Kagoshima	255	365
Komatsu	320	457
Matsuyama	295	420
Nagasaki	224	320
Nagoya	275	393
Nigata	313	448
Oita	224	320
Okayama	237	338
Okinawa	510	758
Osaka	282	402
Sapporo	351	502
Sendai	524	749
Takamatsu	293	419
Tokyo	210	301
Toyama	390	557

The Korean cities of Busan and Jeju each have international flights to four cities in Japan (Tokyo, Fukuoka, Nagoya and Osaka). And, at least on an experimental basis, there is now one flight a week between Daegu and Osaka.

Singapore
A good place to buy low-cost air tickets in Singapore is Airmaster Travel Centre. Also try STA Travel (☎ 737 7188), 2-17 Orchard Parade Hotel, 1 Tanglin Rd. Other agents advertise in the *Straits Times* classified columns.

One-way/return Singapore-Seoul tickets start at US$450/650.

Taiwan
Discount travel agents advertise in Taiwan's three English-language newspapers; the *Taiwan News*, *China Post* and *Taipei Times*. Don't believe the advertised rock-

bottom fares – most are elusive 'group fares' which are not accessible to the individual traveller.

A long-running discount travel agent with a good reputation is Jenny Su Travel (☎ 02-2594 7733), 10th floor, 27 Chung-shan N Rd, Section 3, Taipei. Wing On Travel and South-East Travel have branches all over the island, and both have good reputations and offer reasonable prices.

Bottom-end tickets on the Taipei-Seoul route start at US$250/400.

OVERLAND
Despite the fact that digging invasion tunnels under the so-called 'Demilitarised Zone' is a favourite preoccupation of North Koreans, you can forget about entering South Korea by land.

SEA
A 10% student discount is available on most ferries. Almost any kind of student ID seems to be acceptable.

Readers will notice that there is a broad gamut of classes available on boats. At the risk of over-generalising, 3rd class is a huge dormitory (only for the strong of stomach); 2nd class is a shared room of between four to 10 bunks; 1st class is a shared room of two bunks; and VIP class is a private room. Variations on the theme, like 3A and 3B (two varieties of 3rd class), are not much different (in either price or standards).

China
International ferries connect the South Korean port of Incheon with six cities in China: Shanghai, Tianjin, Qingdao, Weihai, Dalian and Dandong. Weihai and Qingdao are in China's Shandong Province (the closest province to South Korea). Tianjin is near Beijing. Shanghai is the furthest Chinese port from Incheon. Dandong and Dalian are both ports in China's bleak Liaoning province (north-east China).

To reach the international ferry terminal in Incheon, take the Seoul-Incheon commuter train (subway line No 1 from central Seoul) and get off at Dong Incheon station. The train ride takes 50 minutes. From Dong

Incheon station it's either a 45 minute walk or five minute taxi ride to the ferry terminal. You must arrive at the terminal at least one hour before departure (two hours is preferable) or you won't be allowed to board.

In Seoul, tickets for all boats to China can be bought from International Union Travel Service (☎ 02-777 6722, fax 777 4971), room 707, 7th floor, Daehan building, 340 Taepyeongro 2-ga, Jung-gu, which is just across the street (south) of Deoksugung Palace. In China, tickets can be bought at the pier or from the Beijing branch of the China International Travel Service (CITS) (☎ 010-6512 0508) or China Travel Service (CTS) (☎ 010-6512 2514). However, it's faster to buy tickets from the ferry companies in the relevant seaports (as follows).

Incheon-Shanghai Boats are run by the China Shipping Company. Phone numbers for the company are: Shanghai (☎ 021-6596 6009); Incheon (☎ 032-886 9090); and Seoul (☎ 02-777 8080). The ferry runs once weekly in each direction and the journey takes about 40 hours. Departures from Incheon are on Friday at 3 pm, while departures from Shanghai are on Tuesday at 3 pm. The fares are: 2B class US$70; 2A class US$75; 1B class US$85; 1A class US$115; special B class US$145; special A class US$180.

Incheon-Weihai The phone numbers for the Weidong Ferry Company are: Seoul (☎ 02-3271 6753); Incheon (☎ 032-886 6171); and Weihai (☎ 0631-522 6173). The trip takes approximately 14 hours. Departures from Incheon are on Tuesday, Thursday and Saturday at 6 pm. Departures from Weihai are Wednesday, Friday and Sunday at 5 pm. The fares are: 2nd class US$110; 1st class US$130; special class US$180; royal class US$220; and royal suite class US$300. There is a 5% discount on a round-trip ticket.

A warning about this particular boat – it tends to be filled with Chinese traders carrying tonnes of 'luggage' (herbal medicine from China, electronics from Korea). Don't be surprised if every cubic centimetre of space in your cabin is filled with TV sets or deer antlers. Your fellow passengers may even ask you to carry some of their bags through customs (so they can avoid tax) – not a good idea.

Weihai is a dull place to hang around, so if you arrive there it's best to hop on the first bus to Qingdao. If that's not available, take a bus to Yantai and then to Qingdao.

Incheon-Qingdao Boats are operated by the Weidong Ferry Company with offices in Seoul (☎ 02-3271 6753), Incheon (☎ 032-886 6171) and Qingdao (☎ 0532-280 3574). This journey takes about 20 hours. Departures from Qingdao are on Monday and Thursday at 5 pm. Departures from Incheon are on Wednesday and Saturday at 2 pm. Fares are exactly the same as on the Incheon-Weihai route (see previous listing).

Incheon-Tianjin Boats are operated by the Jinchuan (also spelled Jinchon) Ferry Company. Phone numbers are: Seoul (☎ 02-517 8671); Incheon (☎ 032-888 7911); and Tianjin (☎ 022-2311 2842). The schedule for this ferry is a little irregular. It departs once every four days. The journey takes a minimum of 28 hours. You get what you pay for – 3rd class on the boat is a huge vault with around 80 beds and horrid toilets. Departures from Tianjin are at 11 am. The boat departs from Incheon at 1 pm. The fares are: 3B class US$120; 3A class US$130; 2B class US$150; 2A class US$160; 1st class US$180; and VIP class US$230.

The boat doesn't dock at Tianjin, but rather at the nearby port of Tanggu. Accommodation in Tianjin and Tanggu is expensive, and the best advice for a budget traveller to avoid staying here. Tanggu has trains and minibuses directly to Beijing.

Tickets can be purchased in Tianjin from CITS (☎ 022-2835 0092) or the Tianjin ferry company office (☎ 022-2311 2843). Tickets can also be bought in Tanggu at the ferry company office (☎ 022-2579 5694) or at the Tanggu ferry terminal (☎ 022-2570 6728).

Incheon-Dalian Boats on this route are run by the Da-in Ferry Company with offices in

Seoul (☎ 02-3218 6550); Incheon (☎ 032-888 2611); and Dalian (☎ 0411-270 5082). The journey takes 18 to 21 hours depending on the currents and tides. The boat departs Incheon on Wednesday and Saturday at 6.30 pm. It departs Dalian at noon on Tuesday and Friday. The fares are: 2B class US$120; 2A class US$125; 1st class US$150; special class US$180; royal suite US$230.

Incheon-Dandong The Dandong Ferry Company can be contacted in Seoul (☎ 02-713 5522), Incheon (☎ 032-881 2255) and Dandong (☎ 0415-714 2438). Departures from Dandong are on Sunday and Thursday at 3 pm, arriving in Incheon the next morning at 8 am. Departures from Incheon are on Monday and Friday at 5 pm, arriving the next morning at 9 am. Expect this schedule to get knocked back somewhat during the frigid winter season. Fares are: economy US$120; deluxe C US$130; deluxe B US$150; deluxe A US$160; deluxe special US$190; suite US$210; royal suite US$230.

Japan

There are several ferries linking Japan with South Korea. Purchasing a round-trip ticket gains you a 10% discount on the return half, but fares from Japan are higher and there is a Y600 departure tax in Japan. Korea-Japan-Korea tickets work out to be the same or less than a straight one-way Japan-Korea ticket. So for the numerous travellers who work in Japan and need to make visa runs, consider taking a one-way ticket to Korea the first time if you intend to cross the waters more than once a year.

If you'll be doing much travelling in Japan, it's worth buying a Japan Rail Pass before you depart Korea. This can be bought in from travel agencies in Seoul or even at the port office. There is also a cheaper Kyushu Rail Pass if you'll just be confining your rail journeys to the island of Kyushu.

Busan-Shimonoseki Boats run by the Pukwan Ferry Company are slow but will save you one night's accommodation. The one-way journey takes 14½ hours. Daily departures from Busan are at 6, 7 or 8 pm depending on the season, arriving in Japan the next morning. From Shimonoseki (Japan) departure is always at 6 pm and arrival is at 8.30 am. Fares on tickets bought in Korea for 2nd class are US$50; 1st class costs US$85. Students can receive a 20% discount and bicycles are carried free. Tickets are available at Shimonoseki (☎ 0832-243 000) and from Busan (☎ 051-463 3165) or Seoul (☎ 02-738 0055).

Busan-Hakata (Fukuoka) Jetfoils connect Busan with Hakata. The journey takes only three hours and costs US$120. The schedule is complicated – during the summer months there are at least two departures daily. These jetfoils (called 'Beetles') are operated by Korea Marine Express (Busan ☎ 051-465 6111; Seoul ☎ 02-730 8666; Hakata ☎ 092-281 2315).

Korea Ferry operates boats three times weekly between Busan and Hakata. Because these ferries are so much slower than the jetfoils, the are losing market share. The journey takes 14½ hours and costs US$50 in 2nd class, or US$100 in 1st class. Departure from Hakata is at 7 pm on Monday, Wednesday and Friday from April to August, and at 5 pm from September through to March. Departures from Busan are at 6 or 7 pm on Tuesday, Thursday and Sunday. Call Korea Ferry for bookings (Busan ☎ 051-466 7799; Seoul ☎ 02-775 2323; Hakata ☎ 092-262 2324).

Sticky Cure

On ferries heading into or out of Korea, you'll almost certainly notice a few people who seem to have some small pieces of sticky plaster stuck behind their ears. This is *kimitae*, which is touted as a cure for seasickness. It's available from almost any pharmacy in Korea. The locals claim it works wonders, and there's no harm in trying it. However, if you're really prone to seasickness, you might consider the virtues of flying.

Note that in Hakata, the name of the wharf for Busan (and for boats to Okinawa) is Chuo Futoh and it is across the bay, a long walk from Hakata Futoh (bayside place) where domestic boats are moored.

Combination Tickets There are some wonderful combination ferry-train tickets. For example: express train from Seoul to Busan, jetfoil to Hakata, plus a rail ticket to Osaka. Seoul-Osaka costs from US$129 (slow ferry, unreserved train seat) to US$142 (jetfoil, reserved train seat). All sorts of combinations are possible: Seoul-Tokyo, Daegu-Kobe, Daejeon-Hiroshima and so on. Buying one of these combination tickets offers considerable savings over buying your ferry and rail tickets separately.

Tickets are sold at Aju Tours in Korea and Nippon Travel in Japan. Tickets can be obtained as late as two days in advance. Aju Tours has an office in Seoul (☎ 02-753 5051, 754 2221) and Busan (☎ 051-462 6661). Nippon Travel has an office in Osaka (☎ 06-312 0451).

ORGANISED TOURS
It is best to leave the booking of organised tours till after you arrive in Korea. See the Organised Tours section in the Getting Around chapter for additional information on what's available.

Getting Around

In terms of public transport, South Korea is a dream come true: apart from being frequent, on time and comfortable, it's also reasonably cheap. But when you get to where you want to go, finding the address can be a real chore.

Korean people are very helpful to lost-looking travellers, so if you stand around looking bewildered with a map in your hands, someone will probably offer to assist you. However, if you hand a Korean person your map and ask directions, be sure that they don't have a pen in their hands – they will draw and write directions all over the map until it becomes illegible, the same applies to dictionaries or your Lonely Planet book!

AIR

South Korea has two domestic carriers – Korean Air (Daehan Hanggong) and Asiana Airlines (Asiana Hanggong). Service and

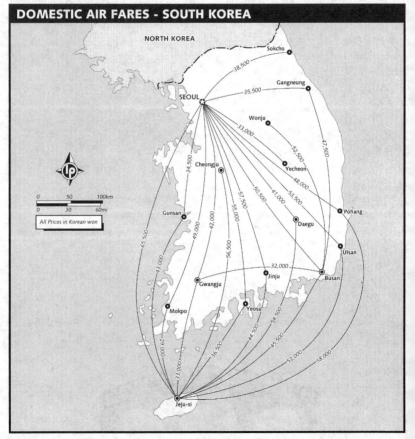

DOMESTIC AIR FARES - SOUTH KOREA

air fares on the two airlines are virtually identical.

Officially, you don't need your passport to board a domestic flight, but some travellers have run into overzealous officials who insisted one was necessary. To be on the safe side, bring your passport.

Air fares are lowest from Monday through Thursday – fares are 10% higher from Friday through Sunday. There are additional surcharges during major public holidays such as the lunar new year and Juseok (see the Public Holidays section in the Facts for the Visitor chapter).

The airlines offer 10% discounts to students. Children under two years of age travel free and those between two and 13 years old travel at 50% of the adult fare. Military personnel get a 30% discount. There is no financial penalty for cancellation if you do so at least three hours before departure time.

To all domestic air fares you must add a domestic departure tax of W3000, which will be included in the price when you purchase a ticket.

BUS

South Korean bus travel is fast, frequent and on time. Buses depart even if there's only one passenger on board.

In some parts of Korea you are likely to encounter the annoying ticket machines. Rather than buying tickets from people, you've got to first feed notes into a machine and then press buttons (which in most cases are all in Korean) for your destination. The machines accept W1000, W5000 and W10,000 notes. This contraption does give change, though you may need to press the coin return button (also labelled in Korean) before the machine will cough up your cash. You may find that half your notes are rejected because they have a few creases or dirt on them. The whole procedure is complicated and error-prone if you can't read *hangeul* (Korean script). There is currently an effort underway to add English to these machines. However, many travellers will still need the assistance of a local Korean when it comes to purchasing a ticket.

If the bus driver doesn't take the ticket off you when you board the bus, then hang onto it – some bus companies want you to turn in the ticket to the driver when you disembark.

Smoking is prohibited on all buses and the rules are generally enforced.

Classes

Most Korean cities and even some obscure towns have at least two bus stations, an express bus terminal (*gosok beoseu teomineol*) and an inter-city bus terminal (*si-oe beoseu teomineol*). Bus terminals are often named after the point of the compass at which they are located: *bukbu* (north), *nambu* (south), *dongbu* (east) and *seobu* (west).

Logically, you might conclude that express buses are faster and more expensive, while inter-city buses are slower and cheaper. However, in most cases the express doesn't save much time. Express buses travel point to point, with no stop-offs to pick up or discharge passengers, except of course for 10-minute rest stops about once every two hours. All passengers must be seated on express buses.

By contrast, the inter-city buses will stop to pick up and discharge passengers along the route, but these stops are combined with rest stops so it hardly takes much longer than the so-called 'express'. Inter-city buses typically make at least three stops en route, but they can also stop at designated bus stops (not only bus terminals) and accept standing passengers for short distances. Some people use these buses to commute to work, which can make them quite crowded during rush hour.

Express buses come in two flavours – 1st class (*udeung*) or 2nd class (*jikhaeng*). The 1st class buses cost 50% more than 2nd class – you pay a lot for the comfy seats. The 1st class coaches are luxurious with plenty of legroom. Some of these buses are even equipped with mobile pay-phones, though none as yet have on-board toilets.

Local (*wanhaeng*) buses constitute the 3rd class. These buses operate on short, set routes and will pick up and drop off anywhere. There are no reserved seats, often as many

Just Give Me the Fax

There's a good reason why most hotel name-cards in Korea include a map on the reverse side – it's because addresses are impossible to find. One reason why fax machines have become so popular in Korea is because Koreans often have to fax maps to each other to locate addresses.

In Korea, an 'address' exists in name only. In the entire country, there are almost no signs labelling street names. Indeed, most streets do not have names at all. Nor do houses have numbers attached to the outside, though every house does in fact have an official number. Unfortunately, even these 'secret numbers' mean little – numbers are assigned to houses when they are built, so house No 27 could be next to house No 324, and so on. Even Koreans find it close to impossible to locate an address.

The government has hinted at reforms, but no one's holding their breath. In the meantime, there is a skeletal addressing system of sorts and it helps if you learn it. A province is a *do*. Thus we have Gangwon-do, Gyeonggi-do, etc. *Buk* means 'north' and *nam* means 'south', and there are a few provinces where knowing this is useful – Jeollabuk-do is 'Jeolla North Province' and Jeollanam-do is 'Jeolla South Province'. Provinces are subdivided into counties, or *gun*, for example; Chuncheon-gun. A *myeon* is a village, a *ri* is a hamlet. Thus, we can have an address like this: 366 Gangchon-ri, Namsan-myeon, Chuncheon-gun, Gangwon-do.

It gets a lot more complicated in cities. A *gu* is an urban district only found in large cities like Seoul and Busan. A *dong* is a neighbourhood smaller than a gu. Seoul presently has 22 gu and 494 dong. Thus, an address like 104 Itaewon-dong, Yongsan-gu, means building No 104 in the Itaewon neighbourhood of the Yongsan district. However, you could wander around Itaewon for hours in search of this building with no hope of finding it, even with the help of a Korean friend. This is the time to make a phone call to the place you are looking for and get instructions or find a local police box, tourist information booth or – best of all – a fax machine.

The word for a large street or boulevard is *no* or *ro*. So Jongno means Jong St, Euljiro is Eulji St, etc. Also worth knowing is that large boulevards are divided into sections called *ga*. Thus, you'll see on the Seoul subway map that there is a station for Euljiro 3-ga, Euljiro 4-ga – these are just different sections of a street named Eulji St. A *gil* is a smaller street than a no/ro – Sambonggil is one such example. Many larger buildings have names – knowing the name of the building will often prove more useful than knowing the address.

You might speculate as to how or why the Koreans ever came up with such a chaotic system for addressing houses. The simple answer is that the Koreans borrowed the system from Japan during the colonial era. Given the fact that the Koreans are not generally fond of the Japanese, one has to wonder why they would want to borrow such a dysfunctional system from their former colonial masters. Posing this question to Koreans, we've received the surprising answer that it was the Japanese who borrowed the system from Korea. If true, then the Koreans have gotten their revenge against Japan after all

standing as sitting passengers, and all but the bulkiest of freight may be squeezed on. You will not be using these for long-distance travel, but you might occasionally need to take one to a remote spot.

Reservations

On the express buses, you'll be sold a ticket with a reserved seat and a guaranteed time and date of departure. But miss the bus and you're out of luck.

The inter-city buses are *usually* not sold with a particular time, and seating is open. If you miss your bus you can board the next one on a space available basis. However, you are supposed to use the ticket the same day you bought it.

In most cases, you won't need an advance ticket, but seats are hard to come by on weekends and holidays. At such peak times, you might have to queue for hours to buy a ticket in Seoul. Things are easier in smaller cities and towns, but travel during holidays means packed-out buses.

Costs

Bus fares are certainly reasonable in Korea. The first class coaches cost approximately W55 per km, while regular inter-city buses are W35. Just about the longest bus ride you can take is Seoul-Busan (432km), which costs W15,700 for 2nd class and W23,400 for 1st class.

TRAIN

South Korea has an excellent railway network connecting all major cities and the ticketing system is computerised. Few ticket clerks speak English, but some of the larger stations have English signs indicating special ticket windows for foreigners. There is also an information phone number (☎ 02-392 7811) which is supposed to be staffed by English speakers.

With advance notice, you can buy train tickets from the Korean National Tourist Organisation (KNTO) in Seoul (most expensive class only). You can also buy train tickets from numerous travel agencies.

There's a monthly timetable available from bookshops – this contains schedules for all forms of transport throughout the country, but only the rail portion is in English. The Korean name for the timetable is *Sigakpyo*.

The Korean National Railroad (KNR) Web site is at www.korail.go.kr and has current route, timetable and fare information in English. You can also book train tickets on the Web, though at the moment this service is only available in hangeul. How do you pay for a ticket that you've booked online? You must first purchase a debit card from KNR for W20,000 – a bit of a hassle, but could be worthwhile if you travel frequently by rail.

The KNR Web site also has information about the Korean Rail Pass (KR Pass). This allows users to have unlimited access to KNR transport across the country for a designated period (three, five, seven or ten days). The passes are only issued to foreign visitors, but unfortunately you must first purchase a voucher abroad (not in Korea). Such vouchers can only be bought from the offices of America Tour Consulting in North and Central America, though in future other countries may have them for sale. Once you've obtained a voucher, you exchange it for a rail pass at one of seven designated train stations in Korea (Seoul, Yeongdeungpo, Daejeon, Dongdaegu, Busan, Gyeongju or Gwangju). For information, contact America Tour Consulting in the USA (☎ 703-256 8944, 800-535 7552) or Seoul (☎ 02-773 2535).

Classes

There are four classes of trains. Fastest are the *saemaul* (new community) express trains. Then come the limited-express *mugunghwa* (flower of Sharon) trains. Similar, but not air-con, are the *tongil* (reunification) trains – the best deal for budget travellers. Finally there are the 4th-class (local) trains known as *bidulgi* (pigeon) and *kkachi* (magpie) – despite being named after birds, they travel at the speed of a tortoise and only make short runs. Seats on the 4th-class trains cannot be booked, indeed you'll be hard pressed to find anyone willing to sell you a ticket on these clunkers. The saemaul trains have 1st and 2nd class carriages; the two middle-range trains have 1st and economy-class seats and standing tickets. There is a

Clean Living - Saemaeul Movement

Teaching proper manners. Organising volunteers. Protecting the environment. Caring for the elderly. Promoting kindness and cleanliness. And, most importantly, preparing for Korean reunification. The term *saemaeul* ('new community') is more than just the name of Korea's most luxurious express trains.

It's also more than just a slogan. Founded in 1970, the Saemaeul Movement, Saemaeul Undong, is a real government-funded program. Like so much in modern Korea, it was the brainchild of former president Park Chung-hee. Dictator though he was, Park instituted a number of important programs. Samaeul Undong was a sincere effort to improve life in the countryside.

Apart from promoting such ideals as proper manners and good clean living, there were more practical programs, such as a credit union and farmers' cooperatives. It also won kudos for breeding 'Suwon 264', a high-yield rice.

President Chun Doo-hwan, who took over the government in 1980, ran the country as a family affair, appointing his close relatives to positions of power. The president's younger brother, Chun Kyung-hwan, was made head of Samaeul Undong. It wasn't long before rumours of improprieties began to surface, and in 1987 Chun Kyung-hwan was arrested and charged with stealing at least US$9.3 million, much of it embezzled from Samaeul Undong.

For an organisation that emphasised such virtues as honesty and voluntarism, the scandal was a near-fatal blow. Nevertheless, Saemaeul Undong lives on, though its significance has been further diminished by the fast pace of urbanisation in modern South Korea. Nowadays, young Koreans head for the bright lights of Seoul or Busan, leaving agricultural communities increasingly populated by elderly pensioners.

Reunification with North Korea would undoubtedly give Saemaeul Undong a new lease on life – if there ever was a country in need of rural development, or any kind of development, North Korea is it. Should reunification ever happen, it would fulfil a dream of the late President Park: 'With thatched roofs replaced, with village roads widened, so goes the song of saemaeul' (words and music by Park Chung-hee).

tendency to sell foreigners the most expensive tickets – if you want economy class, you'd better say so.

The Koreans are constructing a new super high-speed train between Seoul and Busan (foreigners call it the 'bullet train'). No word yet on what tickets will cost, but presumably it will be cheaper than flying.

Reservations

There are no reservations as such, but you can purchase train tickets up to three months in advance. However, as long as you don't need to travel during weekends or holidays, there should be no need to buy a ticket in advance. However, on non-working days, seats are as rare as desert penguins. Indeed, even the standing-room tickets sell out on holidays! If you really get stuck, your only alternative will be to queue for the buses.

Costs

Saemaeul trains cost approximately W60/km, mugunghwa trains W40 and tongil trains W25. Based on this, Seoul-Busan (445km) by a saemaeul train should cost W26,700, mugunghwa W17,800 and tongil W11,125.

BULLET TAXI

Long-distance share taxis are affectionately known as 'bullet taxis' (*chong-al taeksi*) because the drivers tend to drive like maniacs. These taxis can be found at two places: at some major tourist sites and at bus or train stations. For example, they often meet incoming ferries, such as the boat on Soyangho near Chuncheon. You can also find them around the Seoul Express Bus Terminal at night when the regular buses stop running.

Meters are not used, so you must negotiate the fare in advance. Try to find a group of Koreans and let them do the bargaining.

CAR & MOTORCYCLE

The car revolution has arrived in Korea with a vengeance. The vast increase in motor vehicles has wrought all the usual environmental problems, including a severe shortage of parking spaces in Korea's crowded cities. The Koreans – who in former times got along well with their neighbours – often come to fisticuffs with the family next door about who can park in front of whose house.

It makes little sense to rent a car in South Korea. Aside from cost and traffic jams, you take on considerable legal liability. If an accident occurs, there is a tendency to always blame the foreigner.

Driving in the larger cities in particular is not recommended. However, if you confine your driving to rural areas, having a car does allow you the freedom to explore the backwaters at a leisurely pace. Rural roads are generally excellent and have little traffic, except during holiday times when Koreans head for the hills.

Motorcycles are seldom available for hire, so if you need one you'll have to buy your own.

If you're going to drive on the expressways, keep plenty of change handy – there are hefty tolls to pay. Recently, Korea has started to experiment with magnetic toll debit-cards.

A detailed road atlas is essential, and these are readily available from major bookshops.

Road Rules

Driving is on the right side of the road. The speed limits vary considerably and there are not that many signs indicating what they are. In general, the limits are 110km/h on expressways, 80km/h on main highways, 60km/h on provincial roads, and 50/60km/h in urban areas. Speed cops raise a small fortune for the government and they're out in force at weekends and holidays. Drivers coming in the opposite direction will often

indicate the presence of a speed trap ahead of you by flashing their lights.

The police do spot checks for drunk drivers. If you're stopped and there's evidence that you've been drinking, they'll breathtest you and the fines are heavy.

Traffic jams and accidents are disturbingly frequent, and you shouldn't expect much consideration from other drivers. Nevertheless, Korean road warriors *do* respect traffic lights, and they are supposed to respect pedestrian crossings even when these are not controlled by lights. In general, if a car hits a pedestrian, bicycle or even a motorcycle, the police (and courts) usually blame the driver of the car regardless of fault. Under Korean law, one cannot be criminally prosecuted for an accident if a monetary settlement is made with the other party, so lawyers often advise drivers to make some sort of settlement regardless of how innocent he or she is.

In major cities, there is virtually no legal parking other than in private garages (which can cost up to W6000 an hour in downtown Seoul).

It is required by law that the driver and front seat passengers wear seat belts. Safety helmets are mandatory for motorcyclists, though many dare to ignore this rule. Likewise, liability insurance is required, but there are many who drive without it (a major problem if you get into a collision with an uninsured driver).

According to South Korean law, if an uninsured driver hits a pedestrian, the driver is obliged to take the injured party to hospital and foot the bill. I was hit by a truck while walking and the driver was uninsured. I was then forced by accident witnesses into the cabin of the truck with the drunk driver who had just hit me. As an exciting epilogue to the story, I should add that the driver managed to avoid paying my hospital bill by refusing to take me! We drove to the nearest town and there he insisted on me getting out of his vehicle, whereupon he sped off.

Richard Watson

Rental

Cars are available for hire in Seoul, Busan, Incheon, Gyeongju, Gwangju, Jeju, Daegu,

Daejeon and Ulsan. See those city sections for details.

At the minimum, you need an international drivers licence to rent a car in Korea. Ironically, if you've obtained a Korean drivers licence, you still cannot rent a car until you've had that licence for at least one year (but this requirement is waived if you also have an international driver's licence). Renting a car is easier if you have a credit card but that isn't essential (especially in backwaters like Jeju).

Only Korean cars are available for hire. Inquire about discounts – you'll be surprised what can be negotiated, especially during weekdays, off-season (winter) or for long-term rentals. The following rental rates (in Korean won) will give you some idea of what to expect:

model	10 hrs (w)	24 hrs (w)	1 week (w)
Tico	32,000	44,400	248,640
Sonata 1.8	49,600	68,900	385,840
Grandeur 3.0	114,800	145,300	813,680
12-seater bus	70,900	89,700	502,320

BICYCLE

While riding a bicycle in Seoul means almost certain death, it's not a bad way to move around in rural areas if you're experienced in this kind of travel. Besides urban traffic, there are a few other obstacles to consider – remember that the summer is often very wet. Bike lanes are a rarity, and expect some big hills. A safety helmet is recommended.

Bike rentals are available in just a few resort areas (kudos to Gyeongju). Long-term rentals are difficult to find, but good multi-speed bikes can easily be purchased in Korea.

HITCHING

Hitchhiking is not customary among the Koreans, and indeed, they have no particular signal for it. Nevertheless, Koreans in general are kindly disposed to foreigners, and if you're standing by the roadside waving and looking like you need assistance, Korean drivers will often stop to see if you need assistance. However, they may not think you're hitching just to save money,

and will often take you to a bus station in the nearest city!

There are parts of Korea where public transport is poor, especially in rural backwaters (including the national parks). In such a situation, hitching may be your only option.

Is hitching safe? Unfortunately, there is no clearcut answer. Hitching is probably safer in Korea than in many Western countries, but there are no guarantees. A single woman hitching by herself is taking a greater risk than a man. Use your best judgement, just as you would in your own country.

BOAT

Korea has an extensive network of ferries that service the offshore islands (and several lakes).

The city of Incheon (to the west of Seoul) is the departure to numerous islands in the Yellow Sea, including Jakyakdo, Mu-uido, Yeongheungdo, Deokjeokdo and Baengnyeongdo. To the south, Jejudo (Korea's largest island) can be reached by both car and passenger ferry from Mokpo, Wando, Busan and Incheon. If you want to explore the smaller islands of the south-west then Mokpo and Wando are the main departure points. On the east coast, you can get ferries to remote Ulleungdo from Pohang, Hupo and Donghae but those from Hupo and Donghae only operate on a daily basis during the summer months.

Boats servicing lakes can be found in the province of Gangwon-do (Paroho and Soyangho), and farther south on in Chungcheong-do.

During rough weather the ferries can be cancelled, and it is wise to book in advance during the summer months.

LOCAL TRANSPORT
City Bus

Inside cities and their outlying suburbs, buses are classified as ordinary (ilban) and seated (jwaseok). Recently, some cities have added gogeup (high-class) jwaseok. The ilban buses generally cost W600 regardless of distance but they get crowded at rush hours. A jwaseok bus over the same route will cost you W1200, or W1300 for gogeup jwaseok.

Rechargeable magnetic 'transportation cards' (*gyotong kadeu*) are used in large cities and cost W10,500. They can also be used on the subway (if the city in question has a subway system).

All city buses carry a route number and a destination on the front and the sides. Bus stops, likewise, carry panels on the post indicating the route served, but none of these are in English.

Subway

Seoul, Busan, Incheon and Daegu have subways, and they are a very convenient and cheap way of getting around. Signs for both the trains and the stations are in Korean and English. Tickets are bought at vending machines or at ticket windows. For more details, see under the Getting Around sections in the specific chapters.

Smoking is prohibited on trains and stations. Littering or spitting carries a fine of W70,000. Eating is legally permitted, though it violates a Korean social norm that condemns munching in public places. Sneaking on the train without purchasing a ticket can land you a penalty 30 times the ticket price.

Taxi

The two official types of taxis are 'regular' and 'deluxe'. Flagfall for the regular taxis is W1300. That takes you 2km; thereafter it is W100 for every 210m. At speeds under 15km/h, W100 for every 60 seconds is added to the basic fare. Fares are raised 20% between midnight and 4 am (and taxis can be hard to get during these hours). You can also be charged an extra 20% if you take the taxi outside of its 'normal operating area'. Paying the tolls for the expressway, bridges or tunnels is also the passenger's responsibility.

A deluxe taxi *(mobeom taeksi)* is black with a yellow sign on the roof and the words 'deluxe taxi' written in English on the sides. The designation 'deluxe taxi' not only means that the vehicle is very comfortable inside, but also that the driver wears a crisp uniform, white gloves, speaks some English and is polite to a fault. Flagfall is W3000, which takes you 3km, then W200 for each additional 250m (or 60 seconds when the speed drops below 15km/h). There is *no* late-night surcharge for the deluxe taxis. The driver will issue a receipt, and some of the newer taxis even are equipped to accept credit cards. The passenger must still have to pay tolls when applicable.

Taxis can be hailed by telephone. There is no extra charge for this service other than an expected tip (normally, tipping is not customary). There are usually separate phone numbers for regular and deluxe taxis.

There are complaint forms available from the Ministry of Transport, and the public have been encouraged to record details of taxi drivers who drive dangerously or attempt to charge more than the amount on the meter. However, the authorities won't entertain any complaint about taxis not stopping for you.

In the countryside, many taxis are not metered, so you'll have to negotiate the fare before you set off.

If you take a metered taxi to a place where the driver won't necessarily get a return fare (to a temple outside a town, for instance), he will usually demand beforehand that you pay 1½ times what the meter indicates at the end of the journey.

ORGANISED TOURS

There are a wide variety of tours available, and they can be booked at the Seoul KNTO office, major hotels and some travel agencies. The current repertoire of travel agencies (all based in Seoul) catering to foreigners include:

Korea Travel Bureau (☎ 02-778 0150,
    e tour@ktbinc.co.kr) or see their Web site
    www.ktbonline.com
Global Tour (☎ 02-776 3153)
Grace World Travel (☎ 02-332 8946)
Star Travel (☎ 02-569 8114)
Kim's Travel (☎ 02-323 3361);
Theme Tours Korea (☎ 02-777 7003)
Chung-ang Express Tour (☎ 02-2266 3350)

Some travellers have praised the tours, but others have been less impressed. Like most group tours, much depends on your fellow group tourists. If you're lucky, you'll be with a group of people of your own age and interests. If unlucky, it might be a group with whom you have nothing in common. As one traveller to Jejudo wrote:

I ditched the tour on the second day when – 3km away from Sunrise Peak – I was informed that we wouldn't be going there after all but would be heading for a sauna that cost another W4000. The problem was that the tour group was comprised of older Koreans more interested in shopping and saunas than sightseeing.

Deborah Fowler

Just to give a rough idea of what's available, one agency charges US$1600 for a 'Korea In Depth' tour which includes Seoul, the Korean Folk Village, Seoraksan, Songnisan, Beopjusa, Haeinsa, Gyeongju, Tongdosa, Busan, Jejudo and then back to Seoul by air.

The great economist Adam Smith said 'there's no such thing as a free lunch', but you get one anyway on almost all Korean tours (even one-day tours).

The Royal Asiatic Society (RAS; ☎ 02-763 9483, fax 766 3796) – based in Seoul – operates special-interest cultural tours every weekend. The day tours are good value, but overnight trips are not bargain basement because you stay in upmarket hotels rather than cheap yeogwan. The RAS is in room 611 of the Korean Christian building (also called the CBS building) on Daehangno. Office hours are from 10 am to 5 pm on Monday to Friday. Take subway line No 1 to the 5-ga station.

Trek Korea (☎ 02-540 0840) in Seoul organises trekking, cycling, whitewater rafting and other such adventure tours (see their Web site at www.trekasia.com) at reasonable cost. Ditto for Outdoor Korea Travel Center (☎ 02-725 4417) which is in fact the Net House Cyber Cafe. See the Outdoor Korea's Web site at www.korea-travel.com. Another place offering these services is WOW Guesthouse (☎ 02-322 8644). You can see their Web site at www.wowgh.co.kr.

Also in Seoul, the United Service Organization or USO (☎ 02-795 3028, 795 3063) runs tours at bargain prices. You don't have to be a member of the US military to join.

Finally, you could try to hire your own guide for a personalised tour. Travel agencies and KNTO can introduce guides. In Korea, professional guides are well-paid – W80,000 per day is typical. A student guide costs considerably less – figure on maybe W30,000. In some cases, it is possible to get a student volunteer to work for free in exchange for the benefit of practising English. If you decide to hire your own guide, money matters should definitely be discussed first before embarking on a journey.

Seoul

SEOUL

Highlights

- The royal palaces of Gyeongbokgung, Changdeokgung, Changgyeonggung and Deoksugung
- The shrine Jongmyo, the resting place of the ancestral tablets of the Yi kings
- Inwangsan, a dramatic mountain hike close to the centre of the city
- The War Memorial, a reminder of Korea's bitter past and the unresolved future
- Seoul Tower, in Namsan Park
- Namdaemun Market, a mecca for bargain hunters
- Yongsan Electronics Arcade, a gathering ground for technophiles

Ornate pagodas are a feature of Seoul's traditional gardens.

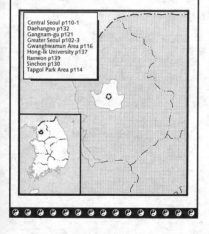

Central Seoul p110-1
Daehangno p132
Gangnam-gu p121
Greater Seoul p102-3
Gwanghwamun Area p116
Hong-Ik University p137
Itaewon p139
Sinchon p130
Tapgol Park Area p114

☎ 061 • pop 10.3 million

Seoul, the capital of South Korea, is a city of incredible contrasts. It was flattened during the Korean War but has risen from the ashes to become a modern metropolis. By some estimates, Seoul rates as the fifth-largest city in the world. Although Korea's capital now boasts high-rise buildings, 12-lane boulevards and urban problems to match, the centuries-old royal palaces,

temples, pagodas and imposing stone gateways set in huge traditional gardens remain timeless and elegant.

Seoul is the political, economic and educational hub of the country, to a dangerous degree. Much of the country's wealth, industry and technology is concentrated here. Even the Defence Ministry is headquartered in Seoul. With this in mind, former president Chun Doo-hwan made an attempt to move some government ministries out of the capital. However, Chun met with fierce opposition and had to drop the plan.

As far as Koreans are concerned, Seoul is *the* place to live because of its educational and economic opportunities. Another factor is prestige – residents gain 'face' by having a Seoul address on their namecard.

Seoul is also a magnet for foreigners, most of whom are more interested in economic opportunities than prestige. Even if the motive for your visit is sightseeing instead of job-hunting, Seoul is still worth your time. However, once you've taken in the major sights, you'd be well advised to get to a bus or railway station and see what the rest of Korea has to offer, something many travellers never do.

SEOUL

GREATER SEOUL

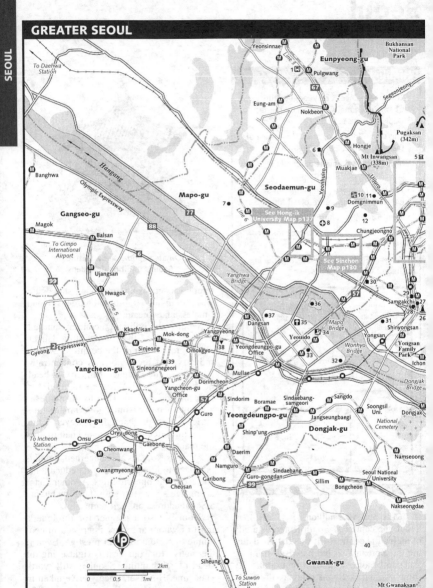

Yeonsinnae

Bukhansan
National
Park

Eunpyeong-gu

To Daehwa
Station

Line 3

1 Pulgwang

67

Eung-am

Nokbeon

Segeoljeong

Hongje

Pugaksan
(342m)

6

Mt Inwangsan
(338m)

5

Muakjae

Banghwa

Hangang

Mapo-gu

7

Seodaemun-gu

10 11

Domgnimmun

9

Olympic Expressway

Gangseo-gu

Magok

88

77

See Hong-ik
University Map p137

8

12

Chungjeongno

To Gimpo
International
Airport

Balsan

6

Line 6

See Sinchon
Map p130

Ujangsan

99

Yanghwa
Bridge

30

29

Hwagok

Line 5

27

Samgakchi

28

26

Kkach'isan

36

31

Shinyongsan

Yongsan

57

Mok-dong

Yangpyeong

37

Dangsan

35

Mapo
Bridge

34

Yongsan
Family
Park

Ichon

Sinjeong

Omokgyo

38

Yeongdeungpo-gu
Office

Yeouido

Wonhyo
Bridge

Dongjak
Bridge

Gyeong

2 Expressway

Sinjeongnegeori

Line 2

33

32

Yangcheon-gu

Mullae

Yangcheon-gu
Office

Dorimcheon

57

Sindorim

Boramae

Sindaebang-
samgeori

Sangdo

Soongsil
Uni.

Dongjak

Guro-gu

Guro

Yeongdeungpo-gu

Jangseungbaegi

National
Cemetery

To Incheon
Station

Onsu

Oryu-dong

Gaebong

Shinp'ung

Dongjak-gu

Cheonwang

Daerim

Namseoong

Gwangmyeong

Line 7

Namguro

Garibong

Sindaebang

Seoul National
University

Cheosan

Guro-gongdan

Sillim

Bongcheon

Nakseongdae

40

Siheung

Gwanak-gu

To Suwon
Station

Mt Gwanaksan
(632m)

Anyang-shi

0   1   2km

0   0.5   1mi

For more detailed subway information see
Seoul Subway Map between pages 112 - 113

SEOUL

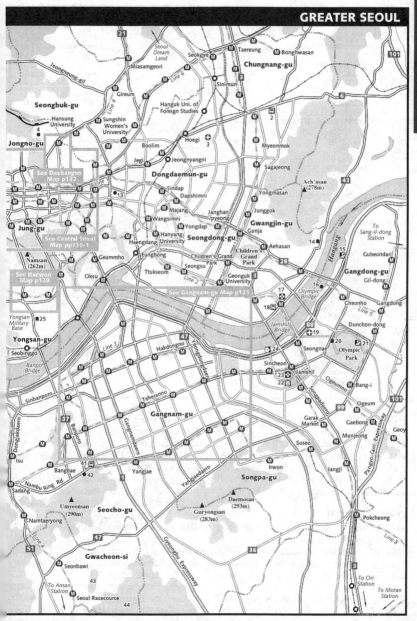

GREATER SEOUL

GREATER SEOUL

PLACES TO STAY
6 Swiss Grand Hotel
  스위스그랜드호텔
14 Sheraton Walker Hill
  Hotel
  쉐라톤워커힐호텔
20 Olympic Parktel
  Hostel
  서울올림픽파크텔
25 Crown & Capital hotels
  크라운호텔,캐피탈호텔
29 Kaya Hotel
  가야호텔
30 Holiday Inn
  홀리데이인서울

PLACES TO EAT
38 Costco (hypermart)
  코스트코홀세일

OTHER
1 Seobu Bus Terminal
  서부시외버스터미널
2 Sangbong Bus Terminal
  상봉시외버스터미널
3 Adventist Hospital
  서울위생병원
4 Sungkyunkwan
  University
  성균관대학교
5 The Blue House
  청와대
7 World Cup Stadium
  월드컵주경기장
8 Severance Hospital
  세브란스병원
9 Seoul Foreign School
  서울외국인학교

10 Bongwonsa Temple
  봉원사
11 Seodaemun Prison
  History Hall
  독립문원
  서대문형무소
12 Ehwa Women's
  University
  이화여자대학교
13 Hwanghak-dong-
  Flea Market
  황학동시장
15 Swimming Area
  광나루유원지
16 Water-skiing Area
  한강시민공원
  수상스키
17 Techno Mart
  테크노마트
18 Dong-Seoul Bus
  Terminal
  동서울종합터미널
19 Asan Medical Centre
  서울중앙병원
21 Olympic Park Indoor
  Swimming Pool
  올림픽공원수영장
22 Nori Madang
  Theatre
  서울놀이마당
23 Lotte World
  롯데월드
24 Jamshil Ferry Pier
  잠실선착장
26 War Memorial
  전쟁기념관
27 USIS Library
  미국문화원

28 United Service
  Organisation
  (USO)
  유에스오
31 Yongsan Electronics
  Arcade
  용산전자상가
32 KLI 63 Building
  대한생명63빌딩
33 Korea Stock
  Exchange
  증권거래소
34 Swimming Pool
  수영장
35 Full Gospel Church
  여의도순복음교회
36 Bamseom Islet
  밤섬(철새도래지)
37 National Assembly
  Building
  국회의사당
39 Immigration Office
  출입국관리소
40 Seoul National
  University
  서울대학교
41 Nambu Bus
  Terminal
  남부시외버스터미널
42 Seoul Arts Centre
  예술의전당
43 Seoul Horse
  Race Track
  서울경마장
44 Seoul Grand Park
  서울대공원

HISTORY

Seoul dates from the establishment in AD 1392 of the Yi dynasty, which ruled Korea until 1910. During this time, when Korea was largely closed to the outside world, the shrines, palaces and fortresses that still stand today were built.

ORIENTATION

The Hangang flows from east to west and bisects the city. There are 25 urban districts (*gu*) and 527 neighbourhoods (*dong*).

Jung-gu is the central district around the City Hall area and Myeong-dong, south to Namsan Park.

Jongno-gu stretches from Jongno ('Bell Rd') northwards to the Gyeongbokgung area. This district, which incorporates the Gwanghwamun and Tapgol Park areas, has most of the budget hotels and the city's best sights. Further to the west on subway Line 2 are Sinchon and the adjacent Hong-ik University area, the best student nightlife areas.

Itaewon is a neighbourhood in Yongsan-gu on the south side of Namsan Park. It's home to an enormous US military base and famous for shopping, bars and nightlife.

Daehangno means 'University St', the name given to the lively area just north of central Seoul surrounding the Hyehwa station on subway Line 4.

Gangnam-gu – the district on the south side of the Hangang – is the most prestigious area to live as far as Koreans are concerned, but the sterile modernism leaves many foreigners cold.

INFORMATION
Tourist Offices

The best source of information about Seoul itself is at Seoul City Tourist Information (☎ 2236 9135; open 9 am to 10 pm) in the soccer stadium at Dongdaemun Stadium (Central Seoul map). Take subway Line 2, 4 or 5 to Dongdaemun Stadium station.

Information kiosks around town are:

Airport Terminal 1 (☎ 665 0088)
Airport Terminal 2 (☎ 665 0986)
Deoksugung Palace (☎ 756 0045)
Euljiro(☎ 731 6933)
Express bus terminal (☎ 537 9198)
Gwanghwamun (☎ 735 0088), in front of the Kyobo building
Itaewon (☎ 794 2490), near the Hamilton Hotel
Jongno 5-ga (☎ 272 0348)
Korea City Air Terminal (☎ 566 4331),
Sanseong station on subway Line 2
Myeong-dong (☎ 757 0088)
Namdaemun Market (☎ 752 1913)

You can get information about Seoul and the rest of Korea at the Korean National Tourist Organisation (KNTO, Tapgol Park map; ☎ 757-0086) in the basement of the KNTO Building near the Jonggak subway station on Line 1. There are touch-screen computers where you can choose a destination and find out about transportation, accommodation, things to see etc. KNTO is open daily from 9 am until 6 pm (9 am to 5 pm from November through February).

It's also worth trying the USO (United Services Organization; Greater Seoul map; ☎ 795 3028, 795 3063) in Yongsan-gu. It's opposite the US army's Yongsan military base and very close to Namyeong station on subway Line 1. The USO is an information, entertainment and cultural centre that serves the US army base, though you don't have to join the military to get in. Office hours are daily from 8 am to 5.30 pm, closed Sunday.

Money

You can change money seven days a week at Gimpo Airport. Exchange counters open

two hours before the first aircraft departure and close one hour after the last arrival.

On departure, do *not* believe anyone when they tell you that there's a money changer in the airport transit area (the boarding area after you've passed through immigration). Yes, there is a money changing booth there, but it's often closed and cannot be relied upon.

During regular business hours, any one of Seoul's numerous foreign exchange banks and legal moneychangers can accommodate you.

Post & Communications

Poste restante is on the third floor of the Central Post Office (CPO; Central Seoul map). All incoming letters are entered into a logbook, which you have to sign when you pick up a letter or package – look over this logbook carefully for your name.

The telecommunications building is just behind the CPO – fax and telephone service are available.

Seoul is in the midst of converting from seven-digit telephone numbers to eight digits. Some of the seven-digit phone numbers in this book might not work (you'll get a recorded message in Korean), so try adding a '2' to the beginning of the number.

Mobile phones are easiest to rent at the airport. If you failed to do so but would like one now, you can try calling:

Asiana (☎ 3472 1600)
Comtel (☎ 597 8950)
HPR (☎ 525 0558)
SK Telecom (☎ 666 4244, 666 4055)
Sky Rental (☎ 854 4152)

Internet Resources

Seoul Focus (www.metro.seoul.kr) is run by the Seoul Metropolitan Government and provides lots of useful information.

The Seoul Tour home page (www.seoul tour.com) gives a good, if somewhat abbreviated, synopsis of what's happening in and around Seoul.

Cyber Cafes

You can cruise cyberspace at the Net Cyber Cafe (Gwanghwamun map; ☎ 733 7973, fax 738 5794). See their Web site at www.net.co.kr. This was the first cyber cafe in Seoul to cater to foreigners, and it's still the favourite hangout for backpackers in the central area. The cafe features a notice board, a fax machine for customers' use and special discounts for members. Operating hours are weekdays from 9.30 am to 11 pm, Saturday 11 am to 11 pm and Sunday from noon to 10 pm. The cafe is on the 2nd floor of a small building in an alley adjacent to Kyobo Book Centre.

Another alternative is Net House (Central Seoul map; ☎ 725 4417, fax 725 4419). Their Web site is at www.korea-travel.com. This is more Korean, but has a quiet setting (like a library coffee shop) and the staff speak English. The nearest subway stations are Gwanghwamun on Line 5 (exit 2) or Anguk on Line 3. Look for the building with a large Coca-Cola and Fanta sign on top – the cyber cafe is on the ground floor.

In Itaewon, there is Cyberia (☎ 3785 3860), check out www.cyberia.co.kr.

South of the river is Net Plaza (☎ 501 3007) which is open daily. It's on the 3rd floor above Ponse Coffee Shop, in an alley on the north-east corner from the Gangnam subway station on Line 2.

Also on the south side is La Puta Internet Cafe (☎ 508 8261). It's south of the Gangnam subway station on Line 2.

Over in the Daehangno area is the Forest Cyber Cafe (☎ 765 4588, 745 6281). It's on the 3rd floor of the Ujeong Building. It's open daily from 10 am until midnight.

Travel Agencies

There are hundreds of travel agencies in Seoul, however English is not widely spoken by staff, and they are unlikely to be accustomed to westerners' preoccupation with getting the cheapest price.

Joy Travel Service (☎ 02-776 9871), 10th floor, 24-2 Mukyo-dong Chung-gu (directly behind City Hall; Central Seoul map), offers good deals and has English-speaking staff.

The YMCA building on Jongno 2-ga next to Jonggak station (Tapgol Park map) houses two discount travel agencies. On the 5th floor (and also in the basement) is Top

Travel (☎ 739 4630), said to have the cheapest fares in Seoul (but no English-speaking staff). Also on the 5th floor (Room 505) are discounters the Korean International Student Exchange Society (KISES; ☎ 733 9494).

Bookshops

Seoul has a number of excellent everything-under-one-roof book shops. Kyobo Book Center (☎ 397 3500) is the largest, and even boasts an English-language information desk. There is one whole room in the back of the shop that is stacked floor to ceiling with books in English (and a few other European languages). Kyobo is next to Gwanghwamun subway station on Line 5.

The Huge Jinsol Book Center is the best in the Gangnam area. This place has a superb collection of computer books. Jinsol is one block south-east of the Gangnam subway station on Line 2.

Also in the Gangnam area is Kim & Johnson, which only sells ESL books. Anyone teaching English in Korea should seriously check out this place. It's on the 3rd floor above Restaurant Marche Movenpick near Gangnam subway station.

Eulji Book Center (☎ 757 8991) has a good collection. It is almost hidden in the bowels of the Euljiro 1-ga subway station, just next to Lotte Department Store.

Youngpoong Bookstore (☎ 399 5600) has some paperbacks and English-teaching materials, but the collection is not stunning. Youngpoong can be entered from the Jong-gak subway station on Line 1.

Jongno Book Centre (☎ 733 2331) is a multi-level fire trap that is difficult to navigate, but has a small section of good English paperbacks on the 5th and 6th floors. Jongno is opposite the YMCA, by the Jonggak subway station on Line 1.

The Foreign Bookstore (☎ 793 8249) in Itaewon has a treasure trove of new and used books, mostly in English but a few other languages. It's closed on Tuesday. Also in Itaewon, Nashville Bar has a take-one leave-on policy on used paperback books.

The Royal Asiatic Society, (RAS; ☎ 765 9483), has the widest selection of books on Korea, but nothing on other topics. Members get a 10% discount. Another drawcard is that it puts out a publications list of information on virtually every book relevant to Korea. You'll find the RAS in Room 611 of the Korean Christian Building on Daehangno. (Central Seoul map; take subway Line 1 to Jongno 5-ga station and walk north). It's open Monday to Friday from 10 am to noon and 2 to 5 pm.

Seoul's major bookshops are open from 10 am to 9 pm on weekdays, or until 8 pm on Sunday and holidays. Some bookshops are closed every 2nd and 4th Sunday.

Libraries
The USIS (United States Information Service ☎ 732 2601) has without doubt the best English-language library in Seoul. The USIS is on the Yongsan military base, but civilians of all nationalities may use the facilities. However, non-military visitors cannot borrow books. The library is directly opposite the USO. The nearest subway station is Namyeong on Line 1.

The National Central Library (☎ 535 4142) is the largest in the land, though the majority of the books are in Korean. The nearest subway station is Seocho on Line 2. The library is open from 6 am to 9 pm.

Universities
Three of Korea's biggest universities are just west of the centre and easily reached by subway Line 2. The big three in this neighbourhood are Ehwa Women's University, Hong-ik University and Yonsei University. This is also a very active nightlife district.

In the centre near Namsan Park is Dongguk University, which boasts a couple of interesting museums on campus. Take subway Line 3 to Dongguk University station.

Down in the south end of town and also reached on subway Line 2 is Seoul National University, which also boasts a museum and some nearby hiking areas.

Schools for Foreigners
Foreign children are permitted to attend Korean schools, but there are several private schools in Seoul catering for the children of expats. They are as follows:

French School (☎ 535 1158) 97-2, Banpo-dong, Seocho-gu
Seoul Academy, Yeong-dong (☎ 554 1690) PO Box 85, Gangnam-gu, Seoul 135-600
Seoul Foreign School (☎ 335 5101) 55, Yeon-hui-dong, Seodaemun-gu
Seoul German School (☎ 792 0797) 4-13, Hannam-dong, Yongsan-gu, Seoul 140-210
Seoul International School, Songpa (☎ 233 4551) PO Box 47, Seoul 138-600

Cultural Centres
For anyone with an interest in Korean culture, planning to base themselves in Seoul for an extended period, it would be worth looking into the activities offered by the Royal Asiatic Society (☎ 765 9483). You can write to the RAS at CPO Box 255, Seoul, see Bookshops, earlier.

Seoul's various foreign cultural centres often have videos for rent, along with other odd events such as occasional stage dramas, parties and cooking classes. For information, contact the following:

British Cultural Centre (☎ 737 7157) next to Deoksugung Palace
French Cultural Centre (☎ 734 9768) east side of Gyeongbokgung Palace
Goethe Institute Yongsan-gu (☎ 754 9831) a short walk south of the Namsan public library
Italian Cultural Centre Yongsan-gu (☎ 796 0634)

Left Luggage
Left-Luggage Rooms Gimpo international airport has bonded baggage facilities. If you leave anything in bonded baggage, you will not be able to gain access to that luggage until you depart the country. Needless to say, it will also be necessary to depart from the same airport.

After passing through customs, there are a few additional left-luggage rooms. In both international terminals, one is on the arrival floor, and another is in the departure hall. There is also one in the domestic terminal. These rooms are marked 'baggage deposit'. They open at 7 am and close 30 minutes before the last flight departure.

Outside the airport, left-luggage rooms are exceedingly rare. However, there are lockers at most major railway, subway and bus stations.

Lockers High-tech computerised lockers have been installed throughout Seoul, especially in the subway stations. Unfortunately, these new 'smart lockers' are much less intuitive to use than the old 'dumb' ones, and all the instructions are written entirely in Korean.

The price is W900 to W1500 per day, depending on size, and you cannot leave your luggage in the locker for more than three days or it will be impounded.

Put your bag into an empty locker, then push the green button next to the computer screen – the screen will show you which lockers are available. Then press the number (two digits) of the locker where you put your bag – for example, if your locker number is '9' then you press '09'. Then insert the fee (probably W900) – the machine accepts W100 and W500 coins, as well as W1000 bills. Finally, turn the key of your locker to the left and remove the key. To reclaim your goods from the locker, press the yellow button, press your locker number (two digits) – if an additional fee appears on screen, you have to pay it (this will happen if you withdraw your bag after midnight). Finally, turn your key to the right.

Below the yellow button (next to the computer screen) is a red button – this button simply means 'cancel'.

Two other buttons are above the keypad, red is 'go ahead' and green is 'go back'.

You can also find two lights on the locker to the right of the coin slot. Yellow indicates that your request is being processed; red glows when nothing is being processed.

Medical Services

Seoul has a number of good hospitals with English-speaking doctors, but most are overcrowded. To avoid the crowds, visiting a small private clinic is not a bad idea.

Adventist Hospital (☎ 210 3241), Dongdaemun-gu. Take subway Line 1 to Hoegi station.
Asan Medical Centre, International Clinic (☎ 224 5001) in Songpa-gu (subway Line 2 to Seongnae station). The clinic is open from 8.30 am to 5.30 pm on Monday, Wednesday and Friday.
Chiropractic Clinic (☎ 3443 0527), Apgujeong-dong (subway Line 3 to Apgujeong station).
International Clinic (☎ 790 0857) in the heart of Itaewon.
Kangbuk Samsung Hospital International Clinic (☎ 723 2911, 735 2129) is in Jongno-gu (Seodaemun station on subway Line 5).
Kyonghee University Herb Hospital (☎ 961 0114). This hospital is notable because acupuncture and other traditional medical techniques are practiced here. It is a 10-minute walk east of Anguk station on subway Line No 3.
Samsung Medical Centre, International Clinic (☎ 3410 0200), Gangnam-gu (take subway Line 3 to Irwon station).
Seoul Foreign Clinic (☎ 796 1871) Seongdong-gu (subway Line 3 to Oksu station).
Seoul National University Hospital (☎ 762 5171), Hyehwa-dong (subway Line 4 to Hyehwa station). This is Korea's largest and most advanced medical facility. The staff here speak some English, but the hospital is usually horribly crowded.
Severance Hospital, International Clinic (☎ 392 3404), in Sinchon. Take subway Line 2 to Sinchon station.

Emergency

If you are in need of urgent medical attention, Asia Emergency Assistance (AEA; ☎ 790 7561) is an organisation that operates 24 hours a day, and will act as an intermediary between foreigners and Korean hospitals. AEA charges for its services but also offers a health plan for expats.

During office hours, you might be able to get a call for help relayed through the Seoul City Tourist Information Centre (☎ 2236 9135) or KNTO (☎ 757 0086). However, don't count on it if your life (or someone else's) is in danger.

If an emergency occurs out on the street, look for a police box. There seems to be one on every second street corner.

Lost & Found

The lost and found (☎ 2299 1282) is operated by the Seoul Metropolitan Police

Bureau, 102 Hong-ik-dong, Seongdong-gu, but don't count on an English speaker answering the phone. If you leave something valuable in the back of a taxi, there is some modest hope of recovering it here.

There are several subway lost and found offices:

Line 1 Guro station (☎ 869 0089)
Line 2 City Hall station (☎ 753 2408)
Line 3 and 4 Chungmuro station (☎ 2271 1170)
Line 5 Wangsimni station (☎ 2298 6767)
Line 7 Taereung station (☎ 949 6767)
Line 8 Jamsil station (☎ 418 6768)

There is an airport lost and found at Gimpo airport terminal No 1 (☎ 660 2664) and terminal No 2 (☎ 660 2673).

Immigration
The main headquarters of the Seoul Immigration Office (☎ 653 3041) covers both Seoul and the nearby province of Gyeonggi-do. It's inconveniently located in Yangcheon-gu out near Gimpo airport. You can get there by taking subway Line 5 to Omokgyo station, and then walking southwest for about 15 minutes.

Fortunately, there is a much more convenient branch in the city centre (☎ 732 6214) on the 5th floor of the Jeokseon Hyeondae Building. This is easily reached by taking subway Line 3 to Gyeongbokgung station. When walking out of the station, take exit No 7 (look for the sign 'Seoul Metropolitan Police Administration').

GYEONGBOKGUNG 경복궁
The palace Gyeongbokgung, at the far north end of Sejongno has had its ups and downs. It was built by the first Yi dynasty king Taejo when he relocated the capital to Seoul. The palace was the hub of royal power, and the royal residence for around 200 years. Before the Japanese Hideyoshi invasion, the grounds housed some 500 buildings. The Japanese onslaught of 1592 (see the History section in the Facts about Korea chapter) saw most of these destroyed. The palace was neglected until an ambitious reconstruction scheme commenced during

An elaborate 10-storey pagoda on the grounds of the Gyeongbokgung. One of the few such buildings to survive the Japanese occupation.

the reign of King Gojong (1864–1907). By 1872 some 200 buildings had been completed. Yet another Japanese occupation (1910–45) plus the Korean War resulted in wholesale destruction – only 10 buildings at Gyeongbokgung survived these disasters.

The Koreans have vowed to restore the entire complex to the splendour it enjoyed during the time of King Gojong. This major reconstruction effort started in 1995 and is scheduled for completion in the year 2020.

The palace grounds are open for viewing from 9 am to 6 pm from March to October, 9 am to 5 pm November to February (closed Tuesday). Admission for adults costs W700.

NATIONAL FOLK MUSEUM
국립민속박물관
This museum is on the grounds of the palace Gyeongbokgung. The collection comprises items from the daily lives of Koreans through history – everything from

SEOUL

CENTRAL SEOUL

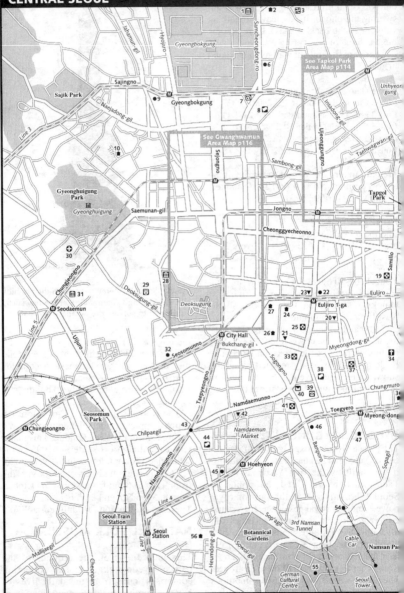

Gyeongbokgung

See Tapkol Park
Area Map p114

Unhyeon
gung

Sajingno

Sajik Park

Naejadong-gil

Jahamun-ro

Hyoja-ro

Samcheongdong-ro

Gyeongbokgung

Ujeonggungno

Imsadong-gil

Line 3

Sejongno

See Gwanghwamun
Area Map p116

Sambong-gil

Taehwagwan-gil

Tapgol
Park

Gyeonghuigung
Park

Gyeonghuigung

Saemunan-gil

Jongno

Cheonggyecheonno

Samilro

Chungjeongno

Deoksugung-gil

Deoksugung

Euljiro

Euljiro 1-ga

Myeongdong-gil

Seodaemun

Uljiro

Line 5

City Hall
Bukchang-gil

Seosomunno

Sogongno

Chungmuro

Line 2

Seosomun
Park

Chilpaegil

Taepyeongno

Toegyero

Chungjeongno

Namdaemunno

Namdaemunno

Namdaemun
Market

Myeong-dong

Bamporo

Sopagil

Malijaegil

Line 4

Hoehyeon

Cheonparo

Seoul Train
Station

Line 1

Seoul
Station

Heumdong-gil

Botanical
Gardens

Sop'agil

Sowol-gil

3rd Namsan
Tunnel

Cable
Car

Namsan Pa

German
Cultural
Centre

Seoul
Tower

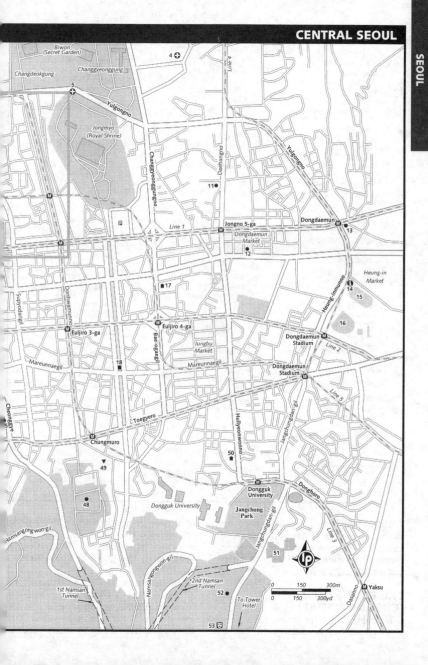

SEOUL

SEOUL

CENTRAL SEOUL

PLACES TO STAY
2 The Nest
네스트
10 Inn Sung Do
성도여관
17 Traveller's A Motel
A모텔
18 Poongjun Hotel
풍전호텔
24 Lotte Hotel
호텔롯데
26 Westin Chosun Hotel
조선호텔
27 President Hotel
프레지던트호텔
36 King Sejong Hotel
세종호텔
47 Pacific Hotel
퍼시픽호텔
50 Sofitel Ambassador
소피텔앰배서더호텔
51 Shilla Hotel
호텔신라
56 Hilton Hotel
힐튼호텔

PLACES TO EAT
20 OK Corral
21 Tony Romas
토니로마
23 La Cantina
42 Wang Mandu
왕만두
49 Korea House
한국의집

OTHER
1 National Folk
Museum
국립민속박물관
3 Lotus Lantern Buddhist
Centre
연등회관
4 Seoul National
University Hospital
서울대학교병원

5 Kyonghee University
Herbal Hospital
경희대종로한방병원
6 French Cultural
Centre
불란서문화원
7 Net House Cyber
Cafe
네트하우스
8 Japanese Embassy
일본대사관
9 Immigration Office;
KYHA
적선현대빌딩
11 Royal Asiatic Society
로얄아시아협회
12 Backpacking Equipment
Shops
등산장비상가
13 Dongdaemun
(Heunginjimun) Gate
흥인지문
14 Seoul Tourist
Information Centre
서울관광안내소
15 Football Stadium
축구장
16 Baseball Stadium
야구장
19 Printemps Department
Store
쁘렝땅백화점
22 Eulji Book Centre
을지서점
25 Lotte Department
Store
롯데백화점
28 Seokjojeon (Museum)
석조전
29 Jeongdong Theatre
정동극장
30 Gangbuk Samsung
Hospital
강북삼성병원
31 Agricultural Museum
농업박물관

32 Korean Air (KAL)
대한항공
33 Metro Midopa
Department Store
미도파백화점
34 Myeongdong Cathedral
명동성당
35 Myeongdong Sauna
명동사우나
37 Utoo Zone Department
Store
유투존
38 Chinese Embassy
중국대사관
39 Central Telephone
Office
중앙전화국
40 Central Post
Office (CPO)
중앙우체국
41 Shinsegae Department
Store
신세계백화점
43 Namdaemun
(Sungnyemun) Gate
숭례문
44 Irish Embassy
아일랜드대사관
45 Backpacking Equipment
Shops
등산장비상가
46 Asiana Airlines
아시아나항공
48 Namsan Hanok Village
남산한옥촌
52 Jangchung Tennis
Courts
장충테니스장
53 National Theatre
국립극장
54 Namsan Cable
Car Station
남산케이블카매표소
55 International Union
Travel Service
국제연합여행사

kitchen utensils to items associated with shamanistic rituals. Altogether there are about 10,000 items housed in nine display rooms. Admission costs W700 and the museum is closed Tuesday.

THE BLUE HOUSE (CHEONGWADAE) 청와대
One could say that the former royal palace Gyeongbokgung is actually still the seat of power in South Korea. Just beyond Shinmumun (the north gate of Gyeongbokgung) stands the Blue House (Greater Seoul map), the home of South Korea's president.

On 21 January, 1968, a squad of 31 North Korean commandos were caught just 500m from the Blue House – their mission was to assassinate South Korean president Park Chung-hee. Obviously, security remains

Seoulites compare it with Manhattan – New Yorkers might disagree. Yeouido, the island district

Sun Pyong-hui, Tapgol Park

Jongno 2-ga, central Seoul

Careworn charm in old Seoul

Floodlit, Seoul's great gates are awesome sights.

Expats dig in: Itaewon, home to a US army base

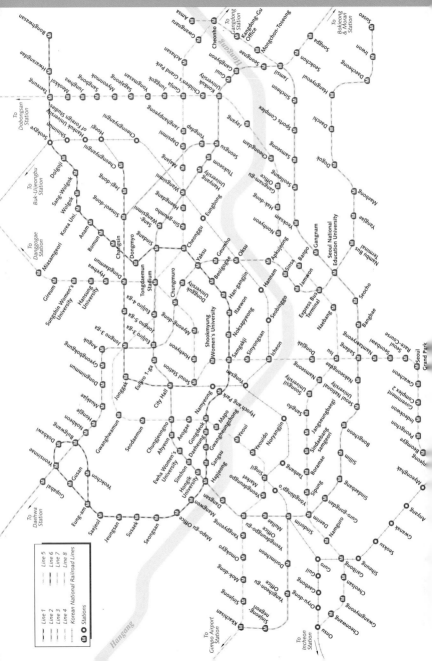

tight and the Blue House itself is not open to the general public. However, the tree-lined street in front of the Blue House has been open to the public ever since President Kim Young-sam was inaugurated in 1993.

JONGMYO 종묘

Moving east, the royal shrine Jongmyo was built concurrently with Gyeongbokgung to enshrine the ancestral tablets of the first Yi king, Taejo. Today, with the exception of two kings of some disrepute, the ancestral tablets of all 27 Yi kings are enshrined here. There are two shrines on the grounds: **Jeongjeon** and **Yeongnyeongjeon**.

Jongmyo is connected by a footbridge to the palace complex Changgyeonggung, and it makes sense to continue on into the grounds of the latter (there is no additional admission fee). Jongmyo is open from 9 am to 6.30 pm March to October, 9 am to 5.30 pm November to February (closed Tuesday). Admission for adults is W700.

CHANGGYEONGGUNG 창경궁

Changgyeonggung was originally a Goryeo dynasty summer palace, built in 1104. In the early 1390s the first Yi king, Taejo, lived here while Gyeongbokgung was completed. During the Japanese occupation, the palace was demoted to a park, a colonial-style red building built, and a botanical garden and zoo moved here. The zoo has since been relocated to Seoul Grand Park.

Changgyeonggung is open daily from 9 am to 6 pm from March to October, 9 am to 5 pm November to February (closed Tuesday). Admission for adults is W700 and this fee also gets you into Jongmyo if you cross the footbridge.

CHANGDEOKGUNG 창덕궁

A brief walk to the west of Changgyeonggung is the palace Changdeokgung. There are tours of the palace which include a visit to **Biwon** (the 'Secret Garden'). Tours take around 90 minutes. English-language tours are only available at 11.30 am, 1.30 and 3.30 pm. There are Korean-language tours on the hour from 9 am to 5 pm. Joining a Korean-language tour is no problem as all the sights have English explanations posted. The tours cost W2200 for adults or W1100 for persons aged 24 or under. If you'd rather not have the tour, you can enter the grounds of Changdeokgung for W700, but you will not be able to visit Biwon. Changdeokgung is closed on Monday.

TAPGOL PARK 탑골공원

Planted in between Jonggak and Jogno 3-ga subway stations is Tapgol ('pagoda') Park. There are always crowds of bored but friendly old age pensioners sitting around here and it's very easy to strike up a conversation with them (quite a few speak English). In the vicinity of the park are roadside vendors and occasionally the Seoul City bloodmobile. Attractive young women are hired to persuade Koreans (and anyone who looks Korean) to donate blood – if you have a Western face, they'll assume you have AIDS and will leave you alone. In the evenings fortune tellers set up shop in small candle-lit tents in the same area.

Tapgol Park is named after the 10-tier **marble pagoda**, now housed inside an ugly protective glass and steel structure. The **statue** in the park is Sun Pyong-hui, leader of the independence movement. On 1 March 1919, Sun Pyong-hui and other Korean dissidents drew up a declaration of independence. The declaration was read aloud in the park two days later. It unleashed a torrent of anti-Japanese passion, and the *Sam-il*, or March 1 Movement was born.

JOGYESA 조계사

Buried in the alleys south-east of Gyeongbokgung is by far the largest Buddhist temple in Seoul, Jogyesa. It is named after the Jogye sect (the major Buddhist sect in Korea), to which it belongs. In the vicinity of Jogyesa, out on the main road, are a number of **Buddhist supply shops** selling everything from alms bowls to tapes of Buddhist meditation chants.

UNHYEONGUNG 운현궁

This was the private housing compound of Heungseon Daewon-gun (1820–98), the father of King Gojong (1852–1919). Gojong

TAPGOL PARK AREA

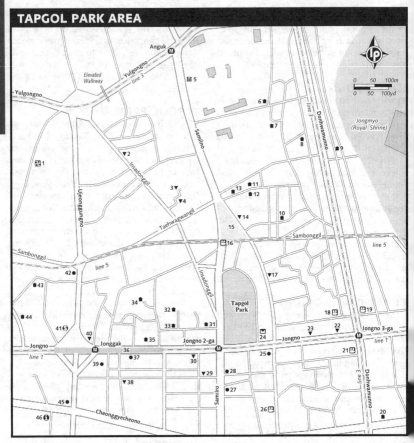

was born in this compound and lived here until age 12.

Unhyeongung is open from 9 am to 7 pm in summer, and from 9 am to 5 pm in winter (closed Monday). Admission costs W700. The palace is close to Anguk subway station on Line 3.

BOSINGAK 보신각

On the south-east corner of Jongno and Ujeonggungno is a belfry, Bosingak. Jongno, which means 'Bell Street', derives its name from its city bell. The old city bell, dating from the mid-15th century, is in the National

Museum, and a newer model is hung in Bosingak. The bell, which was once struck daily at dawn and dusk to signal the opening and closing of the city gates, is now only sounded to usher in the new year and mark Independence Movement Day and National Liberation Day. The pavilion area is fenced off and there's not a lot to see, but the place is packed on New Year's Eve.

GWANGHWAMUN INTERSECTION 광화문

The major intersection lying due south of Gyeongbokgung (Gwanghwamun Area map)

TAPGOL PARK AREA

PLACES TO STAY
6 Munhwa Yeogwan
문화여관
7 Motel Jongrowon
종로원여관
8 Seahwa-jang Yeogwan
세화장여관
9 Sunchang Yeogwan
순창여관
10 Green Field Motel
그린필드모텔
11 Yongjin Yeogwan
용진여관
12 Hwaseong-jang Yeogwan
화성장여관
13 Emerald Hotel
애머랄드호텔
20 Central Hotel
쎈츄럴호텔
31 Inseong Yeogwan
인성여관
32 Wongap Yeogwan
원갑여관
33 Jongno Yeogwan
종로여관
34 Taewon Yeogwan
대원여관
35 YMCA
와이엠씨에이
43 Sejong-jang Yeogwan
세종장여관
44 Seoul Hotel
서울호텔

PLACES TO EAT
2 Youngbin Garden
Restaurant
영빈가든

3 Sanchon Vegetarian
Restaurant
산촌식당
4 Airirang Restaurant;
The Old Teahouse
옛찻집다실
14 Rice Cake Shops
종로떡집
17 Doutor Coffee
Shop
도토루
22 Jongno Gimbap
Restaurant
종로김밥
23 Seoul Gimbap
Restaurant
서울김밥
29 Nutrition Centre
영양센타
30 Sinpouri Mandu
신포우리만두
38 Tokomo Japanese
Restaurant
도꼬모
40 Jongno Tower; World
Food Court; Top Cloud
Cafe
종로타워

OTHER
1 Jogyesa Temple
조계사
5 Unhyeon Palace
운현궁
15 Nakwon Elevated Arcade
낙원상가
16 Hollywood Cinema
허리우드극장

18 Picadilly Cinema
피카디리극장
19 Danseongsa
Cinema
단성사극장
21 Seoul Cinema
Town
서울시네마타운
24 Tapgol Post
Office
탑골우체국
25 Musicland
유직랜드
26 Cine Plaza Cinema
시네프라자극장
27 T-Zone Computers
티존
28 Tower Records
타워레코드
36 Jonggak
Underground
Arcade
종각지하상가
37 Chongno Book
Centre
종로서점
39 Boshingak
보신각
41 Jeil Bank
제일은행
42 Jung-ang Map
& Atlas
중앙지도
45 Youngpoong
Bookstore
영풍서점
46 KNTO
한국관광공사

is Gwanghwamun, named after a **gate** (Gate of Radiant Transformation) one block to the north. It's the only intersection in Seoul from which each of the four radiating roads have different names. Slightly to the north of the intersection, in the middle of Sejongno, is a **bronze statue** of probably the most revered figure in Korean history. Yi Sun-shin was a masterful military strategist and the inventor of the 'turtle ship' (see the History section in the Facts about Korea chapter). By cladding the wooden ships of the time in sheets of armour, he was able to achieve stunning victories over Hideyoshi's numerically and militarily stronger Japanese navy.

To the right of Yi Sun-shin's statue is the tiny **Bigak Pavilion**. It was built in 1903 to commemorate the enthronement of King Gojong.

DEOKSUGUNG 덕수궁
Deoksugung was built in the mid-15th century by King Sejo for his grandson, Prince Wolson. It has twice served temporarily as the royal abode: once for 15 years, after Hideyoshi's 1592 sacking of Seoul; and on a second occasion, from 1897 to 1907, when King Gojong made it his residence when he emerged from a year-long asylum in the Russian legation.

Towards the back of the compound is the white-columned **Seokjojeon** (Stone Hall). Inside Seokjojeon is the **royal museum**, which has on display some possessions of the royal family. It also features

SEOUL

an annexe of the **National Museum of Modern Art**.

The entrance to Deoksugung (Central Seoul map) is through one of the city's great gates, **Daehanmun** (near City Hall). Deoksugung is open from 9 am to 6 pm from March to October, 9 am to 5 pm November to February (closed Monday). The entrance fee is W700.

Visitors flock to see the changing of the guard ceremony at Daehanmun. This is performed daily except Monday at the following times: during July and August from 3 to 4.30 pm; 25 March through 31 December from 2 to 3.30 pm. The ceremony is not performed from 1 January to 24 March.

NAMDAEMUN 남대문

South of the City Hall is Namdaemun (Great South Gate), also known as Sungnyemun. It was once Seoul's chief city gate, in keeping with the principles of geomancy that determined the layout of the Yi palaces. It is still an impressive sight, though somewhat diminished by adjacent skyscrapers and roaring traffic. The gate was built in the late-14th century, and has been designated 'National Treasure No 1'.

POSTAL MUSEUM 우체국박물관

Strictly for the keen philatelist, the Postal Museum is on the 4th floor of the CPO (Central Seoul map). It has an extensive collection of 19th-century stamps and items related to the postal industry. The museum is closed on Sunday and public holidays.

NAMSAN PARK 남산공원

Seoul's main peak, Namsan (Central Seoul map), once marked the farthest southern extent of old royal Seoul – remains of the city walls can still be seen in the park's wooded grounds.

The peak was once crowned with defensive fortifications, though these have now been replaced by Seoul Tower.

In the western section, not far from Namdaemun market, the tropical **Namsan Botanical Gardens** (W300) are enclosed by a large greenhouse – a great place to warm up on a winter's day.

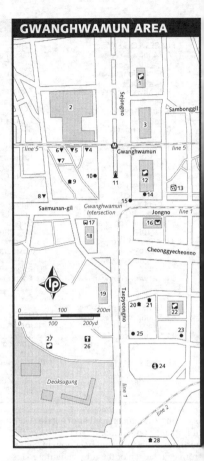

GWANGHWAMUN AREA

At the top of Namsan is **Seoul Tower**. With the help of the mountain, the tower reaches 483m above sea level, though minus the mountain it's a mere 240m. Still, it's the third tallest tower in the world and Seoul's most visible landmark. There's a revolving restaurant, but most visitors settle for the observation deck. Other attractions in the tower include the Photo Exhibition, Global Village Folk Museum, the Game Room, Fairy Land and World Musical Animal Land(!). If you enjoy this kind of tourist-oriented action, an all-inclusive ticket costs W7000. If you're content

GWANGHWAMUN AREA

PLACES TO STAY
9 Inn Daewon
　대원여관
19 Koreana Hotel
　코리아나호텔
20 New Kukje Hotel
　뉴국제호텔
21 New Seoul Hotel
　뉴서울관광호텔

PLACES TO EAT
4 Gabongru Chinese Restaurant
　가봉루반점
5 Sapporo Japanese Restaurant
　삿뽀로우동
6 Paris Baguette
　파리바게뜨
7 Dongseonggak Chinese Restaurant
　동성각반점

8 Goryeo Supermarket
　고려쇼핑

OTHER
1 US Embassy
　미국대사관
2 Sejong Cultural Centre
　세종문화회관
3 Gwanghwamun Telephone Office
　광화문전화국
10 Asiana Airlines
　아시아나항공
11 Yi Sun-shin Statue
　이순신장군동상
12 Kyobo Building (Australia & NZ Embassies)
　교보빌딩
13 Net Cyber Cafe
　넷카페
14 Kyobo Book Centre
　교보서점

15 Bigak Pavilion
　비각
16 Gwanghwamun Post Office
　광화문우체국
17 Airport Bus Stop
　공항버스정류장
18 Gwanghwamun Building (Taiwan Visas)
　광화문빌딩
22 Canadian Embassy
　캐나다대사관
23 Joy Travel Service
　죠이항공
24 City Hall & Tourist Information Centre
　시청
25 Korea Press Centre
　신문회관
26 Anglican Church
　대한성공회대성당
27 British Embassy
　영국대사관

with just the view, it can be yours for W2000.

You can reach the tower either by walking from the botanical garden area (an exhilarating 15- to 20-minute climb), taking a taxi or by cable car. The cable car runs at 30-minute intervals from 9 am to 10 pm from March through October, or 9 am to 8 pm November through February.

The cost is W1400 one way, or W2100 for a round trip. Seoul Tower is open from 9.30 am to 11.30 pm.

Namsan Hanok Village is at the northern end of Namsan Park, and a short walk from the Chungmuro subway station on Lines 3 and 4. The houses in this traditional village are the genuine article, though they had to be relocated from other parts of the city. It's quite fascinating and really worth a look around, and English-speaking guides are available. The village is closed on Tuesday.

JANGCHUNG PARK
At the eastern end of Namsan Park and just behind the Shilla Hotel is Jangchung Park. The park is unusual in that it's well-adorned with magnificent sculptures set out amongst the woods. Take subway Line 3 to Dongguk University station.

DONGDAEMUN
At the east end of Jongno 6-ga is Dongdaemun (East Great Gate). It dates from 1869, though it had to be renovated after it was damaged during the Korean War.

AGRICULTURAL MUSEUM
농업박물관

The Agricultural Museum contains seven rooms displaying 2400 agricultural implements. The displays range in antiquity from the stone age to modern times. As long as you're there, the *gimchi* section is also worth a look. The museum is in the old National Agricultural Cooperative Federation (NACF) Building on Chungjeongno 1-ga. Admission costs W300. Take subway Line 5 to Seodaemun station.

RAILWAY MUSEUM 철도박물관
Seoul station has a nice railway museum (admission W500), a good place to pass the time if you're waiting for a train.

YEOUIDO 여의도
Subway Line 5 can bring you to the island of Yeouido (Greater Seoul map), in the river Hangang. Though touted as Seoul's answer to Manhattan, there are a few sights here but nothing to hold your interest for

long. During office hours the streets are eerily deserted. However that changes dramatically on Sunday, when the parks fill up with Seoulites who couldn't get a seat on the packed buses fleeing the city.

The best way to explore Yeouido is on foot. Things to see include the **National Assembly** building, **Full Gospel Church** and the **Korea Stock Exchange** (free observation room on the 4th floor, with English explanations provided by phones).

Towards the south-eastern end of the island is Yeouido's **KLI 63** building. Despite the name, it's only 60 storeys tall (three levels in the basement are counted to make it seem higher). Nevertheless, it is Korea's tallest building. The top floor has an observation deck. The building also contains an **aquarium** and the **Imax theatre**. The ground level sports a wide selection of **restaurants**.

Along the island's north-east shore is **Riverside Park** (Hangang Simin Gongwon), a vast expanse of lawn (pity the poor soul who has to cut it). It can be packed with picnickers on Sunday when the weather is fine – be careful at such times or you risk being impaled on a barbecue skewer. There is a large outdoor **swimming pool** in Riverside Park which operates during July and August only. During the spring and autumn, the pool is emptied and becomes a roller skating rink – from December through February it's an ice skating rink.

Along the shoreline you'll also find a pier where there are **boat cruises** of the Hangang. There are several routes. Nature lovers will probably enjoy the cruises that take in the islet of Bamseom, a nesting area for migratory birds.

The cruises are operated by Semo Corporation (☎ 785 4411), which you can contact for reservations and information. In the summer peak season, boats run from 10 am to 9.20 pm.

The routes change often, but at the time of writing were as follows:

Yanghwa Bridge – Hangang Bridge – Yanghwa Bridge; 70 minutes; 6800W
Yeouido – Yanghwa Bridge – Dongjak Bridge – Yeouid;70 minutes; 6800W

Ttukseom Riverside Park – Dongho Bridge – Ttukseom Riverside Park; one hour; W6000
Jamsil Ferry Pier – Dongho Bridge – Jamsill Ferry Pier; one hour; 6000W

Along the island's north-east shore is a bicycle path that follows the south bank of the Hangang for 36km (far beyond Yeouido). The path is now being extended to the river's north shore, eventually to create a bicycle loop trail about 80km in length. In summer, there are bicycles for rent in Riverside Park.

Along the south-west shore of Yeouido, on a street called Yunjungno, is a thick grove of **cherry trees** that are spectacular during the brief cherry blossom season in early April.

WAR MEMORIAL 전쟁기념관

Despite the name, this is a fully-fledged museum and certainly one of the best in Seoul. The War Memorial traces the history of war in Korea, from the Three Kingdoms Period to the Korean War. Many younger travellers are surprised by the exhibit on the Vietnam War – it's often forgotten that the South Koreans participated in this war at the urging of their No 1 ally, the USA.

This large museum houses over 13,000 items, including a number of large aircraft, parked outside. The 'great victories' are discussed in all the English translations. The defeats suffered at the hands of the Japanese are only mentioned in Korean script.

Operating hours are 9.30 am to 6 pm and 9.30 am to 5 pm in winter (closed Monday). Admission costs W2000. The War Memorial is north-west of the Yongsan military base, very close to Samgakji subway station on Line 4.

YONGSAN FAMILY PARK
용산가족공원

This park, to the south of Itaewon, was the former golf course for the Yongsan military base. At the moment, it's basically a landscape of trees, grass and shrubs, but the Koreans apparently have big plans for the place. If all goes well, they say, the new **National Museum** will open soon. The old National Museum was torn down in 1996 – the priceless artefacts are currently housed in temporary buildings in the Gyeongbokgung (see the boxed text, below).

BONGWONSA 봉원사

West of the city centre in Seodaemun-gu, the Buddhist temple of Bongwonsa dates back to the late 9th century. It was destroyed during the Korean war and has been subsequently rebuilt. It is now the headquarters of the Taego sect of Korean Buddhism. This is an interesting sect, insofar as it allows its monks to marry; a vestige of the Japanese administration and a controversial issue among Korean Buddhists. The temple can be reached by taxi from Sinchon station

on subway Line 2, or Dongnimmun station on Line 3 (Greater Seoul map).

SEODAEMUN PRISON HISTORY HALL 독립봉원서대문전시장

Patriotic resistance against the Japanese is a theme the Koreans never seem to tire of, and one place to pursue the matter further is Seodaemun Prison History Hall at **Dongnip Park**, due east of Bongwonsa. The park was built on the site of a former prison where patriotic Koreans were martyred during the Japanese occupation of 1910–1945. The city government has left several Japanese-era buildings standing, including the execution

---

The Musical Chairs Museum

While arguably the best museum in Korea, the main problem with Seoul's National Museum is figuring out where to put it. Until 1995, it was housed in the former Capitol building on the grounds of Gyeongbokgung. In 1996, the building closed its doors for good and work crews began tearing it down.

There is a story behind all this. The Japanese built their Capitol building, in 1926, on the grounds of Gyeongbokgung for a specific purpose. It was deliberately constructed in this position to intersect the geomantic axis of power that flowed from the throne hall through the Gwanghwamun (Gate of Radiant Transformation), and the building was constructed in the shape of the Japanese character for Japan. All this was to reinforce the notion that Korea was now part of Japan. Needless to say, many Koreans were less than happy about this and have long vowed to get rid of this symbol of Japanese imperialism.

Not everyone, however, felt that demolishing the National Museum was a great idea. The preservationist lobby argued that the building was an important part of Korea's history. Aside from the Japanese era, much post-liberation history happened here (it was the capital for the Rhee, Park and Chun administrations). Taxpayers noted that building a new National Museum would be very costly. And pragmatists suggested that at least it would be wise to preserve the old museum until a new one could be built to take its place.

In the end, national pride won the day. Once President Kim Young-sam made the decision to demolish the old building, it was done swiftly. As the wrecking crews moved in, the priceless collection of art treasures had to be shifted around between various annexe buildings in the Gyeongbokgung compound. Unfortunately, those buildings have been undergoing renovation at the same time, and none is large enough to display the museum's entire collection. As a result, displays of selected art objects have had to be rotated.

And the new National Museum? It's currently under construction at the Yongsan Family Park, adjacent to the military base. The project has faltered on financial questions and arguments over choosing an architect. Some wanted to open the design competition to international bidding – after lengthy haggling, a Korean architect was chosen.

Behind schedule and way over budget, optimists now say the new museum will (hopefully) open by the year 2003. Meanwhile, the national treasures keep getting shifted around to temporary quarters. To find out just where this mobile collection might be at any given time, ask KNTO (Tapgol Park map; ☎ 757-0086). The museum – wherever it is – is closed on Monday.

chamber. Admission costs W1100. The site is closed on Monday.

Adjacent to the park is **Dongnimmun** which was built in 1898. It's claimed that the gate was modelled after the Arc de Triomphe in Paris, though in fact it looks nothing like the French original.

Dongnip Park can be reached by taking subway Line 3 to Dongnimmun station (Greater Seoul map).

BONG-EUNSA 봉은사

Slightly north of the Korea Exhibition Centre, Bong-eunsa has been relocated to sterile Gangnam-gu, in southern Seoul (no doubt kicking and screaming all the way). A collection of important wood-block scriptures are housed in a small wooden structure next to the main temple. The original temple dates from the 8th century and in its time was an important Zen centre.

OLYMPIC STADIUM 올림픽주경기장

The 1988 Seoul Olympics was an event of great consequence for South Korean national pride, and the auspicious numbers '88' crop up everywhere – there is an 88 Gymnasium, 88 Golf Club, 88 Swimming Pool, 88 Rent-A-Car and even a popular brand of cigarettes called 88. Some of the tourist literature still touts the slogan 'keep the Olympic torch burning', even though it's getting long in the tooth.

Despite the hype, the Olympic Stadium is just what its name suggests: a stadium. However, it's occasionally the venue of rock concerts – probably the most interesting time to visit. The best way to get to the stadium is from Seoul Sports Complex subway station (Gangnam -gu map) on Line 2.

OLYMPIC PARK 올림픽공원

Not far from the Olympic Stadium is Olympic Park (Greater Seoul map) – a more interesting destination. The grounds contain numerous world-class sporting facilities from the '88 Olympics. There are also the remains of the Three Kingdoms-period Mongchontoseong (Earthen Fortress).

Within the park's ground are some 200 sculptures, which offer a serene if somewhat bizarre sight with the sporting facilities in the background.

The park is a short walk from the Mongchon-toseong subway station on Line 8, or the Olympic Park station on Line 5.

There is no admission fee for the park itself, but the **Olympic Cultural Center** charges W4000 for puppet shows, W4500 for its Space & Dinosaur Hall and W8000 for its sledding slope.

LOTTE WORLD 롯데월드

If you are a fan of mall culture, you'll love Lotte World. It's a city in a building, with an ice skating rink, Hotel Lotte World, Lotte Department Store, Lotte Super Store, Lotte World Shopping Mall, Lotte World Sports, Lotte World Swimming and Lotte World Plaza. If this is not enough, there's a Disneyland look-a-like next door in Lotte World Adventure, which includes Magic Island and the Lotte World Folk Museum.

It would easily be possible to spend an entire rainy day exploring the place, and it would be ideal for children (you could probably leave them here for good, and they'd never miss you – providing they had enough money).

The vast majority of Lotte World's shops and the department store are closed on Monday, though the ice skating rink and restaurants around it remain open.

The basic admission fee to Lotte World Adventure doesn't include the rides or the Folklore Museum which all carry steep surcharges. One can purchase an 'all-around ticket' for W22,000, a 'Big 5' ticket for W16,000 or a basic admission ticket for W7000. There are discounts for students and children, and tickets are half-price after 6 pm. Lotte World Adventure is open from 9.30 am to 11 pm.

The Jamsil subway station on Line 2 has clearly marked signs showing the way to Lotte World (Greater Seoul map).

WORLD CUP STADIUM
월드컵주경기장

With a price tag of US$166 million and seating for 61,000 persons, the octagon-shaped stadium is Seoul's latest feel-good

GANGNAM-GU

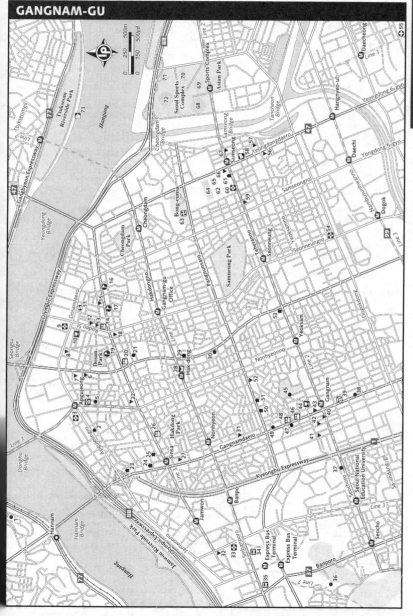

SEOUL

GANGNAM-GU

PLACES TO STAY
23 Samhwa Hotel
삼화호텔
24 Hangang-jang
Yeogwan
한강장여관
25 Pink Motel; Inha-jang
Yeogwan
핑크모텔·인하장여관
29 Amiga Hotel
호텔아미가
50 Ritz-Carlton Hotel
리츠칼튼서울호텔
51 Novotel Ambassador
Hotel
노보텔앰배서더호텔
53 Seoul Renaissance Hotel
서울르네상스호텔
61 Inter-Continental Hotel
호텔인터콘티넨탈

PLACES TO EAT
6 Italianni's
7 Chili's Grill & Bar
칠리
8 Uno Chicago Bar & Grill
우노
12 Bennigan's Chicago
베니간스
13 Coco's California
코코스
15 Hard Rock Cafe
하드락까페
18 TGI Friday's
22 Tony Roma's
토니로마스
27 Pho Hoa Vietnamese
Noodles
31 Outback Steak House
아웃백
32 Kim's Club (mega-store)
김스클럽
40 Restaurant Marche
Movenpick; Kim &
Johnson's ESL Books
41 Carne Station; Bennigan's
Las Vegas
까르네스테이션·베니간 스
42 Spaghettia; Tony Roma's
43 Starbucks
52 OK Corral
56 Hanmiri Korean
한미리
57 Coco's California
코코스
59 Carne Station
까르네스테이션
66 Bennigan's Seattle
베니간스

67 Ponderosa Steak House
판다로사

OTHER
1 UN Village
유엔단지
2 Chang-a Sports Centre
창아스포츠센타
3 Hyundai Department
Store
현대백화점
4 Shinsa Telephone
Office
신사전화국
5 Chunjiyun Sauna
준지윤사우나
9 Galleria Department
Store
갤러리아백화점(서관)
10 Nightlife Area
유흥가
11 CITIBANK
시티은행
14 Kinema Cinema
키네마극장
16 New Seoul Golf Driving
Range
뉴서울골프장
17 Hyoseong Golf Driving
Range
효성골프장
19 Jeonghwa Golf Driving
Range
정화골프장
20 Cine House Cinema
씨네하우스극장
21 Gangnam Mud Sauna
강남진흙사우나
26 Broadway Cinema
브로드웨이극장
28 Yeong-dong
Post Office
영동우체국
30 YMCA Gymnasium
YMCA체육관
33 New Core Department
Store
뉴코아백화점
34 Seoul Express Bus
Terminal (Gyeongbuseon
Building)
서울고속버스터미널
(경부선)
35 Seoul Express Bus
Terminal (Honam-
Yeongdongseon
Building)
서울고속버스터미널
(호남선·영동선)

36 National Central Library
국립중앙도서관
37 Han's Cooking Institute
38 Jinsol Book Centre
진솔서점
39 La Puta Internet Cafe
라푸타
44 Woodstock II Pub;
Net Plaza Cyber Cafe
우드스탁·넷프라자
45 Gukgiwon Taekgwondo
국기원
46 City Cinema
씨티극장
47 Tower Records
타워레코드
48 Dong-a Cinema
동아극장
49 Korean Air
대한항공
54 Grand Department
Store
그랜드백화점
55 Samsung Medical Centre
삼성서울병원
58 Russian Embassy
러시아대사관
60 Hyundai Department
Store
현대백화점
62 Korea City Air
Terminal
도심공항터미널
63 Bong-eunsa Temple
봉은사
64 Korea Exhibition Centre
한국종합전시장
65 Korea World Trade
Centre (KWTC); COEX
종합무역센타
68 Baseball Stadium
야구경기장
69 Students' Gym
학생체육관
70 Indoor Swimming
Pool
실내수영장
71 Gymnasium
실내체육관
72 Olympic Stadium
올림픽주경기장
73 Ttukseom Ferry
Terminal
뚝섬선착장

project (see the boxed text Soccer Wars in the Facts for the Visitor chapter). You'll find it in Mapo-gu, close to the not-yet-opened Seongsan station on subway Line 6 (Greater Seoul map).

SEOUL DREAM LAND 서울드림랜드
The largest amusement park within the city limits is Seoul Dream Land (Greater Seoul map; ☎ 982 6800). Popular facilities here include the dragon coaster, cycle monorail, skyrider, mini-train, haunted house, swimming pool and miniature-golf course. It's open from 9 am to 7.30 pm from March through October and 9 am to 6 pm November through February. General admission for adults is W2000, but the rides cost extra. The amusement park is in Dobong-gu, in northern Seoul. Take subway Line 4 to Suyu station, then bus No 9 to the park.

CHILDREN'S GRAND PARK 어린이대공원
Out in Seongdong-gu, in eastern Seoul, the Children's Grand Park has plenty of atractions guaranteed to keep the kids amused for a day. There are rides, play areas, fountains and ponds, and even a small zoo.

Children's Grand Park is open daily from 9 am to 7 pm. Entry costs W1000 for adults, W500 for teenagers over 12 and is free for children under 12 year olds. To get there, take subway Line 5 to Achasan station or Line 7 to Children's Grand Park station (Greater Seoul map).

ACTIVITIES
Archery (Gungdo)
The organisation to contact is the Korea Amateur Sport Association (☎ 420 3333).

Buddhist Studies
The Lotus Lantern Buddhist Center (☎ 735 5347) is the place to meet the expat Buddhist community for worship and study. There are Buddhist ceremonies in English every Sunday at 6.30 pm.

Computer Club
The Seoul Computer Club is an English-speaking organisation in the US military

base in Yongsan. You don't have to be a member of the military to participate.

Cooking Classes
Han's Cooking Institute (☎ 592 3783) in Gangnam-gu is one of the few such schools in Seoul that offers cooking classes taught by English-speaking instructors. To reach the institute, take subway Line 2 to Seoul National Education University station, exit 4. From there it's a five-minute walk.

Cycling
The Korean Mountain Biking Association, or KMTBA (☎ 967 9287) is a friendly organisation that arranges outings.

Golf
There are 48 golf courses in the province of Gyeonggi-do, but only two 18-hole courses within the Seoul city limits. Most accessible are Namsungdae (☎ 403 0071) and the neighbouring Dong Seoul (☎ 480 5600). Both are in the hills of south-eastern Seoul. Take subway Line 5 to Macheon station, then a 2km taxi ride.

There are also five driving/putting ranges within the city limits of Seoul In Gangnam-gu, the Jeonghak, Hyoseong and New Seoul golf driving ranges are all fairlclose to Apgujeong station on subway Line 3.

Health Clubs
Private clubs that provide exercise machines, racquetball courts, swimming pools and so on can be found all over Seoul. Some places charge by the day, others insist on a monthly membership fee. The Chang-a sports club near the Apgujeong subway station on Line 3 is one such club, but there are many others. These places advertise in the phone book, but in Korean only, so ask a local to help you find these facilities.

Hiking
English is the lingua franca of the International Outdoor Club (☎ 319 9917, 777 4188), which runs hiking, sightseeing and other outdoor excursions. There are also 'cross-cultural' talks held twice weekly.

San Ki Suk (☎ 924 1769, cell phone 011 9006 3054, e sankisuk@yahoo.co.kr) is an organised trekking company which is trying to specialise in day hikes for foreigners. The fee for arranging a trip with an English-speaking guide is W20,000 per person for a half day, or W30,000 for a full day.

A less expensive option is to go with one of the Korean-speaking hiking clubs. The USO (☎ 795 3028) also has a hiking club. The cheapest alternative, of course, is to strike out on your own.

While most of the really good hikes are further out of town, there are several worthy mountains within the city limits of Seoul. Consider the following:

Inwangsan There are a number of approaches to the summit (Greater Seoul map), but the easiest way is to first follow the road (Inwangsangil) on the west side of Sajik Park (Central Seoul map), then as you get to within sight of the peak take one of the obvious paths off to your left. Along the route you'll probably encounter a few soldiers or plainclothes police – the area is a little bit sensitive because it overlooks the Blue House, where the president lives. If you reach the summit (338m) and the weather cooperates, you'll be rewarded with sweeping views of the city.

Don't be tempted to climb the mountain from the Muakjae subway station, even though it appears close on the map – your ascent will be halted by a wire fence!

Gwanaksan Straddling the southern boundary of metropolitan Seoul and Gyeonggi-do, Gwanaksan (Greater Seoul map) is a popular hiking spot. The summit is a moderate 632m above sea level, but the mountain is extremely rocky.

You reach the peak starting from the campus of Seoul National University, due south of the mountain. To get there, take subway Line 2 to Seoul National University station, then a bus about another 2km to the campus. From the campus, Gwanaksan is the large, obvious-looking peak towards the south-east. There are many hiking trails and students will easily point you the way.

Ice Skating
Lotte World offers year-round indoor ice skating, but avoid it on weekends when the ice is hidden under a mass of squirming arms and legs.

From mid-December to mid-February, there is outdoor ice skating on the swimming pools in Riverside Park (see the Yeouido section, earlier in this chapter) and in Olympic Park (see the Olympic Park section, earlier). For Yeouido, take subway Line 5 to Yeouinaru station. For Olympic Park, take subway Line 2 to Jamsil or to Sports Complex station.

The Hyatt Hotel has an indoor skating rink. You don't need to be a guest to use it.

Paragliding
Several companies run paragliding expeditions. Contact Mirae (☎ 773 4267) or KRA (☎ 585 3002) for information.

Saunas
Seoul has plenty of plush saunas, and prices for a basic steam are very reasonable, considering the fine facilities.

One place to try is Myeong-dong Sauna (☎ 774 9555). It's a five-minute walk from Myeong-dong station (Sejong Hotel exit) on subway Line 4.

Gangnam-gu is a happy hunting ground for saunas. Perhaps the easiest to find is the Chunjiyun Sauna (☎ 549 8013) near the Apgujeong station on subway Line 3. Not far away is the intriguing Gangnam Mud Sauna (☎ 544 1060) – management claims that if you can't find the place, call from nearby and they'll come to pick you up.

Hotel saunas are relatively easy to find and you don't have to be a hotel guest to use the facilities (but you must indeed pay). You can try the Poongjun, Pacific, Tower, Holiday Inn, Crown, Capital, King Sejong and Sheraton, Lotte, Lotte World and Seokyo hotels. The saunas inside the Swiss Grand, Inter-Continental and Hilton are for hotel guests and members only.

Special Events
Seoul Citizens Day This is held on 28 October, every year. It's a big, free gala

held in a stadium (not necessarily the same stadium every year). Since 1996, part of the festivities have been a 'Festival to Entertain Foreign Residents' at Daehangno (Hyehwa station on subway Line 4), including a Parade of Foreign Residents in their 'traditional costume' (your one chance to dress like a slob and be applauded for it).

Seokcheonje This is a fascinating ceremony to watch. It's held twice a year in accordance with the lunar calendar (first day of the second moon, and first day of the eighth moon). The ceremony is only staged in the courtyard of the Confucius Shrine at Sungkyunkwan University in the north of Seoul. Performances are done by a traditional court orchestra and full costume rituals are enacted. To get to the university, take the subway to Hyehwa station. The schedule for the next five years is as follows: 23 February & 17 September 2001; 14 March & 7 September 2002; 3 March & 28 August 2003; 20 February & 14 September 2004; 10 March & 4 September 2005.

Jyongmyo Daeje The Royal Shrine Rites are a homage to the monarchs of the Joseon kingdom. Full costume parades are held, accompanied by court music. They take place in Jongmyo on the first Sunday of May.

Taegwondo
The headquarters of the World Taegwondo Federation (☎ 561 9528) is at **Gukgiwon**, a beautiful park-like compound near Gangnam subway station (Gangnam-gu map). The organisation has information on taegwondo schools and tournaments.

An English-speaking organisation is Home of Korea Information Taegwondo (HOKI; ☎ 336 6014), which maintains a Web site at www.taekwontour.com.

PLACES TO STAY
Budget
The definition of 'budget' in Seoul should be any hotel where it is possible to get a room for W30,000 or less.

Gwanghwamun Urban renewal has swept through central Seoul, taking with it a lot of the old buildings and the cheap yeogwan once common in this area. The oldest remaining yeogwan is *Inn Daewon* (☎ 738 4308). Oxygen-free hovels cost W13,000, and all 20 rooms share one dingy washroom. Despite this, it's a popular place to stay, mainly thanks to the small courtyard where travellers sit and swap yarns. And you can't beat the location.

Gyeongbokgung Area (Central Seoul map) The same family that operates Inn Daewon also runs the *Inn Sung Do* (☎ 737 1056). This place is in considerably better condition than its close cousin and is only slightly more expensive. Doubles with shared bath cost W13,000, while private bath raises the tab to W20,000.

A hostel that packs in the backpackers is *The Nest* (☎ 725 4418), a lovely spot just east of the National Folk Museum. This very clean and charming accommodation is owned and operated by the proprietors of Net House Cyber Cafe, at the southern end of Gyeongbokgung, and you should stop in there first to see if rooms are available. Dorm beds cost W10,000, with breakfast thrown in free. This hostel can also arrange trekking tours and other outdoor activities.

Tapgol Park Area Another place that receives the backpackers' seal of approval is *Munhwa Yeogwan* (☎ 765 4659). Pleasant single rooms with shared bath cost W15,000, and a few doubles have private bath for W20,000. The beautiful traditional courtyard here is a major attraction, making it easy for travellers to socialise.

Just a few doors south of Munhwa Yeogwan is the *Motel Jongrowon* (☎ 745 6876). Beautiful rooms with bath go for W20,000.

A little north of the Jongno 3-ga station and just west of Jongmyo (Royal Shrine) is an alley where you'll find *Sun Chang Yeogwan* (☎ 765 0701). At W15,000, it's cheap – but the rooms are tiny. There is a small courtyard and the owner is very nice.

As you face the YMCA, on the right side of the building you'll find an alley. If you head up this alley, you'll find a sign indicating the route to the *Daewon Yeogwan* (☎ *730 6244*). Doubles with shared bath at this popular place cost W15,000.

Other alleys behind the YMCA contain a thick concentration of yeogwan which almost all charge W25,000 for a double with private bath. The selection include the *Wongap Yeogwan* (☎ *734 1232*), *Inseong Yeogwan* and *Jongno Yeogwan*.

The *Yong Jin Hotel* (☎ *765 4481*) is on an alley on the east side of the Nagwon arcade. Tiny rooms with private bath cost W20,000. Directly opposite it is the *Hwaseong-jang Yeogwan* (☎ *765 3834*), which charges W25,000.

On the same alley you'll find the *Emerald Hotel* (☎ *743 2001*). A comfortable double with bath is W25,000. This place distinguishes itself by having table and chairs in the rooms (distinctly lacking in most yeogwan). Cable TV is a feature.

In the next alley south of the Emerald is the clean and modern *Green Field Motel*, again charging the standard W25,000. There are many other yeogwan in this alley.

To the west of Donhwamunno, the *Seahwa-jang Hotel* (☎ *765 2881*) houses many foreigners working in Seoul. Rooms with attached bath cost W20,000 per night, but it's W500,000 per month which works out to a very reasonable W16,600 when calculated on a daily basis. It's a good place for long-termers.

In an alley next to the Seoul Hotel is the excellent *Sejong-jang Yeogwan* (☎ *732 7856*). Rooms cost the standard W25,000.

Sinchon If nocturnal bar-hopping is one of your habits, Sinchon (Seoul's premier nightlife area) is an ideal place to stay. At least you'll be able to walk back to your room at 4 am when the subway is closed.

There are over 20 yeogwan and motels in the alleys just to the north-east of the Sinchon subway station on Line 2. Some reasonably good ones include *Hyeondae Yeogwan* (☎ *313 6871*), *Minjin-jang Yeogwan* and *Hotel Prince* (☎ *313 5551*). There

are many others just as good, and most are in the W25,000 bracket.

Hong-ik University This is also an ideal location for late-night raging, but budget accommodation is surprisingly scarce. One possibility is *WOW Guest House* (☎ *322 8644*), hidden in an alley close to TGI Friday's. A dorm bed is W15,000, or splash out for your own room at W30,000. This hostel also arranges trekking tours and other outdoor adventures.

Dongdaemun (Central Seoul map) *Travellers A Motel* (☎ *2285 5511*, e *pricky@ hitel.net*), despite the name, is more like a hostel than a motel. It's near Ulchiro 4-ga subway station on Line 5 (exit 1), hidden in an alley just off a major street lined with shops peddling sewing machines. Beds cost W12,000 per person, and double rooms are W30,000. Other features include a small kitchen, cable TV, free coffee and tea plus a laundry service.

Itaewon Right in the heart of the action, at the top of that infamous stretch of alley affectionately known as 'hooker hill', is the *Hilltop Motel* (☎ *793 4972*), where there are 15 Western-style doubles with attached bathroom, colour TV and air-con costing W25,000. The sign is in English and some English is spoken by the staff. This place is a favourite with travellers.

Just down the hill from the Hilltop is an alley where you'll find the *Gwangseon-jang Yeogwan*. Rooms cost W25,000.

Back on the main drag is the *Mido Hotel* which is in fact a yeogwan. Closet-like hovels with private bath cost W25,000. Not recommended.

At the western end of Itaewonno, up on a hill, is the *Ihwa-jang Yeogwan*, which is also W25,000.

Daehangno *Trek Korea* (☎ *743 7631*) is a very clean, very pleasant place to stay. As the name implies, trekking tours of Korea's mountains can be arranged here. There are two dormitory rooms and three private rooms. Dorm beds cost W15,000, the private rooms are W25,000. Take subway Line 4 to Hyehwa station.

Gangnam-gu The *Olympic Parktel Hostel* (*Greater Seoul map;* ☎ *410 2114*) with 1234 beds is the only genuine youth hostel in Seoul, but it's hardly worth seeking out. While the facilities are comfortable, it's inconveniently located and not worth the price at W13,000 a bed. Take subway Line 2 to Seongnae station and walk 500m. The building is closed from 10 am to 3 pm.

The area around Sinsa station on subway Line 3 is a good place to look for cheap accommodation. West of the station are *Pink Motel* and *Inha-jang Yeogwan*. Just to the north of the station is the *Hangang-jang Yeogwan*. A bit further north near the big cloverleaf intersection are *Sewon-jang* and *Gangbyeon-jang* yeogwans. Rooms in all these places cost W25,000.

Mid-Range
Gwanghwamun The *Seoul Hotel* (☎ *735 9001*) – a three-minute walk from Gwanghwamun station on subway Line 5 – has a superb location with 102 rooms priced from W65,340 to W83,490.

The *New Seoul Hotel* (☎ *735 9071*) offers singles/doubles for W90,000/120,000 and twins (Western and Korean syle) for W120,000 to W150,000. Facilities include a sauna. Rated three stars (136-rooms).

New Kukje Hotel (☎ *732 0161*) has 130 Western-style and six Korean-style rooms. Singles/doubles cost W80,000/103,000. This place has a sauna and karaoke. Rated three stars.

Tapgol Park Area The low end of mid-range has to be the *YMCA* (☎ *734 6884*) near the Jonggak station on subway Line 1. Check out the basement where you'll find a coffee shop, beauty salon, discount travel agency and even the Boy Scout Shop. Rooms at the Y are no better than the nearby yeogwan, but some of the staff do speak English. Singles/doubles are W31,404/37,190, twins W42,975.

The 72-room *Central Hotel* (☎ *265 4121*) is one block south of the Jongno 3-ga

station on subway Line 1. Singles cost W38,500, doubles (Western and Korean syle) are W44,000, twins (Western-style) are W49,500 and suites are W80,000. The sauna is its trump card. Rated one star.

Myeong-dong (Central Seoul map) The 120-room *Pacific Hotel* (☎ *777 7811*) is a two-minute walk from Myeong-dong station on subway Line 4. Doubles/twins cost W100,000/120,000. Rated three stars.

The 172-room *Poongjun Hotel* (☎ *266 2151*) is a five-minute walk from Euljiro 4-ga station on subway Line 2. It has doubles (Western and Korean syle) for W100,000, twins for W110,000 and suites for W170,000 to W200,000. Rated three stars.

Sinchon The *Mirabeau Hotel* (☎ *392 9511*), a three-minute walk from Ehwa Women's University subway station on Line 2 has Western-style twins for W65,900 and Korean-style rooms at W80,600. Rated two stars.

Hong-ik University The 104-room, three-star *Seokyo Hotel* (☎ *333 7771*) is a two-minute walk from Hong-ik University subway station on Line 2. Twins/suites go W110,000/200,000, Korean-style rooms go for W120,000.

Itaewon The 50-room *Kaya Hotel* (*Greater Seoul map;* ☎ *798 5101*) is a two-minute walk from Namyeong station on subway Line 1. It's not actually in Itaewon proper, but just a stone's throw from the USO. The Kaya gets very good reviews from travellers. There is a sauna and a good restaurant. Singles/doubles cost W40,000/43,000, twins W50,000 and Korean-style rooms are W43,000. Rated one star.

The 170-room *Crown Hotel* (*Greater Seoul map;* ☎ *797 4111*), is just south of the Itaewon tourist zone. Doubles and twins (both Western and Korean syle) cost W100,000. Facilities include a sauna and indoor golf driving range. Rated three stars.

The 139-room *Hamilton Hotel* (☎ *794 0171*) is in the heart of Itaewon. Doubles cost W121,000. Facilities include Korean, Indian and Western restaurants, an outdoor swimming pool and (of course) a shopping arcade. Rated three stars.

Gangnam-gu The *Samhwa Hotel (☎ 541 1011)* – just north of Sinsa station on subway Line 3 – distinguishes itself by being more Korean syle than usual, even boasting *ondol* (traditional Korean) suites. Western and Korean-style doubles are W49,000. Rated one star.

The 195-room *Amiga Hotel (☎ 3440 8000)*, is a 15-minute walk from Seonleung station on subway Line 2 (or catch bus No 235 at Seonleung station). The hotel has received much praise from foreign travellers, and the hotel bakery deserves an award. Twins (Western and Korean syle) go for W210,000, while suites are W330,000 to W550,000. Facilities include tennis courts, game room and disco. Rated two stars.

Top End
Gwanghwamun/Central Seoul The 280-room *Koreana Hotel (Gwanghwamun map; ☎ 730 9911)* towers over the Gwanghwamun intersection, a two minute walk from the Gwanghwamun subway station on Line 5. A recent renovation has left this place with four good restaurants. Doubles cost W145,000. Rated four stars.

The *President Hotel (☎ 753 3131)* with 303 rooms is a five-minute walk from City Hall station on subway Line 1 and 2. Singles/twins cost W95,000/140,000. Facilities include a game room and a good shopping arcade. Rated four stars.

The *Lotte Hotel (☎ 771 1000)* is a two-minute walk from Eulji 1-ga station on subway Line 2. With 38 floors and 1318 rooms, it's the largest hotel in Korea. The hotel is attached to the equally enormous Lotte Department Store. Doubles/twins cost W230,000/250,000. Rated five stars.

The 480-room *Plaza Hotel (☎ 771 2200)*, is officially known as the Radisson Seoul Plaza. It's a two-minute walk from City Hall station on subway Line 1 or 2. Singles/doubles are priced at W210,000/230,000. Rated five stars.

The *Westin Chosun Hotel (☎ 771 0500)*, with its 460-room, is a two-minute walk from City Hall station on subway Line 1 or 2. Twins cost W223,000. Facilities include O'Kim's Irish Pub and Sports Bar, an Italian restaurant, health club, sauna, swimming pool and business centre. Rated five stars.

The *King Sejong Hotel (☎ 773 6000)* is opposite Myeong-dong station on subway Line 4. This 231-room hotel has singles/doubles for W140,000/180,000. Facilities include four restaurants (Western, Japanese, Korean and Korean buffet), a health club, sauna, game room and shopping arcade. Rated four stars.

Itaewon The *Itaewon Hotel (☎ 792 3111)* is on Itaewonno, the main tourist street. The 121-room hotel has doubles for W52,600. Facilities are good but you can find everything you need in life just outside the hotel's main entrance. Rated three stars.

The 605-room *Grand Hyatt Hotel (Greater Seoul map; ☎ 797 1234)* is *the* prestigious address in Itaewon, though in fact it's not truly in Itaewon – you have to walk up a rather large hill to reach it (though at these rates you can probably afford a taxi). Doubles/twins are W220,000/270,000. Facilities include some of Seoul's more popular restaurants and pubs (The Terrace, Hugo's, JJ Mahoney's). Rated five stars.

The *Capital Hotel (Greater Seoul map; ☎ 792 1122)* is south of the main Itaewon tourist zone. There are 287 rooms – twins cost W164,000. Facilities include a coffee shop, bakery, bar, Korean-Japanese buffet restaurant, health club, indoor swimming pool, tennis courts, night clubs, shopping arcade, indoor golf driving range and sauna. Rated four stars.

Gangnam-gu The *Novotel Ambassador Hotel (☎ 567 1101)* is a 10-minute walk from Gangnam station on subway Line 2. This 338-room hotel has twins (Western and Korean syle) for W180,000 to W200,000. Facilities include a Korean-Japanese buffet restaurant, health club, sauna, indoor swimming pool and golf practice range. Rated four stars.

The face of enterprise: billboards and street stalls

Early morning, Jagalchi Fish Market, Busan

A national obsession. Acres of gimchi (and pickles) for sale at Dongdaemun Market, Seoul

Central Seoul: Admiral Yi Sun-shin (1545–98) stands guard before the Gwanghwamun intersection.

PATRICK HORTON

If all roads lead to Seoul, this is where they meet.

JOHN BORTHWICK

See anything you like? Namdaemun Market

The 495-room *Seoul Renaissance Hotel* (☎ 555 0501) is a five-minute walk from Yeoksam station on subway Line 2. Twins are W210,000 to W260,000; Korean-style rooms are W210,000 to W490,000. Facilities include buffet restaurants (Korean, Chinese and Italian food), health club, indoor pool, tennis court, sauna, shopping arcade, indoor golf driving range, games room and business centre. Rated five stars.

The *Inter-Continental Hotel* (☎ 555 5656) is a three-minute walk from Samseong station on subway Line 2. It was already one of Seoul's largest hotels when it had 597 rooms, but at the time of writing is was about to double in size, thanks to a new annexe which should be opening soon. Deluxe rooms (Korean and Western) are W205,000, executive rooms are W250,000 and suites are W300,000. There is also a late check-out option (4 pm) which presumably costs a few *won* more. Creature comforts include a health club, indoor pool, night club, sauna, shopping arcade and busy business centre. Rated five stars.

The *Ritz-Carlton Hotel* (☎ 3451 8000), near the Yeoksam station on subway Line 2, has 400 rooms priced all the way from W230,000 to W3,000,000. A neat new feature is broadband Internet access in every room, which the management claims to be the first in Asia. Rated five stars.

Miscellaneous Areas The *Sofitel Ambassador Hotel* (*Central Seoul map;* ☎ 275 1101) is a three-minute walk from Dongguk University station on subway Line 3. The hotel has 435 Western-style and five Korean-style rooms. Singles/doubles cost W180,000/200,000. Facilities include a coffee shop, bakery, Korean restaurant, sauna, swimming pool, health club and large outdoor car park. Rated four stars.

The enormous *Shilla Hotel* (*Central Seoul map;* ☎ 233 3131) – a five-minute walk from Dongguk University station on subway Line 3 – has a scenic setting at the base of Namsan Park. The 500-room hotel has twins for W235,000. Aside from the usual plush amenities, this place boasts an open-air sculpture park. Rated five stars.

The 218-room *Tower Hotel* (☎ 236 2121) is a 10-minute walk from Dongguk University station on subway Line 3. The hotel distinguishes itself with an outdoor theme, helped considerably by its location in the north-east section of Namsan Park. Other amenities include an outdoor swimming pool, tennis courts, golf driving range and golf shop. Singles/doubles cost W121,000/169,400. Rated four stars.

The *Hilton Hotel* (*Central Seoul map;* ☎ 753 7788) has everything you expect from the Hilton chain, plus the added convenience of being a five-minute walk from the Seoul train station. The 700-room hotel has singles/twins for W240,000/260,000. Rated five stars.

The *Sheraton Walker Hill Hotel* (*Greater Seoul map;* ☎ 453 0131) is 2km east of Children's Grand Park, about a 10 minute walk north of the Gwangnaru subway station on Line 5. The hotel has 617(!) Western-style and six Korean-style rooms. Twins cost W200,000. Rated five stars.

The *Swiss Grand Hotel* (*Greater Seoul map;* ☎ 3216 5656), in the north-west part of Seoul, is a 10-minute walk from Hongje station on subway Line 3. This place boasts a Swiss-style setting at the base of scenic Baengnyeonsan (216m). Another feature worth yodelling about is the unique apartment-style suites, which include a kitchen. The hotel has 397 Western-style rooms, three Korean-style rooms and 111 apartments. Singles/twins cost W220,000/250,000. Rated five stars.

Holiday Inn (*Greater Seoul map;* ☎ 717 9441) is a 10-minute walk from the Mapo subway station on Line 5. There are 363 Western-style and four Korean-style rooms. Singles (Western and Korean syle) cost W120,000 to W132,000. Facilities include everything – plus an indoor golf putting range. Rated four stars.

The 505-room *Lotte World Hotel* (*Greater Seoul map;* ☎ 419 7000) is a two-minute walk from Jamsil station on subway Line 2. The main feature here is the adjacent Lotte World shopping mall-cum-amusement park. It is a bonanza if you have children and need to keep them entertained. Twins cost W215,000. Rated five stars.

PLACES TO EAT

With many thousands of restaurants scattered throughout every neighbourhood of the city, the biggest problem facing the intrepid gastronome ·in Seoul is knowing where to begin. Small restaurants dishing up Korean food are, of course, ubiquitous. For the less adventurous, the familiar Western fast-food barns are easily found near the larger subway stations. Looking for fine Western food takes more effort – your best bets are in central Seoul, Itaewon and Gangnam-gu.

For a night out, maybe try a banquet with traditional-style Korean floor show thrown in at one of Seoul's theatre restaurants (see the Entertainment section, later in this chapter).

Budget

Gwanghwamun The *Koryeo Supermarket* (the sign for which is not in English – see map for Korean script) is worth a look. The lunch counters are hidden in the back and to your right. The food is exclusively Korean style and you can eat well for around W3000. The Koryeo Supermarket is the best in the neighbourhood.

Sapporo Restaurant is a small place dishing up simple Japanese food. It's behind the Sejong Cultural Centre.

Tapgol Park Area The ground floor and basements of the bizarre-looking Jongno Tower building are known as Millennium Plaza. In the first basement you'll find the *World Food Court* – with tremendous variety and good prices. The second basement has the best supermarket in the neighbourhood. You can enter the basements directly from the Jonggak subway station.

Restaurants dishing up *gimbap* (Korean sushi: see the Food section in the Facts for the Visitor chapter) are numerous, but there are a few that are outstanding. Near the YMCA are *Seoul Gimbap* and two branches of *Jongno Gimbap*. Both have very unusual variations on this quintessential Korean dish (tuna gimbap, cheese gimbap etc).

Shinp'ouri Mandu has a tricky name to pronounce, and there is no sign in English (see map for Korean script). Nevertheless, it's definitely worth seeking out. The Korean

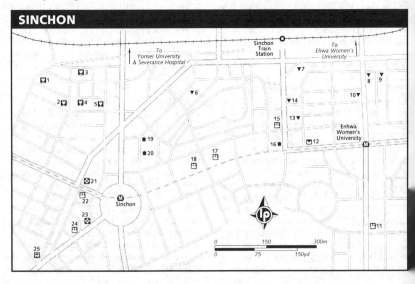

SINCHON

PLACES TO STAY
16 Mirabeau Hotel
미라보호텔
19 Hyeondae, Minjin-jang
Yeogwans
현대여관,민진여관
20 Hotel Prince
호텔프린스

PLACES TO EAT
6 La Vecchia Stazione
스타찌오네
7 Spaghettia Restaurant
8 Starbucks
9 Jessica's Pizzeria
제시카피자리아
10 Amato Pizza Buffet
피자부페
13 Bennigan's New York
베니간스
14 Sweet Heaven Bakery

OTHER
1 Free Crockadiles Pub
악어를풀어놔봐
2 The Doors Pub
도어스클럽
3 Blue Monkeys Pub
4 Woodstock Pub
우드스탁
5 Voodoo Bar
부두바
11 Yeonghwanara Cinema
영화나라극장
12 Post Office
우체국
15 Sinchon Art Hall   Cinema
신촌아트홀극장
17 Sinyeong Cinema
신영극장
18 Noksaek Cinema
녹색극장
21 Hyundai Department
Store
현대백화점
22 Sinchon Cinema
신촌극장
23 Grand Mart
그랜드마트
24 Sinchon Grand Cinema
신촌그랜드극장
25 Sinchon Bus Terminal
신촌시외버스터미널

food is amazingly good and you can eat your fill for less than W5000. As an added bonus, you needn't grapple with the language as the menu has pictures.

Despite the name, the ***Nutrition Center*** is not a health food store: it serves delicious ginseng chicken soup, rice and vegetables for W8000. The lunch special is W5500.

Myeong-dong (Central Seoul) The basement of the Lotte Department Store has a good ***food court***, but it's very crowded.

The ***Utoo Zone*** is a department store with a difference – 60 independent vendors in one large building. The 4th floor, called the ***Z-Side***, has a number of small restaurants. Even more important is ***Myeong-dong Food Alley*** behind Utoo Zone, which has easily Myeong-dong's densest collection of restaurants.

The area around the Chinese Embassy in Myeong-dong is a good place to look for Chinese food. This small collection of restaurants and one or two bookshops is about as close as Seoul gets to a Chinatown. ***Shillawon Chinese Restaurant (☎ 752 2396)*** is a favourite with the embassy staff and features (surprise!) an English menu.

Sinchon Yonsei University has student ***cafeterias*** where you can eat well for about W1500 to W2000. This doesn't apply at the aristocratic Ehwa Women's University, where the food is pricey and the portions are stingy. University cafeterias are normally open from about 10 am to 6 pm, but some only serve food from noon to 1 pm and 5 to 6 pm.

Near the entrance of Ehwa Women's University is an eminent historic site – Korea's very first ***Starbucks***. It might seem odd to call this place 'budget' – until you look at the prices that the typical Korean coffee shops charge.

Jessica's Pizzeria does more than just pizza – check out the exquisite spaghetti and lasagne.

Sweet Heaven Bakery is a good place for a quick caffeine fix and a pastry snack.

Hong-ik University ***Khan Antique Pub*** specialises in Korean food. This chain store has branches all around Seoul, but the signs are in Korean only (see map for Korean script).

SEOUL

Itaewon The *USO* (☎ 795 3028) is operated by the US military but you don't have to join the army to eat there. The food is American style all the way, and this may well be the only place in Seoul that dishes up chilli dogs. This place only does breakfast and lunch, and is closed on Sunday. The USO is outside the main Itaewon area, but within walking distance of the Namyeong station on subway Line 1.

The *Inca Restaurant* looks like a corner cafe, but has great breakfasts and some really fine Western meals.

Daehangno The *Fresh Supermarket* is the best place in this neighbourhood if you want to attempt self-catering. Just opposite the supermarket is a branch of the scrumptious Korean fast-food chain *Shinp'ouri Mandu*. Nearby is another good chain, *Coco Fried Rice*.

Golden Gate Chinese Restaurant, on the big traffic circle, offers tasty meals from the low to mid-range level.

Coffee shops are a Daehangno institution, and they tend to be open late into the night. However, some of these places open early and offer a reasonable choice for a no-frills breakfast. At the bottom of the food chain is *Dunkin' Donuts*, but there is also a *Starbucks*. More exquisite is the *French Cafe & Bakery*. *Mozart Coffee Shop* is more of a socialising place, but you can get something to eat here.

Gangnam-gu Buried deep within the bowels of the Gangnam subway station (south side of the river) is *Holly's Coffee*. The views aren't great, but some locals claim that it offers the best coffee in Seoul. If a view is important, there is a *Starbucks* just outside the station.

The *Hyundai Department Store,* by the World Trade Centre, has restaurants of various levels of elegance with prices adjusted accordingly.

Pho Hoa, near the Sinsa subway station, specialises in tasty Vietnamese noodle soup. This is actually a Vietnamese-American chain – if you've tried it in Los Angeles, you've got the idea.

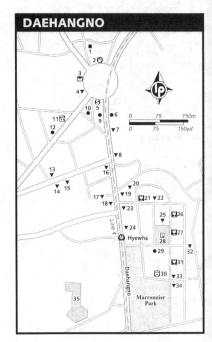

DAEHANGNO

Kim's Club, near the Express bus terminal station on subway Line 3, is a hypermart and appeals to long-term expats and other people who do their cooking at home.

Yeouido (Greater Seoul map) The logical place to start in Yeouido is the *KLI 63 building*. The first basement has several Korean restaurants dishing up noodles, ginseng chicken soup and dumplings. The same floor also has *Mongnyon Chinese Restaurant* and branches of fast food chains.

Miscellaneous Areas On the northern side of Namdaemun Market is the small but ever-popular *Wang Mandu (Central Seoul map; ☎ 752 2765)*. No English is spoken here but there is an English menu. The speciality is, of course, *mandu* (dumplings) but there are several noodle dishes. If you're a fan of spicy food, try the gimchi mandu.

If you do your own cooking, you could consider shopping at Costco (Greater Seoul

SEOUL

DAEHANGNO

PLACES TO STAY & EAT
1 Trek Korea Hostel
  트렉코리아

PLACES TO EAT
4 Golden Gate Chinese
  Restaurant
  금문중국집
7 Bennigan's Boston
  베니간스
8 Coco's California
  Restaurant
  코코스
13 Fresh Supermarket
  후레쉬마켓
14 Coco Fried Rice
  코코볶음밥
15 Sinpouri Mandu
  신포우리만두
16 Family Mart
  훼미리마트
17 Vietnamese Restaurant
18 Dunkin' Donuts
  던킨도너츠
19 TGI Friday's
  야 금요일이다

20 Naksan Garden
  낙산가든
22 Hudson Ristorante
  Italiano
  허드슨
23 French Cafe & Bakery
24 Starbucks
25 Romano's Pub
  Restaurant
32 Cafe Fusion Food
33 Gold Rush Restaurant
  골드러쉬
34 Mozart Coffee Shop
  모짜르트

OTHER
2 Petrol Station
  주유소
3 Hyehwa Post Office
  혜화우체국
5 Hanvit Bank
  한빛은행
6 Doore Bowling Centre
  두레볼링장

9 Billiards Room
  2F
10 Colossus Hof
  콜로서스
11 Forest Cyber Cafe
  포리스트
12 Heavy Rock MTV Club
  엠티비
21 Wild Bills Pub
26 Manchan Beer Garden
27 Boogie Boogie Bar
  부기부기
28 Car Park
  주차장
29 Bier Halle
  비어할레
30 Munye Theatre
  문예회관
31 New Yorker
  Pocket Club
35 Seoul National University
  Medical College
  서울대학교의과대학

map), a hypermart which offers excellent savings. The catch is that you have to buy many items in large quantities, and this is a members-only store (W30,000 per year). By way of compensation, you can use the membership card at any Costco hypermart worldwide. Take subway Line 2 or 5 to Yeongdeungpo Office station (about 2km west of Yeouido).

Mid-Range
Gwanghwamun *Dongseonggak Chinese Restaurant* is a fine eatery in an alley just south of the Sejong Cultural Centre.

Kabongru Chinese Restaurant, near Sejong Cultural Centre, is one of the more upmarket Chinese restaurants in this neighbourhood, but still very reasonable.

Tapgol Park Area *Tokomo Japanese Restaurant* is a large place with elegant decor and a good selection of Japanese delicacies.

Myeong-dong (Central Seoul map)
OK Corral (☎ 771 2771) does a Western buffet, and is also known for steaks and a

fine bakery. There is a branch in Myeong-dong. The closest subway stop is Euljiro 1-ga on Line 2 (take exit 5).

Tony Roma's (☎ 771 6164) is a Western-style restaurant, and is known for its tastey prime rib dinners. You'll find it in a side street, just south of the Lotte Department Store.

Sinchon *La Vecchia Stazione (☎ 363 2160)* is an Italian coffee shop with considerable cosmopolitan charm. The decor is something like an old train station, and classical music is played continuously in the background.

Bennigan's New York (☎ 393 6700) is the name of the Sinchon branch of the American Bennigan's chain.

Hong-ik University *TGI Friday's (☎ 322 6321)*, a superb American-style restaurant, has a branch close to Hong-ik University station on subway Line 2. There are some Mexican dishes on the menu as well.

Almost in the same league (not quite) as TGI Friday is *Coco's California Restaurant*

(☎ 335 1874), not to be confused with a similarly named fast-food chain.

Ponderosa Steak House (☎ 3141 3473) is a family restaurant. Besides steak, the menu features Mexican food, spaghetti, seafood and chicken. If you want to splurge, check out the buffet meals. Typical costs are W12,000 to W24,000. Open 11 am to 11 pm.

Itaewon *Pancho's (☎ 792 4767)* claims to be the best Mexican restaurant in Seoul, and it would be hard to argue. Aside from the expected nachos, enchiladas and burritos, it's a good place for drinks. The restaurant is hidden just off Itaewonno, on the 3rd floor.

Ho Lee Chow (☎ 793 0802) is an international chain restaurant known for its 'Hong Kong-style' Chinese food – even though the chain started in Canada. It's now come to Korea, and the food tastes just like the Chinese food in Toronto – not bad.

La Cucina (☎ 794 6005) is Itaewon's premier Italian eatery. Check out the fettuccine or the lasagne.

One of the few genuinely Korean restaurants in the area is the *Itaewon Restaurant (☎ 797 1474)*. It has a pleasant atmosphere and is not as expensive as it looks.

The *Thai Orchid Restaurant*, next to the Itaewon Hotel, is one of the finest Thai restaurants in the city.

Daehangno For Western food you might want to choose the local branches of the aforementioned *TGI Friday's*, *Bennigan's Boston* or *Coco's California Restaurant*.

If you're looking for something a little more exotic, there is *Cafe Fusion Food*, offering the best Korean-Californian cuisine in this part of town.

In an alley just off Daehangno, there is a charming little Vietnamese restaurant with the creative name *Vietnamese Restaurant*. It offers good food and charming decor.

Gold Rush Restaurant qualifies as a 'spaghetti western' with Texas-cowboy decor and an Italian menu.

Gangnam-gu *Restaurant Marche Movenpick* is a good place for foreigners with no Korean language – there are no menus,

you just point to what you want. You're given a card which gets stamped by staff as you pick up your dishes. Western food is on offer including a salad bar (W3000), lasagne (W6000), steak and some Mexican food. The restaurant is near the Gangnam subway station.

Uno Chicago Bar & Grill (☎ 547 4111) is an attractive restaurant specialising in Chicago pizza, steak, hamburgers and other Western cuisine. It's east of the Apgujeong subway station on Line 3.

Ponderosa Steak House (☎ 565 1021) is part of a chain (see the preceding Sinchon section for details). The restaurant is open from 11 am to 11 pm.

Carne Station has two branches in the south of Seoul: Gangnam-gu branch *(☎ 557 1239)* is near Gangnam subway station on Line 2; Daechi branch *(☎ 562 1239)* is near the Inter-Continental Hotel and the Samseong subway station on Line 2. Both are all-you-can-eat Korean-Western buffet and table barbecue. Prices are just under W30,000.

OK Corral (☎ 565 2778) is a Western chain. The steaks and buffet meals are superb and the portions are huge. The restaurant is about a seven-minute walk from Gangnam station on subway Line 2.

Chili's Grill & Bar has a branch in Apgujeong *(☎ 3443 7272)* (near Apgujeong subway station on Line 3). The restaurant boasts of its 'American south-west' cuisine, though it's not really that spicy. Some dishes to try include the grilled chicken pasta and the Monterey chicken. Don't forget to try the Margaritas. Chili's is open daily from 11 am to 11 pm.

Just south of Chili's in Apgujeong is *Italianni's (☎ 548 1611)*, the best Italian restaurant this side of Naples.

Southern Seoul has several branches of *TGI Friday's*, the American bistro known for good food and far-out interior decorating (aeroplane parts, baby carriages etc). The Gangnamyeok branch *(☎ 3477 0321)* is almost adjacent to Gangnam subway station on Line 2. The Nonhyeon branch *(☎ 512 7211)* is close to Sinsa subway station on Line 3.

Tony Roma's (☎ *3443 3500)* is a superb upmarket Western restaurant. You'll find it on Dosandaero, about halfway between the Apgujeong and Sinsa stations on subway Line 3.

Outback Steak House (☎ *3445 4701)* pretends to be Australian, though it's really an American chain. It's a short walk south of the Sinsa subway station on Line 3, or north of the Gangnam subway station on Line 2.

Coco's California Restaurant has two convenient branches in the area. The Sinsa branch (☎ *548 6904)* is in the Apgujeong area, and the Daechi branch (☎ *561 1112)* is close to the Inter-Continental Hotel.

Bennigan's is another popular Western chain restaurant with a high profile in Seoul. In the Apgujeong area is *Bennigan's Chicago* (☎ *517 5007)*. In the courtyard next to the Inter-Continental Hotel you can find *Bennigan's Seattle* (☎ *567 8600)*.

Yeouido (Greater Seoul map) The *Fountain Plaza* (☎ *789 5731)*, on the ground floor of the KLI 63 Building, is a huge buffet dining hall – capacity 600 people! Food is mixed Korean and Western.

Top End
Tapgol Park Area *Youngbin Garden* (☎ *732 3863)* is the epitome of an upmarket, traditional Korean restaurant. Set in a lovely wooden house in a courtyard in Insadong, this is one place to get a great *galbi* (barbecue) meal and other traditional cuisine.

Top Cloud Cafe (☎ *2230 3000)* is on the 33rd floor of the peculiar-looking Jongno Tower building. No matter what you think of the weird architecture, you can't complain about the views. The cafe serves mostly Western cuisine, and is open from 10.30 am to 2 am (though food is only served from noon until 10 pm). There is live jazz every evening from 6.30 pm to 1 am.

Myeong-dong (Central Seoul map) The Westin Chosun Hotel (see the Places to Stay section, Top End) is home to a number of interesting restaurants. The lunch specials can be considered mid-range (around W10,000 to W20,000), but top dinners can

be pricey. Restaurants here include: *O'Kim's* (Irish food), *The Ninth Gate* (Western food), *Yesterday's* (Italian food), *Sushi Cho* (Japanese food), *Sheobul* (Korean food) and *Hokyungjeon* (Chinese food).

Just opposite the Lotte Hotel is *La Cantina* (☎ *777 2579)*, an outstanding Italian restaurant with an intimate atmosphere and English-speaking staff.

Itaewon A few restaurants here offer specialty foreign foods. The major ones are *Ashoka* (☎ *792 0117)* on the 3rd floor of the Hamilton Hotel, *Moghul* (☎ *796 5501)* which is behind the Hamilton Hotel shop and *Taj Mahal* (☎ *749 0316)* near the mosque. They all have buffet lunches for around W20,000.

Up the hill a little, in the direction of the Grand Hyatt, is the *Chalet Swiss* (☎ *797 9664)*, which features such everyday dishes as *fondue bourguignonne* and *huus roesti*. The only thing likely to give you indigestion here is the yodelling session with the Kim Brothers every Thursday to Saturday night. Chalet Swiss is open from noon to 10 pm and reservations are necessary for dinner.

The Grand Hyatt Hotel (Greater Seoul map) is home to several upmarket restaurants. Chief among them is *Akasaka* (☎ *799 8166)*, which offers sizzling teppanyaki and a fine view of the river.

Daehangno *Hudson Ristorante Italiano* is an enormous place with outdoor tables; a superb place to sample pasta and Italian wine under the stars, weather permitting.

Korean food – yes, there are still some places left in Daehangno that serve this exotic cuisine. One of the better-appointed places is *Naksan Garden*.

Gangnam-gu *Hanmiri Restaurant* (☎ *556 4834)* is the place for elegant Korean food.

The Inter-Continental Hotel is just loaded with opulent restaurants. One interesting choice is *Asian Live* on the 2nd floor, which offers a selection of Asian cuisines.

The Seoul Renaissance Hotel chips in with *Kabin Chinese Restaurant* and *Irodori Japanese Restaurant*.

SEOUL

The Ritz-Carlton Hotel, near the Yeoksam station on subway Line 2, has one of Seoul's best dim sum Chinese restaurants, *Chee Hong* (☎ 3451 8273). The ingredients may be Korean but the chefs have been imported from Hong Kong.

Yeouido In the KLI 63 building, the prices rise as you ascend the building – you pay for the view. On the 56th floor you'll find *Wako* (☎ 789 5751), a Japanese restaurant. The 57th floor has *Paengnihyang* (☎ 789 5741), one of the city's upmarket Japanese restaurants. On the 59th floor is *Steak House* (☎ 789 5904), *Sky Pizza* and *Sky View* (☎ 789 5904, Western cuisine). Literally top end is the *63 Roof Garden* (☎ 789 5751), which does Korean and Western food. For vertigo sufferers, there's also a branch on the 4th floor.

Miscellaneous Areas (Greater Seoul map) Seoul Tower, the city's most conspicuous landmark, is home to the *Sky Restaurant*, Korea's only revolving restaurant. Even better, the tower also boasts *Pulhyanggi*, a superb Korean restaurant where you can eat your fill of scrumptious veggie dishes. Prices range from W15,000 to W35,000. A dance show is thrown in at 7.30 pm (7 pm in winter).

The Swiss Grand Hotel is home to *Mitsumomo* (☎ 2287 8391), a high-powered Japanese restaurant which features such everyday delights as Alaska king crab with asparagus. The hotel's other famous eatery is *Yeohyang* (☎ 2287 8189) which does Chinese food. There is also a Korean buffet which offers lunch/dinner for a moderate W27,000/35,000.

Hotel Lotte World not only offers you convenient access to the nearby amusement park rides, but also dishes up some fine food. *Tohlim*, the hotel's Chinese restaurant, features Chinese pheasant under glass at W35,000 to W50,000. Admittedly, it's probably not the biggest pheasant you've ever seen, but it certainly is good. *Mugunghwa*, the hotel's Korean restaurant, does some stunning all-you-can-eat barbecues.

ENTERTAINMENT
Pubs
Gwanghwamun It's not really the neighbourhood for pubs, but the *Boomerang Bar* on the 11th floor of the Kyobo building (next to Kyobo Book Centre) has a friendly atmosphere and is open to all nationalities. It's a good place to meet other foreigners, especially Australians and Canadians. Drinks are moderately priced.

Sinchon The area behind the Hyundai Department Store is flooded with coffee shops and nightclubs. Some clubs are multi-storey affairs, with each floor geared to a certain clientele. For example, one floor may be reserved for well-dressed customers while another floor is kept for those in grubby blue jeans. Furthermore, there are clubs for really young college students, and if you look too old (over 25) you may not be allowed in.

Woodstock (☎ 334 1310) attracts a large foreign clientele with its 1960s rock music. Technoheads should look elsewhere.

Voodoo Bar (☎ 336 5021) is a small, cosy place that gets the thumbs-up from westerners. There is a comprehensive CD collection, and the friendly bar staff will play your requests.

Around the corner is *The Doors*. True to its name, this is the place to hear classic rock on an all-vinyl record collection.

Free Crocodiles is an interesting place. Unfortunately, it has no English sign – you'll have to look for the green Korean characters. Dark beer is hard to find in Korea – this place brews its own and sells it for W2000 a mug. The beer, reasonably priced food and quiet atmosphere all help to make this place a favourite.

Blue Monkeys is a basement dance pub currently in vogue. The music tends to be hiphop, rhythm and blues.

Hong-ik University Without a doubt, this is the most raging neighbourhood in town. Many places charge W5000 cover but that includes one drink.

A good place to start is right from the Hong-ik University station on subway Line 2. Close to the subway is *Macondo Bar*

HONG-IK UNIVERSITY

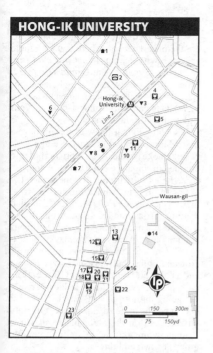

HONG-IK UNIVERSITY

PLACES TO STAY
 1 WOW Guest House
   와우게스트하우스
 7 Seogyo Hotel
   서교호텔

PLACES TO EAT
 3 Coco's California
   Restaurant
   코코스
 6 TGI Friday's Restaurant
   아!금요일이다
 8 Ponderosa Steak House
   판다로사
10 Khan Antique Pub
   칸

OTHER
 2 Sinchon Telephone
   Office
   신촌전화국
 4 Macondo Bar
   마콘도
 5 Bonanza Hole
   보낸자호을
 9 Be Bop Jazz Club
   비밥
11 Saab Disco I
   싸브디스코
12 Myongwolkwan Disco
   명월관
13 Mbimb Techno Pub
14 Hong-ik University
   홍익대학교
15 Ugly Joe Western Bar
   어글리조
16 Underground Cafe
   언더그라운드카페
17 Gold Bar
18 MI Disco
19 Hodge Podge Disco
   흐지부지
20 Joker Red Disco
   죠커레드
21 US 66 Bar; Saab Disco II
   싸브디스코
22 Drug Club
   드러그클럽
23 Pub 101

(☎ 332 5752). It's popular with expats, and justifiably so. The pub is known for dark beer (a rare find in Seoul), Latin-style cuisine and salsa music – with dance lessons every evening at 8 pm (except Monday). Another plus: films are shown every Saturday at 5 pm and Sunday at 6 pm.

Around the corner is **Bonanza Hole**, a live rock venue. There is no cover charge.

Moving slightly south is **Saab Disco I**, a place which does 'mixed dance music' (techno, hiphop, alternative).

A short walk from Saab will take you to the **Be Bop Jazz Club**. It has live bands almost every evening, and every weekend. As it's on the 5th floor it has a good view.

Moving farther south brings you into the heart of technoland. **MBimb Pub** is in a basement. There is a large dance floor: expect loud music and big crowds on Friday and Saturday nights. Beers are W5000.

By contrast to the dance clubs, **Ugly Joe Bar** is much quieter and attracts an older crowd, but that hardly means it's boring. The 'flaming bottle show' is something that can't be described – you'd better go see it for yourself.

Myeongwolgwan Disco is a tricky place to find if you can't read Korean script as there's no English sign (see map for script), but, once you do, take the stairs down to the basement. When you get inside, your next challenge will be finding your way around – it's very dark! This place caters to a techno crowd – plenty of young students and foreigners. Beers cost W5000.

A block to the south is *MI Disco*. This is the most popular place of all with house music, techno and trance. Trendy Korean movie stars come here and the W10,000 cover charge is meant to keep out the riffraff.

The riffraff (including many expats) go to the nearby *Gold Bar*. It's popular because it's cheap. Beer is W1500, and there are harder drinks (tequila etc) which are similarly inexpensive.

Joker Red Disco offers some relief from techno – it's more house music. The DJ is very good.

Even better for techno-haters is *Hodge Podge Disco*. Plenty of good rock music, dancing and no cover charge. Drinks are around W4000. On weekends, expect it to be very busy.

Saab Disco II is also in this neighbourhood. The mixed music is a find and the staff are very friendly.

Next door is *US 66 Bar*. It's a western-style bar with a romantic, quiet atmosphere. It has expensive drinks – but the Korean women customers don't mind the prices and the place is usually very busy.

The *Drug Club* is a Seoul institution. This is *the* venue for live music, with up-and-coming bands often making their debut here. There is a cover charge here (price varies depending on the band) and no booze is served. The Drug Club records live music performances and sells these CDs at the Punk Shop, just above the club.

The *Underground Cafe* is managed by a female westerner who does a lot of parties and special events. Music is mixed techno and alternative, and there's a more friendly (but lively) crowd than in the other places.

The *Pub 101* marks the southern fringe of the techno-action zone. Lots of late-night dancing, young foreigners and even younger Koreans here.

Itaewon Most of Seoul's expat bars can be found in Itaewon. Wandering around this foreign ghetto, it's easy to get the feeling that Itaewon could be a Country and Western themepark – everywhere you look there are bars with names like *Cowboy Club*, *Nashville*, *Stomper* and *Grand Ole Opry*. Most of the cowboy haunts are hole-in-the-wall hostess bars (more on that in a moment) that can burn quite a hole in your wallet if you're not careful.

It's a bit odd that Itaewon doesn't have a much larger number of Japanese and Chinese karaoke venues – a surprisingly large number of Japanese and Chinese tourists come here (quite literally by the busload).

For those after something more exotic there is the *Reggae Pub (☎ 798 5452)* which features African and Caribbean music and dancing. It's open from 4 pm to 2 am (opens at noon on weekends and holidays).

Itaewon's main strip has a few very crowded clubs that have no cover charge and ask W1500 for a bottle of OB beer. The most popular is *King Club*. It doesn't really get going until around 10 pm, but when it does it can be quite an experience. Off-duty GIs descend on the place in droves while Korean women turn up in innumerable groups of two and three.

Hollywood Club (☎ 749 1659) has two dance floors with an excellent sound system (and good DJs). Other entertainment is provided by pool tables, dart games and a plentiful supply of booze. A unique feature is the large collection of Cuban cigars on sale.

Next to *Gulliver Disco* are some stairs which ascend up a hill. At the top of the steps is *Dreamscape* (another disco) and a steep alley. In local parlance this alley is known as 'Hooker Hill' and a stroll up here anytime after 8 pm will make it clear why. The alley is lined with bars, at the top of the alley is *Stomper*, which has no cover charge and inexpensive drinks. Stomper draws in more couples than singles and is a favourite place for a dance.

One other place notable for dancing is *NASA Disco*, which tends to stay open into the wee hours of the morning.

Grand Ole Opry (☎ 795 9155) has Country and Western music (surprise, surprise) on the first floor, but if that doesn't appeal

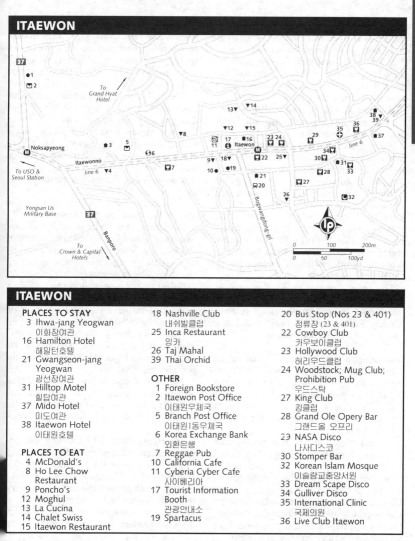

ITAEWON

ITAEWON

PLACES TO STAY
3 Ihwa-jang Yeogwan
  이화장여관
16 Hamilton Hotel
  해밀턴호텔
21 Gwangseon-jang
  Yeogwan
  광선장여관
31 Hilltop Motel
  힐탑여관
37 Mido Hotel
  미도여관
38 Itaewon Hotel
  이태원호텔

PLACES TO EAT
4 McDonald's
8 Ho Lee Chow
  Restaurant
9 Poncho's
12 Moghul
13 La Cucina
14 Chalet Swiss
15 Itaewon Restaurant

18 Nashville Club
  내쉬빌클럽
25 Inca Restaurant
  잉카
26 Taj Mahal
39 Thai Orchid

OTHER
1 Foreign Bookstore
2 Itaewon Post Office
  이태원우체국
5 Branch Post Office
  이태원1동우체국
6 Korea Exchange Bank
  외환은행
7 Reggae Pub
10 California Cafe
11 Cyberia Cyber Cafe
  사이베리아
17 Tourist Information
  Booth
  관광안내소
19 Spartacus

20 Bus Stop (Nos 23 & 401)
  정류장 (23 & 401)
22 Cowboy Club
  카우보이클럽
23 Hollywood Club
  허리우드클럽
24 Woodstock; Mug Club;
  Prohibition Pub
  우드스탁
27 King Club
  킹클럽
28 Grand Ole Opery Bar
  그랜드올 오프리
29 NASA Disco
  나사디스코
30 Stomper Bar
32 Korean Islam Mosque
  이슬람교중앙서원
33 Dream Scape Disco
34 Gulliver Disco
35 International Clinic
  국제의원
36 Live Club Itaewon

go up to the second floor to find some old time rock'n'roll.

All over Itaewon are hostess bars, especially on 'Hooker Hill'. Prices for drinks usually start at W3000, which is not that expensive, but you will inevitably be hit for a 'lady's drink', which will range between W5000 and W10,000 depending on the bar. It's possible to refuse buying one of the girls a drink, but if you do you won't be made very welcome.

On the main drag is *Nashville* (☎ 798 1592), renowned for its superb hamburgers, steaks, dart games and evening movies

SEOUL

shown on a large-size screen. The basement restaurant is open from 9 am to 2 am, the 2nd-floor 'sports pub' is open from 3 pm to 2 am, the blues and jazz club on the third floor is open from 6 pm to 5 am and the rooftop 'beer garden' is open whenever the weather is agreeable.

Woodstock, *Mug Club* and *Prohibition* are known more for good music rather than mini-skirted hostesses.

Itaewon has the only gay and lesbian cafe and bar scene that attracts foreigners and English-speaking Koreans. *California* (☎ 2785 2560) is one of the most popular. It's hidden in an alley – from the south side of Itaewonno, take the stairs down to the entrance. It tends to only do business in the evening, though it may open in the afternoon on weekends. On Friday and Saturday nights, there is a disco in the basement. When the weather is fine, it's relaxing to sit on the outdoor terrace.

The other famous gay/lesbian spot is *Spartacus*, also hidden in an alley south of Itaewonno. It only comes alive at night (chiefly Friday and Saturday) and has a busy bar, disco and pool table.

Daehangno Daehangno is known as Seoul's 'art and culture district'. Street performers set up shop here and live off the donations – look for them in Marronnier Park. The park is also a venue for artists who will be happy to sketch your portrait for a suitable fee.

Up-and-coming bands also get together to give performances. These jam sessions are often held in a small, hot, smoky basement, though there may be a steep admission fee. It's impossible for us to tell you where and when these impromptu concerts will be held. If interested, ask local students. There are posters advertising performances but these are written entirely in Korean.

Daehangno is also known for its playhouses – again, posters in Korean are ubiquitous, but then the dialogue is also in Korean. If you speak the language or bring along a translator, the *Munye Theatre* is perhaps the best place in the whole country to see Western-style dramas.

One specialty of Daehangno is the numerous late-night pubs which feature outdoor tables where you can enjoy beer and snacks while viewing the stars. It's certainly romantic, but unless there is major global warming you probably won't want to try this in January. On the other hand, you don't have to restrict outdoor wining and dining to July and August – the pubs place kerosene heaters next to the tables, which extends the season considerably. Of course, all the open-air pubs do have some indoor tables as well.

Romano's Pub Restaurant is a nice open-air place. Aside from the beer, there are meals priced in the W8000 range. A similar place is the *Manchan Beer Garden*.

Bier Halle is a Tudor-style pub restaurant. Meals cost from W10,000 to W38,000, and they are good, though portions tend to be a bit stingy. The atmosphere is cheery and there are outdoor tables.

Colossus Hof is an indoors place, though it does have a sort of garden ambience. The sound system plays jazz and a pitcher of beer goes for W5000.

Wild Bill's Pub has a 'western saloon' motif, including a 'hitching post' where you can tie up your horse. This large and lively pub also has good music.

The *Boogie Boogie Bar* (☎ 744 3626) is instantly recognisable by the 1956 Chevrolet Bel Air on the roof. There's good music, and a menu with lots of Korean and Western dishes.

The *Heavy Rock MTV Club* has a large-screen video and eardrum-splitting music.

The *New Yorker Pocket Club* is an elegant pub and pool hall venue. If you're looking for something with less frills, you can try *Billiards Room 2F*. Another place where you can get some hands-on entertainment is the nearby *Doore Bowling Centre*.

Gangnam-gu This area is home to **Teheran Valley** (Seoul's answer to Silicon Valley) where new-economy dot com companies thrive. As a result, pricey pubs, discos and coffee houses have set up shop to entertain young, affluent Internet entrepreneurs (affectionately known as 'dot snots').

Teheran (not to be confused with Tehran, the capital of Iran) is the name of a major street. It runs past the Gangnam subway station, an area that is illuminated at night by glittering neon. There are heaps of pubs and restaurants in this area.

Just north-east of Gangnam station is an alley where you can find **Woodstock II**, a pub notable for 1960s rock music.

Within Gangnam-gu, the area around Apgujeong subway station is the most expensive night-time playground in Seoul. The action centres on dozens of so-called 'rock cafes' on 'Rodeo St', near the Galleria department store.

The **Hard Rock Cafe** (☎ 547 5671) offers everything from fried chicken with nachos to shrimp cocktails, served in a super-trendy setting with live music. It's open weekdays from 5 pm to 2 am, or from noon to 2 am on weekends. It's in the Apgujeong neighbourhood, a long walk to the south-east of Apgujeong subway station on Line 3.

Hotel Bars

A trendy location is **JJ Mahoney's** inside the Grand Hyatt (Greater Seoul map). This place is renowned as Seoul's yuppie bar and has a clientele that is about half expat and half Korean.

Pharaoh at the Hilton Hotel (Central Seoul map; just to the east of Seoul station) is a pub and disco. A raging place, though drinks are expensive.

Seoul's one and only Irish theme bar, **O'Kim's** (☎ 317 0357), is in the basement of the Westin Chosun Hotel (Gwanghwamun map). Aside from the booze, there's deluxe food available, such as a six-course dinner for W40,000.

Theatre Restaurants

At Seoul's theatre restaurants you can enjoy power dining while viewing a traditional-style Korean floor show. The most famous restaurant in this class is **Sanchon** (Tapgol Park map; ☎ 735 1900). Sanchon specialises in vegetarian cuisine – the W29,000 special full course allows you to sample 15 courses. There are traditional dance performances every evening from 8

to 9 pm. Seating is by way of cushions on the floor (tough on the back). Sanchon is down a small alley off Insadonggil.

Arirang (☎ 737 2371) is adjacent to Sanchon and offers a similar deal. The main difference is that the meals contain meat and cost W30,000 to W50,000. The shows are at 8.10 pm daily, except the 2nd and 4th Sunday of each month, when the place is closed.

A more upmarket version of the same thing is **Korea House** (Central Seoul map; ☎ 2266 9101). It has seating for 170 people, making it one of the largest theatre restaurants. Dance performances are held here, and it is possible to make a booking for the performance alone (W21,200). The combination show and buffet meal costs W40,700. There are also pricier full-course hanjeongsik (banquet) meals costing up to W62,700. Performances are scheduled twice in the evening from 7 to 8 pm and from 8.40 to 9.40 pm. The restaurant is also open for lunch from noon to 2 pm, but there is no performance then (but the lunch banquet costs only W24,000). Korea House is at the foot of Namsan, and is open everyday except Sunday. Take subway Line 3 or 4 to Chungmuro station.

Kayageum (☎ 450 4555) is inside the Sheraton Walker Hill Hotel (Greater Seoul map). Performances are given twice daily at 4.30 and 7.30 pm. Pigging out on the banquet costs W77,000, budget meals are W63,000 – the dance show is included free with the eats. The champagne show costs W48,000. The Sheraton Walker Hill Hotel is at the far-eastern end of Seoul and the nearest subway station is Gwangnaru on Line 5.

Traditional Arts

The **National Center for Korean Traditional Performing Arts** (Greater Seoul map; ☎ 580 3040) is one place to see performances of traditional opera and dance. The centre houses two theatres, Yeaktang (main theatre) and Umyeondang (small theatre). In Yeaktang, there is a performance every Saturday at 5 pm from February through December. In Umyeondang, there is a performance every third Saturday from

April through June and during September at 3 pm. Admission costs W8000 to W10,000. The National Center for Korean Traditional Performing Arts is a 10-minute walk from the Nambu bus terminal station on subway Line 3. Don't mistake this place with the Seoul Arts Centre, which is just next door.

The National Theatre (*Central Seoul map; ☎ 2264 8448*) offers a full-length *pansori* (traditional opera) performance on the last Saturday of every month at 4 pm. Admission costs W8000 to W15,000. The theatre is on the slopes of Namsan Park behind Dongguk University and right across from the Shilla Hotel. Take subway Line 3 to Dongguk University station, exit 6, and walk for 15 minutes.

Jeongdong Theatre (*Central Seoul map; ☎ 773 8960*) stages modern and traditional performances. There are shows every day at either 4 pm or 8 pm (except Monday), depending on the season – check the Web site for details at www.chong dong.com. Jeongdong Theatre is at the rear of Deoksugung Palace, a five-minute walk from City Hall station on subway Line 1 or 2. Tickets cost W20,000 to W30,000.

Sejong Cultural Center (*Gwanghwamun map; ☎ 399 1516*) does modern performances and exhibitions – classical music, art exhibitions, piano recitals etc. During the warm weather, amateur troupes give free outdoor performances almost daily at noontime for the benefit of office workers. For W3000 to W5000, there is a performance of traditional arts or music on Saturday between 3 and 5 pm.

The *Seoul Nori Madang* (*Greater Seoul map; ☎ 410 3410*) is an open-air theatre for traditional dance performances. It's just behind the Lotte World shopping complex, near the Jamsil subway station on subway Line 2. There are free performances on weekends and holidays with the following schedule: during April and October from 2 to 4 pm; in May and September from 3 to 5 pm; June, July and August from 5 to 7 pm.

Concerts
Western bands occasionally drop in on Seoul. The usual venue for these concerts is

the Seoul Olympic Gym, at *Olympic Park* (*Greater Seoul map; ☎ 700 7500*) or the *Hilton Hotel Convention Center* (*Central Seoul map; ☎ 388 3411*).

The *Seoul Arts Center* (*Greater Seoul map; ☎ 585 3151*) is the best place to go to see Western-style classical orchestras or operas. Take subway Line 3 to Nambu bus terminal station – from there it's about a 15-minute walk.

Cinemas
Plenty of Western movies play in Seoul. The biggest challenge is to find out what's on where and when. The mediocre Friday entertainment section of the English-language newspapers is a good place to start.

In the Tapgol Park area, a small sample of the theatres most likely to be showing foreign films of interest include:

Seoul Cinema Town	(☎ 2269 2700)
Hollywood	(☎ 745 1900)
Piccadilly	(☎ 756 2245)
Danseongsa	(☎ 080 990 8000)
Jung-ang	(☎ 776 8866)
Myeongbo Plaza	(☎ 2274 2121)

In Gangnam-gu, the main theatres are:

Broadway	(☎ 511 2301)
City	(☎ 561 3388)
Dong-a	(☎ 552 6111)
Cine House	(☎ 711 2787)

In Sinchon, check out:

Sinchon Grand	(☎ 332 5107)
Sinyeong	(☎ 392 4450)
Yeonghwanara	(☎ 715 4551)
Noksaek	(☎ 393 5274)

Hard as it is to believe, Seoul has about 10 drive-in movie theatres within the city limits. These are out in the peripheral parts of town and will take some effort to locate.

THINGS TO BUY
Namdaemun Market
Near the Seoul Central Post Office, the Namdaemun (South Gate) Market (Central

Seoul map) is a half-indoor and half open-air market. It's Korea's largest market and a major drawcard for tourists and locals alike. The Koreans say you can get great deals here, but you wouldn't know it by the price tags. Bargaining is necessary, at least for clothing and shoes.

Look for camping gear on the south side of the market (facing the Hoehyeon subway station on Line 4). Two floors under the market you will find Namdaemun, where black market goods (smuggled off US military bases) are sold. It's one of the few places in Seoul where you can buy deodorant, though you pay a premium.

Many of the shops are closed on Sunday, but the street market operates daily.

Dongdaemun Market

This market is just east of the Jongno 5-ga subway station on Line 1 (Central Seoul map). Dongdaemun is more spread out and less 'user friendly' than Namdaemun, but there are bargains to be had. The market is closed on Sunday.

Hwanghak-dong Flea Market

This is perhaps the most important shopping area for newly-arrived shoestring travellers looking to get set up in Seoul. Everything from second-hand furniture to used refrigerators can be bought here. The market is east of Dongdaemun. Take the Line 2 subway to Sindang station and walk north. You will first encounter the Jung-ang Market, which basically sells food (even live chickens and dogs). Continue north for another block and you'll find the flea market – if you've passed the elevated roadway, you've gone too far.

Itaewon

The nearby US military base has turned Itaewon into one big mall, almost a tourist attraction in itself. Prices are good here if you are selective – not every shop offers bargains. One attraction of Itaewon is that shopkeepers speak English. On the downside, every third person you encounter in this neighbourhood greets you by saying 'leather jacket?' or 'custom-made suit?'. Another

speciality are T-shirts with unusual slogans like 'North Korea – Where's the Beef?'.

Insadong

The proper name is Insadonggil (*gil* meaning 'street'), but just call it Insadong. This traditional shopping alley north of the YMCA (Tapgol Park map) is the premier place in Korea for buying antiques, arts and crafts, and for hanging out in trendy tea shops. Some of the prices charged for artwork could bankrupt a third world country, but if you poke around awhile you should find some affordable memento of Korea.

Insadong is closed off to traffic every Sunday from 10 am to 10 pm, and vendors set up tables in the street to display their wares. This makes for very pleasant strolling if the weather is cooperative. During the summer months, various Sunday festivals are organised (traditional dance, food festivals etc).

Electronics Markets

Without a doubt, the premier place to go for computers and other electronic items is the Yongsan Electronics Arcade (Greater Seoul map). Part of this burgeoning market is in one enormous building (a former bus terminal), but the market now spills out into many side streets as well. In total, there are over 5000 shops in 21 buildings. Take subway Line 1 to Yongsan station, and from there follow the elevated walkway over the tracks. You can also take subway Line 4 to Sinyongsan station and walk through the underpass. Most shops operate from about 10 am to 8 pm. The market is closed on the 1st and 3rd Sunday of every month.

Another paradise is Techno Mart (Greater Seoul map), a 10-storey mall filled with electronics shops. The 9th floor has a good food court and there is a cinema complex on the 10th floor (with good views of the river). Techno Mart is open from 10 am to 8 pm. Take subway Line 2 to Gangbyeon station.

T-Zone is a computer chain store with several locations around town. A convenient branch is just south of Tapgol Park.

Music Tapes & CDs

Musicland (Tapgol Park map; ☎ 278 2422) is probably the best source of CDs in Seoul. The selection is large, prices are low and all the CDs are well-organised for browsing. You'll find Musicland in the basement of the towering ELS building on Jongno 2-ga.

The basement of the Metro Midopa department store (Central Seoul map) has one of the best collections for CD buyers, and prices are good.

Among the bookshops, Kyobo Book Center (Gwanghwamun map) has the best assortment of music CDs and tapes.

Tower Records, a London-based company, (☎ 552 0460) has one of the widest selections of CDs in Korea, but prices are high. There are two stores: the central branch is near Tapgol Park close to Jongno 2-ga in the centre; the southern branch (Gangnam-gu map) is near the Gangnam station on subway Line 2.

Department Stores

Although not the cheapest place to buy things, the large department stores, located near the Central Post Office, are worth checking out – without doubt, the 'everything under one roof' philosophy does save a lot of running around.

The densest assemblage of large department stores is clustered on the fringes of Myeong-dong (Central Seoul map). These include the Lotte World, Metro Midopa, Shinsegae, Utoo Zone and Printemps department stores.

COEX Mall

Underneath the huge Convention & Exhibition Center (COEX) building (Gangnam-gu map) the Koreans have built what is claimed to be the largest underground shopping complex in Asia. To get there, take subway Line 2 to Samseong station.

GETTING THERE & AWAY

It's said that about two million Seoulites depart their city every Saturday for various destinations around the country, only to return on Sunday. It's like an immense tidal wave that rolls out and rolls back in again.

Name Chops

When the Koreans adopted the Chinese writing system, they also borrowed the concept of a *dojang* – a seal, or name chop. The traditional name chop has been in use in China for thousands of years.

In ancient Korea, a chop served both as a form of identification and as a valid signature. All official documents needed to be stamped with a chop to be valid. Naturally, this made a chop quite valuable, for with another person's chop it was possible to sign contracts and other legal documents in their name.

Today, chops are no longer recognised as a valid signature on legal documents in Korea, though they still are used this way in China. Nevertheless, traditions die hard and you will still find plenty of shops in Korea which carve name chops. When stamping your 'signature' with a name chop, only red ink is used. On traditional Korean watercolour paintings and decorative scrolls, you will always find the telltale red chop mark which identifies the artist.

There are many different sizes and styles of chops – prices vary wildly depending on the material used. You can easily have one carved as a souvenir, but first get your name translated into hanja (Chinese, as opposed to hangeul, Korean) characters.

The city itself is nearly deserted on weekends and holidays, but every bus, train and plane resembles a moving sardine can.

Air

There are direct flights between Seoul and many other Korean cities. See the Getting Around chapter for domestic flight details.

If you've arrived in Korea with an onward ticket, you need to reconfirm your reservation at least 72 hours before departure. Most airlines have a customer service office in Seoul and at the airport check-in counters. Those airlines which have facilities at the airport permit you to check-in at the Korean Air or Asiana desk in their respective terminals.

angwon-do: Seoraksan (Snowy Crags Mountains) National Park, Korea's most spectacular park

maisan, Maisan Provincial Park, Jeollabuk-do

Naejangsan National Park, Jeollabuk-do

Cheongnyangsan Park, Gyeongsangbuk-do

JULIET COOMBE

A traditional craftsman with lathe, Gyeonggi-do

ERIC L WHEATER

Luridly painted temple guard, Gyeonggi-do

ERIC L WHEATER

Paragon of elegance and refinement: a Buddhist temple in the Korean Folk Village, Gyeonggi-do

There are *two* international terminals at Gimpo airport, with an equal spread of international carriers in each. For bookings and reservations, the airlines prefer that you call their Seoul city numbers, which are as follows:

terminal 1

Air India (AI)	☎ 737 8112
All Nippon (NH)	☎ 666 8700
American (AA)	☎ 734 8820
Asiana (OZ)	☎ 669 8000
Cathay Pacific (CX)	☎ 773 0321
China Eastern (MU)	☎ 518 0330
China Southern (CZ)	☎ 798 6212
Continental (CO)	☎ 720 4946
Dalavia Far East (H8)	☎ 777 2900
Japan Air Sys (JD)	☎ 752 9090
Japan Airlines (JL)	☎ 757 1711
KLM (KL)	☎ 755 7040
Lufthansa (LH)	☎ 538 8141
Northwest (NW)	☎ 666 8700
Qantas (QF)	☎ 777 6871
Sakhalinski (HZ)	☎ 753 7131
United (UA)	☎ 757 1691
Uzbekistan (HY)	☎ 754 1041

terminal 2

Aeroflot (SU)	☎ 551 0321
Air Canada (AC)	☎ 779 5654
Air China (CA)	☎ 774 6886
Air France (AF)	☎ 3788 0400
Alitalia (AZ)	☎ 560 7001
China Northern (CJ)	☎ 775 9070
Garuda (GA)	☎ 773 2092
Kyrgyzstan (KGA)	☎ 3141 1174
Korean Air (KE)	☎ 656 2001
Krasnoyarsk (7B)	☎ 777 6399
Malaysian (MH)	☎ 777 7761
Mongolian (OM)	☎ 756 9761
Philippine (PR)	☎ 774 3581
Singapore (SQ)	☎ 755 1226
Thai (TG)	☎ 3707 0011
Trans-Asian	☎ 777 4864
Vietnam (VN)	☎ 775 7666
Vladivostok (XF)	☎ 733 2920

Bus

The main bus station is the Seoul express bus terminal (*Seoul gosok teomineol*; Gangnam-gu map), also called Gangnam

express bus terminal. It's on the south side of the river – take subway Line 3 and get off at Express Bus Terminal subway station. The terminal is well organised, with signs in English and Korean over all the ticket offices and bus bays. This huge terminal consists of two buildings; Kyeongbuseon (☎ 782-5552) and Honam-Yeongdongseon (☎ 592-0050). Kyeongbuseon is a ten-story building with everything useful on the first floor, while Honam-Yeongdongseon building is a two-stories, with ticket offices and platforms on the 1st floor and a cafeteria on the 2nd floor. These two buildings are placed about 200m apart.

From Seoul express bus terminal you can catch the following buses from in front of the Kyeongbuseon building. If you wish to travel 1st class, add about 50% to the express bus fares):

destination	price (W)	duration	frequency
Busan	15,700	5¼ hrs	15 mins
Cheonan	3300	1 hr	15 mins
Cheongju	4800	1¾ hrs	10 mins
Daegu	11,100	4 hrs	10 mins
Daejeon	6000	2 hrs	10 mins
Gyeongju	13,400	4¼ hrs	30 mins
Jinju	15,300	5½ hrs	20 mins
Kongju	5100	2½ hrs	30 mins
Pohang	14,100	5 hrs	25 mins

From Seoul express bus terminal there are the following buses from the Honam-Yeongdongseon building:

destination	price (W)	duration	frequency
Busan	10,300	3½ hrs	50 mins
Chungju	5600	2½ hrs	30 mins
Donghae	10,700	4½ hrs	45 mins
Gangneung	9200	4 hrs	15 mins
Gimje	9300	3¼ hrs	1hourly
Gunsan	9500	3¼ hrs	20 mins
Gwangju	11,000	4¼ hrs	5 mins
Incheon	2800	1 hr	25 mins
Jecheon	6000	3¾ hrs	45 mins
Jeongeup	10,000	3¼ hrs	30 mins
Jeonju	8900	2¾ hrs	10 mins
Mokpo	14,100	5¼ hrs	40 mins
Sokcho	11,700	5¼ hrs	30 mins
Wonju	4700	1¾ hrs	15 mins

Yeoju	3400	1¼ hrs	35 mins
Yeosu	15,900	6 hrs	50 mins
Yong-in	1600	1 hr	25 mins

In addition to the preceding, there are some night buses from Seoul to major cities like Busan, Daegu and Gwangju, plus a few minor cities like Sokcho and Jinju. For definition purposes, a 'night bus' is one which departs between 10 pm and 1 am. As of yet, there are no night buses between 1 am and 5.30 am, but that could change. These buses are priced about 10% higher than the most expensive daytime buses. All night buses depart from Seoul express bus terminal.

Dong Seoul (East Seoul) bus terminal (Greater Seoul map; ☎ 446 8000) is also very useful, especially for getting to places on the east coast or the central part of the country.

To reach Dong Seoul bus terminal take subway Line 2 to Gangbyeon station. The bus schedule here includes:

destination	price (W)	duration	frequency
Andong	15,800	3½ hrs	20 mins
Busan	16,100	5¼ hrs	1 hourly
Cheongju	5300	1¾ hrs	20 mins
Chuncheon	5400	1½ hrs	15 mins
Chungju	5500	2½ hrs	20 mins
Daegu	11,600	3¾ hrs	35 mins
Daejeon	6400	2 hrs	1 hourly
Danyang	9200	2½ hrs	12 daily
Donghae	10,700	4¼ hrs	2½ hrs
Gangneung	9200	3½ hrs	30 mins
Gongju	5700	2¼ hrs	10 daily
Guinsa	10,600	3½ hrs	19 daily
Gwangju	12,200	4 hrs	45 mins
Incheon	3500	1 hr	1 hourly
Jeongeup	10,500	3¼ hrs	90 min
Jeonju	9300	3 hrs	45 mins
Sokcho	13,700	4½ hrs	21 daily
Songnisan	9700	3½ hrs	15 daily
Wonju	4700	1¾ hrs	10 mins
Yeoju	3300	1½ hrs	1 hourly

Sangbong bus terminal (Greater Seoul map; ☎ 435 2122), in the eastern suburbs, is most useful to people heading east. The terminal is connected by bus with Cheongnyangni railway station (next to Cheongnyangni subway station on subway Line 1). From Cheongnyangni it takes 15 minutes to reach Sangbong on bus No 38-2, 165, 165-2, 166 or 522-1; or 50 minutes by bus from Jongno 1-ga on bus No 131 or 131-1.

From Sangbong terminal there are buses to dozens of obscure towns – the following lists the major destinations only:

destination	price (W)	duration	frequency
Cheongju	5100	1¾ hrs	6 hourly
Chuncheon	5200	1¾ hrs	44 daily
Daejeon	6400	2 hrs	1 hourly
Gangneung	13,000	4¾ hrs	3 daily
Gwangju	12,200	4 hrs	45 mins
Jeonju	9300	3 hrs	2 hrs
Sokcho	13,700	4½ hrs	18 daily
Wonju	7000	2¼ hrs	14 daily
Yeoju	5200	1¾ hrs	29 daily

Other bus terminals, in descending order of usefulness, include:

Sinchon bus terminal (☎ 324 0611). Non-stop bus services to Ganghwado every 10 minutes from 5.40 am to 9.40 pm. To reach the terminal, take subway Line 2 to Sinchon station and ask directions (it's a five-minute walk).
Nambu (south) bus terminal (Greater Seoul map; ☎ 521 8550). Buses to more than 80 destinations south of Seoul, mostly smaller cities and towns. You can reach Nambu bus terminal by taking subway Line 3 to Nambu terminal station.
Seobu (west) bus terminal (Greater Seoul map; ☎ 356 3516) is easily accessible from subway Line 3, and runs buses bound for the northwestern quarter of Gyeonggi-do, which includes Gwangtan, Munsan, Ilsan, Beobwon-ri, Jeokseong and Uijeongbu.

Train

Most long-distance trains departing from Seoul leave from Seoul station (Central Seoul map). The one important exception is the train heading east towards Chuncheon. For this, go to Cheongnyangni railway station (Greater Seoul map), which you reach by taking subway Line 1.

GETTING AROUND
The Airport
Gimpo airport Both domestic and international flights are currently handled at

Gimpo airport, 18km west of the centre. An easy way to get there (and avoid Seoul's traffic) is to take subway Line 5. From the centre, this costs W600 rather than the usual W500 fare.

At present, there are five kinds of buses going there charging different prices. Some buses are express, but it makes little difference – traffic jams basically determine how long a journey takes. However, the fancier buses do offer fancier facilities and extra room to store luggage.

Local buses are cheapest. These cost W600 and are more frequent than express buses. The No 63 bus stops next to Deoksugung and just north of the Koreana Hotel at the Donghwa Duty-Free Shop. The No 68 bus also stops close to City Hall and Midopa Department Store. The disadvantage of both is that they will allow standing passengers and there is very little room for baggage. However, note that there is a fancy new blue and white bus (No 63), which costs W1200. It goes directly to the airport and does not accept standing passengers.

It's more comfortable to take bus No 1002, which costs W1200. It follows much the same route as the No 63 and stops at the same spots in the centre. The service is once every 12 minutes from 7.35 am to 10.20 pm.

Bus Nos 600 and 601 are express buses and guarantee a seat for all. Officially, they run every 10 minutes from 5 am to 10 pm, but don't bet your life on it. You could easily wait 30 minutes for one to come along. The No 601 bus goes into central Seoul, stopping at Sinchon subway station, the Koreana Hotel, Deoksugung, Seoul station, Namdaemun, Jongno 3-ga, Jongno 6-ga and on to the gate Dongdaemun. The No 600 bus goes from Gimpo into the areas south of the river, stopping at the National Cemetery, Palace Hotel, Seoul express bus terminal, Yeongdong market, Nam Seoul Hotel, World Trade Centre, Seoul Sports Complex and Jamsil subway station.

There is also bus No 600-2, following the same route as the 600 but terminating at Seoul express bus terminal; fare is W1300.

The Creme de la creme of Seoul's airport transport is the KAL limousine bus. There is no savings in time, but you get cushy seats, air-conditioning, videos, mobile phones and mobile fax machines – just the thing for the venture capitalist on the go. All that's missing is the sauna. The price tag for this luxury is W5000. These buses run from 7 am to 10 pm, once every 15 to 30 minutes. There are four routes covering 17 luxury hotels – ask at the airport information desk (or your hotel service desk) if interested.

A special airport limousine bus also travels between Gimpo airport and the Korea City Air Terminal (KCAT) in the World Trade Center in Gangnam-gu. This service costs a cool W5000 and (officially) there is a bus every 10 minutes. Buses depart from the airport from 7 am to 10.15 pm; from KCAT departures begin at 5.55 am and finish at 8.50 pm.

A note about Korea City Air Terminal – you can actually complete your entire check-in procedure here (as opposed to checking in at the airport), but it depends entirely on which airline you are flying. The airlines offering this service change periodically, so ring up first (☎ 551 6102) – you can bet your last *won* that Asiana and Korean Air are on the list. You can only check-in on the day of departure, and service begins at 5.30 am.

Taxis are convenient, if you don't mind paying for one. There are often traffic police handing out official complaint forms at the taxi ramp outside the airport to discourage naughty behaviour from the drivers, and most now seem resigned to using their meters. The trip into town should take around 40 minutes and cost W12,000 in a regular taxi, or W23,000 in a deluxe taxi.

One of the confusing things about Gimpo airport is that there are three terminals – two international and one domestic. It's difficult to walk between them on the surface – go into the underground subway if you want to walk. Otherwise, take the free shuttle bus that zips around the airport every few minutes. It's useful to know that buses heading into the airport first stop at international terminal 2, then the domestic terminal and finally international terminal 1 – tell the bus driver which one you want to get off at.

SEOUL

Incheon airport To judge from the amount of money that's being spent, the Koreans are building an ultra-modern new international airport that will knock your socks off. It was still under construction at the time of writing, but it's anticipated to open during the life span of this book.

The exact date for the big ribbon-cutting ceremony is still secret, but one thing is known for sure – the high-speed rail system that will connect Incheon airport to Seoul will *not* be open for several more years. In the meantime, a new expressway is being built and a safe guess would be that Incheon airport to central Seoul will take about 40 to 50 minutes by express bus. Alternatively, there should be buses from the airport to Incheon station – from there you can hop on a subway train for a 50-minute ride to Seoul station.

Bus

City buses run from approximately 5.30 am until midnight. There are three types: ordinary *(ilban)* buses costing W600 (exact change please), seat *(jwaseok)* buses for W1200 and deluxe buses which are W1300.

Of major interest are the magnetic 'transportation cards' *(gotong kadeu)*. These are useful even if you don't ride the bus, since they can also be used in the subway. They can be purchased (W10,500) and recharged at newsstands near all the major bus stops. Using these cards nets you a 10% discount on both the buses and the subway.

At the newsstands near the bus stops, you can also purchase a bus route guide *(beoseu noseon annae)* for W1000. Unfortunately, for most tourists it's not worth its weight in gimchi since it's written entirely in Korean.

Underground

The Seoul subway system is modern, fast and cheap, but can be so crowded that if you drop dead, you'll never hit the ground. There are eight Lines, though Line 6 was still under construction at the time of writing and some of the other Lines were being extended. When all eight Lines are fully completed, the Seoul subway system will be one of the largest in the world.

The system is very user-friendly, and finding your way around should be no problem at all. Trains run every two to six minutes from 5 am until midnight.

The basic charge is W500 for Zone 1, which includes most of the city. The fare rises to W600 if you cross into Zone 2 – the machines where you buy tickets have a self-explanatory fare map, but you'll only occasionally need to go outside Zone 1 (Gimpo airport is in zone 2). Outside the Seoul city limits, the fare rises – the longest ride possible costs W1000.

If you do much commuting, you might want to buy a multiple-use ticket, which saves you 10%. A W10,000 ticket gives you W11,000 worth of rides, and a W20,000 ticket is a W22,000 value.

Taxi

In preparation for World Cup 2002, Seoul has introduced 'Goodwill Guide' taxis. The drivers speak either English or Japanese, and the fare is the same as for a deluxe taxi. These vehicles (and other deluxe taxis) can be summoned by telephone (☎ 3431 5100). There is a separate phone number (☎ 555 8585) for summoning a less-expensive regular taxi.

Car

Renting a car to get around Seoul is an insane idea, but some brave foreigners view it as a challenge. If you want a 'hands-on' experience in Seoul's traffic, any of these car rental companies can accommodate you:

'88'	(☎ 3661 8881)
Changwon	(☎ 556 8177)
Cheil	(☎ 733 8887)
Eagle	(☎ 322 4422)
Hangang	(☎ 2247 0022)
Hertz Keumho	(☎ 3780 8600)
Joy	(☎ 710 5445)
Korean	(☎ 586 5861)
Korea Express	(☎ 719 7295)
Meister	(☎ 526 0500)
Saehan	(☎ 896 0031)
Sambo	(☎ 591 9977)
Samjee	(☎ 362 3233)
Samsung	(☎ 662 7100)
Seoul	(☎ 474 0011)
VIP Avis	(☎ 838 0015)

If you want to travel in style, chauffeur-driven cars go for W144,000 to W510,000 for 10 hours (the price includes the vehicle). You also have to pay for petrol plus the driver's meals and hotels. At least two agencies offer this, Avis (☎ 512 8144) and Korea Car Rental Union (☎ 525 9076).

If you are a new resident of Seoul and wish to apply for a Korean licence, there are four licence-issuing offices in Seoul:

Dobong (☎ 934 7000) window 20, 608 Sanggye-dong, Nowon-gu (Nowon station on subway Line 4)
Gangnam-gu (☎ 555 0743), window 18, 998-1 Daechi-dong, Gangnam-gu, exit No 1 (Samseong station on subway Line 2, exit 1)
Gangseo (☎ 661 0359) window 10, 205 Oebalsan-dong, Gangseo-gu (Kachisan station on subway Line 5, then bus 122). Seobu (☎ 374 6818), window 26, second floor, 338 Jangam-dong, Mapo-gu (Hapjeong station on subway Line 2, then bus 361)

Tours
KNTO, or Seoul City Tourist Information Centre, has the rundown on the latest tour packages. At the bottom of the list are lame half-day tours to places like Namdaemun Market and Lotte World, with a requisite visit to an amethyst shop. Full-day tours will zip you around the city's scenic hot spots for about W65,000. There are even some nightlife tours that take in a banquet with a traditional Korean song and dance show – on most tours, prices range from W60,000 to W90,000.

Gyeonggi-do

Highlights

- Bukhansan National Park, with its incredible granite peaks and the historic fortress of Bukhansanseong
- Seoul Grand Park, home to the National Museum of Modern Art, a zoo, botanic garden and hi-tech rides
- Panmunjeom, a sober reminder that the cold war is not yet over
- Korean Folk Village, a tastefully done recreation of Korea's ancient past
- Baengnyeongdo, a remote island just off the coast of North Korea
- Everything in Gyeonggi-do is an easy day trip from the busy metropolis of Seoul

Bukhansan National Park p152

Incheon p160
Suwon p156

☎ 031 • pop 11.5 million

The province of Gyeonggi-do surrounds Seoul, and even pokes into North Korea. You have about as much chance of visiting the moon as you do of crossing the DMZ (of course this could change) but you can at least have a look at it from here.

One of the bonuses of Gyeonggi-do is that all parts of the province can be reached from Seoul in a day trip.

BUKHANSAN NATIONAL PARK 북한산국립공원

Just to the north of Seoul is **Bukhansan** ('North of the Hangang Mountain'). This national park boasts massive white granite peaks, forests, temples, rock-cut Buddhist statues and tremendous views from various points.

Bukhansan (837m) is the highest peak in the area, but there are at least 20 others within the park boundary. Other notable peaks near to Bukhansan itself (and connected to it by ridges) include Insubong, Mangyeongdae, Baek-undae, Nojeokbong, Bohyeonbong and Bibong. Insubong (812m), Mangyeongdae (800m) and Baek-undae (836m) form a triangle which is named Samgaksan (Triangle Mountain). The rugged granite face of Insubong is a challenge to rock climbers, who turn out in force whenever weather permits.

Insubong offers some of the best multi-pitch climbing in Asia for free climbers. It has been referred to as Asia's 'Little Yosemite' and has routes of all grades. The local climbers are extremely friendly and enthusiastic, eager to introduce newcomers to their mountain. It is possible to hire a guide through one of the climbing shops in Seoul or through the mountaineering clubs. Information is available from KNTO – it's on the computer there too.

Darren DeRidder

At the northern end of the park is **Dobongsan** (740m), which is joined by ridges to the peaks Jaunbong, Manjangbong, Seoninbong and Obongsan.

At the southern end of the park is **Bukhansanseong**. The fortress was built during the Baekje dynasty but the present walls date from the time of the Yi king, Sukjong, who rebuilt the battlements in the 16th century following invasions from China. Sections of the wall were destroyed during the Korean War but have since been restored.

As national parks go, it's relatively small (about 78 sq km) but still large enough to get

150

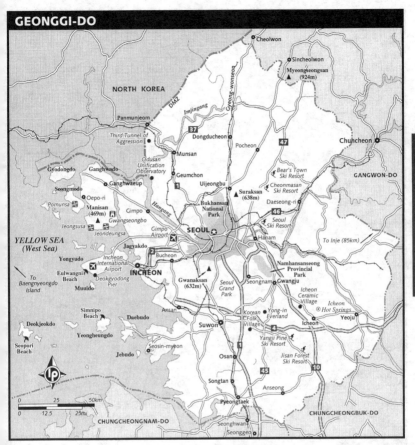

GEONGGI-DO

GYEONGGI-DO

lost in. There are a variety of well-marked trails which lead up into the park and along the ridges – staying on the trails is mandatory to prevent environmental damage (and to prevent falling off a cliff). There are seven huts where simple accommodation is available (bring your own bedding) as well as a limited selection of canned and packaged foodstuffs. There are 32 officially recognised campsites. Water is available at the huts as well as at many other points along the trails. You get a free map when you enter the park (if you ask for it), or you can purchase detailed topographical maps from Jung-ang Atlas Map Service in Seoul (☎ 02-730 9191). Entry to the national park costs W1000 for adults. The admission gates are open from 7.30 am to 6 pm on weekdays, 6.30 am to 6 pm on weekends.

Some of the recommended hiking routes include:

South Area (Samgaksan)
North-South Route 1 (9.1km) U-i-dong, U-i Hut, Baek-undae, Daedongmun, Gugi-dong
North-South Route 2 (8.5km, 3½ hours) Jeongneung Resort, Bogukmun, Yong-ammun, Nojeokbong, Baek-undae

GYEONGGI-DO

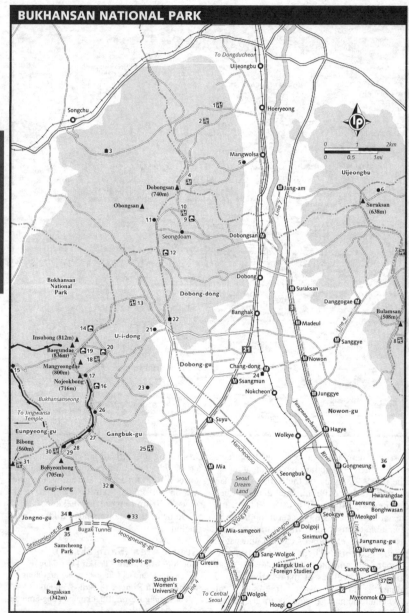

BUKHANSAN NATIONAL PARK

BUKHANSAN NATIONAL PARK

PLACES TO STAY
3 Songchu Resort
송추유원지
9 Dobong Hut
도봉산장
12 Bomun Hut
보문산장
14 Insu Hut
인수산장
20 U-i Hut
우이산장
22 U-i-dong Resort
우이동유원지
24 Green Park Hotel
그린파크호텔
32 Jeongneung Resort
정릉유원지
34 Bugak Park Hotel
북악파크호텔
35 Olympia Hotel
올림피아호텔

OTHER
1 Seokcheonsa
석천사
2 Horyongsa
호룡사

4 Mangwolsa
망월사
5 Jangsuwon
장수원
6 Naewonam Hermitage
내원암
7 Heungguksa
흥국사
8 Bulamsa
불암사
10 Cheonchuksa
천축사
11 Gwaneumam Hermitage
관음암
13 Yongdeoksa
용덕사
15 Daeseomun
대서문
16 Bukhansan Hut
북한산장
17 Yong-ammun
용암문
18 Doseonsa
도선사
19 Baegun Hut
백운산장

21 E-Mart
이마트
23 4.19 Memorial Tower
4.19탑
25 Hwagyesa
화계사
26 Daedongmun
대동문
27 Bogukmun
보국문
28 Daeseongmun
대성문
29 Daenammun
대남문
30 Munsusa
문수사
31 Seunggasa
승가사
33 Kukmin University
국민대학교
36 Seoul Women's University
서울여자대학교
37 Sangbong Bus Terminal
상봉시외버스터미널

Circular Route 1 (7.1km) U-i-dong, Baek-undae, Bukhansan Hut, Jeongneung Resort
Circular Route 2 (8.1km) U-i-dong, Bukhansan Hut, Baek-undae, U-i-dong
Circular Route 3 (6.3km, 3½ hours) U-i-dong, Doseonsa, Baek-un Hut, Baek-undae, Nojeok-bong, Yong-ammun, U-i-dong Resort
Circular Route 4 (5km) Gugi-dong, Daeseongmun, Daedongmun, 419 Memorial Tower
Circular Route 5 (7.5km, 4 hours) Segeom-jeong Resort, Munsusa, Daenammun, Boguk-mun, Jeongneung Resort

North Area (Dobongsan)
East-West Route 2 (8.5km) Dobong-dong, Gwaneum-am Hermitage, Obong Peak, U-i-dong
East-West Route 3 (7.9km) Dobong-dong, Dobong Hut, Gwaneum-am Hermitage, U-i-dong
East-West Route 4 (8.3km) Dobong-dong, Gwaneum-am Hermitage, Obong, U-i-dong
Circular Route 6 (6.7km) Dobong-dong, Cheonchuksa, Mangwolsa, Jangsuwon

Getting There & Away

Getting to Bukhansan by public transport is easy, though there are a number of entrances to the park. You can take subway line No 3 to Gupabal station, then go the last 3km north-east towards the park by bus, taxi or on foot. Another approach is subway line No 4 to Suyu station, then another bus or taxi. Subway line No 7 to Dobongsan station gets you close to the northern end of the national park, where there are trails leading to the summit of Dobongsan.

SURAKSAN 수락산

To the east of Bukhansan National Park is Suraksan (638m), which is another attractive climbing area. It's not a national park, but it's still mobbed with weekend Seoulites trying to get away from it all.

Suraksan is just north of the Seoul city limits, but is connected by a ridge to **Bulamsan**

(508m) which is in Seoul. It's well work hiking along the ridge between the two peaks.

Access to Suraksan is possible from several different angles, and it's not a bad idea to ascend and descend the mountain by different routes. An easy way to begin would be to take subway line No 4 to Sanggye station – Bulamsan is 2km to the east of this station. From Bulamsan you can follow the ridgeline north about 7km to Suraksan. Along the way you must cross a small highway, and just off to the east is an interesting temple, **Heungguksa**, which is worth the small detour. From here there are several obvious trails down – one leads north-west to Uijeongbu, from where there are trains back to Seoul. Whichever route you take, you're in for long walk; it will take a full day, so start early.

SEOUL GRAND PARK 서울대공원

In the suburbs of Seoul proper is Seoul Grand Park (Seoul Dae Gongwon), a huge sprawling affair with a number of attractions. Although it's largely geared towards kids, there are also some sights for adults too. If you don't want to be fighting crowds all day, it is best to visit on a weekday. The basic admission fee for the park is W1500.

There is more to the Grand Park than just a park. Nearby is **Seoul Land** (☎ 504 0011), a full day outing in itself. This high-tech amusement park has plenty of rides of the white-knuckle variety, as well as theme concepts like Tomorrow Land, Fantasy Land and Adventure Land. The attached **zoo** has a good collection of animals, many of them in attractive roomy enclosures. There is even an ant ground. Dolphin shows take place three times daily at 11.30 am, 1.30 and 3.30 pm. The basic admission fee to Seoul Land is W6000 for adults. There are additional charges for the rides and exhibits, or you can purchase an all-inclusive ticket for W22,000. Some discount coupons floating around (ask at KNTO) can net you a 20% discount. The park is open daily from 9.30 am to 7 pm from April to October, and until 6 pm from November to March.

Tucked in the hills behind the amusement park is the **National Museum of Contemporary Art** (☎ 503 9671). This museum has been migrating southwards over the years. It was originally at Gyeongbokgung Palace, then Deoksugung Palace and currently resides near Seoul Grand Park – at this rate it should reach Jejudo in about 100 years. There's an extensive collection of Korean and Western modern art in a variety of mediums, including video movies. Concerts, plays, traditional dance shows and films are on view here, but the schedule varies. There are also a number of bizarre outdoor sculptures. A shuttle bus runs every 20 minutes between the museum and the Seoul Grand Park subway station. The museum is open from 10 am to 6 pm, or until 5 pm during winter. Admission costs W700 (closed Monday).

Getting There & Away

Seoul Grand Park is on subway line No 4 south of Seoul Grand Park station.

From the city, the fare is W600 rather than the usual W500.

SEOUL EQUESTRIAN PARK
서울경마공원

Amid Seoul's sprawling megalopolis, it's reassuring to find a place where one can ride a horse. The Seoul Equestrian Park (Seoul Seungma Gongwon) has basic riding facilities. It's open from Wednesday through Sunday, and costs W15,000 per hour. It's best to call (☎ 509 1357) before heading out there.

Within the confines of the park is the **Seoul Race Course**. Horse racing is one of the very few legal gambling activities open to Koreans, and has become a major cash cow for the government. Races are held every 30 minutes, Saturday and Sunday from 11 am to 6 pm (until 9 pm during July and August). Races may be cancelled during extreme weather. Admission costs W900 and bets range from a minimum of W100 to a maximum of W100,000. To give more of a family image to this activity, baby carriages and children's bicycles are available for hire at the track (but cannot be ridden on the track!). The races can also be viewed on large-screen TVs located at betting offices in downtown Seoul.

The race course is home to the **Equine Museum**. Admission is free.

The race track is close to the already-mentioned Seoul Grand Park. Take subway line No 4 to the Seoul Race Course station.

NAMHANSANSEONG PROVINCIAL PARK 남한산성도립공원

Like Bukhansan, Namhansan is topped by a fortress (Namhansanseong). This park is about 25km south-east of Seoul. Although it doesn't offer the hiking trails that Bukhansan does, Namhansanseong does have a very impressive section of walled **fortifications** that date back to the 17th century. The wall, which winds sinuously over the Namhansan peak and foothills for around 5km, has been touted as Korea's answer to China's Great Wall. Of course, in terms of scale, there's no comparison, but at certain points along the Namhansanseong wall there's more than a vague resemblance.

Historians maintain that there was an earthen fortress on the present-day site of Namhansanseong as long as 2000 years ago. The walls that remain today date from 1621. They were built as a line of defence against the Manchus. When the Manchus invaded Korea in 1635 the Korean king of the time retreated here, only to be forced into surrender shortly after the Manchus laid siege to the fortress. It was an act that led to the Joseon dynasty being forced to accept the suzerainty of China.

The fortress area once accommodated nine temples, as well as various command posts and watch towers. Today a single command post, **Seojangdae**, and a single temple, **Changgyeongsa**, remain. There are other more recent temples on the path up to the south gate and fortress walls. The north, south and east gates have been restored.

Entry to the park costs W500, and don't forget to ask for a free map at the entrance station. In the park itself, a few places sell instant noodles, soft drinks and coffee.

Getting There & Away

The nearest town to Namhansanseong is Seongnam, south-east of Seoul, to the west of Namhansanseong. Subway line No 8 has a station at Namhansanseong and one at Dandae, both within a few kilometres of the fortress. From either station, taxis can drive you up the mountain into the fortress for about W7000. From Namhansanseong station you can take bus No 88 or 88-1, which lets you off at the park entrance at the bottom of the hill.

SUWON 수원
pop 910,000

Suwon is an ancient fortress city 48km south of Seoul and the provincial capital of Gyeonggi-do. The fortress was known as Suwonseong, but has recently been renamed Hwaseong. The **citadel** was completed in 1796 by King Jeongjo in an unsuccessful attempt to make Suwon the nation's capital. The walls once surrounded the whole city but urban expansion has seen the city sprawl far beyond the enclosed area.

The walls, gates, a number of pavilions and an unusual water gate have all been reconstructed. It's possible to walk around the entire length of the wall – this will take a good two to three hours. The best point of entry is Paldalmun (South Gate). From here, steps lead straight up to the pavilion at the top of Paldalsan. If you head off from here first to Hwaseomun (West Gate) followed by Janganmun (North Gate) and Jangyongmun (East Gate), you'll see most of the principal features of the fortifications.

Places to Stay

One of the least-expensive places to stay is the dingy-looking **Ginseong Yeoinsuk,** down a small alley opposite the train station.

The yeogwan near the bus terminals are more salubrious. A good example is the **Eunha-jang Yeogwan** and neighbouring **Ssangyong-jang Yeogwan**, both of which cost W25,000. Also close by is the **Hayateu Motel,** which is W28,000. There are at least a dozen other good places in the adjacent alleys, such as the **Gwibin-jang**.

Moving upmarket, the **Seoksan Hotel** has a good central location and costs about W50,000. Nearby is the **Brown Hotel** (☎ 246 4141) which is rated first class and has doubles for W70,000.

The plushest place to stay in Suwon is the **Castle Hotel** (☎ 212 8811), which is rated

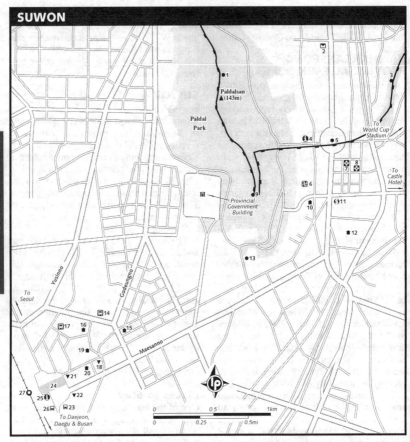

SUWON

four stars and even has its own golf course. However, it's in a suburban area over 4km from Suwon station, so don't stay here if you need to be where the nightlife is.

Places to Eat
As in any Korean city, you'll be spoiled for choice. Descend into the underground arcade facing the train station and you'll find a dozen food stalls selling exactly the same thing – noodles and *gimbap* (Korean 'sushi') – not inspiring, but it's fast and cheap.

Back on the surface, you'll find a branch of the *Khan Antique Pub* chain, which has

some really delicious Korean dishes for W3000 to W4000.

Also fronting the train station is a branch of *Paris Baguette*, which has (surprise!) baguettes and coffee.

Just down the road is *Nashville Pub Restaurant,* whose meals are more elaborate than Khan's.

Getting There & Away
Subway To get to Namhansanseong, take subway line No 1 heading south all the way to the last stop, making sure the train is marked 'Suwon' (*not* Incheon or Ansan).

SUWON

PLACES TO STAY
10 Seoksan Hotel
   석산호텔
12 Brown Hotel
   브라운호텔
15 Gwibin-jang Yeogwan
   귀빈장여관
16 Hayateu Motel
   하야트모텔
19 Eunhang-jang Yeogwan;
   Ssangyong-jang Yeogwan
   은하장여관,
   쌍용장여관
20 Ginseong Yeoinsuk
   진성여인숙

PLACES TO EAT
18 Nashville Pub Restaurant
   내슈빌
21 Paris Baguette
   파리바게뜨

22 Khan Antique Pub
   칸
24 Underground Arcade
   지하상가

OTHER
1 Seojangdae Command Post
   서장대
2 Post Office
   수원우체국
3 Bongdon Tower
   봉돈
4 Tourist Information
   관광안내소
5 Paldalmun
   팔달문
6 Paldalsa
   팔달사
7 Nammun Department Store
   남문백화점

8 Simin & Clover Department Stores
   시민백화점,크로바백화점
9 Hwayangnusa
   화양루
11 Joheung Bank
   조흥은행
13 Confucian School
   향교
14 Kolon Express Bus Terminal
   고속버스터미널
17 Inter-City Bus Termianl
   시외버스터미널
23 Shuttle Bus to Korean Folk Village
   민속촌셔틀버스정류장
25 Tourist Information
   관광안내소
26 Bus No 37 to Korean Folk Village
   정류장
27 Train Station
   수원역

The journey from Seoul takes about 45 minutes and the fare is W950.

Bus Forget the bus if you're just going to or coming from Seoul – the subway is faster, easier and cheaper. However, buses can get you from Suwon to many other destinations in Korea. The Kolon express bus terminal has buses to:

destination	price (W)	duration	frequency
Daegu	10,500	3 hrs	6 daily
Daejeon	5200	1¾ hrs	1 hourly
Gwangju	11,200	4 hrs	35 mins

The inter-city bus terminal has buses to smaller cities and towns including:

destination	price (W)	duration	frequency
Andong	15,200	5 hrs	7 daily
Bupyeong	3000	1 hr	20 mins
Buyeo	8400	2½ hrs	8 daily
Chuncheon	7500	2½ hrs	20 daily
Gangneung	11,700	3½ hrs	10 daily
Incheon	3200	1 hr	15 mins
Pohang	17,900	5 hrs	9 daily
Sokcho	15,500	5 hrs	8 daily
Songnisan	9900	3½ hrs	7 daily

Train Suwon is on the country's busiest railway. Trains head southwards to Daejeon, Daegu and Busan several times an hour.

KOREAN FOLK VILLAGE
한국민속촌

The Korean Folk Village (Hanguk Minsok Chon) rates as one of the best day outings from Seoul. Most people visit the village expecting large-scale tourist kitsch, but instead find a surprisingly tasteful reconstruction of a traditional Korean village.

The kitsch is across the lake (accessible by footbridge). This is the **Family Park**, a Disney like amusement zone complete with a small roller coaster, mini-train and 'volcano'.

There are twice-daily performances of various sorts. The farmers' dance – to the sounds of gongs and drums – takes place at noon and 3 pm. At 12.30 and 3.30 pm is the acrobatics

GYEONGGI-DO

and tightrope dance. There is a 'traditional wedding' in house No 9 at 1 and 4 pm. Over in the Family Park area is a traditional magic and acrobatic show at 11.30 am, 2, and 4 pm.

The Korean Folk Village is open daily from 9 am to 5.20 pm in winter, and until 6.30 pm in summer. In summer, the Family Park stays open until 9 pm.

Admission costs W8500 for adults, but both the Folk Museum and Haunted House each charge an extra W2500. Look at the Web site at www.koreanfolk.co.kr for further information.

Getting There & Away

The first thing to do is get to Suwon, a suburb to the south of Seoul. Take subway line No 1 southbound to the last stop (make sure the train says 'Suwon' on the front, not 'Incheon'). As you come out of Suwon station you'll see the ticket office and bus stop on the right-hand side on the same side of the street. Buses to the village go every hour on weekdays and every half hour on weekends, from 10 am to 3.30 pm. The last free bus back from the village is at 5 pm on weekdays and 6 pm on weekends and public holidays, but you can also take local bus No 37 and pay the W700 fare. These regular buses run once every 20 minutes until 9 pm. Of course, you can always take a taxi.

From Jamsil intersection in Seoul (next to Lotte World), you can catch bus No 100-2 or 1116 directly to the Korean Folk Village.

There are several bus companies in Seoul which offer tours of the village. Lotte Travel (☎ 399 2300) offers a half-day tour for W38,000. Korea Travel Bureau (☎ 585 1191) has a full-day itinerary costing W62,000 (but at least you get a free lunch).

EVERLAND 용인에버랜드

In the town of Yong-in (north-east of Suwon) is Everland (☎ 320 9040), brought to you by the ever-enterprising jaebeol Samsung. This is Korea's largest amusement park, divided into three subsections: Festival World, Caribbean Bay and the Everland Speedway.

Attractions include a botanic garden, a zoo, a safari park and a host of gut-gripping

rides like the 'double loops & corkscrew'. You can ride a sled (in winter), or go surfing in the 'big wave pool' during summer. Everland Speedway offers auto racing, motorcycle racing and mountain bike racing.

Somewhat surprising is the **Hoam Art Museum** near Caribbean Bay, a private collection of Korean art that was owned by Lee Byung-chul, the late founder of Samsung. The museum is closed on Monday.

You can spend the night at the plush *Everland Youth Hostel*. There are even log cabins for rent.

There are various kinds of admission tickets available. Basic admission to Festival World (no rides included) costs W11,000 for adults. An all-inclusive ticket for adults is W40,000 in summer, or W30,000 in winter. Teenagers get a 30% discount and children get 60% off.

The Everland complex is open daily from 9 am to 6 pm (10 pm during summer).

From Suwon station, take bus No 66 direct to Everland. From Seoul, catch bus No 1500 in front of Yangjae subway station (on line No 3) to Yong-in bus terminal, then take bus No 600 to Everland. There are also buses every 20–30 minutes from the Seoul express bus terminal from 6.30 am to 9.30 pm going to Yong-in bus terminal (the journey takes one hour). There are buses from Incheon bus terminal direct to Everland.

There are two special shuttle buses (☎ 575 7710, 759 1305) – one starts from the Westin Chosun Hotel and the other from the Inter-Continental Hotel.

ICHEON 이천
pop 180,000

Just 50km south-east of Seoul is the historic village of Icheon. Though perhaps it won't be much longer before the Seoul megalopolis swallows it up, at present Icheon presents a semi-rural setting with several moderately interesting sights.

Icheon Ceramic Village 이천도예촌

This is perhaps a specialised interest, but the Icheon Ceramic Village (Icheon Doye Chon) does attract a small but loyal following of pottery buffs. The Icheon region – and nearby Gwangju – has been the centre of the Korean ceramics industry, going back at least to the Joseon dynasty (1392–1910). White porcelain is still an export item of Korea, though these days there is heavy competition from innumerable low-wage sweatshops in China. You can find celadon pottery for sale in Icheon for a fraction of what it costs in Seoul.

Icheon is also the home of the Haegang Ceramics Museum (☎ 634 2226) – admission is W1000.

Icheon Hot Springs 이천온천

Though not the most spectacular hot springs in Korea, it's certainly one of the most accessible to Seoul. Water temperatures are a moderate 30°C. Icheon Hot Springs gained popularity during the (unpopular) Japanese colonial period from 1910 to 1945.

Places to Stay

The only reason to stay would be to take advantage of one of the two hot spring resort hotels.

The less expensive of the two is the 84-room *Seolbong Hotel* (☎ 635 5701) which costs a mere W75,000 to W180,000.

Just across the street is the 165-room, four-star *Miranda Hotel* (☎ 633 2001) where doubles cost W140,000 to W242,000. The huge spa here is impressive.

Both hotels are a short walk from the Icheon inter-city bus terminal.

Getting There & Away

There are at least two options for getting to Icheon. Perhaps easiest is from the Seoul express bus terminal – buses run once every 20 minutes from 6.30 am until 9.20 pm, taking just over an hour to make the journey. Buses are once-hourly from the Dong Seoul bus terminal and take one hour to do the trip. The fare is W2800 from the Seoul express bus terminal, or W3500 from Dong Seoul.

You must tell the driver if you want to get off at the Icheon Ceramic Village rather than Icheon itself, which is about 4km further down the highway. Local bus No 114 goes right past the Ceramics Village, which

is actually almost halfway between Icheon and Gwangju. Some tours take in both Everland and the Icheon Ceramic Village in one trip for W75,000.

If going to the hot springs, take a taxi from central Icheon.

YEOJU 여주

pop 102,000

About 2km to the east of the town of Yeoju is **Sileuksa**, a magnificent temple built around 580 AD. The temple is open from 8 am to 4 pm.

A short bus ride to the west of Yeoju is Yeongneung, where you can find the **Tomb of King Sejong**. The tomb site is open from 8.30 am to 6 pm, and there is a small museum on the grounds.

Yeoju is to the south-east of Seoul. You can get there by bus from Seoul's Sangbong bus terminal.

INCHEON 인천

☎ 032 ● pop 2.5 million

Incheon became briefly famous in 1950 when the American General Douglas MacArthur led UN forces in a daring landing here behind enemy lines. Military experts doubted such a tactic could succeed, but it did and within a month the North Koreans were all but defeated. Unfortunately for the allies, the tide turned again in November of the same year when Chinese troops stormed across the border. (See the History section in the Facts about Korea chapter.)

Today, the Chinese are still storming across the border, though now they have tourist visas. Many of the Chinese 'tourists' are here to buy and sell. You may also see sailors from Russia and elsewhere – Incheon is a very cosmopolitan city.

Along with Busan, Incheon of one of Korea's two largest seaports. As might be expected, it's not a port with quaint wooden sailing ships and fishing piers. Rather, it's a world of container ships and high-rise apartment blocks that look as if they were built with Lego.

Nevertheless, the city does have its charms. Thanks to foreign trade Incheon is booming, and some of the money has gone

GYEONGGI-DO

into remodelling the cityscape. Land is being reclaimed from the sea, seaside amusement parks are being developed, a new subway system has started operating, spiffy new shopping malls are springing up and Korea's largest airport is nearing completion. An attempt is being made to turn on the local culture with theatres and arts centres – the municipal government has even dusted off a few historical sites.

Jayu Park 자유공원

At the centre of Jayu (Freedom) Park is a heroic statue of General MacArthur, who led the famous Incheon landing during the Korean War. The park is right next to Incheon harbour.

Munhaksanseong 문학산성

The fortress of Munhaksanseong was the seat of government of the old Baekje kingdom. Within the perimeters of the old fort is a small lighthouse which rises to a modest height of 3m.

The park that surrounds Munhaksanseong has an outdoor swimming pool.

The park is on the south side of the city in an area called Nam-gu.

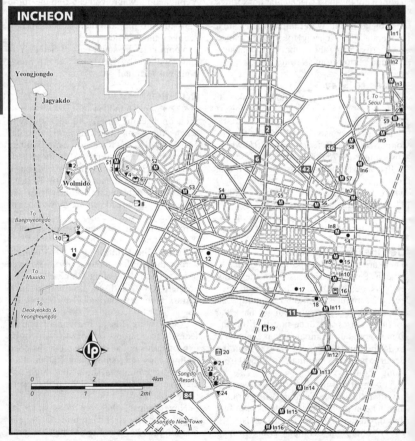

INCHEON

PLACES TO STAY
2 Shangseria; NewStar;
  Sepian; Utopia;
  Samhae-jang Motels
  샹제리아, 뉴스타,
  세피안, 유토피아,
  삼해장여관
3 Olympos Hotel
  올림프스호텔
13 High Park; Ribae;
  Swiss Motel
  하이파크모텔,
  리배모텔, 스위스모텔
22 Alps, Baegakgwan;
  Hilltop Motel
  알프스모텔,
  백악관모텔,
  힐탑호텔
23 Songdo Beach Hotel
  송도비치호텔

PLACES TO EAT
1 Hemingway; Hurricane;
  San Francisco; Dock
  Side
  헤밍웨이, 허리케인,
  샌프란시스코,
  도크사이드
4 Chinatown
  중국인촌
24 Green Tomato & Songdo
  Multeombeong
  그린토마토,
  송도물텀벙

OTHER
5 Jayu (Freedom) Park
  자유공원
6 Central Post Office
  인천우체국
7 Sinpodong
  Underground Arcade
  신포동지하상가
8 International Ferry
  Terminal
  국제여객터미널

9 Ocean Park
  해양광장
10 Yeon-an Pier (Domestic
  Ferries)
  연안부두
11 Incheon Total Fish
  Market
  인천종합어시장
12 Inha University
  인하대학교
13 City Hall
  시청
15 Culture & Arts Hall; CVG
  Multiplex
  종합문화회관
16 Bus Terminal
  종합버스터미널
17 Seowonl
  향교
18 Munhak Sports
  Stadium
  인천문학경기장
19 Munhaksanseong
  문학산성
20 Incheon Municipal
  Museum
  인천시립박물관
21 Incheon Landing
  Memorial Hall
  인천상륙작전기념관

KNR (SEOUL SUBWAY)
S1 Incheon
  인천역
S2 Dong-Incheon
  동인천역
S3 Dowon
  도원역
S4 Jemulpo; Underground
  Arcade
  제물포역
S5 Juan
  주안역
S6 Ganseok
  간석역

S7 Dong-am
  동암역
S8 Baegun
  백운역
S9 Bupyeong; Underground
  Arcade
  부평역

INCHEON SUBWAY
In1 Gayasan
  가야산
In2 Office Of Bupyeong-
  Gu
  부평구청
In3 Bupyeong Market
  부평시장역
In4 Bupyeong
  부평역
In5 Dongsu
  동수역
In6 Bupyeong Samgeori
  부평삼거리역
In7 Ganseok Ogeori
  간석오거리
In8 Incheon City Hall
  인천시청역
In9 Arts Hall
  예술회관역
In10 Terminal
  터미널역
In11 Munhak Sports
  Complex
  문학경기장역
In12 Seonhak
  선학역
In13 Sinyeonsu
  신연수역
In14 Woninjae
  원인재역
In15 Dongchun
  동춘
In16 Dongmak
  동막

Incheon Munhak Stadium
인천문학경기장

Incheon is one of the 10 Korean cities that, in partnership with co-host Japan, will host the 2002 soccer World Cup.

The venue for this momentous event is the Incheon Munhak Stadium, which is close to the *Hyanggyo* (Confucian school). To get there, take the Incheon subway to the Incheon Munhak Sports Stadium station.

Hyanggyo (Confucian School)
향교

This first opened in the Goryeo dynasty. Its salad days were during Joseon dynasty (1392–1910). It was later annexed to a Confucian temple. These days the school serves as a shrine and no classes are held.

The hyanggyo is just to the north-west of the aforementioned Incheon Munhak Stadium.

Incheon Municipal Museum
인천시립박물관

There are about 1200 ancient artefacts on display here, including some large temple bells from China. Next to the museum is the Landing Commemoration Hall, another reminder of MacArthur's landing at Incheon.

The Municipal Museum is at the south end of town, just east of Songdo Amusement Park.

Culture & Arts Hall   예술문화회관

This cultural centre has both indoor and outdoor performance halls for Korean dancing, drama, drum shows and the like. Art exhibits are also regularly presented here. The Culture & Arts Hall is easily reached by Incheon subway to the Arts Center station.

Shopping Malls

This is what people really come to Incheon for. Inspired by Seoul's Lotte World, Incheon has adopted mall culture with a vengeance. The brightly lit shopping arcades are like Aladdin's Caves: stocked to the rafters with goodies – tourist attractions in themselves. You can often see foreign sailors here window shopping, looking for that special memento (or black market item) which can be sold for profit back home.

If you exit the subway at Dong Incheon station and descend through the Incheon Department Store, you will find yourself in one of Korea's longest underground malls, the Sinpodong Underground Arcade. About 2km to the east is the city's second such creation: the Jemulpo Underground Arcade, at the Jemulpo subway station. The newest arcade to adopt this theme is the Bupyong Underground Arcade at Bupyong station.

Another hot prospect for smart shoppers is the CVG Multiplex (at the Culture & Arts Hall) which also boasts good restaurants, billiard halls and cinemas all rolled into one.

Wolmido   월미도

This was once an island, but land reclamation has made it into a peninsula (at least until global warming turns it back into an island). Wolmido is a very trendy spot, on summer weekends boasting everything from art galleries to street opera. The large amusement park has plenty of traumatic rides. The waterfront is lined with plush, outrageously expensive restaurants and there is a small booth here dishing out tourist information. There is a surprisingly good nightlife scene – lots of pubs. A number of yeogwan at the northern end of the waterfront offer reasonable accommodation possibilities, though they can be chock-a-block on weekends.

Two large sightseeing cruise ships, *Cosmos* and *Harmony* (☎ 764 1171), dock at Wolmido and offer Western buffet meals (not recommended if you're prone to sea sickness). The boat costs W7000 (half price for children) for a one-hour cruise. On weekdays, departures are once every 90 minutes between 11 am and 8 pm. On weekends and holidays, departures are every 50 minutes. This schedule gets pulled back somewhat during the off season (winter).

The Incheon city government has plans to construct an Incheon Tower in this area to rival the one in Seoul, perhaps not the wisest idea given Wolmido's proximity to the new international airport.

Wolmido is a one hour walk or a five minute taxi ride from Incheon station. You can also catch bus No 2, 15, 23, 60, 101 or 550 from either Incheon station or Dong Incheon station.

Eulwangni Beach   을왕리해수욕장

The only offshore island you can reach by boat from Wolmido is Yeongjongdo. Or is it? Due to land reclamation, Yeongjongdo has been attached to Sammakdo and Yongyudo to create runways for Incheon International Airport. In other words, three little islands have been merged into one big one. Perhaps this unnamed landmass ought to be called 'Gonghangdo' (Airport Island)? Don't forget – you read it here first.

The west side of 'Airport Island' is officially still called Yongyudo. Here you'll find Eulwangni Beach, the nicest beach in the Incheon area. Windsurfing is possible here, though the heavy tides make it too challenging for beginners.

Boats to Yeongjongdo depart from Wolmido once hourly between 8 am and 9 pm and the sea journey takes 15 minutes. The boat drops you off at Yeongjongdo pier, where there is a wonderful fish market (especially active in the morning). From the pier you have to take a local bus (40 minutes) to Eulwangni Beach on what is still officially called Yongyudo. There are no yeogwan at Eulwangni but minbak are available.

Yeon-an Pier 연안부두

About 300 fishing boats dock here (not all at one time though), and nearby is the Incheon Total Fish Market. You'll also find a street with numerous raw fish restaurants, and a field for drying fish (hold your nose).

Yeon-an Pier is where you catch ferries to the numerous small islands off the coast of Incheon.

Probably of most interest to foreign visitors is that the Incheon International Ferry Terminal will eventually move to Yeon-an Pier. The new terminal building is currently under construction. From here you'll be able to catch ships to China.

The government has big plans to turn the Yeon-an area into a seaside park to rival Wolmido and Songdo (see the next section). With this in mind, they've constructed **Ocean Park**, which is where you catch cruise ships operated by Hyundai (☎ 882 5555). The cruises last for one hour. First departure is at 11 am on weekdays, 11.30 am on weekends and holidays. The last boat is at 5.30 pm. Again, expect the schedule to get knocked back during winter.

A new and somewhat bizarre trend has been the proliferation of 'seawater bathhouses'. Believing that salt water can relieve fatigue and cure various skin ailments, a number of bath houses have set up shop here. The only advantages it offers over just simply going swimming at the beach is that the water is heated and you can bathe nude (frolicking in the nude is not generally acceptable at Korea's public beaches).

Songdo Resort 송도유원지

This is southern Incheon's answer to Wolmido. Songdo is the city's other big amusement park centre. Features include two artificial lakes and even an artificial beach. Think of it as a place for rowboats, paddleboats, drown-proof swimming and cotton candy.

Don't confuse the resort area with the adjacent Songdo New Town. This is being built on reclaimed land in the harbour, and when finished is destined to be a new high-tech industrial park along the lines of Silicon Valley.

Places to Stay

Wolmido At least when the weather is balmy, Wolmido is the most pleasant neighbourhood to stay. There are plenty of motels charging around W30,000 on weekdays, W35,000 on weekends. Among the choices are the *Shangseria Motel* (☎ 773 9955), *Newstar Motel* (☎ 765 7047), *Sepian Motel* (☎ 773 0202), *Utopia Motel* (☎ 764 6365) and the *Samhae-jang Motel* (☎ 772 3939).

Songdo The other interesting part of town is the area surrounding Songdoho – Songdo Resort. Overlooking the lake is the four-star *Songdo Beach Hotel* (☎ 832 1311). Less expensive places to stay in the area include the *Alps Motel* (☎ 832 2233) at W25,000, *Baegakgwan Motel* (☎ 831 0904) also priced at W25,000 and the *Hilltop Hotel* (☎ 834 3500) at W30,000.

City Centre Ironically, the city's main four-star hotel is in a rather unattractive neighbourhood. The *Olympos Hotel* (☎ 762 5181) is near Incheon station. It was built in the old days when the only reason to visit Incheon was to cut business deals with jaebeol kingpins. Rooms on the upper floors offer a nice view of the container ships.

Bupyeong If you don't need to be by the waterfront or the city centre, the area just to the north-east of the Bupyeong subway station has a fine collection of clean and inexpensive 'motels' (ie, yeogwan). Places to try here include the *High Park Motel*, *Ribae Motel* and *Swiss Motel*. Everything around here ranges in price from W25,000 to W30,000.

GYEONGGI-DO

Places to Eat

Incheon offers the usual cornucopia of small Korean-style restaurants and Western fast-food traps. If you're looking for something more interesting, the fashionable seaside resorts are good places to explore.

Wolmido 'Wolmido Culture St' (the waterfront) is decked out with plush restaurants that boast a sea view. Your selection of cuisine here is limited only by the size of your wallet.

Perhaps the best example of the genre is *Hemingway* (☎ 763 0409) which is owned by Korean pop star Lee Soo Man. The least expensive meal is spaghetti, for W8000. The 'Hemingway special dinner' is W15,000 to W20,000, or you can go for lobster and steak for a cool W35,000.

Other restaurants here with a similar motif to Hemingway include *Hurricane* (☎ 772 1325), *San Francisco* (☎ 762 4554) and *Dock Side* (☎ 772 2132).

Songdo Restaurants in this touristy neighbourhood tend to be more Korean than Western. Just opposite the fancy Songdo Beach Hotel is *Green Tomato* (☎ 833 2064), a Western restaurant which indeed gives you plenty of tomatoes (not always green) in your tossed salad. If you'd prefer a *bulgogi* (Korean barbecue), look just across the street to find *Songdo Multeombeong* (☎ 832 3900).

Chinatown The Koreans have as been hospitable to their Chinese minority as the Japanese have been towards ethnic Koreans living in Japan – which is why most of them have emigrated elsewhere. However, Incheon retains a small Chinatown, which consists of around a dozen Chinese restaurants. Prices are reasonable, though there is a wide variation between simple fried rice (W5000) and fancier dishes like assorted seafood with vegetables (up to W35,000).

Chinatown is almost directly opposite the Olympos Hotel near Incheon station.

Getting There & Away

Train Subway line No 1 has trains departing Seoul for Incheon every four minutes

from 5.10 am to 11.30 pm. The ride takes about 50 minutes and costs W900.

Bus From Seoul, it's faster to take the subway to Incheon. However, if you want to get from Incheon to other Korean cities such as Busan or Daegu, there is no reason to go Seoul first. From Incheon bus terminal (☎ 430 7100) you can get a bus to:

destination	price (W)	duration	frequency
Busan	16,300	6¼ hrs	6 daily
Buyeo	10,300	3 hrs	30 daily
Cheongju	7300	2 hrs	23 daily
Chuncheon	8500	3 hrs	15 daily
Daegu	11,800	5 hrs	8 daily
Daejeon	6800	2¾ hrs	30 mins
Everland	3700	1½ hrs	7 daily
Gangneung	13,100	4 hrs	12 daily
Gongju	8000	2½ hrs	9 daily
Gwangju	12,600	4¾ hrs	hourly
Seoul station	2400	1¼ hrs	10 mins
Sokcho	12,000	5½ hrs	2 hrs

Getting Around

Subway Some confusion is caused by the fact that when the Seoul subway reaches Incheon, it's no longer considered a subway – it's a KNR train – but most people still call it 'Seoul subway line No 1'.

Incheon has one subway line, running in a north-south direction. It intersects with the KNR line at the massive Bupyeong station.

Boat Wolmido is where you can take a cruise on the good ship *Cosmos*. This costs W4500 for a one-hour cruise and the official departure times are as follows: 11 am, 12.30, 2, 3.30, 5, 6.30 and 8 pm. It's entirely possible that this schedule would get pulled back somewhat during winter.

Car If the only driver you trust is yourself, consider renting a car from one of the following companies: Avis (☎ 886 5263); Kyeong-In (☎ 525 4444); New Incheon (☎ 882 0106); Paldo (☎ 864 8686).

YELLOW SEA ISLANDS

There are dozens of islands in the Yellow Sea which are technically part of the Incheon municipality, even though it can take hours to reach them by boat. The islands are mostly rocky, though there are a few excellent sandy beaches hidden in coves. On some islands you can see some rare smooth stone beaches. The stones are called *mongdol*, and it takes centuries of tidal action to produce them. It is illegal to collect these stones, so don't try to take any home with you.

For the Koreans, a major reason to visit the islands is to indulge in a raw fish (*saengseon hoe*) culinary safari. Island restaurant menus typically include vinegared rice with raw fish (*saengseon chobap*), broiled fish (*saengseon gui*) and spicy fish soup (*maeun tang*). If seafood appeals to you, be sure to ask the price first – the species of fish as well as the season and the cooking (or non-cooking) method greatly influences the price, which can vary from reasonable to outrageous.

Before embarking for the islands, stock up with sufficient cash – money-changing facilities and even ATMs are next to nonexistent in this far-flung corner of Korea.

Jagyakdo 작약도
In summer the landscape of this tiny island is decked out with peonies (*jagyak*), thus the island's name. The island is also heavily forested with pines.

Jagyakdo is just 3km north of Wolmido, but you don't get the boat from there. Rather, you must take a ferry from Incheon's Yeon-an Pier. There are eight to 10 sailings per day.

If you'd like to spend the night, there is one yeogwan and 15 bungalows for rent on the island.

Muuido 무의도
This small island is less than 500m off the south-west shore of the airport island of Yongyudo. Hanakge Beach, on the island's west side, is the big attraction and boasts a small resort village. Somewhat small but still nice is Silmi Beach, on the north-west corner of the island. The Incheon municipal government has big plans to develop this into an international resort complete with a golf course, marina, theme park and con-

vention centre. With these improvements – along with the jet aircraft screaming overhead from the new airport – it ought to be quite a peaceful place.

Probably the best place to get a view of the aircraft will be from the summit of **Guksabong** (240m), the island's main peak.

There are two ways to get to the island. The most frequent boats are from Deokgyodong Pier on Yongyudo (south of Eulwangni Beach); there are ferries to Gunmuri Pier on Muuido (a 10-minute journey) with four to eight sailings per day. You can ring up for exact times (☎ 891 0011).

The other alternative is to catch a ferry from Yeon-an Pier in Incheon, which drops you off at Muuido's Saemgumi Pier (a 50-minute journey). Unfortunately there are only two boats a day, though possibly more on summer weekends. These depart Incheon at 9.30 am and 2.30 pm – departures from Muuido are at 10.30 am and 3.30 pm. The boats stop at Somuuido en route. Korean speakers can ring up Won-gwang Shipping Company (☎ 884 3391) for the latest schedule information.

Yeongheungdo 영흥도
Simnipo Beach, at the north-west corner of the island, is 30km from Incheon. The beach has a 4km-long pebbly stretch and a 1km sandy stretch.

Ferries to Yeongheungdo depart Incheon about three times daily. Korean speakers can call Won-gwang Shipping Company (☎ 884 3391) for the current schedule. Ferries to Yeongheungdo (and most other small islands) leave from the Yeon-an Ferry Terminal on the south side of the harbour.

Deokjeokdo 덕적도
This is one of the most scenic islands that can be reached from Incheon, though it's a bit far for a day trip from Seoul. Fortunately, the new high-speed ferries make a one-day excursion possible.

The island is 77km from Incheon, and along it's southern shore is **Seopori Beach**, which is 2km long and is lined with a thick grove of pines. The beach is spectacular, and easily the most popular on the island.

The island has a large number of impressive rock formations, and it's worth climbing the highest peak, Bijobong (292 m) for a view. There are 11 *yeogwan* at Seopori Beach and at least 40 *minbak*. There is an information phone number for minbak (☎ 032-886 7772, 888 0154). There is also a *camping ground* where tent rentals are W1000 to W2000 per night.

The ferries to Deokjeokdo depart from Incheon's Yeon-an Pier. There are two kinds of boats: the fast ferries (W16,700) that make the trip in 50 minutes, or the slow ships (W11,400) that take almost two hours. In summer, the fast ferries sail five to seven times daily, but during winter they make three trips daily. The slow ships only run in summer, three or four times daily.

No matter which boat you take, you will be dropped off at Jinri Pier on Deokjeokdo. From there, it's a 20-minute bus ride to Seopori Beach.

For Korean-language information, try calling the Won-gwang Shipping Company (☎ 884 3391).

Baengnyeongdo 백령도

Far to the north-west of Incheon and within a stone's throw of North Korea is Baengnyeongdo, a scenic island that is attracting an increasing number of tourists. The island is the westernmost point in South Korea and is notable for its remote location and dramatic coastal rock formations. Baengnyeongdo is 12km in length and about 7km wide.

Korean speakers can try contacting the Baengnyeongdo Government Office (☎ 436 0006) for information.

There is a significant military presence on the island, a necessity with North Korea so close. This shouldn't interfere much with your enjoyment of the place – just don't climb over any barbed-wire fences.

A tour around the island by boat is one of those 'must do' activities.

Sagot Beach is one of Baengnyeongdo's unexpected sights. The beach is 3km long and consists of sand packed so hard that people can (and do) drive cars on it. In contrast, some of the other beaches in the area have a surface consisting of pebbles. The Koreans like to walk barefoot on the pebbles or even lie down on them because they believe that the resulting 'acupressure' is good for ones health.

Aside from seafood, the island produces buckwheat, which is used to make Korean buckwheat noodles. Fields of buckwheat flowers blooming in springtime can be a fantastic sight.

Yeogwan, yeoinsuk and minbak are easy to find – you should have some offers upon arrival at the ferry pier. *Hwanghae Yeoinsuk* (☎ 436 0333) is one of the cheapest, at W20,000. Other places to consider are the *Ongjin Yeogwan* (☎ 436 0163) and *Harbour Motel* (☎ 436 0354), at W25,000.

In summer there are seven or eight boats daily between Baengnyeongdo and Incheon (Yeon-an Pier). Some of these boats also stop briefly at Daecheongdo and Socheongdo, two smaller islands further south. Just be sure that you don't get off at the wrong island. The one-way Incheon-Baengnyeongdo journey takes four hours and costs from W30,500 to W43,200, depending on class. For the latest schedule, Koreans speakers can call Jindo Transportation Company (☎ 888 9600).

PANMUNJEOM 판문점

Situated 56km north of Seoul, the 'truce village' of Panmunjeom is the only place in the DMZ where visitors are permitted. This is the village established on the ceasefire line at the end of the Korean War, in 1953. It's in a building here that the interminable 'peace' discussions continue.

There's nowhere else in South Korea where you can get quite so close to North Korea without being arrested or shot, and the tension is palpable. In 1968, the crew of the American warship *USS Pueblo* (kidnapped at sea by the North Koreans 11 months earlier) were allowed to cross to the South here. In 1976, two American servicemen were hacked to death with axes by the North Koreans at Panmunjeom. It was also here that an American soldier peacefully defected to North Korea in 1983, and has never been heard from again. Just a year later, a Russian tourist defected to the South at Panmunjeom, triggering a gun battle that killed three North Koreans and one South Korean soldier.

Panmunjeom was also in the news in mid-1989. It was here that Lim Soo-kyong, a Hanguk University student, and the Reverend Moon Gyu-hyon, a Catholic priest, were finally allowed to return to South Korea, after protracted negotiations, following Lim's visit to the Youth Festival in Pyongyang earlier in the year. Both were promptly arrested, whisked off to Seoul by helicopter and charged with violating the national security laws. Lim, a radical fervently committed to the reunification of Korea, has been made into something of a hero in North Korea.

It's perhaps overrated as a 'tourist attraction', but that doesn't seem to stop the hordes flocking here to gawk at this tense 'truce village', learn the history of the DMZ and come face to face with the stern-looking North Korean soldiers.

Part of the ongoing cold war between North and South is the existence of two civilian villages at Panmunjeom. On the southern side is Daeseong-dong (Great Success Village), but the Americans call it 'Freedom Village'. It isn't terribly free for the villagers, as they must be out of the fields after dark and in their homes with doors locked by 11 pm. By way of compensation, it's a very prosperous agricultural community by South Korean standards – the villagers have plentiful land (though they don't own it), large homes and they are exempt from taxes. On the north side is Gijong-dong, which the Americans call 'Propaganda Village'. It differs from its southern counterpart in that it's uninhabited. However, it would be fair to say that both villages exist mainly for no other purpose than propaganda. On the north side you can clearly see what is claimed to be the largest flagpole and flag in the world.

While you are permitted to take photos and use binoculars, there are a number of restrictions that visitors must adhere to. You must bring your passport; children under 10 years of age are not allowed; and Korean nationals are not allowed unless special permission is obtained (a formidable bureaucratic procedure which takes over a month). You are supposed to 'dress decently', which means no shorts or sandals. Furthermore, civilians are warned:

• Visitors must remain in a group from the beginning to the end of the tour and will follow all instructions issued by their tour guide.
• Any equipment, microphones or flags belonging

The War Underground

A brass plaque in Panmunjeom gives this account of the North Koreans' tunnelling activities:

On 15 November 1974, members of a Republic of Korea Army (ROKA) patrol inside the southern sector of the DMZ spotted vapour rising from the ground. When they began to dig into the ground to investigate, they were fired upon by North Korean snipers. ROKA units secured the site and subsequently uncovered a tunnel dug by the North Koreans which extended 1.2km into the Republic of Korea. On 20 November, two members of a United Nations Command (UNC) investigation team were killed inside the tunnel when dynamite planted by the North Koreans exploded. The briefing hall at Camp Kitty Hawk is named after one of the officers killed, Lieutenant Commander Robert N Ballinger. In March 1975, a second North Korean tunnel was discovered by a UNC tunnel detection team. In September of 1975, a North Korean engineer escaped and provided valuable intelligence concerning the communist tunnelling activities. Acting on the information, a tunnel detection team successfully intercepted a third tunnel in October 1978, less than 2km from Panmunjeom. Today, the North Koreans continue to dig tunnels beneath the DMZ. The UNC and ROKA have fielded tunnel-detection teams which drill around the clock in hope of intercepting these tunnels of aggression.

to the communist side in the MAC (Military Armistice Commission) conference room are not to be touched.

- Do not speak with, make any gesture toward or in any way approach or respond to personnel from the other side.
- Firearms, knives or weapons of any type cannot be taken into the Joint Security Area.

Getting There & Away

Access to Panmunjeom is permitted for tour groups only – this is not a do-it-yourself trip. In all cases, you must have your passport or you won't be allowed to board the bus. Your Korean tour guide will accompany you to Camp Bonifas on the southern side of the DMZ, where your group will eat lunch and have the opportunity to play slot machines (the military must really need the money). You are then given a slide show and briefing by an American soldier, who will then accompany your group on a military bus into the Joint Security Area of Panmunjeom. All things considered, it's a good party.

Not all the tours are the same. Some tours take in a visit to the 'Third Tunnel of Aggression', which the North Koreans dug, presumably to attack the South. The discovery of a fourth tunnel was announced in 1990 – this one large enough to accommodate trucks and tanks. Visiting one of the tunnels is worthwhile and you should make sure it's included in the tour before handing over the cash.

The cheapest tours by far to Panmunjeom are offered by the USO (☎ 795 3028), the US Army's cultural and social centre near the Yongsan base in Seoul. They have at least one tour (usually two) weekly and it costs US$25 or the equivalent in *won*, but doesn't include lunch or a visit to the Third Tunnel of Aggression. However, there are separate USO tours to the tunnels which are worthwhile, and Korean nationals may go on these. Because USO tours are cheap, they tend to be very heavily subscribed and you should book a few weeks in advance.

Commercial tours are available but they're somewhat expensive at W60,000 (though lunch is thrown in for free). Only Korea Travel Bureau (☎ 585 1191) is authorised to bring visitors into the Joint

DMZ National Park?

The Demilitarised Zone (DMZ) separates North and South Korea. It is 4km wide and 248km long, surrounded by tanks and electrified fences, and is virtually sealed off to all human beings. Ironically, this has made it something of an environmental paradise. No other place in the world with a temperate zone climate has been so well preserved. This has been a great boon to wildlife – for example, the DMZ is home to large flocks of Manchurian cranes. Environmentalists hope that the day the two Koreas cease hostilities, the DMZ will be kept as a nature reserve.

Security Area, but their tour excludes visits to the Third Tunnel (though they offer such a separate tour for W48,000). Other agencies which go to the DMZ and the Third Tunnel (but not the Joint Security Area) include:

A-One Travel	☎ 701 0947
Global Tour	☎ 335 0011
Grace Seoul Travel	☎ 332 8946
Hanwha Travel	☎ 757 1232.
Star Travel	☎ 564 1232

For all tours, you're expected to arrive at the pick-up point 20 minutes before departure time.

ODUSAN UNIFICATION OBSERVATORY 오두산통일공원

The Unification Observatory (Tongil Jeonmangdae) at Odusan is as close as most Korean civilians can get to the DMZ. Panmunjeom, north of Seoul, is actually inside the DMZ and can be visited by foreigners, but Koreans are not normally allowed there.

Since the Unification Observatory does offer South Koreans a rare peak at the forbidden North, tourists by the bus load turn up here daily throughout the summer months. It isn't quite the same as going to Panmunjeom – there's little of the palpable tension evident at Panmunjeom's 'Truce Village', since the Unification Observatory isn't actually in the DMZ but a few kilometres away. If you want to see anything at all (such as the UN post, the North Korean post – only just – and the North's propaganda signs) then you have to use the available pay telescopes for viewing. It's essentially a non-event but it's a pleasant day out, there are no dress or age regulations, it's a little cheaper than going to Panmunjeom and the government even lays on a free slide show. There is a shop here selling goods made in North Korea (goods which the average North Korean cannot buy).

Admission to the Unification Observatory (☎ 945 3171) is W1500 for adults and W1000 for students and seniors. It's open from 9 am to 7.30 pm in summer, or until 6 pm in winter.

Getting There & Away From Seoul's Seobu bus terminal in Bulgwang-dong, take a bus to Geumchon (buses to Munsan stop in Geumchon). These buses run every 40 minutes and the ride takes 50 minutes. Or from Seoul station, take a train to Geumchon – these depart hourly and take one hour. From Geumchon bus station, take a local bus to the Unification Observatory (these buses are marked Songdong-ri). The local buses depart once every 40 minutes and take half an hour.

GANGHWADO 강화도

Technically part of the Incheon municipality, Ganghwado is a large rural island which has played a significant part in Korean history. It's where the Goryeo court took refuge during the Mongol invasions of the 13th century (see the History section in the Facts about Korea chapter), and where the Koreans resisted American and French troops in the late-19th century.

Being an island fortress, Ganghwado has seen its fair share of fortifications, palaces and the like, but it's overrated as a tourist attraction. The tourist literature and some guide books to Korea rave on about Ganghwado's attractions giving you the impression that the island is littered with fascinating ruins and relics. To a degree it is, but you have to be a real ruins and relics enthusiast to make the effort. However, the island is worth visiting for different reasons – there are some good hikes with beautiful views, plus the opportunity to take a few short ferry journeys. Ganghwado is a laid-back rural place, and if you're looking to get away from the madness of Seoul, the island will do nicely.

Ganghwa-eup 강화읍

The main town on the island, Ganghwa-eup is the gateway to the island. Despite the hype, the city is uninspiring, though it is worth taking a quick look around to appreciate its historic significance.

Ganghwa-eup got its start as a fortress in 1231, when the Mongols invaded Korea and the Goryeo king fled here to take refuge. By 1270 the threat had abated – the royal family abandoned Ganghwa-eup and the fortress fell into disrepair. It was thoroughly rebuilt in the early 1600s, in anticipation of an invasion from Manchu dynasty China. In 1636, Manchu troops destroyed the fortress and blew up the city gates. The fortress was rebuilt for the second time, but Admiral Roze's French Asiatic squadron – which came to Korea to retaliate for the killing of nine French Catholic missionaries – burnt the fortress in 1866.

Today, only fragments of the original structures remain. The Koreans are slowly rebuilding the fortress once again, though this time more in the interests of promoting tourism rather than resisting a foreign invasion. Unfortunately, the restoration efforts are proceeding slowly and it will be many years before the project is finished.

Perhaps the best sights at the moment are the three city gates (a fourth, destroyed, gate is yet to be rebuilt). Similarly, the city's enclosing wall has mostly disappeared, but there are plans to reconstruct it.

The site of the Goryeo castle, where the king lived, has a couple of traditional buildings of slight interest. Again, not much is left of the original structure, and if your time is limited you can skip it without feeling a traumatic sense of loss.

Other than that, there is a seowon (Confucian school), two mineral springs (whose waters are said to have healing power) and, of more practical interest, a good farmers' market.

On the south side of town is a big traditional 'five-day market', which is indeed worth visiting. But it only functions on the 2nd, 7th, 12th, 17th, 22nd and 27th day of each month. The market is open during daylight hours only, starting from around 8 am.

On your way back to Seoul, it might be worth dropping by the Ginseng Center (Ganghwado claims to produce South Korea's best ginseng). Aside from ginseng, this is the place to buy a *hwamunseok*, a large rush mat with beautiful floral patterns. This is a Ganghwado speciality and makes a functional souvenir if you don't mind lugging it home.

Places to Stay There are a number of yeogwan in the centre. Probably the easiest to find is the *Keumho-jang Yeogwan* (just opposite the Ganghwa county office) where rooms are W25,000.

The *Namsan Youth Hostel* (☎ 934 7777) has pleasant surroundings, mainly because it's not right in the centre of Ganghwa-eup. From the bus terminal, it's about a 20-minute walk to the south-west. Dorm beds are W10,000 and private rooms cost W35,000.

Getting There & Away Buses to Ganghwa-eup leave from the Sinchon bus terminal in the western part of Seoul. Buses leave every 10 minutes from 5.40 am to 9.40 pm, take one hour and cost W3300.

Gwangseongbo 광성보
This fortress, on the south-eastern part of the island, was built in 1658 to defend against invaders intending to sail up the river towards Seoul.

In October 1866, Korean defenders fought fiercely against Admiral Roze's French Asiatic squadron.

In 1871, an American fleet sailed into Korea hoping to open the country to foreign commerce. Then, as now, the Koreans weren't keen on free trade and a ferocious battle ensued at Gwangseongbo. The US marines eventually managed to take this fort and a few others, but they eventually withdrew from the island and their mission was considered a failure.

Admission to Gwangseongbo costs W2700.

Manisan 마니산
At the south-west tip of the island is Manisan (469m), 14km from Ganghwa-eup. On the summit is a 5m-tall altar called **Chamseongdan**. This is dedicated to Dan-gun, the mythical first Korean, born in 2333 BC.

It's a 3km walk one-way from the bus stop to the summit. The climb takes about one hour for the ascent and about 40 minutes for the descent. The concrete path with stone steps is easy enough to follow, but many people descend by a separate route which takes them past Jeongsusa.

The entrance gate to the mountain (where you pay W1000 admission) is 500m east of the bus stop in Hwado-myeon. Buses between Hwado-myeon and Ganghwa-eup run every 20 minutes from 6.45 am to 8.50 pm and cost W1100. The journey takes 40 minutes.

Jeondeungsa 전등사
This is one of the oldest temples in Korea, having originally been constructed in the 4th century. Needless to say, there have been numerous reconstructions and renovations since then.

The temple also has great historical significance, mainly because it was here that the second set of the Tripitaka Koreana was carved. The Tripitaka Koreana consists of 81,258 wooden blocks which spell out the Buddhist sutras (see the boxed text in the Gyeongsangbuk-do chapter). The blocks were carved at Jeondeungsa in the 13th century, but were later moved to Haeinsa Temple near the city of Daegu, in Gyeongsangbuk-do. Only 120 of the blocks still remain at Jeondeungsa.

The temple is found within a larger complex, Samnangseong (admission W1500).

The fortress is 1km south of Onsu-ri. Buses between Onsu-ri and Ganghwa-eup run every 20 minutes from 6.30 am to 8.40 pm, cost W900 and take 25 minutes for the journey.

Oepo-ri 외포리

The village of Oepo-ri, on the western side of the island, is the launchpad to Songmodo and other obscure islands in the Yellow Sea. Oepo-ri has a much more rural and relaxing feel to it than Ganghwa-eup, and you should consider spending the night here if you want to explore Ganghwado as more than just a day trip.

Getting There & Away Take a bus from Ganghwa-eup bus terminal. These depart every 20 minutes from 7.15 am to 6.40 pm, cost W900 and the ride takes 20 minutes.

Places to Stay At the bottom end is the *Kanghwa Youth Hostel (☎ 933 8891).* This small hostel has only 32 beds and charges W7000 for a dorm bed, or W40,000 for a 'family room'. There is an on-site restaurant, though you hardly need to limit yourself to eating there.

Sohae Shimto (☎ 933 4056) is a pleasant yeogwan two minute's walk from the ferry pier. Double rooms cost W25,000.

Kanghwa Haesu Oncheon-jang (☎ 933 1479) boasts 'seawater hot springs'. Both Western-style and Korean-style rooms are available for W30,000.

The *Santaruchia Hotel (☎ 933 2141)* is the top-end place in town but is still very reasonable, with rooms priced from W30,000 to W35,000.

Bomunsa 보문사

This important temple sits high up in the mountains on the island of Songmodo off the western coast of Ganghwado. The compound is relatively small but there is some superb and very ornate painting on the eaves of the various buildings, especially those of the bell pavilion. The famous grotto here is quite plain and uninteresting, though it is a cool place to be on a hot summer's day. One of the most interesting sights here is the 10m-high **rock carving** of Gwaneum Bosal, the Goddess of Mercy, which stands below a granite overhang high above the temple compound.

It's a steep walk up to the temple from where the bus drops you and there's a small tourist village with souvenir shops and restaurants at the bottom of the hill.

The bus from Ganghwa-eup to Oepo-ri will probably drop you off at a ferry terminal. However, this terminal caters only for long-distance ferries and is not the one you want. Walk through to the front of the terminal, turn right and continue down the waterfront for about 100m. You'll see a concrete ramp going down to the water and another ferry terminal on the right. From here ferries run daily to Seokmo-ri on Songmodo approximately every hour from 7 am to 7 pm and they take both people and vehicles. It takes 10 minutes to cross the straits. On the opposite side there are buses to Bomunsa which take about half an hour. In order to take the ferry, you must fill out a silly form in which you state your name and passport number – the reasoning is that Ganghwado is close to North Korea. Keep your passport on hand in case anybody wearing a (South Korean) uniform wants to check it.

SONGTAN 송탄

To the south of Suwon and along the main rail line is the town of Songtan. Songtan's main claim to fame is that it's outside the enormous Osan US Air Force base.

In the not-too-distant past when South Korea was poor, Songtan had a notorious reputation as a red-light district. However, times change – Korea has become wealthy and the brothels have shut down, though many Koreans still believe (mistakenly) that Songtan is a den of iniquity. Perhaps this is why the Korean government decided to wipe Songtan from the map – officially it's now part of Pyeongtaek, a municipality 10km to the south.

Although the vice has mostly vanished, there is still a very active nightlife scene in Songtan. Many Koreans (male and female) come here to party along with the US military personnel. Expat civilian party animals come down on Friday and Saturday too. Songtan is also a better place for shopping than Itaewon.

In the confines of about a six block square area there are about 25 to 30 expat bars, reputed to be the least expensive in Korea. On the main street outside the base is the **Golden Gate**, **Dragon Lodge**, **Eagle Club** and **Stereo Club**. On several side streets radiating off from the main road there are many others including *Juliana's*, *Phoenix*, *Youn Chun* and the *UN Club*. Aragon Alley has a number of respectable bars that periodically have live music on weekends.

Getting There & Away

Songtan is on the main rail line and has a station, but passenger trains no longer stop there. You have to take a train to Pyeongtaek (45 minutes from Seoul or 15 minutes from Suwon), then bus No 1 or 1-1 which stop just outside the Osan base main gate.

Even more convenient is to catch a bus from Seoul's nambu terminal (on subway line No 3). Buy a ticket to Songtan, not Pyeongtaek. From the Songtan bus station, walk on the street up the hill (west) from the bus station, proceed on the bridge across the train tracks until the road ends (about 400m of walking). The main gate of Osan and the bars are immediately to the right.

SKI RESORTS 스키장

For half a day of skiing, prices for equipment hire are typically W22,000 and lift tickets are W26,000. For a full day, equipment hire costs W26,000 and lift tickets are W38,000. All ski resorts have a representative office in Seoul. The five ski resorts in Gyeonggi-do are as follows:

Seoul Ski Resort (☎ 02-959 0864, 0346-591 1230) Season: 10 December to late February. Three slopes (beginner, intermediate, advanced), a sledding hill and three lifts. Accommodation: one hotel (66 rooms). The resort is 40 minutes east of Seoul at Baekbongsan, Namyangju-gun. From Seoul's Cheongnyangni station on subway line No 1 (exit No 2) take city bus No 165, 165-1, 330, 765 or 1330 (30 minutes).

Bear's Town Resort (☎ 02-594 8188, 0357-532 2534) Season: late November to early March. During summer, Bear's Town is a golf resort.

There are 11 slopes (three beginner, five intermediate and three advanced), two sledding hills and nine lifts. Accommodation includes one youth hostel (48 rooms) and condominiums (533 rooms). The condominiums boast a heated indoor swimming pool, sauna, bowling alley, game room and tennis courts. There are ski lessons for foreigners (English-speaking instructor) from 10 am to noon and from 2 to 4 pm. Night skiing is available. The resort is 40 minutes north-east of Seoul in Pochon-gun. From Seoul, take a bus to Gwangreung or Ildong departing from Sangbong bus terminal. Travel agencies in Seoul offering shuttle buses (for W11,000, round-trip) include Lotte (☎ 733 0201), Ojin (☎ 739 1211), Smile (☎ 730 5111) and Seil (☎ 739 1261). The USO runs inexpensive weekend trips and sells tickets for the shuttle buses.

Yangji Pine Ski Resort (☎ 02-542 8700, 0335-338 2001) Season: December 10 to late February. Seven slopes (one beginner, four intermediate, two advanced), one sledding hill and six lifts. Accommodation includes the *Pine Villa Hotel* (60 rooms) and *Pine Resortel Condominium* (302 rooms) – the latter has a heated swimming pool and bowling alley. The resort is at the town of Yong-in, near the Korean Folk Village, 50 minutes south-east of Seoul. From Seoul's nambu bus terminal, take a bus to Yangji (40 minutes) and then a free shuttle bus (five minutes) to the resort. Travel agencies offering shuttle buses from Seoul (W11,000, round-trip) include Kumho Express (☎ 730 8811), Seoul (☎ 564 1311) and Seil (☎ 739 1261).

Chonmasan Ski Resort (☎ 02-2233 5311, 0346-594 1211) Season: 9 December to early March. Five slopes (one beginner, two intermediate, two advanced) and seven lifts. Ski lessons for foreigners are twice daily from 10 am to noon and from 2 to 4 pm. Accommodation: one hotel (40 rooms) with a heated swimming pool. It's 50 minutes north-east of Seoul, close to Namyangju. From Seoul's Cheongnyangni station on subway line 1 (exit No 2), take bus No 30, 330 or 765-1 to Mukyeon-ri – then it's a 10-minute walk to the resort.

Jisan Forest Ski Resort (☎ 02-3442 0322, 0336-638 8460) Nine slopes (two beginner, four intermediate, three advanced), snow boarding and four lifts. Ski lessons for foreigners three times daily. It's at Icheon, 50 minutes south-east of Seoul. For accommodation, see the Icheon Hot Springs section. From Seoul take a bus from the Dong Seoul bus terminal to Icheon (50 minutes), then city bus No 12 (20 minutes) to the resort. Travel agencies offering shuttle buses include Ojin (☎ 739 1211) and Sang-il (☎ 2215 0707).

Gangwon-do

☎ 033 • pop 1.6 million

The north-east province of Gangwon-do is one of the least populated, most mountainous and scenic in South Korea. Historically, the province has been isolated due to its rugged terrain, and during the Korean War it was the site of many fierce battles for strategic mountain tops. After the war, the area's rich natural resources, including coal and timber, were developed, bringing roads, rail and harbour connections. With the closure of many of the mines during the 1990s, the province was forced to create alternative employment opportunities. Tourism was the solution.

Outdoor activities reign supreme here, with spectacular mountain and valley hiking, swimming at beautiful white-sand beaches, down-hill and cross-country skiing, white-water rafting, and plenty of peaceful fishing spots, all of which are reasonably accessible.

Public transport is not too bad, but having your own car or bike would make travelling more scenic and convenient. In fact, outside of summer the roads are probably the quietest in the country. Many of the most beautiful parts of the province are found in obscure valleys with dramatic gorges, raging rivers and dense forests.

CHUNCHEON 춘천
pop 250,000

Chuncheon is the provincial capital of Gangwon-do and the urban centre of Korea's northern lake district, which includes the lakes of Chuncheonho, Uiamho, Soyangho and Paroho. It's a very beautiful mountainous area and one of the principal attractions here is the boat trips on the lakes. The town itself is fairly pleasant and is a major educational centre.

A visit to Chuncheon makes a good stopover en route to Seoraksan National Park, especially if you'd prefer the boat and bus combination to taking a bus all the way.

Orientation & Information

Nam (South) Chuncheon train station is the main station, but it's a long way from the centre and the bus terminal. There is a large tourist information centre next to the Folk Museum, which is near the express bus terminal. A smaller office is near the lake, Uiamho.

Jungdo 중도

There are ferries that run out to the recreational island, Jungdo, from a small jetty

GANGWON-DO

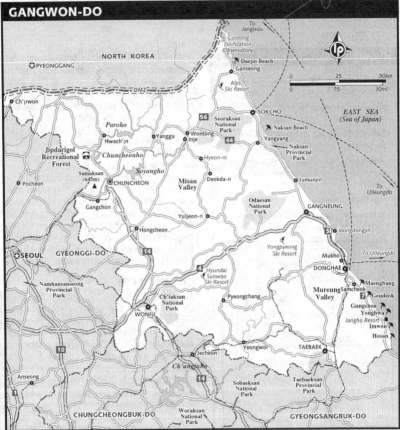

near Chuncheon Bears Hotel. The island is a popular weekend picnic and recreational retreat for locals who come here to eat, rest and play. Boating, cycling, swimming, windsurfing and other activities are available.

You can overnight on Jungdo. See the Places to Stay entry for more information.

To get to the ferry jetty, catch either bus No 65 or 74. Entry is W2700 and a return boat ticket costs W1800.

Samaksan 삼악산

For a panoramic view of Chuncheon and Uiamho, you can make the steep climb up

to the peak Samaksan (654m, 1¼ hours). The hike will take you past the temple **Sangwonsa**. After walking 20 minutes down the other side of the peak, you pass another temple, **Heungguksa**, and enter a beautiful, narrow gorge. Follow it down to **Deungseonpokpo** (50 minutes), a humble waterfall. From Deungseonpokpo it's just 10 minutes to the road from where you can catch a local bus (any will do) back upstream to Chuncheon. Entry to the park costs W1600.

Bus No 81 or 82 stops on the other side of Uiam Dam for access to Sangwonsa.

Places to Stay

If you feel inclined to stay on the island, Jungdo, *camping* and *minbak* are the primary lodging facilities. Make arrangements on the island.

There are plenty of options around the inter-city bus terminal in Chuncheon, including some yeogwan. Try *Dajeong Yeoinsuk* (☎ 254 2528), where rooms cost W10,000. *Taewon-jang* (☎ 254 4244) has good rooms for W30,000. Nearby is *Nobel-jang* (☎ 242 0942), where doubles are W25,000.

Close to the city centre, try *Hill House* (☎ 241 0331) or the nearby *Grand Motel* (☎ 243 5021), which both have decent rooms for W25,000. The *Chuncheon Tourist Hotel* (☎ 255 3300, fax 255 3372) has decent mid-range rooms from W46,200, or W61,600 on weekends

Chuncheon Bears Hotel (☎ 256 2525, fax 256 2530) looks out over Uiamho. It has doubles from W72,600 and *ondol* rooms, with heated floors, from W96,800. Rates at this hotel are reduced by 20% on weekdays and another 30% with phone bookings.

Places to Eat

Chuncheon is famous for *dakgalbi*, or spicy barbecue chicken. To try this delicious meal head to *Dakgalbi-geori*, a food street in the centre of town, where there are restaurants upon restaurants dishing the stuff up. You will need a minimum of two mouths and it's a good idea to order rice or noodles to mop up the leftover sauce.

Hajugol (☎ 256 7963) serves a very tasty set meal, *hanjeongsik,* for W9000 and is worth the extra effort required to get to it. Catch bus No 91 to Mancheonno. The restaurant is close to the local *(sinae)* bus terminal.

Osumul Makguksu (☎ 242 4714) is a friendly family restaurant, famous in Chuncheon for serving up a tasty bowl of *makguksu* (buckwheat noodles; W3000). It also serves up a tasty *bossam* (pork wrapped in lettuce, with a special radish gimchi; W15,000) and *dotorimuk* (acorn bean jelly; W5000). This eatery is a little off the beaten track in Sinjeon-eup, half way to Soyangho. Bus No 17 passes the restaurant, just ask the driver to let you off there.

Getting There & Away

Bus Departures from the express bus terminal include:

destination	price (W)	duration	distance
Daegu	13,900	5½ hrs	378km
Gwangju	14,700	5½ hrs	401km

From the inter-city bus terminal:

destination	price (W)	duration	distance
Cheongju	12,100	3¾ hrs	223km
Daegu	19,900	5¾ hrs	390km
Dong Seoul	5400	1¾ hrs	86km
Gangneung	11,300	4 hrs	190km
Seoul Sangbong	5200	1½ hrs	82km
Sokcho	10,900	3¾ hrs	160km
Wonju	48 00	1¾ hrs	104km

Train Trains to Chuncheon depart from Seoul's Cheongnyangni station (W4100, two hours, hourly) at the terminus of subway line No 1. Unfortunately, Chuncheon's two train stations in town are both equally far from the bus terminal, so you'll need to deal with the city buses, take a taxi or walk about 1.5km.

Getting Around

Bikes can be hired near the Uiamho tourist information office and anywhere near the boat wharves on the lake.

AROUND CHUNCHEON 춘천
Gangchon 강촌

Gangchon is a popular resort, well known by Koreans for the 'membership training' that takes place here among university students. This training is an important part of academic life for Korean students, who get together and head off to the hills and have a good time. Due to the popularity of Gangchon and the nearby waterfall, **Gugokpokpo**, there are plenty of **bicycles** for hire, *bars* and *yeogwan*. Despite the large numbers of youth, it makes for a pleasant day trip from Chuncheon, or even Seoul, with its beautiful mix of forests, mountains, rivers and hiking trails.

There are two main **hikes**. The first one to the peak, Bonghwasan (478m), goes via Gugokpokpo and the village of Bunbae-maeul

GANGWON-DO

CHUNCHEON

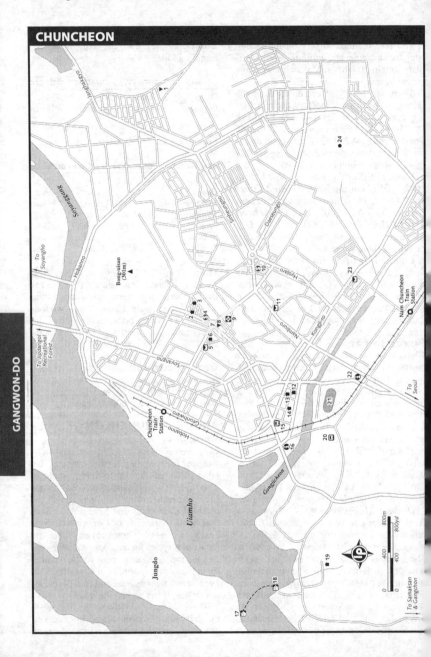

CHUNCHEON

PLACES TO STAY
2 Hill House
   힐하우스모텔
3 Grand Motel
   그랜드모텔
6 Chuncheon Tourist
   Hotel
   춘천관광호텔
12 Dajeong Yeoinsuk
   다정여인숙
13 Noble-jang
   노벨장
14 Daewon-jang
   대원장
19 Chuncheon Bears
   Hotel
   춘천베어스타운
   관광호텔

PLACES TO EAT
1 Hajugol
   하주골

8 Dakgalbi-geori
   닭갈비거리

OTHER
4 Jeil Bank
   제일은행
5 Post Office
   우체국
7 Underground Arcade
   지하상가
9 Midopa Department
   Store
   미도파백화점
10 Korea Exchange Bank
   외환은행
11 Post Office
   춘천우체국
15 Inter-City Bus
   Terminal
   시외버스터미널
16 Tourist Information
   Centre
   관광안내소

17 Jungdo Pier
   중도선착장
18 Jungdo Ferry
   Pier
   중도선착장
20 Express Bus
   Terminal
   고속버스터미널
21 Sports Complex
   종합운동장
22 Tourist Information
   Centre & Folk
   Museum
   민속박물관,
   관광안내센터
23 Post Office
   우체국
24 Gangwon
   University
   강원대학교

(two hours). The second path passes by Gu-gokpokpo, Bunbae-maeul, Geombongsan and continues down to the temple **Gangseonsa** (3½ hours). Both paths start from the far end of the car park. Entrance to the waterfall costs W1600.

The best way to get to Gangchon is to catch bus Nos 50, 51, 56, 57 or 55 (W600, 20 minutes, hourly) from opposite the inter-city bus terminal in Chuncheon. It's a 15-minute walk to the waterfall from the bus drop-off point.

Every train running between Seoul's Cheongnyangni station and Chuncheon stops at Gangchon, from where you can hire a bike and ride up to the falls along the bike path.

Soyhangho 소양호

This huge artificial lake north of Chuncheon is Korea's largest and was the largest dam in Asia when it was built in 1973. Ferries tour the lake and also head over to the temple **Cheongpyeongsa** (W1500, 15 minutes, every 30 minutes), where you can make an assault on the peak **Obongsan**.

Sightseeing boats run for most of the year around the lake (W5000, one hour, on demand). From December to March, however, the part of the lake near Junchyekgyo

bridge and Bupyong-ri is completely frozen and you can see people ice fishing here. For those looking for a more challenging and scenic route to the east coast and Seoraksan pier, an interesting option is to catch a ferry to Yanggu pier (W4400, one hour, hourly), from where you can catch a local bus into Yanggu (13km). Then catch an inter-city bus to Sokcho (W7600, three hours, 123km, hourly). If you want to visit the temple Baekdamsa in Seoraksan National Park, or Sibiseon-nyeotang Valley, just ask the bus driver to let you off there.

Ferries for Yanggu pier leave from Soyang Dam wall. To get there from Chuncheon you must take bus No 11 or 13, which runs up Soyangno, in the city centre (W600/950, 25 minutes, every 10 minutes). The bus will drop you at the top of the dam wall and it's then a short walk down to the ferry piers.

Jipdarigol Recreational Forest
집다리골자연휴양림

This peaceful forest 23km north-west of Chuncheon is a great place to escape from the city. A variety of accommodation options are available, including *camping* (W2000 to W3000), basic *log cabins*

GANGWON-DO

Yeongwol Dam Conflict

In 1996, the Korean government proposed to build a 98m-high dam wall across the Donggang, an upper tributary of the Namhangang in Gangwondo's Yeongwol county. The dam was proposed as a result of the destructive floods that swept through Danyang, Yeongwol and even Seoul in 1990. It was planned to control flooding and also generate electricity. However, it became one of the most controversial environmental issues of the last decade.

The proposed construction of the dam caused a gradual swelling of opposition over four years and a number of new alliances were forged to oppose it. From timid local-resident protests, the movement eventually involved a coalition of Korean environmental NGOs, several international NGOs, the media, local politicians and a groundswell of concerned people from across the country. Arguments opposed to the dam included technical questioning of structure, safety and necessity, social questioning of base democratic values, and environmental questioning of the impact to the river's environment.

Throughout most of the campaign, President Kim Dae-jung sided with the Ministry of Construction, which was the main backer of the dam. However, as the coalition of opponents to the dam increased and the media began to support the dam opposition, the president started to waver – reflecting the internal conflicts, the varying levels of government and the strength of the opponents' campaign. Eventually, an international inquiry was carried out, which concluded that the dam should not be built.

In June 2000, Kim Dae-jung announced the cancellation of the dam project and the protection of the river's flora and fauna. This decision has been marked as a turning point for the country's environmental movement and for increasing the awareness of environmental values among Korea's general public. On a grander scale, some believe the issue resulted in a maturing of Korea's democracy.

(W20,000) and well equipped and comfortable *apartments* (W120,000). In addition to the nearby streams, waterfalls and thick forests, there are a couple of **hiking trails** up into the surrounding mountains. If you don't feel like cooking there are even a couple of *restaurants* and shops nearby.

Transport is a problem as most people drive here, but it's also possible to catch bus No 38 (1½ hours) from Chuncheon. The forest's facilities are only open from 1 May to 30 November. For information call the park authority (☎ 243 1442/3).

BANGTAESAN NATURE FOREST
방태산자연휴양림

This beautiful valley is most easily reached by car, but it is also possible to catch a local bus from Hyeon-ni to either Bangdong-ri or Jindong-ri (W570, 10 minutes, every 1½ hours) and then hike the last 2.5km from the turnoff at the bridge in Bangdong-ri.

Log cabins (W50,000 and W60,000) and *camping* (W3000) are available and there are two walks into hills above the valley.

Bookings can be made on ☎ 743 8066. Entry to the forest costs W1000.

MISAN VALLEY (HWY 31) 미산계곡
The road from Inje to the hamlet of Yujeon-ri follows the Naerincheon, a beautiful meandering river. For most of the year it is a pleasant flowing river, but in summer it is transformed into a raging torrent that is a great place to ride the cascades and rapids with some **white water rafting**. There are a couple of outfits along the river that cater to this activity. In Hyeon-ni, it costs about W20,000 per person (eight people per raft). Just ask around, as there are dozens of small outfits catering to this growing sport, or contact the Korea National Tourist Organization (KNTO).

For the less adventurous the river is an ideal route for a **bike ride**. The road is relatively quiet and wide enough for a pleasant pedal.

Buses connect Hyeon-ni with Inje (W3100, every 1½ hours), Hongcheon (W4700, four daily) and Seoul (W10,700, every 1½ hours).

SOKCHO 속초
pop 89,000

Sokcho is a sprawling town north-east of Seoraksan National Park almost entirely surrounding a lagoon that has a narrow outlet to the sea. Fishing used to be the major industry, but tourism has proved far more lucrative and is now the No 1 cash cow. The town is a useful base for exploring Seoraksan and has a couple of attraction. For a good vista of Sokcho's harbour, wander around past all the seafood restaurants and up the steep staircase to the **lighthouse** at the end of Jungsimno Point.

The express bus terminal is 5km farther south, and you may actually find it more convenient to stay in this area as it's closer to Seoraksan and the beaches – the downside is that it's pricier. Yeogwan are everywhere in Sokcho, and there is an abundance of places to eat. For Koreans, the seafood restaurants are a major draw card.

Places to Stay

The heavy volume of tourist traffic tends to keep accommodation pricey, though the tariff drops in the winter season. Room rates go up 50% throughout Sokcho during summer.

Most of the cheap yeoinsuk are clustered around the inter-city bus terminal in the centre of town. Expect to pay around W15,000. *Seoul-jang Yeogwan* is clean and friendly, despite its wan facade. It charges W25,000. *Daerim-jang Yeogwan* (☎ 633 3685) is good value and friendly, with ondol rooms for W20,000 and doubles for W25,000. *Guwol Park* (☎ 636 3640) is opposite the bus terminal and has good rooms for W30,000. The new *Daebo-jang* (☎ 637 2789) is also nearby, and has good rooms with tables, air-con and fridge for W30,000.

The area near the express bus terminal has accommodation convenient to the beaches. *Duk Won Motel* (☎ 635 6481) has rooms for W30,000 to W40,000. Just opposite is *Motel Royal Beach* (☎ 633 5599), with more overpriced rooms from W35,000. If you'd really like to throw your cash around, *Rocustel* (☎ 633 4959) has rooms for W40,000 and W50,000.

Places to Eat

Subinine Sundubu is just off the main road and has some outdoor tables. It serves a bit of everything, but specialises in tofu. Try *sogogi dubu dwenjang jeongol* (tofu beef hot pot) or *haemul dubu dwenjang jeongol* (tofu seafood hot pot).

Beach Hoejip is in the middle of **Dongmyeong raw fish market** and serves up *modeumhoe* (a large platter of mixed raw fish) from W50,000 to W70,000. It is possible to order a smaller serving if you're travelling solo or in a pair.

You can get a good bowl of *naengmyeon* (cold buckwheat noodles; W5000) at either *Hanyang Myeonok* or *Ijo Myeonok*, which are next to each other near the express bus terminal. These eateries are pretty busy on the weekend, so you might have to wait for a table.

Getting There & Away

Air Korean Air is the only carrier flying Sokcho to Seoul (W38,500, three times daily). Yangyang airport will replace Sokcho airport in 2002. Contact KNTO for details on transport arrangements.

Bus Buses from the express bus terminal connect Seoul and Dong Seoul (W11,700, 4½ hours, 302km, every ¾ hour).

Departures from Sokcho's inter-city bus terminal include:

destination	price (W)	duration	distance
Busan	26,300	7½ hrs	431km
Chuncheon	10,900	3¾ hrs	174km
Gangneung	4600	1½ hrs	73km
Seoul Sangbong	13,700	4¾ hrs	240km

All the buses listed here can also be picked up at Yangyang, south of Naksan.

Local buses to Seorak-dong and Naksan also start from the inter-city bus terminal, but you can easily pick them up anywhere along their route, including outside the express bus terminal.

Boat Depending on demand, there are boats to Ulleungdo from Sokcho during the

GANGWON-DO

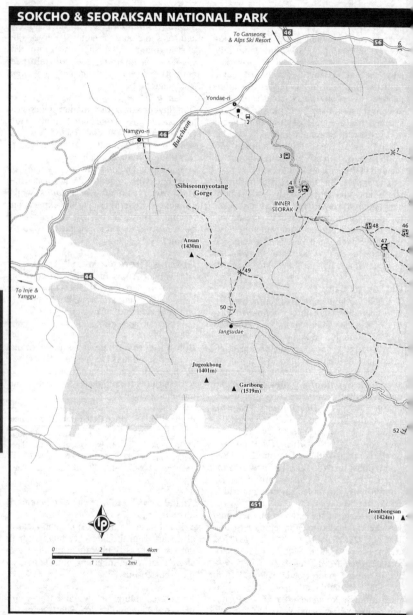

SOKCHO & SEORAKSAN NATIONAL PARK

SOKCHO & SEORAKSAN NATIONAL PARK

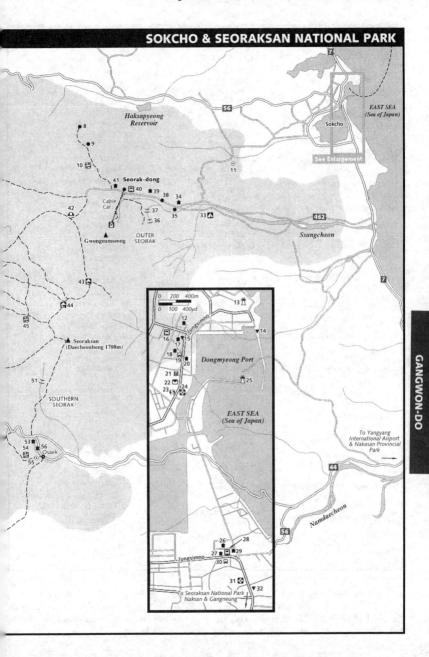

EAST SEA
(Sea of Japan)

Sokcho

See Enlargement

Haksapyeong
Reservoir

8

9

10

41 Seorak-dong
40

39
38 34

42

37
36

35

33

Cable
Car

Gwongeumseong

OUTER
SEORAK

Ssangcheon

462

7

43

44

45

Seoraksan
(Daecheonbong 1708m)

0   200   400m
0   100   400yd

Jungsimno

13

14

12

16
15

17

18

19
20

Dongmyeong Port

21
22
24
23

25

EAST SEA
(Sea of Japan)

51

SOUTHERN
SEORAK

53
54 56
55 Osaek

To Yangyang
International Airport
& Nakasan Provincial
Park

44

Namdaecheon

56

26   28

27 29

Jungsimno   30

31   32

To Seoraksan National Park
Naksan & Gangneung

GANGWON-DO

SOKCHO & SEOROKSAN NATIONAL PARK

PLACES TO STAY
1 Posijeun
포시즌
5 Baekdam Shelter
백담산장
12 Guwol Park
구월파크
17 Daerim-jang Yeogwan
대림장여관
18 Seoul-jangYeogwan
서울장여관
20 Daebo-jang
대보장
26 Duk Won Motel
덕원모텔
27 Motel Royal Beach
모텔로얄비치
29 Rocustel
로커스텔
33 Camping Ground
야영장
34 Garden Motel;
Bandalgom Sanjang;
Seorak Crystal Hotel;
Tulip Sanjang
가든모텔；반달곰산장；
크리스탈호텔；
튜울립산장
39 Kensington Hotel
켄싱턴호텔
41 Seorak Tourist Hotel
설악관광호텔
43 Yangbuk Hut
양북대피소
44 Huiungak Shelter
희운각대피소
47 Suryeomdong Shelter
수렴동대피소
53 Osaek Green Yard Hotel
오색그린야드호텔
56 Hyundai, Winners &
Hotel Seorak Oncheon-
jang
현대，위너스，
호텔설악온천장

PLACES TO EAT
14 Beach Hoejip
비치횟집
32 Hanyang Myeonok;
Ijo Myeonok
한양면옥；이조면옥
15 Subinine Sundubu
수빈이네순두부

OTHER
2 Shuttle Bus &
Car Park
셔틀버스，주차장
3 Shuttle Bus
셔틀버스
4 Baekdamsa
백담사
6 Misiryeong Pass
미시령
7 Jeohangnyeong Pass
저항령
8 Ulsanbawi
울산바위
9 Tottering Rock
흔들바위
10 Naewonam
Hermitage
내원암
11 Cheoksan Hot Springs
척산온천
13 Lighthouse
등대전망대
16 Sokcho Inter-City Bus
Terminal
시외버스터미널
19 Bus Stop
버스정류장
21 City Hall
속초시청
22 Post Office
우체국
23 Hanvit Bank
한빛은행
24 Supermarket
수퍼마켓
25 Lighthouse
등대전망대
28 Sokcho Express Bus
Terminal
고속버스터미널
30 Bus Stop
버스정류장
31 Supermarket
수퍼마켓
35 Park Office
공원사무소
36 Biryongpokpo
비룡폭포
37 Yukdampokpo
육담폭포
38 Park Entrance
공원입구
40 Seorak-dong Bus
Terminal
버스터미널
42 Geumganggul (Cave)
금강굴
45 Bongjeong-am
Hermitage
봉정암
46 Oseam Hermitage
오세암
48 Yeongseoam
Hermitage
영서암
49 Daeseungnyeong (Pass)
대승령
50 Daeseungpokpo
대승폭포
51 Seorakpokpo
설악폭포
52 Sibipokpo
십이폭포
54 Seongguksa
성국사
55 Osaek Mineral Water
오색약수

summer months. The timetable for departures varies. Contact the Sokcho passenger terminal (☎ 636-2811). Alternatively, advance bookings and news about cancelled ferries can be obtained in Seoul (☎ 514 6766) or check with KNTO for details. Some travel agents also make reservations and sell tickets.

Getting Around
To/From The Airport Two buses run out to the airport, though bus No 5 is irregular and for bus No 9, you'll need to walk about 800m to the terminal. A taxi costs between W7000 and W10,000.

NORTH OF SOKCHO
Beaches 해수욕장
There are a number of sheltered sandy coves and beaches north of Sokcho and they're far less crowded than those to the south, though you're only allowed onto them at certain points and only at certain times of year. In the low season that endless razor wire fence that stretches along the whole of the eastern coast of Korea, separating North from South, is firmly sealed and you'll be arrested (or, worse, shot at) if you venture onto the beaches.

The best of the coves are to be found at **Daejin**, **NOM** north of Ganseong. Daejin is a small fishing village that also doubles as a laid-back resort during the summer months. You can rent a room at a *minbak*, plus there are a few, relatively cheap *yeogwan* with the usual facilities. The nearest sandy beach to Daejin is **Geojin Beach**. It can be reached by bus from Sokcho via Ganseong (W2700, 1¼ hours, 43km, every ½ hour).

Goseong Unification Observatory
통일전망대

On Korea's west coast there is a Unification Observatory (at Odusan, near Panmunjeom). Now the east coast has one too. If you've already seen Panmunjeom, then don't be afraid to give this place a miss.

The **Unification Hall** is to your left as you enter the complex surrounded by a sort of tourist village, with souvenir shops (there are plenty of Korean flags on sale), restaurants and the like, and a vast car park. Binoculars are available for voyeurs wanting a closer look at the forbidden North. As long as war doesn't break out, it's a good party. Entry is W2000.

Catch bus No 1 (W3700, 1½ hours) from Sokcho to the last stop. There is an 'education centre' here and then you are whipped up to the observatory by shuttle bus (W2000, 20 minutes).

SEORAKSAN NATIONAL PARK
설악산국립공원

Top of the charts in the Korean national park scene, Seoraksan (Snowy Crags Mountains) is spectacular. It's a land of high peaks, lush forests, tremendous waterfalls, hot springs, boulder-strewn whitewater rivers, old temples and hermitages whose roots go back to the Silla era. The park is at its colourful best in mid-October, when the leaves begin to change hue and the mountainsides are transformed into a riot of colour. Actually, a visit is rewarding at any time of the year. The nearby coast has some of Korea's best beaches.

Unfortunately, Seoraksan's attractiveness is its biggest problem. It's easily Korea's most popular national park, and on holidays you could be forgiven for thinking that they should have named this place Seoraksan National Car Park. Even beyond the highways, the crunch of hikers can be oppressive. At times you will literally have to queue to get on the various trails leading to the waterfalls and peaks. Under the impact of so many feet, the park service has had no choice but to build concrete paths and steps – it's wilderness with handrails and public toilets.

The peak season is summer, though the mid-October leaf-changing show also attracts busloads of weekend trippers. If you prefer to take in nature in more tranquil conditions then you have little choice but to visit during non-holiday times when the students are still in school. You can also escape some of the crowds by heading for remote trails far from the entrance roads.

Despite all this, persevere! About an hour of hiking up the paved trails, and suddenly the terrain gets rough and most of the daytrippers disappear.

Information & Orientation
The park office is before the park's main entrance and has detailed topographic maps with all the trails marked. A new visitor centre is planned here, with some information about the park's flora and fauna.

GANGWON-DO

The park is divided into three sections: Outer Seorak, Inner Seorak and South Seorak. Inner Seorak is farthest inland, while Outer Seorak is closest to the sea – the two are divided from each other by a jagged ridge of mountains. South Seorak is divided from the rest of the park by Hwy 44.

Outer Seorak is the most accessible spot and therefore the most crowded area of the park. The chief town is Seorak-dong, a modern tourist resort in every respect, with deluxe hotels, restaurants and souvenir shops (see Places to Stay, later in this section).

Inner Seorak is the least commercialised area of the park, though no doubt the day will come when the developers move in. There are three entrance points to Inner Seorak. Most accessible is Jangsudae, on Hwy 44. The second most popular entrance is by Baekdamsa, a remote temple area hidden in a large valley. The third entrance point is at Sibiseonnyeotang Valley, which is reached by a hiking trail that runs off Hwy 46 at the north-west corner of the park.

The main tourist spot in **South Seorak** is the **Osaek** (Five Colours) area because of its proximity to **Osaek Hot Springs**. This is the major hot springs resort in the park. Aside from its springs, the Osaek area is famous for its impressive peaks, thick forests and numerous waterfalls.

The goal of many hikers is the highest peak in the park, **Daecheonbong** (1708m). It is reached most easily from either Seorak-dong or Osaek Springs – it's a very long way from Inner Seorak. However, even by the shortest route it's still a strenuous hike – start out early if you plan to get back before dark!

If the weather is cold, you'll almost certainly see kiosks down at the lower elevations renting strap-on ice cleats for about W1000. These are absolutely necessary in the cold season as the higher elevations get icy and dangerously slippery.

The entry fee to Seoraksan National Park varies depending on where you enter (W1000 to W2200).

Gwongeumseong 권금성

Almost everyone begins their tour at Outer Seorak, and a good way to get an introduction is to take the 1100m cable car to the peak, Gwongeumseong. It's good value at W1500/2800 one way/return, and you'll be rewarded with absolutely amazing views. Cable cars run every 20 to 30 minutes. From the cable car drop-off point, it's a 10-minute walk to the summit of the mountain.

Heundeulbawi (Tottering Rock) 흔들바위

This is another of those 'must-see' spots in Outer Seorak. It's famous because it can be rocked to and fro by just one person. In fact, it's surprising it hasn't been completely rocked off its base by now as half the population of Korea must have had a go! Almost adjacent to the rock is **Gyejoam**, a small cave temple.

The hike up to the rock via Naewonam from Seorak-dong takes 1½ hours.

Sinheungsa 신흥사

To the west of downtown Seorak-dong is Sinheungsa, the oldest continually used Zen meditation temple in Korea. It was first constructed in AD 653, later burnt to the ground, and was rebuilt in 1645. A giant, seated bronze Buddha is located between the temple and the main tourist plaza – rather garish!

Ulsanbawi 울산바위

From Heundeulbawi you can climb another 40 minutes to Ulsanbawi. More than just a rock, it's in fact a mountain (873m) that presents a huge granite cliff face that can be seen from many parts of the park. A steel staircase has been built up the cliff face and, although it's hard going, the summit offers some spectacular views. The summit actually consists of six separate peaks.

Yukdampokpo 육담폭포 & Biryongpokpo 비룡폭포

A 45-minute walk from Seorak-dong brings you to these impressive waterfalls. The trail to a third waterfall, **Towangseongpokpo,** is currently closed, which means you'll miss out on a spectacular sight. The rest of the trail is well marked and involves crossing many suspension bridges and climbing flights of steel stairs. The most convenient entrance to the trail is across the bridge that spans the river a few hundred metres before you get to the cable car station.

Baekdamsa 백담사

In the relatively quiet north-western section of the park lies Baekdamsa (Hundred Pools Temple). The name aptly reflects the abundance of beautiful pools scattered along the valley.

Buses run from the car park 4km up the valley (W800, every 20 minutes). It's another 3km hike to the temple (50 minutes). The hike beyond the temple along **Suryeomdong Valley** to *Suryeomdong Shelter* (another two hours) is highly recommended. Entry costs W2000.

Sibiseonnyeotang Valley

This is probably revered as the most beautiful valley in the park. Strewn with waterfalls, cascades, pools and large boulders, the 2½ hour walk to the waterfall, **Dumunpokpo,** at the end of the valley is a real treat. You can continue on up to **Ansan** (1430m), which is a farther 2½ hours walking.

Osaek Hot Springs Resort 오색

Osaek is in the southern part of the national park, approached by a different route (Hwy 44) than the one to Seorak-dong (Hwy 462). Osaek boasts both a **cold mineral spring** (for drinking) and a **hot mineral spring** (for soaking). The hot spring is arguably the best in Korea! There may be other spas in the country that claim to have fancier facilities (probably true) or better quality water (debatable), but none can match Osaek's combination of delightful hot springs and great scenic beauty. As elsewhere in Korea, the hot springs have been taken over by hotels and you won't find natural bathing pools in the wilderness. Nevertheless, there is little to complain about. The **Greenyard Hotel** is acknowledged to have the best bathing facilities, and you do not need to be a hotel guest to use the pools (W5000).

There are also spectacular hiking opportunities in the vicinity. You can make an assault on the peak, **Seoraksan Daecheongbong** (four hours), from here. It is also possible to continue up the valley to the waterfall, **Sibipokpo** (1½ hours). The great attraction of the Osaek area is that you can hike to your heart's content and then collapse into a steaming pool of hot water. Not surprisingly, there are several restaurants in the area that lay on big meals of health food featuring wild mountain herbs.

Hiking

There are dozens of treks in the area, and the national park map provides a good enough reference, with even some English used. Ensure that you check which trails are closed.

There are seven *shelters* at various points along the hiking trails where you can stay overnight. Accommodation is on bare boards and costs W3000 per night (W5000 in Seorak Shelter). Blankets are occasionally available but don't count on it. In most cases you'll have to do your own cooking too, so come prepared. A limited range of canned, dry and bottled goods are for sale. Plenty of water is available at all the huts – either pump-fed or spring-fed. The shelters are marked on the tourist maps of the area. You need to book them in advance if staying on weekends or holidays. Ring ☎ 636 7700 or visit the park's Web site (www.npa.or.kr).

Skiing

Alps Ski Resort (☎ 681 5030, fax 681 2788) was opened in 1984 and is nowhere near as large as the nearby Yongpyeong Ski Resort (see Yongpyeong section, later in this chapter) but it is still quite a good location for skiing. The resort receives the heaviest snow falls of any resort in Korea and has some of the most spectacular scenery, due to the proximity of Seoraksan National Park. There are currently eight slopes and five lifts in operation, offering a good range of slopes for the beginner and intermediate skier. The season runs from late November to late March.

Ski-lift tickets range in price from W5500 for a single use to W33,000 for a whole day. Ski rental prices range from W13,500 for the morning to W26,500 for a full day. Group skiing lessons are available for beginners and range from a basic course (W53,000) to a more intensive course

(W17,500). Contact the ski resort to find out how to book English-language lessons. Discounts are available for children.

Most people organise a ski and accommodation package deal, due to the discounting. Prices for accommodation are a bit limited below the slopes, starting from W140,000. Otherwise it is possible to find some *yeogwan* within walking distance of the slopes. During the ski season, room rates generally start from W50,000.

Transport to the resort is possible from either Seoul's Sangbong inter-city bus terminal (W13,700) or from Sokcho (W3500) on buses bound for Ganseong via Jinburyeong. There are only a few departures for these routes, so check their times. During the ski season, free shuttle buses also make the run from Sokcho's airport. This service will probably continue after the airport moves to Yangyang (scheduled to happen in 2002).

Places to Stay

A big drawback to visiting Seoraksan during peak season (July, August and mid-October) is that the cost of accommodation skyrockets and you'll find yourself having to pay up to three times the normal rates. Even a simple room in a minbak can cost you W40,000.

Camping is available throughout the year at Jangsudae, Seorak-dong and at Osaek. A site costs W3000 and there are cold-water shower and toilet facilities. It's a bit like a rock festival site – with about a metre of space between tents.

Seorak-dong You need to get off the bus at Sorak-dong if you want to stay in a yeogwan or motel. The price of accommodation varies according to popularity. From mid-July to the end of August rates double everywhere. Off-peak rates range from W20,000 to W30,000, with summer prices rising to W60,000 to W70,000. Bookings are like the rest of Korea, essential during summer.

The first place you'll see is *Garden Motel* (☎ 636 7474), which has standard doubles and ondols from W25,000. Suites are W35,000. In summer, rates rise from

W35,000 to W50,000, respectively. They have a kitchen on the ground floor where you can cook your own meal.

Seorak Crystal Hotel (☎ 636 7626) has a pleasant beer garden out the front and rooms from W25,000. Higher up the road you will find *Bandal Gom* (☎ 636 8400), which has rooms with balconies from W20,000. *Tulip Sanjang* (☎ 636 7233) also has rooms for W20,000.

Halfway between Seorak-dong and Sokcho is *Kensington Hotel* (☎ 636 7131, **e** *kensing@chollian.net*), probably the best top-end option around with very reasonable rates outside of summer. Information and reservations are available at their Web site (www.kensing.com).

Osaek Try *Hyundai Oncheon-jang* (☎ 672 4088), *Winners Oncheon-jang* (☎ 672 4111) and *Hotel Seorak Oncheon-jang* (☎ 672 2645), which all have rooms for W25,000, or W50,000 in summer.

The nicest place to stay and the top-end option is *Osaek Greenyard Hotel* (☎ 672 8500), which has two buildings, one of which lacks cooking facilities. Prices range from W55,000 (family room B) to W420,000 (royal suite). They offer a 50% discount off some rooms during the low season.

Baekdamsa Access to the temple Baekdamsa is by way of the small village of **Yongdae-ri**, where *minbak* and *restaurants* are aplenty. On the southern bank of the river is *Posijeun*, which has rooms for W25,000. It is also possible to stay at *Baekdam Shelter* (W3000).

Getting There & Away

The main entry to Outer Seorak is via the tourist village of Seorak-dong, which is at the end of the road branching off from the coast road, about half way between Naksan and Sokcho. There are frequent buses both from Yangyang and from Sokcho (No 7) every five to 10 minutes. If you're not planning on overnighting in Seorak-dong, but only visiting for the day, get off the bus at the very last stop, which is about 3km beyond the main part of the tourist village. This will save you a fair bit of walking. There are also direct buses to Seoul three times daily.

Local buses running between Yangyang and Inje stop at Osaek, in southern Seorak. The same buses also stop at Jangsudae, which is the southern entrance point for Inner Seorak. From Osaek's bus terminal there are inter-city buses to: Seoul (W12,400, every 1½ hours), Sokcho (W2600, every 15 to 20 minutes), Chuncheon (W8400, every two hours) and a local bus to Yangyang (W1200, hourly), from where you can transfer to bus No 9 to Sokcho.

You can also enter Inner Seorak via the village of Yongdae-ri (Baekdamsa). Local buses run from Wontong every 1¾ hour (W1200, 20 minutes). From Yondae-ri there are also buses to: Chuncheon (four times daily, at 9.30, 10 am, 2.50 and 4.50 pm); Sokcho (every 30 minutes); and Seoul (every 20 to 30 minutes). Sokcho-Chuncheon long-distance buses follow Hwy 46 and stop at Yongdae-ri – tell the bus driver you want to get off at Baekdamsa *ipgu* (entrance). Sokcho-Chuncheon buses also stop at Namgyo – tell the bus driver you want to get off at Sibiseonnyeotanggyegok ipgu.

NAKSAN PROVINCIAL PARK
낙산도립공원

This park is famous for the temple Naksansa and its huge white statue of Gwaneum, the goddess of mercy, which looks out to sea from atop a small, pine-covered rocky outcrop. The temple was built originally in AD 671, rebuilt in AD 858 and burned to the ground during the Korean War. It was reconstructed in 1953, following the original design. The 15m-high statue of Gwaneum is more recent and was completed only in 1977. At the entrance to the temple, the stone arch, with a pavilion built above it, dates from 1465.

Entry to the park costs W2200. It's a beautiful spot and very peaceful in the early mornings before the tour groups arrive. Naksansa is also one of the very few Korean temples that overlooks the sea. Don't forget to visit the pavilion, Uisangdae, which sits right on top of an ocean cliff shaded by an old and ailing pine tree. This is one of the most famous sunrise-viewing spots on the east coast.

Down below the temple is **Naksan Beach**, which is one of the best in the area, but it gets unbelievably crowded during July and August.

The nearby town of Naksan is a pleasant albeit crowded summer coastal resort, east of Seoraksan. There are heaps of good yeogwan here.

Naksan Youth Hostel (☎ *672 3416*) is situated next to the provincial park in very scenic surroundings. Unfortunately, it does not offer dorm accommodation, but only has ondol rooms, geared mainly to groups, for W25,000. It's a short walk to the nearby temple and beach.

Getting There & Away
Bus No 9 runs between Sokcho and Yangyang and costs W600 (every 15 minutes). There are direct buses to Dong Seoul and Sangbong Seoul bus terminals (W13,700, 4½ hours).

GANGNEUNG 강릉
pop 232,000
Gangneung is the largest city on the northeast coast of Korea and is worth a visit during the annual Dano Festival. The main tourist office is inside the bus terminal and there is a smaller booth in front of the train station.

Dano Festival 단오제
Probably the only time you would come to Gangneung for its own sake is to see the shamanist **Dano Festival**, which takes the city by storm for a whole week on the 5th day of the 5th lunar month (for exact dates, see the 'Public Holidays & Special Events' section in the Facts for the Visitor chapter).

People flock into the city from all over the surrounding area and a tent city rises to accommodate them. There are circus and carnival acts, shamanist rituals, folk operas, farmers' bands and all manner of stalls and hawkers. It all creates an atmosphere redolent of a medieval fair. It's also likely to be the nearest you'll get to seeing aspects of Korea's original religion.

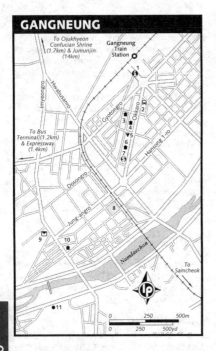

GANGNEUNG

1 Information Centre
  관광안내소
2 Bus Stop to Jeongdongjin
  & Airport
  정동진 .공항버스정류장
3 Hilton Motel
  힐튼모텔
4 Seung-a-jang Yeogwan
  승아장여관
5 Buldak (Korean Chicken
  Grill)
  불닭
6 Dongbaek-jang Yeogwan
  동백장여관
7 Hanvit Bank
  한빛은행
8 Jung-ang Market
  중앙시장
9 Central Post &
  Telephone Office
  우체국 ,전화국
10 Royal Hotel
  로얄호텔
11 Dano Festival Area
  단오장

During the Dano Festival, an information stall with multi-lingual staff and guides is set up in the middle of all the stalls.

Ojukheon Confucian Shrine
오죽헌

About 3.5km north of Gangneung, Ojukheon Confucian Shrine is the birthplace of Shin Saimdang (1504–51) and her son, Yi Yul-gok (or Yi-yi) (1536–84). Shin Saimdang was an accomplished poet and artist, while Yi Yul-gok was one of the most outstanding Confucian scholars of the Joseon period.

Yi Yul-gok learned the classics from his mother at a very young age and subsequently won first prize in the state examinations for prospective government officials in 1564. After that he served in various government posts. Along with his contemporary, Yi Toegye, another famous Confucian scholar, he wielded great influence among the various political factions

at the royal court and was instrumental in advising the king to raise an army of 100,000 men to prepare for a possible invasion by Japan. His advice was tragically ignored – only eight years after he died, the Japanese did indeed invade, and the peninsula was devastated.

Gangneung Municipal Museum forms part of the complex and houses painting, calligraphy and embroidery executed by Shin Saimdang and Yi Yul-gok.

The **Yulgokje Festival** is held annually at the shrine on 26 October when traditional rituals are enacted and classical Korean music is played.

Entry costs W1000 (9 am to 6 pm). Bus Nos 19-7 (W600) from the train station will take you to the shrine from Gangneung city centre.

Places to Stay & Eat

In 1996 Gangneung's bus terminal moved to a new facility far from the centre. As a result, there are not as yet any yeogwan near the terminal, though no doubt this will change. Almost all the hotels and guesthouses are to be found in the vicinity of the now defunct bus terminals, which are not far from the train station.

Dongbaek-jang Yeogwan (☎ 647 7758) has clean and well-kept rooms for W25,000. *Seung-a-jang Yeogwan* (☎ 645 1110) is reasonable value with ondol rooms for W25,000 and doubles for W30,000. *Hilton Motel* (☎ 647 3357) is a bit newer and upmarket, with rooms from W30,000.

Within walking distance of the Dano Festival action, *Royal Hotel* (☎ 646 1295) has ondol rooms for W35,000, and doubles/twins for W40,000/60,000.

As its name suggests, *Buldak* (Korean chicken grill) serves up a variety of tasty grilled chicken dishes. Pictures on the wall make ordering easy.

Getting There & Away

Air Asiana and Korean Air both have flights connecting Gangneung to Seoul (W35,500) and Busan (W47,500).

Bus Gangneung's express bus terminal and inter-city bus terminal are both in the same building, a shiny new facility near the expressway entrance.

Express bus departures include:

destination	price (W)	duration	distance
Dong Seoul	9200	3½ hrs	232km
Seoul	9200	3½ hrs	230km
Wonju	4900	2¼ hrs	119km

Inter-city departures include:

destination	price (W)	duration	distance
Busan	21,700	6/7½ hrs	358km
Chuncheon	10,600	4 hrs	190km
Donghae	2200	½ hr	39km
Jinbu*	2600		
Sokcho	4600	1¼ hrs	73km
Taebaek	6800	2½ hrs	107km

*change here for hourly local bus to Woljeongsa and Sangwonsa

Train Five daily limited-express mu-gunghwa trains and one saemaeul express train connect Gangneung with Seoul's Cheongnyangni station (6 to 7 hours).

Getting Around

Bus No 19-7, 21 or 48 connects the train station and bus terminal. Bus No 28 goes to the airport (W600, 25 minutes). If you catch a taxi to the airport you must pay double the meter.

AROUND GANGNEUNG
Jumunjin 주문진

The busy fishing port of Jumunjin is just 23km north of Gangneung and is a good place to see the hustle and bustle of a typical Korean fish market.

In the north of town past the creek is Jumunjin Beach, an interesting mix of sandy beach, barbed wire, power lines and a smaller fishing village. To reward your visit, have a drink and snack at the *Cove Cafe* (also known as *Got Cafe*) an interesting place by the beach. Prices are more-or-less typical of Korean cafes, with a mug of coffee from W3500, but you couldn't ask for a more bizarre setting.

Bus No 31 (W600) runs regularly from Gangneung and will get to you both the fish market *(eosijang)* and the beach.

Jeongdongjin 정동진

If you want to see everything that can go wrong when a local government uses all its powers to set up a tourist resort, then come to Jeongdongjin. In addition to foetid, polluted water and uncontrolled construction, you will find: a train station on the beach; a memorial to the first landing of the North Koreans during the Korean War; an enormous ship on the top of a hill; the largest hourglass in the world (a memorial to the Korean soapie *Hourglass*, which shot a scene here); a Drama & VID Memorial Center (another memorial to the same soapie); and even an invading North Korean submarine (perhaps the North Koreans had seen the soapie in Pyongyang). If this is too much to handle, then just enjoy this place from the safety of the train window.

GANGWON-DO

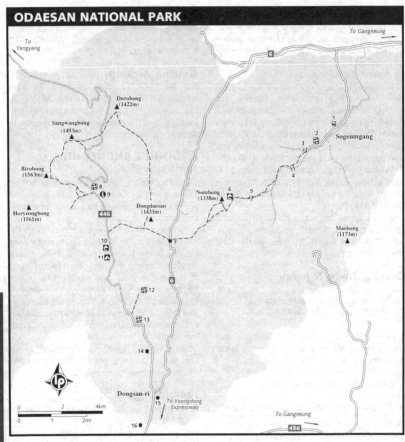

ODAESAN NATIONAL PARK

Bus No 11 or 12 (W600) goes to Gangne-ung, or you can catch any train to/from Gangneung.

ODAESAN NATIONAL PARK
오대산국립공원

Like the peak Seoraksan, Odaesan (Five Platforms Mountain) is another high-altitude massif where nature reigns supreme. The park has excellent hiking possibilities and superb views. It also hosts one of Korea's foremost winter ski-ing resorts at Yongpyeong, south of the park. Deep inside the western section of

the park are two prominent Buddhist tem-ples, Woljeongsa and Sangwonsa.

Birobong (1563m) is the highest peak in the park. It is connected by a **ridge trail** to the beautiful valley of Sogeumgang. The hike takes you via the peaks of Sangwang-bong (1493m), Durobong (1421m), Dong-daesan (1433m) and Noinbong (1338m). This is a long hike, and should take around 15 hours. Rather than complete the whole track in one day, you may choose to stay at either *Odae* or *Noinbong shelters* (W3000).

As with Seoraksan, the best times to visit are late spring and early to mid-autumn,

ODAESAN NATIONAL PARK

PLACES TO STAY
6 Noinbong Shelter
노인봉대피소
10 Odaesan Shelter
오대산장
11 Dongpigol Auto-
Camping
동피골야영장
14 Minbak Village
민박촌
16 Odaesan Hotel
오대산호텔

OTHER
1 Bus Stop to Gangneung
버스정류장
2 Geumgangsa
금강사
3 Cheongsimdaepopko
청심대폭포
4 Guryongpopko
구룡폭포
5 Nagyeongpopko
나경폭포
7 Jingogae Rest Area
진고개휴게소
8 Sangwonsa
상원사
9 Information
안내소
12 Gwaneumam
관음암
13 Woljeongsa
월정사
15 National Park Office
국립공원관리사무소

when the colours of the landscape are at their best. Entry to Odaesan National Park costs from W1000 to W2200.

Woljeongsa

This temple was founded in AD 645 by the Zen Master Jajang-yulsa during the reign of Queen Seondeok of the Silla dynasty to enshrine relics of Sakyamuni (the historical Buddha). Over the next 1300 years or so, it went through various trials and tribulations and was destroyed by fire on at least three occasions. Yet today you would hardly suspect these disasters had ever occurred. Reconstruction work took place in 1969 and again in 1996. The result is simply magnificent and the internal painting in the main hall containing the Buddha image is a masterpiece of religious art. Not

even in Tibet will you find anything quite as intricate, well-balanced and spellbinding as this.

Luckily, not everything was destroyed in the various disasters that have befallen this temple over the centuries. Prominent remains from the Goryeo era include a kneeling – and smiling! – stone Bodhisattva and a number of interesting stone stupas. There's also the unique, octagonal, nine-storeyed pagoda Palgak, dating from the same period, which is classified as a national treasure.

Sangwonsa

A further 10km beyond Woljeongsa, at the end of a well-maintained road, is the temple Sangwonsa, a popular trailhead for hikers. It's from here that you can ascend Birobong and complete a circuit walk passing Sangwangbong (five hours). There is also an information booth here.

Aside from the hiking possibilities, the temple is a famous attraction in its own right. Like Woljeongsa, it has seen its share of hard times – it was last burned to the ground in 1949 but was reconstructed the following year. There's a **gold-plated Buddha statue** here, as well as four bronze ones. One image is of Mansuri (the Bodhisattva of Wisdom), but the temple's most famous possession is its **bronze bell**, one of the oldest in Korea and the second largest (after the Emille Bell at the Gyeongju National Museum). It was cast in AD 663, one year after construction of the temple commenced.

Sogeumgang 소금강

The most beautiful section of Odaesan National Park is hidden away in the north-east corner. This is also the most developed section, with a heavy flow of visitors all year round. Despite this the valley remains a beautiful hike.

About one hour of walking from Sokeumgang brings you to a small temple, **Geumgangsa**. After that, the route is an orgy of waterfalls, cliffs and boulders (about two hours' walking). Stunning! If you've still got the strength, it's another 2½ hours hard climbing up to the summit of **Noinbong** (1338m).

GANGWON-DO

If you're overnighting, *Noinbong Shelter* is just before the peak. Basic necessities are available, including blankets, but bring everything else you need. From Noinbong, you can head down by a different route to Jingogae Rest Area (70 minutes) or continue on to *Odaesan Shelter* (another 2½ hours). Doing this whole walk in one day would really be a killer – day-trippers should probably head back after the waterfall orgy.

Places to Stay

The main *camping ground* is at Sogeumgang, with 1200 sites and good facilities, including showers. Sites cost W4500. It is also possible to camp near Odae Shelter at *Dongpigol auto-camp grounds* (free in low season, W3000 in summer). Only basic facilities are available. The two shelters, *Noinbong* and *Odae,* are also available (W3000). To avoid disapointment, on weekends and during the holidays you should reserve a place (☎ 332 6417, fax 333 5461, e odae@npa.or.kr).

Minbak are available at the park entrance below Woljeongsa and there are even more at Sogeumgang.

At the time of writing there was a new hotel complex being built south of Dongsan-ri that will offer deluxe accommodation. The 15-storey *Odaesan Hotel* (☎ 330 5000, fax 330 5123) is farther south again and has deluxe rooms from W145,200 and suites from W250,000.

Getting There & Away

Bus No 7 or 7-7 connects Gangneung and Sogeumgang (W600, one hour, hourly). Other buses involve a change at Chinbu, just off the expressway.

There are direct buses from Gangneung to Woljeongsa every 30 minutes (W4,500, 1½ hours). These buses will have Woljeongsa on their destination indicator, but terminate in Pyeongchang. Alternatively, take an inter-city bus from Gangneung to Jinbu (W2600, every five minutes). From Jinbu, local buses run to Sangwonsa via Woljeongsa (W1600, hourly, 30 minutes).

YONGPYEONG SKI RESORT
용평스키장

With world-class facilities, Yongpyeong Ski Resort is one of Korea's best. It has one of the longest ski seasons in the country, running from late November to early April. These slopes were the first to open in Korea, back in 1975, but have recently been expanded, with more trails on the back mountain. A new gondola connects the more advanced slopes to the 5km-long Rainbow Road.

The resort has good services and facilities for foreigners, including English-language ski lessons and assistance with hiring. For a better price, it's a good idea to buy your tickets and passes at the village below the resort, or even arrange a package deal (with accommodation).

The park authorities have just opened a new cross-country area just adjacent to the resort. It has plenty of enjoyable and challenging runs.

Keep an ear out for the special **festivals** that are organised for Korea's expat and tourist populations. Most visitors recall lots of good fun during these occasions.

A variety of ski lift tickets are available, including two day (W60,000), full day (W32,500), half day (W25,500), night-time (W17,000) and single use (W4500). Season tickets are available and discounts are provided to children. Equipment hire is reasonably priced from W13,000 for a half day.

For more information regarding costs and the provision of English skiing lessons either visit their Web site (www.yongpyong.co.kr/english/) or call or fax (☎ 335 5757, fax 335 5769).

Places to Stay

Decent accommodation is available, including condos, hotels and a youth hostel, all with ski-in and ski-out access. *Yongpyeong Youth Hostel* (☎ 335 5757, fax 335 0160) has dorm accommodation for members from W6500 and rooms from W42,000. Rates for non-members start from W60,000. The deluxe *Dragon Valley Hotel* (☎ 335 5757, fax 335 0160) has comfortable rooms from W150,000 and suites from W300,000.

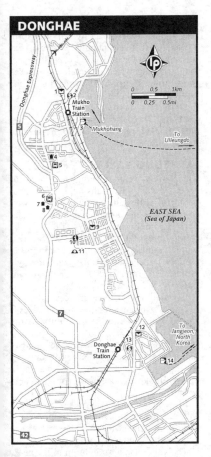

DONGHAE

1 Mukho Post Office
묵호우체국
2 Hanil Bank
한일은행
3 Mukho Ferry Terminal
(To Ulleungdo)
묵호여객터미널
4 Cheongwon-jang
청원장
5 Express Bus Terminal
고속버스터미널
6 Inter-City Bus Terminal
시외버스터미널
7 Noble Tourist Hotel
노블관광호텔
8 New Donghae Tourist
Hotel
뉴동해관광호텔
9 Post Office
우체국
10 Tourist Information
관광안내소
11 Cheongokcheonyeon
Donggul
천곡천연동굴
12 Post Office
우체국
13 Gangwon Bank
강원은행
14 Donghae Ferry Terminal
(To Jangjeon, Nth Korea)
금강산관광선터미널

Getting There & Away

Getting to Yongpyeong Ski Resort is pretty easy. Either catch an inter-city bus from Gangneung to Hoenggye (marked 'Pyeongchang', every 30 minutes), from where a free shuttle bus drops you at the resort, or use the resort's shuttle bus from Gangneung airport (6 daily).

DONGHAE 동해

pop 104,000

This small and pleasant east-coast city is mostly visited by travellers planning to catch a boat to Ulleungdo from Mukho harbour. It's a quiet and relaxing place to be. The nearby Mureung Valley is also very much worth a visit. There is a tourist information booth at the entrance to Cheongokcheonyeondonggul.

Cheongokcheonyeondonggul
천곡천연동굴

Right in the centre of town, these caves are home to some impressive stalactites and stalagmites, as well as a colony of bats. There are also some beautiful calcified limestone waterfalls and an enormous cavern. The caves are about 1.4km in length. Entry costs W1500.

GANGWON-DO

Places to Stay

Donghae's guesthouses are fairly expensive, at least during the summer tourist season, when it's hard to find anything for under W30,000. There are a couple of cheaper places near the express bus terminal. *Cheongwon-jang* (☎ 533 4429) is a good choice, with rooms for W25,000. Summer rates vary between W30,000 and W50,000.

Noble Tourist Hotel (☎ 532 1600, fax 532 6730) is next to the inter-city bus terminal. It has traditional-style rooms going for W40,000 and doubles/suites for W45,000/90,000.

New Dongnae Tourist Hotel (☎ 533 9125, fax 533 1919) is also near the inter-city bus terminal and has good doubles/suites from W50,000/90,000, plus 20% tax.

Getting There & Away

Bus Donghae sits on the main east-coast highway, so bus connections are fairly good. Express bus destinations include: Seoul and Dong Seoul (W10,700, 4¼ hours, 269km, hourly).

Inter-city bus destinations include:

destination	price (W)	duration	distance
Busan	19,500	5 hrs	324km
Daegu	19,000	6¾ hrs	311km
Gangneung	2200	40 mins	34km
Samcheok	950	20 mins	18km
Sokcho	6800	2¾ hrs	107km
Taebaek	4600	3¼ hrs	127km
Uljin	5500	2 hrs	89km

Train Donghae train station is very far from the centre – if you arrive by train, get off at Mukho station. Five daily mugunghwa trains connect Seoul's Cheongnyangni station and Donghae (W15,000, six hours). There is an extra mugunghwa and saemaeul (W21,300) service on weekends and holidays.

Ferry The main reason to visit Donghae is to catch the ferry to Ulleungdo. For information on this boat, see the Getting There & Away entry under Ulleungdo in the Gyeongsangbuk-do chapter.

Hyundai's North Korean Geumgangsan tour ferries also depart from Donghae to the North Korean port, Jangjeon. Despite being just a brief tour of a tiny part of North Korea, it's still very popular with expats as it is at present the only way to visit the spectacular Kumgangsan mountain range. (See the Getting There & Away section in the North Korea chapter.)

Getting Around

Bus no 21-1 runs between Donghae city centre and the town of Mukho (W950).

MUREUNG VALLEY 무릉계곡

This valley west of Donghae is considered by many Koreans to be *the* most beautiful valley in the country! Just why the place is not a national or provincial park is something of a mystery. To make things more confusing, the whole area, which is not a park, is named Suinumsan County Park. (Incidentally, the first syllable 'suin' is unique in the Korean language.)

Gwaneumsa, at the entrance to the valley, is the largest temple and features a seated **golden Buddha** just outside the main hall.

A hiking path leads to another temple, **Samhwasa**, though if you take this route it's an up and back trip. The waterfall, **Yongchupokpo**, is one of the park's notable features.

Mureung Valley stretches 2.5km from Mureungbanseok to **Yongchupokpo**. At the end of the valley, **Mireukam Hermitage** has particularly good scenery.

The valley leads straight up to the peak, **Cheongoksan** (1404m), and to the southeast of that is **Dutasan** (1353m). You can hike the valley and both peaks in one very full day – and it's definitely worth the effort. Entry to the valley costs W1000.

Accommodation is available at *Mureung Plaza Motel* (☎ 534 8855) and the neighbouring *Cheongok Sanjang* (☎ 534 8866) for W25,000. Most of the restaurants also double as minbak.

Getting There & Away

City buses run from central Donghae to the park entrance, via both bus stations (W600,

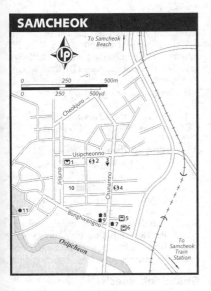

SAMCHEOK

SAMCHEOK

1 Post Office
   우체국
2 Kookmin Bank
   국민은행
3 Hanguk Hoegwan
   한국회관
4 Hanvit Bank
   한빛은행
5 Local Bus Terminal
   시내버스터미널
6 Samcheok Bus Terminal
   삼척버스터미널
7 Hanil-jang
   한일장
8 Hwasin-jang
   화신장
9 Crown Motel
   크라운모텔
10 Central Market
   중앙시장
11 Jukseoru Pavilion
   죽서루

25 minutes, every 10 minutes). You can also take city buses from Samcheok.

SAMCHEOK 삼척
pop 85,000

Samcheok is a pleasant town south of Donghae. Of mild interest are the *hyanggyo* (Confucian school) and the pavilion, Jukseoru; however the big drawcard is the sheltered coves that dot the coast from Samcheok south almost to Uljin, Gyeongsangbuk-do.

This is one of the most mountainous stretches of coastline in Korea – steep cliffs and rocks make most of the coast too rugged for swimming, but in miniature coves there are very scenic stretches of white, sandy beach. In most cases there is a tiny town adjacent to the beach where you can find meals and a minbak if you wish to spend the night.

Even if you don't care to swim, this scenic coast should not be missed. Hwy 7 hugs the coastline and makes for an interesting drive. Ideally, you should have your own transport, stopping off at every scenic cove. There are local buses for those who don't have their own set of wheels, but sometimes you've got a long wait for one to come by. A bicycle would be a great

way to travel, but do be careful on the narrow and twisting highway. Traffic is not heavy here (except on holidays), but it only takes one cement truck to ruin your whole day. Unfortunately, nobody seems to be renting bicycles, so you'll need to bring your own.

From north to south, a rundown of the beaches follows in the Around Samcheok section. Bear in mind that there are more beaches than detailed here – not all of them have a name nor are all of them developed.

Jukseoru 죽서루

Probably named after a famous local *kisaeng* (female hostess, like a geisha), Jukjukseonnyeo. This pavilion was built during the Goryeo period and is perched on a cliff above the river, Osipcheon. It's a peaceful park with some pleasant bamboo groves. Entry costs W550.

Samcheok Beach 삼척해수욕장

This beach is 2km north of the town centre. Though not the prettiest beach in the area, it's the most accessible. You could walk there if you're ambitious, otherwise simply get there by taxi. Buses run from Samcheok (W600, five daily).

GANGWON-DO

Places to Stay & Eat

Obviously, it's much more interesting to stay in a minbak out by one of the beaches, but for convenience sake there are plenty of yeogwan in Samcheok within easy walking distance of the bus station.

Hanil-jang (☎ 574 8277) is next to the bus terminal and has rooms for W28,000. Opposite is *Hwasin-jang (☎ 574 7571)*, where good double and ondol rooms are W25,000 to W35,000. Next door, *Crown Motel (☎ 574 8831)* has rooms for W30,000.

For a bite to eat try *Hanguk Hoegwan*, which serves up a tasty *dolsot bibimbap* (stone pot vegetables and rice; W6000).

Getting There & Away

Bus Departures from Samcheok's express bus terminal include Seoul and Dong Seoul (W11,200, 4½ hours, 284km, every 30 to 60 minutes).

The inter-city bus schedule is almost identical to the Donghae schedule. See the Donghae section, earlier, for details.

Train The schedule is the same as the Donghae schedule, although trains from Seoul arrive in Samcheok about 15 minutes earlier than they do in Donghae.

AROUND SAMCHEOK
Hwanseondonggul 환선동굴

These caves are named after a monk who led a monastic life here. They are quite incredible: with enormous caverns, beautiful streams and waterfalls. There are plenty of 'close one eye and blur the other' attractions, creating images of white turtles, bald heads, a hanged sheep and, of course, the ubiquitous sleeping dragon. Perhaps the 'bridge of love', 'reunification square', 'penitence bridge (where you can cast away your sins)', and the skeletons hanging above 'hell bridge' might be going a bit overboard, but they certainly spice up the walk for the ajumma after they've indulged in a little of the local soju.

The caves are located in a beautiful valley with waterfalls, cascading streams and **bark shingle houses**. Presently, 1.6km of the caves are open of an estimated 6km. Entrance costs W4300.

There are a couple of **walks** behind the caves that all start from the car park. The easiest goes to Hwanseongul (1.3km, 25 minutes); or you could try a more challenging hike to Deokhangsan (1070m, 4.5km, two hours) and, if you have any strength left, continue on to Jigeuksan (1058m, 3km, 1½ hours).

Buses run to the caves from Samcheok (W1600 or W1900, every 1½ hours).

Maengbang Beach 맹방해수욕장

About 12km down the coast from Samcheok is Maengbang Beach, one of the more popular spots. The water is very shallow here, making it a big hit with families with young children. There is also a small freshwater creek nearby, which is OK for light swimming. Local buses from Samcheok run about once every 20 minutes.

Geundeok Beach 근덕해수욕장

Just south of Maengbang, Keundeok Beach is where Hwy 7 moves decidedly inland. Getting to the beach requires a short drive or walk from the main road. The scenery is terrific.

Gungchon Beach 궁촌해수욕장

One of the larger developments on this section of coast, Gungchon is trying to become a classy resort. It's got a long way to go. The resort is about 20km down the coast from Samcheok. Minbak are available. There are buses to Gungchon from Samcheok (40 minutes, 15 daily).

Yonghwa Beach 용화해수욕장

This pine-tree-lined beach is 25km south of Samcheok. The beach is 800m in length and there is a freshwater stream here. There are plenty of *minbak*, and seafood is a local specialty.

Jangho Resort 장하해수욕장

This is the most developed of the beach areas along this stretch of coastline. The beach has a crescent shape and is well-protected from the wind. Buses from Samcheok depart every two hours.

Sacred Mountains

All of Korea's mountains are sacred in some sense – each has its own *sansin* (mountain god). Of course, some mountains are more sacred than others. Mountains with major temples are more sacred to Buddhists, though the sacredness of temples changes with the course of historical events. To get some idea of which mountains are most sacred to Buddhists, look on a good map for mountains dotted with temples. Good examples would be Namsan in Gyeongju or Palgongsan, north of Daegu.

For shamanists Paekdusan, in North Korea, is now the most venerated, due to its large volcanic crater-lake, the legend of Dangun and also because of the reunification issue (see the North Korea chapter). Hallasan, on Jejudo, is considered by some as a Southern counterpart to Paekdusan, because it too is an old volcano with a small lake. Jejudo also has a rich tradition of shamanism.

Taebaeksan, in the south-east of Gangwon-do, is very holy to shamanists. As long as North Korea is closed to ordinary South Koreans, it's a temporary spiritual home for many of shamanists and an alternative site for the Tan'gun legend.

Other mountains famous for shamanism, magical events and powerful mountain gods are Myohyangsan and Geumgangsan, in North Korea; Jirisan, at the intersection of three southern provinces; Gyeryongsan, west of Daejeon; Moaksan, in Jeollabuk-do; Mudeungsan, outside Gwangju; Inwangsan, in west-central Seoul; Bukhansan, to the north of Seoul; Manisan (the third major Dangun-worship site), on the island of Ganghwado, Gyeonggi-do.

These mountains are important to Buddhists too, except for Hallasan, Mudeungsan, Inwangsan and Manisan.

Imwon Beach 임원해수욕장

This small beach is only 200m long, but has a dramatic setting in a cliff-lined cove. Nearby is Hwabanggul sea cave and a pretty little pavilion, Sobongsanjeong. There is also a freshwater creek nearby, and some *minbak*, for refreshments, in the vicinity. Buses from Samcheok run every 1½ hours.

Hosan Beach 호산해수욕장

The southernmost beach in Gangwon province, Hosan is about 1km in length and has good white sand. There is a pine tree grove next to the beach, and *camping* in the area is popular. Two buses from Samcheok run daily.

TAEBAEKSAN PROVINCIAL PARK 태백산국립공원

Taebaeksan (Big White Mountain) is the sixth-highest mountain in South Korea. The mountain actually consists of the twin peaks, Janggunbong (1568m) and its neighbour, Munsubong (1546m). The town of Taebaek is just north of the park.

Taebaeksan is also one of Korea's three most sacred mountains for shamanists. On the summit is the **Cheonjedan Altar**, where religious ceremonies are occasionally held.

Not surprisingly, the park has a number of **temples**, including Manggyeongsa, Baektansa, Yuilsa and Mandeoksa.

The village of Danggol, situated in a large valley, is the park's main entrance and also a magnet for pilgrims. There is a shrine here called Tan-geumseong, dedicated to Dan-gun, the mythical progenitor of the Korean race.

The Taebaek region was once a bustling coal mining area and the Coal Museum traces its local history – and even includes a simulated cave-in. The museum is just inside the park entrance (free entry).

Places to Stay

There are many *minbak* inside the park at Danggol. For *yeogwan* and *hotels* you have to stay in the town of Taebaek.

Getting There & Away

Bus From Taebaek, just north of the park, it's another 20 minutes to the park from the

GANGWON-DO

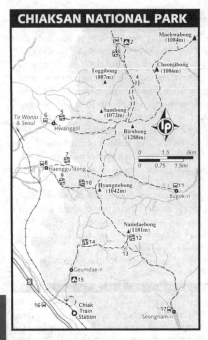

CHIAKSAN NATIONAL PARK

1 Bus Stop (No.41)
  버스정류장
2 Geumdae-ri Camping
  Ground
  금대리야영장
3 Guryongsa
  구룡사
4 Seryeompokpo
  세렴폭포
5 Beommunsa
  범문사
6 Bus Stop (No.82)
  버스정류장
7 Gwaneumsa
  관음사
8 Bus Stop
  버스정류장
9 Gukhyangsa
  국향사
10 Bomunsa
  보문사
11 Bus Stop
  버스정류장
12 Sangwonsa
  상원사
13 Spring
  쌍룡수
14 Yeongwonsa
  영원사
15 Guryongsa Camping
  Ground
  구룡사야영장
16 Bus Stop
  버스정류장
17 Bus Stop (No.21)
  버스정류장

bus terminal on local bus No 33 (W600, every 10 minutes).

Taebaek is well connected to the outside world, with bus services to many places including:

destination	price (W)	duration	distance
Andong	9800	2¾ hrs	134km
Daegu	14,800	5½ hrs	242km
Gangneung	6800	2½ hrs	107km
Samcheok	3600	1½ hrs	53km

Train Trains depart from Seoul's Cheongnyangni train station, including one daily saemaeul service (W17,200, 4¼ hours) and eight mugunghwa services (W11,800, 4¾ hours).

WONJU 원주
pop 265,000
Wonju is a large town but for the traveller probably holds little of real interest and nothing to detain you for long. Its real value

is as a useful transport hub for visiting nearby Chiaksan National Park.

Places to Stay & Eat
To find a couple of decent places to stay and a few restaurants, as you exit the bus terminal turn right at the first street off the main road. If you are hungry, check out *Buffet Nammae Galibi*, where an all-you-can-eat barbecue will set you back W7000 per person.

Getting There & Away
Bus Express buses depart from Wonju to:

destination	price (W)	duration	distance
Dong Seoul	4700	1¾ hrs	120km
Gangneung	7200	2½ hrs	116km
Seoul	4700	1½ hrs	122km

Inter-city bus destinations include:

destination	price (W)	duration	distance
Cheongju	6700	1¾ hrs	141km
Chuncheon	12,700	4½ hrs	200km
Daegu	14,500	3½ hrs	
Suwon	5500	1¾ hrs	110km
Taebaek	11,300	4 hrs	159km

Train Trains to Wonju, including saemaeul services (W7600, 1½ hours, four daily) and mugunghwa services (W5100, 1¾ hours, 17 daily), depart from Seoul's Cheongnyangni train station.

CHIAKSAN NATIONAL PARK
치악산국립공원

Chiaksan (Magpie Crags Mountains) is just east of Wonju. The highest peak is Birobong (1288m), but there are also a number of other high peaks, which are lined up along a north-south axis. These include Birobong, Hyang-nobong and Namdaebong. Chiaksan is close enough to Seoul to attract the usual horde of rock climbers, who come for the challenge of the unusual rock formations in the park.

A popular **hike** is from Guryongsa up to Birobong (six hours) and back to either Guryongsa (six hours) or down to Hwang-gol (five hours). All the hikes are pretty rigorous and steep. There are no shelters inside the park and camping outside of the grounds is prohibited.

In the northern part of the park is the fairly large temple, **Guryongsa**. Another notable temple is **Sangwonsa**. This would have to be the highest temple in Korea, located just below Namdaebong (1181m). The temple, perched on a 50m-high cliff, commands a breathtaking view over the valley. It's about three hours' hike from the Seongnam-ri ham-let and it's another 20 minutes up to Nam-daebong from the temple.

Entry to the Guryongsa area costs W2000, while other areas of the park cost only W1000.

Places to Stay
Camping is available at both *Guryong* and *Geumdae camping grounds*. Sites cost W3000 It is necessary to book ahead during summer months and holidays (☎ 732 5231, e chiak@npa.or.kr).

There are dozens of minbak below the temple at Guryongsa charging between W20,000 and W25,000 a room.

Getting There & Away
Bus From Wonju, you can catch bus No 41 to Guryongsa (¾ hour, every 25 minutes), No 82 to Hwanggol or No 21 to Geumdae-ri and Seongnam-ri (one hour, every two hours).

Gyeongsangbuk-do

Highlights

- Gyeongju, the historic ancient capital of the Silla kingdom. Strewn with temples, caves and ruins set against a backdrop of verdant beauty

- Andong, where much of Korea's traditional culture is still intact

- Haeinsa, the repository of the Tripitaka Koreana

- Juwangsan Provincial Park with its fine mountains and beautiful valleys

- Ulleungdo, a remote, rugged and incredibly scenic island in the storm-lashed sea between Korea and Japan

Ulleungdo p238 ●
Dodong -ri p240

Andong p228 ●
Juwangsan National Park p232
Palgongsan Provincial Park p207
Pohang p235
Central Daegu p204
Central Gyeongju p209
Daegu p202
Gyeongju p216-17

☎ 054 • pop 5.6 million

A province endowed with more than just scenic attractions, Gyeongsangbuk-do is home to some of the most fascinating remainders of Korea's cultural, historical, scientific and religious heritage.

The most famous and popular place is definitely Gyeongju. This former capital of the Silla period (57 BC–AD 935) is a treasure trove of historical relics. North of Gyeongju is Andong, another city surrounded by interesting cultural and historical

sites. Over 130km out to sea, towards Japan, is the rugged island of Ulleungdo. Farther out still is Korea's final frontier, Dokdo, a contested rocky outcrop that has focused the strong nationalism of the Korean people. Both islands have become popular tourist destinations in recent years.

Gyeongsangbuk-do was one of the first provinces to reap the benefits of Korea's rapid post-war development and growth. A large proportion of the country's wealth and industry is based here, and the province is well represented in Seoul. Due to its strong historical and political links, the province evokes a strong sense of regionalism.

DAEGU 대구

☎ 053 • pop 2.5 million

As the country's third largest city, Daegu is of significant economic importance as an industrial and commercial centre. The city itself has little to offer in terms of scenic attractions. However, Daegu is a useful staging point for reaching one of the country's most famous temple-monastery complexes, Haeinsa in Gayasan National Park.

Information

There is a new tourist information centre which is very well resourced and even has a library, computers for Internet browsing, a cafe and souvenir shop. The centre is inconveniently located in the south-west of town. Ring them (☎ 627 8900) for details. More convenient for travellers is the tourist information booth at Dong Daegu Station, or the one in the centre of town, a short walk from Jung-angno subway station.

Bookshops

A good place to find English-language books is at the Jaeil Book Center, near Jung-angno subway station.

Daegu Museum 대구박물관

This museum houses a fine collection of relics that trace the history of the Daegu

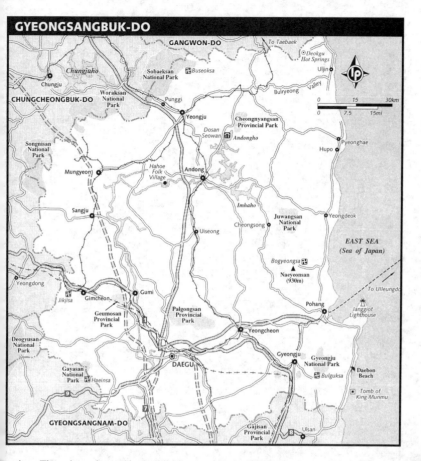

GYEONGSANGBUK-DO

region. There is an interesting exhibition examining the life of *seonbi* – the Confucian literati who rivalled the Yi kings for power – their ceremonies, clothing and customs.

The musum also an exhibition room where they often present local artists' paintings, making for a sharp contrast to the older exhibits A special interactive room gives visitors the chance to play some traditional instruments, like the geomungo (zither), buk (drums) and kkwaenggwari (gong). On special occasions, pottery classes are held here as well – contact the museum for more de-

tails (☎ 768 6051). Entry costs W400 (9 am to 5 pm, closed Monday).

Bus Nos 415 and 514 run from Dong Daegu Station to the front of the museum.

Yasigolmok 야시골목

This is the heart of Daegu's shopping district: a hive of clothing and fashion outlets catering to Daegu's youth; bustling day and night.

Herbal Medicine Market 한약시장

In the central area, about 1km south of Daegu station, is the Herbal Medicine

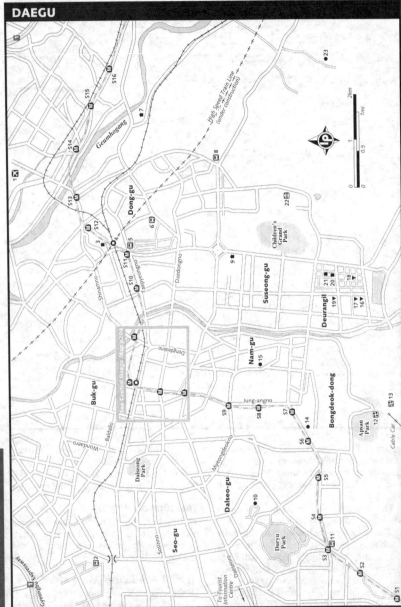

DAEGU

DAEGU

PLACES TO STAY
3 Cheongho-jang; Motel
Buel Jang
청호장; 모텔뷰엘장
7 The Park Hotel
파크호텔
9 Grand Hotel
그랜드호텔
20 Mani-jang Yeogwan
마니장여관
21 Ace-jang Yeogwan; Libera
Hotel
에이스장여관; 리베라호텔

PLACES TO EAT
16 Geumgok Samgyetang
금곡삼계탕
17 Hantibulnak
한티불낙
18 Cheonghakgol
Hanuchon
청학골; 한우촌
19 Songhakgui;
Miseongbogeo
송학구이; 미성복어

OTHER
1 Airport
대구공항
2 Bukbu (North) Inter-City
Bus Terminal
북부시외버스터미널
4 Dongdaegu Train Station
동대구역

5 Express (Gosok) Bus
Terminal
고속버스터미널
6 Dongbu (East) Inter-City
Bus Terminal
동부시외버스터미널
8 Nambu (South) Inter-City
Bus Terminal
남부시외버스터미널
10 Daegu Tower
대구타워
11 Seobu (West) Inter-City
Bus Terminal
서부시외버스터미널
12 Daeseongsa
대성사
13 Daedeoksa
대덕사
14 Camp Walker
15 Camp Henry
22 Daegu Museum
국립대구박물관
23 Daegu Sports Complex
(World Cup Stadium)
대구종합운동장

SUBWAY STATIONS
S1 Wolchon
월촌
S2 Songhyeon
송현
S3 Seongdangmot
(Seobo Bus Terminal)
성당못

S4 Daemyeong
대명
S5 Anjirang
안지랑
S6 Hyeonchungno
현충로
S7 Namdaegu
남대구
S8 Yeongseon
영선
S9 Myeongdeok
명덕
S10 Dong Daegu Station
동대구
S11 Big Pass (Keungogae)
큰고개
S12 Ayanggyo
아양교
S13 Dongchon
동촌
S14 Haean
해안
S15 Bangchon
방촌
S16 Yonggye
용계

Market (Yangnyeong Sijang). This is one of the largest such places in Korea, and if you've missed the one in Seoul, then you should come here for a look. Stock up on everything from lizard's tails to magic mushrooms.

The **Yangnyeong Exhibition Hall** is a good place to start exploring this area. There is a wholesale oriental medicine market on the ground floor which comes to life every five days. Upstairs are some displays of various herbs and medicines, as well as some of the production processes involved. Entry is free (closed Sunday).

Apsan Park 앞산공원

At the far southern end of Daegu is Apsan Park, which at 17 sq km is Daegu's largest. The most notable attraction here is the cable car running 800 metres to the summit of Apsan, but you can walk up by following a 4km trail. Near the base of the cable car ride is the Memorial Museum of Victory in Nakdonggang, or Nakdonggang Seungjeonginyeomgwan, which celebrates a victorious (for the South) battle by the Nakdonggang during the Korean War.

Bus Nos 424, 750 and 910 head out to the park from the centre of town.

Jagalmadang-gu

Jagalmadang-gu is something of a bizarre tourist attraction. A red-light district, it's one of the 'big three' such places in Korea, the other two being Wansol-dong in Busan and Cheongnyangni in Seoul. All three cater to domestic business – there's scarcely a foreigner in sight. Taking a look at these

GYEONGSANGBUK-DO

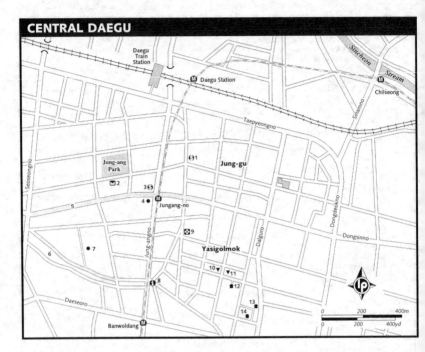

CENTRAL DAEGU

can be an interesting experience, even for women. The brothels look like nothing you've seen in the West – you might describe them as 'display cases'. Each one fronts the street with a huge plate-glass window beyond which, under intense pink lighting, sit up to two dozen women, fully made up in traditional Korean costume, waiting for clients to choose them. These are not strictly *gisaeng*, the Korean equivalent of the Japanese geisha, since real gisaeng would be horrified by such indiscretion. Nevertheless, this is no bawdy sleazebag environment – everyone is on their best behaviour (after all, they are Korean).

Places to Stay

Just to the north of Dong Daegu Station are *Chongho-jang* (☎ 942 4661) and *Motel Buel Jang* (☎ 955 5545), where doubles cost W25,000.

In central Daegu there are couple of OK options. *Silla-jang Yeogwan* (☎ 424 4220)

is conveniently located near all the bars and restaurants downtown, but a little difficult to find. Look for the large Kenzo billboard. The hotel is just off the street. It has decent rooms from W23,000 to W25,000. Just nearby is *Maeil-jang* where reasonable rooms go for W25,000. Also nearby is *Serin-jang Yeogwan* which has clean rooms also for W25,000.

In the Teurangil district are a large number of new abodes. *Ace-jang Yeogwan* (☎ 765 6703) has clean and comfortable rooms for W25,000. Next door, *Libera Motel* offers the same deal and is also new and clean. Around the corner is *Mani-jang Yeogwan* (☎ 763 5100), where doubles are also W25,000.

Most of Daegu's deluxe hotels are spread around the suburbs. The *Grand Hotel* (☎ 742 0001, fax 742 0002) is south of Dong Daegu Station and has decent doubles from W140,000. The *Park Hotel* (☎ 952 0088, fax 953 2008) is in the east of town, near

CENTRAL DAEGU

1 Korea First Bank
제일은행
2 Daegu Post Office
대구우체국
3 Korea Exchange Bank
외환은행
4 Jaeil Book Centre
제일서점
5 Central Underground
Arcade
중앙지하상가
6 Herbal Medicine Market
한약시장
7 Yangnyeong Exhibition
Hall
약령전시관
8 Tourist Information
관광안내소
9 Daegu Department Store
대구백화점
10 Gimgane
김가네
11 Gaejeong
개정
12 Silla-jang Yeogwan
신라장여관
13 Serin-jang Yeogwan
세린장여관
14 Maeil-jang
매일장

Mangudang Park. Very comfortable doubles/
suites start from W80,000/W240,000.

Places to Eat

Around the Yashigolmok district are literally
hundreds of cafes, bars and nightclubs, also
the popular and respected *Gaejang*, which
specialises in a chewy and very tasty
naengmyeon (cold noodles, W5000). Other
tasty dishes include *mandu* (dumplings;
W3500) and a couple of varieties of *bibimbap* (spicy rice with vegetables and meat;
W5000 to W7000). To make ordering easy
they even have a descriptive English menu.

Still in the central area is *Kimganae,* a
gimbap (Korean sushi) chain restaurant that
serves tasty and inexpensive meals like
gimbap, mandu and naengmyeon.

Deurangil is a newly developed restaurant
and hotel district. There are literally hundreds
of restaurants and dozens of places to stay.
The quality is fairly good, but high patronage

is always a good indicator. The only thing
this area lacks is atmosphere. There are a
couple of places worth trying. *Cheonghakgol Hanuchon* is a traditional Korean restaurant serving up delicious *amso galbisal*
(barbecued eye fillet, W12,000), *amso seok-
soegui* (grilled eye fillet, W8000), and
saenggogi (fresh meat, W10,000 per person).

Around the corner is *Geumsan Samgyetang,* which is open 24 hours and serves
up a tasty bowl of ginseng chicken
(W7000). Look for the big yellow chick on
the billboard. If you miss this outlet, there
is another just 100m away. Just next door is
Hantibulnak where you'll find Japanese
chobap (sushi). Also try their *nakjijeon-
munjeom,* a spicy octopus hotpot.

Just a bit farther north is *Songhakgui*, a
second generation restaurant specialising in
grills. It is also open 24 hours.

Getting There & Away

Air Asiana and Korean Air have frequent
flights between Daegu and Seoul and Daegu
and Jejudo. Korean Air has a Sokcho-Daegu
flight, though it is in fact via Seoul. There is
also a daily Korean Air flight to Osaka

Bus Daegu is something of a transport
nightmare. There are five bus terminals
spread around the city, each one offering
buses to different destinations. You can easily spend over an hour hassling with city
buses trying to get from one terminal to the
next. The five bus stations are as follows:

express bus terminal
dongbu (east) inter-city bus terminal
seobu (west) inter-city bus terminal
nambu (south) inter-city bus terminal
bukbu (north) inter-city bus terminal

Daegu's new subway system now connects
most of the important bus terminals and is a
lot easier than catching the wrong bus.

Departures from the express bus terminal
include:

destination	price (W)	duration	distance
Busan	5300	1¾ hrs	135km
Cheongju	8500	3¾ hrs	220km

GYEONGSANGBUK-DO

destination	price (W)	duration	distance
Daejeon	5800	2 hrs	149km
Dong Seoul	11,600	3¾ hrs	
Gwangju	8400	3¾ hrs	219km
Gyeongju	2600	50 mins	60km
Jinju	5600	2¼ hrs	143km
Seoul	11,100	3¾ hrs	297km

Departures from the dongbu inter-city bus terminal include:

destination	price (W)	duration	distance
Gangneung	21,200	7½ hrs	343km
Gyeongju	2600	50 mins	65km
Pohang	5100	1½ hrs	87km
Sokcho	25,800	7 hrs	419km

Departures from the seobu inter-city bus terminal include:

destination	price (W)	duration	distance
Haeinsa	3200	1¼ hrs	60km
Tongyeong	8800	2¾ hrs	167km

Departures from the bukbu inter-city bus terminal include:

destination	price (W)	duration	distance
Andong	5100	2 hrs	102km
Chuncheon	19,900	5¾ hrs	391km
Gimcheon	3600	1¼ hrs	59km
Guinsa	13,000	5 hrs	222km

Train Daegu station serves mainly local trains, and unless you want to stay in the downtown area, don't get off the train here! The Dong Daegu station, on the eastern side of the city, is where express trains stop, and in most cases this is where you should get off.

There are regular connections to Busan and Seoul. *Mugunghwa* (limited express) trains run every 30 minutes to Seoul (W14,600, 3½-4 hours) and Busan (W5400, 1½ hours).

Getting Around

The Airport Daegu's airport is north-east of the city, about 2km from the express bus terminal. Bus No 401 (W600) winds a circuitous route to the airport and can take 45 minutes. Bus No 104 (W1200) is a bit better. A taxi from the airport to the centre will cost around W2500 and takes about 20 minutes.

Bus Green local buses (W600) are usually standing-room only and orange buses (W1200) are seated buses.

Bus Nos 402, 407, 814 and 900 run south from Dong Daegu Station through Deurangil via the Grand Hotel.

Subway The subway is a fast and efficient way of getting around and conveniently connects the major bus terminals. Tickets cost W600 or W700. Presently, Daegu has one subway line and is constructing No 2 line, which hopefully will reach the World Cup Stadium by 2002 and be completed in 2004.

PALGONGSAN PROVINCIAL PARK 팔공산도립공원

Just 20km north of Daegu's urban sprawl is Palgongsan Provincial Park. It was originally called Gongsan, and Buak, but changed its name at the end of the Silla period, when eight generals saved the founding king of the Goryeo kingdom, Wang-Geon. As a result of this good deed, the park was named Palgongsan, or the 'mountain of eight meritorious officers'.

Palgongsan (1192m) is the highest peak in the park, and is connected by ridges to Dongbong (1155m) and Yeombulbong (1021m). However, this is not a wilderness park, and the splendid scenery is somewhat marred by an 18-hole golf course, numerous luxury hotels and a large cable car.

A major feature of the park is **Donghwasa**, a large temple with a history stretching back over 1000 years. The temple is a careful balance of old and new architecture but the noticeable feature is **Tong-ildaebul** or Medicinal Buddha. Many hikers commence their hike from here and continue up to the ridge and along to **Gatbawi** (Seokjoyeoraejwasang), a 33m-high stone statue sitting atop Gwanbong calling for the peaceful reunification of Korea. This squatting and flat-hatted stone Buddha is

PALGONGSAN PROVINCIAL PARK

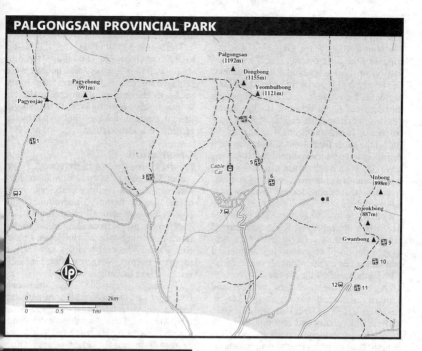

PALGONGSAN PROVINCIAL PARK

1 Pagyesa
 파계사
2 Bus Stop
 버스정류장
3 Buinsa
 부인사
4 Yeombulam Hermitage
 염불암
5 Budoam Hermitage
 부도암
6 Donghwasa
 동화사
7 Bus Stop
 버스정류장
8 Country Club
 컨츄리클럽
9 Gatbawi
 (Seokjoyeoraejwasang)
 갓바위(석조여래좌상)
10 Gwaneumsa
 관음사
11 Boeunsa
 보은사
12 Bus Stop
 버스정류장

the main pilgrimage destination on the mountain; it is said to grant all visitors one wish. Naturally, a long line ensues all day long. It takes about 40–50 minutes to walk up the stone steps to Gatbawi from the tourist village.

The **Palgong Skyline Cablecar** (W4700 return trip) is the quickest way to ascend Palgongsan. The 1.2km long ride drops you at the observatory (820m) which affords a panoramic view of Daegu.

There is an information booth at Donghwasa where you can pick up a map of the mountain.

Getting There & Away

Bus No 104 (W1200) runs between Dong Daegu station and the tourist village that sits below the peak Gatbawi. Bus Nos 105 and 131 connect Dong Daegu and Donghwasa. These buses run at least once every 30 minutes and take 50 minutes to complete the journey.

GYEONGJU

pop 2.9 million

For almost 1000 years, Gyeongju was the capital of the Silla dynasty (see the History section in the Facts about Korea chapter). For nearly 300 years of that period, following Silla's conquest of the neighbouring kingdoms of Goguryeo and Baekje in the 7th century, it was the capital of the whole peninsula. It had its origins way back in 57 BC, at the same time Julius Caesar was subduing Gaul, and survived until the 10th century AD, when it fell victim to division from within and invasion from without. A time-span like that is rare for any dynasty anywhere in the world.

Following its conquest by Goryeo in AD 918, when the capital of Korea was moved far to the north, Gyeongju fell into a prolonged period of obscurity. It was pillaged and ransacked by the Mongols in the early-13th century and by the Japanese in the late-16th century. Despite these ravages and centuries of neglect, the city survived to experience a cultural revival which began early in this century and continues today. A great deal of restoration work has been accomplished, all of it close to original specifications, and practically every year archaeologists uncover more treasure troves of precious relics which help throw light on life during Silla times.

Today Gyeongju is an expanding city, though still relatively small; its major drawcard is that it's literally an open-air museum. In any direction you care to walk you will come across tombs, temples, shrines, the remains of palaces, pleasure gardens, castles and Buddhist statuary. It's an incredible place, where the examples of Silla artistry in the valley are only the most conspicuous and accessible of the sights. Up in the forested mountains that surround the city are thousands of Buddhist shrines, temples, inscriptions, rock carvings, pagodas and statues. Enthusiasts can, and do, spend weeks wandering around these places – less enthusiastic visitors might grow tired of expending such a major effort to visit what appears at first glance to be mediocre rubble. Just how much you enjoy Gyeongju really depends on your interests.

The dictator Park Chung-hee did his bit to preserve Gyeongju – he set up strict limits on building heights, and houses were required to retain the distinctive curly roofs. In this era of democracy, the restrictions have been relaxed, to the delight of real estate developers but much to the chagrin of traditionalists.

Orientation

Central Gyeongju is a fairly compact city. About 5km east of town is Bomunho, a resort area with a country club, lake, golf course, luxury hotels, condominiums and posh restaurants with all the trimmings.

A 16km drive from the centre to the south-east brings you to Bulguksa, one of Korea's most famous temples and a major tourist drawcard. Next to the temple is the resort village of Bulguk-dong.

Gyeongju National Park surrounds Gyeongju. It's not one contiguous park, but numerous separate districts: to the east is the largest district, Tohamsan; due south is Namsan; to the west are Hwarang and Seoak; and to the north-east is Sogeumgang. Other pieces of the park lie farther afield on the coast, near Daebon.

Information

There is a tourist information kiosk outside the express bus terminal with English-speaking staff. This place also dishes out decent maps of the area. There is a similar information booth in front of the train station. There are lockers in the bus terminals and train station.

If you are interested in the legends, the detailed history and current archaeological debate surrounding the Silla remains, then it's worth getting hold of a copy of *Korea's Golden Age* by Edward B Adams. This is a beautifully illustrated guide to all known Silla sites written by a man who was born in Korea and who has spent most of his life there. The book is difficult or impossible to buy in Gyeongju, so pick up a copy at one of the large bookshops in Seoul.

Central Gyeongju

Tumuli Park Right in the heart of central Gyeongju is a huge walled area containing 20 tombs of the Silla monarchs and members of their families. Many of them have been excavated in recent years to yield fabulous treasures, which are on display at the National Museum. One of the tombs, the **Cheonmachong** (Heavenly Horse Tomb), is now open in cross-section to show the method of construction. This huge tomb, 13m high and 47m in diameter, was built around the end of the 5th century AD and is the only one excavated so far which contains a wooden burial chamber. Facsimiles of the golden crown, bracelets, jade ornaments, weapons and pottery found here are displayed in glass cases around the inside of the tomb. Entry is W1500.

Noseo-dong Tombs Across the other side of the main road and closer to the city centre is the Noseo-dong district, where there are other Silla tombs for which there is no entry fee. Seobongchong and Geumgwanchong are two adjacent tombs built between the 4th and 5th centuries AD. They were excavated between 1921 and 1946.

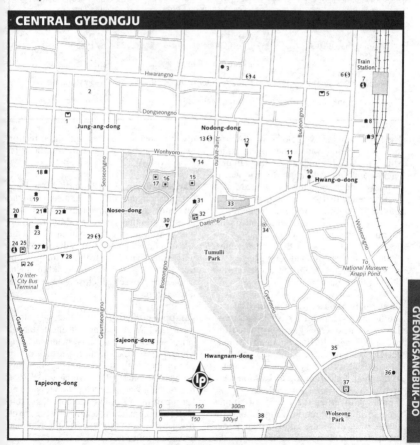

CENTRAL GYEONGJU

CENTRAL GYEONGJU

PLACES TO STAY
- 8 Jeil Yeoinsuk
  제일여인숙
- 9 Arirang-jang Yeoinsuk
  아리랑장여인숙
- 18 Lotte-jang Motel
  롯데장모텔
- 19 Cheonjimokyoktang Motel
  천지목욕탕모텔
- 20 Yeongbin-jang Yeogwan
  영빈장여관
- 21 Hanjin Hostel
  한진여관
- 22 Taeyang-jang Yeogwan
  태양장여관
- 23 Royal-jang Yeogwan
  로얄장여관
- 27 Gyeongju Park Tourist
  Hotel
  경주파크관광호텔
- 31 Sarangchae B&B
  사랑채

PLACES TO EAT
- 11 Nolboo Restaurant
  놀부레스토랑
- 12 Pyeongyang Naengmyeon
  평양냉면

- 14 Terrace
  테라스
- 28 Dukkeobi Bulgogi House
  두꺼비식당
- 30 Donghaegwan
  동해관
- 35 Ssambap restaurants
  쌈밥거리
- 38 Wonpung Sikdang
  원풍식당

OTHER
- 1 Small Post Office
  우체국
- 2 Jung-ang Market
  중앙시장
- 3 Gyeongju Map Centre
  경주지도센터
- 4 Hanvit Bank
  한빛은행
- 5 Post Office
  우체국
- 6 Korea First Bank
  제일은행
- 7 Tourist Information Kiosk
  관광안내소
- 10 Yurim Teahouse
  유림

- 13 Korea Exchange Bank
  외환은행
- 15 Geumnyeongchong;
  Bonghwadae
  금령총
- 16 Geumgwanchong
  금관총
- 17 Seobongchong
  서봉총
- 24 Tourist Information Kiosk
  관광안내소
- 25 Express Bus Terminal
  고속버스터미널
- 26 Bus Stop for Bulguksa
  불국사행버스
- 29 Nonghyeop Bank &
  Supermarket
  농협·수퍼마켓
- 32 Beopjangsa
  범장사
- 33 City Hall
  시청
- 34 Tchoksaem Spring
  쪽샘
- 36 Cheomseongdae
  첨성대
- 37 Performance Stage
  야외공연장

The finds included two gold crowns. Across the road is Bonghwadae, the largest extant Silla tomb at 22m high and with a circumference of 250m. Adjoining Bonghwadae is Geumnyeongchong. Houses covered much of this area until 1984, when they were removed. It's tempting to climb to the top of these tombs, but if you do you'll have park guardians chasing you and blowing whistles! And that's despite the fact that hundreds of similarly minded people have done just that, judging from the tracks up the sides of the tombs.

Cheomseongdae A few hundred metres south-east of Tumuli Park is Cheomseongdae, a stone observatory constructed between AD 632–46. Its apparently simple design conceals an amazing subtlety. The 12 stones of its base symbolise the months of the year and, from top to bottom, there are 30 layers – one for each day of the month. Altogether there are 366 stones used in its construction, roughly one for each day of the year. There are numerous other technical details relating to the

tower's position, angles and the direction of its corners in relation to certain stars. Entry costs W300.

Banwolseong A little farther on from Cheomseongdae on the right side at the junction with the main road is Banwolseong (Castle of the Crescent Moon). Banwolseong was once the royal castle and the site of a fabled palace which dominated the whole area. There's hardly anything left of this fortress today except Seokbinggo or 'Stone Ice House' which was once used as a food store.

Anapji Pond Across the other side of the main road, Wolseongno, on the left hand side, is Anapji Pond, constructed by King Munmu in 674 AD as a pleasure garden to commemorate the unification of Silla. Only remnants of the palace which once stood here remain, but when the pond was drained for repair in 1975 thousands of relics were dredged up, including a perfectly preserved royal barge now displayed in the National Museum. Entry is W1000.

National Museum Continuing a little further up along Wolseongno you come to the National Museum. This beautiful building, whose design is based on classical Korean architecture, houses the best collection of historical artefacts of any museum in Korea, including the National Museum in Seoul.

Outside the main building in its own pavilion hangs the **Emille Bell**, one of the largest and most beautifully resonant bells ever made in Asia. It's said that its ringing can be heard over a 3km radius when struck only lightly with the fist. Unfortunately, you won't be allowed to test this claim! The museum is open during the same hours as Tumuli Park. Entry is W400 (open 9 am to 5 pm, closed Monday).

Bunhwangsa Completing this circuit is the pagoda Bunhwangsa (Gyeongju map). It was built in the mid-7th century AD during the reign of Queen Seondeok, and is the oldest datable pagoda in Korea. It originally had nine storeys but only three are left today. The magnificently carved Buddhist guardians and stone lions are a major feature of the pagoda.

To get there follow the willow-lined road across from the National Museum until you reach the first intersection. Turn right at the intersection and then take the first lane on the right. The walk will take about 20 to 25 minutes. Entry is W1000.

East Area
Bomunho Resort This artificial lake area has become a popular recreational resort area and is home to many of the top-end hotels and condominiums. The lake and extensive parklands are a fantastic place to take a stroll or ride a bike around. Expos and conferences are often held here and the area is more an entertainment than cultural district.

In addition to all the hotels and restaurants, there are a couple of sites worth visiting. The **Seonje Museum of Contemporary Art** is just in front of the Hilton Hotel and holds a diverse range of exhibitions throughout the year. They have three exhibition rooms where some of their permanent collections of

paintings and sculptures from overseas and Korea are displayed. Entry costs W2000 (open 10 am to 6 pm, closed Monday).

Traditional dancing and musical performances are held on a regular basis throughout the year at **Bomun Outdoor Performance Theater,** below the information centre by the lake. If you're lucky enough to be in Gyeongju during a festival then many of the main events take place in and around Bomunho and down at the expo site.

South-East Area
Bulguksa Built on a series of stone terraces about 16km south-east of Gyeongju is Bulguksa ('Buddha Nation Temple'), the crowning glory of Silla temple architecture. It really is magnificent. Korea has never gone in for huge, monolithic (though magnificent) temples like the Potala Palace in Lhasa; instead it concentrates on the excellence of its

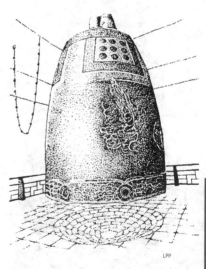

LPP

The massive Emille Bell, created in AD 771, is one of the world's largest and oldest temple bells. Legend has it that a child was thrown into the molten bronze when the bell was cast, and the sound the bell makes when struck evokes the child's cries to its mother (Emi).

carpentry, the incredible skill of its painters and the subtlety of its landscapes.

Originally built in AD 528 during the reign of King Beop-heung, and enlarged in 751, it survived intact until destroyed by the Japanese in 1593. From then until the recent past it languished in ruin and though a few structures were rebuilt it never regained its former glory until 1970, when the late President Park Chung-hee ordered its reconstruction along the original lines. Work was completed in 1972.

Standing on the highest level and looking down you are presented with a rolling sea of tiles formed by one sloping roof after another. The painting of the internal woodwork and of the eaves of the roofs should be one of the Seven Wonders of the World. Down in the courtyard of the first set of buildings are two pagodas which survived the Japanese vandalism and which stand in complete contrast to each other. The first, **Dabotap**, is of plain design and typical of Silla artistry while the other, **Seokgatap**, is much more ornate and typical of those constructed in the neighbouring Baekje kingdom. (There are also copies of the two pagodas standing outside the main building of the Gyeongju National Museum.) Entry to Bulguksa costs W3000.

Seokguram Grotto High up in the mountains above Bulguksa, reached by a long, winding sealed road, is the famous grotto of Seokguram, where a seated image of the Sakyamuni Buddha looks out over the mountainous landscape towards the distant East Sea (Sea of Japan). Constructed in the mid-8th century out of huge blocks of granite – quarried far to the north at a time when the only access was a narrow mountain path – it bears striking resemblance to similar figures found in China and India (especially those at Badami, north of Mysore).

When the Goryeo dynasty was overthrown and Buddhism suppressed during the Yi dynasty, Seokguram fell into disrepair and was forgotten until accidentally rediscovered in 1909. This was the time of the Japanese occupation and, had the regional governor had his way, it might very well have ended up in a Japanese museum. Fortunately, the local Korean authorities refused to cooperate in its removal and in 1913 a two-year restoration was undertaken. However incompetence resulted in the destruction of much of the superstructure, and it was not until 1961 that a more thorough restoration was begun under the auspices of UNESCO (United Nations Educational, Scientific & Cultural Organisation). It was completed three years later.

The only disappointing thing about Seokguram is that the Buddha is encased in a shiny, reflective glass case and photographs are not permitted. Entry to the grotto costs W2500.

Unfortunately, both Bulguksa and Seokguram Grotto are generally crawling with tourists every day of the week during

Stone temple lion guarding the approach to Dabotap, Bulguksa.

the summer months, at which time the place can take on the air of a mass barbecue, so don't expect a wilderness experience.

To get to the grotto from Bulguksa, take one of the frequent tourist buses which leave from the tourist information pavilion in the car park below the temple. The buses terminate at a car park and from there it's a 400m walk along a shaded gravel track to the grotto. You get 40 minutes to visit the grotto before the bus returns, but if you miss it you can take any bus back without paying an additional fare. Alternatively, there's a well-marked hiking trail from the grotto to Bulguksa (about 3.2km long), which is a much more interesting way to return.

West Area

Tomb of King Muyeol The main tomb of the Muyeol group is that of King Muyeol. In the mid-7th century he paved the way for the unification of Korea by conquering the rival Baekje kingdom. Just as you enter the tomb compound there is an interesting monument to his exploits: a tortoise carrying a capstone finely carved with intertwined dragons, symbolising his power. Entry is W500.

Tomb of General Kim Yu-shin Back towards town and along a branch road which initially follows the river is the tomb of General Kim Yu-shin. He was one of Korea's greatest military heroes, leading the armies of both Muyeol and his successor, Munmu, in the 7th-century campaigns which resulted in the unification of the country. Though smaller in scale than the tomb of King Muyeol, the tomb of General Kim is much more elaborate and surrounded by finely carved figures of the zodiac. The tomb stands on a wooded bluff overlooking the city. Entry is W500.

Places to Stay

The *Hanjin Hostel* (☎ 771 4097, fax 772 9679), also known as the *Hanjin-jang Yeogwan*, is two blocks north-east of the express bus terminal and easily identified by a large English sign on the roof. The congenial owner, Mr Kwon Young-joung, speaks good English and Japanese, hands

The lavish detailing of Silla temple architecture extends to every corner of the building – even individual roof tiles are works of art.

out free maps and is very knowledgeable about local sights. Simple rooms are compensated for by the helpful owner, who provides a fridge, hot water, a kitchen, a meeting room for socialising with other travellers and a courtyard where you can hang out in the evening and watch the stars. Humble doubles with shared bath are W18,000, doubles with private bath cost W25,000.

There are heaps of other yeogwan near the express bus terminal, all charging similar or higher prices. *Lotte-jang Motel* (☎ 772 1204) is quite good value with doubles for W25,000. *Taeyang-jang Yeogwan* (☎ 773 6889) is 20m from Hanjin Hostel and is new, clean and pleasant with air-con rooms for W25,000. Also near the bus terminals are *Royal-jang Yeogwan* (☎ 775 8822) and *Yeongbin-jang Yeogwan*, which both have rooms from W30,000. The fancy looking *Cheonjimokyoktang Motel* (☎ 776 2002) has decent rooms for W35,000. *Kyeongju Park Tourist Hotel* (☎ 742 8804, fax 742 8808) has doubles from W52,280 and large twins for W116,160.

Divinity under glass: the Sakyamuni Buddha of
Seokguram Grotto

Budget options near the train station include **Jeil Yeoinsuk** and **Arirang-jang Yeoinsuk**, which have rooms from W9000 to W12,000 with common shower and toilet.

For those looking for a more authentic and personal experience, try **Sarangchae** (☎ 773 4868, e Silla7@chollian.net), a traditional Korean-style house with rooms for W25,000 and breakfast available for an extra W3000. There is a small courtyard and the rooms are tastefully decorated. Bookings are essential. It's just to the west of a small temple, Peopchangsa.

Most of the classier hotels sit along the lake at Bomunho. If you stay here ensure that you have a room with a lake vista. **Hotel Hyundai** (☎ 748-2233, fax 748-8234) is one of the best choices and they often have reasonable package deals available. Walk-in rates start from W193,000 for doubles, while suites start at W363,000.

Another good deluxe choice is the **Gyeongju Hilton** (☎ 745 7788, fax 745 7799), sitting right on Bomunho. Comfy double rooms are a spicy W229,900 and suites start at W338,800.

Places to Eat

There's an excellent choice of restaurants in Gyeongju, with a wide range of international cuisines from which to choose, including Korean, Chinese, Japanese, Western and seafood.

Pyeongyang Naengmyeon serves up a tasty bowl of chewy cold noodles for W4,500. **Wonpung Sikdang** specialises in *hanjeongsik* (Korean banquet) for W9000. There is a street of **ssambap restaurants** on the southern side of Tumuli Park. Ssambap is a variety of lettuce and other leaves served with lots of tasty side dishes, which you wrap up with the leaf and accompanied perhaps by a barbecue.

Nolboo Restaurant is a *cheolpan* (hot-plate dish) restaurant serving up a variety of hot-plate beef, pork and chicken dishes with a rich, spicy sauce and vegetables (W5000). **Donghaegwan** is another hanjeongsik restaurant charging from W10,000 to W15,000.

Opposite the bus terminal is **Dukkeobi Sikdang**, which serves up a cheap pork barbecue for W2500. Look for the English sign out the front, 'Roast Beef Restaurant'.

The **Terrace** coffee shop and restaurant has an open area where you can sit outside (during the warmer months), look out over Bonghwadae, enjoy a barbecue and drink a cold beer. They also serve some Western food.

For the more indulgent try either **Hotel Hyundai** or the **Hilton Hotel** in Bomunho for their lavish breakfast buffets (W19,500).

If you'd prefer a non-alcoholic drink, **Yurim Teahouse** is off the eastern end of Daejeongno in a small alley.

Entertainment

There are outdoor traditional dance and music performances every Saturday during April, May, September and October (3 to 5 pm) on the stage in Wolseong Park. More regular traditional performances are held at Bomunho between April and November. In April and November, these performances are held at 2.30 pm and during summer are held in the evenings at 8.30 pm. Check with KNTO for more details.

This tortoise stele at the tomb of King Muyeol depicts his power and achievements.

Getting There & Away
Air There is no airport at Gyeongju itself, but the busy airports at Busan and Ulsan are readily accessible. Ulsan's airport is closer and therefore preferred, though you'll have to go to Busan for flights to Japan. See the following Getting Around section for information on airport transport.

Bus Gyeongju has an express bus terminal and inter-city bus terminal, conveniently adjacent to one other. Buses depart the express bus terminal for:

destination	price (W)	duration	distance
Busan	3100	one hour	79km
Daegu	2600	1 hr	66km
Daejeon	8300	2¾ hrs	214km
Seoul	13,400	4¼ hrs	362km

Buses depart from the inter-city bus terminal to:

destination	price (W)	duration	distance
Andong	8800	3 hrs	134km
Busan*	3100	1 hour	84km
Gangneung	17,900	6 hrs	281km
Pohang	1800	40 mins	29km
Uljin	10,100	3 hrs	157km

*This is the bus to take if you intend to visit Tongdosa, a temple halfway between Gyeongju and Busan

Train There are trains connecting Seoul's Cheongnyangni to Gyeongju. Mugunghwa services run once daily (W15,800). There is also one mugunghwa from Seoul (W16,200). There are four daily saemaeul from Seoul (W23,600). There are more services on weekends and holidays. There are also trains between Busan and Gyeongju, but buses are more frequent.

Getting Around
The Airport Direct buses now link Gyeongju with both Ulsan airport (W4500, every 2½ hours) and Busan's Gimhae airport (W9000, hourly).

Bicycle Hiring a bicycle for a day or two is an excellent way of getting around the sites in the immediate vicinity of Gyeongju. There are some bike trails around Namsan and Bomunho, which make for pleasant riding. In general, most of the roads are quite safe and there are plenty of bicycle trails. The most danger you may encounter is from other riders.

There are bicycle rental shops everywhere and the rates are standard. A mountain bike costs about W3000 per hour or W10,000 per day and a tandem is W6000 per hour and W20,000 per day. Bike rentals are available near Gyeongju's train station and bus terminals and at Bomunho.

Bus Many local buses terminate in the road outside the inter-city bus terminal, alongside the river, but these are mostly relatively long-distance local buses. For the shorter routes (eg, to Bulguksa), buses can be picked up along Sosongno and Daejeongno.

Bus Nos 10 (which runs clockwise) and 11 (counter-clockwise) run a circuit of most of the major sights, including Bulguksa, Namsan, Bomuho, bus terminals and Gyeongju train station (W600, every 15 minutes). Bus No 150 departs from the train station to the East Sea (Dong-hae) sights, via the Bomunho Expo arena (every 30 minutes). Local buses cost W600, or W920 seated.

Public tour buses are a good way of seeing all the sights and depart from the inter-city bus terminal at 8.30 and 9.50 am and 1.20pm (W10,000, seven hours). For

GYEONGJU

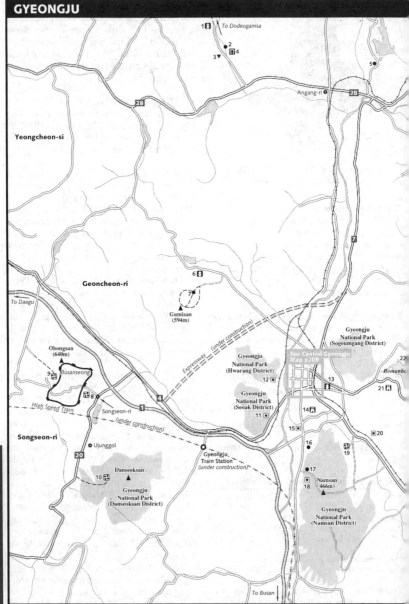

To Dodeogamsa

Angang-ri

Yeongcheon-si

Geoncheon-ri

To Daegu

Gumisan
(594m)

Expressway (under construction)

Gyeongju
National Park
(Sogeumgang District)

Bomunho

Obongsan
(640m)

Busanseong

Gyeongju
National Park
(Hwarang District)

See Central Gyeongju
Map p209

Gyeongju
National Park
(Seoak District)

High Speed Train

Songseon-ri

(under construction)

Songseon-ri

Ujunggol

Gyeongju
Train Station
(under construction)

Danseoksan

Gyeongju
National Park
(Danseoksan District)

Namsan
(466m)

Gyeongju
National Park
(Namsan District)

To Busan

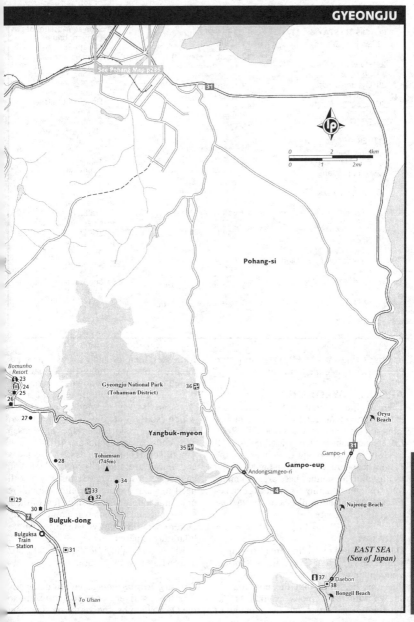

GYEONGJU

See Pohang Map p235

Pohang-si

0   2   4km
0   1   2mi

Bomunho
Resort
23
24
25
26
27

Gyeongju National Park
(Tohamsan District)

36

Yangbuk-myeon

35

28

Tohamsan
(745m)

34

33
32

29

30

Bulguk-dong

Bulguksa
Train
Station

31

To Ulsan

Oryu
Beach

Gampo-ri

Gampo-eup

Andongsamgeo-ri

4

Najeong Beach

EAST SEA
(Sea of Japan)

37 Daebon
38
Bonggil Beach

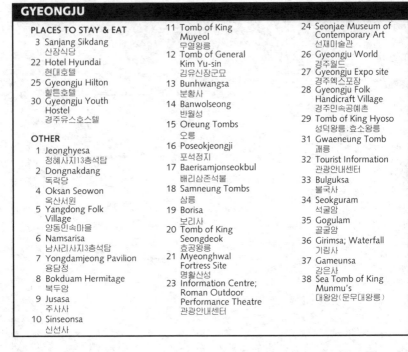

GYEONGJU

PLACES TO STAY & EAT
3 Sanjang Sikdang
  산장식당
22 Hotel Hyundai
  현대호텔
25 Gyeongju Hilton
  힐튼호텔
30 Gyeongju Youth
  Hostel
  경주유스호스텔

OTHER
1 Jeonghyesa
  정혜사지13층석탑
2 Dongnakdang
  독락당
4 Oksan Seowon
  옥산서원
5 Yangdong Folk
  Village
  양동민속마을
6 Namsarisa
  남사리사지3층석탑
7 Yongdamjeong Pavilion
  용담정
8 Bokduam Hermitage
  복두암
9 Jusasa
  주사사
10 Sinseonsa
  신선사

11 Tomb of King
  Muyeol
  무열왕릉
12 Tomb of General
  Kim Yu-sin
  김유신장군묘
13 Bunhwangsa
  분황사
14 Banwolseong
  반월성
15 Oreung Tombs
  오릉
16 Poseokjeongji
  포석정지
17 Baerisamjonseokbul
  배리삼존석불
18 Samneung Tombs
  삼릉
19 Borisa
  보리사
20 Tomb of King
  Seongdeok
  효공왕릉
21 Myeonghwal
  Fortress Site
  명활산성
23 Information Centre;
  Roman Outdoor
  Performance Theatre
  관광안내센터

24 Seonjae Museum of
  Contemporary Art
  선재미술관
26 Gyeongju World
  경주월드
27 Gyeongju Expo site
  경주엑스포장
28 Gyeongju Folk
  Handicraft Village
  경주민속공예촌
29 Tomb of King Hyoso
  성덕왕릉, 효소왕릉
31 Gwaeneung Tomb
  괘릉
32 Tourist Information
  관광안내센터
33 Bulguksa
  불국사
34 Seokguram
  석굴암
35 Gogulam
  골굴암
36 Girimsa; Waterfall
  기림사
37 Gameunsa
  감은사
38 Sea Tomb of King
  Munmu's
  대왕암(문무대왕릉)

bookings ring (☎ 743 6001) or drop into
their office inside the terminal.

AROUND GYEONGJU
There are literally thousands of relics from
the Silla kingdom scattered over the mountains and the plains around Gyeongju. Relic
finders can hunt to their hearts' content all
the way from Gyeongju to Pohang, on the
eastern seaboard, to Daegu in the west, and
to Busan in the south. There are also many
other of interest dating from the Joseon period – not to mention places of spectacular
geographical beauty.

Namsan
One of the most rewarding areas to explore
within easy reach of Gyeongju is Namsan,
a mountain south of the city. Not only is
this area beautiful, but the mountain is
strewn with royal tombs, pagodas, rock-
cut figures, pavilions and the remains of

fortresses, temples and palaces. There are
hundreds of paths alongside the streams
which come tumbling down the mountain
that you can follow; there is also the
'Namsan Skyway', a winding gravel road
which starts out close to the bower
Poseokjeongji, skirts the ridges of Namsan
and ends up at Namsan village near
Tongiljeon (Unification Hall). The paths
and tracks are all well-trodden and you
cannot get lost, though at times you will
need to scout around for relics which are
not immediately visible, since few of them
are signposted. Whichever point you decide to take off from you're in for an exhilarating experience.
  Bus Nos 11, 500, 501, 503, 505, 506, 507
and 591 all pass by Namsan.

Oreung Tombs Going south from the city
over the first river bridge you will come to
the Oreung tombs, five of the most ancient

Day Trip No 1

If your time is limited, you could try this full-day itinerary.

Take a bus from the inter-city bus terminal and get off at **Poseokjeongji** on the west side of Namsan (or at the Samneung tombs if you've already visited Poseokjeongji). From Poseokjeongji, walk to the **Samneung tombs** (about 1km) via the Sambulsa triangle. From the Samneung tombs take the track that follows the stream to the crest of Namsan. On the way up there you will pass many free-standing and rock-cut images and a small **hermitage** near the summit (where an old bearded monk lives). Follow the trail along the saddle until it joins the Namsan Skyway – the views from the saddle might inspire you to start your own hermitage.

Carry on south along the Skyway towards Namsan village for about 500m until the road makes a sharp turn to the left. If you continue on a straight course from this point it will bring you to two **pagodas**. Neither of these are visible from the road and the trail leading to them is somewhat indistinct. Also, the pagoda furthest from the road is not visible until you are just past the first, so it's easy to miss. From here, backtrack to the Skyway and continue on down to Namsan village, where you should visit the twin pagodas and **Seochulji** (a pavilion with adjoining pond). The latter is an idyllic little spot described in legends going back to the early days of Silla. If at this point you've had enough for one day you can catch a local bus back to Gyeongju from Unification Hall. If not, you could carry on south past Namsan village to the seven Buddha reliefs of **Chilbul-am**. From there you would have to return to Namsan village and take a bus back to Gyeongju.

Day Trip No 2

Here's another possibility for a full-day trip.

Take local bus No 11 and get off as soon as the bus crosses the river about 2.5km past the National Museum. From here it is a short trip to the Mireauk Valley, where you can visit **Borisa**, a beautifully reconstructed nunnery set amid old conifer trees with a number of ancient freestanding images. It is possible to make your way over the hill at the back of this temple to Pagoda Valley but it's a rough climb. If you don't have the right footwear it's perhaps easier to backtrack down to the bridge over the river and turn left there. Take the track along the west side of the river for several hundred metres until you come to a small village. Turn left here and head up Pagoda Valley. The first temple you come to is **Okryongsa**. Just beyond it you will find the greatest collection of **relief carvings** anywhere in Korea, as well as a pagoda.

Returning to the river bridge and looking across to the main road to Ulsan you will see two stone **pillars** standing in a thicket of trees in the middle of paddy fields. These pillars are all that remain standing of what was once a huge temple complex during Silla times. If you like fossicking for ancient reliefs then this is the spot to do it. If that doesn't particularly interest you then head off down to Namsan village and take any of the trails which lead up into the mountains.

jeongji, a banquet garden set in a glade of shade trees where there remains a fascinating reminder of Silla elegance: a curious granite bower carved in the shape of an abalone through which a stream once flowed. The stream is still there but its course is now too low to feed the bower. Entry costs W500.

Baerisamjonseokbul (Triple Buddhas)

Less than 1km down the road from Poseok-jeongji, on the left hand side of the road, are three mysterious statues known as the Baerisamjonseokbul. Discovered only in

tombs in the area, including the 2000-year-old tomb of the kingdom's founder, King Hyeokgeose. Entry costs W300.

Poseokjeongji Farther down the road – quite a walk, in fact – is the bower Poseok-

1923, it's not known how they came to arrive here: they are not of Silla origin and display the massive boldness characteristic of the Goguryeo style.

Samneung Last on this circuit, just a few minutes' walk past the Baerisamjonseokbul, are a group of four tombs known as Samneung. The one which stands separate from the rest is the burial place of King Gyeonggae, who was killed when a band of robbers raided Poseokjeongji during an elaborate banquet. Nearly 1000 years separates these tombs from those in the Oreung compound.

Girimsa

There are a number of interesting places to visit along or not far off the road between Gyeongju and Daebon, located on the east coast, and the road which takes you there passes through a beautiful and thickly forested section of Gyeongju National Park.

Once you've descended from the pass which takes you through Gyeongju National Park in the Tohamsan district, you will reach the turn-off to Girimsa, the first place of interest west of the park. The temple was one of the largest complexes in the vicinity of the Silla capital and its size (14 buildings in all) compares with that of Bulguksa, yet it is rarely visited by foreigners. You can enjoy this temple in peace and quiet as you will certainly never come across the picnic multitudes common at Bulguksa.

The temple has its origins back in early Silla times, when a monk named Gwangyu arrived from India and acquired a following of some 500 devotees. Known originally as Imjongsa, its name was changed to the present one in AD 643 when the temple was enlarged. The present buildings date from 1786 when Girimsa was rebuilt.

There are the beginnings of a small tourist village at the entrance to the temple and minbak rooms are available if you want to stay for the night. Entry costs W2000.

Getting There & Away Getting to Girimsa requires a degree of perseverance since there are no direct buses from

> ## Bottoms Up
>
> Legend has it that the king, in the company of concubines and courtiers, would sit beside the Poseokjeongji bower while dancers performed in the centre. One of the favourite games played here was for the king to recite a line of poetry and command one of his guests to respond with a matching line, at the same time placing a cup of wine on the water. If the guest couldn't come up with a matching line by the time the cup reached him then he was required to drain the cup to the last drop. Though there are records of similar entertainment in imperial China, Poseokjeongji is the only banquet garden left in the world.

Gyeongju. What you have to do is take a bus from the inter-city bus terminal in Gyeongju to Gampo-ri or Yangbuk-myeon (No 100 or 150) and ask the driver to drop you off at Andongsamgeo-ri, where the turn-off to the temple goes off on the left hand side. From here to the temple it's 4.5km along a paved road. There are local buses from Andongsamgeo-ri to the temple but they only go past four times daily, at 6.30 and 12.30 am and 1.30 and 5.20 pm, on their way to Pohang. For the rest of the day you'll either have to walk, hitch a ride or take a taxi.

Gameunsa

About 1km back from Daebon Beach, along the main road to Gyeongju, stand the remains of what was in Silla times a large temple. All that is left are two three-storey pagodas – among the largest in Korea – and a few foundation stones. The pagodas are prototypes of those constructed following the unification of Silla. A huge bell, some four times larger than the Emille bell in the National Museum at Gyeongju, once hung in Gameunsa but was stolen by the Japanese during their 1592 invasion, who tried to take it back to their homeland. They didn't get far and the bell was lost in the ocean close to Daebon. A search was made for the bell several years ago by a team from

Gyeongju National Museum but it was un-successful. There are plans to try again.

Sea Tomb of King Munmu

The small, rocky islet located 200m off the coast at Daebon is the site of the famous underwater tomb of the Silla king, Munmu (AD 661–81). It's perhaps the only underwater tomb in the world and at low tide it can be seen through the clear water of the pool in the centre of the islet.

Munmu had made it known that on his death he wished his body to be burned and the ashes buried at sea close to Gameunsa. The idea behind these unusual funeral rites was that his spirit would become a dragon and protect the eastern shores of the Silla kingdom from Japanese pirates. His wishes were carried out by his son, Sinmun, who became the next Silla king.

The tomb was not rediscovered until 1967. There is speculation that the rock visible in the centre pool is actually a stone coffin. Most experts dismiss this as a flight of fantasy, though no investigations have been carried out.

North of Daebon is **Daebon Beach**, and to the south is **Bonggil Beach**. Both are popular with Koreans, especially during the summer holiday period, but there's nothing special about this stretch of coastline. Like the rest of the east coast, too, the inevitable barbed wire fence lines the beach.

Getting There & Away To get to Daebon from Gyeongju you need to take a bus going to Gampo (W2400, one hour, 44km, every 20 minutes).

Yangdong Folk Village

The places of interest north of Gyeongju are perhaps best seen as two separate day trips, though it's just possible to see them all in a single day, as long as you make an early start.

Having steeped yourself in Silla history, it's now time to immerse yourself in an-other period that escaped the ravages of modernisation. Yangdong fits the bill perfectly. Here is a beautiful and peaceful Yi-dynasty village full of superb traditional wooden houses and mansions. It's been designated as a preservation area, like Hahoe outside of Andong and Seong-eup on Jejudo, so it's an excellent opportunity to soak up the atmosphere of what life was like in most Korean villages before the advent of concrete and corrugated iron.

The village was established in the 15th and 16th centuries and consists of around 150 large and small houses typical of the *yangban* class – a largely hereditary class based on scholarship and official position, as opposed to wealth. It was the birthplace of Son-so (1433–84), a scholar-official who was one of the key figures involved in quashing the revolt against King Sejo in 1467. It was also the birthplace of Son Chung-ton (1463–1529), otherwise known as Ujae, and of Yi Eon-jeok (1491–1553), a famous Confucian scholar during the early years of the Yi era but more widely known by his pen name of Hoejae.

Most of the houses here are still lived in, so you need to observe the usual courtesies when looking around, but the larger mansions stand empty and are open to the public. There's a plaque outside the more important structures on which you'll find the name of the building and an account of who built it in and what year. Most of these mansions are left open but there may be one or two which are locked. If that's the case, ask for the key at the nearest house. There are no entry fees to any of the buildings.

Of the larger buildings, make sure you see the Yi Hui-tae, Simsujeong and Hyang-dam houses. There's a booklet with map and descriptions available from the tourist offices in Gyeongju. A half-hour's walk from the village stands Korea's second largest Confucian study hall, which was built in honour of Yi Eon-jeok and completed in 1575.

It rarely features in any of the tourist literature, and possibly as a result of that the people who live here are very friendly. It's easy to strike up a conversation and even to be invited for tea and snacks. You should plan on spending several hours here.

Yuhyangdasil is just behind the church and is a friendly restaurant serving tea, wine, snacks and small meals. There are also two general stores where you can buy snacks and cold drinks.

Getting There & Away From Gyeongju, bus Nos 200, 201, 202, 203 and 206 will all get you to within 1.5km of Yangdong. These buses go to Andang-ri. From where they drop you, follow the train line and then go under it. You can't get lost as there's only the one road into the village.

To get back to Gyeongju from Yangdong, simply walk back to the turn-off where the bus originally dropped you. There are plenty of buses from there back to Gyeongju. Alternatively, if it's early enough in the day, take a bus to Angang-ri from the turn-off and another bus from there to Oksan Seowon, west of Angang-ri.

Oksan Seowon

A *seowon* is a Confucian academy. Oksan Seowon was once one of the two most important academies in Korea and, like its counterpart Tosan Seowon outside of Andong, one of the few seowon to escape the destruction wrought on them by the father of King Gojong in the 1860s. It was established in 1572 in honour of Yi Eon-jeok (1491–1553) by another famous Confucian scholar, Yi Toegye, and enlarged in 1772. A fire accidentally destroyed some of the buildings here early this century so that today only 14 structures remain.

Oksan Seowon has a sublime setting surrounded by shade trees and overlooking a stream with a waterfall and rock pools – an ideal place for contemplation and study. The main gate is usually unlocked, so you can wander at will through the walled compound. It is a little run down and only one building is presently occupied by the family which looks after the place. There's no entry fee.

During the summer holiday period the banks of the stream are a popular camping spot and swimming is possible in the rock pools below the waterfall.

If you didn't bring a picnic, then cross the stream and on the other side of the road that heads up to Donghakdang is *Sanjang*

Sikdang, which specialises in free range duck and chicken dishes. If there are three or four of you try the tasty *tojongdak baeg-suk* (W25,000), a whole chicken with rice porridge. It's possible to sit outside and enjoy the scenery.

Dongnaktang A 10-minute walk beyond Oksan Seowon along the main road up the valley will bring you to Dongnaktang, a beautiful collection of well-preserved buildings, built in 1516 as the residence of Yi Eon-jeok after he left the government service. Like the seowon, it has a timeless and relaxing atmosphere to it, as well as a beautiful pavilion which overlooks the stream. The walled compound is partly occupied by a family which looks after the place. Due to past vandalism, the family would prefer if you booked a time with the tourist offices to visit and they will open up the rooms and answer any questions.

Jeonghyesa Just 400m beyond Dongnakdang and off to the left, surrounded by rice fields, is the huge 13-storey stone pagoda of Jeonghyesa. It's origins are somewhat obscure but it's generally agreed that it dates from the unified Silla period. The temple of which the pagoda once formed part was destroyed during the Japanese invasion of 1592.

Dodeogam About 1.75km beyond Dongnakdang, high up in the forested mountains near the end of the valley, is the small temple of Dodeokam. It's a beautiful place perched on a rock outcrop from which two springs emerge. The views are magnificent. There are five buildings in all, including a tiny hermitage above the temple complete with its own ondol heating system. It's a steep walk up from the main road along a well-worn path but definitely worth the effort. It's about as far as you can get from the madding crowd and hardly anyone ever comes up here except the monks and the family who look after the cooking and cleaning. If male travellers were to bring their own food and drink, the monks would undoubtedly offer them somewhere to sleep.

Seowon

When *seowon* (Confucian academies) were first established in the 1500s, they quickly became the centres of learning of the Yi empire; their alumni numbered in the thousands. They were also centres of political intrigue. Indeed, they rapidly became so powerful that the Yi kings lost their supremacy over the Confucian scholars who thenceforth effectively controlled the entire country. Were a scholar to commit a crime, he was tried not by the state, but by the Confucian college.

During the 18th century there were over 600 seowon across the country. This was even more schools than in China, the birthplace of Confucianism. In the 1860s, the monarchy refused to stand for Confucian dominance any longer and conducted an anti-seowon campaign which was fatal to the academies.

These days, although they no longer function, the seowon are regarded as an important part of the country's cultural heritage since it was in their halls that most of the calligraphy and paintings of the Yi dynasty's last three centuries were produced.

The scholarly adjuncts to seowon were the *hyanggyo*, or Confucian schools, which served as preparatory schools for the seowon.

To get to Dodeokam, take the main tarmac road up the valley past Dongnakdang and the dam wall. From the dam wall follow the left stream for another 600m from where the tarmac ends and you'll see a rusty sign on the left with a small car park. Turn left and follow the zigzag path up the mountain. It's about 900m from here to the temple. It's possible to hitch a ride with trucks along the main tarmac road as there's a rock quarry up near the end of the valley – if you pass the quarry you have gone too far. Don't be put off by the steepness of the path as it gets gentler farther up. You'll know you're on the right track when you come across a rock in the middle of the track saying (in Korean), 'Dodeokam 700 metres'. There's a similar sign at the 500m point.

Getting There & Away Bus No 203 (every 30–40 minutes) to Angang-ri connects Gyeongju train station and Oksan Seowon. From Angang-ri, bus No 57 also runs up to the bridge below Oksan Seowon.

Tomb of King Heundeok

The farthest of the royal tombs from central Gyeongju, this was also one of the last ones constructed during the Silla dynasty. It's one of the most complete tombs and has a pretty setting among the trees.

The tomb is 4km north of Angang-ri, about halfway between Oksan Seowon and Yangdong Folk Village.

Yongdamjeong

Along a minor road in the countryside stands Yongdamjeong, the temple of the Cheondogyo (Heavenly Way) religion. This unique Korean religion was founded by Choe Che-woo in 1860. The religion incorporates aspects of Confucianism, Buddhism and Taoism. Choe was regarded by the Yi dynasty authorities as a subversive at a time when Korea was attempting to shut out foreign influences. He was martyred in Daegu in 1864. At the same time, the original buildings of this temple were razed. His followers were a determined bunch, however, and, despite further repression, rebuilt the temple only to have it burned yet again. The most recent reconstruction was in 1960, this time with government assistance, after the area had been made part of the Gyeongju National Park.

It's a beautiful, tranquil area of wooded mountains and terraced rice fields where farmers continue to cultivate the land in the traditional manner. In fact the surrounding forests are much more interesting than the two pavilions. Continue along the path past the pavilions up to Guimisan (594m) and take the left path at the top and you will return to the car park (2½ hour round trip). Another path that joins up with this path starts from behind the caretaker's house. If you want to view inside the pavilions then you will need to borrow the keys from the caretaker.

To get there take bus No 230 from near the inter-city bus terminal in Gyeongju and ask the driver to drop you at the turn-off for the temple. It's a 1.4km walk along a gingko-lined road up to the temple entrance.

Bokduam

Reaching this place involves a steep hike up the thickly forested mountain Obongsan. Close to the summit is Bokduam, a hermitage where you will find a huge rock face out of which 19 niches have been carved. The three central niches hold a figure of the historical Buddha flanked by two bodhisattvas (Munsu and Bohyeon), while the remainder house the 16 *arhat* monks who have attained Nirvana. The carving is recent and although there's an unoccupied house up here, the actual hermitage was burned down in 1988 after an electrical fault started a blaze. There's also a recently erected statue of Gwanseeum, the Goddess of Mercy, just beyond the rock face.

Just below the hermitage is a stunning viewpoint from the top of a couple of massive boulders. It's a great place for a picnic lunch.

The trail is well maintained and easy to follow, but bring your own liquid refreshments as there are no springs along the way. The walk up will take around an hour, and somewhat less coming back down.

From the bus stop in Songseon, follow the creek up along the dirt road to the small temple. The trail starts just to the left of this temple and is well marked with Korean characters painted on rocks. It's impossible to get lost.

If you continue over the small bridge and on up the dirt track you will eventually come to the fortress Busanseong and to Jusaam.

Jusaam

This temple is on the opposite side of the valley from Bokduam, high up on the ridge Obongsan (640m). The temple was founded some 1300 years ago by monk Uisang and has since provided a home for a number of famous monks.

To get to this temple, use the same buses to get to Songseon-ri as you would for Bokduam and take the same gravel road up into the valley, but instead of turning off at the concrete causeway, continue on over it and up the other side of the valley. About halfway between the causeway and Jusasa, some 200m off the main gravel road, is Mangyo-am hermitage.

Sinseonsa

Located a further 3.8km up the road from Songseon-ri, this remote temple near the top of Danseoksan (827m) was used as a base by General Kim Yu-shin in the 7th century. It has seen a bit of renovation work since then. About 50m to the right as you face the temple are some ancient rock carvings in a small grotto – it's believed to be one of the oldest cave temples in Korea. It's about a 1½ to two-hour circuit walk from the bus stop.

Just up from the bus stop, *Danseok Sanjang* is a good place to pick up some drinks or a bite to eat.

Getting There & Away Bus No 350 (W1050, every 40 minutes) from Gyeongju passes Songseon-ri, for Bokduam, and continues up past Ujunggol, where you need to hop off for Sinseonsa.

GAYASAN NATIONAL PARK
가야산국립공원

Gayasan National Park is part of the Sobaek range. It is sacred to Buddhists and shamans and it straddles the border between two provinces, Gyeongsangbuk-do and Gyeongsangnam-do.

Hikers will no doubt want to challenge **Gayasan** (1430m), a pretty peak. However, the most famous attraction in the park is **Haeinsa**, on the Gyeongsangnam-do side of the border. Haeinsa is one of the ten great temples of the Avatamsaka sect. This is also the repository of the Tripitaka Koreana - more than 80,000 carved wood blocks on which are the complete Buddhist scriptures, as well as many illustrations remarkably like those one sees in Nepal. Like Bulguksa,

Strewn with temples and ruins, blessed with fertile arable lands, Gyeongju, Gyeongsangbuk-do

PATRICK HORTON

Gyeongju: traditional methods of rice farming

PATRICK HORTON

Woman in chilli pepper field, Gyeongsangbuk-do

MARTIN MOOS

The 'samaeul' vision: a prosperous traditional rural house (in the fertile lands of mainland Jeollanam-do)

MARTIN MOOS

Rocky peaks rise over the plains: Wolchulsan (Rising Moon Mountains) National Park, Jeollanam-do.

Slung with steel stairways and suspension bridges, Wolchulsan makes for a spectacular day hike.

near Gyeongju, UNESCO has declared Haeinsa an international treasure. The blocks are housed in four enormous buildings complete with a simple but effective ventilation system to prevent their deterioration. Also housed in the halls are an additional 2835 blocks from the Goryeo period containing more Buddhist scriptures, literary works and an illustration of Avatamsaka Sutra.

The buildings are normally locked, and although it's possible to see the blocks through the slatted windows one of the friendly monks may open them up for you if you show an interest. Even if you don't manage to get into the library there's plenty of interest in the other buildings of the complex.

The wood blocks which you see today are actually the second set and they were carved during the 14th century when the Goryeo dynasty king, Gojong, was forced to take refuge on Ganghwado during the Mongol invasion of the mainland. The first set, completed in 1251 after 20 years' work, was destroyed by the invaders. The Tripi-taka was moved from Ganghwado to Haeinsa in the early years of the Yi dynasty.

Haeinsa itself has origins going back to the beginning of the 9th century, when it was founded by two monks, Suneung and Ijong, following many years of study in China. It was not until the early days of the Goryeo dynasty in the mid-10th century that it attained its present size.

The main hall, **Daegwangjeon** was burnt down during the Japanese invasion of 1592 and again (accidentally) in 1817, though, miraculously, the Tripitaka escaped destruction. The hall was reconstructed again in 1971. Other reconstruction has been undertaken since then, principally on the monks' quarters, and all of it, naturally, along traditional lines.

As well as being one of the most significant, Haeinsa is one of the most beautiful temples in Korea and part of its beauty lies in the natural setting of mixed deciduous and coniferous forest. It's a romantic's paradise in wet weather, when wisps of cloud drift at various levels through the forest.

Tripitaka Koreana

The Tripitaka Koreana, also known as the Goryeo Buddhist canon, is one of the most significant complete Buddhist sacred texts in the world. Tripitaka literally means 'three baskets', representing the three divisions of Buddhism: the Sutras (scriptures), Vinaya (laws) and the Abhidharma (treatises).

The Tripitaka Koreana has been preserved on more than 80,000 beautifully carved woodblocks, their extraordinary workmanship further emphasising their importance. The carving of the woodblocks took 16 years to complete. Every stage of the process was carried out so as to ensure their future preservation. From carefully selecting appropriate birch wood, then soaking it in brine and boiling it in salt before drying it, to locating and constructing a sophisticated repository, the techniques involved were so complex and the artwork so intricate that they remain an inspiration today. The woodblocks are housed and preserved in the 15th-century Janggyong Pango, a masterpiece of remarkable ingenuity in its own right. Despite the ravages of Japanese invasion and fires that destroyed the rest of the temple complex, the repository remained standing, with the woodblocks preserved intact.

During the 1970s, President Pak Chung-hee ordered the construction of a modern storage facility for the woodblocks. The facility was equipped with advanced ventilation, temperature and humidity control. However, after some test woodblocks began to grow mildew the whole scheme was scrapped. Today, the four storage halls and woodblocks are inscribed on the World Heritage List to ensure their continued preservation. In a bold attempt to ensure accessibility to more people, Haeinsa's monks have completely transcribed the complete works onto a single CD-ROM and are presently working on translating the classical Chinese of the text into modern-day Korean.

For more, check out the Web site at www.ocp.go.kr/IRS/docs/english/world/haeinsa_intro.html.

Entry to the park and temple costs W2500. The temple is about 25 minutes' walk from where the bus drops you.

Places to Stay

Most people visit as a day trip from Daegu, but it is pleasant and worthwhile to spend the night. Accommodation is available in the tourist village below the temple, and ranges from minbak to yeogwan. You won't have to look hard – ajummas meet arriving buses with offers of places to stay. In the off-season, you can easily do some productive bargaining. Camping is available, 500m from the bus terminal.

Probably the nicest place to stay is the traditional style *Sanjangbyeol-jang Yeogwan (☎ 932 7245)*. The rooms are quite simple, but large and cost W40,000 or W50,000 including a meal. Reservations are necessary. Walk up the road from the post office and it's on your left after all the restaurants. *Haeinsa Tourist Hotel (☎ 933 2000, fax 933 2989)* is farther up the same path and is the top-end option. Comfy doubles with nice views range from W55,000 (weekdays) to W68,000 (weekends & holidays) and suites start at W180,000.

Getting There & Away

Daegu is the most convenient access point to Gayasan (W3200, every 20 minutes), but there are also buses to Busan (W9500, one daily) and Jinju (W6600, 2½ hours, every 1½ hours).

GIMCHEON 김천
pop 152,000

Gimcheon is a useful staging point to visit the nearby temple, Jikjisa. There's little of cultural interest in Gimcheon itself since it was completely destroyed during the Korean War and is now totally modern, but it's pleasant enough for spending the night. Gimcheon has both an express bus terminal and a more popular inter-city bus terminal. The train station is sandwiched in between the two bus terminals, and all three places are within walking distance of each other.

Getting There & Away
Bus Departures from the inter-city bus terminal include:

destination	price (W)	duration	distance
Andong	7900	3 hrs	125km
Daegu	3600	1¼ hrs	88km
Daejeon	4300	1¼ hrs	88km
Gochang*	4600	1¼ hrs	65km

*for Haeinsa & Gayasan National Park

Train Gimcheon is 50 minutes from Daegu, on the way to Seoul – and shares most of the same trains.

JIKJISA 직지사

Jikjisa is one of Korea's largest and most famous temples. Situated in the foothills of Hwang-aksan, west of Gimcheon, it was first constructed during the reign of the 19th Silla king, Nul-ji (AD 417–58), which makes it one of the very first Buddhist temples built in Korea. It was rebuilt in AD 645 by priest Jajang, who had spent many years studying in China and brought back to Korea the first complete set of the Tripitaka Buddhist scriptures. Further reconstruction was done in the 10th century but the temple was completely destroyed during the Japanese invasion of 1592. Though there were originally over 40 buildings at Jikjisa, only some 20 or so remain, the oldest of which date from the reconstruction of 1602.

Jikjisa's most famous son is priest Samyeong or Son-gun, a militant monk who spent many years in Geumgangsan (the Diamond Mountains, in North Korea). He organised troops to fight against the Japanese in 1592 and later became the chief Korean delegate to the Japanese court when a peace treaty was negotiated in 1604. Following the completion of the treaty, Sa-myeong returned to Korea with over 3000 released prisoners of war.

Entrance costs W2000. The extensive temple complex is a pleasant 15-minute walk from the bus stop.

Places to Stay & Eat

There's a well-established tourist village down where the buses stop with a range of minbak, yeogwan and restaurants. It's peaceful and pleasant, making for a good place to stay.

Getting There & Away

Local bus Nos 11 (W600) and 111 (W920) head out to Jikjisa (20 minutes 13km every 10 minutes). The bus stop is just to the right as you exit the train station. From the inter-city bus terminal, cross over the road towards the train station and continue up over the footbridge. These same buses pass the express bus terminal on their way to the temple.

ANDONG 안동

pop 186,000

Andong is roughly in the middle of Gyeongsangbuk-do. The whole area surrounding Andong is peaceful and rural and notable for having preserved much of its traditional character. Though Andong itself is not a particularly interesting town, there are numerous interesting places to visit in its vicinity.

Most of Andong's sights are outside the city – some of them a considerable distance away – and getting to them requires a series of bus rides. There are also a few interesting spots right on the edge of town. Having your own transport, either a bike or car, would make visiting the sites a lot more pleasant.

Information

There are two useful tourist offices in town. The most convenient is to the left as you exit the train station. A newer and better resourced office is tucked away to the north of the station.

Musil Folk Village & Museum
무실민속마을,박물관

Almost within walking distance of Andong proper is the Musil Folk Village. It's nowhere near as large as its cousin outside of Suwon, south of Seoul, but it serves a different purpose. Musil Folk Village was built to house all the cultural assets which were moved to prevent them from being submerged by the construction of Andong Dam in 1976.

Here you'll find a series of relocated and partially reconstructed traditional-style buildings ranging from simple thatched peasants' farmhouses to the more elaborate mansions of government officials and the like, with their multiple courtyards.

Where this village differs from the one at Suwon is that many of the houses are also restaurants, and for atmosphere and quality of food it cannot be beat. Koreans have already discovered this, and it's a very popular place to go for lunch or dinner. You'll find both the people who run the restaurants and their guests to be very friendly indeed. Musil Folk Village has to be *the* place to meet people in Andong. Not only that, but the prices for the meals here are very reasonable, with the two simpler restaurants near the top of the hill being the cheapest. For starters, try Lee Cheen black noodles *(geonjinguksu nureunguksu – jobapgyeomyong)* at **Ichunchoga,** just above the thatched roof houses. Equally good is the *minsokeumsikjeom* (traditional-style dishes and service) at **Pakpunseom Kkachigumeongjip** next door.

Just next door to the folk village is Andong's **Folklore Museum** *(Andong Minsok Bangmulgwan).* It's quite interesting with clear and fascinating descriptions introducing Korea's folk traditions from birth through to death via a series of educational displays. There are also some displays illustrating Andong's particular folk gatherings, like the *dongchaessaum, notdari palgi* (bridge-crossing olay), *wonnoleum* (county magistrate's game), *Hahoe byeolsingut talnori* (Hahoe dance drama), *uiseonggamassaum* (sedan-chair game) and *hwajeonnori* (picnic day for ladies). Entry costs W550 (open daily 9am to 6pm).

The village is situated about 3km to the east of Andong, close to the dam wall on the opposite side of the river from the road which runs alongside the train track. To get there catch bus No 3 (every 35 minutes) and hop off at *minsokchon* (folk village). A taxi will cost W2500.

If you're walking or have your own transport stop off at the Silla period 7-storey **brick pagoda,** which is largest and oldest brick pagoda in Korea.

GYEONGSANGBUK-DO

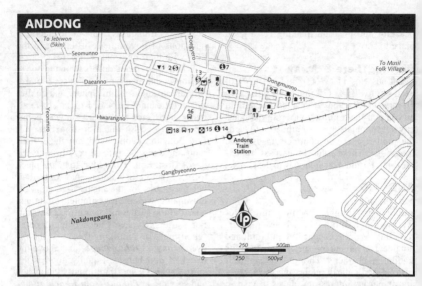

ANDONG

1 Dongmyeong
Songuksujip
동명손국수집
2 Jutaek Bank
주택은행
3 Joheung Bank
조흥은행
4 Mammoth Bakery
맘모스베이커리
5 Post Office
우체국
6 Bando Motel
반도모텔

7 Tourist Information
관광안내소
8 Jaerim Galbi
재림갈비
9 Seoul Galbi Sikdang
서울갈비식당
10 Grand-jang; Namgeong-
jang Yeogwan
그랜드장
11 Hilton-jang Yeogwan
힐튼장여관
12 Gwandong Yeoinsuk
관동여인숙

13 Andong Park Tourist Hotel
안동파크관광호텔
14 Tourist Information
관광안내소
15 Life Shopping Centre
라이프쇼핑센터
16 Bus Stop (Hahoe Folk
Village & Jebiwon)
버스정류장
17 Bus Stop (Dosan Seowon)
버스정류장
18 Andong Bus Terminal
시외버스터미널

Bongjeongsa 봉정사

This Silla-period temple. located 16km to
the north-west of Andong, is home to the
ornately decorated Geungnakjeon (Paradise
Hall), possibly the oldest wooden structure
in Korea (according to the literature). The
walls and ceilings of the temple and adjacent halls are all beautifully adorned with a
distinctive style of mural called dancheong.
Entry costs W1300.

Bus No 51 (40 minutes, every 1½ hours)
runs out to the temple.

Jebiwon (Amitaba Buddha)
제비원

Andong is also famous for the huge rock-
carved Amitaba Buddha known as Jebiwon
(Icheon-dong Seokbulsang), some 5km
north of Andong on the road to Yeongju.
The body and robes of this Buddha are
carved on a boulder over 12 metres high,
on top of which are the head and hair –
carved out of two separate pieces of rock.
Interestingly, the head was actually added
at a later date.

Catch bus No 54 (every 30 minutes). Ask the driver to drop you off at Jebiwon. Local buses to Yeongju can also drop you off at Jebiwon.

Andong Mask Dance Festival This festival, in early October, is a great time to visit Andong. It brings together a colourful array of national and international mask dance troupes. It is usually held in tandem with Andong's folk festival, showcasing many traditional performances of music and dance. Check with KNTO for more details.

Soju Museum 소주박물관
The *soju* of Andong may not be to your taste, but its significance has been preserved with its designation as a provincial intangible cultural property. A few cups of this wicked brew (made with rice, yam or tapioca) and you will start to understand. With 45% alcohol content you will need to keep the lid on tight to avoid evaporation. Andong's soju museum houses a couple of displays that detail the distilling process, the drinking ceremony and a history of soju labels.

The museum (closed Sunday) is in the south of Andong, across the Nakdonggang, and best reached by taxi (W2000).

Places to Stay
There are plenty of inexpensive yeoinsuk around the bus terminal, although most are pretty grotty affairs. Closer to the train station is *Gwandong Yeoinsuk* (☎ 859 2487) which seems okay. Rooms are W10,000.

Hilton-jang Yeogwan (☎ 857 6878) has clean doubles and ondol rooms for W25,000. Opposite, the *Grand-jang* is a bit newer, but the price is the same. Also nearby is *Namyeong-jang Yeogwan* (☎ 857 8160) where doubles and ondols are W25,000.

A good mid-range option is *Bando Motel* (☎ 841 3563) where good and clean rooms are W30,000. The hotel is on a corner. The entrance is a little obscure, the hotel is on the 3rd, 4th and 5th floors of the building.

The top-end place in town is the *Andong Park Tourist Hotel* (☎ 859 1500) where twins cost W65,000 and suites are W87,000, plus 20% tax and surcharge.

Places to Eat
Dongmyeong Songuksujip lacks atmosphere but is popular with Andong's youth. They serve a variety of tasty dishes, like *yeolmu* or *bibim naengmyeon* (curried vegetables and cold noodles; W4000), *dolsot bibimbap* (stone pot mixed vegetables; W4000), and mandu (W2500). Pay first and they will bring your food to you. Look for the yellow and green sign. Also in town is *Jaerim Galbi*, one of the best *galbi* restaurants in Andong. Another good choice for a barbecue is *Seoul Galbi Sikdang*, where they serve up generous servings of the local specialty of beef galbi (W10,500).

For self-caterers *Life Shopping Center* is conveniently located between the bus terminal and the train station. As its name suggests *Mammoth Bakery* has a great range of pastries.

Getting Around
The tourist office hands out a very helpful local bus timetable with English explanations. The town is small enough to get around on foot, and the local buses serve all the sights. Naturally, you would do well if you had a car or bike.

Getting There & Away
Bus The bus terminal serves both express and regular buses. Some of the buses to Seoul also stop at Danyang in Chungcheongbuk-do, a useful destination for exploring central Korea. From Andong, there are buses to the following destinations:

destination	price (W)	duration	distance
Busan	12,100	3¾ hrs	209km
Cheongsong*	3500	1 hr	50km
Daegu	5100	2¼ hrs	102km
Daejeon	12,600	4 hrs	
Pohang	9300	2½ hrs	135km
Seoul	15,600	5¼ hrs	277km

*for Juwangsan National Park

Train Trains running between Seoul's Cheongnyangni train station and Andong include three daily saemaeul (W17,600, four hours) and six mugunghwa (W12,100, 4½ hours).

HAHOE FOLK VILLAGE
하회민속마을

Hahoe Folk Village (Hahoe Maeul) is some 24km west of Andong and is as close as you'll find to a 16th-century Korean town. This village has to be one of Korea's most picturesque. Apart from the refrigerators, TVs and various other electrical appliances in the houses, precious little has changed for centuries. Not only do the residents want to keep it that way but the government actually funds the costs of preservation and restoration. As a result, you'll be hard pressed to find anything quite as earthy and traditional as Hahoe and, unlike the folk village at Suwon which is basically a tourist production, this is a genuine village with roots going back some 600 years. There are about 130 traditional houses here.

Every weekend at 3 pm from May to October you can see traditional Hahoe dances performed in a small stadium near the car park. The performances are just fabulous and are a must-see. There is no charge, but donations are demanded by a poor and hard working *halmeoni* (grandmas).

There is a helpful tourist information booth at the entrance to the village. Entry costs W1600. You can visit various houses which are open to the public, but remember to respect people's privacy if you step beyond the entrance gates. These are their homes, after all. The most important of the houses usually have a sign outside describing its history.

Two kilometres back towards Andong is the **Hahoe Mask Museum**, which houses a mix of traditional Korean masks, in addition to a collection from around the globe: from Zaire to Nigeria and Papua New Guinea. The museum also has a shop selling a variety of masks and other tourist products. Entrance costs W1100.

There are a number of minbak available in Hahoe, which cost W15,000 to W20,000 per room on average. This is certainly a better choice than staying in Andong. Some have signs, but if you're not sure then ask around. Dinner can usually be provided on request.

Bus No 46 (W1050; 50 minutes; every 1½ hours) runs out to Hahoe from Andong.

Byeolsingut Talnori

Despite its ease of access from Andong, Hahoe Folk Village is surrounded by fields and enshrined in a gentle rustic atmosphere.

This remote and peaceful village is the home to one of Korea's most entertaining mask dances, Byeolsingut Talnori. The notoriety of this dance and the strength of traditional values in Hahoe Maeul have helped to preserve the locals' way of life.

Byeolsingut Talnori was created by the common folk for the common folk. Its role is to mock and satirise the establishment. The performance is an amusing combination of popular entertainment and shamanism. Each of the characters in the dance represent respective social classes and the conflicts that exist between them. Accompanying the dance are the sounds of *nong-ak*, a traditional farmers' musical percussion quartet.

DOSAN SEOWON 도산서원
This Confucian academy is located some 28km to the north of Andong on the road to Taebaek and Donghae. It was founded in AD 1557 by Yi Toegye, Korea's foremost Confucian scholar (whose portrait appears on the W1000 banknote), during the reign of King Seonjo. It functioned for several centuries as the most prestigious school for those who aspired to high office in the civil service during the middle years of the Yi dynasty. It was here that the qualifying examinations for the civil service took place. Some of Yi's most famous expressions include: 'When you are alone, behave decently' and 'In practicing virtue one should perform it with perseverance, suppressing one's desires'. Yi Toegye was also a prolific writer, publishing dozens of volumes summarising and explaining the Chinese classics.

Confucianism is no longer taught at the seowon and the buildings and grounds have been converted into a museum which is open to the public every day. It's a particularly beautiful spot and often used by Korean film directors for making historical documentaries and the like. Entry costs W1100 (9 am to 6 pm).

Nearby are **Ocheon-ri Traditional Houses** (Ocheon-ri Yujeokji), which are in the same direction as Dosan Seowon. By car, the seowon is about 25 minutes from Andong.

Getting There & Away

Bus No 67 (W700, 40 minutes) runs out to Dosan Seowon, but you should check with the driver as only half the buses drive the extra 2km down to the seowon. Otherwise you'll have a pleasant walk (15 minutes). You can catch a boat from Andong dam when the water level is high (July to September).

CHEONGNYANGSAN PROVINCIALPARK 청량산도립공원

Just to the north of Dosan Seowon is Cheongnyangsan Provincial Park. The most notable feature in the park is the mountain Cheongnyangsan, the summit of which is Geumtapbong (870m). There are 11 other scenic peaks, eight caves and a waterfall, Gwanjanpokpo. The largest temple in the park is Cheongnyangsa, and there are a number of small hermitages. Built during in AD 663, the temple is quite scenic: sitting in a steep valley below the cliffs. Ansimtang, at the base of the temple, is a pleasant place for some tea drinking.

The parks boasts some spectacular views, with tracks wandering along cliff precipices. There is a spider web of tracks radiating out from Cheongnyangsa – most are well signposted and marked. It takes about five hours to complete a round trip of the peaks and return to the bus stop; or just over an hour to the temple and back again. Entrance to the park is W800.

Sanseong Sikdang is the only restaurant and minbak at present serving *hansik* (W5000) and *dotorimuk* (acorn jelly; W4000) or *pajeon* (Korean pancake; W5000). A simple room costs W20,000. Try washing your meal down with some of their local *dongdongju* (W5000). There is also a small store near the restaurant.

It's a 2km walk from where the bus drops you up a new road to the restaurant and first trail. Next to where the bus stops there are

plans to develop a tourist village and folk museum of sorts. Bus No 67 (hourly, 1¼ hours) continues past Dosan Seowon for another 20 minutes to the park.

BUSEOKSA 부석사

Another out-of-the-way place that's worth visiting is Buseoksa (temple of the floating stone), a temple about 60km north of Andong, between Yeongju and Taebaek. This beautiful temple was established in AD 676 by monk Uisang after he had returned to Korea from China, bringing with him the teachings of Hwaeom Buddhism. Though burnt to the ground in the early-14th century by invaders, it was reconstructed in 1358 and escaped destruction during the Japanese invasions under Hideyoshi at the end of the 16th century.

This stroke of good fortune has resulted in the preservation of the beautiful main hall (Muryangsujeon) to this day, making it one of the oldest wooden structures in Korea. It also has what are considered to be the oldest Buddhist wall paintings in the country, as well as a unique gilded-clay sitting Buddha. It's also worth visiting the small exhibition room, which houses some of Korea's oldest paintings of Indra, Brahmadeva and four Deva kings.

There is a small tourist village below the entrance with restaurants and minbak. Entrance costs W1000.

Getting There & Away

Transport to Buseoksa is from Yeongju or Punggi, in either case taking about one hour (W1500, hourly).

JUWANGSAN NATIONAL PARK 주왕산국립공원

Far to the east of Andong and almost by the coast is Juwangsan National Park. In the past, Juwangsan was known as Seokpyeongsan, or 'Stone Screen Mountain'. The park is dominated by the impressive limestone pinnacles that seem to appear from nowhere. Beautiful gorges, waterfalls and cliff-face walks also feature strongly. Sadly, the charm of the waterfalls is reduced by the restricted walkways to keep people

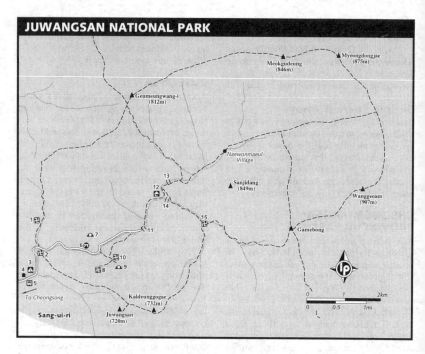

JUWANGSAN NATIONAL PARK

Myeongdongjae
(875m)

Meokgudeung
(846m)

Geumeungwang-i
(812m)

Naewonmaeul
Village

Sanjidang
(849m)

Wanggeoam
(907m)

13
12
14
15

1
7
6
11
3
2
10
4
8
9
5

To Cheongsong

Gamebong

Kaldeunggogae
(732m)

Sang-ui-ri

Juwangsan
(720m)

0   1   2km
0   0.5   1mi

from polluting the water catchment. One of the nicest and quietest places to stay is Naewonmaeul, a tiny artists' village within the park at the end of the valley. Most visitors just see the waterfalls and caves, but for a more rigorous experience try hiking up from Daejeonsa to Juwangsan (1¼ hours), along the ridge to Kaldeunggogae (15 minutes) and then down to Hurimaegi (50 minutes), before following the valley back to Daejeonsa (1¾ hours). On the way down take the side trip to Juwanggul: the track first passes Juwangam Hermitage, from where a steel walkway takes you through a narrow gorge to the modest cave.

There is a national park information centre on the 2nd floor of the bus terminal. You can pick up a map here and learn about the park. Park entrance is W2000.

Places to Stay
There is a *camping ground* on the other side of the stream (W3000) and a *minbak*

village (minbakchun) opposite the bus terminal. Rooms are W15,000. The most up-market hotel near the park is the Juwangsan Grand Hotel (☎ 872 6801) which has doubles from W45,000. The hotel is 2km below the park entrance.

Getting There & Away
Cheongsong is the main access point to Juwangsan (W1200, every 30 minutes). From Cheongsong it is possible to catch buses to:

destination	price (W)	duration	distance
Andong	3500	1 hr	61km
Busan*	12,300	3¼ hrs	
Dong Daegu	8600	2¾ hrs	
Dong Seoul	20,200	5¼ hrs	313km

*via Yeongdeok on the east coast

ULJIN 울진
pop 67,000
Uljin is a quiet, pleasant little one-street town sitting on the East Sea in the far north

JUWANGSAN NATIONAL PARK

1 Gwangamsa
  광암사
2 Daejeonsa
  대전사
3 Camping Ground
  야영장
4 No 20 Juwangsan Minbak
  (Minbakchon)
  20호주왕산민박
5 Bus Terminal; Park
  Information Centre
  버스터미널·공원안내센터
6 Picnic Ground
7 Yeonhwagul
  연화굴
8 Mujanggul
  무장굴
9 Juwanggul
  주왕굴
10 Juwangam
  주왕암터
11 Jeilpokpo (1st Waterfall)
  제일폭포
12 Shelter
  대피소
13 Jesampokpo
  (3rd Waterfall)
  제삼폭포
14 Jeipokpo (2nd Waterfall)
  제이폭포
15 Hurimaegi
  후리매기

of Gyeongsangnam-do. The main attractions here are Buryeong Valley, the caves at Seongnyugul and the Deokgu Hot Springs. Uljin is also famous (infamous?) for being the home of four of Korea's nuclear power plants.

The bus terminal is in the south of town with the main shopping area on the north side of the stream. If you need to cash up, the Nonghyup Bank in the centre of town has a foreign exchange service.

Places to Stay
There are several yeogwan spread throughout the town, all of which are of reasonable standard. In summer, however, most double their rates. Just to the north of the bus terminal is *Daerim-jang Yeogwan* (☎ 783 2131) which has rooms for W25,000. Still close to the bus terminal and just before the bridge to the town centre is

Sinseong-jang Yeogwan (☎ 782 1777) where double and ondol rooms are W25,000. At the northern end of town, *Yongkkum-jang* (☎ 783 8844) has good-value rooms from W25,000.

Getting There & Away
You can catch inter-city express buses from Uljin to:

destination	price (W)	duration	distance
Busan	14,000	4 hrs	243km
Daegu	13,400	4½ hrs	219km
Seoul	22,000	5¾ hrs	344km
Gangneung*	7800	2½ hrs	138km
Gyeongju	10,100	3¼ hrs	157km
Pohang	8300	2¼ hrs	129km

*via Samcheok; W4600

AROUND ULJIN
Seongnyugul 성류굴
This limestone cave was the first cave to be developed for tourism in South Korea. It is adorned with impressive stalagmites and stalactites, as well as having a number of large caverns and pools. The cave is nearly 500m in length and sits alongside a picturesque river near the foreshore. Entrance is W2200.

The easiest way to get there is to catch a taxi (W4500) from Uljin, otherwise hop on one of the Bulyeongsa buses.

Bulyeongsa 불영사
Bulyeongsa (Buddha's Shadow Temple) is located in the beautiful Bureyong Valley, a 15km winding valley of forests, streams and impressive gorges.

Buses connect Uljin with the temple (W1800, 25 minutes, hourly) but the best way to get around is independently: riding a bike or driving a car.

Deokgu Hot Springs 덕구온천
Deokgu ia a relatively undeveloped and unspoilt area. It has some good walks further up the valley to Eungbongsan, also known as Maebongsan. A 12km circuit trail follows Deokgu valley past Yongsopokpo, the original hot springs and up to

Eungbongsan (999m), returning via Minssimyo (5 hours)

The main hot springs are inside ***Deokgu Hot Springs Hotel*** (☎ 782 0671) where you can either have a dip in their tubs (W4000) or stay the night. Comfy singles and doubles are W55,000. There are a couple of other yeogwan below, which only charge W25,000 a night and have mineral springs on tap. Buses connect Uljin and the hot springs (W1950, one hour, hourly).

Beaches 해수욕장
Running north and south from Uljin are a number of pleasant sandy beaches, some of them developed, with attendant restaurants and minbak, while others remain fishing villages. Local buses run along the coast, but are few and far between. The best way to travel is to either ride or self-drive. Mangyang, Gusan and Bongpyeong are three of the most popular.

POHANG 포항
☎ 0562 • pop 514,000
Pohang is the largest city on the east coast and an important industrial centre. The city's claim to fame is POSCO (Pohang Iron and Steel Company), the world's second-largest steel maker. Unless you have a particular interest in steel smelters, you are only likely to use Pohang as a transit point to Ulleungdo or Bogyeongsa. Most of Pohang's life revolves around the two intersections, Ogeori and Yukgeori, literally '5-road junction' and '6-road junction'. The market is always a hive of activity and most of Pohang's youth hang out to the north of these intersections, where most of the cafes, clothing stores, hofs (bars), restaurants and DDR games parlours are located. Another entertainment strip runs along Bukbu Beach.

Information
There is a pretty useless information booth outside the inter-city bus terminal; hopefully things will improve in the future.

Songdo Beach 송도해수욕장
The closest beach to the centre, this is something of a local summer resort area. A

row of pine trees have been planted next to the beach, making for an attractive background. There are complete facilities here, including lifeguards and a resort hotel. Seafood restaurants can dish up raw fish which costs the earth. Bus No 103 runs out to the beach via the inter-city bus terminal.

Bukbu Beach 북부해수욕장
This beach, 3km to the north of Pohang, is 1.7km long, making it one of the longest sandy beaches on Korea's east coast. Bus Nos 105 and 200 go to Bukbu Beach from the inter-city bus terminal.

Bogyeongsa 보경사
This temple, 30km north of Pohang, is a gateway to a beautiful valley boasting 12 splendid waterfalls, gorges spanned by bridges, hermitages, stupas and the temple itself. There are a number of good hikes, including ascending **Naeyeonsan** (930m). The summit itself is called Hyangnobong, and the return trip from Bogyeongsa is about 20km (around six hours).

The temple is 15 minutes' walk from where the buses from Pohang terminate and there's a tourist village with a collection of souvenir shops, restaurants, minbak and yeogwan. Entry to the area costs W2000.

The trail to the gorge and waterfalls branches off from the tourist village and is well maintained. It's about 1.5km to the first waterfall, **Ssangsaengpokpo**, which is five metres high. The sixth waterfall, **Gwaneumpokpo**, is an impressive 72 metres high and has two columns of water with a cave behind it. The seventh waterfall is called **Yeonsanpokpo**, and is a respectable 30 metres high.

As you head farther up the trails, the going gets difficult and the ascent of Hyangnobong should only be attempted if the day is young.

Buses run hourly between the temple and the northern end of Pohang's inter-city bus terminal (25 minutes). If you miss your bus then a 5km taxi ride to Songna (on the east-coast highway) costs W6000. It is possible to visit Bogyeongsa as a day trip from Gyeongju.

POHANG

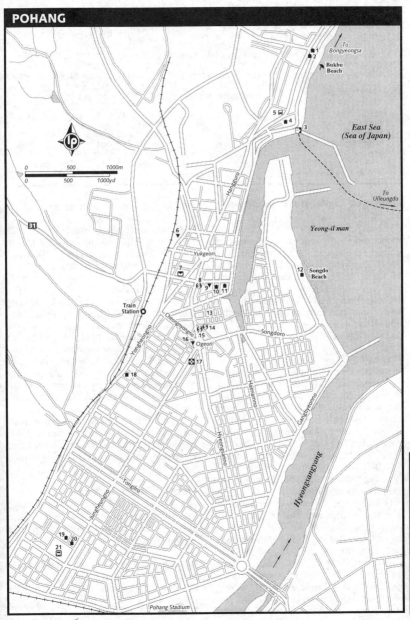

To Bongyeongsa

Bukbu Beach

East Sea (Sea of Japan)

To Ulleungdo

Yeong-il man

Songdo Beach

Hanggoro

Train Station

Yukgeori

Cheongnyongno

Yonghûngno

Ogeori

Songdoro

Hanamno

Hyeongsanno

Gangbyeonno

Hyeongsangang

Jungheungno

Tongilro

Pohang Stadium

POHANG

1 Motel City Yeogwan 모텔시티여관	8 Joheung Bank 조흥은행	15 Korea First Bank 제일은행
2 Miseagull Hotel 미시갈호텔	9 Pyeonghwa Ssambap 평화쌈밥	16 Gohyang Naengmyeon 고향냉면
3 Ulleungdo Ferry Terminal 울릉도여객터미널	10 Suan-jang Motel 수안장모텔	17 Taebaek Shopping Centre 태백쇼핑센터
4 Maenseuta Motel 맨스타모텔	11 Useong Yeoinsuk 우성여인숙	18 Cygnus Hot Springs 시그너스온천
5 Bus Stop 버스정류장	12 Songdo Resort 송도국민관광지	19 Namjin-jang Yeogwan 남진장여관
6 Jung-ang Super Galbi 중앙수퍼갈비	13 Jukdo Market 죽도시장	20 Ibeu-jang Motel; Goemong-jang Yeogwan 이브장모텔
7 Post Office 우체국	14 Korea Exchange Bank 외환은행	21 Inter-City Bus Terminal 시외버스터미널

Janggigot Lighthouse Museum
장기꽂등대박물관

This museum houses a large collection of memorabilia relating to lighthouses in Korea and overseas (9 am to 6 pm, free entry). The lighthouse and museum are on the tip of Janggi-got, a natural cape that protects Pohang's harbour.

Catch either bus No 200 or bus No 250 from either bus terminal to Guryongpo. Hop off and then catch a bus going to Daebo (every 30 minutes).

Places to Stay

There are a couple of neat little yeogwan in the streets behind the ferry terminal. Maenseuta Motel (☎ 244 0225) has nice and new rooms (W30,000) with great views. Miseagull Hotel (☎ 242 8400) is perfectly located, looking out as it does over Bukbu be ach. Double rooms are W50,000, twins W70,000 and ondols W60,000. Just a bit farther north is Motel City Yeogwan (☎ 249 5533) which has good rooms for W30,000.

There must be about two dozen yeogwan around the inter-city bus terminal with rooms typically going for W25,000. *Ibeu-jang Motel* (☎ 283 2253) and *Geomong-jang Yeogwan* (☎ 277 3033) both have good rooms for W25,000.

Down near the old ferry terminal is the friendly *Useong Yeoinsuk* (☎ 247 5266), which has decent rooms for W13,000. Just around the corner is *Suan-jang Motel*

(☎ 241 3111), which is quite new and has good rooms for W25,000.

Cygnus Hot Springs Hotel (☎ 275 2000, fax 275 2218) is the top-end abode, with doubles and twins from W115,000 and suites for W230,000.

Places to Eat

Heading up Ogeori you'll find *Gohyang Naengmyeon*, which serves up a tasty bowl of chewy cold noodles for W5000. *Jung-ang Super Galbi* serves a variety of delicious barbecue dishes, including dwaeji galbi (pork ribs; W4500) and galbi sal (fresh beef ribs; W9000). *Pyeonghwa Ssambap* does a line in scrumptious *ssambap* (side dishes wrapped in lettuce leaves) for W6000.

If you'd like to try some fresh seafood then you need look no farther than the Ulleungdo ferry terminal. There is a string of restaurants with your meal waiting in their tanks.

Getting There & Away

Air Asiana and Korean Air both have Seoul-Pohang services (W50,000). Asiana also operates a flight between Pohang and Jejudo (W60,000).

Bus Destinations from the inter-city express bus terminal include Gwangju (W11,400, 2½ hours, 321km, every 2½ hours) and Seoul (W14,100, five hours, 399km, every 20 minutes).

Buses from Pohang include:

destination	price (W)	duration	distance
Andong	9300	2¼ hrs	136km
Busan	5700	1½ hrs	113km
Daegu	5100	1¾ hrs	78km
Gangneung	16,000	4½ hrs	251km

All inter-city buses bound for the cities of Busan, Daegu and Seoul go via Gyeongju, so you can take any of these to Gyeongju. The journey takes 40 minutes.

Train There are a few trains from Pohang. Destinations include Seoul (saemaeul train: W25,200, five hours, twice daily) and Busan (mugunghwa train: W11,200, three hours, every 30 minutes).

Ferry For details of the ferries to Ulleungdo, refer to the Ulleungdo section, which follows.

Getting Around
Local buses cost W600 (standing) or W920 (seated). Bus No 200 makes its way out to the airport from the inter-city bus terminal.

ULLEUNGDO 울릉도
pop 11,000
Isolated about 135km east of the Korean peninsula, this spectacularly beautiful island is all that remains of an extinct volcano towering over the storm-lashed Donghae (East Sea).

The island was captured from pirates after an order from King Yeji, the 22nd king of the Silla dynasty, in order to secure the east coast of the peninsula. From then until 1884 this small volcanic island remained essentially a military outpost, but from that year on migration to the island for settlement was sanctioned by the government.

Rugged, forested mountains and dramatic cliffs rise steeply from the sea, so don't expect sandy beaches. Snorkelling and scuba diving off the rocks is stunning, thanks to the clear water and abundant sea life, but the rip tides can be powerful and the water is always cold. Diving in Ulleungdo is not an activity for a novice.

Thanks to the rugged topography and isolation, the island is only sparsely inhabited and farms are tiny. Most of the people are concentrated in small villages along the coast and make their living harvesting fish and summer tourists. Everywhere you look there are racks of drying squid, seaweed and octopus (and summer tourists). Another industry is the production of pumpkin taffy, which is on sale in all the souvenir shops. Wood carvings made from native Chinese juniper are also big business – you can see these offered for sale at the island's many tourist shops.

A popular slogan of the local chamber of commerce is that Ulleungdo lacks three things: thieves, pollution and snakes.

Information
The information booth by the Dodong-ri ferry terminal will soon have English maps and brochures available, hopefully with ferry and bus timetable information. More-detailed maps of the island can be purchased from tourist shops. You can change money at the Nonghyup Bank.

Dodong-ri 도동리
Dodong-ri is the island's administrative centre and largest town. Like a pirate outpost, it is almost hidden away in a narrow valley between two craggy, forested mountains with a very narrow harbour, making it visible only when approached directly. This is also the main tourist thoroughfare and for some, the number of tourists can become a little overwhelming.

There is a spiral staircase behind the ferry terminal which leads around the base of the cliffs to a lighthouse. There is a small kiosk here where you sit back have a beer and watch the boats and seagulls go past. A similar walkway runs around the other side of the harbour, but abruptly ends.

Jeodong-ri 저동리
Jeodong-ri remains a fishing village despite the impact of tourism. The town retains a laid-back feeling and the harbour is still a bustle of fishing activity when the boats return. Accommodation is also of better quality and price than in Dodong-ri.

Boat Trips

A round-island tour is a great way to see the island and admire its dramatic landscape. The tour takes around two hours and costs W13,000. Outside of summer the tours depart only once or twice daily, but during August there are tours departing every two hours.

A submarine tour follows the same course as the round-island boats, but you get to choose either above or below deck. Departures depend on demand, but ask at the main ticket office inside the ferry terminal (W15,000, two hours).

At both Dodong-ri and Jeodong-ri, you'll see plenty of fishing boats docked during the daytime. They don't generally take tourists on board, but it is interesting to watch them in the evening when they head out to sea with their brilliant lanterns glaring. The bright lights draw the squid to their doom, just as a moth is drawn to a candle.

Hiking

Seong-inbong is the highest peak (984m) on the island and is the summit of a now-dormant volcano. There are various pathways leading to the summit. The main route to the top is to take the path from Dodong-ri to Daewonsa – just before you reach the temple there is a fork in the trail and a sign (in Korean only) pointing the way to Seong-inbong (a steep 4.3km). From the peak head down to Cheonbu-ri (7.1km) via Nari-dong.

A good circuit trip involves catching an early ferry to Seommok, from where the local bus to Hyeonpo drops you off in Cheonbu-ri. From here it's a steep climb up to Nari-dong following the main road up past the primary schools. From Nari-dong, follow the main road, but ask for directions just to be sure. As you leave Nari-dong and enter the forest there are many side tracks, keep to the central track and you will soon arrive at the chrys-

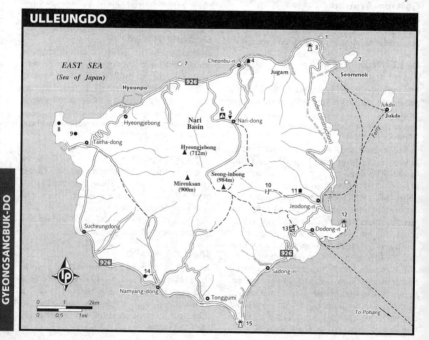

ULLEUNGDO

EAST SEA
(Sea of Japan)

Cheonbu-ri

Jugam

Seommok

Hyeonpo

926

Jukdo

Hyeongjebong

Nari Basin

Nari-dong

Taeha-dong

Hyeongjebong
▲ (712m)

Seong-inbong
(984m)

Mireuksan
(900m)

Jeodong-ri

Dodong-ri

Sucheungdong

926

Namyang-dong

Sadong-ri

Tonggumi

To Pohang

0   1   2km
0   0.5   1mi

thanthemum forest. Farther on you'll pass some more traditional homes. Finally, at the entrance to the virgin forest area and picnic ground, you will begin the steep ascent of Seong-inbong (one hour) through a forest of Korean beech, Korean hemlock and Korean lime. Just below the peak as you descend to Dodong-ri is a trail off to the right. Either continue to the left to Dodong-ri (one hour) or follow the other trail down to Namyang-dong (1½ hours).

Camping is available in Nari-dong. In Cheonbu-ri, there are *Cheongrim-jang Yeogwan* (☎ 791 6028) and *Saengsu-jang Yeogwan* (☎ 791 6108).

Bongnaepokpo 봉래폭포
This waterfall is 25m high and is quite spectacular during the summer. But don't expect a wilderness experience. With a concrete path running along a concreted river bed you will finally come to a concrete lookout.

ULLEUNGDO

1 Samseonam Rock
   삼선암
2 Gwaneumdo
   관음도
3 Lighthouse
   등대
4 Jeongrim-jang Yeogwan;
   Saengsu-jang Yeogwan
   정림장여관, 생수장여관
5 Sanma-eul
   산마을
6 Camping Ground
   야영장
7 Gong-am (Elephant Rock)
   공암
8 Chinese Juniper Forest
   향나무자생지
9 Wind Turbine
10 Bongnaepokpo
   봉래폭포
11 Ulleung Beach Paradise
   Hotel
   울릉비치파라다이스호텔
12 Lighthouse
   등대
13 Daewonsa
   대원사
14 Sunset Point Pavillion
   일몰전망대
15 Lighthouse
   등대

Just below the falls is a kiosk. Entrance is W1200. It's a steep 1.5km walk from Jeodong-ri or you can catch every 2nd local bus between Dodong-ri and Jeodong-ri.

Mineral Spring Park 약수공원
Just above Dodong-ri you will find a rock-climbing **rack cliff**, Ulleungdo's **historical museum**, the impressive **Dokdo Museum**, a **mineral-water spring** (yaksu gwangjang) and a **cable car** up to Manghyangbong (316m). There is no set order to partake in all these facilities, but you might like to call here either earlier or later in the day to avoid the masses of tour groups.

The mineral water has a distinctive flavour and some claim drinking it has all sorts of medicinal benefits. However a couple of travellers, including yours truly, only experienced mild diarrhoea.

The main highlight of the park is the Dokdo Museum. No effort has been spared on this centerpiece of Ulleungdo culture. It's an interesting cartographic experience and, in addition to the usual nationalistic indoctrination, there is some useful information on the need to conserve the natural environment of both Ulleungdo and Dokdo. Next door to the main museum is a smaller history museum displaying artefacts from early residents of Ulleungdo. This folk museum is a mere shadow of the towering Dokdo Museum. Entry costs W1200.

A ride on the cable car offers a stunning vista of the sea and the cluster of houses and yeogwan in Dodong-ri (one way W3500, return W4500).

Jukdo 죽도
This island, just 4km from Jeodong-ri, rises dramatically from the sea, with cliffs on every side. It makes for a pleasant day trip and is home to a *restaurant*, picnic ground and *camping ground*. Ferries depart every two hours from Dodong-ri's harbour, taking 15 minutes (one way W2000, return W4000). Entry costs W1200.

Dokdo 독도
If you're disappointed with Ulleungdo and are looking for something more rugged and

inhospitable, then catch a boat to Dokdo. An interesting island that also goes by the Japanese name of Takeshima. (See the boxed text Japan's Discomfort in the Facts about Korea chapter.)

Tour boats chug out to Dokdo every 2nd day during the warmer months and daily in July and August (W37,000, 1¾ hours one way).

Nari Basin 나리분지

This valley is on the northern slope of Seong-inbong. It's the only place on the island that's reasonably flat, so there are several farms here and a couple of reconstructed traditional thatched roof houses made from timber, straw and mud. All around the valley are thickly-forested slopes and it makes for a very photogenic sight.

Minbak are available at *Nari Sanjang* (☎ 791 6546). There are also a couple of restaurants in Nari-dong. *Sanmaeul* serves up a tasty *hanjeongsik* (Korean banquet; W5000) or you might try either *gamja buchim* (a potato pancake; W5000) or *sanchae deodeokjeon* (mountain vegetable pancake; W5000) and wash it down with some local *dondongju* (rice wine; W5000). Camping is also available.

Namyang-dong 남양

The small fishing village of Namyang, on the south-west corner of the island, is worth a visit if you're in the area.

Half the fun is just getting there – the road from Dodong-ri follows a tortuous path along the coastal cliffs for the whole way. This could raise the hair on your head or cause you to go prematurely grey, but there's no denying that the views are spectacular. The journey can be made by public bus or taxi. Along the way there are opportunities to stop off in Sadong-ri and Tonggumi.

Sunset Point Pavilion (*Ilmoljeon Mangdae*) is a steep 15-minute walk above the town, commanding great views of the ocean and yes, of the sunset. Follow the western creek out of town and cross the bridge after the school. A small trail continues up to the pavilion.

Places to Stay

Yeogwan prices in Ulleungdo rise steeply in the summer peak season (July and August) when the island throngs with holidaymakers. But even on a Saturday night you'll find a place to stay, though top end accommodation tends to book out with tour groups.

Every ferry is met by a gaggle of ajummas, all of them extolling the virtues of their minbak. By all means, go and look at what's on offer but don't take anything you're not satisfied with – there's plenty of good choices. Minbak generally charge W20,000, but in summer the skies are the limit.

Camping is available on the beach at Namyang, Naessujeon and Sadong. Toilets and showers are available at the latter two during summer.

Dodong-ri Visitors should book in advance, especially for places close to the harbour. *Paldo-jang Yeogwan* (☎ 791 3207) just above the harbour can get a little noisy.

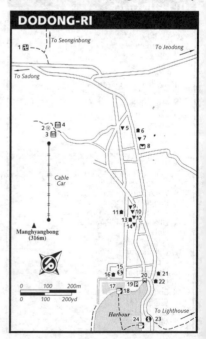

They have both rooms with/without toilets (W25,000/W20,000). In summer, prices rise to W30,000 and W35,000, respectively. Nearby, *Gurin-jang Yeogwan* (☎ 791 3204) and *Hanil-jang Yeogwan* (☎ 791 5515) have good rooms for W25,000 or W35,000 in summer. *Sanchang-jang Yeogwan* (☎ 791 0552) has good clean rooms for W25,000; W35,000 in summer. *Daegu-jang Yeogwan* (☎ 791 2314) has clean rooms ranging from W25,000 with common toilets to W30,000 with shower. Bookings are needed. *Jung-ang-jang Yeogwan* (☎ 791 3036) has clean pleasant rooms for W25,000 to W30,000. *Ulleung Hotel* (☎ 791 6611, fax 791 5577) is a good mid-range option with standard doubles from W40,000 and larger rooms for W80,000.

Jeodong-ri There are a couple of yeoinsuk in town, but as with Dodong-ri they are fairly grotty. All of these places are just behind the fish market and bus stop. *Jangsil-jang Yeogwan* (☎ 791 3261) has good budget-priced rooms for W15,000 or W20,000 in summer. *Daehwa Yeogwan* (☎ 791 2497) is another reasonable option with rooms for W20,000. *Nakwon-jang Yeogwan* (☎ 791 0580) has a similar standard of rooms for W25,000.

Jeil-jang Motel (☎ 791 2637) is above the town on the way to Bongnaepokpo and has good doubles for W25,000.

Also on the way to Bongnaepokpo, above Jeodong-ri, there will soon be the luxurious *Ulleung Beach Paradise Hotel*, which will be an enormous resort with plenty of expensive rooms and a swimming pool or two.

Places to Eat
Outdoor seafood stalls are so ubiquitous in Ulleungdo that you have to be careful not to trip over a squid. If you want to see lots of squid then visit during autumn, especially during October.

Dodong-ri Downstairs from the hotel of the same name, *Sanchanghoe Sikdang* specialises in *honghapbap* (mussel rice porridge; W10,000) and *mulhoe* (raw fish; W10,000). If you prefer outdoors, restaurants have tables fronting the harbour where you can watch the boats unload squid for the women to clean and sell. *Sanrok Sikdang*'s specialty is mixed seafood: *honghapbap* (W10,000) and *ttaggaebibap* (W10,000). They are geared to tour groups, but that doesn't detract from the flavour. *Hyangto Sikyuk Sikdang* (specialises in bibimbap), *Sanchanghoe Sikdang* and *Ulleunghoetjip* all serve decent food at a reasonable price.

At *99 Sikdang*, ttaggaebibap (W13,000) is the house speciality. If you want more spice, try *ojing-eo bulgogi* (spicy fried squid; W5,000). *Seoulwangmandu* is a

DODONG-RI

PLACES TO STAY
6 Ulleung Hotel 울릉호텔
11 Jung-ang-jang Yeogwan 중앙장여관
13 Daegu-jang Yeogwan 대구장여관
16 Paldo-jang Yeogwan 팔도장여관
21 Hanil-jang Yeogwan 한일장여관
22 Gurin-jang Yeogwan 구린장여관

PLACES TO EAT
5 Saekggalinneun Namgwayeo 색깔있는남과여

7 Sanrok Sikdang 산록식당
9 99 Sikdang 99식당
10 Ulleunghoetjip 울릉횟집
12 Sanchanghoe Sikdang; Sanchang-jang Yeogwan 산창회식당.신창장여관
14 Seoulwangmandu 서울왕만두

OTHER
1 Daewonsa Temple 대원사
2 Dodong Mineral Springs 도동약수터
3 Ulleungdo Museum 울릉도박물관

4 Dokdo Museum 독도박물관
8 Post Office 우체국
15 Nonghyeop Bank 농협
17 Park 공원
18 Ferry to Jukdo 죽도여객선선착장
19 Car Park 주차장
20 Bus Stop 버스정류장
23 Information Booth 관광안내소
24 Ferry Terminal 여객선터미널

GYEONGSANGBUK-DO

good place to pick up a cheap meal of *mandu* (dumplings), *naengmyeon* (cold noodles) or gimbap for around W4000. There are also a few scattered gimbap shops where you can eat for as little as W2500.

Jeodong-ri *Gyeongju Sikdang* serves up a tasty *yaksu bulgogi* (marinated beef; W9000), but you have to order a minimum of 2 serves. Their mixed vegetable dishes, *naengmyeon* (W4000) and *sanchae bibimbap* (W6000), are just as tasty. Adjacent, *Byeoljang Garden* has a similar menu.

Entertainment
In Dodong-ri *Saekkkalinneun Namgwayeo* is a pleasant cafe to relax or to enjoy a drink later in the evening. The cafe is on the 2nd level above Soul clothes shop.

Karaoke create a bit of noise pollution during the summer months. It can be fun if you're into it, though most westerners swear that the wailing sounds like a sonic representation of the island's chief product – squid.

Getting There & Away
You should carry your passport, in case you have to register your arrival on Ulleungdo.

Helicopter Citiair flies helicopters between Gangneung, on the Korean peninsula, and the islands of Guam and Ulleungdo. For bookings and prices call Seoul (☎ 3272 8120), Gangneung (☎ 648 7626) or Ulleungdo (☎ 791 1146). The same company also offers an aerial tour of the island.

Boat You can get to Ulleungdo by ferry from Pohang and Mukho (via Donghae). The catamaran service to Pohang is least likely to be cancelled due to weather or poor demand. Ferries from Hupo and Sokcho may only run during July and August. The timetable for departures varies month to month and ferries can be delayed for a week due to rough conditions. Fares between Pohang and Ulleungdo are W49,000 (ordinary) and W54,000 (1st class). From Mukho the trip costs W34,000. Concessions are available for children aged 2 to 12, students, seniors over 65 or to residents of the island.

It is best to reserve all your tickets to and from the island, especially during summer. Otherwise you can buy your ticket at the boat terminal first thing in the morning but you may go on a waiting list if there is a surge of tour groups. Advance bookings and news about cancelled ferries can be obtained in Seoul (☎ 514 6766), Ulleungdo (☎ 791 0801), Pohang (☎ 242 5111) and Mukho. You can also ring up the passenger terminals at the various ports: Pohang, Hupo (☎ 7872 8112), Donghae and Sokcho (☎ 636 2811). Ring KNTO for more details.

Some travel agents make reservations and sell tickets.

Getting Around
Bus Buses between Dodong-ri and Jeodong-ri run every 30 minutes (W700, 10 minutes). Other local buses run between Dodong-ri and Namyang (via Sadong and Tonggumi, every 1½ hours) and from Seommok to Hyeonpo via Cheonbu-ri (meets the ferry in Seommok). For an up-to-date timetable, ask at the tourist booth or try and decipher the one at the bus stop in Dodong-ri or Jeodong-ri.

4WD Taxis Taxis regularly ply between Dodong-ri and Jeodong-ri – wave them down if a seat is empty (W1900 per person).

The ring road which circumnavigates the island is 4km long, but has not yet been totally completed. 4WD taxis can be chartered (at negotiable prices) for a tour over most of the island's roads.

Boat There is only one last 4.4km section between Jeodong-ri and Seomok to be completed before there is a circuit road around the island that both local and tour buses will be able to use. Until then there are two car ferries operating to Seomok via Jukdo, one from Dodong-ri and one from Jeodong-ri. Boats depart every 2 hours from 8 am to 6 pm from Jeodong-ri and Dodong-ri. It takes 15 minutes to reach Jukdo and 10 minutes more for Seomok. Tickets are sold on the boat (W2500). When the island ring road is completed this service will cease.

Gyeongsangnam-do

Highlights

- Busan, South Korea's largest and most bustling seaport
- The bird sanctuary of Eulsukdo, seasonal home to over 100,000 migratory birds
- Tongdosa, one of Korea's largest and most famous Buddhist temples
- The rugged and picturesque coast of Hallyeo Haesang National Park
- Jinju's majestic and historic fortress
- Jirisan, Korea's first national park, a favourite for mountaineers

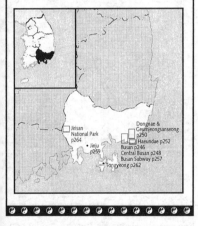

☎ 055 ● pop 8.4 million

To many people, Gyeongsangnam-do simply means Busan, the large port city that dwarfs its surroundings just as Seoul overshadows Gyeonggi-do. And yet, if you are prepared to dig a little deeper, Gyeongsangnam-do can offer some real surprises – including beautiful temples, rugged coastlines and islands, pleasant beaches, hot springs and scenic mountains. The coastline's proximity to Japan has shaped much of the province's past and continues to play a strong role today.

BUSAN 부산
☎ 055 ● pop 3.8 million

Busan is the second-largest city and principal port of South Korea. It is also the only major Korean city to have escaped capture by the communists during the Korean War – at the time its population was swelled by an incredible four million refugees.

Busan has a superb location, nestled between several mountain ridges and peaks. Many travellers regard it as just a place from which to take the ferries to Yeosu, Jejudo or Shimonoseki (Japan), or to catch international and domestic flights from Gimhae Airport. This is a great pity since it has a cosmopolitan ambience all of its own, quite distinct from Seoul. Busan does not have the old temples and palaces surrounded by areas of wooded tranquillity right in the heart of the city, like Seoul, however it can grow on you if you're prepared to spend the time exploring it. If you're looking for wooded tranquillity, then there are endless possibilities in the mountains that separate the various parts of the city.

Busan's distinct ambience results from constant exposure to sailors from all over the world. As seaports go, it's a *relatively* safe place to explore, but you should exercise a bit of caution in the central area at night.

Orientation

The central part of the city is squeezed into a narrow strip of land between a series of mountain peaks, steep slopes and the harbour. The ferry terminals, central business district, Busan train station, and a collection of hotels and yeogwan can be found in this area. The main subway stop here is Jungang-dong, which means 'Central District'.

Nampo-dong, in central Busan, is the trendy shopping and eatery district. It is packed with cinemas, restaurants, and designer fashion stores.

A little to the north is Dongnae, Busan's hot springs area and gateway to the fortress Geumjeongsanseong. Dongnae is also

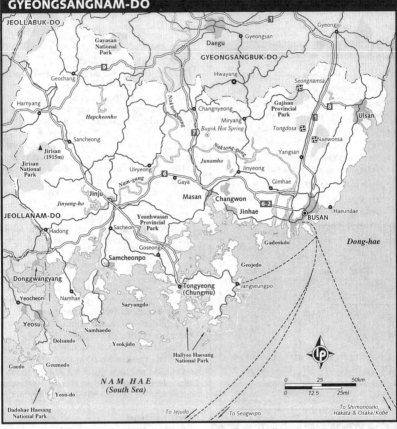

GYEONGSANGNAM-DO

home to Busan's dongbu (east) inter-city and express bus terminals. The third and least-used terminal, seobu (west), is out in the north-west of town.

If you fancy a spell at the 'Korean Riviera', Busan's beaches are north-east of the city centre. Haeundae Beach is the most popular in Korea.

The quickest and easiest way to get around Busan is to use the subway. Well-developed bus connections from subway stations make getting around the city very easy. The main line of the subway follows Busan's geographical features, and a new

line serving Haeundae Beach is under construction (due to open in 2001).

For luggage, there are lockers at the train station and at the bus terminals.

Information

Busan is well served by a number of tourist offices, with the main office near the International Ferry Terminal. This office has stacks of brochures, as well as Internet access and a place to read newspapers. Branches can also be found at Gimhae airport, Haeundae Beach and in front of Busan train station.

The Internet carries a lot of informative and interesting details about Busan. Probably the most reliable and useful of sites is at www.pusanweb.com. The site includes everything about living in or visiting Busan. It also has a lot of great links. The city government also has a Web site (www.metro.pusan.kr).

Consulates

The Chinese consulate is located on 9th floor of the Cheil Jedang Building. It takes three days to a week to process a visa. It's open 9.30 to 11.30 am, Monday to Friday. Take exit No 14 at Choryang subway station.

The Japanese consulate (☎ 465 5101) is at 1147-11 Choryang-dong, Dong-gu, just north of the Chinese consulate. It's open from 10 am to noon and from 1.30 to 3.30 pm, Monday to Friday.

The Russian consulate (☎ 441 9904) is on the 8th floor of the Korea Exchange Bank Building, 89-1 Jung-ang-dong 4-ga, Jung-gu. It's open from 9.30 am to 12.30 pm, Monday to Friday.

Bookshops

Busan's bookshops, when compared with the abundance of Seoul, offer lean pickings in English-language literature. The market seems to be sewn up by Young Kwang Bookstore in Seomyeon. They have a wide range of magazines, books and educational material. Take exit No 9 from Seomyeon subway, and from the top of the stairs the bookshop is straight ahead.

Opposite the main Busan post office is the Ilgwang Map Centre, which is a good place to pick up topographic hiking maps.

Beomeosa 범어사

Surrounded by a peaceful deciduous forest, Beomeosa is one of the largest temples in Korea – and one of the most beautiful. This is perhaps the best sight in Busan.

Beomeosa was founded in AD 678 by priest Uisang during the reign of King Munmu, one of the most enlightened rulers of the Silla dynasty. Uisang spent some 10 years of his life studying in China following his entry into the priesthood, and is revered as one of the greatest of the early Buddhist scholars.

Despite its proximity to Busan, Beomeosa is a world away from the concrete jungle down at sea level. The gate, **Jogyemun**, the **belfry** and the **main hall** in particular, are all sublime examples of Korean Buddhist art and architecture. A visit here on Buddha's Birthday is an absolute must! Buddha's Birthday (or the Feast of the Lanterns) will fall on the following dates: 30 April 2001; 19 May 2002; 8 May 2003; 26 May 2004; and 15 May 2005.

Much of the original temple was destroyed during the Japanese invasion of 1592–93, but not before a priest by the name of Seosan had defeated a Japanese army at this very same spot. Quite a few things remain from the Silla period, including pagodas, stone lanterns and pillars. The rest of the temple was reconstructed in 1602. Renovations took place in 1613 and 1713.

Getting there is simple enough. Take the subway and get off at Beomeosa station. From there it's a distance of about 2.5km. Bus No 90 (W1000, every 30 minutes) runs up to the temple – catch this bus from a small terminal just one block west of the subway station. Entry costs W1000.

Immortality for a Mere W5000

At major temple sites you may see stacks of large black tiles piled up near the side of the buildings. Each tile has some writing painted on it, usually in hangeul but sometimes in Chinese characters or (rarely) in English.

The tiles are in fact building materials, needed by the temples for their continuous maintenance and expansion plans. The white writing is simply the names of those who donated the money to buy the tile. You can have your name written on a tile for W5000, but if you can't afford this then two people (or a group) can share one tile. Your small donation will immortalise your name within the temple structure, and no doubt earn you some good karma.

BUSAN

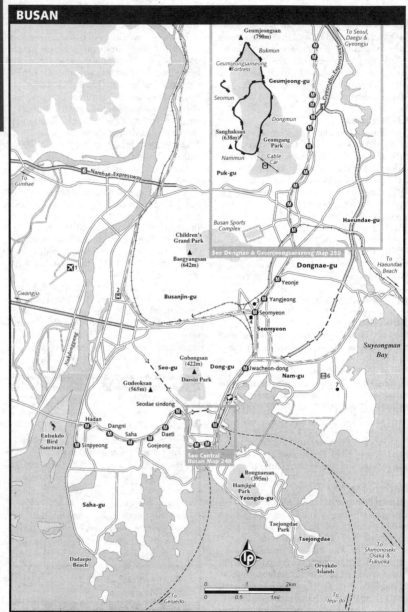

Geumjeongsan
(790m)

Bukmun

To Seoul,
Daegu &
Gyeongju

Geumjeongsanseong
Fortress

Geumjeong-gu

Seomun

Dongmun

Sanghaksan
(638m)

Geumgang
Park

Nammun

Cable
Car

Puk-gu

Haeundae-gu

To
Haeundae
Beach

Busan Sports
Complex

See Dongnae & Geumjeongsanseong Map 250

Children's
Grand Park

Dongnae-gu

Baegyangsan
(642m)

Yeonje

To Gimhae

Namhae Expressway

Gwangju

Busanjin-gu

Yangjeong

Seomyeon

Seomyeon

Nakdonggang

*Suyeongman
Bay*

Gubongsan
(422m)

Seo-gu

Dong-gu

Jwacheon-dong

Nam-gu

Daesin Park

Gudeoksan
(565m)

Seodae sindong

Hadan

Dangni

Saha

Daeti

Eulsukdo
Bird
Sanctuary

Sinpyeong

Goejeong

See Central
Busan Map 248

Bongnaesan
(395m)

Hamjigol
Park

Yeongdo-gu

Saha-gu

Taejongdae
Park

Taejongdae

Dadaepo
Beach

To
Shimonoseki,
Osaka &
Fukuoka

Oryukdo
Islands

To
Geojedo

To
Jeju-do

0   1   2km
0   0.5   1mi

BUSAN

1 Gimhae International Airport
김해국제공항
2 Seobu Inter City Bus Terminal
서부시외버스터미널
3 Younggwang Bookstore
영광도서
4 Lotte Hotel & Department Store
부산롯데월드:롯데호텔
5 Japanese Consulate
일본영사관
6 Municipal Museum &
Cultural Centre
부산시립박물관,문화센터
7 UN Cemetary
유엔묘지

Geumjeongsanseong 금정산성

The city's walled mountain fortress, Geum-jeongsanseong, sits high on the ridges of Geumjeongsan (790m) and Sanghaksan in the north-west of Busan. To see it properly you really need to put aside a whole day, though you could combine it with a visit to Beomeosa (see previous entry), a little beyond the northern extremity of the fortress.

This impressive walled fortress, with four imposing gates in traditional style, is the largest in Korea. Construction began in 1703 and was not completed until 1807. It's a popular place for weekend picnics and, weather permitting, the views from various points are terrific. There are rest and picnic areas inside the fortress at Dongmun (East Gate) and Nammun (South Gate).

There are plenty of trails leading to entrances to the fortress. The most accessible entrances are Dongmun, Beomeosa and Nammun (above the subway station of Myeongnyun-dong).

A hiking path starts from the left of Beomeosa and runs up to Bukmun (North Gate). If you're heading down from Buk-mun, then continue past the temple to the restaurants and car park for the No 90 bus to Beomeosa subway station.

Down at the park entrance there's a Buddhist temple, an aquarium, a zoo, a folk art exhibition hall, botanical gardens, pavilions, restaurants and a children's playground. There is also a cable car to take you to the top. The ride takes you to a height of 540m over a total distance of 1.26km. Otherwise it is a steep walk up to the summit (50 minutes). It's another 50 minute hike to Nammun. From here you can continue along the fortress wall to Dongmun (50 minutes) and Bukmun (a further 1½ hours).

Dongnae Hot Springs 동래온천

Being a large hot spring right in the middle of a major city, it's perhaps not surprising that Dongnae has been overdeveloped to such an extent that the water temperature of the spring has dropped. Despite this, a trip to the public bathhouse **Heosimcheong** will be a memorable experience. This place is big, possibly the largest hot springs bathhouse in Asia. It has an enormous variety of tubs to soak in, including different herbal infusions, mud baths, coal baths and all the facilities you could want for a completely indulgent time: massage waterfall, dry saunas, a mini-pool and a sleeping area. If your fingers and toes have turned into prunes, then coffee and snacks are available on the 3rd floor, but don't forget to wear the robe provided. Open daily (5.30 am to 9 pm, last entry 8 pm). Entry costs W6600, or W4400 before 8 am.

Busan Tower 부산타워

If you've seen Seoul Tower, you've got the idea. Busan Tower (118m) in Yongdusan Park is a good place to get your bearings. Activities include watching pigeons, getting your photo taken, eating ice cream cones and buying tacky souvenirs alongside *halabeojis* and *halmeonis* (grandpas and grandmas).

Admission to the tower costs W2500 (8.30 am to 10 pm). The tower is right in central Busan, a five-minute walk from Nampo-dong subway station.

Jagalchi Fish Market 자갈치어

Busan's huge fish market is worth a visit for those who enjoy watching catches unloaded from the boats, and the haggling that goes on between the boat captains and the buyers. The fish market is on the harbour, south of the central business district. Get there *early* though! Most of the action takes place before 6 am. There are also many *seafood restaurants* here specialising in sashimi.

GYEONGSANGNAM-DO

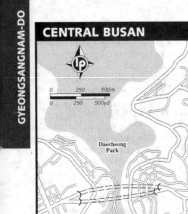

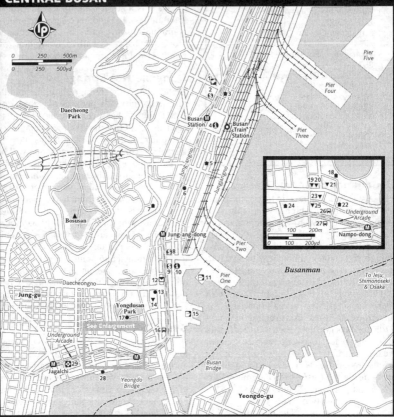

Every year in early October the **Jagalchi Festival** is held, featuring shamanist rituals and prayers, as well as traditional farming music and dance. Keep an eye out for the eel skinning, raw fish slicing and bare-handed fish-catching demonstrations.

Haeundae Beach 해운대해수욕장

Some 14km north-east of the city centre are Busan's beach resorts, the main one being Haeundae. It is the most popular beach in Korea. So popular, in fact, that you'll have to slither through a mass of squirming bodies greased with suntan oil (could be fun) to reach the water. No doubt the beaches are a welcome sight for those who live and work in Busan, but this certainly isn't Bali. Haeundae Beach is 1.25km long and is equipped with all the usual facilities, from changing rooms to hot dog vendors.

The annual summer **Haeundae Festival** is held in August and includes many colourful sporting events, as well as an outdoor film festival on the beach and fireworks.

In 2001 the four-storey **Haeundae Aquarium** will open right on the beach, with fish tanks displaying deep-sea fish, sharks, reptiles and penguins.

CENTRAL BUSAN

PLACES TO STAY
3 Dongbaek-jang
   Yeogwan
   동백장여관
5 Monaco Yeogwan
   모나코여관
7 Commodore Hotel
   코모도호텔
18 Royal Hotel
   로얄호텔
22 Seoul Yeogwan
   서울여관
24 Phoenix Hotel
   피닉스호텔

PLACES TO EAT
14 Lee Daegam
   이대감
19 Sigolbapsang
   시골밥상
20 Sahaebang
   사해방
21 Bisabeol
   비사벌

23 Wonsan Myeonok
   원산면옥
25 Huirak
   희락

OTHER
1 Chinese Consulate (Cheil
   Jedang Building)
   중국영사관
2 Kookmin Bank
   국민은행
4 Tourist Information Kiosk
   관광안내소
6 KAL Building
   대한항공빌딩
8 Korean ExchangeBank;
   Russian Consulate
   외환은행,러시아영사관
9 Busan Bank
   부산은행
10 Tourist Information Centre
   관광안내소

11 International Ferry
   Terminal
   국제여객터미널
12 Central Post Office
   부산우체국
13 Ilgwang Map Centre
   일광지도센타
15 Coastal & Tezroc Ferry
   Terminal
   부관훼리터미널
16 Bus Stop for Eulsukdo
   Bird Sanctuary
   을숙도버스정류장
17 Busan Tower
   부산타워
26 Bus Stop
   버스정류장
27 Bus Stop
   버스정류장
28 Jagalchi Fish
   Market
   자갈치어시장
29 Nonghyup Supermarket
   농협수퍼마켓

There are also sightseeing boats to the islets of **Oryukdo,** which depart from the eastern end of the beach.

Windsurfing on Suyeongman Bay, which faces Haeundae Beach, has become a popular summer activity (equipment is available for rent).

If you don't like the crowds, then not far east of Haeundae is a less well-known beach, **Songjeong**. It looks more or less like Haeundae, but is less famous and therefore less crowded.

Behind the Westin Chosun Beach Hotel is a pretty circuit road that cuts through **Dongbaek Park**. The road is famous for its profusion of camellias, which bloom in April.

Busan Metropolitan Art Museum is well worth a visit. The museum is very contemporary in collection and design, but it also houses a large number of traditional works. In addition to conventional displays, it has indoor and outdoor sculptures. The museum is open Tuesday to Friday (W700, 10 am to 6 pm) and is a five-minute walk from Seungdang subway station.

To get there, take bus No 31, 200 or 200-1 (W1000, 40 minutes) from Nampo-dong.

Taejongdae Park 태종대

If the 'Korean Riviera' doesn't appeal, try a day out at Taejongdae Park on Yeongdo, just across the bridge from City Hall. Once past the suburbs, it's a very pleasant place with beautiful views out to sea. It's not a national park so there are no entry fees. To get there, take bus No 30 from the city centre (20 minutes). Bus No 8 or 8-1 from the seobu terminal or No 88 from the train station goes to Taejongdae.

Eulsukdo Bird Sanctuary
을숙도철새도래지

South-west of Busan, this large, flat sedimentary island in the mouth of the Nakdonggang is home to over 100,000 migratory birds. Over 50 species winter here, including the white-necked crane, the spoonbill and the white-tailed eagle. The area is well-known to international bird watching groups such as the Audubon Society. There are several islands in the sanctuary, the largest and most accessible can be reached by a bridge.

If you contemplate coming here, remember that birds will be birds – their migratory patterns are seasonal and they

GYEONGSANGNAM-DO

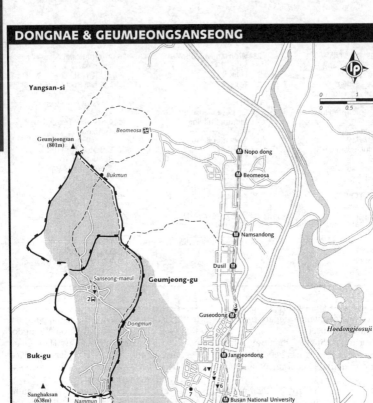

DONGNAE & GEUMJEONGSANSEONG

Yangsan-si

Geumjeongsan
(801m) ▲

Beomeosa ⊞

Ⓜ Nopo dong

Ⓜ Beomeosa

Bukmun

Ⓜ Namsandong

Dusil Ⓜ

Sanseong-maeul
1
2

Geumjeong-gu

3
Guseodong Ⓜ

Hoedongjeosuji

Dongmun

Buk-gu

Ⓜ Jangjeondong

Sanghaksan
(638m) ▲

Nammun

4 ▼
5 ▼
▼ 6
7 ●

Ⓜ Busan National University

🚡 *Cable Car*

8 ▼

Dongnae-gu

9 ●
10 ●   Ⓜ Oncheonjang

▲ 11
12 ■
14 ⊡ 13 ■   Ⓜ Myeongnyundong

⊡ 15

Ⓜ Dongnae

▼ 16
▼ 17

Busan Sports Complex

Ⓜ Busan University of Education

N 0 1 2km
0 0.5 1mi

DONGNAE & GEUMJEONGSANSEONG

PLACES TO STAY
9 Gangnam-jang Motel
강남장모텔
11 Oncheon Motel
온천모텔
12 Miseong-jang Yeogwan
미성장여관
13 Daedeok-jang Yeogwan
대덕장여관

PLACES TO EAT
1 Sanseong Daemunjip
산성대문집
3 Baebijang
배비장
4 Won Chon
원촌
5 Crossroads
크로스로드
6 Monk
멍크
8 Hyeondae Sutbulgalbi
현대숯불갈비
16 Dongnae Halmae Pajeon
동래할매파전
17 Hamgyeong Myeonok
함경면옥

OTHER
2 Bus Stop
버스정류장
7 Busan National University
부산국립대학
10 Heosimcheong
허심청
14 East Inter-City Bus Terminal
동부시외버스터미널
15 Express Bus Terminal
고속버스터미널

won't pose for the camera. Your chance of seeing some interesting creatures depends on the time of year, the time of day, the weather and luck. Don't forget your binoculars and telephoto lenses.

Korea being Korea, and the construction industry being the main economic stimulant, there is a massive reclamation project taking place in the area. This is despite Eulsukdo Bird Sanctuary being a protected nature reserve.

The Eulsukdo rest area, which is on the main island, is a 20-minute walk west across the bridge from Busan's Hadan subway station. Bus No 58, 58-1 or 300 stops

at the rest area and leave from Chungmu-dong. Most of the birds are south of the rest area – follow the rough road and hug the estuary for about a kilometre.

Other Attractions

The **Busan Municipal Museum** is not stunning, but it does have a good collection of ancient Korean artefacts (W200, 9 am to 6pm, closed Monday). The museum is right beside the **UN Cemetery**. This cemetery is the final resting place for 2,293 foreign soldiers who were killed during the Korean War (1950–53) and the only cemetery in the world managed by the UN.

The **Busan Cultural Centre** has regular traditional and contemporary dance and music performances, and is also nearby.

For all three sights, take bus No 134 from Busan train station or bus No 78 from the express bus station. Ring the KNTO for more details.

Places to Stay

There are just as many places to stay in Busan as there are in Seoul, however, for the budget traveller in Busan the choices are fairly limited. There are plenty of yeogwan around the inter-city bus terminal, but around the express bus terminal it is mostly low standard and not very convenient for visiting the sights. Nampo-dong and the area around the central Busan train station is the most central. In many respects, the Seomyeon and Dongnae area is a more attractive place to stay than central Busan. Staying out at Haeundae is great if you are in Busan to spend time on the beach.

Central Busan *Monaco Yeogwan* (☎ 463 6265) is south of the train station and has friendly staff, and good rooms for W25,000. *Dongbaek-jang Yeogwan* (☎ 463 5504) is north of the station and has okay rooms for W30,000.

Seoul-jang Yeogwan (☎ 247 3111) is in Nampo-dong on the 3rd and 4th floor above the cafeteria, Seoul Kkakttugi. Rooms are a reasonable W25,000. A good mid-range option is the *Royal Hotel* (☎ 241 1051,

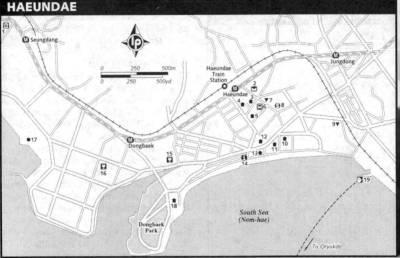

fax 241 1161), where decent rooms are W39,000 and suites are W88,000.

Just on the fringe of downtown Busan, the landmark *Hotel Commodore* (☎ 466 9101, fax 462 9101) has standard doubles from W98,000, superior rooms from W125,000 and deluxe rooms from W145,000, plus 20% tax.

Seomyeon 서면 **& Dongnae** 동래 The shopping and business centre of Busan, Seomyeon is convenient to all major areas of the city. Most major tourist landmarks are within 15–40 minutes of the area.

Probably the best place to stay in Busan is the *Lotte Hotel* (☎ 810 1100, fax 810 5110, ⓔ pusanrp@hotel.lotte.co.kr). This place is very impressive. From flash and comfy rooms to the Jungle Cafe, the Lotte Hotel has it all. All of this comes at a price: doubles start at W160,000 and suites at W280,000. The hotel is next door to the Lotte department store, just four minutes from Seomyeon subway.

Just next door to the bathhouse, Heosim-cheong, is *Gangnam-jang Motel,* where doubles go for W30,000. They don't take bookings, so just rock up and try your luck.

Across the road from the inter-city bus terminal and opposite Myeongnyun-dong subway station is *Oncheon Motel* (☎ 552 5394), which has rooms for W25,000 Around the corner and down the lane on the left is *Miseung-jang Yeogwan*, which is newer and cleaner inside and also charges W25,000 a room. In the same lane on the right is *Daedeok-jang Yeogwan* (☎ 554 7130), where double rooms are W25,000.

Haeundae This is where most of Busan's top-end hotels are located, but there are also plenty of budget and mid-range options available.

The cheapest options are down a small lane opposite the Riviera Hotel. Here you'll find *Daeheung-jang* and *Gwangwang Yeoinsuk* which both have a range of rooms from W15,000, with higher prices in summer. *Samseong Yeoinsuk* (☎ 746 6240) is in the same lane and has singles/twins from W10,000/15,000 with common showers. In summer expect the price to double. The lane is just at the end of a strip of restaurants.

The *Riviera Hotel* (☎ 740 2111, fax 740 2100) has discounted room rates and is worth a look. Standard doubles are W50,000

HAEUNDAE

PLACES TO STAY
3 Samseong Yeoinsuk
삼성여인숙
4 Daeheung-jang; Gwangwang Yeoinsuk
대흥장.관광여인숙
5 Hotel Riviera; Riviera Department Store
리베라호텔.리베라백화점
10 Paradise Beach Hotel
파라다이스호텔
11 Marriott Hotel
메리오트호텔
12 New Beach Hotel
뉴비치호텔
18 Westin Chosun Beach Hotel
웨스턴조선비치호텔

PLACES TO EAT
7 Ops Bakery; Sinheunggwan
신흥관
9 Daecheongmaru
대청마루

OTHER
1 Busan Metropolitan Art Museum
부산시립미술관
2 Post Office
우체국
6 Local Bus Terminal
시내버스터미널
8 Busan Bank
부산은행
13 Haeundae Aquarium
해운대수족관
14 Tourist Information
관광안내소
15 Ocaen Tower & Nightclub
오션타워
16 Sun Plaza (Bali Night Club)
썬프라자
17 Busan Yacht Club
부산요트경기장
19 Orukdo Ferry Terminal
미포선착장

Larger rooms are also available. *New Beach Hotel* (☎ 742 8877) is just back from the beach and has double rooms from W40,000, and in summer W70,000.

The *Paradise Beach Hotel* (☎ 742 2121, fax 742 2100) has standard doubles and ondol rooms from W140,000. Make sure you ask for a beach vista at this price. Another comfy choice is the nearby *Marriott Hotel* (☎ 743 1234, fax 743 1250), the largest hotel in Haeundae, with rooms ranging from W150,000 to W1,200,000, plus 20% tax. You can book online through their Web site: www.marriott .com (use the keyword 'Pusan').

Also with a grand Haeundae Beach vista, the *Westin Chosun Beach Hotel* (☎ 749 7201, fax 742 0515) has standard doubles from W193,000 and ondol rooms from W242,000.

Places to Eat
Central Busan Nampo-dong in central Busan offers plenty of restaurants to choose from and all within walking distance of each other. *Huirak* is a Japanese restaurant serving delicious *udong* (thick wheat) noodles, ranging in price from W3500 to W7000. Their tempura costs W9000. The restaurant is on the 2nd floor (closed Sunday). *Wonsan Myeonok* is a popular restaurant with the masses and serves up tasty *naengmyeon* (cold buckwheat noodles). The restaurant is down a small lane from the triangular junction, and could require a bit of hunting down.

Just east of this same junction is *Bisabeol,* which serves *dolsot bibimbap* (iron-pot mixed vegetables and spicy sauce on rice; W4000). The restaurant is in the basement, down the stairs off the street. On the second floor of the triangle junction is *Sahaebang*, a restaurant that specialises in Chinese mandu. You might have to fight for space around lunch time. Just behind is *Sigolbapsang,* which serves up tasty Korean staples like *doenjang tchigae* (tofu and vegetables in a bean paste soup).

Lee Daegam, near the Busan post office, specialises in *hanjeongshik* (Korean banquet), which will cost between W20,000 and W30,000. The restaurant is a little upmarket, but their prices are still reasonable and worth a visit just for the amazing decor.

Dongnae The Dongnae area is famous for *Dongnae pajeon* (traditional-style pancakes) and the most famous restaurant is the 4th generation *Dongnae Halmae Pajeon*. In fact, this place is famous throughout Korea, and has even received a certificate for preserving and upholding the pajeon culinary tradition from the Ministry of Culture. Its pajeon is so good that the late president Park Chung-hee made a pilgrimage to the restaurant. At Dongnae Halmae Pajeon they only use a small amount of rice flour, then they add egg, spring onions, lots of seafood, beef and Japanese parsley. The pajeon comes in two sizes and costs W15,000 or W20,000. Washing it down with a bowl of *dongdongju* (fermented rice wine, W5000) is recommended. The restaurant is a traditional-style building down a small lane. Ask for directions.

If you're still hungry *Hamgyeong Myeonok* is just around the corner and is reputed to serve the best naengmyeon in Busan. For W4500 you will receive a small serving of very tasty and chewy noodles.

On the other side of the subway line and near Oncheonjang station is *Hyeondae Sutbulgalbi* (☎ 513 2266), one of Busan's best galbi restaurants. Its fresh beef (W9000) is succulent and is served with an array of fresh side dishes. Upstairs is quieter than downstairs, but the food is the same. *Baebijang* is just next to Kuseodong subway station. It serves tasty *makguksu* (spicy cold noodles) and *bossam* (boiled pork with wrapping vegetables) and is worth the trek.

The local speciality in Sanseongmaeul (an area within the walled fortress Geumjeongsanseong) is worth the hike up the mountain. It consists of *yeomso bulgogi* (barbecue goat) served with dongdongju and *makgeoli* (traditional rice wine). *Sanseong Daemunjip* (☎ 517 8900) is a good place to try goat (W20,000). One serving is enough for two people. The dongdongju is called *tosanju* and costs W5000 for a large bowl (enough for four).

Haeundae *Ops Bakery* is a good place to sit down for a coffee and enjoy some of the tasty cakes available. Just next door, *Sinheunggwan* serves up some tasty Chinese and Sichuanese cuisine for a reasonable price. Also in Haeundae is *Daecheongmaru*, the locality's best galbi restaurant.

Entertainment

The small lanes in front of Busan University are home to dozens of restaurants, bars, cafes and clothes shops. If you're looking for youth hustle and bustle, then you will find it here.

Monk and *Crossroads* are popular bars that play a variety of music and sometimes have live bands. Upstairs from Monk is a coffee shop and gallery that is popular with expatriates. There are also plenty of cheap galbi restaurants here, usually hidden down small lanes. Close to Crossroads is *Won Chon*, a traditional-style soju bar decorated with folkcraft and antiques. Try a bowl of dongdongju with pajeon (the traditional-style pancake).

The most popular nightclubs in Busan can be found at Haeundae. For starters, try *Bali Night Club* in Sun Plaza, between the Chosun Hotel and the Yacht Club. Or you could try *Ocean Tower Night Club* on the top floor of Ocean Palace, opposite the Westin Chosun Beach Hotel.

The annual Busan Film Festival is usually held in October. It is constantly growing and features a variety of films from across the globe. Films are presented at cinemas all around town. For more details contact KNTO.

In the 'Russian sector' (just west of Busan station), gaggles of heavily made-up, miniskirted girls hang around outside the doors to the clubs. To the uninitiated, this might suggest the raucous beer-swilling fleshpots of Thailand or the Philippines. Actually, not many of these places are fronts for prostitution. Most of these clubs simply push pricey food, beer and vodka on their clients.

Shopping

The **Gukje Market** is Busan's answer to Namdaemun in Seoul. It's definitely worth a stroll. Just nearby is the trendy shopping and eatery district of **Nampo-dong**. It is packed with cinemas, restaurants, designer fashion stores, galleries, jewellery shops and more. This is the heart of Busan and a great place to just take in the scenery.

The enormous **underground arcade** between Jung-ang-dong and Jagalchi subway stations is like one big fashion parade – row after row of clothing stores.

The **Choryang Foreigners' Shopping Area** mainly caters to the Russian market. In former times, this was the haunt of American soldiers and was known as 'Texas Street'. These days Russian traders and sailors are the most enthralled about the place, and you'll see plenty of signs written in Cyrillic script. You can watch the sailors hauling away everything from fake Reeboks to Swiss watches and Mitsubishi refrigerators. However, there isn't really much of interest here to the average backpacker.

Getting There & Away

Air Busan is served by Gimhae Airport (☎ 972 3010). International flights are mostly to Japan (Tokyo, Nagoya, Osaka and Fukuoka), but also include Bangkok and Shanghai. As in Seoul, be sure to reconfirm onward flights. Three international carriers fly from Busan: Asiana (☎ 465 4000), Korean Air (☎ 973 2168) and JAL (☎ 469 1215).

As for domestic flights, the Seoul-Busan route is one of Korea's busiest. There are also flights between Busan and Jejudo (W45,500), Gwangju (W33,500), Wonju (W52,500), Mokpo (W40,000) and Gangneung (W47,500).

Bus The express bus terminal and the dongbu inter-city bus terminal are out in a Dongnae suburb, a long way from the city centre. The dongbu(east) inter-city bus terminal is quite convenient, being right next to Myeongnyun-dong subway station. The express bus terminal is about a kilometre west of Dongnae subway station.

There is one other bus terminal and that is the seobu (west) inter-city bus terminal, about halfway to Gimhae Airport. The only time you'd be likely to use this station is if you want to go to the small towns and cities to the west of Busan (especially Jinju). The subway connects the dongbu and seobu inter-city bus terminals.

Destinations from the express bus terminal include:

destination	price (W)	duration	distance
Cheongju	12,000	4½ hrs	319km
Daegu	5300	2 hrs	135km
Dong Seoul	16,100	5¼ hrs	445km
Gwangju	10,100	4½ hrs	268km
Gyeongju	3100	1½ hrs	79km
Jeonju	17,800	5¼ hrs	323km
Jinju	4500	2¼ hrs	115km
Seoul	15,700	5¼ hrs	432km

Some departures from the dongbu inter-city bus terminal include:

destination	price (W)	duration	distance
Andong	12,100	4 hrs	209km
Gangneung	21,800	6½ hrs	358km
Gyeongju	3100	1 hr	78km
Pohang	5700	1¾ hrs	107km
Sokcho	26,300	7½ hrs	431km

Departures from the seobu inter-city bus terminal include:

destination	price (W)	duration	distance
Daewonsa*	7900	1½ hrs	155km
Hwaeomsa*	10,600	3¼ hrs	202km
Jinhae	3000	1 hr	57km
Jinju	14,600	5¼ hrs	276km
Ssanggyesa*	9600	2¾ hrs	202km

*in Jirisan National Park

Train The Seoul-Busan line is one of Korea's busiest. Two trains travel this route – the saemaeul (W26, 300, every 30 to 60 minutes) and the mugunghwa (W18, 100, every 15 to 30 minutes). Trains also connect Busan to Mokpo via Gwangju (W17,700, twice daily). One mugunghwa train connects Busan to Gangneung on weekends and public holidays (W20,400).

If you're heading for Japan, a Korea-Japan Through Ticket has been devised to provide discounted travel between the two countries. This ticket covers your travel by train to Busan, the ferry crossing between Busan and Shimonoseki and then a train to your destination in Japan. It's a good way to save a few pennies. For more information, contact Korea Rail at Busan train station.

Ferry Details of the international ferries from Busan to Shimonoseki and Hakata (Fukuoka) can be found in the Getting There & Away chapter at the beginning of this book. Details of ferries between Busan and Jeju are in the Jeju-do chapter (Getting There & Away section).

Ferries leave from the domestic ferry terminal to Jangseungpo (W13,650, every one to two hours) on Geojedo.

Getting Around

To/From the Airport KAL runs two airport limousine buses (☎ 973 2168) to Gimhae Airport from the city's main tourist hotels (W4,500, every 30 minutes). Route one includes Gimhae Airport, the Commodore Hotel, the KAL Building, the area opposite the Busan train station, and the Seorabeol Hotel. Route two links the airport and Haeundae, stopping at the Westin Chosun Beach Hotel, Hyatt Regency Hotel, Paradise Beach Hotel and Haeundae train station.

Local buses (W1000, every 10 to 20 minutes) take a bit longer and are more inconvenient if you have a lot of baggage. Bus No 201 (Busan station), 300 (Dong-A University), 307 (Haeundae) or 310 (Nampodong) all run out to Gimhae Airport.

There are also buses directly from the airport to Gyeongju (see the Gyeongsangbuk-do chapter, Gyeongju section for details).

A taxi from the airport to the city centre takes around 30 minutes and will cost between W8000 and W10,000. Right outside the airport terminal is a large sign in English indicating the current taxi fares to various points in the city.

Subway The subway is an excellent way of getting around Busan. Fares depend on the distance travelled – W500 for up to 10km or W600 for longer. If you are spending a longer time in Busan, then investing in a *hanaro* card (W12,000) is not only expedient, but it provides a 10% discount on bus and train travel. Eventually, taxis are to be included in the hanaro network.

Busan will have a much more extensive subway network in place by 2005.

GAJISAN PROVINCIAL PARK
가지산도립공원

This park has three separate sections. The northernmost section is not far from Gyeongju and is known for it's rocky terrain. This is where you'll find **Gajisan** (1240m), the highest peak in the park. The park has some good walks; most hikers start their ascent to Gajisan from Seongnamsa.

Seongnamsa 석남사

Located in the far north of the park, this monastery is the centre for Zen monks of the Buddhist Bhiksunis. Most of the buildings are 20th-century reconstructions, but the beauty of the surrounding scenery more than compensates.

A good 20km walk (around 12 hours) runs from Seongnamsa to Gajisan, returning via Oksan, Daebisa and Unmunsa. The hiking trail to Gajisan (6.4km) begins just below the temple. There are markers and maps, but they are in Korean only.

Admission to the park and temple complex costs W1000.

Getting There & Away

Buses connect Seongnamsa and Eonyang (W550, 30 minutes, every 30 minutes). Bus No 370 or 317 (W550 or W1000, 1½ hours, every 30 minutes) depart from Ulsan train station and pass the inter-city bus terminal before going to Eonyang and terminating in Seongnamsa. Two buses run to Eonyang from Busan's dongbu inter-city bus terminal (W900, two hours, every 15 minutes; or W2200, 50 minutes, every 20 minutes).

Tongdosa 통도사

This Buddhist temple, the largest and most famous in Korea, is in the park's middle section. It is a traditional Zen temple, Tongdo meaning 'Reaching Enlightenment'. It was founded in AD 646 during the reign of Queen Seondeok of the Silla dynasty. The temple's founder, priest Jajang, studied Buddhism for many years in China before returning to Korea and making Tongdosa the country's foremost temple. He also brought back from China what were reputed to be part of the Buddha's ashes and 400 cases of the *Tripitak* (Buddhist holy scriptures). The ashes were enshrined in the elaborate tomb known as the **Seokga Sari-tap**, which is the focal point of Tongdosa.

Andong, Gyeongsanbuk-do: Flooding the rice paddies in spring in preparation for the next harvest

Scenes from yesteryear, Andong

mille Bell pavilion, Daegu, Gyeongsangbuk-do

Parked in Hahoe Folk Village, Gyeongsangbuk-do

A traditional 'ondol' underfloor heating system

Rural labour ages as the youth head for the city.

Interior of a traditional rural dwelling in the reconstructed Korean Folk Village, Gyeonggi-do

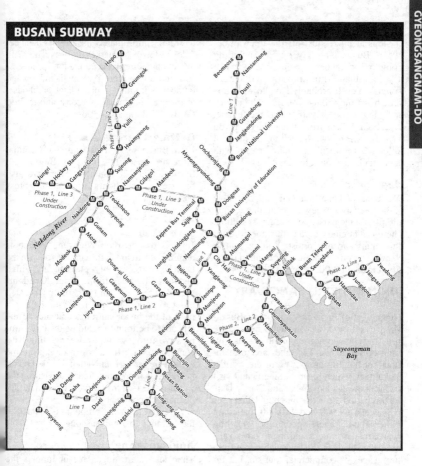

BUSAN SUBWAY

Like many other Buddhist temples in Korea, Tongdosa is situated in beautiful surroundings amid forested mountains and crystal-clear streams. There are some 65 buildings in all, including 13 hermitages scattered over the mountains behind the main temple complex.

There are some exceptionally beautiful structures here and it's well worth making the effort to stop off between Busan and Gyeongju. There are usually around 200 monks in residence, so it's more than likely that a ceremony or chant will be going on when you arrive. Entry costs W2000.

Definitely worth a visit is the impressive new **Seongbo Museum**, near the main car park. It houses more than 30,000 Buddhist relics and hundreds of Buddhist paintings. The Buddhist Painting Hall, inside, is only open four hours a day. Entry costs W2000 (open 9 am to 6 pm, closed Tuesday).

Getting There & Away
To get to Tongdosa, take the Busan-Daegu inter-city (not express) bus from either Busan dongbu (W1800, every 20 minutes) or Gyeongju. Tell the ticket office where you want to go and they'll make sure you

get on the right bus, which makes a number of stops at places just off the freeway between Busan and Gyeongju, including Tongdo. From where the bus drops you off, it's less than 1km into the village of Tongdo. You'll probably have to walk this stretch. At the village you have the choice of taking a taxi or walking to the temple. It's about 1.5km from the village. If you have the time it's worth walking, as the road follows a beautiful mountain stream with many rock carvings along the way.

Naewonsa 내원사
South-east of Tongdosa on the opposite side of the freeway is Naewonsa, another temple complex in the park's southernmost section. There is a nunnery here with some 50 Buddhist nuns and one priest. You can get to Naewon by bus from Busan's dongbu inter-city terminal (W900, every 15 minutes).

JUNAMHO BIRD SANCTUARY
주남호
To the west of Jinyeong on the main Busan-Masan highway you will find a remarkable bird sanctuary, comprised of three lakes covering 602 hectares. The lakes are most famous for holding up to 80% of the world's Baikal teal, which breed in Siberia and visit the lake between November and March. During this period the lake's bird population rises to between 50,000 and 150,000, including white-naped cranes, spoonbills, whistling swans, mallard ducks and many other varieties. This place is still reasonably free from the ravages of commercial tourism, but for how much longer? Don't forget your binoculars and a warm jacket.

Getting there isn't easy if you don't have your own transport. Local bus No 21-5, 6, 8, or 391 runs from Masan's inter-city bus terminal and bus No 92-4 leaves from Changwon's inter-city bus terminal. Regular buses connect Busan, Jinju, Jinhae and Tongyeong to Masan and Changwon. Otherwise, catch a taxi from Jinyeong (W6000).

BUGOK HOT SPRINGS 부곡온천
A major tourist resort in the countryside, Bugok is one of the hottest of Korea's hot springs (water temperatures range from 58°C to 78°C). Unfortunately the area has been developed for mass market tourism. The main attraction is **Bugok Hawaii**, a hot springs resort and amusement park with indoor and outdoor swimming pools, a huge bathhouse, a theatre, botanical gardens and a zoo (W6000, 7.30 am to 7.30pm).

Getting There & Away
From Busan's seobu inter-city bus terminal there are buses that pass by Bugok Hot Springs every 30 minutes. There are also buses every two hours from Seoul express bus terminal.

JINJU 진주
pop 342,000
Jinju is on the river Namgang, which is dammed upstream at the confluence with the Dokcheon. It's a pretty, pleasant city with a history going back to the Three Kingdoms period. There's a large, partially forested hillock overlooking the river. It's here that most of the historical relics and sites of the city are to be found, including the city's impressive fortress, **Jinjusanseong**. Jinju is a convenient base from which to explore the eastern side of Jirisan National Park. Gurye, however, is more convenient for visiting the western side (see the Gurye section in the Jeollanam-do chapter).

A tourist information booth is located at the entrance to Jinjusanseong.

Jinjusanseong 진주성
The most interesting place in Jinju is the hillock, which is actually the remains of Jinju's fortress. This was once a walled fortress, built during the Goryeo dynasty, but it was partially destroyed during the Japanese invasion of 1592–1593. It was here that one of the major battles of the campaign was fought, in which some 70,000 Korean soldiers and civilians lost their lives. The wall was rebuilt in 1605 by the provincial commander-in-chief, Lee Su-ill, and it's the remains of this which you see today.

Inside the walls are several places of interest as well as a number of traditional gateways and shrines. Overlooking the river

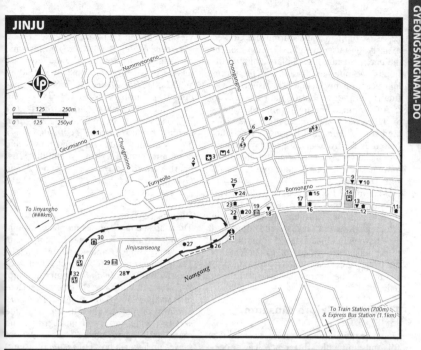

JINJU

JINJU

PLACES TO STAY
11 Dongbang Hotel
   동방호텔
12 Greece Motel
   그리스모텔
15 Yeongnam Yeoinsuk
   영남여인숙
16 Hite Motel
   히트모텔
17 Byeoksan Gungjeon
   벽산궁전
20 Hamyang Yeoinsuk
   함양여인숙
22 Hanil Yeoinsuk
   한일여인숙
23 Gyeongnam Yeoinsuk
   경남여인숙

PLACES TO EAT
2 Hanguksidae
   한국시대
9 Kimgane
   김가네
10 Samgyetang
   삼계탕

13 Hapdong Sikdang
   합동식당
18 BBQ Eel Restaurants
   장어구이식당
24 Dongaya Ugaya; Donto
   돈가야우가야; 돈토
25 Seoul Seolreongtang
   서울설렁탕
28 Kiosk
   매점

OTHER
1 Seobu Market
   서부시장
3 Police Station
   경찰서
4 Post Office
   우체국
5 Seoul Bank
   서울은행
6 Underground Market
   지하상가
7 Jung-ang Market
   중앙시장

8 Jeil Bank
   제일은행
14 Inter-City Bus Terminal
   시외버스터미널
19 Taejeong Folklore Museum
   태정민속자료관
21 Information Booth
   관광안내소
26 Righteous Rock
   의암
27 Chokseongnu Pavillion
   촉석루
29 Jinju National Museam
   잔주국립박물관
30 Cheonggye Seowon
   청계서원
31 Changnyeongsa
   창령사
32 Hoguksa
   호국사

is **Chokseongnu**, a large pavilion which was first built in 1368 during the Goryeo dynasty, and used as an exhibition hall for the poems of famous scholars and civil officials. Despite having survived the turbulent years of the Japanese invasion, it was finally burnt down during the Korean War.

Also worth noting are the impressive gates to the fortress, including **Seojangdae, Bukjangdae** and **Yongsam Bojongsa**. The latter served as the front gate for the Gyeongnam provincial government during the days of the Yi dynasty, when its headquarters were inside the fortress.

Also inside the fortress is the **Jinju National Museum**, a modern structure built in traditional style. The museum specialises in artefacts from the Gaya period, though it also has many objects dating from the time of the Japanese invasion of 1592 (W500, 9 am to 6 pm, closed Monday).

Entry to the fortress costs W500 (open daily).

Taejeong Folklore Museum
태정민속자료관

Opposite the entrance to Jinjusanseong is a folk museum with a difference. The collection includes a beautiful array of early 19th and 20th century furniture and brassware, and hundreds of silver, brass and copper plates and *jangseok* (escutcheon). The displays are visually informative, but all information is in Korean. Entry costs W1000 (open daily, 9 am to 7 pm). The collection is on the 2nd level above a tourist shop.

Jinyangho 진양호
About 5km west of Jinju is the huge Namgang Dam, which was constructed from 1962 to 1969. On the northern side of the dam is a recreational and resort area known as Jinyangho. There are lookout platforms, hotels, coffee shops and restaurants. You can hire motor boats and launches on the lake.

To get there from Jinju, take local bus No 26 from opposite the bus terminal.

Places to Stay
A delightful thing about Jinju is the line of yeogwan along the riverfront, close to the inter-city bus terminal. Rooms with a river view usually cost a bit more.

Greece Motel (☎ 741 6723) is clean and conveniently located next to the inter-city bus terminal. Rooms cost W30,000 to W35,000. *Hite Motel* (☎ 748 6606) has decent doubles for W30,000 and W35,000. *Byeoksan Gungjeon* (☎ 741 7738) has rooms for W25,000. *Yeongnam Yeoinsuk* and *Hamyang Yeoinsuk* (☎ 741 3818) are not bad with clean rooms and common showers for W10,000. Just nearby, *Hanil Yeoinsuk* (☎ 743 6422) and *Gyeongnam Yeoinsuk* (☎ 745 6444) have rooms for W10,000.

Places to Eat
There are a couple of decent places around the bus terminal. *Kimgane* is just opposite and serves cheap and tasty light meals. Their *naengmyeon* (cold buckwheat noodles; W3500), *mulmandu* (dumpling soup; W3500) and wide variety of *gimbap* (Korean sushi; W3000) are all good. *Hapdong Sikdang* is next to the bus terminal and serves a wide variety of inexpensive and reasonably tasty dishes. *Samgyetang* serves up a warm bowl of *insam* (ginseng) and garlic chicken with *insamsul* (ginseng wine) for W7000.

Donto and *Dongaya Ugaya* are cheap galbi restaurants next to each other. Across the road is *Seoul Seolreongtang*, which specialises in its namesake *seolreongtang* (beef broth with rice; W4500).

Along the waterfront near Jinjusanseong are a string of restaurants specialising in *minmuljang-eogui* (barbecued fresh water eel). They are all much the same in price and quality.

Hanuksidae is an upmarket option specialising in galbi and *hanjeongsik* (Korean banquet). The restaurant is opposite the police station.

Getting There & Away
Air Jinju's airport is in Sacheon. There are flights to Jinju from Seoul (W57,500) with both Asiana and Korean Air. There is also a Jejudo-Jinju flight with Korean Air (W44,500).

Bus Both the train station and the express bus terminal are in the section of the city south of the Namgang, about 1.5 kilometres from the centre. Take local bus No 15 if you don't want to walk.

Destinations from the express bus terminal include:

destination	price (W)	duration	distance
Busan	4500	2¼ hrs	115km
Daegu	5600	2¼ hrs	143km
Gwangju	6300	2¾ hrs	165km
Seoul	15,300	5 hrs	419km

Departures from the inter-city bus terminal include:

destination	price (W)	duration	distance
Daewonsa	2900	1¼ hrs	43km
Hadong	3200	2 hrs	49km
Haeinsa	6600	2½ hrs	13km
Namhae	3500	1½ hrs	61km

Train One daily mugunghwa train connects Busan and Jinju (W6000, two hours). Between Seoul and Jinju there are four daily mugunghwa trains (W20, 100, 6½ hours) and one daily saemaeul train (W29, 100, six hours).

Getting Around
To/From the Airport Local buses connect Jinju to the airport (W900, 35 minutes, every 10 minutes). These buses leave from the eastern end of the inter-city bus terminal.

TONGYEONG 통영
pop 139,000
Situated at the southern end of Goseong Peninsula, three sides of Tongyeong are surrounded by the sea. The city is sandwiched between the two beautiful islands of Namhaedo and Geojedo, and is a good place from which to explore Korea's rugged and scenic southern coastline. Tongyeong is considered the 'Naples of the Orient', due to its attractive little harbour and bustling small streets. It is often referred to as Chungmu because of the historical association with

Admiral Yi Sun-shin, Korea's greatest general (Chungmu was naval headquarters). The title *Chungmu* was bestowed upon Admiral Yi and literally means 'loyalty-chivalry'. Today, Tongyeong is a sprawling city, which still retains the charms of a busy fishing port.

For a good vista of the harbour, it's worth wandering up to **Nammangsan Sculpture Park**. For more information, especially about the city's festivals, see their Web site (http://city.tongyong.kyongnam.kr).

Sebyeonggwan 세병관
One of the oldest wooden structures in the country, this 1603 open residence used to be the headquarters of a large naval base. Up until recently, it was all that was left standing. However, in 1999 the authorities began rebuilding the whole complex and it is expected to be completed in 2002. Sebyeonggwan is just five minutes walk up the hill from the harbour.

Folklore & History Museum 민속박물관
This small museum includes a large number of relics and documents relating to Tongyeong's intimate relationship with the sea. The beautiful displays include cannons, lacquered boxes, maps, military documents, ancient ceramics and a number of traditional costumes. A descriptive pamphlet is available. The museum is opposite Sebyeonggwan. Admission is free (closed Monday).

Tonyeong Haejeo Tunnel 통영해저터널
Built in 1932 under the direction of the occupying Japanese, this 483m-long tunnel runs under Seoho harbour. The tunnel took 5½ years to complete and was the first of its kind in Korea. It is no longer used by cars, but is still used by pedestrians and bicycle riders.

Places to Stay & Eat
Accommodation is a little pricey down near the harbour. The farther away from the waterfront you go, the cheaper the rooms. *Naporee* (☎ 646 1155) is a good waterfront option. It has ondol rooms for W30,000 and Western-style doubles for W35,000. On the

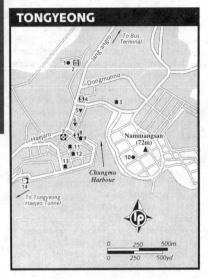

TONGYEONG

PLACES TO STAY
3 Naporee
   나포리
9 Namyang-jang Yeogwan
   남양장여관
11 Deokseong Yeogwan
   Yeoinsuk
   덕성여관,여인숙
12 Deungdae-jang Yeogwan
   등대장여관
13 Daeung-jang
   대웅장

PLACES TO EAT
5 Ritz
   리츠
6 Chungmu Gimbap
   Restaurants
   충무김밥

OTHER
1 Sebyeonggwan
   세병관
2 Folklore & History
   Museum
   향토역사관
4 Korea First Bank
   제일은행
7 Supermarket
   수퍼마켓
8 Kukmin Bank
   국민은행
10 Nammangsan Sculpture
   Park
   남망산조각공원
14 Ferry Terminal
   여객선터미널

opposite side of the harbour is ***Namyang-jang Yeogwan*** (☎ 645 2829) where harbour-view rooms cost W30,000.

Tucked in behind the harbour and the ferry terminal is ***Deokseong Yeogwan Yeoinsuk*** (☎ 645 3695), which has rooms from W15,000 to W25,000. Nearby, ***Deungdae-jang Yeogwan*** (☎ 643 5350) has clean and comfortable rooms for W30,000. ***Daeung-jang*** (☎ 648 0919) is also a good choice with rooms from W30,000 to W35,000.

Around the bus terminal are some good options, including ***Sapa-i-eo-jang*** (☎ 648 2369) and ***Suite-jang*** (☎ 642 6381) which are both reasonably new and have rooms from W25,000.

Tongyeong is famous for its gimbap, better known as Chungmu gimbap, which is rice rolled in a sheet of *kim* (seaweed) and served with a plate of hot and spicy squid. Quite tasty and just the treat after being out at sea for a couple of days. A street of ***Chungmu gimbap restaurants*** lines the harbour, all serving the same dishes for the same price.

For those preferring a coffee and a snack, then *Ritz* is a pleasant place to have a drink and enjoy watching the movement in the harbour.

Getting There & Away

Air The nearest airport is in Sacheon, where there are daily flights to Seoul (W57,500) and Jejudo (W44,500). Buses to the airport depart from the inter-city bus terminal (W3400, one hour, 54km, six daily).

Bus Express buses go to Seoul (W16,100, hourly), inter-city buses from Tongyeong to Jinju (W4300, 1½ hours, hourly) and Busan (W7100, 2 hours, 125km, every 30 minutes).

Ferry The ferry terminal is in the south of town and has regular ferries to the surrounding islands of:

destination	price (W)	duration	freqeuncy
Bijindo	5950	1 hr	2 daily
Jejudo	5650	1½ hrs	2 daily

Jeseungdang	3100	30 mins	8 daily
Maemuldo	9850	1 hr	2 daily
Saryangdo	9850	1 hr	2 daily
Yeonhwado	12,700	1 or 4 hrs	5 daily

GEOJEDO 거제도
pop 173,000

Korea's second-largest island, Geojedo is a mountainous and rugged place that bears the full brunt of the summer monsoons. Geojedo is also well known in Korea for being the home of two enormous shipyards: Daewoo's Okpo Bay and Samsung's Gohyeon. More interesting for the political scientist perhaps is that the island is the birthplace of former president Kim Young-sam. His home is now a sacred place where pilgrims come from all over Gyeongsangnam-do to pay homage.

The main city on the island is Geoje, but most travellers visit via the port of **Jangseungpo**, where ferries run to Busan.

The best way to appreciate the full beauty of this island is to either ride, catch a bus or drive around the coastal road. This road would have to be one of the most scenic coastal roads in Korea.

The southern tip of the island is particularly rugged and is called **Haegeumgang**, after the spectacular mountain range in North Korea. Most of this area is included in the **Hallyeo Haesang National Park**, and it is the part of the park most visited by Koreans. Tourists can get a tour boat around the barnacled rocks with a brief stopover on **Oedo** (Paradise Island). If you enjoy travelling on the peak-hour subway in Seoul, then this is the boat trip for you. Be prepared for the shouting of superfluous details about strange-shaped rocks over the loudspeakers. You will need to part with a large amount of cash to wander around an artificial island, packed with too many species of plants. Brace yourself for the constant queues of excited bodies that resemble a supermarket-aisle jam rather than a nature experience. If this is your style, then boats to Haegeumgang and Oedo depart on demand from Jangseungpo, Wahyeon, Gujora, Hakdong and Dojangpo.

Transport around the island is quite easy, with a regular local bus running the circuit of the island and returning to Geoje, and other buses coming from Tongyeong.

Getting There & Away
Ferries connect Jangseungpo to Busan (W13650, eight daily). The main bus terminal is in Jangseungpo, up the hill from the ferry terminal. Departures include: Tongyeong (W2800, every 10 minutes), Jinju (W7200, every 30 minutes) and Seoul (W20,900, 7½ hours, 496km, every three hours).

NAMHAEDO 남해도
pop 62,000

Not unlike Geojedo, Namhaedo shares a beautiful and rugged coastline. The island is further endowed with a beautiful mountain, **Geumsan**, and a couple of sandy beaches. On the northern tip of Namhaedo is Korea's equivalent to the Golden Gate Bridge, the main point of entry to the island **Geummungyo**. Next to the bridge is the small fishing village of **Noryang**. This village would not otherwise be very remarkable, except that it is famous for marking the site of death of Korea's greatest general, Admiral Yi Sun-shin (AD 1545–98). It was during the retreat of the fleeing Japanese ships that a stray arrow killed the Korean admiral. The small shrine, **Chungnyeolsa**, sits above the village and is dedicated to Admiral Yi.

Geumsan
This sacred mountain area is part of Hallyeo Haesang National Park. It features the pretty temple Boriamsa and the peak, Ku (681m). It is possible to catch a local bus from Namhae bus terminal to the park entrance at Bokgok. Shuttle buses run from here up to the temple or you can walk along the road (1½ hours). From the temple, a hiking trail continues down to the beach at Sangju (1½ hours). Half-way down is the main road, which you follow for 1km before reaching the beach.

Sangju
This is one of the most popular sandy beaches on the island, and during summer is a mass of beach umbrellas and inflatables.

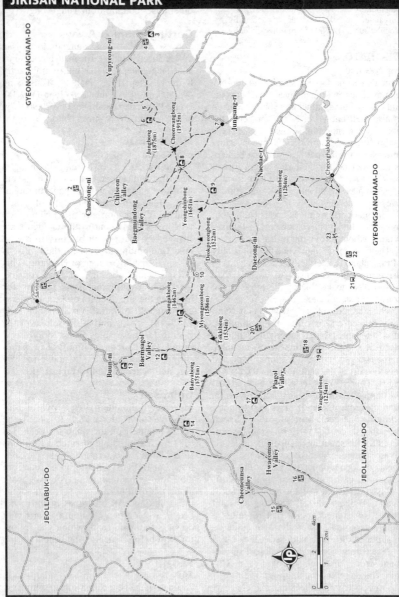

JIRISAN NATIONAL PARK

JIRISAN NATIONAL PARK

PLACES TO STAY
3 Camping Ground
   야영장
6 Chibatmok Shelter
   치밭목산장
8 Jangtemok Shelter
   장터목산장
9 Seseok Shelter
   세석산장
11 Yeonhacheon Shelter
   연하천산장
12 Byeongpungso Shelter
   병풍소
13 Takyongso Shelter
   탁용소
14 Yongso Shelter
   용소
17 Piagol Shelter
   피아골산장

OTHER
1 Silsangsa
   실상사
2 Byeoksongsa
   벽송사
4 Daewonsa
   대원사
5 Mujaechigipokpo
   칼바위
7 Kalbawi Boulder
   무재치기폭포
10 Spring
   샘
15 Cheoneunsa
   천은사
16 Hwaeomsa
   화엄사
18 Yeongoksa
   연곡사
19 Bus Stop (To Hadong)
   버스정류장
20 Chilbulsa
   칠불사
21 Bus Stop (To Hadong)
   버스정류장
22 Ssanggyesa
   쌍계사
23 Bulilpokpo
   불일폭포

Plenty of accommodation is available, with yeogwan and minbak all charging ridiculous prices in July and August. Buses connect Sangju and Namhae via Geumsan (W1400, every 40 minutes, 21km, 40 minutes).

Getting There & Away
The main bus terminal is in Namhae which has connections with:

destination	price (W)	duration	distance
Busan	8300	2¼ hrs	161km
Jinju	3500	1¼ hrs	62km
Seoul	22,600	5½ hrs	475km
Suncheon*	3700	1½ hrs	64km

*stops at Noryang

JIRISAN NATIONAL PARK
지리산국립공원

Straddling the border of three provinces is Jirisan National Park, which offers some of Korea's best hiking opportunities. This was Korea's first national park, and is still one of the best.

Mountaineers are delighted with the place. Jirisan is honeycombed with well-maintained trails which take hikers up to the ridge forming the backbone of the park. Many peaks are over 1500m high, including South Korea's second highest mountain, **Cheonwangbong** (1915m).

If you're going to do some hiking in this park, get a copy of the National Park's map titled *Jirisan National Park*, which has detailed topographic information on the area. It also indicates road-heads, trails, camp sites, springs, shelters, temples and other points of interest. It's sufficiently accurate for most people's purposes.

There are three principal areas of the park, each with its own temple. Two of the three temples, **Ssanggyesa** and **Daewonsa**, lie in Gyeongsangnam-do. Another temple, **Hwaeomsa**, is approachable from Gurye in Jeollanam-do province (see the Hwaeomsa section in the Jeollanam-do chapter for details).

Daewonsa 대원사

At the eastern edge of Jirisan National Park is Daewonsa. The Daewonsa entrance to the park offers a challenging route for the assault on Cheonwangbong, Jirisan's highest peak. The route goes via the shelter *Chibalmok Sanjang*, and the peaks **Sseori-bong** (1642m) and **Jungbong** (1875m). From Cheonwangbong you could descend for the night to shelter at *Jangteomok Sanjang*. This hike would require about eight to nine hours' hard slog. It is 10.7km from

Yupyeong-ni to Cheonwangbong. Entry to the park at Daewonsa costs W1000.

Ssanggyesa 쌍계사

In the south-eastern part of the park is Ssanggyesa, one of the principal temples of the Jogye Order of Korean Buddhism. The temple was originally built in AD 722 to enshrine a portrait of monk Yukjo that was brought back from China by two Silla monks. The temple was originally named Okcheonsa, but received its present name around 886, in tribute to the Zen monk Jingam-seonsa. It was monk Jingam-seonsa who enlarged the temple in 840 after he returned from studying in China. He was also responsible for establishing the tea plantations on the slopes of Jirisan, using seeds that he brought back from China. The temple has been renovated several times by a number of prominent monks, and several important artefacts are kept here.

This temple has a sublime setting amid steep forested hillsides and is entered by a series of massive gateways housing the various guardians of the temple. Entry costs W2200.

A crystal-clear rocky stream, spanned by a bridge, divides the Ssanggyesa compound into two halves. If you follow the path which crosses this stream farther up into the mountain, it will take you to the impressive waterfall of **Bulilpokpo** (2km, one hour).

Above the temple on the way to *Seseok Sanjang* is **Gallim Valley**, a beautiful valley with roaring cascades. It is an ideal spot for a break or for a swim in the refreshing stream. From Jageunsegaegol to Gallim Valley the path follows a spectacular river valley full of waterfalls, cascades and rock pools.

Buses to Ssanggyesa terminate in a small village on the opposite side of the main river from the temple. To get to the temple, cross the river bridge. There are restaurants, souvenir shops and minbak, both in the village where the buses stop and along the road which leads to the temple beyond the ticket office. Bus tickets should be purchased from the restaurant by the bridge.

Hiking

It would be almost impossible to describe the myriad of trails and possible hikes within this great park. If you embark on an ascent, then a large amount of your time will be spent traversing the steep ridge. You will have to devote at least a full day, or even two, to your hike. There are many half-day hikes along incredible valleys that channel into the mountain. These include Daeseonggol, Jungsanni Valley, Daewonsa Valley, Baekmudong Valley, the famous Baemsagol Valley and Hwaeomsa Valley. For those looking for the most challenging course then you could walk from east to west (Daewonsa to Hwaeomsa) or vice versa. This hike supposedly takes 24 hours, but this doesn't include breaks or photo shots, so realistically you will need about three or four full days.

Places to Stay

Camping Camping is available below Daewonsa, Nodong-ri , Jungsan-ni, Baengmudong and Hwaeomsa. Sites generally cost W3000 and facilities are basic.

Shelters There are seven shelters within the park where it is possible to crash for the night when undertaking a one to three-day hike (W3000 to W5000). All of these shelters are situated along the mountain ridge which forms the backbone of the park. *Jangteomok Sanjang* has enough space for 140 tired bodies, and has a wide range of supplies available, including film, torches, noodles and drinks. *Seseok Sanjang* is the largest shelter, with 240 beds. There used to be a camping ground here, but the land has since been reclaimed.

You should still bring your own bedding, food and tea/coffee, as there is a limited range of canned and packaged foods for sale at some of the shelters. In general blankets (W1000) are also available if you haven't brought your sleeping bag. All the shelters have access to spring water. Bookings are essential on weekends and during holidays. See the national park's Web site (www.npa.or.kr) for further details.

Minbak & Yeogwan This is the most common option for those wanting to stay at the entrances to the park. The rates vary according to the season. Generally, minbak charge from W15,000 to W20,000 and yeogwan charge from W20,000 to W40,000. In recent years, more mid-range and top-end accommodation has been developed around the park, with rates of W40,000 and up.

Getting There & Away

Buses connect Daewonsa with Jinju (W2900, 1¼ hour, 43km, every 40 minutes). All the buses that go to/from Ssanggyesa stop in Hadong (W1600, 35–60 minutes, 24km, every 40 minutes), making it a convenient transfer point. Buses connect Ssanggyesa with Jinju via Hadong (every 2½ hours) and directly to Gurye (W1300, 35 minutes, 21km, hourly).

Buses also depart Cheonghak-dong to Hadong (W2700) at 7 and 10 am and 12.30

and 5 pm and to Jinju at 9 and 11 am and 3 and 6 pm (W6000).

Buses run to Jungsan-ni from Jinju (W3200, 1½ hours, every 30 minutes).

On the northern side of the park buses connect Baekmu-dong with Namwon (W3000, one hour, 49km, hourly) and Hamyang (W2200, one hour, 61km, every 30–40 minutes).

The 24km road from Hadong to Ssanggyesa is lined with glorious cherry blossom trees and is regarded as one of the most scenic drives in Korea. The road makes its way along the Seomjingang, a river famous for *jaecheop*, a small fresh-water or estuarine shellfish that is cooked into a soup called *jaecheopguk* (supposedly a good hangover drink).

Jeollanam-do

Highlights

- Dadohae Haesang National Park, a marine park consisting of over 1700 islands and islets
- Hwaeomsa, a temple which has survived five major devastations and was last rebuilt in 1636
- Jogyesan Provincial Park, home to Songgwangsa, the main temple of the Jogye Buddhist sect
- Duryunsan Provincial Park, where you'll find Daeheungsa, a major Zen meditation temple
- Jindo, a scenic island known for its bizarre 'Landing Tide Phenomenon'
- Bogildo, an island boasting three nice, sandy beaches

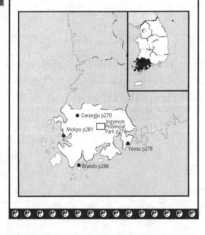

☎ 061 • pop 3.5 million

This province in the south-west corner of Korea is notable for its dramatic rocky coastline and thousands of islands. It contains rich agricultural lands, but it was one of the last provinces to share in Korea's rapid post-war development. Jeollanam-do is also well-known for its rocky politics – political dis-

sent has a long history here. All this has its roots in a long history of exploitation and neglect of the Jeollas and a tradition of voicing their dissatisfaction with the harsh rule.

Leaving aside its deep regionalism, the province is a great place to visit. There is plenty of beachside scenery as well as the requisite Buddhist temples and hermitages.

History

Over the past couple of decades, Jeollanam-do has acquired a reputation for its student and industrial worker radicalism, with at least one annual riot every May 18, the anniversary of the infamous Gwangju Massacre.

A series of events here in 1980 (described in the History section in the Facts about Korea chapter) led to large-scale student protests against the government. On 18 May, 1980, the military moved into Gwangju – the soldiers had no bullets, but they used bayonets to murder dozens of protesters. Outraged residents broke into armouries and police stations, and used the seized weapons and ammunition to drive the military forces out of the city. The city of Gwangju enjoyed nine days of complete freedom before the brutal military response came. On 27 May, soldiers armed with loaded M16 rifles retook the city, and most leaders of the protests were summarily shot. Some put the death toll at over 2000, but the government has always contended that about 180 people died. An independent count, made after President Kim Young-sam came to power, put the death toll at around 200, and this figure has even been accepted by the opposition. At present, 130 bodies have been accounted for and are buried in a special commemorative cemetery.

The chief culprits behind these tragic events were two generals, Chun Doo-hwan and Roh Tae-woo, both of whom later were to serve as president. Student protesters have long made prosecution of these two men their key demand. As a result, Gwangju

Massacre riots have been staged annually in the central area of the city on 18 May.

The province's most famous export, and dissident, is probably Korean president and Nobel Peace Prize laureate Kim Dae-jung. In early 1998, Kim Dae-jung pardoned Chun Doo-hwan and Roh Tae-woo in a widespread amnesty to most political prisoners. The people of Jeollanam-do hope he will be able to help rebuild the province after a history of neglect and injustices from Seoul.

GWANGJU 광주
☎ 062 • pop 1.4 million
Information
There are tourist information offices at Gwangju airport, in the bus terminal, at the train station and at the foot of Mudeungsan.

Special Events
Though Gwangju has been the provincial capital of Jeollanam-do for centuries and

is the fifth largest city in Korea, there is precious little left of its traditional heritage. This is a sprawling, all-modern, concrete-and-glass city that is firmly placed in modern Korea. In an attempt to lift its cultural profile, the city has hosts a biennial (ie, occurring every two years) festival. During this time the city is jam-packed full of colourful and interesting performances, displays, lectures, exhibitions and music. This is the best time to pay a visit to Gwangju.

Gimchi Festival Every year, in October, Gwangju hosts a three-day *gimchi* (spicy vegetable dish) festival for all those fans of this unique Korean delight. If you want to partake in making, tasting, purchasing or just enjoying the visual sensation of the many gimchi varieties, then this is the time to visit Gwangju. The venue changes from year to year. Wherever it is held, shuttle buses will run between the venue and the

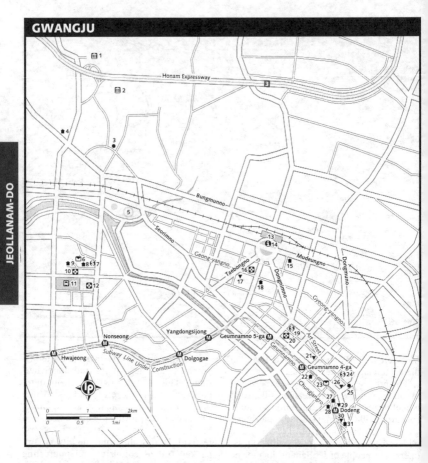

GWANGJU

airport, train station and bus terminal. Contact KNTO for more details.

Gwangju National Museum & Folk Museum 광주국립박물관,민속박물관

The Gwangju National Museum was mainly built to house the contents of a Chinese Yuan dynasty junk which sank off the coast some 600 years ago and was only rediscovered in 1976. Exhibits include celadon vases, cups and apothecaries' mortars and pestles, almost all of them in perfect condition. The rest of the museum is taken up by 11th to 14th-century Buddhist relics, scroll paintings from the Yi dynasty and white porcelain.

Entry costs W400 (open 9 am to 6 pm, closed Mondays).

Like many of Korea's folk museums, this one also follows the traditional culture from birth until death and beyond. There are also displays on festivals, clothing, food and folk paintings.

Entry costs W440 (open 9 am to 5.30 pm, closed the day after national holidays).

The museums are to the north of the city centre, a pedestrian bridge over Honam Expressway connects the two museums.

GWANGJU

PLACES TO STAY
4 Prince Hotel
  광주프린스호텔
8 Baekrim-jang Yeogwam
  백림장여관
9 New Seoul-jang Yeogwan
  뉴서울장여관
15 Parangsae Motel
  파랑새모텔
18 Young Bin Hotel
  영빈각호텔
22 Gwangju Palace Tourist Hotel
  광주팔레스관광호텔
27 Mokhwa-jang Yeogwan
  목화장여관
28 Gwangju Grand Hotel
  광주그랜드호텔
31 Chungnam Yeogwan
  충남여관

PLACES TO EAT
17 Yeongyang Duck
  영양오리탕
21 Eunhye Bunsik
  은혜분식

26 Mimirak
  미미락
29 Minsokchon
  민속촌
30 Songjukheon
  송죽헌

OTHER
1 Gwangju National Museum
  광주국립박물관
2 Gwangju Municipal Folk Museum
  광주민속박물관
3 Biennale Exhibition Hall
  비엔날레전시장
5 World Cup Stadium
  월드컵경기장
6 Post Office
  우체국
7 Gwangju Bank
  광주은행
10 Nonghyeop Supermarket
  농협수퍼마켓
11 Bus Terminal
  버스터미널

12 Shinsegae Department Store
  신세계백화점
13 Train Station
  광주역
14 Tourist Information Kiosk
  관광안내소
16 Hyundai Department Store
  현대백화점
19 Gwangju Bank
  광주은행
20 Lotte Department Store
  롯데백화점
23 Central Post Office
  중앙우체국
24 Korea First Bank
  제일은행
25 May 18th Democratic Plaza
  5.18민주광장

From Gwangju Station, catch bus No 1, 16, 19, 26, or 101 and from Gwangju Bus Terminal hop on bus No 23 or 25 to the Folk Museum.

Shopping

Gaemi, or **Art Street**, is the place to come for artwork or art supplies or even traditional handicrafts. This street in the middle of town is full of art galleries, antique and souvenir shops and framing shops. It also hosts a weekend market. To get here catch bus No 9 from the bus terminal or No 17 from the train station.

Chungjangro is Gwangju's trendy shopping street and is where you will find all the popular bars and nightclubs, a couple of bookshops and all of the fast-food giants. The street is closed to traffic and is bustling with young hip people every evening.

Places to Stay

The bus terminal area in the west of town is most convenient for places to stay. Just to the north of the bus terminal and across the street is a plethora of yeogwan tucked away in the small alleys. Some are fairly expensive (W35,000 for cushy rooms), but you can do all right for W25,000 at *New Seoul-jang Yeogwan* and *Baekrim-jang Yeogwan* (☎ 363 0356).

Parangsae Motel (☎ 511 8080) is just around the corner from the train station and has rooms for W25,000. In the same neighbourhood, *Young Bin Hotel* (☎ 526 8550) has ondol rooms from W35,000 and suites from W45,000.

Down the same obscure little lane as Songjukheon (see Places to Eat) is *Chungnam Yeogwan* (☎ 226 8826). This place is is one of the cheapest places in town. It has a selection of no-frills rooms for W20,000. Chungnam Yeogwan is next door to the restaurant Songjukheon.

In the centre of town, down a narrow corridor, is *Mokhwa-jang* (☎ 222 8119) which has rooms for W25,000. Look for the Yeogwan symbol (see the Accommodation section in the Facts for the Visitor chapter). *Gwangju Grand Hotel* (☎ 224 6111) is just nearby and has doubles from W64,000 and suites for W130,000.

Gwangju Palace Tourist Hotel (☎ 222 2525) has doubles ranging from W82,000

Gwangju Biennial

The Gwangju Biennial is an international exhibition of contemporary art which runs for over two months. It attracts artists to Gwangju from both Korea and from around the globe. The last Biennial took place in 2000 under the theme of 'Man + Space', or *'in + gan'*. When the two hanja, *in* and *gan* are brought together (*ingan*) the word 'human being' is created. This theme asked artists to reflect on the relationship between the philosophical, social and environmental factors in relation to human behaviour.

The Biennial provides an opportunity to glimpse contemporary art from around the world and in a number of mediums, ranging from experimental to multimedia. Another interesting feature of the festival are the symposiums, where artists and invited guests analyse the theme of the Biennial and discuss the developments in the contemporary art world with reference to the exhibited pieces.

In addition to the exhibitions, symposiums and seminars, the local tourist authorities also organise traditional folk dancing and musical performances, photographic exhibitions, theatre, fashion shows and workshops. These events take place throughout the Biennial. A special Web site (www.kwangjubiennale.org) provides more details, including dates and locations of the exhibitions.

The 2000 Biennial was sadly marred by planning difficulties that reflect a more general problem in Korea. From under-resourcing facilities for visiting journalists, to inadequate and insufficient translators, the festival highlighted Korea's continuing challenges when hosting international events. The organisers of the Biennial will hopefully share some of their insights and problems with the people involved in the 2002 World Cup. More careful planning will ensure that Korea is able to showcase its rich and colourful culture without unnecessary distractions.

The next Biennial is scheduled for 2002 and will run from 29 March to 29 June, overlapping with the 2002 World Cup.

to W150,000, but they usually offer a 20% discount off these prices.

One of the most comfortable abodes in Gwangju is the *Prince Hotel* (☎ *524 0025, fax 524 0026)* where doubles start from W84,700 and ondol rooms from W96,800. The hotel is near the national museum and is very convenient for visiting Gwangju's Biennial.

Places to Eat

Minsokchon is a popular new restaurant with a traditional folksy appearance: even the waiters are dressed in *hanbok* (a traditional Korean garment). Barbecues are usually sizzling away on most tables, especially *dweji galbi* (pork barbecue, W5800) and *so galbi* (beef barbecue, W10,000). Their *naengmyeon* (cold buckwheat noodles, W4000) are also pretty good. The food is inexpensive and very fresh.

Around the corner from here is *Songjukheon* (☎ *222 4234)*, probably one of Gwangju's most expensive and well-known establishments. Korean banquet is their specialty, but at W50,000 per person you would want to be hungry. This is no ordinary banquet, with a delicious range of food on show. This place is very popular and bookings are essential.

Yeongyang Duck lies on what the locals call 'duck street', due to the large number of restaurants serving *yeongyang oritang* (duck stew), a Gwangju speciality. For something a bit more low key, try *Eunhye Bunshik*, where you can eat cheaply on *mandu* (dumplings) and *gimbap* (Korean 'sushi').

The large Lotte and Shinsegae department stores have all sorts of restaurants. In both their basements is a huge supermarket and a food court.

Getting There & Away

Air Both Asiana and Korean Air offer Gwangju-Seoul and Gwangju-Jeju flights. Asiana also runs a flight between Gwangju and Busan.

Bus Gwangju's bus terminal is a monolithic structure housing both express and inter-city buses, an information desk and easily a dozen restaurants.

The terminal is out west end of town, and city bus Nos 7, 9, 13, 17, 36 or 101 connect the terminal with the train station area.

Express bus destinations include:

destination	price (W)	duration	distance
Busan	10,100	4 hrs	270km
Daegu	8,400	3¼ hrs	219km
Daejeon	6900	3 hrs	185km
Dong Seoul	12,300	4 hrs	331km
Jeonju	4100	1½ hrs	106km
Seoul	11,900	4 hrs	320km

Inter-city buses departing Gwangju include:

destination	price (W)	duration	distance
Baegyangsa*	2700	1 hr	50km
Gurye**	4600	1½ hrs	80km
Haenam***	6300	1½ hrs	96km
Mokpo	4800	1¾ hrs	78km
Wando	9100	2½ hrs	149km
Yeosu	6900	2½ hrs	137km

*Naejangsan National Park
**transfer point for Hwaeomsa & Jirisan National Park
***for Duryunsan Provincial Park

Train Trains to Seoul include: saemaeul (new community express train; W21,300, four hours, six daily) and mugunghwa (limited express train; W14,700, 4½ hours, eight daily). Two daily mugunghwa also connect Busan and Gwangju (W14,200, 6¼ hours).

Getting Around

To/From the Airport Bus No 50 or 999 from the train station and bus terminal regularly runs to the airport (40 minutes). A taxi between the airport and the centre costs about W7500 and takes 20 minutes.

Subway Line No 1 is currently under construction, and will run through Gwangju from the east to the west. There will be subway stations just north of the airport and just south of the bus terminal and throughout the city centre. The first stage is planned to be opened in 2002.

AROUND GWANGJU
Mudeungsan Provincial Park
무등산도립공원

Overlooking Gwangju is Mudeungsan Provincial Park, an undulating mountain range with a spider's web of trails that lead up to the highest peak, **Cheonwang-bong** (1187m). At the base of the mountains is a resort area and, farther up the slopes is **Jeungsimsa**, a Buddhist temple surrounded by a **tea plantation**. This plantation was initially established at the end of the 19th century by the famous Yi dynasty artist, Heo Baek-ryeon (also known as Uijae). It is famous for its green tea and there are two nearby processing factories. Another temple in the park is **Wonhyosa**, and there is also **Yaksa-am**, a small Buddhist hermitage.

Although it's not one of Korea's spectacular parks, Mudeungsan's thick forests offer a splendid display of colours during autumn. There are plenty of streams through the forest and it's popular hiking country.

Just below Jeungsimsa is the new **Uijae Art Gallery** (Uijae Misulgwan), completed at the beginning of 2001. There are two exhibition rooms, one devoted to the artist Uijae and the other to local artists. Opposite the gallery is *Chunseolheon*, a delightful teahouse which backs on to a tea plantation which was started by Uijae. The teahouse is still run by his family and if asked they will even teach you the Korean tea ceremony. The price of a pot depends on the quality and starts from W1500 per person.

To get to the entrance of the park take local bus No 15, 23, 27, 52, 106, 555 or 771, just ask the driver for Jeungsimsa.

Unjusaji 운주사지

Legend has it that 1000 Buddhas and 1000 pagodas were originally scattered around this fascinating temple, 40km south of Gwangju in Hwasun-gun. According to official records, this temple was the only one in Korea to have such a collection. Most of the pieces were believed to have been made during the Goryeo period by local stone ma-

JEOLLANAM-DO

sons. There are some strange and unique statues to be found, including the Goryeo-period back-to-back **twin Buddhas** (Seokbulgam Ssangbaebul Jwasang) with pagodas placed in front of both. It seems that the building of the temple wasn't impressive enough in itself so, according to local legend, all of these Buddhas and pagodas were built in one night.

Today, only 18 pagodas and 70 Buddhas remain, including some prostrate Buddhas, which were the last Buddhas to be made that busy evening: due to an early crow call, the stone masons fled back to heaven before standing the Buddhas upright.

Catch bus No 218 from in front of the bus terminal (W1,000, 1½ hours). The bus stop is ten minutes' walk from the entrance to the temple. Check with the driver that the bus goes all the way, as some buses only go as far as Yiyang. The last bus back to Gwangju passes around 6:40 pm.

Damyang Bamboo Crafts Museum 담양죽공예박물관

North of Gwangju is the town of Damyang, famous for its abundant bamboo forests and bamboo crafts. To celebrate this resource, the town is home to a regular bamboo market and the Bamboo Crafts Museum (☎ 381 4111, W500, 9 am to 6 pm), where you can find baskets, furniture, fans, scoops and other bamboo paraphernalia.

The best time to visit is during the bamboo products market day, which operates on the second, 7th, 12th, 17th, 22nd and 27th day of each month. An annual Bamboo Crafts Festival is also held in May.

Buses to Damyang run from Gwangju's bus terminal (W1400, 40 minutes, 22.3km, every 10 minutes).

GURYE 구례

pop 34,000

Gurye is probably the best gateway to Jirisan National Park. It's a small town just south of the park, connected to all major centres by bus and train. In Gurye, there's a good selection of yeoinsuk, yeogwan, restaurants and shops where supplies can be obtained.

Getting There & Away

Departures from Gurye include:

destination	price (W)	duration	distance
Busan	10,300	3½ hrs	227km
Hadong	2200	40 mins	
Jeonju	4600	2¼ hrs	109km
Seoul Nambu	17,000	4½ hrs	329km
Ssanggyesa*	1300	30 mins	21km
Yeosu	4600	1¾ hrs	76km

*Jirisan National Park

HWAEOMSA 화엄사

One the three famous temples in Jirisan National Park and certainly one of the oldest, Hwaeomsa was founded by priest Yongi in AD 544 after his return from China. It is dedicated to the Birojana Buddha. The temple has suffered five major devastations, including the Japanese invasion of 1592, but luckily not everything was destroyed in those various cataclysms. It was last rebuilt in 1636.

The most famous structure still surviving is a unique **three-storeyed pagoda** supported by four stone lions. It has Korea's oldest and largest stone lantern. The huge two-storeyed hall, **Gakgwangjeon**, whose wooden pillars tower nearly 49m, was once surrounded by stone tablets of the Tripitaka Sutra (made during the Silla era), but these were destroyed during the Japanese invasion. Many of the pieces have since been collected and are preserved in the temple's museum.

It is possible to continue on past the temple and along the valley. After about 2½ to three hours the trail begins to ascend to a shelter, *Nogodan Sanjang* (four hours). From the shelter the trail continues to rise until you are finally on the spine of the Jirisan ridge. For more hiking details see the Jirisan section in the Gyeongsangnam-do chapter.

Entry to Hwaeomsa costs W2400.

Places to Stay & Eat

Jirisan Prince (☎ 782 0740) has nice, friendly staff and good rooms for W25,000, W30,000 and W70,000. It's the large log-cabin-like building. Next door is *Hotel*

Medicinal Water

Korea's mountains are mostly composed of granite, an excellent stone for filtering water. Spring water of excellent quality issues from cracks in the cliffs or from under boulders. Every Buddhist temple or hermitage in rural areas is built around or next to a spring. Visitors may sample the water by employing the plastic ladle hanging there, often scooped from a granite tub carved with dragon designs. Some of the springs, more mineral-rich than most, are thought to have the power to cure various illnesses. There are many famous Korean folk tales of cures involving a monk, sage, or royal figure, led to a spring by magic or prophecy.

Long accustomed to such excellent water, modern city-dwelling Koreans have a particular distrust of the government-supplied variety that issues forth from a pipe. You'll see patient lines of urbanites with large plastic containers filling up at mountain-side springs. Sometimes retired grandparents take on the role of daily water-carrier, to do something useful for the family and get some exercise.

Travellers should sample the waters as they travel around the nation – you may be surprised at the variety of tastes. In general, the higher the altitude, the better the purity. Most mountain springs are referred to by locals and on signs as *yaksuteo* (medicinal water source).

In former times, the Koreans held annual *San Yaksu Je* (Sacrificial Ceremony for the Spring Waters) to offer their gratitude for the continuous gift of pure water. Only one such yearly event is still held, at Hwaeomsa.

Hwaeomgak (☎ 782 9911) where decent rooms are W25,000 and W30,000.

Usually tourist village restaurants serve up the same stuff, but *Ttukbaegi Sikdang* stands out with generous and tasty side dishes, a free *bindaettok* (pancake) and a cup of coffee to see you on your way. Try *sanchae jeongsik* (mixed vegetables set meal, W9000), *dolsot bibimbap* (hotpot mixed vegetables and rice, W600) or *doen-*

jang tchigae (bean curd stew, W6000). The restaurant is up the stairs directly opposite the bus terminal and police box.

Getting There & Away

There are inter-city buses connecting Hwaeomsa with:

destination	price (W)	duration	distance
Gurye	600	20 mins	6km
Hadong	2600	50 mins	33km
Namwon	2300	one hour	51km

There are also direct buses from:

destination	price (W)	duration	distance
Busan	10,600	3¼ hrs	202km
Gwangju	5000	1½ hrs	
Jeonju	6100		
Suncheon	2900	1½ hrs	45km

SUNCHEON 순천

pop 268,000

Suncheon is a pleasant city to the north of Yeosu, but for travellers it's mainly a base for exploring Jogyesan Provincial Park.

Getting There & Away

Air Suncheon shares an airport with neighbouring Yeosu. There are direct flights between Suncheon and Seoul (W55,000) and also Suncheon and Jejudo (W36,500).

Bus Buses departing from the express bus terminal go to:

destination	price (W)	duration	distance
Busan	7600	3 hrs	194km
Daegu	8400	3½ hrs	218km
Seoul	14,600	5 hrs	405km

Departures from the inter-city bus terminal include:

destination	price (W)	duration	distance
Busan	7600	3 hrs	109km
Gurye*	2500	1 hr	39km
Gwangju	4700	1½ hrs	98km
Jeonju	8800	3 hrs	142km
Jinju	4500	1½ hrs	85km
Mokpo	8900	2¾ hrs	140km

JEOLLANAM-DO

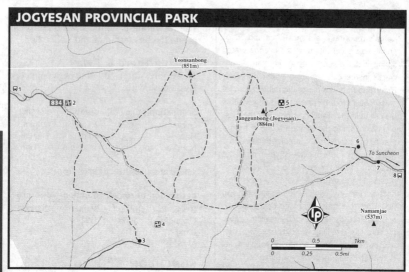

JOGYESAN PROVINCIAL PARK

1 Bus Stop
  버스정류장
2 Songgwang-sa
  송광사
3 Cheonjaam
  천자암
4 Cheonjaamsan
  천자암산
5 Hyangnoam Ruins
  향로암터
6 Seonamsa
  선암사
7 Seungseongyo
  승선교
8 Bus Stop
  버스정류장

destination	price (W)	duration	distance
Ssanggyesa*	3800	2 hrs	58km
Yeosu	2300	50 mins	37km

*for Jirisan National Park

Train The schedule for trains on the Seoul-Suncheon route is virtually the same as it is for Seoul-Yeosu (see Yeosu section, later in this chapter).

JOGYESAN PROVINCIAL PARK
조계산도립공원

This provincial park is somewhat special. **Songgwangsa**, located in the park, is the main temple of the Jogye, the largest faction by far of Korean Buddhists. It is also one of the oldest Zen Buddhist temples in Korea, originally founded in AD 867, although most of the buildings date from the 17th century. The beauty of the monastery is complimented by the attractive surrounding forest.

Songgwangsa represents one of the three jewels of Korean Buddhism. The other two are Dongdosa, in Gyeongsangnam-do and Haeinsa, in Gyeongsangbuk-do. The temple is home to a community of monks, or *sangha,* who have devoted their lives to the study and preservation of the teachings of Buddha.

Between July and August the temple runs five-day programs enabling people to learn about and experience temple life, Korean Buddhism and meditation. For details contact the temple (☎ 755 0107, fax 755 0408). Entry costs W1800.

On the other side of the mountain is another temple, **Seonamsa**. There is a spectacular hike over **Janggunbong** (884m), the peak which separates the two temples. The walk takes six hours if you go over the peak (the northern route), or four hours if you go around it (the southern route). Either route is fantastic.

Seonamsa is much smaller and not as spectacular as Songgwangsa. Below the temple is **Seungseongyo**, one of the most exquisite ancient granite bridges in Korea, with a dragon's head hanging from the top of the arch.

Entry fees are W1800 for Songgwangsa, or W1200 for Seonamsa.

Accommodation and *restaurants* are available by the car park at Songgwangsa. All yeogwan charge W20,000 for musty rooms and minbak range from W10,000 to W15,000. The restaurants and temples are busier near Seonamsa and are probably a better choice.

Getting There & Away
From Gwangju there are buses to Songgwangsa (W4400, 1½ hours, 57km, hourly) and to Seonamsa (W51000, once at 7.50 am).

From Suncheon and Yeosu there are buses to Songgwangsa (every 40 minutes). From Suncheon, local bus No 111 (W950, 1¼ hours, hourly) heads out to Seonamsa from the train station, via the bus terminal. From the bus terminal, turn left as you exit and turn right at the main road, then walk another 50m to the bus stop.

NAGAN FOLK VILLAGE
낙안민속마을

This folk village, 12km west of Suncheon, is housed inside a Chosun-period **walled fortress**. Inside the restored walls are a variety of traditional houses, including *umjip* (a dugout hut), *choga* (thatched roof house) and some *giwajip* (tiled roof houses). There is also a **folk museum** that houses a variety of tools and other exhibits, detailing traditional customs, practices and rites.

Festivals according to the lunar calendar are held here in spring (15th day of the new year and on the sixth and seventh day of the fifth month). The annual Namdo Food Festival is usually held here in early October. There are traditional cultural events put on, along with displays of about 300 kinds of

Korean food. Eating contests liven up the atmosphere. Typically, at least 200,000 people attend and the numbers grow every year. Check with KNTO for exact dates and more details. Entry costs W1100.

Traditional *minbak accommodation* is available (W10,000, or in winter W15,000).

Catch bus No 63 from Suncheon (W600, 40 minutes, every 1½ hours).

YEOSU 여수
pop 327,000
The city of Yeosu lies about halfway along the mountainous and deeply-indented southern coastline of Korea. It's a spectacularly beautiful area peppered with islands and peninsulas.

Information
There is a tourist information booth at the entrance to the island Odongdo.

Orientation
Due to the mountainous terrain of the peninsula on which Yeosu stands, the city is divided into a number of distinct parts, though the centre essentially consists of the area between the train station and the ferry terminal. The bus terminal is a long way from the centre (about 3.5km) along the road to Suncheon, so you'll need to take a local bus or taxi between the bus stop and the city centre. The airport is even farther out, but a shuttle bus operates into the centre whenever there are flights.

Jinnamgwan 진남관
Right in the centre of town stands the huge Jinnamgwan, one of the longest pavilions in Korea. It's a beautiful old building, with massive poles and beams. It was originally constructed for receiving officials and holding ceremonies, and later used as military quarters.

In the summer months it's used a lot by the old men of the town as a place to gather and talk and perhaps throw down a bottle of soju. They're a friendly bunch and will probably draw you into conversation since very few westerners ever visit Yeosu. Entry costs W440.

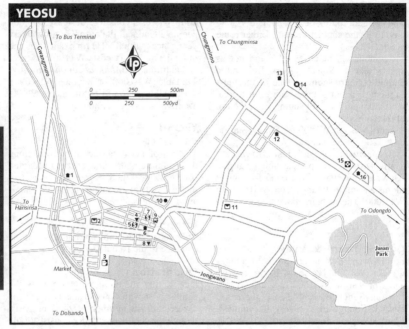

Chungminsa 충민사

High up on the hill which overlooks the area between City Hall and the train station is the Chungminsa, dedicated to Admiral Yi. It was built in 1601 by another naval commander, Yi Si-ŏn, though it has been renovated since then. There are excellent views over Yeosu and the harbour area but it's a steep climb.

Odongdo 오동도

Another popular spot in Yeosu is Odongdo, an island which is linked to the mainland by a 730m-long causeway. It's a craggy, tree- and bamboo-covered island with a lighthouse, picnic spots and walking trails. Entry costs W1000.

Admiral Yi's Turtle Ship 거북선

Yeosu's historical claim to fame is in connection with Admiral Yi, who defeated the Japanese navy on several occasions in the 16th century (see History in the Facts about Korea chapter). On display in Yeosu is a full-size re-creation of one of the admiral's famous iron-clad war vessels, known as turtle ships (geobukseon).

The ship can be found on the island of Dolsando, which is south of town and connected to the mainland by an enormous suspension bridge. Many travellers are disappointed with this boat and believe the one in the Gwangju National Museum is a lot more interesting and authentic.

Places to Stay

Most yeogwan and yeoinsuk are clustered along the road which connects the harbour front to the train station. The cheapest places to stay near the train station are the *Oseong Yeoinsuk* and *Daedong Yeoinsuk*.

Three good yeogwan next to the bus station are *Deokwon-jang Yeogwan*, *Bo-eun-jang Yeogwan* and *Nasangak*.

On the Yeosu side of the bridge from Odongdo is *Golden Park Motel*, a favourite

YEOSU

PLACES TO STAY
1 Yeosu Beach Hotel
   여수비치호텔
6 Haedong-jang
   해동장
12 Yeosu Tourist Hotel
    여수관광호텔
13 Oseong & Daedong
    Yeoinsuks
    오성여인숙,대동여인숙
16 Golden Park
    골든파크

PLACES TO EAT
4 Jeonju Sikdang
   전주식당
8 Gubaek Sikdang
   구백식당

OTHER
2 Gyodong Post Office
   교동우체국
3 Ferry Terminal
   여객터미널
5 Exchange Bank
   외환은행
7 Korea First Bank
   제일은행
9 Bus Stop to Dolsan-do
   돌산도행버스정류장
10 Jinnamgwan Guest House
    진남관
11 Yeosu Post Office
    여수우체국
14 Train Station
    여수역
15 Supermarket
    수퍼마켓

haunt of tour groups, but arguably the best bet in town. Rooms start at W30,000.

In town, **Haedong-jang** (☎ 662 5577) has good rooms for W20,000 and W25,000. **Yeosu Beach Hotel** (☎ 663 2011, fax 663 1625) is on the west side of town, and not on the beach at all, but is still an okay place to stay. Doubles cost W50,000, twins W55,000 and suites W90,000. The **Yeosu Tourist Hotel** (☎ 662 3131, fax 662 3491) is near the train station. Twins are W36,000 to W45,000 and suites cost W63,000.

Places to Eat

Gubaek Sikdang serves a very filling meal at a reasonable price. Popular with the locals, it's a good place to try some of the local catch. Try their *saengseongui* (grilled fish, W10,000) and *agutchim* (spicy fish with bean sprouts, W10,000).

Jeonju Sikdang serves a variety of Korean meals in a pleasant environment.

Getting There & Away

Air There are direct flights between Yeosu and Seoul (W55,000) and also Yeosu and Jejudo (W36,500).

Bus The express and inter-city bus terminals are next to each other on the western side of the city on the road out to Suncheon and the airport.

Express buses go to Seoul (W15,900, 5½ hours, 444km, every 30–40 minutes) and Busan (W8700, six hours, 227km, every two hours).

Inter-city buses go to:

destination	price (W)	duration	distance
Gurye*	4800	2¼ hrs	76km
Gwangju	6900	2 hrs	135km
Hadong**	5000	2¼ hrs	82km
Mokpo	11,200	3½ hrs	179km

*for Hwaeomsa
**for Jirisan National Park

Train Trains from Seoul include saemaeul (W26,300, 5½ hours, three daily) and mugunghwa (W18,100, six hours, hourly).

Boat All boats into and out of Yeosu dock at the large passenger ship terminal at the western end of the old fishing dock. You can get boats here to many of the islands off the south coast and to the east of Yeosu. There are no ferries to Jejudo from here.

Getting Around

The Airport The airport is 7km north of town, on the way to Suncheon. The airport is served by local buses and there's no need to take a taxi – simply walk the few metres from the terminal buildings to the road and wait for a bus.

Getting Around The express and inter-city bus terminals are in the far north of town. City bus No 3, 5, 6, 7, 8, 9, 10, 11, 13 or 17 goes past the two bus terminals but probably the most useful is bus No 11, which connects the bus terminals with the train station via the centre of town.

AROUND YEOSU
Hyang-ilam 향일암

This hermitage is perched above the cliffs on the southern tip of Dolsando. It is a great place to catch the sunrise, with superb view over the clear blue seas. The hermitage sits in a forest of old camellia trees that usually blossom in March and April. Entry is W1200.

If you need some more exercise then continue on up to **Geumosan** (323m), a rewarding and pleasant hike above the temple. There is a circular track that starts next to a **temple** and returns to the temple road 200m further down the track.

Below Hyang-ilam is a small tourist village where you can find plenty of restaurants serving spicy meals. One place that stands out is *Hwangtobang*, a restaurant and hotel that looks out over the sea. There is a great outside area where you can eat and drink while watching the sea change colours. *Haemul doenjang tchigae* (seafood and beancurd stew, W6000) and *haemultang* (a seafood hot pot, W30,000) are the most popular dishes. Rooms are W30,000.

Bus No 101, 108, 111 or 111-1 runs every 30 minutes from Yeosu. If you want to catch the sunrise, the first bus departs Yeosu at 5am.

Hansansa 한산사

If you're up to a more substantial trek, try Hansansa, a temple high up on the wooded mountain slopes to the west of Yeosu. The temple was built in 1194 by a high priest named Bojo during the reign of the Goryeo king, Myeongjong.

The **trail** up to the temple is well marked and the views are superb. The best view of all is not from the temple itself, but from a point about five minutes walk away.

To get to the **lookout**, take the trail through the woods to the right of the temple as you face it and descend onto a small platform where the local people do their washing (here you may be lucky enough to come across a shamanistic performance). Then turn left up through an area dotted surrealistically with gym equipment and posters telling you how to do push-ups, and on to the highest point – a grassy cliff-top. The views are practically 180°.

Manseong-ri 만성리

The beach at Manseong-ri is almost unique in Korea because of its black sand. The black sand soaks up the sun's summer rays and gets quite hot. Koreans are fond of burying themselves up to the neck and letting themselves cook – this is supposed to relieve aches and pains. Whether or not you wish to bake yourself in a sand cast, the beach is about 300m-long and good for swimming. Manseong-ni is 3km north of Yeosu and can be reached by frequent city buses (W600).

MOKPO 목포
pop 246,000

The fishing port of Mokpo is at the end of the train line near the south-western tip of mainland Korea. Mokpo is the departure point for Jejudo and for the ferries to the islands west of Mokpo, the most interesting of which is **Hongdo**. It is also possible to catch a ferry to Lianyungang, an industrial city in Jiangsu, China. Korea's impressive new National Maritime Museum is appropriately located in Mokpo, and is definitely worth a visit.

If you have some time to spare, it's worth wandering along the **waterfront** near the ferry terminal to see the incredible number of octopuses that are for sale – kept alive writhing and slithering in aerated plastic tubs.

Information

A tourist information booth sits opposite the Maritime Museum and is usually staffed by a friendly English-speaking guide. For more details see their Web site at http://city.mokpo.chonnam.kr/english/.

National Maritime Museum
국립해양박물관

In 1983, a Goryeo period (perhaps 11th-century) Korean boat was discovered under the sea near the island of Wando. It con-

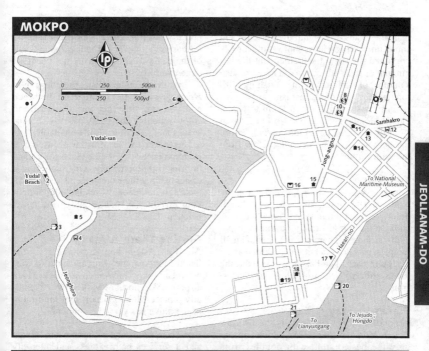

MOKPO

MOKPO

JEOLLANAM-DO

PLACES TO STAY
5 Sinan Beach
  Tourist Hotel
  신안비치관광호텔
11 Minsu-jang
  민수장
13 Baekje Tourist Hotel
  백제관광호텔
14 Dongsan-jang
  동산장
15 Chowon Tourist Hotel
  초원관광호텔
18 Dong-a Yeoinsuk;
  Yeocheon-jang
  Yeoinsuk
  동아여인숙,
  여천장여인숙
19 Chosun Beach Motel
  조선비치모텔

PLACES TO EAT
2 Hemingway's
  Café
  헤밍웨이
17 Seafood
  Restaurants
  해산물식당

OTHER
1 Mokpo Maritime
  University
  목포해양대학
3 Ferry Tour
  Jetty
  관광선선착장
4 Bus Stop
  버스정류장
6 Sculpture Park
  조각공원

7 Changpyeong
  Post Office
  창평우체국
8 Hanvit Bank
  한빛은행
9 Train Station
  목포역
10 Gwangju Bank
  광주은행
12 Airport Bus Stop
  공항버스정류장
16 Post Office
  우체국
20 Ferry Terminal
  (Jejudo & Hongdo)
  여객터미널
21 International Ferry
  Terminal
  국제여객터미널

tained a large cache of ceramic ware. This pottery and the skeletal remains of the boat have been preserved and a small scale replica are all on show in the National Maritime Museum. A Chinese Yuan dynasty

boat has also been excavated along with its contents, including over 20,000 pieces of ceramic ware. The museum is currently restoring this boat and the workshop is open to the public.

There are a large number of historical maritime maps of Korea in the museum and some interesting early photos of Korea's ports and waterfront settlements at the beginning of the 20th century. There are also a number of exhibits looking at fishing folklore and the role of shamanism.

Entry costs W600 (open 9 am to 6 pm, closed Monday). Catch bus No 111 from in front of the train station or bus No 7 from the harbour. A taxi will cost W2500 from the train station.

Yudalsan 유달산

Sitting in western Mokpo, overlooking the harbour, Yudalsan (229m), with the beach below, is a popular recreational area. A walk to the top affords good views, especially at sunset. There are a couple of small temples, pavilions, a botanical garden and a sculpture park. The beach is basic, but the locals still enjoy a stroll along the waterfront.

Places to Stay & Eat

Around the ferry terminals is the *Chosun Beach Motel* (☎ 242 0485), which is probably the best option, with doubles from W35,000. Hopefully some newer places will sprout up after the opening of the international ferry terminal. There are still a couple of yeoinsuk in this area, including *Dong-a Yeoinsuk* (☎ 244 1951) and *Yeocheon-jang Yeoinsuk* (☎ 244 7287), which have basic rooms for W15,000.

Dongsan-jang Yeogwan (244 0109) and *Minsu-jang Yeogwan* (244 5406) both have basic rooms for W25,000.

Baekje Tourist Hotel (☎ 242 4411, fax 242 9550) is a centrally-located mid-range option with decent rooms for W35,000, W40,000 and W60,000. One step up is the *Chowon Tourist Hotel* (☎ 243 0055, fax 243 4472) which has doubles for W85,000 and suites for W140,000. Add another 20% in tax.

Sinan Beach Tourist Hotel (☎ 243 3399, fax 243 0030) is Mokpo's other 1st-class hotel. Rates for doubles and twins are from W90,000 and suites start at W200,000. The hotel is right on Yudal Beach.

Mokpo specialises in seafood dishes, especially sashimi. There is a strip of seafood restaurants along the harbour with tanks full of the day's catch. Prices are not cheap so tread carefully.

If you visit Yudal Beach, then drop in to *Hemingway's Cafe*. It's right on the beach and you can sit either inside or out and enjoy watching the boats pass by. Meals, snacks and refreshments are available.

Next door to the Maritime Museum is *Badatga* (Seaside), a nice place for a meal or drink right on the bay. You might find it easier reading the Korean menu, rather than the English version, which includes 'Fried-king Pnaunl' (W16,000) and 'pank cutlet belchop steak'!

Getting There & Away

Air Both Asiana and Korean Air fly the Seoul-Mokpo route. Korean Air also flies between Mokpo and Jejudo. The new Muan airport, 28km north of Mokpo, will eventually replace Mokpo airport, but the timing of the move has yet to be announced.

Bus There's only one bus terminal in Mokpo and it services both express and inter-city buses. It's a considerable distance from the centre of town, so take bus No 1 to get to it.

Departures include:

destination	price (W)	duration	distance
Busan	18,100	6 hrs	345km
Daedunsa*	3900	1½ hrs	74km
Gwangju	4800	1½ hrs	76km
Haenam*	3300	1 hr	55km
Jindo	4100	2 hrs	97km
Seoul	14,100	5 hrs	383km
Wando	6600	2 hrs	83km

*Duryunsan Provincial Park

Train It's possible to catch a train from Gwangju to Mokpo, though most people will find the bus more convenient. If you're in a hurry, it's possible to catch a train direct from Seoul to Mokpo.

Boat The boat terminal at Mokpo handles all the ferries to Jejudo and to the smaller islands west and south-west of Mokpo. The schedule for the ferries is in the Getting There & Away section of the Jeju-do chapter. Booking in advance for these ferries isn't usually necessary, except during the summer holidays – July to mid-August.

There is presently only one international ferry service: to Lianyungang, in Jiangsu, China. This is a new service and timetables are very flexible, so contact KNTO for more details

Getting Around

Nearly all buses pass by the train station and the bus terminal (W500) Bus No 1, 1-2, 2, 101 or 102 runs to Yudal beach and park.

Airport buses (W2300, 30 minutes) depart from the bus stop near the train station one hour before domestic departure time. They also stop on the main road opposite the bus terminal. Hopefully this service will continue when the airport is moved to Muan.

DADOHAE HAESANG NATIONAL PARK 다도해해상국립공원

Consisting of more than 1700 islands and islets, Dadohae Haesang (Marine Archipelago) National Park occupies the south-west corner of the Korean peninsula. Of course, many of the islets are little more than rocks which appear above the surf occasionally, but others are large enough to support small communities of people who earn their living from fishing and catering to summer tourists.

There are scores of local ferries from Mokpo to the larger of these small islands. The most popular islands with Korean tourists are Hongdo and Heuksando. Indeed, Hongdo is so popular with holidaymakers during July and August that it's often difficult to get on a ferry, and equally difficult finding accommodation. Indeed, during July your only option to get a night's sleep might be camping.

These are not the only islands you can visit, of course, but if you're planning a trip around the less well-known of them then you really need a copy of the national bus, boat, rail and flight timetables booklet (*Sigakpyo*) already mentioned in the 'Getting Around' chapter. Armed with this

booklet (and the coloured maps which it contains detailing boat connections) it's possible to work out a route and an approximate schedule, though you'll need help with translation as the timetables are written in Korean, with a little Chinese. There are a series of maps in the booklet detailing the boat connections. There's no better way to get off the main tourist circuits than to visit some of these less well-known islands. Entry to the park costs W1000.

Hongdo 홍도

Hongdo (Red Island) is the most popular and beautiful of the islands west of Mokpo. It's comparable with Ulleungdo off the east coast in that it rises precipitously from the sea and is bounded by sheer cliffs, bizarre rock formations and wooded hillsides cut by steep ravines. There are also many islets which surround the main island. Sunsets are spectacular on clear days. Where it differs from Ulleungdo is that it is much smaller, being only some 6km long and 2.5km wide, and the main land mass rises to only a third of the height of its eastern cousin. That doesn't make it any the less interesting, but the hitch is that the only way you can see most of it is by boat, because the whole island, with the exception of the villages, is a protected nature reserve; entry is prohibited.

Ferries to Hongdo land at Il-gu, the larger and more southern of the island's two villages which is where the minbak, yeogwan and telephone office are situated. It's also the only village where electricity is available, thanks to a small generator. Entry costs W2000. Like I-gu, its smaller neighbour to the north, there's a tiny cove which provides shelter to fishing boats. A boat connects the two villages. Tour boats operate around the island for about W8500 (two hours, four trips daily).

Places to Stay There's a good choice of minbak, yeoinsuk and yeogwan in Il-gu at the usual prices (except during the summer holiday period, when prices can double). *Royal-jang* (☎ 246 3837) is clean but beware the karaoke downstairs. Rooms range from W20,000 to W35,000 in summer.

Getting There & Away Hongdo is 115km west of Mokpo, and there are four ferries making the Mokpo-Hongdo run between March and July, and eight ferries a day from the end of July to the middle of August. Expect the schedule to be cut back during winter.

Fast ferries take 2¼ hours to make the one-way journey. The fare is W28,100. Slow car ferries require five hours to cross the waters and the fare is W18,650. For more details, you can call Mokpo ferry terminal (☎ 243 0116) or KNTO.

Heuksando 흑산도

Heuksando is a small group of islands to the east of Hongdo, the largest of which is called **Daeheuksando** (Big Heuksando). It is larger and more populated than Hongdo, and like Jejudo, is littered with the stones used to create the dry-stone walls that enclose the fields. Attached to rope, these stones are also used to hold down thatch roofs in windy weather. There are several villages on Heuksando and, since the island doesn't rise anywhere near as steeply from the sea as Hongdo, farming is possible on the coastal fringes. The villages are connected by trails and you can walk around the island in a day if you make an early start.

The largest village **Ye-ri**, has an excellent harbour and was formerly a whaling centre. It's also where the ferries from the mainland dock and where most of the island's accommodation is to be found. There's a sizeable fishing fleet which moors here. The other village is **Jin-ni**.

Places to Stay & Eat Unlike Hongdo, you shouldn't have a problem finding accommodation on this island, even during the summer holiday period. Ye-ri has a good selection of minbak for around W20,000. *Namdo-jang Yeogwan* (☎ 275 9003) and *Uri Minbak* (☎ 275 9634) both have fairly clean rooms with bathrooms for W20,000.

There are also a couple of minbak in Jin-ni. Beach *camping* is possible at Baeranggimi. For W3000 you are supplied with a board on which to set up your tent. Public toilets and water are nearby.

With a substantial fishing fleet, you might expect that cheap seafood is available on Heuksando but, as elsewhere in Korea, it can be very expensive. Be sure to ask the price of a meal before you order.

Getting There & Away All ferries from Mokpo to Hongdo call at Heuksando so you can use any of them to get to this island. The fast ferry from Mokpo takes 1½ hours and costs W22,150. Hongdo–Heuksando on a small boat takes about 30 minutes and costs W5500.

WOLCHULSAN NATIONAL PARK
월출산국립공원

This small national park invites a day of hiking. Wolchulsan (Rising Moon Mountains) is reminiscent of Daedunsan Provincial Park in Chungcheongnam-do. There are crags and spires, steel stairways on the trail and at one point, a steel bridge (52m) crossing a huge gap between rocks. The area boasts some beautiful and rugged rock formations, including the park's highest peak, **Cheonwangbong** (809m). It's small enough to hike from Cheonhwangsa in the east to **Dogapsa** in the west in a day (five hours). The tracks are well signposted; there is currently only one track that links the two temples. The ascent is steep and strenuous, but you'll be rewarded with great views. While the temples are not spectacular, they do add a nice touch to this scenic area. There is a pleasant **teahouse** below Dogapsa, where you can sip a refreshing cup of green tea.

Admission to Wolchulsan National Park costs W2000.

Places to Stay

Camping is available at Cheonhwangsa and should be booked ahead for weekends and holidays (W3000, e wolchul@npa.or.kr). Minbak accommodation is plentiful at the park entrances.

Getting There & Away

The small community of Yeong-am has buses running directly to Cheonhwangsa departing at 10.10 am, 3.20 and 4.30 pm. A taxi costs W4000. To Dogapsa, there are only two daily buses, departing 9.30 am and 4.10 pm. Otherwise there are regular buses to Gurim-ri, which is 4km from the temple (W3500 for a taxi). Double-check with KNTO for bus times.

Buses run from Yeong-am to Gwangju (W3700, one hour, 53km, every 10 minutes) and Mokpo (W2400, 50 minutes, 40km, every 20 minutes).

DURYUNSAN PROVINCIAL PARK
두륜산도립공원
Here you'll find **Daedunsa** (also known as Daeheungsa), a major Zen meditation temple complex. There is also a **museum**, which houses a Goryeo-period bell, some Buddhist treasures, a gallery and a tea ceremony display. The museum's displays are very good, but sadly they lack English descriptions. The temple is popular for Koreans, who visit to pay their respects to the priest So, who led a group of warrior monks against the Japanese invaders (AD 1592–98). The temple is a 40-minute walk from the bus stop, past a string of restaurants.

The highest peak in this park, **Duryunsan** (700m) provides a dramatic backdrop for the temple. If you want to make an attempt on the peak, take a left at the first split in the trail after the temple. It takes 1½ hours to reach the top. You are rewarded with a very picturesque view of Korea's southern coastline. Head back via the other trail and turn right at the first junction (20 minutes). It's another 1½ hours back down to Daedunsa, via Jinbulam.

Places to Stay
There are plenty of options around the bus stop. Half-way up to Daeheungsa is *Yuseol Sikdang & Yeogwan* (☎ 534 6005). This traditional courtyard-style abode has rooms for W25,000 (no showers).

Getting There & Away
Access to the park is from the nearby town of Haenam (W600, 15 minutes, 12km, every 30 minutes).

Bus connections from Haenam include:

destination	price (W)	duration	distance
Busan	16,400	6 hrs	300km
Gwangju	6300	1¾ hrs	97km
Jindo	3400	1 hr	54km
Mokpo	3300	1 hr	57km
Wando	3400	1 hr	55km

WANDO 완도
pop 69,000
The island of Wando lies on the south-western tip of the peninsula. It is famous throughout Korea for the quality of its seaweed (*gim*), at certain times you'll see this seaweed drying on racks around the island, in much the same way as squid are dried on Ulleungdo and along the north-east coast.

The town of Wando has a quiet, rural atmosphere and a look of benign neglect about it. Unfortunately most of the old tiled-roofed traditional buildings have disappeared, but the narrow streets are still there – so narrow that the somewhat decrepit local buses only go down one street. It's a very small town so you can't get lost.

There are both sandy and pebble beaches on the island which is connected to the mainland by a bridge. There is a ferry service to Jejudo.

Jeongdo-ri
Jeongdo-ri is the main pebble beach on the island and is very attractive. To get there from the town of Wando, take a local bus from the centre, close to the ferry terminal, and get off at Sajeong-ri. From there it's a 1km walk to the beach. There's a small cafe, which offers beer and soft drinks, with minbak (W10,000) on the beach.

Gugyedeung
This pebble beach and small nature reserve is a good place for a picnic or a leisurely stroll. There is a minbak on the beach which has great views (W20,000). Buses run every 30 minutes from the bus terminal (W1000).

Myeongsasimri
Myeongsasimri (otherwise known as Myeongsajang) is very beautiful and the

JEOLLANAM-DO

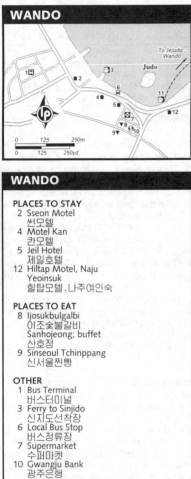

WANDO

WANDO

PLACES TO STAY
2 Sseon Motel
   썬모텔
4 Motel Kan
   칸모텔
5 Jeil Hotel
   제일호텔
12 Hiltap Motel, Naju
   Yeoinsuk
   힐탑모텔, 나주여인숙

PLACES TO EAT
8 Ijosukbulgalbi
   이조숯불갈비
   Sanhojeong; buffet
   산호정
9 Sinseoul Tchinppang
   신서울찐빵

OTHER
1 Bus Terminal
   버스터미널
3 Ferry to Sinjido
   신지도선착장
6 Local Bus Stop
   버스정류장
7 Supermarket
   수퍼마켓
10 Gwangju Bank
   광주은행
11 Ferry Terminal
   여객터미널

main sandy beach on the island of Sinjido. At certain times of the year it's a little harder to get to than Jeongdo-ri, since it involves a trip by local ferry and they'll only sail if there's sufficient demand.

The ferries leave from the local ferry terminal, which is about 1km from the main terminal, which serves the Jejudo ferries.

The fare is W400 and the trip takes 30 minutes (every 30 minutes). In summer, buses wait for the ferries at the far end and take you from there to the beach.

Places to Stay & Eat
Opposite the ferry terminal is *Hiltap Motel* (☎ 555 2566), where reasonable rooms are W25,000, and *Naju Yeoinsuk* (☎ 554 3884), with okay doubles for W13,000 and triples for W15,000.

Close to the bus terminal are quite a few yeogwan and one with a harbour view is *Sseon Motel*, with rooms for W25,000. *Motel Kan* (☎ 554 1061) has decent rooms for W25,000 and some rooms include a harbour view.

The nicest place to stay by far is the *Jeil Hotel* (☎ 554 3251), which has rooms with small balconies that look out over the harbour and the small island of Judo. Rooms are W35,000, but are more expensive during summer.

If you're feeling hungry, then the *hanjeongsik* (buffet) at *Sanhojeong* is worth the W12,000 outlay. Closer to the harbour and on the 2nd level is *Ijosukbulgalbi*, which serves a barbecue *galbi* (pork). They are a little stingy as the minimum serving is for three, but if you're feeling hungry it will be more than adequate. If you would just like a snack or simple and cheap meal, then you can't go past *Sinseoul Tchinbbang,* which serves a great range of dumplings, noodles and *gimbap* (Korean 'sushi').

Getting There & Away
Bus Buses that go to Wando include:

destination	price (W)	duration	distance
Busan	18,700	6 hrs	454km
Gwangju	9100	2¾ hrs	147km
Haenam[*]	3400	2 hrs	54km
Mokpo	6600	2 hrs	110km
Yeong-am[**]	5300	1½ hrs	94km

[*]for Duryunsan Provincial Park
[**]for Wolchulsan National Park

Ferry
Wando is connected to Jejudo by ferry. The schedule for these ferries is in the Getting

There & Away section of the Jeju-do chapter. Other destinations by ferry include Cheongsando, Nokdongdo, Nohwado, Jodo and Seokhwado.

To Cheongsando there is a slow boat (1½ hours) and a fast boat (30 minutes). Similarly, to Nokdongdo there is a slow boat (3½ hours) and a fast boat (2¼ hours). Jodo (3¾ hours) and Seokhwado (one hour) are on the same route.

If you're heading for Mokpo from Wando and would prefer to go by sea rather than by bus, there is a daily ferry which leaves Wando at 8 am and takes seven hours. The ferry calls at many places en route.

Getting Around
The bus terminal is a long walk from the centre of town (about 1.5km). Local buses and taxis run to the centre.

BOGILDO 보길도
pop 3400
An island further to the south of Wando, Bogildo boasts three fine beaches. The sandy spot where everyone heads for is **Jungni Beach**, also known as Bogildo Beach. **Yesong-ri Beach**, at the southern end of the island, is a pebbly beach but is dramatic for its evergreen forest. The island boasts several thick groves of pine trees, and there is also a temple called **Namunsa**. The other beach is called Soanpo Beach.

Bogildo is the old home of Yun Son-do, a famed poet of the Joseon dynasty. The story goes that Yun Son-do took temporary shelter from a typhoon here while on his way to Jejudo. He was so impressed by the beauty of the island that he decided to stay for the next 10 years. During that time, he is said to have built 25 buildings on the island, and penned some of his best poems such as *Fisherman's Prose*. It is also possible to visit his beautiful **gardens**, which are open to the public.

Bogildo is very much a summer resort, which means it can get a bit packed out at such times. On the other hand, visiting during the winter wouldn't be much fun, and most hotels will be closed.

Getting There & Away
There are four ferries daily between Wando and Bogildo, from 8 am to 5.40 pm. The journey takes 1½ hours and costs W6,700. Between 15 July and 20 August, the schedule is increased to eight times daily.

JINDO 진도
pop 43,000
This is another large island south of Mokpo and is connected to the mainland by a bridge. The most remarkable thing to see here is the dramatic rise and fall of the tides. Jindo has some of the largest tides in the world. There is an island far off the southeast coast of Jindo which, in early March of every year, can be reached on foot during low tide by crossing a spit of tidal land 2.8km long and 40m wide.

The experience is officially known as the **Landing Tide Phenomenon** (*Ganjuyuk Gyedo*). This phenomenon was witnessed in 1975 by the French ambassador to Korea, who later described it in a French newspaper as 'Moses' Miracle'. The name easily stuck because South Korea has a very large Christian community. Not surprisingly, large numbers of people come to view this event, and what you often get to see is a line of people 2.8km in length seemingly walking on water! Two miracles for the price of one.

As you will no doubt be told by locals, Jindo is home to a unique breed of dog simply known as the Jindo dog (*Jindo gae*).

Getting There & Away
Buses connect Jindo to:

destination	price (W)	duration	distance
Busan	19,800	6¾ hrs	354km
Gwangju	9700	2¾ hrs	131km
Mokpo	4100	1¼ hrs	106km
Seoul	16,500	6 hrs	458km

JEOLLANAM-DO

Jeju-Do

JEJU-DO

Highlights

- The volcanic peak of Hallasan, South Korea's highest mountain
- Manjanggul, at over 13km in length it's the longest known lava tube in the world
- Seong-eup Folk Village and Jeju Folk Village, for a look at Korea's past
- Ilchulbong, a spectacular volcanic cone with sides plunging vertically into the surf
- Udo, a small but remarkably scenic island where you can see wetsuited women diving for shells
- The Mystery Road, where cars seem to roll uphill
- The warmest beaches in all Korea

☎ 064 • pop 539,000

'Welcome to Paradise', announces a sign in the airport. 'Jejudo – the island of myth and legend', says a glossy tourist brochure. 'Korea's Hawaii', declares a wall poster at a travel agency in Seoul. 'Korea's Disneyland', grumbles an expat English teacher, down for the weekend. Every statement is right in its way.

The Three Jejus

It's worth noting that 'Jeju' is actually three places. There is Jeju-do (the province) and Jejudo (the island, spelled without a hyphen). And finally there is Jeju-si ('si' means 'city'), the island's capital.

To be sure, tourism makes the cash register ring on this island: a large, subtropical province off the southern tip of the Korean peninsula. Packaged tourists are processed through Jejudo like squid through the island's canneries. (The two often meet for dinner at the ubiquitous seafood restaurants for which the island is famous.) As if this weren't bad enough, local officials have rolled out their proposal for the next stage of economic development – turning Jejudo into a 'free-trade zone' somewhat like Hong Kong and Singapore.

Nevertheless, despite the hype and commercialism, there is still much to love about Jejudo. The island boasts many spectacular geographical features. In particular, there is the almost 2000m-high extinct volcano of **Hallasan**, the highest mountain in South Korea. Then there are the beaches dotted around the island, several impressive waterfalls and the spectacular volcanic cone at Seongsan, which rises up sheer from the ocean. Another unusual geographic feature is the rare lava-tube caves, formed when surface lava cools and hardens while molten lava continues to flow like river beneath the surface.

Jejudo's fauna can be just as impressive. At dusk, in the summer months, bats swoop out of their caves in the tens of thousands, sometimes even blackening the sky over Jeju-si.

Jejudo's coastal lowlands are dominated by small fields of barley and vegetables, but further inland there are enormous grazing pastures which support horses and cattle.

288

JEJU-DO

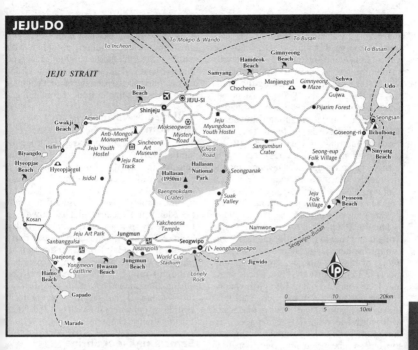

To Incheon · To Mokpo & Wando · To Busan · To Busan

JEJU STRAIT

Iho Beach · JEJU-SI · Shinjeju · Samyang · Hamdeok Beach · Gimnyeong Beach · Gimnyeong Maze · Sehwa · Udo · Chocheon · Manjanggul · Gujwa · Pijarim Forest · Seongsan · Ilchulbong · Goseong-ri · Sinyang Beach

Gwakji Beach · Aewol · Anti-Mongol Monument · Mokseogwon · Mystery Road · Jeju Myungdoam Youth Hostel · Sangumburi Crater · Seong-eup Folk Village

Hallim · Biyangdo · Hyeopjae Beach · Hyeopjaegul · Jeju Youth Hostel · Sincheonji Art Museum · Jeju Race Track · Isidol · Ghost Road · Hallasan (1950m) · Hallasan National Park · Seongpanak · Baengnokdam (Crater) · Suak Valley · Jeju Folk Village · Pyoseon Beach

Kosan · Jeju Art Park · Sanbanggulsa · Daejeong · Yongmeori Coastline · Hwasun Beach · Hamo Beach · Gapado · Marado · Jungmun · Jusangjiolli · Jungmun Beach · World Cup Stadium · Lonely Rock · Yakcheonsa Temple · Seogwipo · Jeongbangpokpo · Jigwido · Namwon · Seogwipo-Busan

0 · 10 · 20km
0 · 5 · 10mi

Jejudo is the only place in Korea where citrus fruit can be grown; though, regrettably, this industry is dying due to cheap imports. Cactus is also cultivated for both ornamental plants and for making cactus tea. The island also produces most of Korea's mushrooms.

The climate here is significantly different from that of the Korean peninsula – you can even find palm trees. But all the subtropical greenery comes at a price – Jejudo is the rainiest place in Korea, typically recording only 60 clear days annually. To avoid this, try to visit during autumn, when downpours are least likely.

As long as the weather cooperates, you'll find plenty of outdoor activities to keep you amused. Physical forms of recreation include hiking, cycling, golf, snorkelling, scuba diving, windsurfing, sailing, fishing, paragliding and horseback riding.

Aside from scenery and sports, another of Jejudo's attractions is its culture. Despite being just 85km from the Korean mainland,

the island was little visited for centuries. As a result, Jejudo acquired its own history, traditions, dress, architecture and dialect. The most obvious sign of this are the *harubang* (grandfather stones), carved from lava rock, whose purpose is still debated by anthropologists. Certainly parallels are easily drawn between these and the mysterious statues found on Easter Island and Okinawa. One thing that can be said for sure is that no other symbol represents Jejudo so completely as the harubang. They are featured in every tourist pamphlet that has ever been produced about the island, and are even painted on the sides of the local buses. Not surprisingly, the production of imitation harubang for sale to visitors has been a lucrative growth industry. You can even find large harubang being used as decorations in some of Seoul's classiest restaurants.

It may have been an isolated provincial outpost until recently, but over the last two decades Jejudo has changed radically. Gone are the days when the locals had to earn their living by fishing or farming. The catalyst, of course, was tourism. Drawn by the warm climate and frustrated by restrictions on obtaining a passport to travel abroad, well-to-do Koreans began taking their holidays in Jejudo. By the 1970s, the island became the favourite honeymoon destination for Korean couples. Although nowadays many young Koreans prefer to take their romantic interlude in Guam, you will still see many honeymooning couples in Jejudo (easily recognisable because honeymooning couples always dress in a matching set of clothes). Not surprisingly, the majority of students studying at Jeju National University are majoring in tourism.

The local chamber of commerce has worked at trying to categorise the rocks: deciding whether they're shaped like dragons, tigers, or pickled ginseng; erecting monuments to immortalise the sites where patriotic locals have resisted foreign invaders. For the most part, you can ignore all this: Jejudo is a beautiful and exciting place, and well worth the visit. If you manage to go during off-peak times (weekdays, any season but summer) you may well conclude that Jejudo is indeed a paradise.

JEJU-SI
pop 274,000
Just to make life difficult, Jeju-si has two parts – Gujeju (old Jeju) and Sinjeju (new Jeju). If you tell a taxi or bus driver that you want to go to Jeju-si, it's generally assumed that you mean old Jeju. Sinjeju has the same sterile charm as Seoul's Gangnam district.

Information
The Jeju Tourism Information Service has an office in the international terminal of Jejudo airport (☎ 742 8866) and at the Jeju Ferry Terminal (☎ 758 7181).

Halla bookshop, east of City Hall, is Jejudo's best. There is no English sign (yet), but look for the noodle-like sculpture over the entrance. The bookshop is in the basement.

If you didn't rent a mobile phone at the airport, you can get one in Jeju-si by calling SK Telecom (☎ 757 5727).

Gwandeokjeong 관덕정
This 15th-century pavilion is one of Jeju's most interesting buildings, complete with harubang. It's the oldest building of its type on the island and draws a steady flow of domestic tourists, out to get the perfect photo of themselves standing in front of something.

Folklore & Natural History Museum 민속자연사박물관
The museum is set in **Sinsan Park** (spectacular during the brief cherry blossom season in April). Inside, there is a recreation of a traditional thatched house in the local style; local crafts; folklore and marine displays. There's also a film about the island (in Korean) which is shown five times daily for no extra charge. Entry costs W770 and the museum is open daily except for Monday from 8.30 am to 6.30 pm (only until 5 pm from November through February). The museum is closed during the Lunar New Year and *Juseok*, the Korean 'Thanksgiving' (see Public Holidays and Special Events in the Facts for the Visitor chapter).

Samseonghyeol Shrine 삼성혈
Adjacent to Sinsan Park is Samseonghyeol, which contains a small cave and an outdoor shrine (dedicated in 1526). According to local legend, the ancestors of the Ko, Pu and Yang clans emerged from the cave and their offspring went on to populate the entire island. On the 10th day of April, October and December, the modern-day descendants of the three clans (the entire population of Jejudo?) gather here for a ceremony to honour their ancestors.

National Jeju Museum
국립제주박물관
The museum was still under construction at the time of writing, but a lot of money is being spent and it should be a humdinger when finished. No word yet on when it will open, so check the tourist pamphlets when you arrive in town. To judge from the construction site, it's going to be significantly larger than the current Jeju Folklore and Natural History Museum.

JEJU-SI

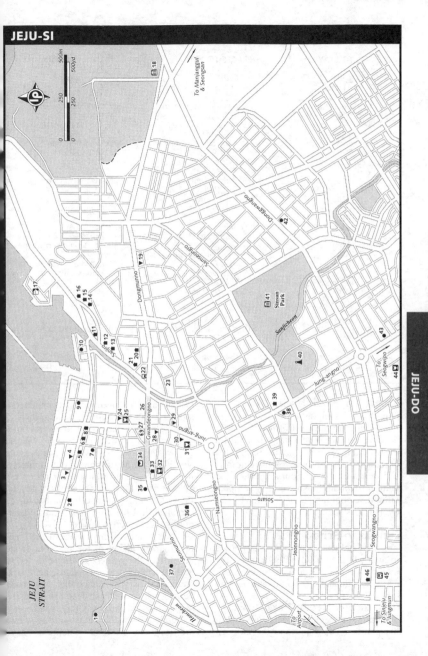

JEJU STRAIT

To Manjanggul
& Seongsan

Donggwangno

Samseongno

Sinsan
Park

Sanjicheon

Jung-angno

To
Seogwipo

Dongmunno

Sanjicheon

Gwandeongno

Jung-angno

Namseongno

Sosaro

Jeonmongno

Seogwangno

Seongmun

Hancheon

To Sineju
& Jungmun

To
Airport

JEJU-SI

PLACES TO STAY
2 Oriental Hotel
제주오리엔탈호텔
5 Palace Hotel
팔레스호텔
6 Jeju Seoul Hotel
제주서울호텔
8 Seaside Hotel
해상호텔
11 Songdo Yeoinsuk
송도여인숙
12 Geumsan-jang
Yeogwan
금산장여관
13 Sujeong-jang Yeogwan
수정장여관
14 Yeon-an Yeoinsuk
연안여인숙
15 Yangsando Inn
양산도민박
16 Hanil Minbak
한일민박
20 Suwon Yeoinsuk
수원여인숙
21 Hanmi-jang Yeogwan
한미장여관
33 Robero Hotel
호텔로베로
36 Lagonda Hotel
호텔라곤다
39 KAL Hotel
제주KAL호텔
46 Olympia Hotel
올림피아호텔

PLACES TO EAT
3 E-Mart
이마트
4 Burger King & KFC
버거킹
19 Jeju King Supermarket
제주킹마트
23 Tongmun Market
동문시장
24 Aida Italian Restaurant
아이다
28 Joong Ang Bakery
중앙베이커리
29 Paris Baguette
파리바게뜨
30 Shinra Chobap Restaurant
신라초밥

OTHER
1 Yongduam Rock
용두암
7 Sunkyong Smart Bicycle
선경자전거
9 Jeju World
제주월드
10 Fish Market
어시장
17 Ferry Terminal
제주항종합터미널
18 National Jeju Museum
국립제주박물관
22 Dongmun Rotary
(Bus Stop)
동문로타리

25 Tombstone Pub
툼스톤
26 Underground
Arcade
지하상가
27 Hanil Bank
한일은행
31 The Playhouse Pub
플레이하우스
32 The Doors Pub
도어스클럽
34 Post Office
우체국
35 Gwandeokjeong
Pavilion
관덕정
37 Confucian School
향교
38 Korean Air
대한항공제주지점
40 Samseonghyeol Shrine
삼성혈
41 Folklore & Natural
History Museum
민속자연사박물관
42 Halla Bookstore
한라서점
43 City Hall
시청
44 Student Pub Zone
45 Inter-City Bus
Terminal
시외버스터미널

Yongduam Rock 용두암

Yongduam ('Dragon's Head') Rock, on the seashore to the west of town, is eulogised in the tourist literature. It's hard to see what all the fuss is about. It might be worth a visit, but only if you have nothing to do for a couple or hours. On the other hand, no Korean honeymoon is complete without a photograph of the newlyweds taken at this spot.

Confucian School 향교

Jeju-si's Confucian school (*hyanggyo*) was originally built in 1392, but it has seen a bit of renovation since then. A ceremony is held here twice annually, in spring and autumn.

Top Land & Ocean Park 탑랜드

Pity the poor speculators who invested in this place – Top Land and the adjacent

Ocean Park have been variously under construction and demolition for more than 15 years. The name has morphed several times – in years past it was known as Jeju World and Waterpia. This waterfront real estate should be worth a fortune – unfortunately, it's reclaimed land which was built on top of sea mud that is inherently unstable. Plans to build high-rise hotels had to be scrapped, lest the buildings wind up leaning like the tower of Pisa.

Attempts are still being made to drill holes in the ground and pump the muck out. In the meantime, the owners continue to try to make it work as a seaside amusement park. At the time of writing, the roller coaster and Ferris wheels were being demolished (for the second time) to make way for...what?

Top Land is worth a look – the sea views are fine and seafood restaurants have opened (in decidedly temporary-looking buildings). In summer, it has great atmosphere – arcade games, cotton candy and balloons for the kids.

Top Land is just to the west of the ferry harbour.

Oiljang (Five-Day Market) 오일장

Oiljang (see Sinjeju map), a long-standing tradition, is held only once every five days on calendar days that end in 'two' or 'seven'. It operates during the daytime only, and opens early in the morning. You can find cheap clothes, food, Jejudo plants, traditional *gimchi* (spicy fermented cabbage) pots, kitchen utensils and animals (alive or contorted by recent, violent death). It's a very large market, so allow some time to explore it.

Mokseokwon 목석원

About 6km south of Jeju-si on the No 1 cross-island highway is Mokseokwon (Jejudo map), a garden of stone and wood. If you've ever found yourself taking home interesting-looking pieces of wood and stone which have been carved by the elements you'll love this place.

The garden was put together over many years by a local resident. It features 'installations' comprised of objects found all over the island, many of them originating from the roots of the Jorok tree, which is found only on Jejudo. The wood of this tree is very dense – it sinks in water – and it was formerly used for making combs and for tobacco boxes. Along with the natural objects, there are many old grinding stones and the requisite harubang. Admission to the gardens costs W2000.

To reach Mokseokwon, take the city bus bound for Jeju National University. The journey from central Jeju-si takes 30 minutes.

Places to Stay

Budget *Yangsando Inn* (☎ 758 9989) used to be a yeoinsuk but has been demoted to minbak status. Nevertheless, it's clean and the owners are very friendly. The bathroom is communal style. Rooms cost W20,000.

In the same category is *Hanil Minbak* (☎ 757 1598). Rooms have fans, showers

are communal and guests can use kitchen facilities. A double room is W20,000.

Also in this same area is *Yeonan Yeoinsuk* (☎ 722 6984) which is clean, quiet and friendly and costs W20,000 for a double.

At the corner of Sanjiro and an alley is *Songdo Yeoinsuk* (☎ 722 3891) with rooms for the usual W20,000. Farther up Sanjiro but hidden in a narrow alley is the squeaky clean *Suwon Yeoinsuk*.

If you want a private bath, you'll have to upgrade to yeogwan standard. *Hanmi-jang Yeogwan* (☎ 756 6555, 756 7272) is a truly excellent place to stay. The *ajumma* (female proprietor) doesn't speak English, but she wears a perpetual smile – she must be the friendliest person on the whole island. Spotlessly clean double rooms with private bath cost W25,000.

If Hanmi-jang is full, just around the corner you'll find similar comforts at *Sujeong-jang Yeogwan* (☎ 758 7076).

By contrast, *Geumsan-jang Yeogwan* is definitely showing it's age and could use a renovation.

The *Olympia Hotel* charges yeogwan prices despite the 'hotel' moniker – W25,000 for a very clean and pleasant room. It's located just across the street from the inter-city bus terminal.

Jeju Youth Hostel (☎ 799 8811) looks like a four-star hotel – marble foyers, immaculately dressed staff, 50m outdoor pool and a gymnasium with mountain bikes for hire. There are 668 beds in both Western and Korean rooms – the Western rooms sleep six in double bunks. The hostel has meals, a coffee shop and grocery store. Dorm beds cost W13,500 and 'family rooms' are W56,000. The big problem with this place is the inconvenient location – the hostel is about 20 minutes west of Jejudo airport. Enquire at the airport information desk about the hostel shuttle bus – otherwise, it's a taxi ride.

Jeju Myungdoam Youth Hostel (☎ 721 8233) is smaller and less well-appointed than its cousin, but it's also cheaper. There are 225 beds here – dorm bunks cost W7500, while private rooms are W37,500. The hostel is about 6km south-east of central Jeju-si.

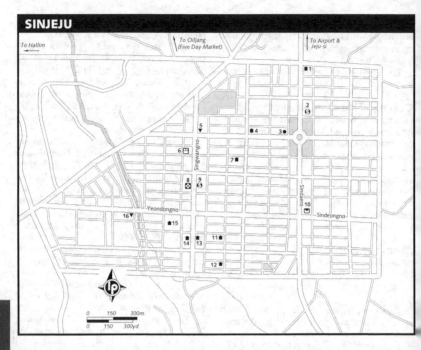

SINJEJU

To Hallim

To Oiljang
(Five Day Market)

To Airport &
Jeju-si

Singwangno

Sindaero

Yeondongno

Sindeongno

0   150   300m
0   150   300yd

Mid-Range You might as well go for a place with a sea view, even if the 'beach' in Jeju-si is only a beach in name, being quite rocky. At the bottom end of mid-range is the *Seaside Hotel* (☎ 752 0091). True to its name, it faces the seaside, overlooking the remains of Top Land. Rooms here start at W40,000.

Just next door is the better-appointed *Jeju Seoul Hotel* (☎ 752 2211) with double rooms at W70,000. This is adjacent to the very slightly better *Palace Hotel* (☎ 753 8811), which comes equipped with a sauna and has rooms starting at W80,000.

If you're afraid of tidal waves, you can move farther inland and stay at the *Robero Hotel* (☎ 757 7111), a modest-sized highrise opposite the pavilion Gwandeokjeong. Doubles start at W75,000.

Over in stodgy-looking Sinjeju, there are a number of nondescript mid-range places to stay with double rooms priced from W80,000. Some of the facilities are: *Green*

(☎ 742 0071) with banquet hall, night club, health club and sauna; *Hawaii* (☎ 742 0061), with cocktail lounge, coffee shop, restaurants and banquet hall; *Island* (☎ 743 0300). With cocktail lounge, coffee shop, restaurants, sauna, game room, karaoke bar, beauty salon and shops; *Marina* (☎ 746 6161). with restaurants and shops but does not have a marina; and *New Crown* (☎ 742 1001) with restaurants, health club.

Top End If you want to be near the water, the *Oriental Hotel* (☎ 752 8222) offers sea views and a chance to admire the ongoing construction project at Top Land. Facilities include a bowling alley and a sauna. Double rooms begin at W210,000. Rated five stars.

Several blocks inland is the old but still cushy *Lagonda Hotel* (☎ 758 2500). Facilities include a sauna and shopping arcade. Doubles here are W150,000. Rated four stars.

Without a doubt, the most comfortable accommodation in old Jeju is the *Jeju*

SINJEJU

PLACES TO STAY
1 Marina Hotel
  마리나호텔
4 Holiday Inn Crowne Plaza
  홀리데이인크라운호텔
7 Royal Lagonda Hotel
  제주로얄호텔
11 Green Hotel
  그린호텔
12 Hawaii Hotel
  하와이호텔
13 New Crown Hotel
  뉴크라운호텔
14 Island Hotel
  아일랜드호텔
15 Grand Hotel
  제주그랜드호텔

PLACES TO EAT
5 Grand Durant Restaurant
  그랜드드랑식당
16 939 Pizza
  939피자

OTHER
2 Jeju Bank
  제주은행
3 Asiana Airlines
  아시아나항공
6 Sinjeju Cinema
  신제주극장
8 Lotte Champion
  Department Store
  롯데참피온백화점
9 Kookmin Bank
  국민은행
10 Post Office
  우체국

KAL Hotel (☎ 724 2001). Situated on a hill, it overlooks the city and the adjacent Sinsan Park. Staying here is worth it just for the health club and indoor swimming pool. And, in case you meet someone interesting, the KAL even has its own wedding hall. Rooms start at W220,000. Rated five stars.

Over in Sinjeju, *Royal Lagonda (☎ 743 2222)* gets the nod with its restaurants, bar, night club and sauna. Doubles begin at W160,000.

Holiday Inn Crowne Plaza (☎ 741 8000) in Sinjeju scarcely needs an introduction. Facilities include a health club, indoor swimming pool and sauna. Doubles from W220,000.

Also in the Sinjeju there's the *Grand Hotel (☎ 747 5000)* where doubles are W200,000.

Places to Eat
Jejudo is famous for certain foods which are difficult to find elsewhere in Korea – horsemeat, for example. If you'd prefer a meal that fights back, there's nothing like live octopus (chew the tentacles fast – otherwise the suckers stick to your teeth). Another treat is live shrimp. Slightly more appealing are raw (but not living) abalone *(jeonbuk hoe)* and sea urchin soup *(songgeguk)*. Wash it all down with a bottle of snake wine.

Budget If the bizarre and exotic fails to tempt you, there is plenty of plainer stuff on offer in Jeju-si. A good place to start is breakfast – *Joong Ang Bakery* is the largest and has tables where you can sit down and enjoy your pastries with coffee, tea or milk. The other bakeries around town are all take aways, but you can find some tasty pastry at *Paris Baguette*.

When it comes to more wholesome meals, a good place to look is *Dongmun Market* which is in a narrow alley behind Dongmun Rotary bus stop. There are dozens of stalls here dishing out everything from *gimbap* (Korean 'sushi') to fried chicken. Aside from food, everything else you need in life is on sale here too.

Supermarkets are worth a look, at least for fruit, snacks, herbal tea and the like. One of the best in town is *Jeju King Supermarket*, on Dongmunno. The other big one in Jeju-si is on the first floor of *Emart*, which is near the waterfront.

Over in Sinjeju, the *Lotte Champion Department Store* has an excellent supermarket in the basement.

Mid-Range *Shinra Chobap Restaurant (☎ 753 0254)* is deservedly popular with both Koreans and the few local expats in Jeju-si. The food is a mixed Korean-Japanese style. Prices on the menu (which is entirely in Korean) run from W8000 to W30,000, but even the W8000 meals are fabulous. No matter what you order, it's pretty hard to go wrong. The restaurant

JEJU-DO

has no English sign outside – look for the fish tanks facing the street.

Aida Italian Restaurant is hidden on the 5th floor of the Youth Desk Building (yes, they really call it that). Some house specialties include pizza, chicken, spaghetti and seafood. There is a good set lunch for W5500, and dinner typically runs to W9000 per person.

You'll find a Harley-Davidson motorcycle parked indoors at *939 Pizza* in Sinjeju. The motorcycle is used by the owner, though not for delivering pizzas. The pizza here is reputed to be the best in town.

Top End Nothing can quite compete with *Sky Lounge* at the KAL Hotel. It's Jejudo's only revolving restaurant. Prices are in the stratosphere, but someone's got to pay the electricity bill. The restaurant is also famous for its cocktails – a Singapore Sling or Blue Hawaii should hit the spot. Take the glass lift for the best view.

You can also hop over to Sinjeju if you want a deluxe meal. *Grand Durant Restaurant* has the best Western food on the island.

Entertainment

The most popular pub in town is *The Playhouse* (☎ 726 9611). Jeju-si's expat English-teaching veterans gather here in the evening to swap war stories. Drinks are reasonable and there is often live music. The pub is just above Chicago Pizza (don't bother eating there).

Another good place to listen to music is *The Doors* pub. This place has a fabulous CD collection. *Tombstone Pub* offers the best cocktails in Jeju-si.

There is a whole group of small pubs in the alleys just opposite City Hall. This is where Jeju's student population hangs out, so if you'd like to practice English with a younger crowd, check it out.

Sinjeju does not have an interesting pub scene, but it does have the *Sinjeju Cinema,* which usually has foreign films.

GETTING THERE & AWAY
Air

Both Korean Air (☎ 752 2000) and Asiana Airlines (☎ 743 4000) operate domestic

flights to Jejudo. Flights connect Jeju-si with Cheongju, Jinju, Gunsan, Gwangju, Mokpo, Pohang, Busan, Seoul, Daegu, Ulsan and Yeosu.

There are international flights to four cities in Japan (Tokyo, Fukuoka, Nagoya and Osaka).

The main Korean Air office is opposite the KAL Hotel on Jung-angno (Jeju-si map). The Asiana Airlines main office is in Sinjeju. However, it's very easy to book tickets from numerous travel agents around town or at the airport.

Ferry

There are ferries from Jeju-si to Mokpo, Wando, Busan, Yeosu and Incheon. On the southern coast there are ferries from Seogwipo to Busan. There are student discounts available on all of the ferries but you have to ask for them. The seas in the straits between Jejudo and the mainland are often quite rough – if you're not a good sailor it might be worth your while taking one of the faster ferries or even flying.

Schedules vary from one season to another. Not surprisingly, boats are most frequent during summer and the following schedules all assume you are travelling during peak times. If travelling during the off-peak season, it's a good idea to ring up first or check the schedule immediately upon arrival in the port city.

Busan-Jejudo There is a choice of four ferries to Jejudo from Busan – two to Jeju-si and two to Seogwipo via Seongsan (on the eastern tip of the island). The timetables at the terminal are in both Korean and English.

The posh *Treasure Island* ferry is large with fantastic facilities – almost like taking a luxury cruise. Somewhat less plush is the *Cozy Island*, but it still beats swimming. Both boats are operated by the Tongyang Express Ferry Company, which has several offices (☎ Seoul 730 7788, ☎ Busan 463 0605, ☎ Jejudo 751 1901). *Treasure Island* departs from Busan at 7 pm on Monday, Wednesday and Friday; departures from Jejudo are at 6.30 pm Tuesday, Thursday and Saturday; travel time is 11½ hours. There are seven classes from economy (W33,000) all the way up to VIP (W210,000). *Cozy Island* departs Busan at 7 pm on Tuesday, Thursday and Saturday; from Jejudo at 7.30 pm on Monday, Wednesday and Friday; fares are somewhat lower, at W21,650 to W210,000. There are no boats on Sunday.

Car Ferry No 3 operates between Busan and Seogwipo. It departs Busan on Monday, Wednesday and Friday at 6.30 pm. From Seogwipo departures are on Sunday, Tuesday and Thursday at 5 pm. The journey takes 15 hours. The one-way fare is W29,950. For information, call the office (☎ Busan 463 0605, Seogwipo 732 0220).

Mokpo-Jejudo The *Seaworld Express* runs daily except Sunday in both directions. Departures from Mokpo are at 9 am while departures from Jeju are at 5.30 pm. The journey takes 5½ hours and costs W14,700 to W40,000. For information you can ring up in Mokpo (☎ 245 1927) or Jejudo (☎ 752 9258).

The *Democracy No 2* departs Mokpo daily at 2 pm, and from Jeju daily at 9.30 am. The journey takes slightly over three hours. Fares are W33,000 to W39,400. For information you can ring up in Mokpo (☎ 245 3235) or Jejudo (☎ 721 2171).

The *Tongyang Express* departs Mokpo daily except Sunday at 3.30 pm. Departures from Jeju are daily except Monday at 7 am. The journey takes 5½ hours and costs from W14,700 to W40,000. For the latest information, call the office (☎ Seoul 730 7788, Jejudo 751 1901, Mokpo 243 2111).

Wando-Jejudo *Hanil Car Ferry No 1* sails from Jeju daily (except Sunday) at 9 am. In the opposite direction it departs Wando at 3 pm daily.

Hanil Car Ferry No 2 departs Jeju at 8.20 am daily except Saturday. It departs Wando at 4 pm daily.

Both boats take 3½ hours to make the crossing. The fare is from W13,850 to W17,700. Call for the latest information (☎ Seoul 535 2106, Jejudo 722 4170, Wando 554 3294).

Incheon-Jejudo It's a long ride, but since the boats depart in the evening you can sleep through half the journey. Departures from Incheon are on Monday, Wednesday and Friday at 7 pm; from Jejudo it's on Tuesday, Thursday and Saturday at 7 pm. The journey takes 16½ hours and costs W39,000 to W72,000 (depending on class). For further information, call Semo Express in Incheon (☎ 884 8700) or Jejudo (☎ 721 2173).

GETTING AROUND
The Airport
Jejudo airport is a mere 2km west of central Jeju-si (W2000 by taxi). At the airport, there are five buses numbered 100, 200, 300, 500 and 600 (just what happened to No 400 is anybody's guess). Although considered 'municipal' buses, some of them journey quite far, even to Seogwipo, on the other side of the island. Buses are claimed to run once every five to eight minutes from 6 am to 10.25 pm. The five routes are :

100 Airport, Sinjeju, inter-city bus terminal, Jung-angno, Dongmun Rotary, ferry pier. The fare is W600.
200 Airport, Sinjeju, inter-city bus terminal, Dongmun Rotary, Gwandeokjeong, Somunro, Yongdam Rotary, airport (circular route). The fare is W600.
300 Airport, Yongdam Rotary, Gwandeokjeong, Dongmun Rotary, inter-city bus terminal, Sinjeju, airport (circular route). The fare is W600.
500 Halla University, Halla Hospital, airport, Somunro, Gwandeokjeong, Jung-angno, Gwangyangro, City Hall, Mokseokwon Garden, Jeju University. The fare is W600.
600 Airport, Crown Plaza Hotel (Sinjeju), Renaissance Hotel, Jungmun Resort (Yeomiji entrance gate, Hanguk Condominium, Shilla Hotel, Hyatt Hotel), New Kyungnam Hotel, Seogwipo wharf, Paradise Hotel, Seogwipo KAL Hotel. Fare to Jungmun Resort is W3000; to Seogwipo W4200.

Bus
There are plenty of buses going to most places of interest around the island. Unfortunately, travelling around the island by bus can be painstakingly slow, and you can't stop wherever you like. However, if you're determined to try it, prepare an ample supply of W100 and W500 coins, plus some

JEJU-DO

W1000 notes. A rough guide to the bus routes is as follows:

Pyoseon via Sangumburi and Seong-eup. Buses terminate at Jeju Folk Village near Pyoseon.
Seongsan via the eastern coast road.
Hallasan and Seogwipo via No 1 cross-island highway.
Hallasan and Jungmun via No 2 cross-island highway.
Daejeong and Hwasun via inland routes.
Jungmun and Seogwipo via inland routes.
Seogwipo via Hallim, Daejeong, Hwasun and Jungmun via the western coastal road.
Hallim and Seogwipo partially via western coastal road and partially via inland routes.

Coastal Road (Soehaeseon Route)
The coastal road going west from Jeju-si (known as the Soehaeseon Route) will give you the best selection of beaches on the island. These include Iho, Gwakji, Hyeopjae and, on the southern coast, Jungmun. Also along this coastal road are the lava caves of Hyeopjaegul and the cave temple, San-banggulsa. All buses along this road stop at both the lava tubes and the grotto.

Coastal Road (Donghaeseon Route)
The coastal road going east from Jeju-si (known as the Donghaeseon Route) will take you to the beaches of Hamdeok and Gimnyeong, the turn-off for Manjanggul.

Cross-Island Highway No 1
This road skirts the eastern side of Hallasan. The road passes three points at which you can start the trek to the summit of Hallasan. It ends up at Seogwipo.

Cross-Island Highway No 2
The road skirting the western side of Hallasan is known as Cross-Island Highway No 2, and it passes two points at which you can start the trek up Hallasan and end at Jungmun. Buses taking this route will have '2' in the window.

Dongbusan Route
This is a minor route which connects Jeju-si with Pyoseon. It branches off from the No 1 Cross-Island Highway on the lower northern slopes of Hallasan and goes past Sangumburi and Seong-eup to end at Jeju Folk Village (near Pyoseon).

A few examples of schedules and fares:

Jeju-si–Seogwipo (via No 1 Cross-Island Highway). There are buses every 12 minutes from 6.10 am to 9.30 pm which cost W3300 and take about one hour). Fares and journey times are proportionally less if you're getting off at the start of the Hallasan trekking trails.
Jeju-si–Jungmun (via the 2nd Cross-Island Highway). There are buses every 20 minutes from 6.20 am to 9.40 pm which take about one hour and cost W2500. Fares and journey times are proportionally less if you're getting off at the start of the Hallasan trekking trails.
Jeju-si–Seong-eup–Pyoseon (via the Dongbusan route). There are buses every 30 minutes from 6 am to 9 pm. The journey to Seong-eup takes about one hour.
Jeju-si–Seongsan (via the eastern coastal road). There are buses every 20 minutes from 5.30 am to 9.40 pm, which take about one hour. These buses will drop you at the turn-off for Manjanggul.

Car
Given the rural nature of the island (though decidedly less so, year by year), renting a car almost makes sense. The cost is not excessive, especially if you can share the vehicle with a few others. The main drawback is the legal liability of renting a car and the numerous speed traps (don't exceed 80km/h anywhere on Jejudo).

Most upmarket hotels have a car-rental desk in the lobby. Or you can deal directly with the car rental agencies, as follows:

Avis	☎ 726 3322
Jeju	☎ 742 3301
Dong-a	☎ 743 1515
Green	☎ 743 2000
Halla	☎ 755 5000
Hanseong	☎ 747 2100
Beomhan	☎ 748 4001
Seokgwan	☎ 748 2800
Seongsan	☎ 746 3260
Woori	☎ 752 9600

Taxi
Hiring a taxi for a full day is not such a ridiculous extravagance as it might seem.

It's a little more expensive than renting a car, but saves you much hassle. If you've got one or two companions to share the cost, so much the better. In most cases, drivers are happy to act as your tour guide, though very few can speak English.

You can figure on about W80,000 (negotiable) plus lunch (also negotiable). It should be discussed in advance about whether or not this fee includes the petrol. Drivers typically expect you to hire them for 1½ days, or perhaps two full days – the rate they quote you may be based on this assumption. If you spend the night somewhere, then you are responsible for the driver's hotel room. Make sure that the details of the journey have all been talked through thoroughly so as to avoid misunderstandings later.

Tours
The most readily available tours are those which can be booked right in Jejudo airport at the information counter. The tours depart daily from the airport at 9.30 am and finish around 6 pm. There are two tours. One covers the west side of the island and costs W32,200 while the other does the east side for W29,700. The tour price is supposed to cover everything, including admission fees to the various sights. If you're with a large group, an English-speaking tour guide can be arranged. Otherwise, you can expect the tour to be conducted in Korean only.

All-inclusive tours (air fare and hotels included) can be booked in Seoul. Korea Travel Bureau, for example, offers a three-day tour for W530,000.

Bicycle
If motorised transport turns you off, consider renting a mountain bike. If you're reasonably fit, you can propel yourself around the island (about 200km) in three or four days and visit all the hot tourist spots. Make sure you have some tools, pump and a patch kit in case you need to repair a flat tyre. A bike cable-lock and rain gear are also necessities.

Bikes are available for rent in Jeju-si at Sunkyong Smart Bicycle (☎ 751 2000, 757 6000), and from Samcheonri Bicycle (☎ 751

0946). There are bike rental shops in Seogwipo, Seongsan, Moseulpo and Hallim.

Horse
Jejudo has been famous for its horses ever since the Mongols raised them on the island in the 13th century. Even as late as the Korean War, horses were still regarded as a practical means of transportation.

Needless to say, times have changed. Most Koreans never get a chance to ride a horse, except for the mechanical kind that accepts W500 coins. Thus, the chance to sit atop a real live horse in Jeju-do to pose for heroic photos is irresistible. If you want the horses for more than just a fast photo opportunity, it can be arranged, for a price. Horses for rent near the Jungmun Resort and Ilchulbong are expensive, but you pay about a quarter of the price in relative backwaters of the island.

Around the Island

BEACHES 해수욕장
The coastline of Jejudo is rocky, and none of the beaches are large. Nevertheless, the island has a number of sandy coves and these can be relaxing places to enjoy the sun and surf. Bear in mind that, being 33½° north of the equator, you'll need a wetsuit unless you confine your swimming to July and August.

Some of the beaches have nearby yeogwan, yeoinsuk or minbak where you can spend the night. Certainly it's more charming than staying in downtown Jeju-si.

See the Jejudo map in this chapter for the locations of the top public beaches.

SANGUMBURI CRATER
산굼부리분화구
Just by the side of the highway, about half way between Seong-eup and Jeju-si, lies the Sangumburi volcanic crater, some 350m in diameter and around 100m deep. This is just one of the 360 so-called 'parasitic cones' (secondary volcanos) found on Jejudo.

This particular parasite charges W2000 for admission – all the other 359 cones can be visited for free, but you'll have to do some climbing. By contrast, Sangumburi crater is an easy walk on flat terrain – without a doubt the most accessible of the craters. There's a trail that allows you to hike along the rim, but you're not allowed down inside the crater itself.

Buses from Jeju-si to Seong-eup and Pyoseon pass right by the crater gate and will stop if you want to get off. You can't miss this place, as it's fronted by a huge parking lot and a tourist village by the entrance gate.

MANJANGGUL 만장굴

East of Jeju-si, and about 2.5km off the coast road from Gimnyeong Beach, are the lava caves of Manjanggul. The cave is 13.4km long, with a height and width varying from 3m to 20m, thus making it the longest lava tube known in the world. If you've never seen one of these before, then don't miss this chance.

Take a sweater with you and a reasonable pair of shoes. It's damp down there (87% to 100% humidity) and the temperature rarely rises above a chilly 9°C. The cave is well-lit as far as a huge lava pillar (about 1km from the entrance) which is as far as you're allowed to go without special permission. The caves are open daily from 9 am to 7 pm, but from November through February hours are 9 am to 5 pm. Entry costs W2200.

Much closer to the turn-off from the main highway, but alongside the road which leads to Manjanggul, are another series of lava tubes, known as the **Gimnyeongsagul**. They are especially unusual because there are actually two tubes, one on top of the other. However these caves are currently not open to the public.

Getting There & Away

To get to Manjanggul, take a bus from Jeju-si going to Seongsan and get off at the Kimnyeong turn-off (signposted for the caves). From here there are local buses to Manjanggul which run every 30 to 60 minutes between 7.50 am and 6.30 pm. There's a full schedule for the buses posted up in the window of the ticket office at the caves. Alternatively, you can hitch a ride or walk.

Beware of Snakes

Jejudo's lava tubes are associated with an ancient legend of a huge snake which dwelled in them. In order to placate the snake and prevent harm befalling the nearby farms and villages, a 15- or 16-year-old virgin girl was annually sacrificed by being thrown into a lava cave. This horrific practice continued until 1514, when it was stopped by a magistrate newly appointed to the area. He persuaded the reluctant villagers to perform the usual ritual but to omit the sacrifice whereupon, so the story goes, the angry snake emerged, was killed by the villagers and burnt to ashes. For his pains, the magistrate inexplicably fell ill and died soon afterwards – but there was no reappearance of the snake.

GIMNYEONG MAZE 김녕미로공원

A short hop from Manjanggul Caves is a hedge maze of the type normally seen in Europe. The maze – which contains 3km of pathways and is designed in the shape of Jejudo – has a short but interesting history.

The founder of the maze is Fred Dustin, an American who first came to Korea in 1952 as a soldier during the Korean War. After the war, he went back to the USA to study, but returned in 1958 and has been an expat ever since. He accepted a teaching position in Jejudo, and started growing the maze in 1987 using *leylandii* shrubs imported from England. Although getting quite advanced in age, Mr Dustin is still manager of the maze, still living on the site and has interesting tales to tell.

Admission to the maze costs W2000.

SEONGSAN ILCHULBONG
성산일출봉

Seongsan (Fortress Mountain) is the village at the extreme eastern tip of Jejudo nestled at the foot of the spectacular volcanic cone known as Ilchulbong (Sunrise Peak). The summit is shaped like a punch bowl, though there's no crater lake here because of the very porous volcanic rock. It is definitely one of Jejudo's most impressive sights.

The sides of the mountain plunge vertically into the surf. Along the rugged shoreline, you can often see Jejudo's famous diving women searching for seaweed, shellfish and sea urchins.

Climbing the summit in time to catch the sunrise is a life-affirming journey for the Korean people – expect plenty of company on the trail. To do the sunrise expedition, you'll have to spend the night at a yeogwan in Seongsan. Most yeogwan owners will wake you up early so you can watch the sunrise. It's best to bring a torch (flashlight) so you don't walk over a cliff in the dark. You could, of course, climb the peak at a more sensible hour. Entry to Ilchulbong costs W2000.

Apart from walking around the crater there are boats (W5000) available to sail you around. However, they only sail when demand is sufficient and the sea is calm enough so that your gimbap stays where it belongs.

Scuba Diving

If you'd rather explore Ilchulbong from below, you can try scuba diving. Sea Life Scuba (☎ 794 9728) in Seongsan-ri has equipment and makes the arrangements.

Places to Stay

Facing the road which leads up to the Seongsan village tourist complex and entrance gate to Ilchulbong is the *Suji Yeogwan,* where you can get a room with bath for W25,000. Around the corner is the *Seongsan Yeoinsuk,* which is somewhat cheaper at W18,000.

Going up in price is *Jaesong-jang Yeogwan,* opposite the post office on the bottom road, which has rooms for W25,000.

Getting There & Away

There are frequent buses to Seongsan-ri departing from Jeju-si. The trip takes about 1½ hours.

Make sure that the bus you get on is going right into Seongsan-ri and not just to Goseong-ri, the town on the main coast road where you have to turn off for Seongsan-ri. If you get dropped here, it's a 2.5km walk into Seongsan.

SINYANG BEACH 신양해수욕장

Near the eastern end of the island, Sinyang Beach is shaped like a half-moon and is about 1.5km in length. It's the most sheltered beach on the island, and for that reason there is a place here that rents sailing boats and windsurfers and gives lessons on how to use them. This is a good staging post for climbing nearby Ilchulbong.

There are yeogwan and minbak in Sinyang-ri, the village adjacent to the beach, and even more in Seongsan-ri, which is about 3km to the north (see previous listing). Rates are typically W25,000.

Buses from Jeju-si do not go directly to Sinyang Beach. First take a bus to Goseong-ri – these run about once every 20 minutes, from 5.45 am to 9.40 pm, and take 1¼ hours. The hard part is the last 2km from Goseong-ri to the beach. You could walk it if your bags aren't too heavy, or take a taxi. Otherwise, there is a bus once hourly from 6.15 am to 9.12 pm, which takes just six minutes.

During the summer months the beach is patrolled by lifeguards and there are small kiosks dishing out drinks, snacks, postcards and other tourist paraphernalia.

UDO 우도

North-east of Seongsan, just off the coast, is Udo (Cow Island) which is still very rural despite it's population of 2000. The number of motor vehicles has increased sharply in recent years, but it's still a very relaxing place. The superb views over to Ilchulbong are rewarding, and there are three **beaches** (one has white sand, one has black sand and the other is coral). An interesting twist is the small community of *haenyeo,* Jeju-do's famous **diving women,** who work in the cove below the lighthouse.

During the summer tourist season, drivers waiting at the ferry pier gather up tourists for a scenic bus tour around the island.

Spending the night on the island at one of the numerous minbak or yeogwan is recommended. Figure on around W20,000.

There is a fabulous *restaurant* on Udo, which you practically walk straight into after you get off the ferry. You can eat your fill of fish and vegetables for around W6000.

JEJU-DO

Getting There & Away

There are ferries to Udo from the port at Seongsan. The ticket office and pier are quite a walk from the centre of Seongsan, so leave yourself enough time (about 15 minutes). Ferries depart at least once an hour, more frequently in the early morning. You have to fill out a silly form (entirely in Korean) stating your name, nationality and passport number (but you don't actually need to show the passport). The round-trip fare is W2000. While it costs a reasonable W500 extra for a bicycle, taking a car is outrageously expensive at W22,000.

SEONG-EUP FOLK VILLAGE
성읍민속마을

A short bus ride north of Pyoseon lies Jejudo's former provincial capital Seong-eup, founded in Goryeo times. It became provincial headquarters in 1423 during the reign of King Sejong and remained such until 1914, when the administrative unit was abolished. Today it's designated as a folk village and its traditional architecture has been preserved with government assistance (W1,000,000 per year for each household).

If you want to see what Jejudo's villages looked like before concrete and corrugated iron transformed the Korean landscape, then Seong-eup is worth a visit. Some modern intrusions include souvenir shops, car parks and a number of tourist restaurants.

The village has a number of sections – take some time to explore. Very likely, your bus, car or taxi will be greeted by a local, offering to take you (and a few others) on a guided tour of the village. These tours are conducted entirely in Korean, but are free – the catch is that they hope you'll buy some things from the village souvenir shop. A major local product is the five-flavours tea (W30,000 a jar).

The tours are interesting, but if you can't understand a word of Korean, just take off down the narrow lanes and discover the place for yourself. There are no entry fees to any of the buildings. Remember that most of the houses are still occupied, so don't barge in and ask the 'staff' if you can cash a travellers cheque.

Haenyeo

Haenyeo, female divers, are found on a number of Korea's outlying islands, including Ulleungdo. However, they are most well-known (and most numerous) in Jeju-do.

Great physical stamina is a prerequisite. The divers use no scuba gear, but are able to hold their breath underwater for two minutes and reach a depth of 20m. Their equipment is decidedly low-tech: fins, a wetsuit, face mask, gloves, basket and net.

At their peak (in the 1950s), there were almost 30,000 haenyeo in Jeju-do. By the 1980s, their numbers were reduced to around 10,000, and by year 2000 there were perhaps only 3000 left. The average age of the divers is increasing – some of the women have continued to dive until they are 75.

That few young women are choosing to go into the diving profession is hardly surprising – it has always been a difficult way to earn a living. These days, far more money can be earned selling food, drinks and souvenirs to tourists.

For the schedule for the buses from Jeju-si to Pyoseon – via Sangumburi and Seong-eup – see the Getting Around section at the end of the chapter.

JEJU FOLK VILLAGE 제주민속촌

This is Jejudo's answer to the Korean Folk Village in Suwon (see Gyeonggi-do chapter).

Just outside of Pyoseon and close to the town's fine beach, the Jeju Folk Village portrays 19th-century Jejudo. It has a shamanistic area and official buildings to house government officials and records. Though essentially a modern creation, all the construction here is authentically traditional and some of the cottages were brought intact from other areas and so are 200 to 300 years old. There's also a performance yard where folk songs and legends are enacted.

The folk village also has diverse flora and fauna, as it contains three habitat zones – coastal, plain and mountain.

Like other such folk villages, there are a number of restaurants offering traditional food such as dried squid, along with the requisite ice cream cones and Coca-Cola.

The Jeju Folk Village is open daily from 9 am to 6 pm and entry costs W4000.

SEOGWIPO 서귀포
pop 86,000
On the southern coast of Jejudo, Seogwipo is the island's second-largest town after Jeju-si and is connected to the rest of Korea by ferries from Busan. It's more laid back than Jeju-si, and its setting at the foot of Hallasan, whose lower slopes are covered with tangerine groves, is quite spectacular.

Jeongbangpokpo 정방폭포
Despite the heavy rainfall, surface water of any kind is a rarity on Jejudo due to the island's porous volcanic rock. Ground water, by contrast, is abundant – Jejudo is basically one big sponge. The Seogwipo area is one of the very few places on the island where the water table makes it to the surface (briefly) before plunging into the sea.

Jeongbangpokpo is 23m high and it's claimed in the tourist literature that it is the only waterfall in Asia which falls directly into the sea. This isn't quite correct since Toroki on the south coast of Yakushima in Japan also does this and is even larger than Jeongbangpokpo. Still, these falls are an impressive sight *if* it's been raining recently. They are a 10-15 minute walk from the centre of town. Entry costs W2000.

Cheonjiyeonpokpo 천지연폭포
This waterfall is on the other side of town at the end of a beautifully forested and steep gorge through which a path and bridge have been constructed. After a heavy rain, the waterfall can be impressive, but at other times it's only a trickle. Cheonjiyeonpokpo is a 10-15 minute walk from the centre of town down by the fishing harbour. Entry costs W2000.

Oedolgae (Lonely Rock) 오돌개
About 2km to the west of Seogwipo is Oedolgae, a 20m tall basalt pillar jutting out of the ocean. It was formed by volcanic

activity, and is the most notable feature of a beautiful cliffside park. Getting down to the ocean looks dangerous and is not recommended, but there's a pleasant hike through the pine forests along the ocean cliffs. Admission to the park is free.

Boat & Submarine Tours
해상유람, 대국해저의유람
There are regular surface boats (☎ 732 1717) shuttling seasick tourists along the coastline for W5000 per person. Or, if you don't mind spending W30,000 for a fish-eye's view of the coral beds around Seogwipo, contact the Daekuk Subsea Company (☎ 732 6060). You'll find both the surface boats and the submarine at Seogwipo harbour.

Scuba Diving 다이빙클럽
If you'd rather explore the sea floor without a submarine, try contacting Manta Scuba (☎ 763 2264) or Poseidon Diving (☎ 733 1294) in Seogwipo.

Places to Stay
Budget If you'd like to stay in the busy market area in the centre of town, you could do not better than *Donghwa-jang Motel* (☎ 762 7141). Some of the friendly staff here speak English and the rooms are excellent value at W25,000.

Just a stone's throw down the street are two other good choices, *Daeseong-jang Yeogwan* and the large (six floors!) *Honey Motel* (☎ 763 6677).

Although staying in the centre of town can be convenient for restaurants and the limited nightlife, the best selection of budget accommodation (with the best views) is down near the ferry terminal.

The bottom-end in the ferry terminal zone is the *Ujeongyeo Yeoinsuk*. It's small but boasts a low price of W18,000, and it's clean.

Just a stone's throw away are *Yurak-jang Motel* and *Useong Motel*. Both offer comfortable rooms with private bath for W25,000, and some rooms have a sea view.

Right along the waterfront at the bottom of the hill are *Namyang-jang Yeogwan* (☎ 762 2021) and *Manbu-jang Motel* (☎ 733 1315), both charging the usual W25,000.

JEJU-DO

JEJU-DO

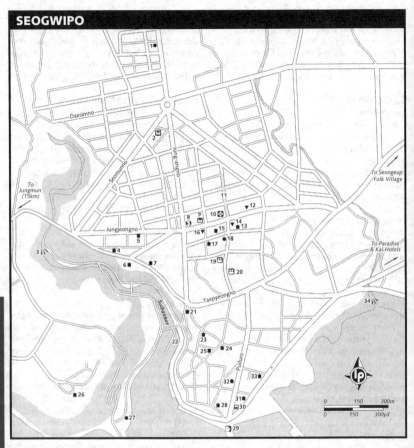

SEOGWIPO

Mid-Range The *Napoli Hotel* (☎ 733 4701) costs W40,000 for a double that is so clean it could pass a military white glove inspection. Some rooms offer a good view of Seogwipo harbour – it's truly excellent value.

The *Hotel Koreana* was undergoing renovation at the time of writing but should open again soon. Prices are anticipated to be in the W50,000 and over range.

The 66-room *Park Hotel* (☎ 762 2161) is a large old place in the process of being renovated. Doubles are W52,000 to W60,000. Facilities include a night club, sauna and indoor swimming pool.

The *Lion's Hotel* (☎ 762 4141), like the others, is also beginning a renovation.

Slightly better is the *Daemung Greenville Hotel* (☎ 732 8311) where doubles will cost you W60,000.

There are a couple of hotels clustered together on the west side of town, including the *New Kyungnam Hotel* (☎ 733 2129) and *Sun Beach Hotel* (☎ 763 3600). Rooms in both places start at W100,000.

Top End All of the top-end hotels are located on the peripheries of town. To the west of town, sitting on a bluff with a view

SEOGWIPO

PLACES TO STAY
4 New Kyungnam
   Hotel
   신경남관광호텔
5 Daemyeong Greenville
   Hotel
   대명그린빌호텔
6 Lion's Hotel
   라이온스호텔
7 Sun Beach Hotel
   호텔서비치
13 Donghwa-jang Motel
   동화장모텔
15 Honey Motel
   허니모텔
17 Daeseong-jang Yeogwan
   대성장여관
21 Napoli Hotel
   나포리호텔
23 Useong Motel
   우성모텔
24 Ujeong Yeoinsuk
   우정여인숙
25 Yurak-jang Motel
   유락장모텔
26 Prince Hotel
   프린스호텔

28 Park Hotel
   파크호텔
31 Namyang-jang Yeogwan
   남양장여관
32 Hotel Koreana
   코리아나호텔
33 Manbu-jang Motel
   만부장모텔

PLACES TO EAT
11 Seogwipo Market
   서귀포시장
12 Chun Restaurant
   준식당
14 Tombstone Restaurant &
   Mokbo Punshik
   톰스톤, 먹보분식
16 Koryo Bakery
   고려제과

OTHER
1 Halla Supermarket
   한라마트
2 Inter-City Bus Terminal
   시외버스터미널
3 Cheonjiyeonpokpo
   천지연폭포

8 Kookmin Bank
   국민은행
9 Post Office
   우체국
10 Dongmyeong
   Department Store
   동명백화점
18 Wonnam Bowling Alley
   원남빌딩,
   원남볼링장
19 Seogwipo Town
   Cinema
   서귀포극장
20 Academy Cinema
   아카데미극장
22 Boat & Submarine
   Pier
   잠수함선착장
27 Submarine
   Ticket Office
   대국해저관광
29 Ferry Terminal
   서귀포항터미널
30 Airport Bus Stop
   공항버스정류장
34 Jeongbangpokpo
   정방폭포

of the ocean, is the luxurious *Prince Hotel*
(☎ 732 9911). Standard rooms here begin
at W150,000.

On the east side of town you will find the
Paradise Hotel (☎ 763 2100). South
Korea's first president, Syngman Rhee,
used to stay here in the 1950s. The hotel
now belongs to the same company that operates the luxurious Paradise Beach Hotel
in Busan. It's worth coming here just to explore the hotel grounds, even if you don't
say. Short hiking trails with spectacular
views overlook the coast. Rooms are available with a variety of motifs – Korean-
style, American, European, Mediterranean,
Scandinavian and even African. Doubles
cost W245,000, or you can splurge on a
suite for W400,000.

The *Seogwipo KAL Hotel* (☎ 733 2001)
is a short distance from the Paradise Hotel.
Although reputed to have the best facilities
in Seogwipo, it does not have a sea view.
Doubles start at W200,000. Facilities include indoor and outdoor swimming pools,
tennis courts, a night club, sauna, shopping
arcade and a golf course.

Places to Eat

The *Koryo Bakery* is the best in Seogwipo,
and will do nicely for a simple breakfast.

The *Seogwipo Market* occupies an alley
in the centre of town and is *the* place to go
if you're looking for food stalls.

Self-caterers will appreciate the huge
Halla Supermarket on the northern fringe
of the city.

In a building just south of the Seogwipo
Market is *Meokbo Bunshik* (☎ 733 0059),
a small Korean restaurant specialising in
delicious dumplings.

Just next door but up on the second floor
is the *Tombstone Restaurant* (☎ 763 4400).
Despite the name, there is nothing fatal
about the food: good Western meals at reasonable prices.

Around the corner from Tombstone and
down in the basement is *Chun Restaurant*
(☎ 732 8086). This place serves both Korean and Western meals.

Entertainment

Seogwipo doesn't have the expat and student nightlife scene that Jeju-si does. As a

JEJU-DO

consequence, you could check to see what's playing at the *Academy Cinema* or *Seogwipo Town Cinema*.

Another possibility is to visit the *Wonnam Bowling Alley* on the 5th floor of the Wonnam Building.

Getting There & Away

Helicopter For a mere W100,000 per person, you can fly for 25 minutes from Jejudo airport to Seogwipo. Presumably, you could rent the helicopter to fly through some of the island's scenic spots – but not caves!

Bus Bus No 600 runs from the airport to Seogwipo (W4200) via the Jungmun Resort (W3000).

From the inter-city bus terminal in Jeju-si, there are buses to Seogwipo (W3300) via Jungmun (W2500) every 12 minutes from 6.20 am to 9.40 pm.

YAKCHEONSA 약천사

One of the most attractive Buddhist temples on the island, Yakcheonsa is of recent origin. It was constructed between 1987 and 1997, and is built entirely from wood. You are free to wander inside as long as you don't disturb the worshippers. The only rules are that this is a shoes-off temple, and flash photography is not permitted (time exposures are OK). Take the stairs to the 4th floor to see the amazing exhibit of 18,000 Buddhist figurines.

The temple complex is about 2km east of Jungmun Beach.

JUSANGJOLLI ROCKS 주상졀리

Less than 1km to the south of Yakcheonsa is a spectacular stretch of coastline known as Jusanjolli. What makes it so spectacular are the hexagonal-shaped rock columns that look almost as if they were stamped out with a cookie cutter. Such bizarre rock formations are the result of rapid cooling and contraction of lava (just what you'd expect to happen when molten lava pours into the sea).

You can admire Jusanjolli from the cliffs above the sea. Climbing down onto the rocks is risky – don't try it without life insurance.

There is no admission charged for entering the area.

JUNGMUN RESORT 중문관광단지

Jungmun is Jejudo's largest resort, with a number of five-star hotels, condominiums, restaurants and sightseeing attractions.

The much-touted beach is OK, but it is awfully crowded during the busy summer holiday season.

A major tourist drawcard is **Cheonjiyeonpokpo** (not to be confused with Cheonbangpokpo in Seogwipo) which is a 20-minute walk back from the beach up to the bridge on the coastal highway. Unless it's been raining heavily recently, you might find the waterfall disappointing.

The resort is also home to the **Yeomiji Botanical Gardens**. This massive complex boasts one of the world's largest greenhouses. Admission costs W5000.

Bird hunters descend on the island from November through to the end of February. Although there are no recorded cases of travellers getting blown away by trigger-happy bird hunters, it's probably no coincidence that the hunting season comes in winter when visitors to Jejudo are fewest. At the Daeyu hunting ground in Jungmun, bird hunting is permitted year round.

Overlooking the beach itself is **Pacific Land**, which contains a dolphinarium, aquarium and restaurantarium. If you're interested in seeing performing dolphins (along with penguins and sea lions), there are shows at 11 am, 1.30, 2.40 and 4.30 pm daily. Entry to the park costs W4000.

Information

There is a tourist information office (☎ 738 0326) inside the Jungmun resort complex.

Places to Stay

This is the territory of the rich and famous. Nevertheless, there are a couple of yeogwan in Jungmun village itself, but it's quite a walk from the beach, and along a busy highway. Unless you intend to splash out the cash for the golf course, tennis courts, horseback riding and other amenities, there's really no reason to stay in Jungmun.

If you do have a Platinum Visa card, then Jungmun can accommodate you in style. The more upmarket places include: *Green Villa* (☎ 732 8311), one of the newer places; and the *Hyatt Regency* (☎ 733 1234), which rests on the cliffs just above impressive Jungmun Beach. The Hyatt does not disappoint – facilities are plush-plus.

Korea Resort Condominium (☎ 738 4000) has facilities that include a disco, outdoor swimming pool and video rental shop.

The *Shilla Hotel* (☎ 738 4466) is very luxurious, and offers a fine view of Jungmun Beach. Li Peng – the Chinese politician most associated with the slaughter of student democracy protesters in Beijing in 1989 – once stayed at the Shilla, and his photo is proudly displayed all around the hotel's lobby. A number of westerners refuse to stay here for this reason.

The newest and largest pleasure palace in Jungmun is the *Lotte Hotel* (☎ 738 7301), named for the *jaebeol* (huge corporate conglomerate) made famous by its chocolate pies. The Lotte offers rooms priced from W225,000 to W3,600,000 – not cheap, but if you sign up for the 'deluxe package' you get free airport pickup, so at least you save on the cab fare. Some nice amenities include the aerobics room, sauna, and indoor and outdoor swimming pools. Honeymooners can take advantage of an advertised 'free wedding gift' plus a wedding cake, not to mention the usual basket of fruit and flowers, with a bottle of champagne thrown in.

Getting There & Away Bus No 600 runs between the airport and Seogwipo, stopping at Jungmun en route. It runs every 15 minutes between 6.20 am and 9.50 pm, and takes 45 minutes for the journey. The fare to the airport is W2200.

From the inter-city bus terminal in Jejusi, there are buses to Jungmun every 12 minutes from 6.20 am to 9.30 pm.

SANBANGGULSA 산방굴사

About 7km east of Daejeong rises the massive volcanic cone of Sanbangsan (395m). Halfway up its southern slope, overlooking the ocean, is a natural cave that was turned into a temple by a Buddhist monk during Goryeo times. It's a steep walk up, and although the grotto itself is only of marginal interest, the views are worth the effort. Lower down, near the entrance, are two temples of recent origin.

Entry to the site costs W2000. The entrance to the grotto is alongside the coast road – buses plying between Daejeong and Seogwipo inevitably stop here.

YONGMEORI COASTLINE
용머리해안

Across the road from Sanbanggulsa, footpaths lead downhill towards the sea. This rocky stretch of coastline is known as Yongmeori. There is a serious proposal afloat to build a massive Disney-like theme park here, though it has run into opposition from local environmentalists. At present, the area is only partially developed, and it's doubtful that it's worth the W2200 admission fee. Nevertheless, fleets of tour buses dock here, and a virtual army of visitors compete for a spot on the rocky coast to pose for that memorable photo.

Perhaps the chief attraction is the **Hamel Monument**, a simple plaque placed on a rocky promontory. It was dedicated by both the Korean and Dutch governments to commemorate the shipwreck of the Dutch merchant vessel *Sparrowhawk* in 1653. Those who survived the wreckage were taken to Seoul by order of the Yi dynasty king and were imprisoned there for the next 13 years for entering Korea illegally. (Then, as now, the Korean immigration authorities have shown zero tolerance towards foreigners who violate visa regulations).

The story had a happy ending. The Dutch prisoners were finally able to escape to Japan in a small fishing vessel. An account of those years, written by Hendrick Hamel, one of the survivors, became a best seller in Europe at the time and was the first accurate description of the Hermit Kingdom that Europeans had received.

JEJU ART PARK 제주조각공원
Built on an open meadow near Sanbangsan on south-west Jejudo, the Jeju Art Park

features more than 180 pieces of sculptured modern art in a naturalistic setting of ponds and trails. The park is open from 9 am to 5.30 pm.

GAPADO & MARADO 가파도, 마라도
South of Daejeong lie the islands of Gapado and Marado – the latter is the most southern point of Korea. Both islands are inhabited. Gapado, the nearest and largest of the two, is flat and almost without trees, and crops have to be cultivated behind stone walls to protect them from the high winds which sweep the island. Many of the inhabitants earn their living by fishing.

Unlike Gapado, Marado rises steeply from the sea and its grassed top supports cattle grazing, though it is only half the size of Gapado and there are only some 20 families living there.

Getting There & Away
There are two daily ferries from Daejeong to Gapado at 8.30 am and 2.30 pm which take about half an hour. To Marado there is one ferry daily from Daejeong at 10 am which takes about 50 minutes.

The ferry terminal in Daejeong is down by the fishing harbour and is about 1km from the centre of town, which is where the buses drop you. There are yeogwan in Daejeong if you prefer to stay overnight in order to catch the morning ferry.

ANTI-MONGOL MONUMENT
항몽유적지
Jejudo was the last redoubt of a faction of the Goryeo army during the time of the Mongol invasion of the 13th century (see the History section in the Facts about Korea chapter). The soldiers were determined to resist the Mongol troops even after King Wonjong had made peace with the invaders and returned to his capital at Gaesong. In 1273, an elite military force built a 6km long dual-walled fortress near what is today the town of Aewol on the north-west coast of the island. The defenders were later slaughtered to a man by the Mongols. Although the effort proved futile,

islanders have honoured their ancestors' bravery by erecting the Anti-Mongol Monument on the site of the battle.

Another relic is that of the temple Wondangsa, or rather a five-story stone pagoda. When Jejudo was under the rule of Mongols, they built their own temple here. The temple was destroyed and today only the pagoda remains.

SHINCHEONJI ART MUSEUM
신천지미술관
Despite the name, the museum is more of an outdoors garden rather than an indoor gallery. Essentially, it's another one of those parks with modernistic outdoor sculptures so common in Korea.

The museum is close to the Anti-Mongol Monument. Admission costs W2000.

HORSE RACETRACK 제주경마장
In case you have excess cash you'd like to get rid of, the Jeju Racetrack is just to the south of Sincheonji Art Museum. The races are a weekend-only event, and well attended by the Koreans. One interesting footnote is that the horses raced here are *jorangmal:* unique, small ponies native to Jejudo.

HALLIM 한림
The main fishing village on the west coast of the island, Hallim is also home to the Hallim Weavers' Village. Visitors are welcome to come view the wool processing operation. This includes everything from shearing sheep to running the wool through various machines and finally churning out 'I Survived Jejudo' sweatshirts, shawls, blankets and other knick-knacks geared towards the tourist industry.

HYEOPJAEGUL 협재굴
About 2.5km south of Hallim, on the north-western side of the island, are a group of lava tube caves, the most famous of which is Hyeopchaegul, which was only discovered in 1981.

Hyeopjaegul is not as long as Manjanggul – think of it as Manjanggul Lite. However, despite it's short length, the cave has an odd feature – it's one of the few lava tubes in the world which has stalagmites and stalactites, usually only found in limestone caves. In Hyeopjaegul, the stalactites and stalagmites are due to the presence of large quantities of pulverised seashells in the soil above the cave, which have been blown up from the sea shore over thousands of years. Visitors to the cave are advised to hire an umbrella in wet weather (available at the cave entrance) – it 'rains' inside the cave.

After walking 100m into Hyeopjaegul, the tunnel splits to form Ssangyonggul (twin dragon cave). However, you cannot go any further. The other caves in this area (none of which are commercialised) include Hwanggumgul, Seochongul and Jogitgul. The largest and most spectacular of these is Seochongul which is some 3km long. Its two entrances resemble a subterranean botanical garden.

Hyeopjaegul is found inside Hallim Park, which supports beautiful luxuriant subtropical plants. There's an extensive tourist complex and a mini folk village around the entrance. There is no admission fee to visit the caves, but entrance to Hallim Park costs W3500.

To get there, take a bus going along the western coastal road. You can't miss the caves, as the entrance is right by the side of the road and all buses stop here.

MYSTERY & GHOST ROADS
신비의도로, 도깨비도로

This is one of the more fun things to see on Jejudo, and you almost wonder why it isn't more heavily hyped in the tourist literature. These two roads are a curiosity because the laws of gravity seem to have been repealed. If you turn off your car's engine and put the gearbox in neutral, the vehicle appears to roll uphill. If you've arrived with a rental car, taxi or bicycle, you can test it yourself. Similarly, if you pour water on the pavement, it flows in the opposite direction you'd expect. The cause is said to be an optical illusion, but it certainly looks convincing.

The main road, called Mystery Road (Sinbi-ui Dolo), is in the hills about 7km south of the airport. Further to the east is

Ghost Road (Dokkaebi Dolo). Locals claim that a third road with this phenomenon has been discovered, though it has not yet been publicised.

HALLASAN NATIONAL PARK
한라산국립공원

Walking (or crawling) to the top of Hallasan is the finest thing you can do on Jejudo. Unfortunately, you may not get the chance – the summit of the peak has been closed to hikers since 1995. This is not, as some have claimed, because the volcano is in danger of erupting (the last eruption was 25,000 years ago). Rather, it's closed to allow the environment a chance to recover from the hordes of day-trippers who have littered the place, chopped wood and built fires to roast hot dogs and marshmallows.

By now, the environment has recovered nicely, and the national park service has said that the summit could be reopened at any time – you'll have to make local inquiries to find out what the current status is. In the meantime, visitors are only allowed to explore the lower slopes of the mountain – the upper sections of the trails are closed, the signs obvious (they are barricaded, with a big warning sign in Korean). Do not attempt to sneak past the barricades – there are big fines for doing so.

If the summit is reopened to hikers and you want to make the climb, make sure you get off to an early start. No matter how clear the skies may look in the morning, the summit is often obscured by clouds in the early afternoon, which is when you should be on the way down. Any reasonably fit person can do this trek and no special equipment is required. Just make sure you have a decent pair of jogging shoes or hiking boots and something warm (it gets remarkably windy and cold up there on top). Rain gear is also advised as the weather is very fickle.

Entry to the national park costs W2000, unless you arrive very early (before the ticket sellers come to work).

On the western side of the mountain are the two shortest **trails** leading to the summit, Yeosil (3.7km) and Orimok (4.7km). It takes the average person about 2½ hours to

HALLASAN NATIONAL PARK

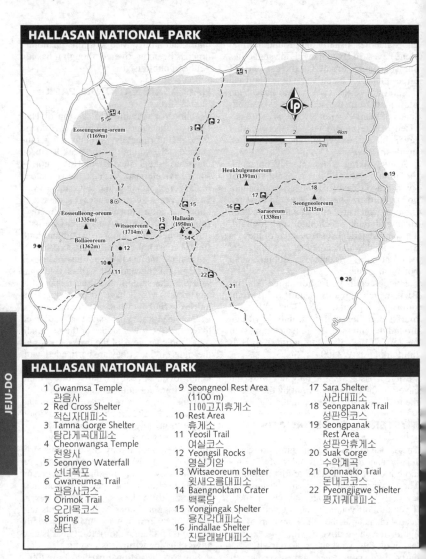

HALLASAN NATIONAL PARK

1 Gwanmsa Temple
관음사
2 Red Cross Shelter
적십자대피소
3 Tamna Gorge Shelter
탐라계곡대피소
4 Cheonwangsa Temple
천왕사
5 Seonnyeo Waterfall
선녀폭포
6 Gwaneuumsa Trail
관음사코스
7 Orimok Trail
오리목코스
8 Spring
샘터

9 Seongneol Rest Area
(1100 m)
1100고지휴게소
10 Rest Area
휴게소
11 Yeosil Trail
여실코스
12 Yeongsil Rocks
영실기암
13 Witsaeoreum Shelter
윗새오름대피소
14 Baengnoktam Crater
백록담
15 Yongjingak Shelter
용진각대피소
16 Jindallae Shelter
진달래밭대피소

17 Sara Shelter
사라대피소
18 Seongpanak Trail
성판악코스
19 Seongpanak
Rest Area
성판악휴게소
20 Suak Gorge
수악계곡
21 Donnaeko Trail
돈내코코스
22 Pyeongjigwe Shelter
평지케대피소

climb to the top along either of these and about two hours to get back down again. The Gwaneuumsa trail (8.7km) from the north and the Seongpan-ak trail (9.6km) from the east require a four to five hour slog to the summit. The Donnaeko trail from the south is the most difficult trail of all and the park service has closed it, perhaps permanently. If you have camping equipment there are several sites where you can pitch a tent. Close to all the ticket offices are places where you can buy soft drinks, snacks and even *soju* (tapioca, yam or rice 'vodka').

If you do reach the summit, you'll no doubt be delighted to find a crater lake. It is, in fact, just about the only lake on Jejudo.

There's a large and active Buddhist monastery – **Gwaneumsa** – close to the trail of the same name.

There are a number of restaurants at the start of some of the trails. The one at the start of the Seongpan-ak trail is open year round as is the one at the '1100 Metre Rest Area' about halfway between the trail entry points on the western side of the mountain (on the 2nd cross-island highway).

To reach Hallasan from Jeju-si, simply decide which trail you want to start off on and then take the appropriate bus along either the 1st or 2nd cross-island highway. Tell the driver or conductor which trail you want to go on and they'll make sure you're put down at the right spot.

Jeollabuk-do

Highlights

- Deogyusan National Park, where you'll find a valley of cascades and waterfalls, as well as the southernmost ski resort on the peninsula

- Moaksan Provincial Park, home to the attractive temple, Geumsansa

- Jeonju, birth place of the Yi dynasty and more recently Korea's only museum devoted to paper

- Naejangsan National Park, a giant amphitheatre-like landscape that is a riot of colour in autumn

- Seonunsan, a stunning provincial park

- Maisan, where a uniquely designed temple is decorated with hundreds of stacked stone formations

Jeonju p314
Deogyusan National Park p318
Byeonsanbando National Park p324
Seonunsan Provincial Park p322
Naejangsan National Park p321
Gangcheonsan County Park p320

☎ 063 • pop 2 million

Despite its small size, the western province of Jeollabuk-do has a large number of natural and cultural attractions. The province's national and provincial parks offer some of Korea's finest day hikes and scenery. It is also reputedly the home of Korea's best rice varieties and tastiest cuisine.

The province is undergoing rapid growth due to its proximity to China, with large development zones opening up to foster trade. The most ambitious of these is the Saemangeum reclamation project, off the coast near Gunsan.

JEONJU 전주

pop 611,000

Jeonju is the provincial capital of Jeollabuk-do. Its principal claim to fame is that it was the birthplace of the Yi, or Joseon, dynasty, which ruled Korea for more than 500 years (AD 1392–1910). Even today, many reminders of this past glory remain scattered around town.

Centrally located, Jeonju makes for a useful base to explore the rest of the province. There are plenty of sites in and around town that justify an overnight stay, including Jeonju National Museum, Moaksan Provincial Park, Hansol Paper Museum, Gyeongijeon, and the city's southern gate, Pungnammun. Another good reason to visit Jeonju is the tasty cuisine. For starters try *kongnamulgukbap* (rice and bean sprout soup) and *Jeonju bibimbap* (Jeonju rice and vegetable pot).

Information

There are information kiosks in front of the express bus terminal and at the entrance to the park, Gyeongijeon. There is also a well-resourced tourist information centre (☎ 322 2201) near the city hall. For more information check out the city's Web site at www.chonju.chonbuk.kr.

Hansol Paper Museum
한솔종이박물관

This beautifully presented museum not only traces the historical development of paper in Korea and throughout the world, but provides an interesting mix of digital and interactive displays. For the curious, it's also possible to try your hand at making paper the traditional Korean way, or even trying

JEOLLABUK-DO

312

Woman and granddaughter harvest sea grass.

Admiral Yi Sun-shin gazes over Busan harbour.

Korea's largest, busiest seaport, Busan harbour

Rising to 118m, Busan Tower in Yongdusan Park

Busan: There's many ways to move freight.

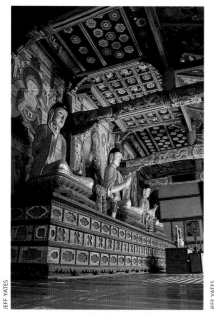

Seonunsa, in a camellia forest, Jeollabuk-do

Seonunsan Provincial Park, Jeollabuk-do

Seonunsan Provincial Park, a 500-year-old camellia forest featuring the temple Seonunsa

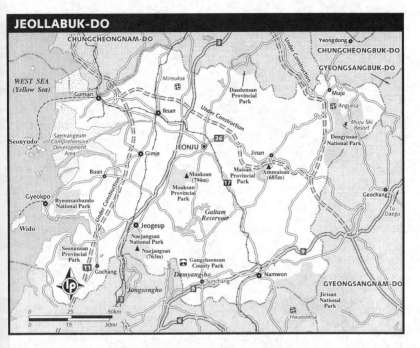

JEOLLABUK-DO

jong-ijeopgi (origami). Despite the lack of English descriptions for the exhibits, most visitors will find this museum visually informative and entertaining (free admission, closed Monday).

Paper making classes and demos are held every day except the 2nd and 4th Friday of the month. For more information see the museum's Web site at www.hansol.co.kr/eng lish/emain/paper.html. The museum is inside the grounds of the Pan Asia Paper Company (PAPCO) in the north-west of Jeonju; catch bus No 165 or hop in a taxi.

Gyeongijeon 경기전
This picturesque urban park contains a hall where a portrait of King Taejo is enshrined, surrounded by a collection of palanquins that were used for official ceremonies. On the same grounds is an intriguing **stupa** and stele where the placenta of King Yejong (1468–69) is buried. Entry to the park costs W400.

Pungnammun
This impressive gate is all that is left of Jeonju's original city wall and four gates. First built in 1398, but destroyed in 1597, 1734 and 1767, the gate maintains a prominent position in the centre of Jeonju.

Jeonju National Museum
전주국립박물관

The museum houses a wide range of historical and archaeological relics, fine arts and folklore displays, which reflect the central place of Jeonju during the Mahan, Baekje and Joseon periods. Entry costs W400 (9 am to 6 pm, closed Mondays).

The museum is 5km south-west of town and can be reached by either bus No 66 or taxi.

Jeonju Confucian School 전주향교
This picturesque complex of Confucian halls and shrines is in a little-visited southeast corner of Jeonju. Two very impressive

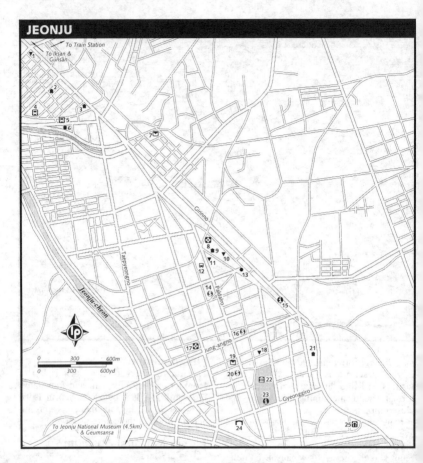

JEONJU

400-year-old gingko trees complement the pretty gardens. The buildings were originally located in the central palace, in the centre of town, but were moved to the hills as a result of complaints from neighbours about the rowdiness of students. The school was later returned to its present location for convenience. Nowadays, calligraphy classes are held only on weekends and public holidays.

The entrance is tucked away at the back to the left, and you may need to knock on one of the main buildings to obtain the key to the rest of the complex.

Deokjin Park & Jeonju Deokjin Art Hall

Located in the north of town, this expansive park was established to improve the geomantic value (see the Geomancy section in the Facts about Korea chapter) of Jeonju. The best time to visit is in August and September when the lake's white lotuses are flowering. The main entrance is on the south-western side of the park (W500).

Just 150m from the park entrance is the Jeonju Deokjin Art Hall, where free traditional music and dance performances are held every Saturday at 3pm.

JEONJU

PLACES TO STAY
2 Hanguk Motel
   한국모텔
3 Sydney Motel
   시드니모텔
6 Munhwatang
   Yeogwan
   문화탕여관
9 Koa Hotel (Core Hotel)
   코아호텔
21 Riviera Hotel
   리베라호텔

PLACES TO EAT
1 Hangukgwan
   한국관
10 Yennaleneun
   옛날에는
11 Gohyang sancheon
   고향산천

18 Waeng-i haejanggukjip
   왱이해장국집

OTHER
4 Express Bus Terminal
   고속버스터미널
5 Inter-City Bus
   Terminal
   시외버스터미널
7 Post Office
   우체국
8 Core Department
   Store
   코아백화점
12 Bus Stop
   버스정류장
13 City Hall
   시청
14 Hanvit Bank
   한빛은행

15 Tourist Information
   Centre
   관광안내센터
16 Korea Exchange Bank
   외환은행
17 Hanareum Department
   Store
   한아름백화점
19 Post Office
   우체국
20 Hanvit Bank
   한빛은행
22 Gyeongijeon
   경기전
23 Information Booth
   관광안내소
24 Pungnammun
   풍남문
25 Jeonju Hyanggyo
   전주향교

Places to Stay

Opposite the inter-city bus terminal, **Munhwatang Yeogwan** (☎ 276 9261) is a little town, but good value at W20,000. There are plenty of options behind the express and inter-city bus terminals, including **Hanguk Motel** (☎ 254 5880) and **Sydney Motel** (☎ 255 3311), which both charge W25,000 for decent rooms.

The deluxe accommodation in town includes **Core Hotel** (☎ 285 1100, fax 285 5707), where twins cost W100,000 and suites range from W145,000 to W500,000 (plus 20% tax and surcharge), and **Riviera Jeonju** (☎ 232 7000, fax 232 7100), with rooms from W145,000 to W190,000.

Places to Eat

Waeng-i Haejanggukjip is a modest affair that only serves one dish, *kongnamulguk-bap*. This is a spicy bowl of beansprouts, egg, squid, onion, *gimchi* (spicy fermented cabbage) and rice brewed in a stock made from seaweed, radish and dried fish (W3000). It's very popular with the locals who drop in around the clock. The restaurant is opposite a large off-white two-storey building.

Yennaleneun..., which means 'Once upon a time...', is easily recognisable by its traditional-style facade and interior. The barbecued *saenggogi* (fresh pork; W5,000)

is succulent and delicious. And, when it's in season, you must try the Jirisan *heuk-dwaeji* (black pig). The prices are reasonable and the servings generous.

Gohyang Sancheon is another sit-down BBQ restaurant that serves a tasty *bulgogi* (Korean barbecue) and *galbi*, which is similar to bulgogi, although it uses short ribs instead of strips of beef. The restaurant is just down a lane, near the Core Hotel.

Hangukgwan specialises in *Jeonju bibimbap* (a bed of rice with gimchi, vegetables, meat and a dollop of hot chilli on top; W6000), which is recognised as one of Korea's three representative dishes (the others being *Pyeongyang naengmyeon* and *Gaesong tangban*, or cold buckwheat noodles). The restaurant is a 10-minute walk from the bus terminals in the northwest of town.

Getting There & Away

Bus Destinations from the express bus terminal include:

destination	price (W)	duration	distance
Daegu	8500	3¾ hrs	220km
Daejeon	3500	1¼ hrs	97km
Dong Seoul	9300	2¾ hrs	246km
Gwangju	4100	1¾ hrs	106km
Seoul	8900	3¼ hrs	232km

JEOLLABUK-DO

Departures from the inter-city bus terminal include:

destination	price (W)	duration	distance
Busan	2800	1 hr	44km
Gochang	3800	1½ hrs	71km
Gurye	5700	2 hrs	113km
Hwaeomsa	6100	3½ hrs	117km
Jinan	2500	50 mins	37km
Muju	5200	2½ hrs	86km

Getting Around

Bus No 79-1 departs from the bus terminal area to Moaksan Provincial Park, but it also travels through the town centre, so it's useful for getting around town. Jeonju's buses take a while to work out – the town is small enough to make the use of taxis affordable and more convenient.

AROUND JEONJU
Moaksan Provincial Park
모악산도립공원

The hike up Moaksan (794m) is quite enjoyable, but the big attraction here is the temple, **Geumsansa**. It can be traced back as far as AD 599. There are a number of unusual buildings on the temple grounds, including the curiously shaped pagoda in front of the main hall, **Mireukjeon**. The hall has endured the usual destruction and repairs, but still retains an air of antiquity, highlighted by the fading murals.

The most popular climbing route to the peak, **Janggunjae**, is a circular trail (three hours) that continues past Geumsansa, along the valley and then up to the peak. Follow the ridge for another 40 minutes up to Moaksan. At the peak there are three main paths, but if you follow the northwestern path and keep to the left, it will take an hour to descend back to the Simwonam Hermitage, and from there to the main trail.

There is a *camping ground* close to Geumsansa, near Maningyo Bridge, or there are plenty of *minbak* and *yeogwan* near the bus stop.

Sanjungdawon, a pleasant teahouse in front of the temple serves up a variety of teas, including *yuja cha* (citron tea, W3000) and *dachu cha* (jujube tea, W4000) accompanied by some *dasik* (small snacks). They even have comfy rocking chairs.

Admission to Moaksan Provincial Park costs W2000. The park is easily reached on bus No 78-1 (25 minutes, half-hourly) from the bus stop near the Core Hotel.

DAEDUNSAN PROVINCIAL PARK
대둔산도립공원

Yet another beautiful park, Daedunsan offers craggy peaks with spectacular views over the surrounding countryside. Although relatively small, it's one of Korea's most scenic mountain areas.

Aside from the views, the climb to the summit of **Daedunsan** (878m) along steep, stony tracks is an adventure in itself. The main attraction for many Korean hikers is the 50m-long cable bridge stretched precariously between two rock pinnacles, followed by an incredibly steep and long steel cable stairway. Vertigo sufferers should stick to the boulder-strewn trail instead!

It's a very popular place on weekends with locals, as well as those from farther afield, huffing and puffing their way to the summit loaded with goodies for the inevitable picnic. On these precarious slopes you'll even meet amazing *halabeoji* (grandfathers) and *halmeoni* (grandmothers) ascending the heights so rapidly that it makes the younger folks lose face (*chemyeoni ansonda*).

There is a refreshing spring *(yaksuteo)* to the right, above the half-way rest area.

The ascent will take between two and 2½ hours for any reasonably fit person and about one hour for the descent. For the less active, a cable car can take you up past the steepest ascent (W2300/3500 one way, return). Entry to the park costs W1300.

Places to Stay & Eat

Free camping is available below the open space next to *Daedunsan Tourist Hotel* (☎ 263 1260, fax 263 8069). This hotel is the most luxurious option available, with hot-spring water pumped into your bath tub. The rooms are clean and spacious. *Ondol* rooms (with underfloor heating) cost W65,000 and twins cost W70,000. If you aren't a guest it's still possible to pay a visit to their sauna (W5000).

Nadeulmoksanjang (☎ 262 7170) has been renovated recently, with rooms starting from W20,000. There are half a dozen other *yeogwan* nearby, with similar prices and standards.

There is the usual string of restaurants serving the usual *sanchae bibimbap* (rice and mountain greens). Snacks like *beondegi* (silkworm larvae) and *mettugi* (grasshoppers) are available or, for the less adventurous, there's always ice cream.

Getting There & Away
By bus, Daedunsan is most easily reached from either Jeonju (W3400, 70 minutes, 52km, every 40 minutes) or Daejeon seobu (W1900, 50 minutes, 38km, every 1½ hours).

MAISAN PROVINCIAL PARK
마이산도립공원

Maisan means 'Horse Ears Mountain', a rough description of the shape of the two rocky outcrops that make up the twin peaks, or Mai-bong. The east peak, Sutmaisan, is considered male and reaches a height of 678m. The west peak, Ammaisan, is regarded as female and is slightly taller at 685m.

Tapsa (Pagoda Temple) is stuck right between the two 'horse ears'. It's a temple of unique design, decorated by hundreds of stone formations of rocks stacked on top of one another.

For the best views, climb up the small path to the summit of Ammaisan, which is to the left of the souvenir stands when descending from the main temple.

Admission to the park costs W1400.

Getting There & Away
Bus transport is via the tiny town of Jinan at the park's entrance. From Jinan buses to Tapsa run every 30 minutes (W500, 10 minutes, 4km). The bus schedule from Jinan is:

destination	price (W)	duration	distance
Daegu	8500	4 hrs	154km
Daejeon	5100	2½ hrs	87km
Jeonju	2500	40 mins	37km
Seoul	10,200	4 hrs	281km

DEOGYUSAN NATIONAL PARK
덕유산국립공원

The main highlights of this park include the ancient mountain fortress of Jeoksansanseong, Gucheon-dong Valley and Muju Ski Resort. Gucheon-dong is the main tourist village, located at the southern (upper) end of a 30km long valley.

From Gucheon-dong, a trail (1¾ hours, 6km) runs south up Gucheon-dong Valley, a beautiful landscape of cascades, pools and waterfalls, to the small temple of Baengnyeonsa. Keep an eye out for the fairies that inhabit this valley. The trail up the valley continues past Baengnyeonsa for a 1½ hour ascent of the fourth highest peak in South Korea, Deogyusan (1614m), or Hyangjeokbong as it's also known. The view from the peak is rewarding and if you visit in spring it is covered in azalea blossoms.

In the north-west of the park is **Jeoksansanseong**, a fortress that dates back to the Goryeo dynasty (918–1392); but most of what you see today was built during the 17th century. Inside the fortress walls is **Anguksa**, some ruins and a reservoir. There are three main entrances to the fortress, with the most challenging following a gruelling zigzag path (two hours) from the town of Jeoksang, which is 8.5km south of the township of Muju.

It is also possible to hike from Gucheon-dong to Anguksa (seven hours, 18km) along a beautiful trail/road. The fortress is certainly less popular than Gucheon-dong, making for a more peaceful visit, but transport can be a problem. Local buses run to Bukchang-ri and Jeoksang from Muju, but you might find a taxi more expedient. Admission to Jeoksansanseong costs W1,000.

Admission to the national park costs W750/1300 for students/adults and W380 for children.

Muju Ski Resort 무주스키리조트
Opened in 1990, Muju Ski Resort (☎ 322 9000, fax 322 9993) has become one of the most popular ski resorts in Korea, attracting both Korean and foreign visitors. Despite being the most southerly resort on the peninsula, the resort has a good range of

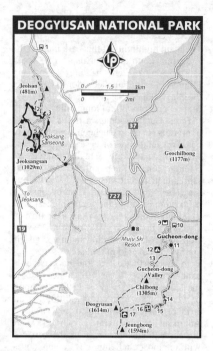

DEOGYUSAN NATIONAL PARK

PLACES TO STAY
8 Tirol Hotel
   티롤호텔
12 Deokyudae Camping
   Ground
   덕유대야영장
17 Hyangjeokbong Shelter
   향적봉대피소

OTHER
 1 Bus Stop
   버스정류장
 2 Bukmun
   북문
 3 Lookout
   전망대
 4 Seomun
   서문
 5 Anguksa
   안국사
 6 Nammun
   남문
 7 Jimok Village
   지목
 9 Post Office
   우체국
10 Bus Stop
   버스정류장
11 Wolhatan Pavillion
   월하탄
13 Spring
   약수
14 Gucheon Rapids
   구천폭
15 Yeonhwa Rapids
   연화폭
16 Baengryeonsa
   백련사

slopes from beginner to advanced, with the longest run over 6km in length. There are 23 ski slopes, including a freestyle course and 15 ski lifts. Snowboarding is presently allowed on all slopes. The two main areas are Mansonbong and the Solchonbong ski ranges. The ski season runs from late November to late March.

An all day skiing package including lift pass, skis, poles and boots starts from W50,000. The ski school conducts day classes in English with prior arrangement. Reasonable ski packages are available from the tourist village of Kucheon-dong.

Free shuttle buses make the run up to the resort hourly from the car park opposite the bus stop at Kucheon-dong.

Places to Stay

The Austrian-style *Tirol Hotel* (☎ 320 7617, fax 320 7609) is *the* abode if you want to stay in comfort. This super-deluxe option has an incredible array of luxury suites available for those willing to splash out, ranging from W270,000 to over W300,000. For the less indulgent, their deluxe and premier rooms are a bit cheaper at W220,000 and W250,000, respectively. Don't forget to add an extra 10% service charge and 10% tax. Packages are available, providing reasonable discounts. The resort also boasts a number of Western-style restaurants and discounts on skiing facilities.

There are two designated camping grounds in the park, one at Samgong-ri near Gucheon-dong (W2200 per person) and a larger one at Deogyu at the eastern edge of the park near Songgyesa. Back-country camping and cooking are prohibited.

Samgong-ri is a kilometre north of Gucheon-dong and there are yeogwan here costing around W15,000.

More expensive *yeogwan* can be found in Gucheon-dong, close to the bus stop and tourist shops. You can expect to pay from W20,000 to W30,000.

Minbak accommodation is on offer and chances are good that you'll be greeted at the bus stop by several *ajumma* (a term of respect for a woman who runs a restaurant or hotel) offering you a place to stay for around W15,000.

Upmarket accommodation is offered at the *Muju Resort* (☎ 324-9000), where rooms cost a mere W150,000. The resort is 4km from Gucheon-dong and accessible by bus.

Getting There & Away

Bus Muju is the main gateway to the park, though you can also get there from Yeongdong in Chungcheongnam-do province. Buses frequently depart Muju for Gucheon-dong (W2300), though you can do this same trip by taxi for around W18,000. Buses to Jeoksang (W600, half-hourly) depart from Muju. If you're heading to Anguksa (W800, eight daily) from Muju, take the bus and get off at Naechang and then walk.

The bus schedule from Muju is:

destination	price (W)	duration	distance
Daegu	8900	2¾ hrs	128km
Daejeon dongbu	4000	2 hrs	65km
Gwangju	9700	3¾ hrs	163km
Jeonju	5200	2¼ hrs	99km
Seoul	8900	3¼ hrs	255km

JEONGEUP 정읍
pop 151,000

The main reason for coming to Jeongeup is to get to neighbouring Naejangsan National Park or to Seonunsan Provincial Park, which is slightly further afield.

Getting There & Away

Bus Jeongeup's express bus terminal and inter-city bus terminal are on opposite sides of the same complex. Express buses depart regularly for Seoul (W10,800, 3¾ hours,

289km, every 50–70 minutes). Inter-city departures include:

destination	price (W)	duration	distance
Busan[*]	2200	40 mins	37km
Daegu	12,700	5 hrs	232km
Daejeon	5400	1¾ hrs	120km
Gimje[**]	2300	1 hr	38km
Gochang[***]	1700	¾ hr	29km
Gwangju	2900	1¼ hrs	58km
Jeonju	2400	1 hr	45km
Sunchang[****]	3300	40 mins	60km

[*]for Byeonsanbando National Park
[**]for Byeonsanbando National Park
[***]for Seonunsan Provincial Park
[****]for Gangcheonsan County Park

Train Trains between Jeongeup and Seoul include Saemaeul (W17,400, three hours, eight daily) and Mugunghwa (W12,000, 3¾ hours, 18 daily).

GANGCHEONSAN COUNTY PARK
강천산군립공원

Close to the Jeollabuk-do border, this small park is home to a very pleasant hike along a scenic valley of cascades, maple and bamboo forests, waterfalls, lakes and the temple, **Gangcheonsa**. Above the temple are steep cliffs crowned with an ancient and crumbling **fortress**.

You can combine all these sights in a popular two-hour walk along the valley and up to the fortress. There isn't any water once you begin ascending, so take some along.

There are a couple of minbak, including *Gangcheonsan Hotel* (☎ 652 9920) in the tourist village. Entry to the park costs W800.

Access to Gangcheonsan is via the small town of Sunchang; from where buses run from the terminal (W600, every 50 minutes). There are also direct buses to the park from Gwangju (W3200, hourly) and Jeonju (W4200, four daily).

NAEJANGSAN NATIONAL PARK
내장산국립공원

It's easy to see why this area was named Naejangsan (Inner Treasure Mountains) – the landscape is formed like an amphitheatre.

JEOLLABUK-DO

GANGCHEONSAN COUNTY PARK

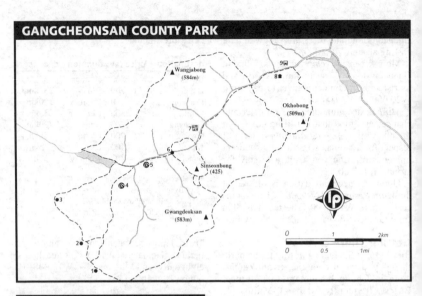

GANGCHEONSAN COUNTY PARK

1 Dongmun
   동문
2 Bukbawi
   북바위
3 Songnakbawi
   송낙바위
4 Biryongpokpo
   비룡폭포
5 Gujanggunpokpo
   구장군폭포
6 Suspension Bridge
   현수교
7 Gangcheonsa
   강천사
8 Gangcheonsan Hotel
   강천산호텔
9 Bus Stop
   버스정류장

There is an interesting visitor's centre below Naejangsa (closed Tuesdays) that has some information on the flora and fauna of the area. Maps are also available here and the staff might recommend some hikes. Admission to the park costs W2000.

A spider web of trails leads up to the amphitheatre rim. One of the most beautiful passes Naejangsa, then continues through Geumseon Valley up to Kkachibong (2¼ hours). Once you've climbed to the rim, you can walk all the way to the other side, though it's strenuous. There are ladders to help hikers master the cliffs, and the views are just amazing all around. It takes at least three hours to walk the circuit, but try to allow for more. There are several trails that approach the ridge, all taking between 40 minutes and an hour.

Temples in the park include **Naejangsa** and **Baegyangsa**. Other sights spread out all over this large park include **Geumseon** and **Wonjeok valleys**, a cave, **Yonggul**, and a **cable-car** ride over the forest canopy.

There is a shuttle bus (W600) that runs the kilometre between the park entrance and Naejangsa, but the walk along the stream is much more pleasant. If your legs are not up to ascending, then catch the cable car (W1700/2500 one way/return) from in front of the information centre up to the pavilion, **Jeonmangdae**. There is a kiosk here that sells food and plastic touristy things.

Places to Stay

There is *camping* (W3000) below the tourist village and just outside the park

The crowning glory of Silla architecture, Bulguksa

Pavilion, Jogyesan Provincial Park, Jeollanam-do

Picturesque Bulguksa, Gyeongsangbuk-do

Detail from a sea of tiled roofs, Bulguksa

Gyeongju: Tongiljeon (Unification Hall)

Beautiful, and crowded: Daedunsan, Jeollabuk-do

You can see forever on the old fortress wall with gate in Gochang, Jeollabuk-do.

NAEJANGSAN NATIONAL PARK

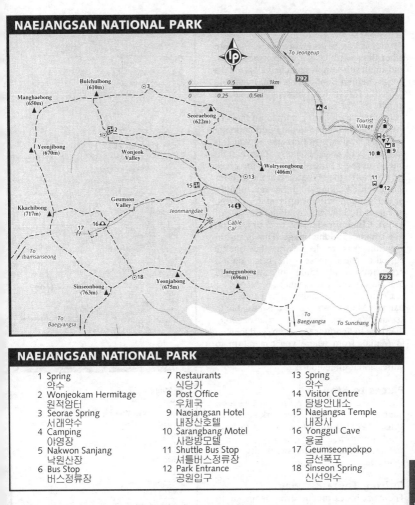

NAEJANGSAN NATIONAL PARK

1 Spring
약수

2 Wonjeokam Hermitage
원적암터

3 Seorae Spring
서래약수

4 Camping
야영장

5 Nakwon Sanjang
낙원산장

6 Bus Stop
버스정류장

7 Restaurants
식당가

8 Post Office
우체국

9 Naejangsan Hotel
내장산호텔

10 Sarangbang Motel
사랑방모텔

11 Shuttle Bus Stop
셔틀버스정류장

12 Park Entrance
공원입구

13 Spring
약수

14 Visitor Centre
탐방안내소

15 Naejangsa Temple
내장사

16 Yonggul Cave
용굴

17 Geumseonpokpo
금선폭포

18 Sinseon Spring
신선약수

boundary. There are dozens of *minbak* above the *restaurants*.

The place with the green roof, *Nakwon Sanjang* (☎ 322 3155), is good value. It's the last yeogwan behind the bus stop up the hill. Rooms cost W25,000 and W35,000. *Sarangbang Motel* (☎ 538 8186) is very clean and new, with rooms for W30,000. *Naejangsan Tourist Hotel* (☎ 538 4140 fax 538 4138) has comfortable rooms from W88,430 to W495,041, plus 20% tax. During the low season you can get 40% off these rates.

Getting There & Away

Naejangsan is best reached from the town of Jeongeup (W750, 25 minutes, 13km, every 20–30 minutes). The Jeongeup-Gwangju bus passes by the temple Baegyangsa on the hour.

SEONUNSAN PROVINCIAL PARK
선운산도립공원

Seonunsan is a gorgeous place. Among other things it boasts a temple, Seonunsa, and small sub-temples perched all around a gorge. Behind Seonunsa is a 500-year-old camellia forest that blossoms around the middle of April.

It is worthwhile to continue up the valley beyond Seonunsa to the **Buddha image** just past Dosulam Hermitage. As you follow the path past Seonunsa, take a right once you see a little shop across the creek (to your left), then take a left at the next intersection. Walking a further ten minutes past Dosulam will bring you to a large image of Buddha engraved into the side of a cliff. Climb the stairway to your right up to a **smaller Buddha image**. This beautiful creation was made during the Baekje period by the Chinese – the artists built a precarious scaffolding of sticks and branches in order to create it.

Continue on beyond the relief to **Gaeippalsan** (345m) from where it is possible to see the West Sea. The path carries on along the ridge to **Seonunsan** (336m) and then on to **Maijal**, from where you can return to Seonunsa. This pleasant circuit walk requires about three hours.

Places to Stay
There is a camping ground plus several minbak and yeogwan in the park near Seonunsa. ***Seonunsan Youth Hostel (☎ 561 3333, sonunsan@lycos.co.kr)*** is quite new and has both dorm rooms and family rooms available.

Getting There & Away
There are buses running from Jeongeup to the park at 9.50 and 10.50 am, and at 1.55, 3.00, 5.10, 6.00 and 6.50 pm. Buses also run between the park and Gochang (W1300, 30 minutes, 22km, half-hourly) and Gwangju (W4200, two hours, 72km, hourly). Do not confuse Gochang with Geochang – the latter is in the province, Gyeongsangnam-do, halfway between Gwangju and Daegu. Connections from Gochang include:

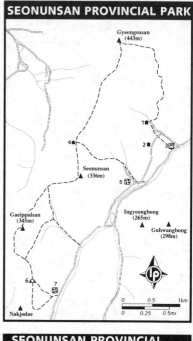

SEONUNSAN PROVINCIAL PARK

SEONUNSAN PROVINCIAL PARK

1 Minbak Village
   민박촌
2 Seonunsan Youth Hostel
   선운산유스호스텔
3 Bus Terminal
   버스터미널
4 Maijae
   마이재
5 Seonunsa
   선운사
6 Yongmungul
   용문굴
7 Dosolam
   도솔암

destination	price (W)	duration	distance
Gwangju	2800	1¼ hrs	47km
Jeonju	3800	1½ hrs	70km
Seoul	10,800	3¾ hrs	290km

BYEONSANBANDO NATIONAL PARK 변산반도국립공원

The park occupies a peninsula in the extreme western part of Jeollabuk-do. It's dotted with temples, such as Naesosa and Gaeamsa. The park's highest peak is Sabyeonsan (492m). The park is divided into Outer-Byeonsan, covering the coastal areas, and Inner-Byeonsan, the mountainous and forested section.

A good day-hike could start at Naesosa and continue up to the peak, Gwaneumbong, and then down to the waterfall, **Jiksopokpo**, before hiking through Bongnae Valley, up to Nakjodae and down to Namyeoji, then carrying on along the road to the bus stop at Jiseo-ri. This should take about five or six hours.

On the north side of the park is **Byeonsan Beach**, one of the cleanest sandy beaches on the west coast. It's absolutely amazing to see the change of tides here – at low tide you can almost walk to distant offshore islands.

Admission to Byeonsanbando National Park costs from W1000 to W2000.

There are *yeogwan* near Naesosa and also at Byeonsan Beach that generally charge W25,000 (or double this during summer). *Camping* is allowed on the beach.

Getting There & Away

From Jeongeup there are buses to Naesosa (W2200, every 40 minutes) or Buan (W2200, every 30 minutes). Buan is a major transit point, with buses to Byeonsan Beach that terminate at Chaeseokgang (W1600, 40 minutes, every 10 minutes). You can get to Buan from Jeonju (W2800, every 10 minutes), Jeongeup (W2200, every 30 minutes) or Seoul (W10,300, every 50 minutes).

GUNSAN 군산

pop 280,000

Gunsan is a rapidly growing harbour city that is at the forefront of the massive

---

Comprehensive Development Area

The Saemangeum project in Byeonsanbando National Park is believed to be world's largest reclamation project, covering an area of over 40,000 hectares. With the construction of a 33km sea wall soon completed, the fate of the project is probably already sealed, much to the disappointment of NGOs opposed to the project. The main proponents of the project are the Ministry of Construction and the regional governments, who hope that the reclaimed land will be used for rice cultivation and an industrial development complex.

The main opposition to the project comes from the Korean Federation of Environmental Movement (KFEM) and the Wetlands Alliance, who are trying to stop the project on environmental grounds. In addition to being an important wetlands for migratory birds, the area is an fish breeding ground that is rich in nutrients, marine resources, and is an enormous storage tank of biomass. However, they have discovered it is hard to stir-up people's emotions about tidal mud flats and migratory birds.

The issue has only been able to garner a small amount of support outside of these two environmental NGOs, which is in contrast to the groundswell of support that rose to oppose the construction of the Yeongwol Dam (see the boxed text 'Yeongwol Dam Conflict' in the Gangwon-do chapter for more details). The Ministry of Environment only recently conducted a survey of Korea's migratory birds and discovered that the Saemangeum area is one of the most important in Korea for a wide range of bird species. However, this arm of government would be discouraged from voicing too many conservation opinions due to the seniority and superiority of the Ministry of Construction in government.

Interestingly, the reclamation project mirrors similar efforts carried out in Japan, where land is equally intensively farmed and there are also enormous resources poured into the country's rice production and construction industry. The reclaiming and landfilling of the Fujimae tidal flats near Nagoya is causing a similar controversy in Japan and it will be interesting to see how the two projects pan out.

For an environmentally aware perspective on the project, visit KFEM and the Korean Wetland's Alliance Web site (wetland.kfem.or.kr).

BYEONSANBANDO NATIONAL PARK

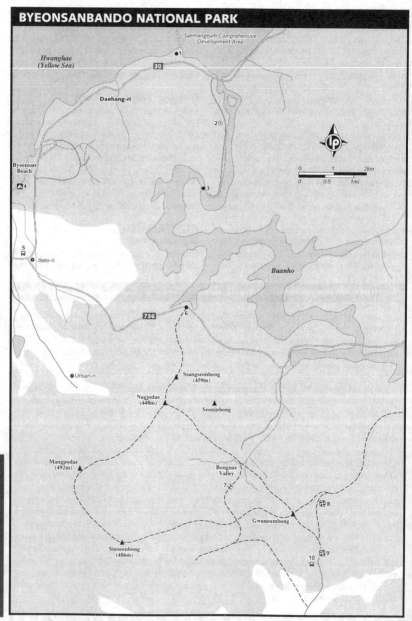

Saemangeum Comprehensive
Development Area

*Hwanghae
(Yellow Sea)*

Daehang-ri

Byeonsan
Beach

Jiseo-ri

Unsan-ri

Buanho

Ssangseonbong
(459m)

Nagjodae
(448m)

Seoninbong

Mangpodae
(492m)

Bongnae
Valley

Gwaneumbong

Sinseonbong
(486m)

JEOLLABUK-DO

BYEONSANBANDO NATIONAL PARK

1 Saemangeum Exhibition 새만금전시장	5 Bus Stop 버스정류장	9 Naesosa 내소사
2 Byeonsan Hot Spring 변산온천	6 Namyeoji 남여지	10 Bus Stop 버스정류장
3 Buan Dam 부안댐	7 Jiksopokpo 직소폭포	
4 Camping Ground 야영장	8 Cheongryeonam 청련암	

Saemangeum reclamation project. The main reason for coming here is to either catch a ferry to Seonyudo or further afield to Weihai in China's Shandong province.

Places to Stay & Eat

Jeil-jang Yeogwan (☎ 446 3227) is behind the bus terminal. Good rooms are W25,000.

Next to the motel are a row of tent restaurant bars (*bojangmacha*) serving up a lot of seafood and a heap of *soju* (yam or tapioca 'vodka') and beer. You will find some cheap and reliable restaurants just opposite the bus terminal.

Getting There & Away

Bus There are bus connections to:

destination	price (W)	duration	distance
Daejeon seobu	5400	1½ hrs	97km
Dong Seoul	9400	3¾ hrs	248km
Jeonju	3000	1 hr	48km

Boat Ferries depart from Gunsan's ferry terminal – Gunsan Yeogaek Terminal – to Seonyudo (W11,700, two hours). The ferry timetable changes monthly according to the tides and demand. Check with the KNTO for more details.

AROUND GUNSAN
Seonyudo 선유도

A 43km ferry trip from Gunsan brings you to the pretty island of Seonyudo. The fine sand of its **beaches** is the main attraction, but there also some enjoyable **hikes** around the island and into its interior. The highest peak on the island, **Mangjubong**, rewards you with great views of the island and the surrounding sea. It is also possible to walk to **Mangjupokpo**, a series of 10 waterfalls.

Seonyudo is connected to the neighbouring islands of Munyeodo and Jangjado by bridge and may eventually be connected with the mainland when the Saemangeum land reclamation project is complete.

The main town is a 10-minute walk from the jetty, where you can find a couple of *yeogwan* and *minbak*. A new large yeogwan has just been built – inquire locally for prices. There are lots of minbak, such as *Jung-ang Minbak* (☎ 465 3450) and *Seohae Minbak* (☎ 465 8787), both of which have rooms with shower and toilet for W20,000. Prices rise during the summer months.

It is possible to walk to most places on the island, or you could hire a fishing boat for the day. This is an affordable option if you join a group (W10,000 per person).

JEOLLABUK-DO

Chungcheongnam-do

Highlights

- Buyeo, a quiet provincial town and site of the last capital of the Baekje kingdom
- Gongju, the second capital of the Baekje kingdom, houses a rich collection of tombs of the Baekje kings
- Gyeryongsan National Park, home of the picturesque temples Gapsa and Dong-haksa
- Gaesimsa, a remote and beautiful temple tucked away in a secluded valley
- Sapsido, a peaceful island where life moves at a stately pace
- Deoksan, a mountain of incredibly varied scenery and home to the historical temple Sudeoks

☎ 041 pop 3.3 million

Chungcheongnam-do was the base of the Baekje kingdom (see the History section in the Facts about Korea chapter). It houses a rich collection of cultural assets from the period in museums, intriguing tombs and fortresses. Scattered across the province are scenic mountain areas, such as Gyeryongsan National Park, which is covered in challenging hiking trails and timeless temples.

DAEJEON 대전

☎ 042 • pop 1.4 million

Promoted as the science and technology capital of Korea, Daejeon's claim to fame was hosting Expo'93. Today, in an attempt to reduce pressure on Seoul, the city is an expanse of high-rise apartments and home to a growing number of public servants. Daejeon is an important transport hub, sitting at the junction where Korea's main north-south train line and expressway split for the south-west and south-east of the peninsula.

Information

There is a tourist information booth inside Daejeon train station that supplies maps of Daejeon and Chungcheongnam-do. There is also a kiosk out the front of the Daejeon express bus terminal, but it seems to keep irregular hours.

Bomunsan 보문산

Daejeon is encircled by a ring of mountains that not only traps most of the city's smog, but fortunately also provides a scenic backdrop. One of the most accessible of these mountains is Bomunsan, a small mountain park on the southern side of town. The park is a popular recreational area for the locals, especially on weekends. In addition to having the highest peak in the province (457m) it has numerous temples, hermitages and fun parks scattered around the area.

Bus No 310 (W630, 10 minutes) from Daejeon train station, brings you to within walking distance. A taxi (W2000) is more convenient as it will drop you at the entrance to the park, saving the ten minute walk from the bus stop. There is an information board at the main entrance with a large, detailed map of the park. The main path to the peak, and to the mountain fortress **Bomunsanseong,** starts just to the left of this board. If you would rather avoid the steep path, then continue along

CHUNGCHEONGNAM-DO

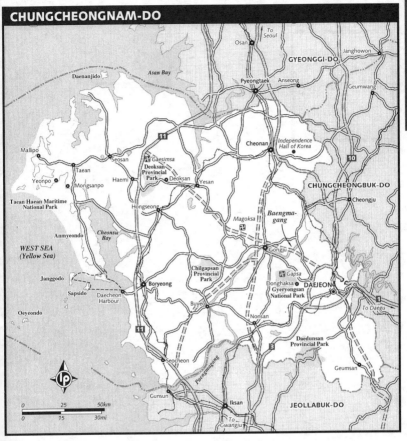

the winding road or ride the cable car up to the **observation lookout**.

Yuseong Hot Springs 유성온천
Just 10km west of downtown Daejeon, near the Honam Expressway, is the hot springs resort of Yuseong. There really isn't much here other than a collection of large, fancy and expensive hotels where you can soak in luxurious indoor pools. If you're not a guest at one of the hotels, you can still have a soak, but expect to pay around W6000. From Daejeon train station you can reach Yuseong in 30 minutes on bus No 102 (W600).

Daejeon Expo Science Park
대전엑스포공원

Although Expo'93 has come and gone, most of its buildings and car parks remain preserved in one form or another. The park has been officially designated a 'special tourism zone' – whatever that means. The best time to visit is during the annual Daejeon Science Festival, which takes place in August – check with KNTO (see Tourist Offices in the Facts for the Visitor chapter) for details. With the exception of public holidays, when there are a trickle of visitors, the park would make a great setting for a B-grade horror film.

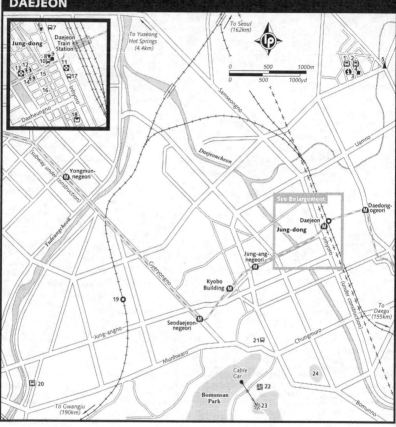

DAEJEON

Budding directors should catch bus No 105 (W600), which passes the train station.

Places to Stay

Most travellers don't stay long in Daejeon but, if you get stuck, there are a couple of reasonable options around the express and inter-city bus stations.

The *Daejeon Park* (☎ 631 2728) is to the left as you exit the express bus terminal and charges W25,000 for good clean rooms with bathrooms. Reception is on the 3rd floor.

Near the train station are a number of yeogwan, all of which compete to look the most run-down. The lane opposite the station is the most yeogwan-congested, with *Hamajang Yeogwan* and *Ilryeok-jang Yeogwan*, both charging a pricey W25,000 a room.

Most of Daejeon's better hotels are 10km to the west of the town centre at Yuseong Hot Springs. The *Adria* (☎ 824 0211, fax 823 5805; Bongmyeong-dong) and the *Riviera Yuseong* (☎ 823 2111, fax 822 0071; Bongmyeong-dong) are top-end hotels. They have doubles going for W100,000 and W140,000, respectively. Both have large mineral spring bathing pools, open to non-guests as well.

DAEJEON

PLACES TO STAY
4 Daejeon Park
대전파크
9 Hama-jang; Ilyeok-jang Yeogwan
하마장여관,일력장여관

PLACES TO EAT
6 Bakery Roma
로마베이커리
8 Bongojang Udong
본고장우동

OTHER
1 Express Bus Terminal
고속버스터미널
2 Dongbu Inter-City Bus Terminal
동부시외버스터미널
3 Tourist Information
관광안내소

5 Daejeon Tower
대전타워
7 Bus Stop for Nos 851,860 & 888 to Express and Dongbu Bus Terminal
버스정류장
10 Bus Stop for Nos 102 & 105 to Yuseong Oncheon and no 841 to Seobu Bus Terminal
버스정류장
11 Agricultural Cooperative Supermarket
농협수퍼마켓
12 Commercial Bank
상업은행
13 Dongbang Mart
동방마트
14 Hanvit Bank
한빛은행
15 Underground Arcade
지하상가

16 Jung-ang Market
중앙시장
17 Bus Stop for No 310 to Bomunsan
버스정류장
18 Central Post Office
중앙우체국
19 Seodaejeon Train Station
서대전역
20 Seobu Inter-City Bus Terminal
서부시외버스터미널
21 Bus Stop
버스정류장
22 Wongaksa Temple
원각사
23 Bomunsan Scenic Lookout
보문산전망대
24 Daejeon Stadium
대전운동장

Places to Eat

Halfway between the river and Inhyoro (the street on which the post office and the train station are situated) is **Jung-ang Sijang** (Central Market). A colourful array of goodies can be found here: anything from chicken's feet to herbal medicine. There are also many different *restaurants* and *street stalls* where you can eat well and cheaply. Common dishes include gimbap, tteokbokgi (sticky rice sticks in a spicy sauce) and *sundae* (noodle, vegetable and pig's blood sausages). If you can read Korean look out for *sacheoltang* or *yeongyangtang*: stewed dog – probably not everyone's favourite. Still, it's a very colourful neighbourhood and worth a stroll even if you aren't hungry.

A good place to pick up some gimbap before a train trip is **Bongojang Udong**. Further north, on the same side of the street, is **Bakery Roma**, which has a good range of dumplings, breads and snacks. For self-caterers and the less adventurous, **Dongbang Mart** has a supermarket on the 1st floor and a food court on the 2nd floor.

If you have some time on your hands and would like to try Daejeon's specialty, *dotorimuk* (acorn jelly), then head out to **Solbat Mukjip** (☎ 935 5686) on the edge of town. Dotorimuk (W2500) is similar in

texture to firm tofu, but is made from acorns. Other tasty dishes include *boribap* (steamed barley) and *tojongdakbaeksuk* (boiled free-range chicken and gruel). Catch bus No 181 from Daejeon train station and ask the driver to let you off at the restaurant.

Getting There & Away

Bus There are three bus terminals in Daejeon: the seobu (west) inter-city bus terminal, the dongbu (east) inter-city bus terminal and the express bus terminal (*gosok teomineol*). The latter two are located side by side on the eastern outskirts of town; they are the terminals most used by travellers.

There are buses departing the express bus terminal for:

destination	price (W)	duration	distance
Busan	10,600	3¾ hrs	283km
Cheonan	2800	1 hr	73km
Daegu	5800	2 hrs	149km
Dong Seoul	6500	2 hrs	167km
Gwangju	6900	3 hrs	179km
Seoul	6000	2 hrs	153km

From the dongbu inter-city bus terminal, destinations include:

destination	price (W)	duration	distance
Cheonan	2800	1 hr	73km
Gongju	2400	1 hr	39km
Hongseong*	7600	2½ hrs	136km
Jeonju	3500	1¼ hrs	97km
Songnisan	4300	1¾ hrs	68km
Taean**	10,600	4 hrs	192km

*for Deoksan Provincial Park
**for Taean Haean National Park

Departures from the seobu inter-city bus terminal include:

destination	price (W)	duration	distance
Buyeo	3800	1¼ hrs	78km
Cheongju	3500	1 hr	61km
Daecheon	6500	2–3 hrs	115km

Train There are two train stations in Daejeon. Daejeon train station, in the centre of the city, serves the main line between Seoul and Busan and all trains en route to either of those cities stop here. The other station, on the west of town, is Seodaejeon train station. This station serves the line to Mokpo, via Ilsan and Jeongeup, though if you're heading for Gwangju you must change at Yeongsanpo.

Saemaeul trains from Seoul to Daejeon run hourly (W9,900, 1 hour 40 minutes) and Mugunghwa run every 15 minutes (W6800, 1 hour 55 minutes).

Getting Around
Bus The most important local bus as far as travellers are concerned is the No 841, which connects the dongbu inter-city/express bus terminals with the seobu inter-city bus terminal via Daejeon train station and the city centre. Bus No 860 also connects Daejeon train station with the dongbu inter-city/express bus terminals, and No 714 connects Daejeon train station with the seobu inter-city bus terminal. The fare is W600 or W1000 on seated buses.

Subway A subway system is currently being built to connect the city centre and Yuseong, but it has encountered funding shortfalls and therefore completion has been delayed. Check with KNTO for an update.

GEUMSAN 금산
pop 65,000
In the south-east corner of Chungcheong-nam-do is the obscure market town of Geumsan. This town wouldn't rate a mention in a guidebook to Korea if it were not for the fact that 80% of the nation's *insam* (ginseng) is collected and marketed here.

Overseas buyers who purchase in bulk come to Geumsan for one-stop shopping. Individual travellers with a particular interest in insam might want to come and take a look. The town's largest and most colourful insam markets are the **Geumsan Ginseng International Market** (Geumsan Insam Gukje Sijang) and **Geumsan Medicinal Herb Market** (Geumsan Hanyak Sijang).

The market functions on the 2nd, 7th, 12th, 17th, 22nd and 27th days of every month.

During September, Geumsan is host to Korea's **Ginseng Festival**, check with KNTO for more details.

Not surprisingly, insam-based foods are a local specialty in Geumsan's restaurants. A heart-warming bowl of *samgyetang* – a whole chicken stuffed with sticky rice, jujubes, chestnuts and ginseng – is a must. A medicinal variety is also popular, but a bit more expensive.

Tents are set up around the market serving samgyetang, or you could try **Wonjo Samgyetang** (☎ 752 2678). The restaurant is 50m east of the International Market. The entrance is via a small arcade (look for the information sign). Go to the 2nd floor. A steaming bowl of samgyetang costs W7000, or W10,000 with extra insam and herbal medicine.

Getting There & Away
The easiest access is from either of Daejeon's inter-city bus terminals (W2300, one hour, 37km, hourly).

GYERYONGSAN NATIONAL PARK

This park's unusual name means 'Rooster Dragon Mountain', apparently because some locals thought the mountain resembled a dragon with a rooster's head. Regardless of what it's called, **Gyeryongsan** (845m) is a worthwhile peak to climb

GYERYONGSAN NATIONAL PARK

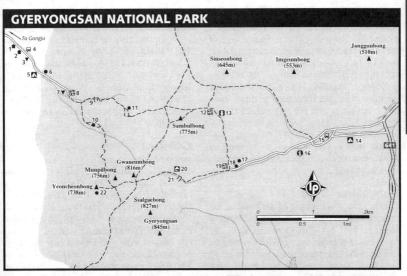

GYERYONGSAN NATIONAL PARK

PLACES TO STAY
1 Gyeryong Youth Hostel
  계룡유스호스텔
2 Gyeryong Sanjang
  계룡산장
5 Camping Ground
  야영장
14 Camping Ground
  야영장
20 Eunseon Sanjang
  은선산장

PLACES TO EAT
3 Restaurants
  식당가
7 Jeontong Chatjip
  전통찻집

OTHER
4 Bus Stop
  버스정류장
6 Park Office
  공원사무소
8 Gapsa
  갑사
9 Yongmunpokpo
  용문폭포
10 Daejaam Hermitage
  대자암터
11 Sinheung-am Hermitage
  신흥암터
12 Gyemyeongjeongsa
  Temple
  계명정사
13 Brother & Sister Pagoda
  오뉘탑

15 Bus Stop
  버스정류장
16 Visitor Information
  Centre; Park Office
  공원사무소 . 탐방안내소
17 Munsuam Hermitage
  문수암터
18 Mitaam Hermitage
  미타암터
19 Donghaksa; Donghak
  Sanjang
  동학사
21 Eunseonpokpo
  은선폭포
22 Dungunam Hermitage
  둥군암터

This area of forested mountains and crystal-clear streams between Gongju and Daejeon is a popular hiking spot. It also contains within its boundaries two of Korea's most famous temples, Gapsa and Donghaksa.

The best way to see the two temples is to set off early in the day and walk from one to the other via the peak Gwaneumbong. This takes about four hours at a comfortable pace. During winter, the hike along the ridge between Sambulbong and Gwaneumbong is justifiably popular. All the official trails are well marked and signposted, although due to its close proximity to Daejeon a large number of unofficial paths have sprouted and are only marked by hiking-club tags. There is a visitor information centre below Donghaksa. Entry costs W2000.

Gapsa 갑사

At the western end of the park, surrounded by beautiful scenery, stands Gapsa, one of the oldest Buddhist temples in Korea, dating back to the unified Silla period (8th to 10th centuries AD). Unlike many of the temples in Korea, which have been either restored or completely rebuilt from time to time, some of the buildings here are original. There is a stunning Silla bronze bell with intricate patterns that was cast in 1584.

Just below Gapsa, by the stream, is *Jeontongchatjip*, a pleasant traditional-style tea house.

Donghaksa   동학사

This temple stands at the eastern end of the park and, although the buildings here are nowhere near as old as those at Gapsa, the complex is a large one and the setting is stunning. As a result of the large number of visitors to the temple, much of it has been closed off to the public. As at Gapsa, there's a small tourist village down the road from the temple with the usual facilities.

Places to Stay

There are small camping grounds at both Gapsa and Donghaksa. It is also possible to stay at the simple 20-bed shelter *Eunseon Sanjang (W3000; gyeryong@npa.or.kr)* but you will need to book during weekends and holidays. Blankets (W2000) and sleeping bags (W3000) are available for hire.

Both temples have the requisite tourist villages with *yeogwans* (W25,000 to W35,000) and *minbak* (W20,000). The *Gyerong Youth Hostel* (☎ 856 4666) at Gapsa has dorm beds from W6500 and ondol rooms for W30,000. Otherwise try *Gyerong Sanjang* (☎ 857 5016), which has reasonable ondol rooms from W25,000.

Donghak Sanjang (☎ 825 4301), just near the Donghaksa parking lot, has both Western and ondol rooms from W35,000.

Getting There & Away

Local bus No 2 (W630, 40 minutes, 19km, every 30 minutes) and inter-city buses (W1200, every two hours) make the run between Gongju and Gapsa. Buses also connect Gapsa with Daejeon seobu inter-city bus terminal (W1900, 40 minutes, hourly).

Donghaksa is best approached by bus No 102 (W1000/630, 40 minutes, every 10 minutes) from Daejeon train station. There are only four buses daily to Donghaksa leaving from Gongju's local bus terminal, at 9.55 and 11 am, and at 1.49 and 4.40 pm. Check with the tourist office in case the times have changed.

GONGJU 공주

pop 137,000

Gongju, established in AD 475, was the second capital of the Baekje kingdom; after the first capital, Han-gang, south of the river near Seoul, was abandoned. More and more is being discovered and excavated from the first capital, however it's only possible to view a few artefacts, preserved in the National Museum in Seoul, at present. At Gongju, however, there are far more tangible remains in the form of a whole collection of tombs of Baekje kings.

The tombs are clustered together on a wooded hillside outside of Gongju. Inevitably, most of them were looted of their treasures over the centuries and nothing was done to preserve what remained until the Japanese carried out excavations there in 1907 and 1933. Even those excavations were marred by the looting which took place once the tombs were opened up. However in 1971, while work was in progress to repair some of the known tombs, archaeologists came across the undisturbed tomb of King Muryeong (AD 501–23), one of the last monarchs to reign here. The find is one of Korea's greatest archaeological discoveries, and the hundreds of priceless artefacts form the basis of the collection at the National Museum in Gongju.

Gongju is today a fairly small provincial market town and educational centre, but its Baekje origins are celebrated every two years with a festival held in mid-October that lasts for three to four days. It includes a large parade down the main street, fireworks, traditional dancing on

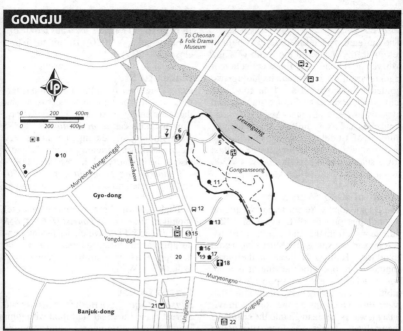

Gongju

GONGJU

PLACES TO STAY
13 Gongju Tourist Hotel
   공주관광호텔
16 Samwon Yeoinsuk
   삼원여인숙
17 Geumho-jang Yeogwan
   금호장여관

PLACES TO EAT
1 Homigwan
   호미관
7 Gomanaru
   고마나루
19 Myeongseong Bulgogi
   명성불고기

OTHER
2 Express Bus Terminal
   고속버스터미널

3 Inter-City Bus Terminal
   시외버스터미널
4 Yeong-eunsa
   영은사
5 Gongbungnu Pavilion
   공북루
6 Information Booth
   관광안내소
8 Tomb of King Muryeong
   백제무령왕릉
9 Gongju Historical Site
   Office
   공주사적관리사무소
10 Tomb of King Muryeong
   Exhibition Hall
   무령왕릉모형관

11 Ssangsujeong
   쌍수정
12 Bus Stop
   버스정류장
14 Local Bus Terminal
   시내버스터미널
15 Korea First Bank
   제일은행
18 Baptist Church
   침례교회
20 Sanseong Market
   산성시장
21 Post Office
   우체국
22 Gongju National Museum
   공주국립박물관

the sands of the Geumgang, traditional games and sports and various other events at local sites. The festival is celebrated in alternate years in Buyeo. Ask KNTO for more details and dates.

Information

There is a tourist information kiosk at the entrance to the west gate of Gongsanseong. There is a Web site at http://city.Kongju .chungnam.kr/eindex.html.

Gongju National Museum
공주국립박물관

The museum, opened in 1972, was built to resemble the inside of the tomb of King Muryeong. It houses the finest collection of Baekje artefacts in Korea, including two golden crowns, part of a coffin, gold, jade and silver ornaments, bronze mirrors and utensils, as well as Bronze-Age daggers, arrowheads and axes, an Iron-Age bell and a number of Buddhist images. Outside the museum are some interesting Buddhist stone statues and a pagoda. Entry is W300 (open 9 am to 7 pm, closed Monday).

Tomb of King Muryeong 무령왕릉

The Baekje tombs are clustered together on the hill just outside of Songsan-ni, a 20-minute walk from the centre of town. By the entrance to the site is the Muryeong Tomb Exhibition Hall. Only three of the burial chambers are open for viewing at present, but models have been set up inside the exhibition hall featuring many of the relics that were discovered inside the tombs. Previously it was possible to go into the chambers themselves – but it was found that moist warm air entering from the outside was causing deterioration of the patterned bricks and tiles inside, so they're now all protected by hermetically sealed glass windows.

Cost of entry is W1200 (open daily, 9 am to 6 pm).

Gongsanseong 공산성

This mountain fortress was the site of the Baekje royal palace, but now it's a park with pavilions and a temple. The castle walls date from Baekje times, but are actually the remains of a 17th-century reconstruction. Entry is W500 (open daily, 9 am to 6 pm).

Korea Folk Drama Museum
판소리박물관

An impressive collection of puppets, dolls, masks and musical instruments – which were mostly collected by the museum founder, Shim Useong – are housed at the Folk Drama Museum. Traditional music and puppet performances are sometimes held here, check with KNTO for details.

The museum is a 15-minute ride on bus No 18 or 20 from Gongju's local bus terminal.

Entry costs W1000 (10 am to 5 pm, closed Monday).

Places to Stay

Across the river from the northern bus terminals is the best place to be based, and there are many reasonable places to stay. This includes *Samwon Yeoinsuk* (☎ 855 2496) on Jung-angeukjanggil, which is very clean and run by friendly people. There's also a shady courtyard. It costs W10,000.

Geumho-jang Yeogwan (☎ 855 1156) on Gogaemaeulgil offers good value rooms for W18,000.

Those looking for a mid-range hotel should try the *Gongju Tourist Hotel* (☎ 855 4023, fax 855 4028) which has recently undergone a much-needed renovation. The new price list will probably range from W40,000 to W70,000.

Places to Eat

Sanseong Sijang is a fresh food market and a great place for street stall food with gimbap, *tuigim* (tempura) and *mandu* (dumplings) for very reasonable prices. If you prefer to sit down, then *Gomanaru* has a wide range of tasty food. For a glimpse of the dishes and prices see their Web site at www.gomanaru.co.kr/food/menu/.

Myeongseong Bulgogi serves up tasty and generous portions of bulgogi for W10,000. The restaurant is next door to an Internet cafe, Fantasia.

Delicious and inexpensive galbi and naengmyeon can be found at *Homigwan*. The restaurant is just around the corner from the inter-city bus terminal, look out for the big green sign, the KBS/SBS stamp of approval or the KIA shop next door.

Getting There & Away

Both the express bus terminal and inter-city bus terminal are on the north side of the river, opposite the town. A taxi between the town centre and the bus terminals costs W1500. Buses going to/from Daejeon also stop in the centre of town at the small kiosk selling bus tickets.

Buses depart from the express bus terminal for Seoul (W5100, 2¼ hours, 132km, every 30–40 minutes).

Departures from the inter-city bus terminal include:

destination	price (W)	duration	distance
Boryeong	4100	1¾ hrs	65km
Buyeo	2300	1 hr	37km
Cheonan	3000	1 hour	46km
Daejeon	2400	1 hr	39km

Getting Around
The local bus terminal is the easiest place to catch a bus to the Gongju Folk Drama Museum, Magoksa, Gapsa (bus No 2) and Donghaksa. Local buses cost W630.

MAGOKSA 마곡사
Another fairly remote and beautiful temple lies north-west of Gongju off the main road to Onyang, Magoksa. It was built by the Zen Master Jajangyulsa during the reign of the first Silla queen, Seondeok (632–647 AD), a major patron of Buddhism who introduced Chinese Tang culture into Korea. The temple was reconstructed during the middle years of the Goryeo dynasty but, since then, apart from additional structures erected during the middle of the Yi dynasty, precious little has changed – so you're in for a real treat of genuine Goryeo religious art.

Magoksa's Cheonbuljeon, a hall with three huge golden Buddhas, is simply incredible, both in size and execution. That beams of this size were lifted into place in the days before cranes is almost beyond belief. Another gem at this temple is **Yeongsanjeon**, with its three golden Buddhas flanked by four smaller Bodhisattvas and backed by a thousand pint-sized white painted devotees – each of them slightly different from the other. Entry to the temple costs W2000.

Three circular hiking trails branch off from behind Magoksa, At a regular pace, the trails take between 1½ and 2½ hours each to complete. The first trail is particularly recommended. It is five kilometres long and includes the two peaks, **Nabalbong** (417m) and **Hwalinbong** (423m). Both trails link

several hermitages scattered throughout the beautiful forest.

There's a small tourist village alongside the river before the entrance gate to the temple. Some *restaurants* are attractively placed, overlooking the river, but there are not many places to stay. If you want to stay overnight, the best place is the *minbak* on the opposite side of the river from the restaurants. It can be reached by a footbridge.

To get to Magoksa, catch local bus No 7 from Gongju (W630, every 30–40 minutes, 37km, 40 minutes).

BUYEO 부여
pop 95,000
Buyeo is the site of the last capital of the Baekje kingdom, Sabi. The capital was moved here from Gongju in AD 538, where it flourished until it was destroyed by the combined forces of the Silla and the Tang (of China) in AD 660. Today, it's a quiet provincial town surrounded by wooded hills and paddy fields, with a friendly and very traditionally minded people. Of the Baekje ruins, not a great deal remains, save for the kings' burial mounds a little way out of town, a few foundation stones of the army's arsenal and food shop on Busosan, and a five-storey stone pagoda – one of only three surviving from the Three Kingdoms period. The main point of interest here is the museum.

Information
There is a tourist information centre by the main entrance to Busosan.

Buyeo National Museum
부여국립박물관

This museum, opened in 1993, has one of the best collections of artefacts from the Baekje kingdom you will find in Korea – as well as other exhibits from later periods in the country's history. It is divided into four galleries: early Korean history, Baekje history, Buddhist art and Baekje pottery. It is home to bronze spearheads, daggers and pottery from the 5th to 4th centuries BC, including Baekje jars, the gilt-bronze Seated Maitreya, Buddha images and examples of roof tiles embossed with various designs; as well as a collection

CHUNGCHEONGNAM-DO

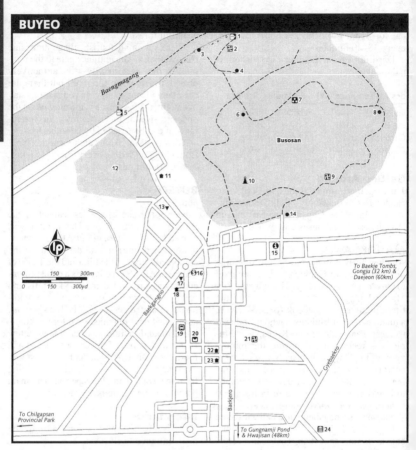

BUYEO

of celadon vases, funeral urns and bronze bells dating from the 6th to 14th centuries (W400, 9 am to 6 pm, closed Monday).

There are also a number of interesting stone relics – steles, baths, lanterns, and Buddha images – in the gardens in front of the museum. If you need a break for fresh air, behind the museum is a pleasant park which is home to a couple of pavilions, a temple and Geumseongsan (121m).

Busosan 부소산

Rising up above Baengmagang is the pine-forested hill of Busosan, which is where the royal palace and fortress of the Baekje kings once stood. It's now a popular park honeycombed with paths and roads. It contains a number of very attractive temples and pavilions with some excellent views over the surrounding countryside. Also on this hill are the ruins of the Baekje army's food store, where it's said that it is still possible to find carbonised rice, beans and barley.

Busosan is associated with the legend of the 3000 court ladies who threw themselves onto the rocks from a high cliff, known as Nakhwaam, above Baengmagang, when the

BUYEO

PLACES TO STAY
11 Samjung Buyeo
   Youth Hostel
   부여유스호스텔
18 Myeongseong-jang
   Motel
   명성장모텔
22 Motel Arirang
   모텔아리랑
23 Mirabo Motel
   미라보모텔

PLACES TO EAT
13 Kudurae Dolssambap
   구드래돌쌈밥
17 Daemyeong
   Sikdang/Minbak
   대명식당

OTHER
1 Ferry
   선착장
2 Goransa
   고란사
3 Baehwajeong
   낙화암, 백화정
4 Sajaru
   사자루
5 Ferry
   선착장
6 Banwolru
   반월루
7 Suhyeolbyeongyeongji
   수혈병영지
8 Yeong-ilru
   영일루
9 Samchungsa
   삼충사

10 Chungnyeongsa
   충령사
12 Kudurae Park
   구두래공원
14 Busosan Main
   Entrance
   부소산입구
15 Tourist Information
   관광안내소
16 Hana Bank
   하나은행
19 Buyeo Bus Terminal
   부여버스터미널
20 Post Office
   우체국
21 Jeongnimsa
   정림사지
24 Buyeo National
   Museum
   부여국립박물관

Baekje kingdom finally came to an end. They preferred death to capture by the invading Chinese and Silla armies. Nakhwaam literally means Rock of Falling Flowers. People come from all over Korea to see this spot and, according to a tourist brochure, ponder the 'steadfast chastity and lofty allegiance of Baekje ladies'. A stroll around this peaceful hillside is a pleasant and relaxing way to spend a morning or afternoon.

Also within the foregrounds of Busosan are three Buyeo county government offices dating from the late-Joseon period. They include the county magistrate's office, his residence and a guesthouse for government officials.

Entry costs W1400.

Jeongnimsa 정림사

This small temple site near the centre of town contains a five-storey pagoda dating from the Baekje period and a weather-beaten, seated stone Buddha from the Goryeo dynasty. The latter is one of the strangest Buddhas you're ever likely to see, and bears an uncanny resemblance to the Easter Island statues.

Gungnamji Pond & Pavilion
궁남지

About 1km past Jeongnimsa, and surrounded by paddy fields, stands a pavilion that was originally constructed by the Baekje king as a pleasure garden for the court ladies. Until a few years ago it stood in virtual ruins, but restoration has been undertaken and the bridge which takes you across the pond to the pavilion is now in good repair. It's a beautiful place to sit and relax and watch the activity in the surrounding paddy fields.

Baekje Royal Tombs 백제왕릉

About 2km from Buyeo along the road to Nonsan stands an extensive collection of Baekje royal tombs (Baekje-wangneung) dating from AD 538–660. These tombs are similar to those at Gongju. Most of them have been excavated and are open for viewing, though all the contents have been removed so they're of limited interest. The wall painting in the 'painted tomb' is actually a modern reconstruction. What is worth seeing here is the museum, which has been designed to resemble a tomb. Inside is a burial urn, as well as a number of scaled-down reproductions of the various tombs showing their manner of construction. Just next door is a large excavation site where farmers discovered some ancient relics in the soil.

Entry costs W700 (open daily, 6 am to 7.30 pm). To get there, take a local Buyeo-Nonsan bus or hire a taxi (W3000). You can't miss the site as it's right next to the road on the left-hand side.

Korean National University of Cultural Heritage 한국문화예술학교

In early 2000, this university (*Hanguk Jeontong Munhwa Hakgyo*) was opened in with the intention of elevating the preservation, knowledge and significance of Korea's rich cultural heritage. It is also hoped the university will revive interest in the Baekje culture. It is part of a national government program to boost tourism in the area.

Places to Stay

Buyeo has some of the best accommodation in Korea with very comfortable yeogwans and motels at reasonable prices. There is also the budget option of **Samjung Buyeo Youth Hostel** (☎ 835 3101, fax 835 3791, **e** *buyeoYH@channeli.net*) with dorm beds from W8900, or twin rooms for W39,900.

Closer to the centre of town, **Mirabo Motel** (☎ 835 9988) stands out with its distinctive pebble-rock facade. It has good rooms for W25,000.

Just opposite, **Arirang Motel** (☎ 832 5656) is of similar standard and price, but lacks the Flintstones facade.

Another good option is **Myeongseongjang Motel** (☎ 833 8855), with very decent rooms for W25,000. The motel is just off the main road running north from the bus terminal.

Places to Eat

Daemyeong Sikdang is the place to come if you're hungry and would like to taste every speciality that Buyeo has to offer. Their *hanjeongsik* (W10,000) is a table d'hôte with as many tasty small dishes that can fit onto your table or into your tummy.

If you would prefer a Korean barbecue, then try the popular **Kudurae Dolssambap** in the north of town. See their illustrated menu at www.kudurae.co.kr/food/menu/.

Getting There & Away

Inter-city buses departing from Buyeo bus terminal go to:

destination	price (W)	duration	distance
Boryeong	2800	1 hr	43km
Daejeon	3800	1½ hrs	61km
Gongju	2300	1 hr	37km
Jeonju	4200	1¾ hrs	74km
Seoul	8600	2½ hrs	166km

BORYEONG 보령
pop 121,000

When Koreans think of this part of the country they think of two things: mud and Moses. The silt and large tidal fluctuations of the Yellow Sea are the source of these two attractions, producing a low-tide phenomenon that resembles the parting of the seas. For those wanting to fulfil their childhood dream of parting the seas, then a trip to Muchangpo Beach is a must.

It is probably true to say the Boryeong Mud Festival and associated mud cosmetic products are more a by-product of the popularity, during the summer months, of **Daecheon Beach**.

Information

The train station and bus terminal are conveniently clustered together, with a tourist information booth in between.

Boryeong Mud Festival
보령머드축제

Held annually in July, the festival's main ingredient is taken from the mineral-rich sediment on the sea-floor. In addition to mud massages, mud pools, mud art, mud games and a mud body-painting contest, you could also just enjoy lying in the sun on the sandy Daecheon Beach.

Sapsido 삽시도

This island, 13km from Daecheon harbour, is a picturesque and peaceful place to escape to for a day trip, or even overnight. It is still possible to see fire flies at night, which are becoming rare on the peninsula.

The island is small enough to walk from one end to the other (40 minutes) and there are enough sights for a pleasant two-day trip. The two main beaches are **Bamseom** and **Geomeolneomeo**. The nicest place to stay on the island is the latter, where some beach huts have been set up just behind the beach. The owner also has a restaurant/minbak in the centre of the village, ***Dongbaek Sikdang/Minbak*** (☎ 932 3738) which is the only accommodation that's open all year round. Despite its drab appearance, the food is good. Rooms range from W20,000 to W40,000, depending on demand.

There is usually a minimum of two boats a day leaving from Daecheon harbour, at 8 am and 4.30 pm, with more services in summer and during the holidays. The first boat stops at Wonsando, Anmyeondo, Godaedo and Janggodo, before arriving at Sapsido. Just taking the boat on a circuit trip of the islands makes for an enjoyable day trip. Due to tidal variations there are two ferry berths on Sapsido, so make sure you confirm where and when to catch the ferry back to Daecheon. Check with KNTO for any changes to the ferry timetable. Regular local buses run from in front of Boryeong station to Daecheon harbour (W950, 25 minutes), just ask for Daejeonhang.

Muchangpo 무창포
This beach, 10km south of Boryeong, has become a popular tourist stopover – due to a low-tide phenomenon which reveals a 1.5km sandbar that connects the beach to the nearby island, Sokdaedo. The event was once likened to the biblical story of Moses parting the seas and has ever since been touted as tourist hot-spot. If you don't want to get wet feet, visit the beach during the neap tide period on the 15th day of the lunar month. Boryeong local buses head out to Muchangpo (W950, 25 minutes) from in front of the Buryeong train station If you get excited about all of this, then you should also check out Jindo in Jeollanam-do.

Places to Stay & Eat
The best place to stay in Boryeong is, without doubt, Daecheon Beach, which is 10km west of the town centre. You will find there an abundance of good yeogwan and hotel accommodation. Most places range in price from W25,000 to W50,000. Particularly recommended is the ***Daecheon Hyatt Motel***

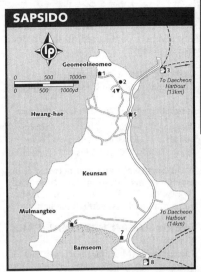

SAPSIDO

SAPSIDO

1 Geomeolneomeo Beach Bungalow
   거멀너머해수욕장 방갈로
2 Sapsido Primary School
   삽시초등교
3 Ferry Jetty
   밤성선착장
4 Restaurant
   식당
5 Dongbaek Shikdang/Minbak
   동백식당/민박
6 Suriminga Minbak
   수림인가민박
7 Jeonmasuldung Minbak
   전마술뚱민박
8 Ferry Jetty
   술뚱선착장

(☎ 934 9007), just by the entrance to Daecheon Beach. It has comfortable rooms for W30,000.

The best place to try the local specialty of *kkotgetang* (spicy crab soup) or *jeonbokjuk* (abalone gruel) is Daecheon harbour (2km north of Daecheon Beach). This is also the place to come if you have a hankering to buy a variety of seaweed, fresh and dried fish or shellfish.

Getting There & Away
Bus Departures from Daecheon include:

destination	price (W)	duration	distance
Daejeon	6500	2¼ hrs	105km
Gunsan	3900	1¼ hrs	62km
Seoul	10,100	3 hrs	181km

Train Saemaeul trains run between Seoul and Boryeong/Daecheon three times daily (W11,400, 2½ hours) and mugunghwa trains run hourly (W7800, three hours).

TAEAN HAEAN NATIONAL PARK
태안해안국립공원

Taean Haean (Maritime) National Park offers some dramatic coastal scenery, four large sandy beaches and about 130 islands and islets. The largest island by far is Anmyeondo, which can be reached by a bridge.

This is the nearest national park to Seoul to offer beachside scenery. Not surprisingly, most of the beaches are jam-packed on weekends and holidays. From north to south, the four main beaches are **Cheollipo**, **Mallipo**, **Yeonpo** and **Mongsanpo**. Mallipo seems to be the most popular.

A 2.5km walk along the main road north of Mallipo is the **Cheollipo Arboretum**, a botanical garden with over 7,000 species of plants from around the globe. Reservations are necessary (☎ 672 9310; open daily, free admission).

Entry to the national park costs W1300.

Places to Stay
There are two *camping grounds (W3000)* bordering Taean Haean National Park, at Mongsanpo and Yeonpo. Both places are equipped with showers and toilets. There are plenty of *minbak* and *yeogwan*, many pushing up right against the beach with no thought for aesthetics. These places can pack out during the July–August peak season, so you will need to book well in advance. Prices range from W20,000 a night

during the cooler months to W60,000 on peak weekends and holidays.

Getting There & Away
Access is from the town of Taean, which is still about 18km from the beach at Mallipo. Local city buses (W1000) run from Taean out to the beaches. There are also buses to Mallipo from Seoul's Nambu bus terminal (W11,100, 3½ hours, 223km, hourly) and Daejeon's dongbu bus terminal (W11,600, four hours, 210km, four times a day).

There are buses from Taean going to the following locations:

destination	price (W)	duration	distance
Cheonan	7000	3 hrs	122km
Daejeon	10,500	4 hrs	193km
Haemi	1800		
Seoul	10,100	3 hrs	205km

HAEMI 해미
pop 9600

The village of Haemi, 10km west of Deoksan, is well worth a stop to see Haemi-eupseong (the old town wall) and to visit nearby Gaesimsa.

Haemi-eupseong 해미읍성
This well-preserved ancient town wall was first built in 1407, during the reign of King Taejong of the Joseon. Originally built to protect the local inhabitants and as a military command, the wall was later used as a prison during the Catholic pogroms of the 1860s. In 1866 alone, about 1000 Catholics were tortured and executed here. Some grim reminders of this persecution still remain within the walls today. The wall is a five-minute walk from the Haemi bus stop in the north-east of town.

If you're feeling peckish, *Haein-kalguksu* is a local favourite that serves up a tasty bowl of *kalguksu* (fettuccine noodle soup; W2500). The restaurant is diagonally opposite the south-west corner of Haemi-eupseong.

Getting There & Away
There are regular buses that pass through Haemi from Hongseong, Cheonan and

Taean. Check the timetable and buy your bus ticket from the general store on the main street.

AROUND HAEMI
Gaesimsa 개심사

Gaesimsa is located in a tranquil valley 8km to the north of Haemi. This is probably one of the most remote and beautiful temples in Korea. This small gem is worth all the effort it takes to find it. The main hall of the temple, **Daeungjeon**, was built in AD 654, making it one of the oldest wooden structures in Korea. In spring, cherry blossoms take over the temple, creating an unforgettable scene. The temple's traditional wooden toilets are a worthy attraction all year round – just follow your nose.

To get to the temple catch the Haemi to Seosan local bus (W760, hourly) from the intersection near the south-west corner of Haemi-eupseong, and hop off in Sinchang-ri. From here follow the sign-posted road under the new expressway up the valley to the dam wall. Continue along the main road around the reservoir until you reach the small car park. The walk takes about 50 minutes. The last bus back to Haemi passes through Sinchang-ri at 7.35 pm.

DEOKSAN PROVINCIAL PARK
덕산도립공원

This park offers pleasant forest scenery and should not be missed if you're in the area. The easy one-hour climb to the top of **Deoksungsan** (495m) rewards you with a panoramic view of the surrounding countryside. A couple of trails split from the main path, but they all meet up at the peak.

On the southern slope of Deoksungsan is **Sudeoksa**, a Buddhist temple known for its large contingent of resident nuns. The main hall at the back of the temple was built 700 years ago and is one of the oldest wooden structures in Korea. There are also a number of hermitages scattered around the temple.

Admission to Sudeoksa is W2000.

Just opposite the ticket office is the traditional style *Sudeok Yeogwan (☎ 337 6022)*, a very humble abode with rooms for W20,000. There are only common bathrooms, however Sudeok Yeogwan serve up tasty food.

Getting There & Away

Inter-city buses connect Hongseong and Sudeoksa (W1270, 40 minutes, 11km, every 20 minutes). Hongseong is easily reached from:

city	price (W)	duration	distance
Boryeong	2100	1 hr	33km
Cheonan	4000	1½ hrs	65km
Daejeon*	7600	2½ hrs	136km

*seobu inter-city bus terminal via Gongju

CHEONAN 천안
pop 403,000

Cheonan is a convenient transit point for visiting Korea's largest museum, the **Independence Hall of Korea** (otherwise known as Dongnipginyeomgwan), which is 14km south-east of the city.

The Independence Hall of Korea

This is the nation's largest museum and definitely worth a visit, if only to marvel at the monolithic architecture. Its many buildings look like a set from a science fiction movie, rather than a patriotic museum.

Behind the main hall is a whole complex which consists of seven exhibition halls, each cataloguing the course of Korean history from the earliest recorded times up until the present. Unsurprisingly, really, there is a strong emphasis on Korea's history of resistance to foreign invaders. The museum is easy to navigate and there are lots of English descriptions. There is a pleasant forest area surrounding the museum containing the Reunification Monument and Patriots Memorial.

The museum also boasts the **Circle Vision Theatre**, which presents a 15-minute film on Korea's scenic beauty, its traditions, customs and development, using the latest high-tech audio-visual techniques (W1500).

Strollers for babies are available at the entrance to the museum, and despite all the stairs there is wheelchair access throughout the complex. There are a couple of tourist

The Independence Hall of Korea

When it comes to nationalism, there is a competition of sorts between North and South Korea. Each have built gigantic statues, monuments, plazas, towers and other feel-good projects which are meant to eulogise the nations' integrity and the uniqueness of its culture. The main difference between them is that North Korea can't afford these projects and South Korea can. When you see the Independence Hall of Korea it becomes apparent that all stops were pulled out to make this an uncompromising totem to national sovereignty.

There's a high propaganda content to many of the exhibits, which chart the course of late-19th and 20th-century Korean history, and the Japanese and North Koreans come in for some particularly virulent condemnation. On any weekday you will see busloads of school children being run through this place accompanied by their teachers. Unfortunately, part of Korea's educational system includes a lengthy hate-mongering campaign against Japan – the 'Japanese Aggression Hall' is the most notorious example of the genre.

The post-colonial relationship between Korea and Japan is a complex and highly sensitive one. It is exacerbated by painful historical memories of their relationship – well before the Japanese occupation of Korea in 1910 – which continues to sour the present. A traveller to Korea would be hard pressed to find a historical site or temple that doesn't mention how many times it was burnt to the ground by invading Japanese. More disturbing for the Japanese is that research supports the idea that Korea's historical influence has been far greater on Japan than the other way round. This isn't news to the Koreans, who have always assumed a superior cultural heritage, but is definitely hard for the Japanese to swallow. In addition to borrowing pottery, advanced iron products (especially armaments), gold and silver jewellery, and even artistic and cultural styles, recent research has suggested that the two races share a common stock. Mounting evidence is tending to show that present-day Japanese originating from Koreans who migrated to the Japanese islands over 2000 years ago. The Japanese response to these theories is mute. They are not in the least interested in demystifying their legendary and ancient roots.

The Japanese have blithely ignored these historical investigations and instead turn to the present to make their point. Not only is Korea running a trade deficit with Japan, the flow of culture now is predominantly one-way. The Korean government is gradually and reluctantly lifting their bans on the importation of Japanese culture. Japanese films, books, comics and art are for the first time legally available in the Korean market. The Koreans were reluctant to lift the bans, which were originally imposed to protest against the imposition of Japanese culture on Korea during the occupation period 1910 to 1945. However, the fact that most young Korean adults grew up on a diet of Japanese animation has resulted in fewer protests than expected to the lifting of the bans. In fact, the sharing of the 2002 World Cup between Japan and Korea seems to be fostering a climate of improved bilateral relations. From official high-level apologies for wartime atrocities and exploitation to giving the vote to Japanese-Koreans, there are signs of an improving climate between these two neighbours. The next challenge is to radically reform the education curriculum of both countries, to ensure that the generations to come are not handicapped by ignorant nationalistic values.

shops selling souvenirs and nick nacks. One is located inside a *restaurant* in the central basement area and the other just in front of the main entrance.

Entry to the Independence Hall costs W1600 (W1100 for students and W700 for seniors and children). The Hall is open every day (except Monday) during April to September from 9 am to 6 pm, and during October to March from 9.30 am to 5 pm.

City buses head out to the museum from Cheonan every five minutes. They depart from in front of the express bus terminal or from in front of the train station (turn right as you exit the station and walk 100m to the bus stop). You can catch any of the following buses: Nos 34 to 49, 420 and 500. The ride takes 20 minutes and costs W500, or W900 seated.

Getting There & Away

Bus The Cheonan bus terminal is located in the basement of the Galleria Department Store, which is 150m north of the express bus terminal, in the north of Cheonan. A selection of useful destinations from Cheonan bus terminal includes:

destination	price (W)	duration	distance
Buyeo	5300	2 hrs	84km
Cheongju	6200	1¾ hrs	98km
Taean	7000	2¾ hrs	111km

Buses depart the express bus station for Seoul (W3300/W4800, one hour, 84km, every 15 minutes) and Daejeon (W2800/W4100, one hour, 73km, every 20 minutes).

Train Cheonan straddles a heavily travelled train line; remember that it can be difficult to get even a standing-room ticket on weekends.

Chungcheongbuk-do

Highlights

- Songnisan, a national park that is home to fine scenery and the magnificent temple of Beopjusa

- Danyang, a beautiful mountain resort where you can boat on a lake, climb forested peaks or visit ancient Buddhist caves

- Sobaeksan, a large, magnificent national park in its own right, but also home to the huge temple of Guinsa

- Suanbo, known for its fine skiing in the winter and superb hot springs

- Woraksan, one of the less-visited national parks, but still home to thick forests that display magnificent colours in the autumn

☎ 043 • pop 1.5 million

A land of small towns, mountains, hot springs and forests, Chungcheongbuk-do is South Korea's most rural province. There are no large cities here, but plenty of opportunities for outdoor recreation. The Sobaek mountain range, which shares a border with Gyeongsangbuk-do, includes the beautiful Songnisan, Woraksan and Sobaeksan national parks. The pleasant city of Danyang is easily the most popular destination in the province, with nearby mountains, caves and lakes.

Chungcheongbuk-do may be landlocked, but a tidal wave of Seoulites pours in on the weekends and during the holidays. At other times, this is one of the most peaceful places in Korea.

CHEONGJU 청주
pop 570,000

Cheongju is the provincial capital of Chungcheongbuk-do and a useful launching pad for nearby Songnisan National Park. The town has a few sights, including the Early Printing Museum, Cheongju National Museum, Myeong-am Mineral Spring and Sangdangsanseong.

Information

There is a helpful tourist office with a large assortment of maps and brochures just next door to the inter-city bus terminal. Just opposite is Magnet department store, where you'll find the express bus terminal, banks and a post office.

Early Printing Museum (Heungdeoksaji) 고인쇄박물관

The museum is located on the ancient site of Heungdeoksa, a temple that was destroyed during the early years of the Goryeo dynasty and only rediscovered by archaeologists in 1985.

The world's oldest existing book printed with movable metal type, *Jikji Simche Yojeol*, was printed at this temple in 1377. This ancient Buddhist text is presently preserved in La Bibliothèque Nationale de Paris. The Early Printing Museum houses some relics excavated from the ruins (ji) of the temple site, as well as wax exhibits outlining the process of both wood block and metal movable-type printing. There is also an interesting display of various hanja and hangeul fonts.

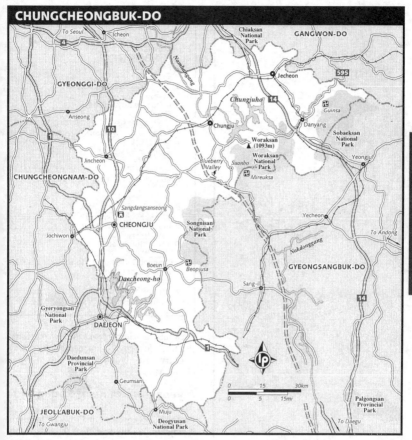

CHUNGCHEONGBUK-DO

Catch bus No 125 from in front of the inter-city bus terminal and get off at Heungdeoksaji. A taxi from the bus terminals costs about W3000. Entry costs W330 (open 9 am to 6 pm, closed Monday).

Yongdusaji Iron Flagpole

용두사지철당간지

Still standing, supported by two large granite slabs, Yongdusaji Iron Flagpole is the oldest banner pole in Korea. Only one other iron flagpole still stands, at Gapsa in Gyeryongsan National Park. According to the inscription at the base of this 13m-high

iron flagpole it was built in AD 962. Traditionally, on festive occasions or during special Buddhist ceremonies banners would adorn the pole.

Cheongju National Museum

This museum is housed in an impressive building on the eastern outskirts of town. It has a wide range of displays detailing the development of tools and pottery vessels in Korea. There is an exhibition of Buddhist arts and crafts and another room tracing the development of printing. The museum also houses a fine collection of relics that were

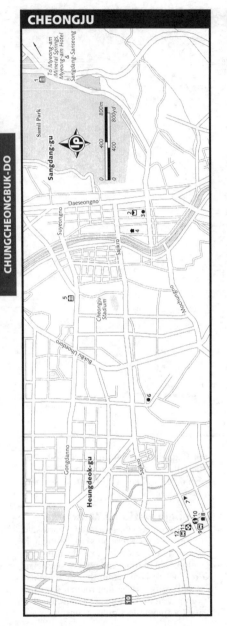

CHEONGJU

1 Cheongju National Museum
청주국립박물관
2 Post Office
우체국
3 Yongdusaji Iron Flagpole
용두사지철당간지주
4 Cheongju Royal Tourist Hotel
로얄관광호텔
5 Early Printing Museum
고인쇄박물관
6 Chungbuk National University
충북대학교
7 Bongchang-i Haemul Kalguksu
봉창이해물칼국수
8 Hilton Hotel; Plaza Park
힐튼호텔, 프라자파크
9 Inter-City Bus Terminal
시외버스터미널
10 Tourist Information
관광안내소
11 Magnet Department Store; Banks; Post Office
마그넷
12 Express Bus Terminal
고속버스터미널

unearthed at Heungdeoksaji (see the Early Printing Museum section, earlier).

Entry costs W400 (open 9 am to 7 pm, closed Monday).

Myeong-am Mineral Spring
명암약수

On the north-eastern outskirts of Cheongju, sitting amid pretty woods, is the reasonably famous and very popular Myeong-am Mineral Spring. People come here to drink and bathe in the spring waters, which are rich in iron and carbonic acid. Having a dip will set you back W5000.

Sangdangsanseong 상당산성

This huge fortress is 3km north-east of Myeong-am Mineral Spring, on the slopes of Uamsan. There are four gates still standing and the wall is in good nick, thanks to a recent renovation. It takes about 40 minutes to walk the length of the wall.

The history of the fortress is unclear. One legend claims that it was built during the Silla dynasty by the father of Kim Yu-shin, who was the leader of a military contingent called the Hwarang. Another story says it was built by Goseong of the Baekje Kingdom. Whoever first built it, the fortress was falling apart until it was renovated in 1716. These days it's past its prime as a fortress, but remains a weekend getaway for Cheongju residents.

Places to Stay & Eat
There are plenty of budget and mid-range yeogwan behind the inter-city bus terminal. Both the *Hilton* and *Plaza Park* have good, clean rooms from W25,000 to W30,000.

Out at Myeong-am Mineral Springs is the 1st-class *Myeong-am Park Hotel* (☎ 257 7451, fax 257 7458). Rates are W58,000 for doubles, W66,000 for twins and W83,000 for suites. In town, another 1st-class option is the *Cheongju Royal Tourist Hotel* (☎ 221 1300, fax 221 1319) with singles/doubles from W49,000/63,000 and suites from W100,000. You need to add 20% for service tax and surcharges for both of these hotels' rates.

If the fast food outlets in the bus terminal don't suffice, then turn right as you exit the bus terminal and walk five minutes to *Bongchang-i Haemul Kalguksu*, which serves a cheap and tasty bowl of seafood noodles.

Getting There & Away
Departures from the express bus terminal include:

destination	price (W)	duration	distance
Busan	1200	4½ hrs	319km
Daegu	7800	2¾ hrs	197km
Dong Seoul	5200	1¾ hrs	137km
Seoul	4800	1¾ hrs	123km

Useful departures from the inter-city bus terminal include:

destination	price (W)	duration	distance
Chuncheon	11600	4 hrs	213km
Chungju	4800	1¾ hrs	70km
Daejeon	2400	35 mins	45km
Danyang	9400	3½ hrs	143km
Jecheon	100	2 hrs	128km
Seoul Nambu	4800	1¾ hrs	126km
Songnisan	4700	1½ hrs	70km

Getting Around
Bus No 150 or 152 leave from in front of the inter-city bus terminal every 30 minutes (W600) and run through the centre of town, passing Cheongju National Museum and Myeong-am Mineral Spring, then terminating at Sandangsanseong.

SONGNISAN NATIONAL PARK
속리산국립공원
Songnisan National Park is one of the finest scenic areas in central Korea. Not surprisingly, there are numerous, excellent walks. A favourite hike leads to the summit of **Cheonwangbong** (1058m), the park's highest summit.

Although the area's great scenic beauty is a major attraction – its name originated from Buddhist philosophy and means 'Remote from the Mundane World Mountains' – Songnisan National Park is really distinguished by **Beopjusa**, one of the largest and most magnificent temple sites in Korea.

Daeungbojeon, with its enormous golden Buddhas, and **Palsangjeon**, the five-roofed wooden pagoda, date back to the Silla dynasty. Both are part of a sanctuary which, at the time of its founding in AD 553, was one of the largest in Korea. Repairs were undertaken in 776, but in 1592 it was burned to the ground during the Japanese invasion. Reconstruction began in 1624, and it's from this time that the present Palsangjeon hall dates, making it one of the few wooden structures at Beopjusa from the 17th century to survive.

Beopjusa is famous for yet another reason. Until 1986, it had the largest Buddha statue in Korea – maybe the largest in all of North-East Asia. The 27m-high concrete statue of the **Maitraya Buddha** dominated the temple compound. It took 30 years to build and was only completed in 1968. It featured prominently in the tourist literature of this area. Unfortunately, by the 1980s the statue had begun to crack, and in late 1986 it was demolished. In its place a new statue has risen

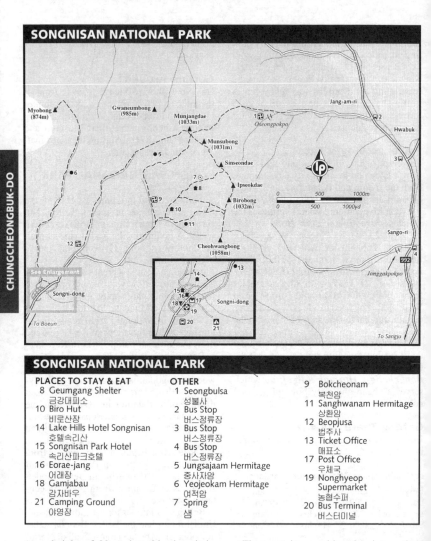

SONGNISAN NATIONAL PARK

PLACES TO STAY & EAT
8 Geumgang Shelter
금강대피소
10 Biro Hut
비로산장
14 Lake Hills Hotel Songnisan
호텔속리산
15 Songnisan Park Hotel
속리산파크호텔
16 Eorae-jang
어래장
18 Gamjabau
감자바우
21 Camping Ground
야영장

OTHER
1 Seongbulsa
성불사
2 Bus Stop
버스정류장
3 Bus Stop
버스정류장
4 Bus Stop
버스정류장
5 Jungsajaam Hermitage
중사자암
6 Yeojeokam Hermitage
여적암
7 Spring
샘

9 Bokcheonam
복천암
11 Sanghwanam Hermitage
상환암
12 Beopjusa
법주사
13 Ticket Office
매표소
17 Post Office
우체국
19 Nonghyeop
Supermarket
농협수퍼
20 Bus Terminal
버스터미널

(to a height of 33m), but this time it is made from 160 tons of brass. The brass component sits on top of a massive, white, stone base containing a ground-level shrine. This gigantic project, which cost about US$4 million, was completed in 1990 and is dedicated to world peace and the reunification of Korea.

There are inumerable other interesting features at Beopjusa, just a few of which are stone lanterns, a seated Buddha hewn out of the rock, a huge bell and an enormous iron cauldron cast in AD 720. The cauldron was used to cook rice for the 3000 monks who lived at Beopjusa during the temple's heyday.

The magnificent temple buildings are surrounded by the luxuriously forested mountains of Songnisan National Park which, although at their best during autumn, are beautiful any time of year. There are well-marked hiking trails in the mountains above the temple and several hermitages where you may be able to stay for the night.

You will require a full day to complete a circuit of the main peaks (Cheonwangbong, Birobong, Munsubong and Munjangdae) via Beopjusa. It is also possible to continue down the eastern side of the park to Jang-am-ri (2¾ hours down or 3½ hours up).

There is a tourist information booth in the bus terminal building, on the northern side. Hiking maps of Songnisan are available from the ticket office. Entry is W2500.

Places to Stay & Eat

There are two *camping* areas that have basic facilities only (toilets) and are free of charge, except in summer when you pay W4000. *Minbak* with shared bathroom go for W20,000, while *yeogwan* boasting a private bathroom start at W25,000. The owners of minbak and yeogwan hang out by the bus terminal and solicit business. There are many nondescript places in town all of which offer pretty much the same price and value. If you are stuck, try *Eorae-jang (☎ 543 3568)*, where rooms for W20,000 are the best value around. Just on the other side of the road is *Songnisan Park Hotel (☎ 542 3900)*, which has comfortable and clean ondol or Western-style rooms for W30,000.

Lake Hills Hotel Songnisan (☎ 542 5281, fax 542 5198) is the most luxurious abode in the park, with stylish rooms affording superb views of the forest. Check out their Web site for a preview at www.lakehills.co.kr. Doubles, twins and ondol rooms are W108,000, or you could indulge with one of their suites, which range from W223,000 to W507,000. A 20% discount is available weekdays outside of July, August, October and November. An American-style breakfast costs W15,000.

Songnisan-dong has an abundant supply of restaurants, mostly serving the same tasty dishes at similar prices, including *sanchae bibimbap* (mountain vegetables mixed with rice; W6000), *pyogo deopbap* (shitake mushrooms, vegetables and mixed rice; W7000) and *haemul pajeon* (seafood pancake; W5000). For a break from the mountain vegetables try *Gamjabau* for a bowl of *kalguksu* (chicken broth with noodles; W3000), *ramyeon* (instant noodles; W2000) or gimbap (W2500).

Getting There & Away

The most useful direct buses go from Song-nisan to:

destination	price (W)	duration	frequency
Boeun	1000W	20 mins	5 mins
Cheongju	4700W	1¾ hrs	15 mins
Dong Daejeon	4300W	1½ hrs	40 mins
Dong Seoul	9600W	3½ hrs	1 hour
Seoul Nambu	9500W	3½ hrs	1 hour

Local buses run to Hwayang Valley from Miwon. To get to Miwon catch a bus from Boeun. On the eastern side of Songnisan is Hwabuk, from where you can catch a bus to Sangju. Buses also run from Cheongju to Hwayang Valley (W3100, every 40 minutes, 1¼ hours) and some of these buses also go to Hwabuk (W4600, 6 times daily, 2 hours).

CHUNGJU 충주
pop 219,000

If you're exploring Chungcheongbuk-do, it's very likely you'll at least pass through Chungju, but unlikely that you will need to spend the night. However, as a transport hub the town is the main jumping off point for Suanbo Hot Springs, Woraksan National Park and Chungjuho.

Getting There & Away

Bus Chungju has only one bus terminal, conveniently located right in the centre of town. There are also local city buses, which can be caught across the street from the terminal, and these travel to some useful destinations, such as Suanbo Hot Springs, Chungjuho and Woraksan National Park.

From the bus terminal itself, some destinations include:

destination	price (W)	duration	distance
Andong	9000	3 hrs	137km
Cheongju	4800	1¾ hrs	66km
Chuncheon	9200	3 hrs	144km
Daejeon	8000	2¼ hrs	116km
Danyang	4700	1½ hrs	54km
Seoul	5500	1¾ hrs	142km
Wonju	3800	1¼ hrs	56km

Train There is one train daily from Seoul to Chungju. It departs from Seoul station at 6.40 pm, and takes 2¾ hours to reach Chungju (W5100).

SUANBO HOT SPRINGS 수안보온천
The town of Suanbo is a resort village at the base of the Woraksan, 21km from Chungju. This is South Korea's pre-eminent hot spring resort, but is also known for its golf courses and skiing facilities. It also happens to be the only government-controlled hot springs resort.

Not surprisingly, Suanbo's amenities are no secret, and the area can be overrun with tourists at any time of the year: on holidays it seems like half of Seoul has migrated to Suanbo in pursuit of pleasure. You'd be wise to schedule your visit when most of the Korean populace is at work. Another peak time is during the Suanbo Hot Springs Festival in October.

The bus terminal is at the northern end of town and the new hotels are at the southern end. There is a helpful information booth just over the creek from the bus terminal.

Blue Valley Ski Resort
Previously known as Suanbo Aurora Valley, Blue Valley Ski Resort (☎ 846 0750, fax 846 1789) is only 2km from the hot springs of Suanbo. The facilities and runs are quite modest in size (seven slopes and three lifts), but it is still a good place for a day trip. The ski season runs from early December to early March, with both day and night skiing available.

A variety of lift tickets are available, ranging from W16,000 (night) to W30,000 (full day). Skis, boots and poles can be rented from the base of the slopes and lessons (in Korean) are also available. There are shuttle

buses running from Suanbo bus terminal during the ski season.

Places to Stay & Eat
Most yeogwan in town are a little dilapidated and the newer and cleaner places don't have hot spring water. If you don't mind the lack of mineral bubbles, then try the *Milran Hotel* (☎ 846 7770), where large doubles are good value at W35,000.

The *Suanbo Sangrok Hotel* (☎ 845 3500, fax 845 7878) is right in the centre of town and is popular with tourist groups. Doubles start from W92,000.

The *Suanbo Park Hotel* (☎ 846 2331, fax 846 3705) has an outdoor mineral spa, and is probably the best place to stay, with doubles from W80,000.

At the base of the ski slopes is the *Blueberry Resort Youth Hostel* (☎ 846 0750), a youth hostel that is only really open during the ski season. For YHA members, a five-person ondol room will set you back W38,000, or W51,500 for non-members Bookings are essential.

Hyangnamu Sikdang is a good place to try *hanjeongsik* (Korean-style banquet). The restaurant is tucked away down a lane at the southern end of town. Ask the locals for directions, as it is a little tricky to find

Getting There & Away
A local bus runs from near Chungju's intercity bus terminal to Suanbo (W1000, 40 minutes, every 1¼ hour). This bus continues on to Songgye-ri, via Mireuksa.

Inter-city buses depart Suanbo to the following destinations:

destination	price (W)	duration	frequency
Andong	7600	2½ hrs	1½ hrs
Cheongju	5500	2¼ hrs	hourly
Dong Seoul	7700	2½ hrs	

Getting Around
Suanbo is small enough to get around on foot there is really only one main street. Taxis are available for daily tours (W100,000) which include Woraksan, Danyang and Chungjuhe

A taxi from Suanbo to Deokjusa will cost you W15,000.

WORAKSAN NATIONAL PARK
월악산국립공원

Woraksan (Moon Crags Mountains) gets relatively few visitors by Korean national park standards. While lacking the dramatic cliffs and spires found in some of Korea's mountains, the park still offers fine hiking through picturesque forests.

On the north slope of the park is **Song-gye**, a valley 6km in length that forms the main entrance to the Woraksan area. At the northern end of the valley is Songgye-ri, a tourist village that offers basic facilities. Further south in Songgye Valley, another valley branches east (Deokju Valley). It harbours a temple, **Deokjusa**.

At the southernmost (upstream) end of Songgye Valley is a scatter of ruins. These are the remains of the temple **Mireuksa**. It's believed that Mireuksa was built in the late-Silla or early-Goryeo period. A five-storey and three-storey stone pagoda are preserved here, as well as a standing stone Buddha.

A circuitous **hiking course** that takes in the major sights could be as follows: Songgye-ri, Songgye Valley, main ridge, Woraksan summit (1093 metres), information board, 960 Peak, Deokjusa, and the entrance to Deokju Valley. The total distance is 9.6km and hiking time about 4½ hours.

The eastern end of Woraksan is approached from Danyang on an entirely different road. Here you will find the much-ballyhooed **Danyang Palgyeong** (Eight Scenic Wonders). Essentially, these wonders are rock formations with names like 'Middle Fairy Rock', and 'Upper Fairy Rock', and can be reached by highway. They are more frequently visited by windshield tourists, but a better view can be gained on foot.

A pleasant walk begins in Deokju and follows a picturesque path up to the new temple Deokjusa. From here the track continues past the Joseon-period fortress gate to the stone Buddha statue. Restaurants and minbak (W20,000) can be found at both Songgye and Deokju.

Entry to the park costs W1000.

Places to Stay & Eat

There are four tiny villages in the park which offer **minbak**. Rooms are priced from W15,000 to W25,000, depending on what the market will bear. The four villages are Worak-ri, Songgye-ri, Mireuk-ri and Bokpyeong-ni. The villages have a small assortment of restaurants and grocery stores. Camping and cooking in non-designated areas are prohibited.

Camping is available at Deokju and Datdonjae for free, except during summer when you pay W3000.

Getting There & Away

Buses run from Chungju via Suanbo passing Mireuk-ri, Deokju (W1100, hourly) and stopping in Songgye (W2850). From Songgye there are more direct buses back to Chungju (W2000, hourly) that travel along the edge of Chungjuho.

JECHEON 제천
pop 148,000

Jecheon is another useful transit point in the northern part of Chungcheongbuk-do, but you aren't likely to come here just to enjoy the town.

Uirimji 의림지

The nearest sight to Jecheon is Uirimji Pond, to the north-west of town. The pond is in fact a small reservoir, about 2km in circumference. It's part of the oldest irrigation system in Korea and has been designated a historic monument.

History aside, the pond is picturesque: surrounded by pines and willows. The scenery is dressed up by two pavilions, **Gyeonghoru** and **Yonghojeong**.

Local city buses run from Jecheon to Uirimji Pond every 10 minutes.

Getting There & Away

Bus Jecheon has two bus stations, the dongbu (east) express bus terminal and the inter-city bus terminal. From the dongbu express bus terminal there are buses to Seoul (W6100, 2¼ hours, 168km, every 40–50 minutes).

From the inter-city bus terminal there are buses to the following places:

CHUNGCHEONGBUK-DO

CHUNGCHEONGBUK-DO

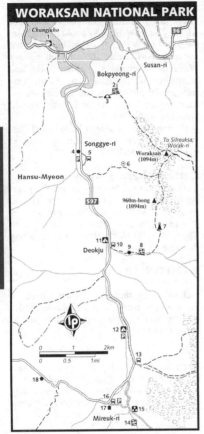

WORAKSAN NATIONAL PARK

1 Ferry
   선착장
2 Bokduam
   복두암
3 Bodeokgul
   보덕굴
4 Park Office
   공원관리사무소
5 Bus Stop
   버스정류장
6 Spring
   샘
7 Maaebul
   마애불
8 Deokjusa
   덕주사
9 Dongmun
   동문
10 Bus Stop
   버스정류장
11 Camping Ground
   야영장
12 Camping Ground
   야영장
13 Bus Stop
   버스정류장
14 Mireukdaewonsa
   미륵대원사
15 Mireuksaji
   미륵사지
16 Bus Stop
   버스정류장
17 Minbak Village
   민박촌
18 Ticket Office
   매표소

destination	price (W)	duration	distance
Andong	8200	3 hrs	119km
Chungju	3000	1 hr	49km
Danyang	1900	50 mins	35km
Dong Seoul	7300	2¾ hrs	168km
Guinsa	3200	1½ hrs	52km
Taebaek	8600	2½ hrs	117km
Wonju	2700	1 hr	42km

Train There is one daily *mugunghwa* (flower of Sharon – a limited-express variety) train connecting Jecheon and Seoul's Cheeongnyangni station (W10,000, three hours).

DANYANG 단양
pop 41,000

Danyang is an up-and-coming resort town nestled between the mountains halfway across the peninsula. It is close to the eastern end of an artificial lake, south of Wonju and north of Songnisan National Park. It's a very relaxing place to spend a few days and there are plenty of interesting things to see and do in the area.

The town itself is a recent creation and completely modern, since the old town of the same name was partially submerged by the waters of the dam. Indeed, Danyang is actually called *Sin* Danyang (New Danyang) while the original place (which partially still exists) is called *Gu* Danyang (Old Danyang).

The lake stretches almost all the way to Chungju in the west. Like Soyangho, east of

The mausoleum-like War Memorial in Seoul. A fitting design for the subject it documents

Golden Goddess, Gyeongju

'Turtle ship' replica, Seoul

Cheomseongdae (AD 632–46)

Painted temple guardian with painstaking detail.

Totem poles at Namsan Park, Seoul

Calligraphy brushes for sale in a Seoul shop

A rural scene, Jongmyo shrine, Seoul

Traditional wooden carvings, including shamanist masks, are popular souvenirs.

Chuncheon, there are boats all along it. There's also a very attractive bridge which connects the town to the eastern shore of the lake, where one of Korea's most famous limestone caves stands and where a very scenic highway (No 595) branches off to Yeongwol and the east coast.

Information & Orientation

There's a tourist information kiosk on the eastern side of the bridge into town (on the way to the cave Gosudonggul – see below).

The ferry terminal for boats to Chungju is on the lake shore in the centre of town. It deals only with boats going to the dam wall (near Chungju).

Sight-seeing boats depart only from Dodam Sambong, a few kilometres north of Danyang.

The train station is on the opposite side of the lake – over the road bridge about 4km west of Danyang (this is a different bridge from the one in the centre of town), where the old town used to stand. Local buses run to the station from Danyang (hourly) from the river.

Places to Stay

A good budget option is *Takhui Yeoinsuk* (☎ 422 2930), with ondol or double beds from W13,000. The rooms have their own shower and there are common toilets. *Hanmi-jang Yeogwan* (☎ 422 2846) has clean and renovated rooms from W20,000 (ondol) to W25,000 (Western). *Sanho-jang Yeogwan* (☎ 422 2619) has doubles with shower for W25,000.

Motel Venice (☎ 421 4400) is a little inconveniently located but is quite new and clean. Double rooms range from W30,000 to 40,000. *Danyang Tourist Hotel* (☎ 423 9911) is the most upmarket option in town. Weekday rates for a double are W63,000, or W90,000 on the weekends.

Places to Eat

Jangdari Sikdang is a popular local restaurant serving a mixture of *sanchae* (mountain vegetable) dishes, including *ondalmaeul solbapjeongsik* (W10,000), a stone pot rice with 15 different ingredients, including

garlic, jujube and gingko fruit. Also worth trying is *sanchae bibimssambap* (W6,000), a wide selection of mountain vegetables that you wrap up in lettuce with mixed grain. A bit more expensive is *song-i bulgogi* (W13,000), which is standard bulgogi with a mixture of wild mushrooms. The restaurant is just down the small lane opposite the bus terminal.

Ohak Sikdang specialises in *mukbap* (acorn jelly with rice) served with side dishes (W4000). It is in the western part of town in the lane behind the post office.

Getting There & Away

Buses connect Danyang to:

destination	price (W)	duration	distance
Andong	6300	2 hrs	91km
Chungju	4700	1½ hrs	54km
Daegu	11,300	3¾ hrs	193km
Guinsa	1900		
Jecheon	1900	50 mins	31km
Seoul	9200	3½ hrs	186km

AROUND DANYANG
Gosudonggul 고수동굴

Just across the bridge from the centre of Danyang is one of Korea's most famous limestone caves. Koreans flock to Gosudonggul in their thousands during the summer holiday period. At that time of year you cannot move for all the tourists, and it will take you an excruciating hour or more to walk around the system.

Gosudonggul is certainly spectacular and extensive cave system – or rather it must have been before the catwalks and miasmic spiral steel staircases were installed up the main vertical galleries. These staircases aid access (or aid commercial exploitation?) and have been thoroughly over-done. A considerable amount of vandalism is also apparent on the tips of stalactites and stalagmites, which are in reach of eager souvenir hunters. Nevertheless, it's perhaps worth visiting the caves if the crowds are not too great.

You should allow an hour, or more depending on the crowds, to get through the caves, which are about 1300m long. Just outside the caves is an extensive tourist

DANYANG RESORT & SOBAEKSAN NATIONAL PARK

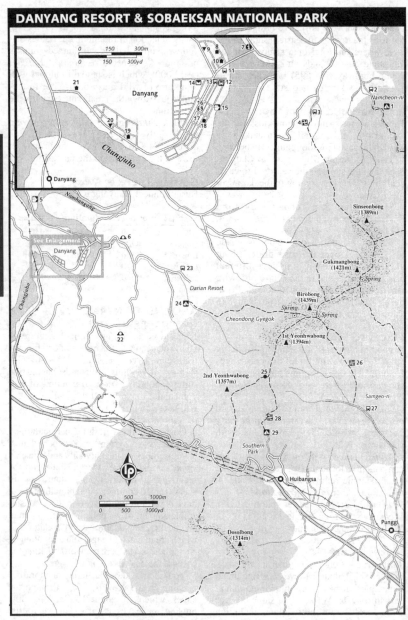

DANYANG RESORT & SOBAEKSAN NATIONAL PARK

PLACES TO STAY
1 Namcheon Camping
  Ground
  남천야영장
8 Hanmi-jang Yeogwan
  한미장여관
10 Takhui Yeoinsuk
  탁희여인숙
18 Sanho-jang Yeogwan
  산호장여관
19 Motel Venice
  모텔베니스
21 Danyang Tourist
  Hotel
  단양관광호텔
24 Darian Camping
  Ground
  다리안야영장
29 Huibang Camping
  Ground
  희방야영장

PLACES TO EAT
9 Jangdari Sikdang
  장다리식당

20 Ohak Sikdang
  오학식당

OTHER
2 Bus Stop
  버스정류장
3 Bus Stop
  버스정류장
4 Guinsa
  구인사
5 Dodamsambong Ferry
  Terminal
  도담삼봉선착장
6 Gosudonggul
  고수동굴
7 Tourist Information Kiosk
  관광안내소
11 Bus Stop for Train Station
  & Huibangsa
  버스정류장
12 Inter-City Bus Terminal
  시외버스터미널
13 Bus Stop to Guinsa &
  Caves
  버스정류장

14 Post Office
  우체국
15 Ferry Terminal
  선착장
16 Joheung Bank
  조흥은행
17 Central Market
  중앙시장
22 Nodongdonggul
  노동동굴
23 Bus Stop
  버스정류장
25 Astronomical
  Observatory
  천문대
26 Birosa
  비로사
27 Bus Stop
  버스정류장
28 Huibangsa; Huibangpokpo
  희방사.희방폭포

CHUNGCHEONGBUK-DO

complex. – with yeogwan, restaurants and shops – which completely obscures the entrance to the caves. Entry costs W3000.

Nodongdonggul 노동동굴
More low-key than Gosudonggul, and less dramatic, this cave is still an interesting journey. Nodongdonggul is the most recently discovered cave in the area, with a length of around 1km. There are the usual steel staircases and catwalks, but nowhere near as many people visit this cave, so you don't get that feeling of claustrophobia that is possible in Gosudonggul. When you finally emerge and have to walk down the hill to the car park, you will appreciate the depth of the cave. There is even a small resident bat population here.

Entry costs W3000. The mornings are usually quieter and make for a more pleasant visit. From Danyang catch a bus going to Janghyeon (6.20 and 9.35 am and 1.55, 5.25 and 7.15 pm).

Chungjuho 충주호
When the water level is high (late summer), Chungjuho is an impressive body of water. It's considerably less impressive in spring when the water level drops, leaving an ugly 'bathtub ring' around the shoreline. In central Danyang the 'lake' reverts to being a river during much of the year. Nevertheless, when the water level *is* high, cruising the lake can be a very appealing prospect.

Pleasure craft are moored at Dodam Sambong, about 3km north of Danyang via the lakeside road.

Timetables vary according to the water level and to demand. Contact the KNTO (see the Facts for the Visitor chapter, Tourist Offices) for more details.

SOBAEKSAN NATIONAL PARK 소백산국립공원
Sobaeksan (Little White Mountain) National Park is one of Korea's largest. It's on par with the better-known Seoraksan National Park, but lacks the latter's dramatic cliffs and rock formations. Nevertheless, the park is rich in flora and offers good hiking trails through thick forests. The climbs are not particularly steep or dangerous, but can be hard work.

Birobong (1439m) is the highest peak in the park and is most easily reached from Cheondong-ni (three hours) in the northwest of the park. This is a picturesque trail that follows the beautiful Cheondong Valley.

From Birobong you can head north to **Guinsa** (5½ hours) via Gukmangbong (1421m) and Sinseonbong (1389m) along a large part of the mountain's ridge. Alternatively, you can go to the park's southern entry via the **Astronomical Observatory**, **Huibangsa** and **Huibangpokpo** (3¾ hours).

Guinsa 구인사

Deep in the mountains stand the isolated headquarters of the Cheontae sect of Korean Buddhism. This order was re-established in 1945, based on an interpretation of the Lotus Sutra made by an ancient Chinese monk named Jijang Daesa. The temple is entirely modern and made from concrete, and the opulence is obvious. The temple complex is squeezed into a steep, narrow, thickly wooded valley, alongside some impressive landscaping and engineering projects.

If you still have some energy left after the steep climb from the car park, then continue up past the temple for about an hour to the tomb of its founder, Sangwol Wongak. Just a bit further up is a rewarding view of the surrounding Sobaeksan range.

The temple is 20km north-east of Danyang and can be easily reached by either local bus or inter-city bus from Danyang. There are also direct buses from Busan and Dong Seoul.

Places to Stay

Camping is available at Darian (W2000), Namcheon-ri and Huibang (W4500). Entrance to the park costs W1000. There are also dozens of *minbak* that charge about W20,000 at all the main entrances to the park.

Getting There & Away

Local buses from Danyang regularly serve all of the main entry points into the park and depart from near the inter-city bus terminal.

North Korea

Highlights

- Pyongyang, the national capital, with its larger-than-life monuments to the exploits of the late Kim Il Sung, the 'Great Leader'

- The mountains of Kumgangsan are one of the most spectacular sights on the whole peninsula and are now a Hyundai resort complex

- The northern side of the Demilitarized Zone (DMZ) at Panmunjeom, your last chance to see the Cold War at full freeze

- Paekdusan, Korea's highest peak and a sacred mountain of outstanding natural features. The mythical and spiritual birthplace of the Korean race and naturally Kim Jong Il, the 'Dear Leader'

- Myohyangsan, a pleasant natural escape from Pyongyang and home to the unbelievably larger-than-life International Friendship Exhibition

- Kaesong, the ancient capital of the Goryeo kingdom. Despite only just surviving the ravages of three wars, a couple of sites of interest remain, including a small section of the city containing some traditional tile-roofed housing

Over 100 years ago, Korea was known as the 'Hermit Kingdom' because the country tried to shut out the rest of the world. These days, South Korea is a mostly open and modern nation, but in the North both the terms 'hermit' and 'kingdom' apply – in strange and novel ways.

While most other formerly hardline Communist countries are opening up to market-based economic systems and some semblance of political pluralism, North Korea remains devoutly mired in a unique and highly-organised way of life. No other country in the world still maintains such a closed, rigid system.

This may not sound like a traveller's paradise. Indeed, it is entirely possible that North Korea hosts fewer Western tourists than any other country on earth. And those who do manage a visit are restricted to seeing certain places and must be accompanied by two government-employed tour guides at all times. While you are in North Korea, you are expected to refrain from criticising the North Korean government and people. You will however discover that you are subjected to nonstop propaganda and criticism of the West which often borders on over-the-top comical. On top of that, North Korea is not a backpacker's budget paradise, the cost of a tour is not ridiculous, but will stretch most travellers.

So why go? Simply put, North Korea is fascinating. Tourists are drawn to this country out of pure curiosity. Furthermore, it's an education you aren't likely to forget – many travellers have commented that their visit to North Korea was easily their most memorable journey. Asked to sum up their impressions of the country, visitors come up with phrases such as 'a Stalinist theme park', 'a dictatorship *par excellence*' or 'too surreal to be believable'. On the other hand, there is no denying that North Korea contains stunningly beautiful mountains surrounded by verdant rural regions that have hardly been touched by commercialised tourism.

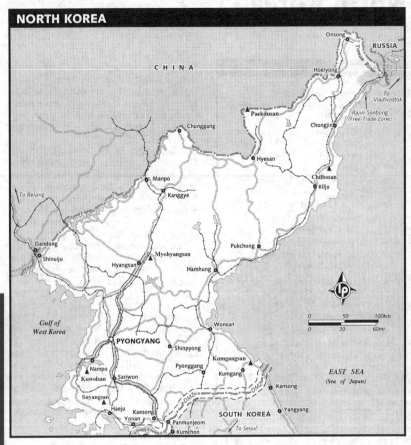

NORTH KOREA

Some travellers come away from North Korea impressed by the cleanliness and orderliness of the society while others are horrified, but most are left with a very memorable experience of socialist 'surrealism'. The big question is whether or not you'll be able to go at all.

North Korea periodically opens and closes its doors to foreign tourists – the only thing predictable about it is its unpredictability. The country is in desperate financial condition and badly needs every bit of hard currency that tourists can bring. But at the same time, North Korea remains the world's most xenophobic country. All foreign tourists are regarded as potential spies and saboteurs. The government is especially paranoid that tourists might try to 'pollute' the people's minds with foreign ideas like free enterprise and democracy.

One might have thought the opening up of eastern Europe and the former Soviet Union would have encouraged some sort of reform efforts in North Korea. However, the opposite has happened: fearing similar turmoil and collapse, the regime has tightened the screws and escalated the war of words. A few grudging and ineffective attempts at economic reform have been made, notably just prior to the death of the Kim Il Sung, but none so far have lasted long.

To the Western press in the 1990s, North Korea was clearly heading for collapse. They repeatedly ridiculed the state of affairs in the country and the absence of visible leadership and predicted a sudden catastrophic collapse. The onset of two years of disastrous flooding followed by a crippling drought were the triggers that left parts of the country in famine and brought about the arrival of the aid agencies. The combination of economic decline, natural disasters and international isolation seems to have brought about a dramatic turn of events starting in 1997. Most of this involved diplomatic communications with South Korea and Western governments, but also limited contact between the DPRK and the Asian Development Bank, the World Bank and the IMF in 1997. The main concern seemed to be aid and low-interest loans, but for the first time hopes were raised that North and South Korea would come together and restart negotiations. This finally occurred at the June 2000 summit. North and South were reunited in the form of the two Kims hugging, chatting and drinking together. The two leaders, Kim Dae-jung and Kim Jong Il had forged a new era of trust and potential cooperation. It is still too early to tell what the full repercussions of this event are, but the fact that both sides were able to amicably come together and discuss the issues separating them was a dramatic advance.

What does all this relate to for tourists wanting to visit North Korea? Despite the improving diplomatic and economic relations North Korea has developed, visiting North Korea still remains a bit hit and miss. Officially tourists are welcome with open arms, but the realities of sudden changes in the political, military and natural climate can easily result in a tour being delayed or cancelled. If you have a tour booked always ensure that you have some contingency plan, so that you are not left stranded in Beijing waiting for the tide to change.

Facts about North Korea

HISTORY

Most Korean history, either Northern or Southern, depicts pre-1945 events in much the same sequence and with the same attached significance. However, in recent years in the North there have been a run of 'discoveries' further explaining the greatness, homogeneity and historical traditions of the Korean people. In one case, the skeletal remains of a Neanderthal man were discovered in Pyongyang. The remains highlighted the continuity of the Korean race in ethnic features, blood line and naturally as a single nation. (For more general Korean history prior to 1945 see the Facts about Korea chapter.)

One thing is important for the traveller to remember is that the Koreans of the north have a history of grievances against the southerners; their current troubles and attitudes are not as Cold War induced as one might think. They have felt politically oppressed, economically exploited and socially marginalised by the southerners for over 1300 years; this is a significant contributing factor to the past 50 years of national division and acrimony.

In AD 668, the far-south-eastern Silla kingdom, in alliance with Tang China, conquered the more sophisticated northern Goguryeo kingdom (comprising the northern half of the peninsula and most of Manchuria), losing most of Goguryeo lands to China in the process. From the northern point of view, this was only the first of a long string of betrayals of the Korean nation to foreign powers by southerners acting for their own benefit. Silla proceeded to oppressively rule what remained of Goguryeo for 250 years, sowing seeds of resentment that still bloom today.

The Goryeo dynasty (918–1392), which succeeded the Silla, was founded by a general of north-central origins, and some northern families gained importance in its government, but for the most part southern clans continued their socio-economic dominance.

NORTH KOREA

Northerners felt especially mistreated by southerners throughout the Joseon dynasty (1392–1910), ruled by a Jeolla-do clan and their mostly-southern cronies in an openly subservient relationship to China. Northerners had less chances to advance to the ruling classes and bore the brunt of frequent raids and invasions from Manchuria; they saw very few benefits return in exchange for their onerous tax payments. With Korea's economy based on rice, the south, being less mountainous, warmer and better-watered, was naturally wealthier. Little was ever done to redress the imbalance, or pull the northern populace back from the brink of starvation during their frequent famines. The government only seemed to acknowledge the worth of the taller, stronger, tougher northern mountain-dwellers when they needed soldiers to fight off another 'barbarian' incursion.

At the end of the Joseon dynasty, after Korea had opened up to foreigners, almost the only successful Western economic venture was a large gold mine north of Pyongyang. By providing difficult and dangerous jobs for northern workers at very low wages, with all profits sent to Seoul and abroad, it came to be seen as south-sanctioned foreign theft of the north's resources. At the same time, American Christian missionaries found the northern regions to be fertile (spiritual) soil, rapidly gaining converts by exploiting the resentment of poor northerners toward the corrupt and exclusive Confucian culture of Seoul.

The Japanese imperial conquest of Korea (1905–1945) was, in northern eyes, the result of yet another sell-out of the national sovereignty by corrupt southern officials. Most of the guerrilla warfare conducted against the Japanese police and army took place in the northern provinces and neighbouring Manchuria; northerners are still proud of having carried a disproportionate burden in the anti-Japan struggle. In fact, modern history books from Pyongyang imply that Kim Il Sung defeated the Japanese nearly single-handedly (with a bit of help from loyal comrades and his infant son).

He led the armed struggle against the Japanese imperialist invaders to victory, and liberated the country on August 15 1945.

North Korean propaganda booklet

North and South Korea have gone to great lengths to portray Kim Il Sung in radically different moulds. Myths abound on both sides. The South suggests that he was an impostor who stole the name and exploits of a famous anti-Japanese guerrilla fighter. History will no doubt reveal more truths and myths about the history of both South and North. So far, more and more evidence is supporting the North Korean line of a well-organised and effective guerrilla leader who operated largely in Manchuria with the strong support of the Korean-Chinese populace.

During the Japanese occupation the south remained mostly agricultural (and better-fed), while Japan partially industrialised the northern regions by exploiting their hydropower, logging and mining potential. This fostered a semi-urbanised, harshly-treated industrial working class in the north. This new class, together with the hungry farmers, both already primed to hopeful idealism by fervent evangelical Protestantism, became again fertile soil for another foreign ideology – Marxism.

The Democratic People's Republic

North Korea's history as a separate political entity begins from the end of WWII. The USA, the UK and the USSR had made a deal just after the Yalta Conference, in the closing days of the war – the USSR was to temporarily occupy Korea north of the 38th parallel, while the USA would occupy the south, with the purpose of disarming surrendered Japanese troops and sending them home. This 'temporary' partitioning was also done to Germany, with the same tragic result.

Kim Il Sung steadily became head of a separate government in North Korea, in defiance of the United Nations plan for nationwide democratic elections. In February 1946 a de facto separate northern administration, called the Interim People's Committee, was established in Pyongyang with quiet Soviet backing. It was initially comprised of communists, socialists and moderate figures, but Kim Il Sung was able to take full control and force the moderates out in less than a year. He created the pro-Soviet and revolutionary Korean Workers' Party as his political vehicle, and deployed police and the military to defend his takeover and implement a socialist revolution. The party together with the armed forces evolved into a government during 1947–48.

In 1948, the south went ahead with UN-sponsored elections when the north refused to let UN personnel enter their territory. Negotiations failed to resolve the problem, and the temporary division became permanent because neither side was willing to yield. The north was aware that the higher population of the south would have ensured victory for the US-installed southern authorities. Northern elections were held on 25 August 1948 in response to the southern elections, and on 9 September 1948 the Democratic People's Republic of Korea (DPRK) was proclaimed as the sole legitimate government on the peninsula. Kim Il Sung took formal office as Premier, one of his lesser titles.

Both the USA and USSR pulled most of their troops out of Korea by the end of 1948. The Soviet withdrawal contrasted with their continuing heavy presence in Eastern Europe. At the same time large numbers of hardened Korean soldiers returned from China after the victory of the communists there in 1949. On 25 June 1950, with US military aid to the Southern government still on the drawing boards, and the US State Department sending out signals that it had little further interest in Korea, the DPRK had assembled a significant army.

The Korean War

Prior to the eventual outbreak of war, North and South were involved in an increasing number of skirmishes along the DMZ (the 38th parallel). It was clear that both governments were eager for the outbreak of war to reunify the peninsula. The problem was who was going to make the first move. Today, both North and South adamantly deny starting the war, despite their open support for war at the time. War was in-

evitable, due to the ardent views and blatant aggressive acts of both sides.

Regardless of who fired first shot, from the first the North Koreans swiftly pushed the South Korean armed forces into a tiny enclave around Busan. The Northern attack was aided by large numbers of guerilla fighters from both the South and North. As a result of the success of these guerillas, the US began burning suspected villages harbouring guerillas and even destroying villages to deprive the guerillas of shelter. The US viewed all civilians as potential enemies and the disturbing results of this approach are only now coming to light. The fact remains, however, that both sides committed horrific atrocities and that civilian deaths outnumbered troop casualties.

Under US prompting, the United Nations passed a resolution calling for other countries to send in troops to try to turn around the war. The war effort took a dramatic turn when a 16-nation UN army, led by already legendary WWII general Douglas MacArthur, landed behind enemy lines at Incheon on 15 September. Within days they recaptured Seoul, cutting their enemy's supply lines; within a month the North Koreans had been pushed back to the Chinese border. The North claims this as a strategic move, or tactical withdrawal, and evidence of the speed of their movement may back this claim.

Fortunes changed again when China's Mao Zedong decided to help the North Korean effort to reciprocate the support the Koreans had provided to the Chinese communist revolution a few years earlier. The Chinese threw 200,000 'volunteers' into the fray and UN forces were pushed back again to the 38th parallel. The war continued as a bloody stalemate in the centre of the peninsula while negotiations for a truce dragged on for two years.

During the entire war the US air force relentlessly bombed Northern territory in a failed attempt to force a surrender, targeting anything and everything, military or civilian. Pyongyang claims that by the end there was hardly a building left standing in all the North; their citizens and soldiers became accustomed to living underground and eating whatever came to hand. This bombing campaign was in fact even heavier than either Japan or Germany had endured in WWII. The North Koreans still recall it with deep bitterness, as a war-crime of the worst sort.

In 1953 the war ended with a negotiated cease-fire only signed by Pyongyang, Beijing and the UN Forces (led by Washington, of course); Seoul refused to sign, protesting that America 'had not finished the job' of complete re-unification. A point that has up until today frustrated South Korea's attempts to discuss security relations with the North. The North believes that future security issues on the peninsula are a matter between themselves and the US.

The Korean peninsula remained divided, split by the Demilitarized Zone (DMZ). The Korean War resulted in over two million deaths, a million separated families, and devastation of both countries' economies and infrastructures – for no political resolution at all. In reality both sides lost the war, and the harsh division of the country continues to challenge the leaders of both North and South.

North Korea, which refers to this conflict as the 'Fatherland Liberation War', gives a different account of how the Korean War started. Your guide and others may tell you repeatedly that American soldiers attacked them massively with tanks and bombers, but that the North defeated the invasion and massively counter-attacked into the South, finally attaining a great victory. One pamphlet has this to say about the war:

The US imperialists, who had boasted of being the strongest in the world, frantically pounced upon the Korean people in league with the south Korean puppet army plus the troops of 15 satellite countries.

'An Earthly Paradise for the People'

However, the American imperialists who were assured of a glorious victory in this grim war were covered all over with wounds and surrendered to the heroic Korean people. As a result, the Korean people and their young People's Army held a military parade in honour of their victory in the presence of President Kim Il Sung, the ever-victorious and iron-willed brilliant commander.

This was a great victory and natural outcome attained under the wise leadership of the great President Kim Il Sung.

Post-War Standoff

In the first 10 years after the war the North Korean economy actually developed quite rapidly, building Soviet-style heavy industry on the foundations the Japanese had laid. North Korean people had some of their first schools, clinics, food reserves, labour rights, recreational facilities; life greatly improved for those not considered 'class enemies', while mortality rates nose-dived. Development was much faster and friendlier to common people than it was in the South during those early days.

The ideology of *Juche* (self-reliance) that Kim Il Sung created and installed as his nation's complete and only guiding thought never meant refusing aid from Moscow and Beijing. In fact Kim Il Sung used it quite successfully to play the two off against each other, gaining massive amounts of assistance in the process while maintaining national sovereignty – something no other Cold-War client nation managed to do, except perhaps Albania.

Using Stalinist-style purges, Kim Il Sung's one-man show evolved steadily away from the wartime collective leadership installed by the Soviets.

Meanwhile the Kim personality cult was rising; soon it began to rival that of Mao Zedong, and then it surpassed even Mao by canonising most of Kim Il Sung's family too – especially his parents, ancestors and oldest son, Jong-il. Even Kim's great-grandfather was declared by North Korean historians to have been the leader of those who massacred the crew of the American ship the *General Sherman* in 1866. Further evidence of a good line of patriotic and revolutionary genes.

Constant provocations and hard-line responses by both North and South kept relations between them at sub-zero levels for nearly 50 years. During this period 'negotiations' were mostly exercises in shrill rhetoric.

The General Sherman

During the 'Hermit Kingdom' phase of the Joseon dynasty, one of Korea's first encounters with westerners was the ill-fated attempt of the American ship the *General Sherman* to sail up the Taedong River to Pyongyang in 1866. It arrogantly ignored warnings to turn around and leave; insisted on trade; carried a Protestant missionary who illegally proselytised; and repeatedly abused riverside inhabitants. When it had the bad luck to run aground on a sand bar just below Pyongyang, locals managed to burn it to the waterline and kill all those on board. An American military expedition later pressed the Seoul government for reparations for the loss and after that, this incident was otherwise virtually forgotten in the south. However northerners have always regarded it with great pride, as being their first of many battles with, and victories over, the hated Yankee imperialist enemy.

Also of great pride to the North Koreans is the 'fact' that none other than the Great Leader's great-grandfather had not only participated in burning the ship down, but had been instrumental in organising the successful defeat of the imperialist Yankees in Pyongyang. Today, all that is left of the *General Sherman* is a plaque commemorating the historical event. The site is over-shadowed by the nearby ship the *Peublo*. This US surveillance vessel was seized by the North Koreans off the east coast of Korea in January 1968 during a heightening of tensions between the North and South. For a fee you can even step aboard and be provided with another interesting lecture on the incessant violations of the cease-fire agreement by the US imperialists.

Incidents of terrorism, assassination, and armed incursion into the DMZ have bedevilled both sides for decades, though Pyongyang consistently and angrily denies having anything to do with them.

The difficulty for the DPRK has been in accepting the growing strength and importance of South Korea in the global arena. The regime was under the firm belief that there was only one sole legitimate state of Korea. According to a 1989 propaganda book *Do You Know about Korea?*

The so-called 'government of the Republic of Korea' in south Korea is a colonial puppet regime which can neither represent the Korean people nor exercise any sovereignty in its relations with other states.

North Korea's position regarding the USA and the South Korean government is further summed up in the following quote from *Women of Korea*, a magazine published in Pyongyang:

The US imperialists have stationed more than 40,000 troops and more than 1000 nuclear weapons in south Korea, and they, with the nearly one million puppet troops, are preparing an invasion against north Korea...Their aim is to create 'two Koreas', to divide Korea permanently and to continuously occupy south Korea as their colony and, using south Korea as a bridgehead, to make an invasion of north Korea and the other countries of Asia.

Post-Cold War Ramifications

The disintegration of the Soviet bloc has left North Korea with very few friends. The former USSR established diplomatic relations with South Korea in 1990, and cut off most aid to the North. China followed suit in 1992, although it continues to grant small amounts of economic aid (and overlooks lots of cross-border movement) to keep their old ally afloat. Both Russia and China now trade far more with the South than with the North, and regularly exchange friendly diplomatic meetings at the highest levels. In the past, Pyongyang has reacted angrily and spitefully to these moves. It is not clear to what extent China or Russia have been able to facilitate the DPRK's recent thaw in its hardline attitude to the South.

In early 1991 the International Atomic Energy Agency (IAEA) declared that North Korea was suspected of developing nuclear weapons from its one reactor near Yongbyon north of Pyongyang. Pyongyang denied this but refused IAEA inspections, counter-claiming that the USA had over 1000 nuclear warheads based in the South. After the crisis slowly escalated all year long, the USA surprised North Korea by withdrawing all nuclear weapons from the Korean peninsula; those based elsewhere are now considered a sufficient deterrent. Western military sources say that North Korea also possesses huge quantities of chemical and biological weapons which could kill millions if ever launched against the South, and are developing long-range missiles.

In spite of this tense international atmosphere, 1991 actually saw the first signs of a thaw in the icy relations between the two Koreas. Their prime ministers held high-level talks in Pyongyang and Seoul, implicitly recognising each other's governments for the first time ever. To the great surprise of the rest of the world, they signed a non-aggression accord at the end of the year, providing for mutual nuclear inspections and various civilian exchanges. Optimists began to talk of the possibility of peaceful reunification of the peninsula.

In the end, it was the pessimists who won the day. North Korea refused to implement their 1991 accord with South Korea Then an inspection team from the International Atomic Energy Agency (IAEA) was denied access to North Korean nuclear facilities, in January 1993. Further pressure from IAEA caused Pyongyang to announce in March that it would withdraw from the Nuclear Non-Proliferation Treaty. Negotiations accomplished nothing, with Pyongyang demanding the total withdrawal of US military forces from the Korean peninsula as the price of cooperation on the nuclear issue, while insisting that their nuclear reactors were for peaceful purposes only.

North Korea's apparent nuclear bomb ambitions brought harsh condemnation from the rest of the world. Pyongyang countered with shrill threats, which resulted in a statement from US President Bill Clinton that a military strike from the North would result in 'the end of North Korea'. Even relations with China, North Korea's one remaining friend, deteriorated. A statement was issued by the United Nations, with Chinese cooperation, in spring 1994, calling on North Korea to comply with the IAEA. Pyongyang rejected the statement. World media speculated whether the two Koreas were sliding towards another 'inevitable' war. After all the media attention died down, the IAEA's inspectors were given access to the alleged nuclear sites and found no conclusive evidence to support the accusations, but were unable to confirm nor deny that any exchange of nuclear materials took place.

A Rising Son

On 29 June 1994, after a personal visit by former American President Jimmy Carter, Kim Il Sung surprised everyone with an announcement that he would freeze North Korea's nuclear program and would meet with South Korean President Kim Young-sam for summit talks. The talks never happened because Kim Il Sung died of a heart attack on 8 July, after ruling the North for 46 years. A new era of even greater uncertainty began.

Kim Il Sung (the Great Leader) had long planned that power should be passed to his son, Kim Jong Il (the Dear Leader). Dynastic succession (feudalism) runs counter to Marxist theory – and this is the first such case in a communist society. If one is to believe the North Korean news media, Kim Jr has indeed smoothly assumed power with no opposition whatsoever from other possible contenders to the throne. However, there are many critical observers in South Korea and the West who doubt this official line (which is nothing new). The fact that Kim Jr has not assumed his father's title has left many wondering if he really is in power, or simply a figurehead.

For the first few years following the death of the Great Leader, the Dear Leader maintained a low profile. This led many outside observers to question not only his authority, but even his basic capacities. In reality little was actually known about Kim Jong Il, but most accounts from outside North Korea questioned his sanity and character. According to these reports Kim Jong Il was lacking in charisma, often appeared dazed and feeble, perhaps in poor health or even handicapped, introverted, an alcoholic, an addict of Western movies and a fancier of tall blondes. It is interesting to note that most of these statements were originally produced by South Korea's intelligence service, who had a lot invested in discrediting North Korea's leadership. The amusing part is how the West picked up on this blatant propaganda as truths fit for dissemination. The whole exercise has only resulted in a large pool of disinformation – further muddied after the June 2000 summit, which resulted in more than a couple of political back-flips by both countries. In fact, the South is currently undergoing a Kim Jong Il craze, with Kim paraphernalia appealing to large numbers of youth, who are going out buying portly little Kim Jong Il dolls replete with glasses, bushy eyebrows and curly hair.

The Second Great Arduous March

As a result of the withdrawal of favourable trading status with the former USSR and communist bloc countries, North Korea was forced to rely more heavily on its Juche ideal of economic self-reliance. The DPRK publicly acknowledged for the first time that they had not met their economic targets for the Third Seven-Year Plan (1987–93). This was the first time that such an acknowledgment had been publicly made, revealing the severity of the situation. This slow-down of the economy was further exacerbated in 1994 by the death of Kim Il Sung and devastating hailstorms and floods. There was little respite, with further damaging floods in 1995 and 1996 leaving the country in a fragile state of affairs. So much so that Pyongyang was forced to ask for a helping hand from the UN and the outside world to avoid a famine, or worse – the collapse of the system.

Economic depression and environmental disasters have resulted in the steady decline of industrial production, the deterioration of infrastructure and social services (particularly health care), persistent food shortages, increased deforestation and land erosion, insufficient fertiliser for agriculture and a severe shortage of essential resources. The extreme difficulties faced by the government have been labelled the 'Second Great Arduous

Sunshine Policy

At the inaugural address of President Kim Dae-jung on 25 February 1997, he announced that South Korea would embark upon a new diplomatic strategy in dealing with the North. This strategy incorporated three guiding principles, later to be labelled the 'Sunshine Policy' (*Haetpyol Chongchaek*): firstly, there would be zero tolerance of armed aggression; secondly, that unification would not follow the German-style absorption method; and finally, that inter-Korean reconciliation and cooperation would be actively promoted with priority given to those areas of mutual interest. This new strategy was based on the premise that change in the North would most likely come about in a 'sunny' environment of positive collaboration rather than through a cold and harsh policy of containment and estrangement.

Gradually, South Korean and overseas politicians, academics, policy makers, journalists and the general South Korean populace began to appreciate the meaning and significance of this policy. The new strategy rapidly produced a string of positive developments in the bilateral relationship, including increased dialogues on trade, tourism, family reunions and cultural exchanges. The process was not without a couple of hiccups of course, highlighted by the West Sea naval fighting in June 1999 (see boxed text, The 14 Minute Conflict), but due to the strength of commitment by Kim Dae-jung the strategy was never derailed.

The most fundamental product of the policy so far has been the June 2000 summit between the two leaders in Pyongyang. This summit not only produced a joint declaration, but also accelerated the trade and cultural exchanges between the two countries and cemented the growing optimism of the South Korean people that the Sunshine Policy was working.

March', reflecting the second challenge to the country since the effort to rebuild from the devastation of the Korean war.

Despite this alarming picture the country has maintained an impressive economic and social resilience. In an attempt to counter the country's hardships, the government has embarked on a number of rehabilitation programs in tandem with various agencies of the United Nations and the Red Cross.

The main fears are that due to its vulnerable state of affairs and to continuing natural disasters, North Korea may sink into a state of dependency. The recurrence of disasters one after another throughout the 1990s to recent times has severely reduced the capacity of the authorities to handle the situation alone. Despite an antipathy towards foreign relief agencies, North Korea has started to work with them in some of the hardest hit regions. The ongoing frustrations of continued decline have forced the government not only into accepting outside help, but has even resulted in a transgression of the fundamentals of Juche.

The flow of refugees and defectors escaping from North Korea to Russia, China and other nations noticeably increased throughout the 1990s. From high-level diplomats to common fishermen, they all brought with them stories of hardship, deprivation and pending turmoil. The Russian government usually allows North Korean defectors to remain in the country. Those North Koreans who escape to China are sometimes not so lucky: the Chinese government has forcibly repatriated some of them, allegedly to face horrific fates of torture and execution. North Korea maintains that no such treatment of returnees occurs, but the difficulty in tracing returnees clouds the issue. China has built a huge refugee camp outside Yanji near the Korean border, to hold the flood of starving refugees. Riots have broken out at this camp as a result of attempted forced repatriations. Some South Korean churches have established aid centres in North-East China close to the border to prevent the repatriation process and give aid to escapees. South Korea is reluctant to take in and support all these refugees, and

recently has been reforming its laws on defectors to cope with the increasing flow.

See-Saw Politics

In mid-September 1996 a UN-sponsored seminar for potential foreign investors was held in the Rajin-Sonbong 'Free Trade Zone', indicating a desire for economic reform and opening up. But at the last minute half of South Korea's delegation was disinvited by Pyongyang, causing the other half to cancel. The North's actions seemed to indicate an absence of desire for reconciliation with the South and for general involvement with the world: the industrial conglomerates of the South are the most willing of any nation to invest in the DPRK, for obvious reasons (Japanese companies are No 2 and the rest of the world comes in a distant third; most companies are waiting for the South Korean concerns to go in first and pave the way).

Relations between the two Korea's plummeted again in late 1996 after a North Korean submarine carrying heavily-armed commandos beached in Gangneung (South Korea). Firefights between the commandos and South Korean troops left several South Koreans dead. Then in 1999 fighting broke out in the West Sea between the two navies, with some of the most dramatic battles since the end of the Korean War. As a result of these conflicts, conservative politicians and social leaders in the South called for a tougher policy against the North, and Seoul briefly suspended all food and energy aid efforts to the North.

The June summit in Pyongyang between President Kim of the South and Chairman Kim of the North was probably the most significant advance towards a peaceful settlement of the divided peninsula since hostilities began. A steady flow of educational, economic and cultural exchanges between the two Koreas were the most visible result of the summit. A major impact of these exchanges for both sides, especially the South, was the realisation that there was a human side to their neighbour. No doubt increasing trade between the two nations will be the greatest result. A major accomplishment was a more

The 14-Minute Conflict

In June 1999, the first ever post-Korean War inter-Korean naval conflict took place in the West Sea. What originally seemed a routine infringement by North Korean fishing vessels over the Northern Limit Line (a maritime extension of the Military Demarcation Line – the 38th parallel) turned into a naval battle that resulted in at least one North Korean naval vessel sunk and injuries and casualties on both sides. The fact that the conflict only lasted 14 minutes didn't diminish the significance of an exchange that in normal circumstances would have placed both countries' defence forces on red alert. As things panned out, however, the consequences of the battle were very slight: the cancellation of family reunion discussions and an increase in US naval reinforcements in the region. Despite the clash, Seoul continued its delivery of fertiliser and rice aid, the Kumgangsan tours bringing people from South to North continued unabated and South Korean economic and trade envoys continued to visit Pyongyang. Most analysts suggested that Kim Dae-jung's Sunshine Policy (see boxed text, earlier) was the main reason that reunification talks weren't sidetracked or completely halted. As for why the conflict occurred in the first place, the reason may never be known. Whether it was a continuation of North Korea's erratic 'diplomacy' or a sign of divided decision-making, the main result was the conclusion that the Sunshine Policy was succeeding in reducing tensions and fostering mutual cooperation and reconciliation on the peninsula.

optimistic assessment of the situation, which up until 2000 was realistically depressing.

North Korea's true situation and intentions remain intensely speculated upon. Anyone who tells you that they know what's *really* going on up there is either a fool or a liar. The truth about North Korea probably lies somewhere between the propaganda of both North and South, though one of the most fundamental changes to the South since the June 2000 summit has been a more

honest reporting of events and developments. The world can only watch and wait as the next act of the Korean drama unfolds.

Engaging with the World

The ideology and experience of the past has in some ways helped the North Korean leadership weather the collapse of the Soviet bloc and the economic difficulties of the 1990s. The government's resolve to strengthen ideological discipline and to continue its isolationist Juche policy grew out of watching the collapse of successive regimes throughout Eastern Europe and the former Soviet Union. It appears that they have been able to carry out an ingenious diplomatic feat that has seen the country break out of five decades of isolation, without compromising its domestic political and social rigidity.

The events of recent years caught many countries and Korea-watchers by surprise. No one expected Kim Jong Il to break out of his domestic shell. In hindsight most are now arguing that he had no choice if he was to avert the collapse of the country.

This recent diplomatic drive can be traced back to 1998, with the beginning of some nuclear and missile brinkmanship. In August 1998 the launching of Taepodong I, a missile that passed over Japan before landing in the sea, resulted in a stunned international response. In early 1999 a US spy satellite sited a suspected nuclear site at Kumchang-ri. The DPRK then threatened to launch Taepodong II, a long-range ballistic missile, in September 1999. These events led to the US embarking on a bit of soul searching. The result was the Perry Report, which called for an extensive review of US policy towards North Korea. The US demanded an end to the missile program and unconditional access to the suspected nuclear site. Pyongyang was forthcoming, but only at a price. Admission to Kumchang-ri would cost $300 million and to scuttle the missile launch US sanctions would have to be dropped and compensation paid. Negotiations were still progressing at the time of writing, but it looks inevitable that North Korea will be removed from the United States' list of

NORTH KOREA

terorist-sponsoring states, US sanctions will be lifted and the US will embark on the signing of a peace treaty.

In the more immediate follow up to this apparent crisis, Pyongyang embarked on a rapid and never-before-seen diplomatic pilgrimage. In just over a year, diplomatic relations were normalised with European Union nations, the Philippines, Australia and Canada, and North Korea was admitted to the ASEAN Regional Forum. There were also promising developments in the bilateral relationship with China and Russia, two strong former allies. With the lifting of US sanctions, the World Bank and the Asian Development Bank will begin to provide aid and soft loans to the North, but only on the basis it will undertake reforms and restructuring to its economy. Up until now, North Korea has been able to strike omnidirectional trade and aid deals without making any reciprocal offers of reforms to the country's economy or society.

North Korea's 'peace offensive' entered a new phase in October 2000, with a visit to the country by US secretary of state Madeleine Albright to discuss, among other things, the scaling back of North Korea's missile program in return for assistance with launching North Korean satellites. The US administration's desire to 'do business' with Kim Jong Il is palpable; whether he is willing to offer returns on their investment is still a matter for intense speculation.

The diplomatic achievements of Kim Jong Il and his regime have been quite miraculous. They have sensed the desires of the international community and cashed in on the emerging global environment. It is still too early to assess the sincerity of these triumphs and whether there is a real interest of the North in participating in the international community. What has clearly been achieved, however, is a dramatic reduction in regional tensions and a gradual increase in the transparency of a country that still keeps many world leaders guessing as to its next move.

GEOGRAPHY

North Korea occupies 55% of the land area of the Korean peninsula, around 122,700 sq km.

It is divided from China to the north by the rivers Amnok (Amur) and Tuman (Tumen), and by the Tuman from a slight sliver of Russia to the extreme north-east. An electrified fence marks the border with South Korea.

North Korea is estimated to be 80% uninhabitable mountains, compared to 70% for the South. The northern and eastern regions of North Korea are mostly rugged mountains with dense forests, and are not well suited to agriculture. The North's food producing regions, its granaries, centre around the great plains of Pyongyang, Hwanghaenam-do, Hwanghaebuk-do, Pyonganbuk-do and Pyongannam-do. Resources include great mineral wealth (soft coal, iron, magnesium, graphite, a little gold), vast forests of both hardwoods and softwoods, hydropower sites and fisheries. Estuaries and marshes teem with migratory birds and other wildlife.

CLIMATE

The weather is similar to South Korea, but colder and drier in winter. There are four distinct seasons. Autumn is the preferred time for a visit, with crisp, dry weather and a chance to see the leaves changing colour. Over 60% of the annual rainfall falls from July to September. Average monthly temperatures for Pyongyang are as follows:

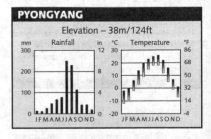

ECOLOGY & ENVIRONMENT

A trip to North Korea makes an interesting comparison to the South. While South Korea suffers from some serious environmental problems, there is little visible pollution in the North. The one thing which strikes most visitors to North Korea is its squeaky-clean appearance. This is a function not just of the lack of consumer goods and their packaging but of determined policies which keep it that way. The streets are washed down twice a week, and before dawn each day street cleaners are out sweeping up any litter or leaves they can find. You'd be hard pressed to find a single piece of paper on the streets, despite the absence of litter bins. Even in the countryside, women are assigned a particular stretch of the main road to sweep up – each and every day.

The other major contrast with the South is the lack of traffic on the highways. Most of what you'll see will be work unit, army or aid agency vehicles. There are very few passenger cars. North Korea has only just started up its first automobile manufacturing plant, with the aid of South Korea. As a result, there's nothing remotely like the traffic congestion and vehicle-exhaust pollution which characterises many South Korean cities.

The main challenges to the environment are from problems that are harder to see. The devastating floods and economic slowdown during the 1990s wreaked havoc not only on property and agricultural land, but also on the environment. Fields were stripped of their top soil which, combined with shortages of fertiliser, forced authorities to expand the arable land under cultivation. Unsustainable and unstable hill-side areas, river banks and road edges were brought under cultivation, further exacerbating erosion, deforestation, fertiliser contamination of the land and rivers and the vulnerability of crops. The government was forced to ask the United Nations Development Program for assistance to improve the rural environment. As a result, attempts have been made to rehabilitate and protect vulnerable agricultural land and water catchment basins. There have been reafforestation programs, and recently a flurry of activity in the construction of fresh-water fish ponds and an increase in goat farming, so as to increase the protein levels of the populace. The environmental effects of such changes are yet to be examined. At present it is difficult to assess the impact of the economic problems on the country's flora and fauna, but it seems logical that enormous pressure has been placed on many species in the nation's search for alternative sources of nutrition and energy.

FLORA & FAUNA

North Korea boasts a diverse range of plants and animals, especially in the northern, more mountainous, regions of the country. The varying climatic regions have created environments that are home to subarctic, alpine and even sub-tropical plant and tree species. Most of the country's fauna is contained within the limited nature reserves around the mountainous regions as most of the lower plains have been converted to arable agricultural land. An energetic reafforestation program was carried out after the Korean War to replace many of the forests that were destroyed by the incessant bombing campaigns. A notable exception being the area to the north of the DMZ, where defoliants are used to remove vegetation for security purposes. The comparatively low population has resulted in the preservation of most mountainous regions.

Only recently has the international community begun to look at assisting the North in assessing and monitoring the country's biodiversity. Three areas of particular focus are the DMZ, the wetlands of the Tumen River and the Paekdusan mountains. For those interested in participating in a tour of North Korea with a greater emphasis on flora and fauna, then it is possible to organise an appropriate itinerary with your Korean tour company. Bird watching visits to some of the wetland habitats of migratory birds are the most popular. These tours, however, often involve greater expenses, especially if a chartered flight is necessary.

Two particular flora species have attracted enormous attention from the North Koreans and neither of the flowers are native. After a visit to Indonesia in 1965, President Sukharno named a newly developed orchid after Kim Il Sung. The name *kimilsungia* was adopted – popular acclaim overcoming Kim's modest reluctance to accept such an honour. Not to be outdone, Kim Jong Il was presented with his namesake, *kimjongilia*, a begonia developed by a Japanese horticulturist, on his 46th birthday. The blooming of either flower is announced annually as a tribute to the two Great Leaders and visitors will

NORTH KOREA

notice their omnipresence throughout official tourist sites.

GOVERNMENT & POLITICS

The North Korean government has divided the republic into nine provinces and five 'special cities' (under direct control of the national government). The Southern government dogmatically holds to the pre-war view that North Korea consists of just five provinces (with no special cities), and so maps of North Korea made by the two sides look quite different (Pyongyang acknowledges the divisions of the South as the Southern authorities have drawn them).

The reason for the expansion of Northern administrative units to match those of the South is to support North Korea's re-unification proposals. Pyongyang proposes that it and the Seoul government share power equally through indirect democracy; having an equal number of provinces and special cities makes the two nations appear politically equivalent despite the South's population being double the North's. Seoul rejects this administrative-division equivalence and insists on a whole-nation direct democracy (in which of course the Southerners would have an overwhelming advantage).

Kim Il Sung totally dominated the politics of North Korea from 1948 until his death in 1994. If there was anyone who outdid Stalin or Mao Zedong in their cults of personality, then it was Kim Il Sung. Huge statues and portraits of him litter North Korean cities, villages and parks; everyone wears a Great/Dear Leader badge; and every home, store and work place has pictures of the Kims mounted on the wall. Not only was Kim Il Sung's word considered the Will of Heaven, but children are taught hymns to him, which they sing daily. He is still referred to as 'Our National Father, Who Shines on Us Like the Sun', 'Ever-Victorious Marshall', 'the Greatest Genius the World has Ever Known', 'Great Comrade Kim Il Sung', 'the *Suryong* (an old Goryeo term meaning 'maximum leader') of Our Party and Revolution' and 'the Fatherly Leader of All Koreans Forever' and so on (and on).

His death created a yawning vacuum that could only be filled by dynastic succession. Kim Il Sung ruled supremely and Kim Jong Il was expected to inherit his mantle. This created the first and only socialist dynastic kingdom on the planet. Kim Jong Il proclaimed that Confucian-style mourning for his father was to run for three years. As a result of this filial piety, Kim Jong Il is said to have 'achieved a new standard of morality that surpasses even our ancestors'. This was the explanation for why Kim Jong Il remained out of public sight and left the thrones of president and chairman of the Workers' Party vacant for three years. Recent slogans have transferred the title of Great Leader to Kim Jong Il and proclaimed that 'Kim Jong Il is the same as Kim Il Sung', a rather heavy-handed attempt to pass the mantle. The title of president is the only position beyond his reach. The late Kim Il Sung was not only proclaimed 'the Sun of the Nation', but was immortalised in the country's constitution, newly named *Kim Il Sung Constitution*, as the 'Eternal President of the Republic'. Kim Jr became general secretary of the Party on October 8 1997, three months after Kim Il Sung's death. No one

Liberator, father, protector, God: Kim Il Sung presides over the national conscience.

knows to what extent the elite, the common people, and especially the military really accept Kim Jr as their leader. If the perennial celebrations that take place in Pyongyang are any clue, then things seem to travelling smoothly for the son of 'the Sun'.

To the extent that any outsider can understand North Korea's political system, the government of North Korea continues as a family affair: consisting of Kim Jong Il and various relatives, a few old hardline comrades-in-arms of Kim Snr, and a few more pragmatic or technocratic friends of Kim Jr. After Kim Jong Il returned to the spotlight in 1997, it seemed that no major changes were afoot. He was instated as the general secretary of the Korean Workers' Party, made no major deviation from the past and smoothly transferred the personality cult across to himself. Despite the economic and natural calamities inflicting the country, the army's position and importance appears to have been maintained, if not enhanced.

ECONOMY

Market freedom does not officially exist in North Korea, although elements of a simple capitalist economy have appeared during the past decade as the mainstream economy has steadily shrunk.

The nominally Marxist centralised command economy established after 1945 has been guided by Juche. The forty-year attempt at isolationist self-sufficiency resulted in the country spurning Western overseas aid and trade, but maintaining trading and economic links with many Soviet bloc states and developing countries in Africa. The focus of economic thinking, including the *Chollima* movement – committing industrial enterprises to productivity 'speed battles' – stressed the pivotal contribution of ideology and monumentalism to economic development. Hence the country has poured its resources into the military, heavy and light industries, grandiose monuments and statues of the Great Leader, while neglecting agriculture and the production of basic consumer goods.

The ironic result of these policies is what has been called the world's most heavily industrialised nation – the industrialisation rate of North Korea's workforce is estimated at an astounding 60% (the Soviet Union at its peak had only 40%, while Western countries average 20% or less).

Unfortunately, steel and bricks are not edible. Furthermore, heavy industries depend on such inputs as fuel and materials, which have grown steadily scarcer. Industry has been in a steep decline ever since subsidies from the former USSR ended in 1990. Credible outside sources claim the economy is continuing to shrink by at least 5% per year on the average, though it is hard to see how the economy can decline much further in the future since it is close to subsistence level. Severe energy shortages have led to the closure of more than half of all factories. The last furnace in North Korea's largest steel mill was shut down in March 1996. The size of the North's total annual foreign trade is smaller than that of most of South Korea's *jaebeols* (conglomerates).

Catastrophic flooding in the summers of 1994, 1995 and 1996 ruined grain crops and destroyed prime agricultural land, resulting in widespread malnutrition; even soldiers are thought to have been desperately short of food. Grain rations are reported to have sunk to around 200g per person per day (the UN's minimum for basic nutrition is 500g), and that is often only coarse corn or millet. While the party elite remain well fed, ordinary citizens have been reduced to foraging the hills for weeds to make soup, and hand-forging bits of scrap metal to make household and garden tools.

Officially unacknowledged, apparently unregulated markets have sprung up in the heart of major cities and towns, devoted mainly to cash sales but also to the bartering of food for goods. The government has officially sanctioned the existence of small neighbourhood-run street stalls selling bread and other basics at unsubsidised prices. There are even some travelling traders, mostly Korean-Chinese, who are becoming a common sight in the far-northern provinces, often accepting household goods and clothing in exchange for Chinese-grown food.

NORTH KOREA

NORTH KOREA

Reunification at Any Price?

You would be hard-pressed to find anybody in Korea who does not support reunification of their divided peninsula. Indeed, if there is anything that both North and South Korea can agree on, it is the 'burning desire of the Korean people for reunification. Furthermore, every Korean agrees that the sooner the two Koreas can reunify, the better...Or do they?

Having witnessed the great financial burden that the former West Germany has incurred while absorbing the East, many South Koreans have started to ask just how much the family reunion is going to cost them. This question has sent economists scurrying for their computers, and the price tag they've come up with has raised more than a few eyebrows.

All figures are rough estimates, but it is thought that the cost of absorbing North Korea into the South Korean economy will cost anywhere from US$770 billion up to $3.6 trillion over a ten year period. The high figures have much to do with the fact that North Korea is in far worse financial shape than the former East Germany ever was. And this is to say nothing of the potential social problems if millions of Northern economic refugees pour into the South to search for better-paying jobs. There are other economists who argue that the sooner reunification takes place the less the burden on the Southern economy. They argue that the divide between the two economies will only continue to widen in the coming years and the cost of bringing their Northern neighbours up to Southern living standards will only continue to grow.

Interestingly enough, the North also has a lot to lose from reunification. The pressure on the communist state to reform may be too much, resulting in its collapse or, worse still for the current leadership, perhaps a calling to account for their years of rule. This stark outcome has forced many in the North to search for a third way. One that won't challenge their grip on power, but will facilitate the large amounts of investment from the South necessary to rebuild and strengthen the Northern economy. Perhaps the Chinese reform program will provide more guidance than a Berlin-style reunification.

While you won't find many South Koreans opposing reunification in the abstract, as it approaches many seem to be having second thoughts about its realities. A recent poll of South Koreans showed that 60% felt that the pace of developments with the North was too fast. In reality, both sides have little to worry about, as it seems evident from the recent developments that neither North nor South are pushing for a reunified Korean state. Instead, they have both agreed in principle to the basic tenant of a peaceful and gradual reunification process.

Even if the Pyongyang regime collapses, maybe that electric fence on the DMZ will be kept in place just a little longer...An increasing number of Southern politicians have been saying that creating one Korean nation out of the two may be 'too expensive' for now and should be postponed until some unspecified time in the future. Many youths now agree, openly saying that they don't want to pay the price.

North Korea owes more than US$10 billion in defaulted loans to European and Japanese banks – the country borrowed the money for manufacturing joint-ventures in the 1970s, then abruptly defaulted on the contracts and kept the technology. As a result, North Korea cannot borrow additional funds for development projects, nor will most countries sell anything to it on other than a cash or barter basis. As for exports, it has little to sell except for weapons (Africa has proven to be a particularly good market). North Korean artworks and antiques, some of 'national treasure' quality, have been quietly appearing for sale in Beijing and other cities of China.

In the early 1990s North Korea passed a number of encouraging foreign investment laws, such as the Foreign Enterprise Act which made it legal for wholly-owned foreign companies to set up operations in authorised 'free-trade zones'. To that end, zones were established, with UN sponsorship, in far north-eastern Korea along the Tuman River bordering Russia and China (called the Rajin-Sonbong region) and at Nampo on the west coast. So far they have failed to attract much interest from foreign companies, with the exception of some Hong Kong and Macau companies, which have opened the area's first casinos. South Korean companies were originally excluded, although they have been the only ones willing to make serious investments there in more recent times.

Despite the near collapse of the North Korean economy, a number of high-priority projects continue, especially power generation and infrastructure projects. Many of these projects receive UN or NGO technical and financial assistance.

Major donor countries, like South Korea, the USA and Japan continue to provide large amounts of humanitarian assistance in the form of rice, wheat and fertiliser. Despite constant rosy assessments of future developments from the UN's agencies, it appears that North Korea will continue to be dependent upon donor assistance for many years to come.

POPULATION & PEOPLE

The population of North Korea is approximately 22.2 million – about half that of the South. The government has controlled population growth, which was estimated at 1.8% annually by the late 1990s. However there are serious concerns that this growth may have slowed due to a rise in infant mortality and deaths from preventable illnesses.

Around 2.2 million people are estimated to live in the capital Pyongyang. Only those who have a stable revolutionary background and are wholeheartedly faithful to the regime are fortunate enough to reside in the capital. More than half of North Korea's population lives in urban centres with strict controls on people's movements and migration between localities.

You need never be in doubt as to whether someone is a North Korean or not. Everybody, young or old, at home or abroad, wears a small metal badge with the face of one of the Great Leaders on it, surrounded by a colour-coded rim indicating the wearer's social rank. After the inauguration of Kim Jong Il as general secretary of the Korean Workers' Party a new badge began appearing with both Leaders on it. There are also badges with just Dear Leader Jr.

You won't see any minority groups in North Korea; both North and South are ethnically almost completely homogeneous and have been for millennia – or so they believe.

ARTS

One thing you have to say for Kim Il Sung – he did indeed promote traditional Korean arts and culture. Kim was a fierce nationalist, relentlessly emphasising the superiority of Korean culture. North Koreans are told they are intrinsically ethnically superior, their country is the best in the world, and Kim Il Sung was the greatest man that has ever lived. The focus on Korea's cultural superiority reinforces the late Kim's position as 'the Greatest Leader of All Time'.

Whatever ulterior motives the regime might have, tourists with an interest in traditional arts can benefit – visits to performances of traditional Korean music, singing and dance can easily be arranged. Some even argue that in terms of traditional culture, the North is the 'real Korea'. Exhibitions of traditional or modern pottery, sculpture, painting and architecture can be viewed on request, and it is highly recommended to include a visit to a cinematic, theatre or opera performance in your itinerary. If one hasn't been pre-arranged for you, your guide should be able to organise a visit to a performance for a token extra charge as long as you give them some warning.

RELIGION

In North Korea, all traditional religion is regarded, in accordance with Marxist theory, as an expression of a 'feudal mentality', an obsolete superstitious force opposing political revolution, social liberation, economic development and national independence. Therefore, it has been effectively proscribed since the 1950s.

NORTH KOREA

See the Facts about Korea chapter, Religion section, for the general religious background of Korea prior to WWII.

The Million Member Movement

By the end of the Joseon dynasty, the Pyongyang area and some other parts of northern Korea were the most successful centres on the peninsula for American Protestant missionary work. One factor in this was the centuries-old poverty and oppression of northern residents, and their resentment of it; this made them more susceptible than southerners to the missionaries' appeals to abandon traditional Buddhist, Confucian and shamanist beliefs in favour of a relatively 'foreign' religion. The Protestant tenant of the equality of all human beings was a revolutionary notion in Korea, and the northerners were growing ripe for revolt against not only foreign occupation, but also the Neo-Confucian elitism, stagnation and corruption that were bringing it about.

Pyongyang was the epicentre of the 'Great Revival' of 1907 and the origin of the subsequent nationwide 'Million Member Movement'. These fevered evangelical outbreaks were partly an emotional response to the surrender of Korea's sovereignty to Japan, which began in 1905; but regardless of the cause they resulted in a heavy concentration of Christians in northern areas.

Until Kim Il Sung came to power, that is. The near total suppression of religion and traditional customs that he imposed from 1946 onwards led to a mass exodus of Christians – especially priests, ministers and lay leaders – to the South before and during the Korean War. Many of those who would not or could not flee were executed outright or died in labour camps. This fuelled a strong anti-communist and anti-Kim Il Sung passion in South Korean Christian churches that persisted until the early 1990s.

Showcase Christians and showcase churches have been exhibited to foreign visitors in the past decade, in an effort to show that North Koreans enjoy religious freedom. These are part of a general strategy to head off human-rights accusations and woo sympathisers in the West. However, reporters and delegations of Christian visitors have noticed that the displayed churches, Bibles and hymnals show few signs of use and the 'Christians' there seem remarkably unencumbered by biblical knowledge or doctrines.

These facts didn't hinder Kim Dae-jung, a Catholic, from asking Kim Jong Il to invite Pope John Paul II to visit Pyongyang. Kim Jong Il apparently agreed in principle to inviting the Pope. An interesting subject for someone wishing to study religion in North Korea would be the relationship between the South Korean Reverend Moon and his financial dealings with the North, which included proposals for a ski resort at Kumgangsan mountains.

Traditional Religions

The northern version of Korean shamanism was individualistic and ecstatic, while the southern style was hereditary and based on regularly scheduled community rituals. As far as is known, no shamanist activity is now practiced in North Korea. Many Northern shamans were transplanted to the South, chased out along with their enemies the Christians, and the popularity of the services they offer (such as fortune-telling) has endured. Together with the near-destruction of southern shamanism by South Korea's relentless modernisation, we have the curious situation where the actual practice of Northern Korean shamanism can only be witnessed in South Korea.

Northern Korea held many important centres of Korean Buddhism from the 3rd century through the Japanese occupation period. The Kumgangsan and Myohyangsan mountain areas in particular hosted large Zen-oriented (*Jogye*) temple-complexes left over from the Goryeo dynasty. Under the communists, Buddhism in the North (along with Confucianism and shamanism) suffered a fate identical to that of Christianity.

Some historically important Buddhist temples and shrines still exist, mostly in rural or mountainous areas. The most prominent among them are Pyohon Temple at Kumgangsan, Pohyon Temple at Myohyangsan, and the Songgyungwan Confucian Shrine just outside of Kaesong. (For more details, see the relevant regional sections, later in this chapter.) For the most part, all these old buildings function only as tourist attractions or museums. Many of the traditional arts associated with them are still practised, on the other hand. Most temples or shrines that a foreign traveller will be able see have been renovated to their original colourfulness.

LANGUAGE
The language of North Korea is essentially the same as that of the South, but the North has developed a sharply different accent and vocabulary, influenced by China and Russia rather than Japan and America. It's getting a bit difficult for citizens of both sides to understand each other's casual speech. There are now more than 8000 foreign words used in South Korea, a large share adopted from either English or Japanese, that their Northern neighbours cannot comprehend. Furthermore, despite both sides agreeing at the time of division to eradicate *hanja* (Chinese characters) from the writing system, only the North has upheld the promise. The South continues to teach hanja as a means of illustrating its cultural and historical past. The North, on the other hand, has actively removed the Chinese influence on Korean words by using words of purely Korean origin. Over the past 50 years of division, the differences in the use of vocabulary, especially jargon, in the areas of economics and politics has become quite significant. In fact, the North has officially refrained from adopting foreign vocabulary. Very few people in North Korea outside of government service speak English or any other foreign language.

Complicating this situation is the adoption of a new style of romanisation in the South. North Korea strictly adheres to the *McCune-Reischauer system*, which the South used to (inconsistently) employ, until it changed systems in 2000 (see the Language chapter for an explanation). Therefore, for this book we have retained the McCune-Reischauer system for the North Korea chapter (but without the diacritical breve and aspirant markers), but we have adopted South Korea's *new* romanisation style for the rest of the book.

The language divide will be an interesting area to watch as the two sides work towards the adoption of standards to reinforce their desire for reunification. Hopefully, the two sides will agree to consult with each other in the future to build on what they have in common. (For the foreigner the adoption of one common romanisation system would also be helpful.) In any case, for the average visitor there is little to worry about, as the guides will be there to assist you every step of the way.

Below is a list of exclusively Northern vocabulary that may be useful during your visit. One of the first differences you will discover is the different word North and South have for 'Korea'. It follows from this that every word that uses 'Korea' will be also be different, including their word for the Korean language and most items of shared cultural heritage.

English	South Korea	North Korea
Korea	Hanguk	Chosen
Korean	hangeul	Chosongul
entry/exit	juripku	nadulmun
traditional clothing	hanbok	chosonot
ballpoint pen	bolpen	wonjupil
juice	juse	chandanmul

The following hip or fashionable expressions are pretty exclusive to the North:

Hello comrade!
  Tongmu (Tongji)!
I wish the Great Leader Comrade Kim Jong Il a long life in good health.
  Widaehan ryongdoja Kim Jong Il tongji-ui mansumugang-ul samga chugwon-hamnida.
It is really Chollima speed.
  Jongmal Chollima soktoimnida.
It is Juche-orientated.
  Igosun Juchejog-imnida.
Here is really people's paradise.
  Yoginun jongmal inmin-ui ragwon-imnida.
It is really a country of morning calm.
  Kwa-yon malgun achimui nara-imnida.

If you want to read more of the same, DPRK-speak books are available from bookshops in hotels and at most tourist sights.

NORTH KOREA

FACTS FOR THE VISITOR

PLANNING
When to Go

Tourists hoping to join tours to catch a glimpse of this unique country are officially welcome. They must keep in mind, however, that sudden crises caused by military or diplomatic factors or natural disaster (all increasingly common these days) may force the cancellation of tours with little or no advance notice. Ensure that you have alternative arrangements in place, such as a tour of Beijing and Xi'an, so as to avoid inconveniences and disappointment.

The best time to plan a trip is during one of Pyongyang's Mass Games or during a national holiday. Special performances, which have been rehearsed for months, can be included in the itinerary. During these periods train and plane tickets are harder to obtain, so ensure that you have booked well in advance. Speak to your tour operator about these possibilities, but always remember that with all the movement that occurs locally during these times the border crossings are more unreliable, and cancellation is highly possible.

North Korea's winters are long and Siberian-cold, and a good time to avoid – especially while energy shortages remain an issue. Summers are generally hot, sticky and rainy. The best months for a visit are April, May, June, September and October.

What to Bring

There is a shortage of basic consumer items, so bring everything you think you'll need, especially pharmaceutical items (medicines, shaving cream, tampons, deodorant etc). Depending on how long you are visiting, it is worthwhile to bring either fresh or dried fruit to eat and share. Fresh fruit won't be a common site during your visit. Korean men smoke like chimneys and foreign cigarettes make good gifts. Marlboro Reds are especially valued since they are not available in North Korea. If you can bring a Polaroid camera, instant photos make a great gift for the North Koreans you meet. Even bringing some photos of your family and friends back home to show is appreciated. Small, modest presents are appropriate for the many guides who show you around the tourist sites. It is always best to ask your main guide first if they think a particular gift is appropriate, just to ensure there are no difficult consequences for your guides.

TOURIST OFFICES

Ryohaengsa, the government tourist agency, is also known as the Korea International Tourist Company (KITC). For information on their domestic and international offices see the Visas and Organised Tours sections.

For details on private tour companies, see the Getting There & Away – Organised Tours section.

VISAS & DOCUMENTS

North Korea began to accept group tourism in 1986, and individual Western travellers in 1989 (although their version of 'individual travel' means constant escort by two government-employed tour guides). USA and South Korean passport holders are still unable to obtain tourist visas, with the exception of those joining Hyundai's Kumgangsan tours, or qualifying for a family reunion. (The situation for US citizens and South Koreans may change in the near future; contact one of the tour companies for details.) US and South Korean citizens aside, all other nationalities are eligible for tourist visas. However business visas are still obtainable by anyone – those willing to invest in joint ventures are especially welcome.

The Do-It-Yourself Option If you choose to apply for a visa and organise a tour by yourself, your best bet is to directly approach Ryohaengsa in Beijing (☎ 6437 6666, fax 6436 9089). Chances are far lower at other North Korean embassies or consulates. You choose a tour program and fill out a visa application, which they fax off to Pyongyang.

While buying your ticket to and from Beijing, keep in mind that success when you go to book your tour directly with the North Korean embassy there is far from automatic. Some travellers have received a warm welcome at the embassy, while others have been told 'the person you need to see won't be back for two months'. They may give you an approval or rejection in 10 minutes, or a week, or a month. In general, a minimum of two weeks' notice is required, but more than a month is preferable. Changes in the precarious economic and political situations in North Korea may bring sudden, unannounced changes in their tourism and visa policies; at times they refuse all prospective travellers, with no reason given. You should have a back-up plan for travel within China in case your bid for a North Korean visa fails.

It is also possible to apply directly to KITC in Pyongyang. This office will forward all the information and forms required and that may be cheaper than going through their Beijing outlet. However, there is the risk of lack of communication between Pyongyang and Beijing, from where you will most likely pick up your visa. If you are organising the tour independently or have been invited by a host organisation, it is recommended that you keep in contact with Ryohaengsa in Beijing to ensure that all the necessary forms and notices have been forwarded and confirmed in Pyongyang. Visas have to be issued by Pyongyang – they are not issued by the North Korean embassy in Beijing, even to applicants with a written invitation from a North Korean host.

If you are organising the tour independently or have been invited by a host organisation, you will require approval and confirmation of your itinerary from the North Korean Foreign Office in Pyongyang. Travellers should check with North Korea's mission to the United Nations in New York or with the North Korean host organisation to ensure that the host organisation has arranged for a visa through the Foreign Office and that a visa is ready for pick-up in Beijing.

One of the first questions you will be asked is 'Are you a journalist?' If you really want to go to North Korea, you'd better say 'No', but we don't recommend

lying to get in. It is illegal to enter North Korea on a tourist visa if you are any sort of journalist or writer, and if caught you could be expelled at your own expense, or worse. Your North Korean guides and your tour company could also get into trouble. The implications for your North Korean guides and/or contacts are more serious than they will be for you, so keep the risk to them in mind. Journalists and other professional writers can apply to Ryohaengsa directly, or through a well-connected travel agent, for a special visa; approval or rejection will be according to their whim.

Ryohaengsa normally issues your visa as soon as you pay the full charge. You must pay for the entire trip in advance in hard currency before your visa is issued, and then arrange your own transport for getting to/from North Korea (see the Getting There & Away section, later in this chapter). Two passport-type photographs are required and there is a US$10 visa fee.

After paying for your tour, your next step is to organise your transport to and from Pyongyang. The normal starting point is your tour company – or if you are in Beijing you can book at China International Travel Service (CITS; ☎ 6515 8562; fax 6515 8603) Beijing Tourist Building, 28 Jianguomenwai Dajie. You must then inform the North Korean embassy of your arrangements. They will call ahead to make sure that your guide is there to meet you and that your hotels are booked and transport within North Korea is arranged.

There are no little tricks, like entering on a transit visa and then extending after arrival, for getting into North Korea. Don't even think about sneaking across a border. This is one country where you dare not thumb your nose at the authorities: you could be accused of 'espionage' and suffer the most severe consequences.

Getting your visa extended while in North Korea is easy, as long as you pay. Just how much your extended stay will cost is subject to negotiation, but include in your calculations your hotel bill, meals, transport and a service charge for your guides and driver. If you want a visa extension and can

NORTH KOREA

come up with the cash, your guide will make all the arrangements.

The visa is not stamped into your passport (which might prejudice future visits to the USA or South Korea) but onto a separate sheet of paper which will be retained by the immigration authorities on leaving North Korea. You can't keep it as a souvenir, unfortunately.

Most likely, you'll be entering and returning through China. This means you should obtain a double-entry or multiple-entry visa for China. Otherwise, you can get a re-entry permit from a CITS office in Beijing before leaving. If you fail to obtain one of these options, you may be turned back from North Korean immigration counters with no refund. In a pinch, some travellers have managed to get a return visa at the Chinese embassy in Pyongyang; this can cost up to US$80 (same day). Your guide will take you to the embassy. You will need to fill out a visa application form and provide two photos and the appropriate money (either Chinese RMB or US$). The embassy is open Monday to Friday until noon. The visa will normally take three or four days to process. Remember that the office will be closed on Korean and Chinese national holidays.

Organised Tours If your time is limited and you want to arrange everything before arriving in China, there are a few tour companies (very few!) who deal with tours to North Korea. Making use of them is highly recommended, both for saving money and for having a smooth and well-organised visit. See Organised Tours under the Getting There & Away section for names, addresses, details and costs.

EMBASSIES
North Korean Embassies & Consulates

North Korea does have tiny embassies in various European countries, notably Austria, Italy and Germany, but these have been useless to prospective visitors. This may change as the DPRK continues to develop its diplomatic relationships. A list of useful embassies

and consular contacts that may be useful to travellers follows:

China (☎ 10-6532 1186/1189, fax 6532 6056; visa section ☎ 6532 4148/6639) Embassy of the DPRK, Ritan Beilu, Jianguomenwai, Chaoyang District, Beijing. This is the most useful embassy in the list. Ryohaengsa travel usually has a worker (☎ 6532 4862) within the consular and visa section of the embassy. The entrance to the consular section is on the east side of the building at the northern end of the fruit and vegetable stalls.
Ryohaengsa main office: (☎ 10-6437 6666/3133, fax 6436 9089) Korean International Travel Company, 2nd floor, Yanxiang, No A2 Jiangtai Road, Chaoyang District, Qionghuating, Beijing. Ryohaengsa also has branches in Dandong, Liaoning Province and in Yanji in Jilin.

Germany (☎ 30-229 3189/3181, fax 229 3191) Glinkastr. 5-7, D-10117 Berlin. An Interest Section for the DPRK is their unofficial embassy in Berlin. It is also possible to contact the DPRK's consular section through this office.

Hong Kong (☎ 2803 4447) Consulate General of DPRK, 20/F Chinachem Century Tower, 178 Gloucester Road, Wanchai, Hong Kong. It may be possible to arrange North Korean visas and tours from here.

Indonesia (☎ 21-521 1081, fax 526 0066) Embassy of the DPRK, Chancery, J1 HR Rasuna Said, Kav X-5, Kuningan, Jakarta 12950, Republic of Indonesia

Russia (☎ 095-143 6249/9063) ulitsa Mosfilmovskaya 72, RF-117192 Moscow *Nakhodka Consulate* (☎ 423-665 5210) ulitsa Vladivostokskaya 1

UK International Maritime Organisation, or IMO (☎ 020-8346 9733, fax 8346 9733) 14 Allandale Avenue, GB-London N3 3PJ, Great Britain North Korea maintains a Permanent Mission to the DPRK to the IMO. UK residents are mean to be approved by this organisation before their application is passed onto Beijing and then finally to Pyongyang for processing.

USA Permanent Representative of the DPRK to the United Nations (☎ 212-972 3105, fax 972 3154) 820 2nd Avenue, New York, NY 10017. At the time of writing, the USA and the DPRK had no diplomatic representatives but North Korea does maintain an office in New York for the United Nations that may be useful for information regarding contacts and other information.

Foreign Embassies in North Korea & China

There are about 25 embassies in Pyongyang, but the only ones of significant size are the Chinese (☎ 390 274) and Russian (☎ 381 3101) embassies. The rest are small offices staffed by one or two persons representing mostly developing nations in Africa, Asia and the Middle East. The only useful Western full-time representative is the Swedish mission, which handles the interests of the USA, Australia and Canada.

Sweden (☎ 2-381 7908 or 382 7908, fax 381 7258) Munsudong District, Pyongyang, DPRK. A translator/interpreter can be contacted on ☎ 381 7485.

Italy, Australia and Canada have recently established diplomatic relations with Pyongyang, but at the time of writing were operating through their Beijing embassies. Their contact details in Beijing are:

Australia (☎ 10-6532 2331, fax 6532 4605) 21 Dongzhimenwai Dajie, Sanlitun, Beijing 100600. Web site: www.austemb.org.cn
Canada Consular Section (☎ 10-6532 3536, fax 6532 5544) 19 Dongzhimenwai Dajie, Chaoyang District, Beijing 100600, People's Republic of China.
 Web site: www.canada.org.hk
Italy (☎ 10-6532 2131~5, fax 6532 4676) San Li Tun 2, Dong Er Jie, Beijing 100600.
 Web site: www.italianembassy.org.cn

The pace of negotiations between Pyongyang and Washington may possibly result in the establishment of an American embassy in Pyongyang in the foreseeable future. If this occurs, then it would be highly likely that other Western nations would follow suit.

USA (☎ 10-6532 3431/3831, fax 6532 4153) 2 Xiu Shui Dong Jie, Beijing, 100600. This is the best place for details regarding US visitors to North Korea.
 Web site: www.usembassy-china.org.cn

CUSTOMS

North Korean customs have received a wide variety of reviews. We were not hassled at all, but some other travellers reported being gone-over quite thoroughly. Bags are sometimes searched on the way in for illegal or 'subversive' materials (which may include religious documents or any products or papers from South Korea). Always be very polite and agreeable with the customs officers, who understand and speak English reasonably well. Besides the usual prohibitions against guns and narcotics, the government lists several other things which you may not bring in:

• Telescopes and magnifiers with over 6x magnification
• Wireless apparatus and parts, including mobile phones, camcorders or video cameras and transistor radios
• Seeds of tobacco, leaf tobacco and other seeds
• Publications, video tapes, recording tapes, films, photos and other materials which are hostile to the North Korean socialist system or harmful to the North Korean political, economic and cultural development and disturb the maintenance of social order

Note that they are very serious about the last of these prohibitions, which may include any foreign-printed information you have about either North or South Korea. It may even include this guidebook, although we have never yet heard of one of our books being confiscated by the North Korean authorities.

Bags rarely seem to be checked on the way out.

MONEY
Currency

The unit of currency is the won. One won equals 100 jon. There are bank notes for W1, W5, W10, W50 and W100, and coins for W1 and jon 1, 5, 10 and 50.

There is not one, but two types of North Korean currency. The first is coloured purple, which is what you receive if you're converting hard currency; this is the only one you are likely to use. The second is local currency for use by Koreans only. Local currency comes in both banknotes and coins, whereas purple currency comes only in banknotes. As a foreigner, you must pay for hotels, restaurants and goods bought in stores in purple banknotes and change will be given only in the same.

You're not likely to need local currency while you're in North Korea: even when you use the Metro in Pyongyang or you want a make a local call, your guide is likely to pay with their own money.

Currency Exchange

Foreigners must exchange money at hotels or at tourist shops. It is possible that your guide will 'assist' you in converting currency. Most Koreans would love to have the 'green' currency, since it can be used to buy rare imported goods.

US dollars are the most easily exchanged and accepted, but Chinese yuan and Japanese yen are becoming equally popular, with the rapid increase in Chinese tourists. It is also easy to exchange Deutschmarks, French francs, Canadian dollars, British pounds and Australian dollars.

Currency declaration forms are usually issued when you get your visa or at the port of entry and you must fill in an exit currency form when you leave. It's probably best to make sure you get a currency form to avoid hassles on leaving, but if you don't it seems that the guides assigned to you can generally sort things out without too much trouble.

All exchange rates are based on the US$, which the Korean won is pegged to at US$1 = W2.13.

The black-market exchange rate in Chinese cities close to the North Korean border demonstrates the true value of the won: in September 1996 it was around US$1 = W180. Anywhere else in the world it is effectively zero. We advise you *not* to buy North Korean currency in China and try to smuggle it in with you – at the least it will be confiscated and at the worst you will be deported.

Costs

It's not going to be a shoestring trip. You're looking at between US$100 and US$250 per day all-inclusive (not including transport to and from North Korea). There are also several price levels depending on the number of persons in your group: one person

(US$200+/day), two persons ($180), three to five persons ($160), six to nine persons ($130), 10 to 15 persons ($100), or 16 and more persons ($70). In some cases you can save up to US$25 per day by choosing 'standard' accommodation rather than 'deluxe' and thus sleeping and eating in lower-class hotels. Discounts may also be offered during the 'low' travel season (November–March); inquire with a tour company.

Transport to/from Pyongyang is not included in your tour fee, but travelling by train instead of plane will save you $66 each way. See the Getting There & Away section for details.

If it's any consolation, they do give very good service for the money.

Travellers Cheques & Credit Cards

These are only useful at the big hotels. When changing money you will get a much better rate for cash rather than travellers cheques. The policy on credit cards seems to change frequently; don't depend on being able to use them.

POST & COMMUNICATIONS
Post

A postcard to Australia costs W1.30. To the USA it's W1.50. The postcards themselves cost about W1 for a packet of 10.

You needn't bother trying to track down the post office, since most major hotels offer a postal service.

You're best off sending postcards since these give the authorities a chance to read what you've said without having to tear open your letters. We haven't experienced any problems with postcards not arriving and the time it takes to arrive at its destination is average. Saying a few nice things about how clean and beautiful North Korea is will increase the chances of your mail getting through.

You can forget about the central post office and poste restante. Given the short time you're likely to be spending in North Korea, it's hardly worth bothering trying to receive any letters. However, if you want to try, the most likely place to receive your mail is at the Pyongyang Koryo Hotel, Tonghung-dong, Central District, Pyongyang; or care of the KITC (Ryohaengsa), Central District, Pyongyang. Just be aware that there is a better-than-average chance that your letters will be opened and read.

Telephone & Fax

It's easy to book an overseas call and send a fax from major hotels, and some even offer international direct dialling (IDD) right from your room. However it is recommended instead that you use the hotel's post office, which in addition to selling stamps and sending faxes can also organise calls. You will probably have to write down the details of the call and they will provide you with an open line. Phone calls usually go through without much trouble. Charges are very high for almost anywhere, except China. Rates per minute for international calls and faxes depend on the hotel, but are consistently expensive. It may be worth calling China and connecting through a telephone card dial-up from there. Approximate charges per minute are:

country	rate/minute
Australia	W23
China	W8
East Asia	W18
Europe	W20
Middle East	W20
USA	W25

Coin-operated public phones are not very common, even in Pyongyang, but you probably won't find too many people to call anyway. They require 10-jon coins, which means you'll need some local money if you want to use them.

If you are dialling direct to North Korea from abroad, the country code is 850, for Pyongyang it's 02. Most Western countries now have direct phone or fax connections with North Korea, but making an IDD call from Beijing or Japan to Pyongyang is very easy. At the time of writing, there were only a dozen official lines connecting the two Koreas. Plans to lay optical fibre links are being mooted and if relations continue to warm between Pyongyang and Seoul, then ringing ones neighbour may even be legalised.

INTERNET RESOURCES

More and more Web sites are sprouting up looking at North Korea. In addition to the large number of travellers to the DPRK who have published their diary and photos on the Web, there are also universities, research institutes and NGOs who publish reports and papers about the changing situation in North Korea.

The DPRK has recently been quite active in establishing Web sites around the globe, with over twenty sites espousing the virtues of the North Korean system, most of which mirror a handful of main sites:

Pan-Pacific Economic Development Association of Korean Nationals An impressive new Web site. It provides a good introduction to the DPRK with an emphasis on encouraging trade and investment, but with useful practical information.
Web site: www.english.dprkorea.com
Korean Central News Agency The official news outlet of the DPRK. A good place to begin learning DPRK-speak.
Web site: www.kcna.co.jp
The People's Korea Web site Includes a summary of recent developments and announcements from Pyongyang. It also has details regarding inter-Korean relations and North Korean history and culture.
Web site: www.korea-np.co.jp/pk

A number of UN agencies and NGOs work in and around North Korea and publish reports and details of their activities. For starters try:

The UN world food program Has reports and updates on the state of the UN's DPRK activities.
Web site: www.wfp.org
The International Federation of Red Cross and Red Crescent Societies Includes DPRK news stories, appeals and relief strategy.
Web site: www.ifrc.org
Relief effort Details and updates for the DPRK.
www.reliefweb.int
Amnesty International An annual report on human rights in Asia, including North Korea.
Web site: www.amnesty.org

NORTH KOREA

Nautilus One of the best sites, it covers recent developments on issues such as energy, relief, diplomacy and peace in the DPRK context. www.nautilus.org/index.html

More and more South Korean Web sites include details and introductions about North Korea, mostly dealing with tourism and photo collections. A visit to some of South Korea's main newspaper's Web sites should also provide a good introduction to recent developments on the peninsula. To start with, try:

The Korea Web Weekly News from the South Includes news announcements and a expansive list of interesting links on ROK and DPRK affairs.
Web site: www.kimsoft.com/korea.htm

Ministry of National Unification Includes propaganda, recent current affairs and developments related to the reunification of the North and South.
Web site: www.unikorea.go.kr

Yonhap News Agency Has an interesting round-up of the weekly North Korean news.
Web site: www.yonhapnews.co.kr

Korea Focus The Korea Foundation journal provides a good summary and analysis of recent inter-Korean events.
Web site: www.kf.or.kr/KoreaFocus/

Contacts A comprehensive listing of useful and relevant contacts relating to the DPRK. http://shops.odien.com/tii/wtto/laender/058.htm

A good source of information is some of the many travellers' reports published on the Web. Just check out any search engine and you will be sure to discover some interesting postcards. Some of those that we found of interest include:

Japanese businessman Has a curious interest in the DPRK, supposedly a communication satellite engineer and clearly an avid golfer.
Web site: www.dpr-korea.com

Postcards from the DPRK Includes amusing music and video segments.
Web site: www.pedropoint.com/dprk/

One of the best sites on the DPRK A great collection of photos detailing every facet of Pyongyang's metro with maps and other details on trams and some useful links.
Web site: www.pyongyang-metro.com/

Leonid A Petrov The Australian National University maintains this site containing some interesting pieces on the relationship between Russia and North Korea.
Web site: www.members.nbci.com/north_korea/index.html

Tour links Useful links to various North Korean tour operators which is regularly updated.
Web site: www. stat. ualberta.ca/people/schmu/nk.html

BOOKS & MAPS
Literature about North Korea remains relatively rare, especially tourist literature. However as a result of the thawing in inter-Korean relations and the diplomatic efforts of the DPRK, more and more literature is emerging. The easiest place to get travel brochures is from the Internet, or from the few travel companies that cover North Korea. The DPRK embassy in Beijing sometimes holds a few bits and pieces, if they are in stock. The consular waiting room – the one dominated by the painting of the Kumgangsan mountains – has a rack that sometimes holds copies of various glossy colour magazines, tourist guidebooks and books by or about Kim Il Sung and Kim Jong Il. You may take these with you when you leave.

Many scholarly works have been written on North Korean history, policies, and leadership; check your local library or university. Most of these can be found in Seoul.

Two more recent, quality works are *Korea's Place in the Sun: A Modern History* by Bruce Cummings and *The Guerilla Dynasty: Politics and Leadership in North Korea* by Adrian Buzo. An older book, but no less relevant is *Korea: The First War We Lost* by Alexander Bevin. Academic journals that often provide interesting analysis of DPRK politics and history are *Asian Survey* and *Korea Focus*.

See the Books section in the Facts for the Visitor chapter at the front of this book for more titles that include discussions and travelogues on the DPRK.

Within North Korea, there are numerous interesting propaganda books and pamphlets. These provide a good insight into the DPRK and perhaps more usefully into the way the DPRK would like to see itself. They also make rare gems for collectors. *Korea Tour: A Land of Morning Calm, a*

Land of Attractions is a very useful guide-book published by the National Tourism Administration in 'Juche 86' (1997). It includes a complete run-down of all the major sights throughout the country, as well as interesting pointers to the DPRK's own version of socialist revolution under the helmsmanship of Kim Il Sungism (Juche). If you are planning a trip to North Korea, then it may be worth asking the KITC to send you a copy to help you plan your itinerary. An earlier version (1991) of the same book is titled *A Sightseeing Guide to Korea*.

Maps of Pyongyang and North Korea can be purchased at major tourist hotels.

MEDIA

The press is centrally controlled. There is no need to be concerned about scandal and sensationalism – everything is completely tedious and bland. Predictable, reassuring stories about happy workers, loyal soldiers, US imperialist aggressors, South Korean puppets, the superhuman feats of Kim Il Sung and 'new discoveries' about Kim Jong Il's mythical childhood make up the lion's share. Likewise, TV programmes are all designed to reinforce the reigning ideology. The improvements in inter-Korean relations and diplomatic developments with the US have resulted in a reduction of the anti-US/ROK tirades. Even the reciprocal broadcasting of North/South news and propaganda across the DMZ has ceased due to the diplomatic thaw. Average North Koreans cannot receive foreign news broadcasts because all radios and TVs are designed to only pick up the government broadcasting frequencies. Information about the rest of the world is hard to come by in North Korea.

Newspapers & Magazines

There are no foreign publications available, so if you want to read any you'll have to bring your own copies. These are hotly sought-after items for the news-starved embassy staff in Pyongyang – you can quickly win some expat friends if you have a few extra magazines and books to give away. Make sure that the publications don't contain any blatant or perceived anti-DPRK

propaganda as they will be confiscated at customs and you will probably be placed under suspicion.

As for local publications in English, the selection is severely limited. There are magazines in a variety of languages available at bookshops, hotels and tourist shops, especially the colourful *Democratic People's Republic of Korea* magazine. This is filled with the usual stories of increased production, great diplomatic advances, scientific discoveries plus articles about the Great Leader and Dear Leader. You'll also learn that 'the Juche idea' is a shining beacon of hope which has swept the world by storm. At the tourist hotels you can find a weekly English-language newspaper, the *Pyongyang Times* but every issue is practically the same.

The *Pyongyang Times* reported that our 500-room hotel with 20 guests in residence was 'always full'.

Ron Gluckman

The Korean-language *Rodong Shinmun* is the official newspaper of the Workers' Party. The main stories usually involve 1) Kim Jong Il urging all citizens to respect faithfully the Kims' ruling ideology and 2) the Party strengthening its role so that it may rebuild the North Korean economy and construct a *kangsong taegeuk* (a strong and prosperous great state).

Radio & TV

The official electronic media outlets are the Central Broadcasting Station and Radio Pyongyang. There are two AM radio stations and two regular TV stations. There is a third TV station which broadcasts cultural events on Sundays and holidays only. The two TV stations broadcast from 6 pm to 10 pm.

A while back, around one hour per week of North Korean TV was permitted in South Korea (heavily edited and with dubbed commentary). When it was first shown, the South Koreans were fascinated, but quickly grew bored with it. It was eventually dropped due to poor ratings. In the lead up to the June 2000 summit, and after, South Korean media were allowed to visit their Northern neighbour. This resulted in their first insightful

NORTH KOREA

and balanced descriptions of what daily life is like in Pyongyang. These shows were highly popular and will probably help to reduce ignorance about the North.

You can rest assured that no South Korean TV shows are shown in the North, except for news clips of student riots and labour violence.

PHOTOGRAPHY & VIDEO
Film & Equipment
You can buy colour print film at reasonable prices from the hard-currency gift shops, but everything else is expensive, so bring what you need. There are modern photo-processing facilities on the 2nd floor at the Koryo Hotel, but you'd probably be better off waiting until you return to China, Hong Kong or elsewhere. This same place can do visa photos in case you need some.

Restrictions
It is always best to ask first before taking photos. Avoid taking photos of soldiers or any military facilities, and obey the reply. In many cases, permission *will* be given. Note that North Koreans are especially sensitive about foreigners taking photos of them without their permission. Not only are Koreans camera shy, they are acutely aware of the political power of an image in the Western press. Your guides are familiar with the issue of tourists taking photos which end up being published in a newspaper article which contains anti-DPRK content. The repercussions of such an event could be quite serious for your guides and the tour company that is sponsoring you.

TIME
The time in Korea is Greenwich Mean Time plus nine hours. When it is noon in Korea it is 1 pm in Sydney or Melbourne, 3 am in London, 10 pm the previous day in New York and 7 pm the previous day in Los Angeles or San Francisco.

Some travellers may be confused by the seeing years such as Juche 8 (1919) and Juche 90 (2001) when they first arrive in Pyongyang. Three years after the death of Kim Il Sung, the government adopted a new system of recording years, starting from Juche 1 (1912) when Kim No 1 was born.

ELECTRICITY
Electric power is 220V, 60kHz, though luxury hotels often have an outlet for 110V. If so, this will be clearly labelled. All outlets are of the US type, with two flat prongs but no ground (earth) wire.

HEALTH
There seems to be no problem with the cleanliness of food and most Koreans drink their water unboiled. You won't have to worry about eating from dirty street stalls either, because there aren't any – well, not officially anyway, and not for tourist eyes.

That said, North Korea doesn't seem like a good place to get sick, since there are shortages of basic medicines. Of course you can try traditional Korean medicine, which is similar to the Chinese variety.

The World Health Organization reports that cholera and typhoid fever can occur in North Korea, but the risk for most travellers is minimal, compared to the risk for relief workers or North Koreans.

If you do get sick while visiting, then you can be sure that your guides will do everything possible to ensure you are adequately looked after and provided for. A hospital staffed by English-speaking professionals is available to foreigners in Mansudong district of Pyongyang.

WOMEN TRAVELLERS
For single foreign women a visit to North Korea is definitely possible and without risks. However, due to the nature of guided travel in North Korea it is always recommended to travel with a friend or in a group just to make the trip more fun. We suggest that you ask your travel agent or Ry ohaengsa to provide you with a female guide as this will probably prove a more workable and pleasant experience. Ry ohaengsa claims that they are available upon request and in recent years there has been a growing number of female guides.

One thing we can say for sure – Korea is a very male-dominated society. It is hard to

ore! The world's most dangerous golf links, Panmunjeom (ROK)

PATRICK HORTON

PATRICK HORTON

nd over the border...the tallest flagpole in the world (DPRK)

Fatigues in civvy street, Seoul

PATRICK HORTON

tatue frieze of South Korean soldiers in action, near the DMZ (Demilitarized Zone)

Forests and gulleys of Myohyangsan are popular with tour groups.

Pohyonsa, Myohyangsan, DPRK

Mansudae hill, Pyongyang

Reunification mural, DPRK

The Tower of the Juche Idea, as seen from Kim Il Sung Square

gauge the real level of equality between the sexes in both North and South, but theoretically it is better in the North. The reality is that old traditions die hard and most Korean men are unashamedly sexist. In spite of the regime's constant attempts to show complete equality between the sexes, there are few women holding positions of importance. There are two North Korean women who *are* revered though: the Great Leader's mother Kang Ban-sok, sometimes referred to as the 'Mother of Korea', and Kim Jong-suk, mother of the Dear Leader.

SENIOR TRAVELLERS

Facilities for tourists are generally very good, and comfortable. The one thing that many travellers complain of is the heavy schedule and lack of time to just watch and think. Koreans normally bestow a large amount of respect on people older than themselves and will usually be very patient and considerate of your needs. It is rare that you will be required to walk long distances as the guides and driver prefer to whip you around in the tour car. If you do prefer to walk more, then ask your guide if it is possible to walk from one sight to the next. He or she will naturally accompany you the whole time. If you require a special diet, then ensure that you let KITC or your tour company know well in advance so that they can make the appropriate arrangements.

DANGERS & ANNOYANCES

For the most part, crime is not a problem. The North Korean criminal laws, crime statistics and penal system are state secrets, but we'd be willing to bet that thieves are dealt with harshly (ie, incarceration or even execution). This doesn't mean you should be careless, but the chance of theft is probably lower than in most countries.

One thing that will get you into serious trouble fast is to insult the Great Leader or the Dear Leader. We know of one Austrian visitor who put out his cigarette butt on a newspaper, right on the face of a photo of Kim Il Sung. The maid found it in his hotel room and informed the police. This resulted in a frightening confrontation, with threats,

shouting, pushing and shoving. The Austrian escaped prosecution but was quickly booted out of the country.

Climbing up into the lap of a Great Leader statue for a photo is just not on (standing in front of it is OK). Try and dress neatly during your visit, as you will be visiting many official tourist sites, many of which are deemed sacrosanct. Avoid expressing disrespect for the nation's leadership in any way until you are safely back in China. You need not be overly paranoid, but assume that your actions are being watched and offensive activities will be reported. Keep in mind that the repercussions of your activities would be more severe for your guides and for the Koreans that you make contact with. At worst you may be detained, but more than likely speedily deported. Assume that walls have ears and keep your political opinions to yourself. The last thing you need in North Korea is to be accused of 'espionage'.

Male travellers should not even think about touching a North Korean woman regardless of how friendly, charming and receptive she might seem to be. Even something fairly innocent like shaking hands could be construed as an 'immoral act' and could result in serious punishment for both parties to this 'crime'. As for relations between North Korean men and foreign women, it's a big unknown. Most North Korean men would probably not dare touch a foreign woman, but given the fact that Korea is a bastion of male chauvinism, it would probably be viewed less seriously than contact between a foreign man and a Korean woman.

Besides thinking about dangers to yourself, give some thought to the Koreans you meet. Giving them gifts like foreign coins or writings might result in quite unpleasant repercussions for them.

In general, if you aren't sure if you should do something or not, ask your guide or just don't do it.

If you want to make an impression while you are in the DPRK, then discard your camera, animate yourself and foster an environment of positive interaction rather than of investigative journalism.

NORTH KOREA

BUSINESS HOURS

Official working hours are Monday to Saturday from 9 am to 6 pm. In practice, business hours will matter little to foreigners.

PUBLIC HOLIDAYS & SPECIAL EVENTS

Public holidays include:

New Year's Day 1 January
Kim Jong Il's birthday 16 February
Kim Il Sung's birthday 15 April
Armed Forces Day 25 April
May Day (international socialist workers' holiday) 1 May
The Death of Kim Il Sung 8 July
Victory in the Fatherland Liberation War 27 July
National Liberation (from Japan) Day 15 August
National Foundation Day 9 September
Korean Workers' Party Foundation Day 10 October
Constitution Day 27 December

Note that North Korea does not celebrate Christmas or the Lunar New Year, or many of South Korea's major traditional holidays.

Foreign tourists are usually not welcome, unless by special invitation, around the birthdays of the Kims (16 February & 15 April).

By all means try to be in Pyongyang during May Day or Liberation Day. Both holidays are celebrated with huge extravaganzas called Mass Games, featuring military-style parades and mass-gymnastics performances. These rank among North Korea's most memorable sights.

WORK

Aside from business opportunities in trade and relief, work opportunities are scarce in North Korea. A handful of foreigners actually have foreign-language teaching jobs in North Korea, but such opportunities are rare. If your country has diplomatic relations with North Korea, then try contacting the Embassy of the DPRK for details.

ACCOMMODATION

You will have to stay at certain designated hotels wherever you go. They are reasonably modern, multi-star hotels which have been built specifically for foreign tourists. It would be illegal for you to stay anywhere else. Since you must stay in these few large tourist hotels, this also limits where in the country you can travel.

FOOD

Despite continuous reports of severe food shortages, foreign visitors eat very well. Your guide will help you order your food. The food is heavily based on meat, fish and poultry, and vegetarians are liable to have a difficult, but not impossible, time. There is a tendency to order Western food for westerners, so if you want Korean food, ask for it. If you have special dietary requirements, then let KITC or your tour company know in advance and they will endeavour to make appropriate arrangements.

DRINKS

Korean beer is not bad, but the hard liquors are often pretty hefty for Western tastes. Try the refined rice-wines and the *insam-ju* (Korean vodka with an *insam* (ginseng) infusion). Blueberry wine from the Paekdu region is quite sickly sweet, but easy to drink and it makes for a good present to take home. Imported liquors are available for high prices. North Korea produces mineral water and some pleasant-tasting carbonated fruit drinks. There are plenty of imported soft drinks available in the hotels and hard-currency shops. Prior to the lifting of US trade sanctions you would be hard pressed to find a can of Coke on the shelves. All has now changed and Coke and its associated bubbly sugar drinks are available for foreign consumption. Don't expect to see Coke vending machines lining the streets of Pyongyang just yet though.

Getting There & Away

AIR

There are flights between Beijing and Pyongyang by the North Korean airline, Koryo

NORTH KOREAN CUISINE

North Korean food is much the same as that found in South Korea, but in general perhaps more salty and not as sweet. The two main ingredients of *dweonjang* (bean paste) and *gotchu* (red chilli) are ubiquitous. One additional characteristic of North Korean food is that most meals will come with several small side dishes, which usually include some pickled vegetables, like gimchi or bean sprouts, and sometimes egg rolls.

In Pyongyang, *tongchami gimchi* is worth trying. With more emphasis on aroma, and lacking chilli, the stock is often used in cold noodles. One of the most famous dishes is *Pyongyang naengmyon* (cold chewy buckwheat noodles). The Pyongyang variety is famous throughout the peninsula and a good place to try these noodles is the **Ongnyu Restaurant** just north of Ongnyu Bridge, over-looking the Taedong River.

Your guides will enjoy taking you out to a couple of banquet meals during your stay, one of which will be *galbi*, or barbecue. Another popular banquet is *sinsollo*; a little like the Japanese *shabu shabu*, sinsollo actually refers to the dish used to boil the dozens of ingredients, which range from vegetables to seafood and various red meats. A bowl of noodles or rice is usually served at the end to help balance off the usual accompaniment of heavy drinking.

Nokdujijim, or green bean pancake, is a tasty snack or side dish. Green bean flour is mixed up with various pickled vegetables, and sometimes meat, and pan fried. A popular dish with many travellers is *pansanggi*, a table d'hôte which always includes an odd number of dishes, usually about 11, served with rice and soup. Kaesong is the home of pansanggi and most people come to the **Tongil Restaurant** to try it.

Kaesong is also famous for its *insam*, or ginseng. Due to ideal soil, water and weather conditions the insam from Kaesong is reputed to be the best on the peninsula. You may see fields of insam growing beside the road covered in dark shade cloth. If you want to continue the healthy trend while in Kaesong, ask your guides if you can have a meal of *yakbap*, or medicinal/healthy glutinous rice mixed with an array of nuts and dried fruit and vegetables. It can either be quite sweet, when mixed with honey, or more salty when soy sauce is used.

A couple of modest rice snacks are also regional specialities, usually consumed during Chuseok, the mid-autumn lunar holiday. One of these, *songpyon*, is made from rice flour filled with various tasty fillings, like red bean paste, jujubes or sesame. *Tok*, or glutinous rice cakes, are a tasty treat eaten during the Lunar New Year period. Tok are steamed and usually coated with powdered nuts, honey, sesame or red bean. Almost as common an accompaniment as gotchu and dweonjang is *soju*, a clear wine, varieties of which are drunk all over the peninsula, made from corn, potato and rice. A common sight on public holidays all over Pyongyang's parks and gardens is groups of picnickers appearing a little overwhelmed by soju.

Air (or Chosonminhang). The flight takes about one hour each way. Koryo Air flies twice weekly, on Tuesday and Saturday, at 11.30 am, arriving in Pyongyang at 2 pm (flight JS152). Returning from Pyongyang, flights are also on Tuesday and Saturday, departing at 9 am and arriving in Beijing at 9.40 am (flight JS151). Tickets cost US$170 one-way, either direction; US$330 return.

There are also two weekly inbound and outbound flights from Shenyang, Liaoning Province, with Koryo Air, on Thursday and Saturday. Flights from Pyongyang to Shenyang depart Wednesday and Saturday. Tickets cost $80 one-way.

Koryo Air's office in Beijing (☎ 10-6501 1557/2288 ext. 2187, fax 6501 2591) is located inside the Swissotel building, Hong Kong, Macau Center, Dongsi Shitau Lijiao, Beijing 100027. This building adjoins the Swiss Hotel, but the entrance is around the back. You must have a visa before you can pick up your ticket. It is possible to arrange for KITC to pick your ticket up for you as they will not require your visa when they present at the counter (you pay the KITC when they hand it over). KITC will charge a 10% commission for the pick-up.

There are flights by Aeroflot and Koryo Air between Pyongyang and the Russian cities of Khabarovsk, Vladivostok and Moscow, going both directions. There are irregular chartered flights to/from Bangkok via Macau and to/from Berlin via Moscow, but Western tourists may not be able to use them. The fact that most travellers are required to pick up their visa in Beijing restricts the use of these flights.

You're advised to book as far in advance as possible. This is especially the case now that the DPRK has embarked on its diplomatic drive. During holidays and festivals, picking up plane tickets can be easier than train tickets. Occasionally, delegations of diplomats descend on Pyongyang for some special event and seats suddenly become scarce. Apparently, there was never a risk of getting bounced by the Great Leader – he was afraid of flying and all his journeys abroad were made overland.

Sunan International Airport is 30km west of Pyongyang, about 20 minutes by car.

TRAIN

There are four trains per week in either direction between Beijing and Pyongyang via Tianjin, Tangshan, Jinxi, Dandong and Sinuiju. They run Monday, Wednesday, Thursday and Saturday. On each day, train No 27 leaves Beijing at 5.48 pm and arrives at Pyongyang the next day at 6.05 pm (about 23 hours). Going the other way, train No 26 departs from Pyongyang at 10.10 am (on the same four days) arriving in Beijing at 9 am. The one-way fare is US$92 for a soft sleeper. In contrast to the plane, it's possible to pick up your train tickets to Pyongyang without a DPRK visa.

The North Korean train is actually just two carriages attached to the main Beijing-Dandong train, which are detached at Dandong (Chinese side) and then taken across the Yalu River bridge to Sinuiju (Korean side), where more carriages are added for local people. Non-Koreans remain in their original carriages.

Customs and immigration on both sides of the border are relatively casual and your passport will be taken away for stamping. The trains usually spend about four hours at the border for customs and immigration – two hours at Dandong and two hours at Sinuiju. You are permitted to wander around the stations, but obey the directives of signs and officials and guides about going outside or taking any pictures.

Sinuiju station will be your first introduction to North Korea and the contrasts with China will be quite marked. Everything is squeaky-clean and there are no vendors plying their goods. A portrait of the Great Leader looks down from the top of the station, and at all other train stations in North Korea. You may wander around the station and take photos, but ask permission first.

Soon after departing Sinuiju, you will be presented with a menu (complete with colour photographs) of what's for dinner. The food is excellent and the service is fine. It's all very civilised. Make sure you have some small denomination US dollar bills to pay for the meal (about US$5), as this is not included in the package deal you paid for in advance. There are no facilities for changing money at Sinuiju or on the train. The dining car is for the use of non-Koreans only.

Your guide will meet you on arrival at Pyongyang train station and accompany you to your hotel. Likewise, when you leave North Korea, your guide will bid you farewell at Pyongyang train station or the airport and you then travel to China unaccompanied.

When leaving North Korea, you can link up with the *Trans-Siberian* at Dandong, China. To make this connection you need to reserve your tickets with CITS or KITC in Beijing beforehand. There's also a chance of crossing directly from North Korea into Russia in the north-east via Hasan and then taking the *Trans-Siberian* to Moscow. KITC will let you know if such is possible.

Russia By Rail by Athol Yates (1996, Bradt Publications, UK) contains much rare and valuable information about train travel in North Korea and the northern Far East in general. For more details and experiences of connecting up with a *Trans-Siberian* trip check out the Web site (www.russia-rail.com) or read *Siberian Bam Railway Guide: The Second Trans-Siberian Railway* by Athol Yates and Nicholas Zvegintzov (2000), or the *Trans-Siberian Handbook* (1998, World Rail Guides) by Bryn Thomas, et al. If you would like to make arrangements of this sort, then either contact CITS in China, your tour company or KITC.

DEPARTURE

If you are travelling without a tour, you should make your reservations for departure from North Korea before you arrive. The government tourist agency, Ryohaengsa, can easily do this for you as long as you inform them in advance. Ensure you reconfirm your departure reservations through your guide.

If departing by air, your guide will accompany you to the airline office so you can buy your ticket, or to reconfirm your outbound flight if you've already bought one. You must pay an airport departure tax of W22, or US$11, at the airport.

Money-changing facilities are available at the airport, but not at the train station. There is no departure tax for the train.

ORGANISED TOURS

Tours booked through a private travel agent are more expensive than booking directly with Ryohaengsa, but only slightly. Travel agents will shield you from all the hassles of dealing with the North Korean bureaucracy and China International Travel Service (CITS) in Beijing. They ensure a smoother, safer tour, acting as a buffer between you and the Pyongyang authorities. Most of the tour companies are able to provide detailed run-downs of DPRK affairs and how they are likely to affect traveller.

Tour prices start from around US$100 per day in a group of 10 people or more. The price gradually increases to over $200 per day for an individual traveller. There is also a $40 per room per night supplement for individual travellers.

These prices seem high by global standards, but keep in mind that they include everything – all meals, most drinks, sightseeing, good-quality accommodation, interpreters, two guides, private cars, trains and entrance fees. A similar-style package tour of South Korea would cost more.

Booking a tour through a tour company or travel agent usually requires a wait of between one and four weeks to process your visa application and confirm your tour, and you may have to leave your passport with them for a few days. Approval or rejection of your visa by Pyongyang can be known in less than a week. To ensure that all goes smoothly, provide your tour company with a minimum of one month's notice. You may need to also supply your resume and a letter from your employer confirming your status. If you are travelling independently, then they may prefer that you join with another group or another independent traveller. This will improve your chances of receiving a visa and also make your time in North Korea more pleasant. Some travellers find travelling independently to North Korea a bit too intense. Having a couple of fellow travellers to share the joys and exploits is definitely worthwhile.

Koryo Tours (☎/fax 10-6418 1722, celular 13621 099 277, ✉ Nicholasbonner@ cs.com) is a British company based in Beijing specialising in North Korea tours. Write to Nicholas Bonner at his office in China at KITC Beijing Office, 2nd floor, Yanxiang Hotel, No A2 Jiangtai Road, Chaoyang District, Beijing 10016, China; or visit their Web site at www.koryogroup .com. This site makes for interesting reading, and offers set-date four-day, eight-day and tailor-made tours, accompanied by their own experienced British guides. Koryo Tours goes beyond the basics of just organising your visa, itinerary and tickets, like most travel agents. Independent tours start at approximately US$1490 per person, minimum of two travellers. Discounts are provided for larger groups. Prices are quite reasonable for their very good service, which includes on-the-ground assistance during your stay in Beijing. One unique

Hyundai's Kumgangsan Tours

Since Hyundai began operating their Kumgangsan tours in November 1998 there has been a steady increase in visitors from South Korea to the mountain resort. Hyundai has invested heavily in the Kumgangsan tours. Not only have they paid a handsome sum to ensure their exclusive rights to develop tourism in the area, but they have constructed port facilities, hotels, provided buses, and improved the basic infrastructure of the area. Hyundai has agreed to pay the North about $1 billion to guarantee their exclusive right to develop the area up until 2005.

In February 2000 the first non-Korean visitors to Kumgangsan boarded Hyundai's cruises from the port city of Donghae. The cost of the four-day tour is around W550,000. It includes hiking in the scenic Kumgangsan, trips to nearby beaches and various sight-seeing trips, as well as a visit to traditional-style hot spas and a performance by a North Korean circus troupe. Restrictions are more severe than for general tourists to North Korea, but the opportunity provided for the mostly South Korean tourists to have a peek at their Northern neighbour seems to make it worthwhile for the many visitors.

Hyundai has also been busily promoting the construction of a railroad from Gansong in Gangwon-do to Onjong-ni in North Korea, so that it will be able to transport its tourists by rail rather than cruise ship. The estimated cost of constructing the 30km line is more than US$220 million. A sign that business is going smoothly, Hyundai continues to bring more cruise ships into the Kumgangsan service. Within eighteen months of starting the tours, over 250,000 tourists had visited the mountains; the tours were often fully booked throughout 2000. Hyundai also has plans to open a casino in its newly opened floating hotel off Changjon port, the port of entry to Kumgangsan. The company hopes to further develop the tourism potential of North Korea by attracting up to 100,000 Japanese tourists annually. Hyundai is also trying to attract other investors into the tourist resort, so that the company can develop the complex into a ski resort and golf course.

To break even on this enormous investment at least 800,000 visitors a year are needed, or 4.9 million during the six year contract term. The company is attempting to expand its exclusive rights to develop the area from the current term up until 2030. With a development of these proportions, you would hope that there weren't any major changes in policy in Pyongyang.

For more details regarding Hyundai's Kumgangsan tours, visit their Web site at www.ilovecruise.com

---

offering of theirs are semi-annual six-day tours arranged to include the May Day or Liberation Day festivities in Pyongyang, at a discount. The advantage of using Koryo Tours is that they are based in Beijing and have good contacts with KITC.

VNC Travel in the Netherlands has been running DPRK tours for a while and, together with Koryo Tours, have been recommended by Lonely Planet readers. They offer a six-day tour costing US$1025 per person for a minimum of two persons sharing a twin room, or $1260 for a single traveller. For more details visit their Web site at www.vnc.nl or contact Mark Meulenbeld at VNC Travel (☎ 30-231 1500, fax 231 0232, ⓔ ind.tours@vnc.nl), Catharijnesingel 70, Postbus 79, 3500 AB Utrecht.

The following is a list by country of other tour companies that may be able to help you arrange your tour:

Australia *Passport Travel*(☎ 03-9867 3888, fax 9867 1055, ⓔ passport@travelcentre.com.au) Suite 11, 401 St Kilda Road, Melbourne 3004. Previously organised North Korean tours, but recently ceased dealing with DPRK tours. They may provide you with some guidance or in fact they may even start up tours again.
Classic Oriental Tours (☎ 02-9261 3988, fax 9261 3320, ⓔ travel@hermes.net.au) 4th Floor, 491 Kent Street, Sydney NSW 2000
Web site: www.hermes.net.au/travel/Dprk1.htm
Canada *Wings of the World* (☎ 416-482 1223, fax 486 4001) 653 Mount Pleasant Road, Toronto, ON M4S 2N2, Canada.

Germany *Marco Polo Reisen* (☎ 061-737 0970, fax 737 635, ⓔ contact@marco-polo-reisen .com) Postfach 13 20, 61468 Kronberg/Ts
Web site: www.marco-polo-reisen.com
Lotte Travel & Trade (☎ 30-6160 9660, fax 6160 9662) Oranienstr. 22, D-10999 Berlin, Germany
Netherlands *VNC Travel* (mentioned previously)
UK *Koryo Tours* (mentioned previously)
Regent Holidays Ltd (☎ 020 7921 1711, fax 7925 4866) 15 John Street Bristol BS1 2HR England
USA *Blue Sea Travel Service* (☎ 310-659 4438, fax 659 4518) 8929 Wilshire Boulevard, Suite 420, Beverly Hills, CA 90211-1953, U.S.A.
Internet *Russia-Rail Internet Travel Service* Web site: www.russia-rail.com.

Getting Around

ORGANISED TOURS

The KITC is Ryohaengsa's representative in North Korea itself (to reach them, phone ☎ 18111 for the English-speaking operator or, to speak with KITC directly, ☎ 817 201, fax 817 607). It is located in Jung District (Central District), Pyongyang. Five-day KITC tours of Pyongyang and Kaesong go for around US$700 all-inclusive (except for travel to/from the country).

Whether you have arranged your visit through the KITC or have had it arranged for you by a tour company, you must be accompanied at all times by two Korean guides – whose fees you will already have paid. These guides work for Ryohaengsa.

For the most part, you will be driven around in a car or a bus; in a few places you are allowed to walk around with your guides (central Pyongyang and a few scenic spots).

Guides are available who can speak English, French, German, Chinese, Japanese and Russian, as well as a number of other languages; at least the guides we encountered all spoke English well. Never try to give your guides the slip or disobey their instructions – both of you could get into serious trouble (and so could your tour company).

There are a number of special interest tours, the per-day costs of which are all generally the same as quoted in the Costs section earlier in this chapter – some may have

higher rates. Special tours include mountaineering (Paekdu, Myohyangsan & Kumgangsan), taegwondo, mud (spa) treatment, Korean language study, educational establishments, dance notation, golf, hunting, and biological or geological survey trips to Paekdusan (these last three would be more expensive). Another possibility is the 'Tour for Traditional Korean Medical Treatment'. This involves acupuncture, moxibustion (suction using vacuum flasks), manipulative (chiropractic) treatment and physical therapy. Cure rates of 90%(!) are claimed for most illnesses. The additional a costs for these treatments vary, but don't expect it to be cheap. Ryohaengsa can supply you with more details.

How much you enjoy your trip largely depends on your guide, so keep a good relationship. A few gifts (a carton of cigarettes, some chocolate bars) given early in the journey will surely smooth relations. North Korean guides earn a pittance – consider giving them a tip at the end of the journey if you received good service.

NON TOUR-GROUP TRANSPORT

Public transport isn't anywhere near as well developed in North Korea as in the South. However you will have few opportunities to use it anyway, and then only in the company of your guide.

One thing you'll notice is the distinct lack of traffic in the cities and countryside. Most of the motor vehicles you'll see will be tourist, departmental, relief or military transports. The majority of the population either walk or hitchhike on the back of trucks.

There are no regularly scheduled domestic flights, only chartered flights.

Air

It is possible to either organise a chartered flight within the country or to join an existing tour that includes one. The costs, however, are quite high. If you want to visit the mountains of Paekdusan, chartered flights go for US3,400 per round trip. The maximum number of passengers is 20. It is difficult to say, but with an increased presence of South Korean and other overseas companies in North

Korea, it may become easier to join chartered flights to other destinations as well.

Bus

There are hardly any public buses in the countryside or between major cities, a reflection of the fact that North Koreans cannot move freely around their country without permission. Most of the time, you'll be travelling by car accompanied by your driver and guide. If you're with a larger group, you'll ride in a specially arranged tourist bus. Naturally, this will limit your chances of meeting local people. On the other hand, if you can't speak Korean then at least it will make things easier, though it does mean you'll stand out a mile as a foreigner.

Being conspicuous is no great disadvantage, and can even be a lot of fun. Children will wave at you as you pass by, while adults will smile and maybe even chat (in Korean) if you happen to stop and get out on the streets. They're naturally curious, and have been encouraged to give visiting foreigners a warm welcome.

Train

It used to be possibly to travel by train from Pyongyang to a couple of sights around town, however with the construction of tourist freeways to Myohyangsan, Nampo and Kaesong, there are few opportunities to do so.

One of the spin-offs of the June 2000 summit has been the announcement that the South will help fund the re-construction of the Seoul-Sinuiju train line across the DMZ, via Pyongyang. The construction of this train line will hopefully open up more opportunities for travellers to continue on through to Europe, via Mongolia or Siberia. This will be a long time in coming, as discussions are still taking place over how to remove the thousands of land mines scattered throughout the DMZ.

Bicycle

A major contrast with China is the distinct lack of bicycles. There are very few in Pyongyang and even fewer elsewhere. Outside of Pyongyang, most people walk. In fact bicycles are barred from the streets of Pyongyang during the working week. Occasionally, you'll come across a few in a department store, usually with no price tags on them. Certainly you cannot rent bikes anywhere.

But even if you did have your own bike, it would create a headache for your guides, who technically have to be with you the whole time. Diplomats and relief workers can be seen riding around Pyongyang, but for the general tourist it is not an option.

Pyongyang

☎ 02 • pop 2.2 million
Being the capital, Pyongyang is a superb example of the regime's determination to project its own image of progress, discipline and the well-being of its citizens. You won't find here the hustle and bustle, the noise and smells of other cities in Asia.

Pyongyang is North Korea's centre of political, cultural, educational and economic activity. 'Pyongyang' translates roughly as 'flat land', reflecting its central location in the low-lying plains of the country's main agricultural bowl. It is the showpiece of North Korea and is peppered with distinctive landmarks and monuments, many of them in honour of the Great Leader: Kim Il Sung Square, Kim Il Sung Stadium, Kim Il Sung University, Kim Il Sung Higher Party School and so on. The city is full of green corridors and large open parks, making a visit during autumn or spring very rewarding. Rather spookily, there is a scarcity of traffic and none of the busy pace one would expect from a national capital.

North Korea's version of the model communist capital city excludes appearances by all things outside the acceptable norm. This includes limiting the public appearances of people with disabilities and the very old, as well as bicycles, animals, street vendors, and even pregnant women. (These restrictions seem to have been relaxed a bit in recent years.) Furthermore, the rules prescribe that only those with the proper 'class background' and proven records of unswerving loyalty to the country's leaders are allowed to live in Pyongyang. Not that you will have the chance to really appreciate these issues, due to the limited time most foreigners spend in the country. What you will see is what is on your itinerary: an impressive list of scenic, bizarre and fascinating sights. There will be little opportunity or time to try and see what really takes place behind the semblance or veneer of normality.

HISTORY

Pyongyang's history goes back to the myth of Tan'gun, who it is claimed was born near the present day city. The authorities have rebuilt a memorial tomb to the legendary founder near the original memorial, which was built in 1429. In 1993, the Korean Central News Agency announced that the skeletal remains of Tan'gun were unearthed near Pyongyang. Where the South Koreans emphasise the greatness of the Silla dynasty, the DPRK instead looks to the Goguryeo dynasty for its historical and cultural beginnings. In 427 Pyongyang became the ancient capital of this powerful kingdom, after it was moved south from the Amnok River. Goguryeo's borders reached deep into Manchuria and the kingdom is fondly remembered by many Koreans for its strength and resistance to outsiders, notably the Chinese.

By the 7th century AD the kingdom of Goguryeo had started to collapse under the strain of successive, massive attacks from Sui and Tang China. Cutting a deal with the Tang Chinese, the Silla kingdom was able to conquer Goguryeo in AD 668, creating the first unified Korea. Later, during the Goryeo dynasty, Pyongyang became the kingdom's secondary capital. The city was to be completely destroyed by the Japanese in 1592 and then again by the Manchus at the beginning of the 17th century. Pyongyang thenceforth remained a relative back water until the arrival of foreign missionaries, who constructed over 100 churches in the city. The city was once again destroyed during the Sino-Japanese War (1894–95) and was to remain in a neglected way until the occupying Japanese began to develop industry in the region. All was lost again

during the Korean War (1950–53) under heavy aerial bombing by the US.

After the Korean War, the Chollima (industrial productivity and speed) campaign was launched to rapidly rebuild the country, with no effort spared in Pyongyang. Today, only a few, rebuilt remnants of the past remain – including a couple of temples and pavilions, the Hyunmoo Gate and a few sections of the Goguryeo kingdom's inner and northern walls.

ORIENTATION

Like Seoul, the city is built on the banks of a major river, in this case the Taedong: a deep and once tidal river whose source is the Nangnim mountains in Hamgyongnam-do. One of the amazing sights here are the two mid-river fountains, which rise to a height of 150m. Your guide will proudly tell you they're the highest in the world, and this may well be true. Most of the major monuments are near the banks of the Taedong.

Since Pyongyang is one of the few places where you are able to freely walk around, accompanied by your guide of course, it's a good idea to walk between the sites on your itinerary (naturally with the consent of your guide). This will give you a chance to get a better glimpse of life in Pyongyang and enjoy the scenic beauty of much of the city.

Instead of traffic lights, female traffic police stand on wooden plinths in the middle of intersections. Another of the charms of Pyongyang, these smartly dressed women in blue direct the traffic in a stiff, robotic fashion.

THINGS TO SEE

Your first day out in Pyongyang will undoubtedly be a guided tour by car. One of the principal monuments is the **Tower of the Juche Idea**, a 170m needle on the east bank of the Taedong River. You can get to the top by express lift for a good view of the city. The ride costs W20, or US$10, but is worth it on a clear day. In an alcove at the bottom are commemorative messages from various parts of the world hewn in stone and brick, extolling the concept of Juche, also referred to on the plaques as Kim Il Sungism.

PYONGYANG

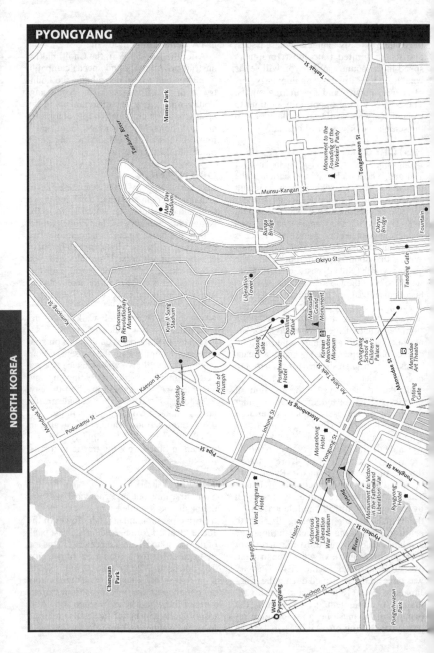

NORTH KOREA

Taehak St

Tudong River

Munsu Park

May Day Stadium

Monument to the Founding of the Workers' Party

Tongdaewon St

Munsu-Kangan St

Runga Bridge

Okryu Bridge

Fountain

Okryu St

Taedong Gate

Chonsung Revolutionary Museum

Kim Il Sung Stadium

Liberation Tower

Mansudae Grand Monument

Kimsong St

Chilsong Gate

Cholima Statue

Korean Revolution Museum

Pyongyang School & Children's Palace

Mansudae St

Mansudae Art Theatre

Arch of Triumph

Ponghwasan Hotel

An Sung Taek St

Potong Gate

Kaeson St

Friendship Tower

Moranbong St

Mundok St

Podunamu St

Inhung St

Pipa St

Moranbong Hotel

Yongung St

Ponghwa St

Ryugyong Hotel

Monument to Victory in the Fatherland Liberation War

Hyoksin St

Changsan Park

West Pyongyang Hotel

Hasin St

Victorious Fatherland Liberation War Museum

Sangsin St

River

West Pyongyang

Sochon St

Pongwhwasan Park

PYONGYANG

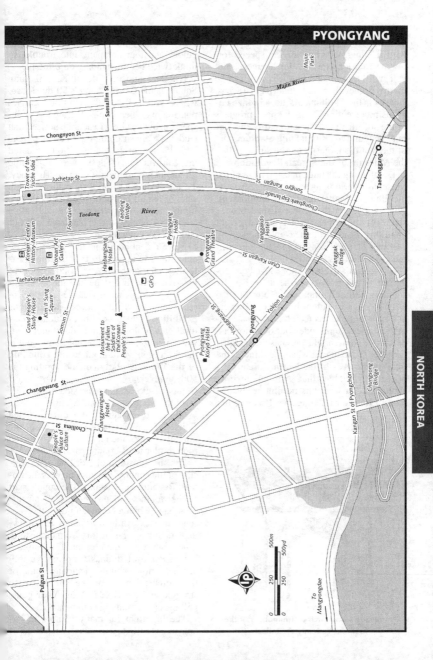

Mujin Park

Mujin River

Saesallim St

Chongnyon St

Juchetap St

Tower of the
Juche Idea

Songyo Kangan St

Chongbaek Esplanade

Taedonggang

Korean Central
History Museum

Fountain

Taedong

River

Taedong
Bridge

Pyongyang
Hotel

Yanggakdo
Hotel

Korean Art
Gallery

Haebangsang
Hotel

Pyongyang
Grand Theatre

Yanggak

Taehaksupdang St

GPO

Otan Kangan St

Yanggak
Bridge

Grand People's
Study House

Kim Il Sung
Square

Monument to
the Fallen
Soldiers of
the Korean
People's Army

Yonggwang St

Pyongyang

Yokjon St

Somun St

Chungsong
Bridge

Pyongyang
Koryo Hotel

Kangan St of Pyongchon

Changgwang St

Changgwangsan
Hotel

Chollima St

People's
Palace of
Culture

Pulgun St

500m

250

500yd

250

To
Mangyongdae

0

0

NORTH KOREA

You will surely be taken to see the **Arch of Triumph**, which marks the spot where Kim Il Sung made his rallying speech following the departure of the Japanese, and you will be reminded that it is a full three metres higher than its counterpart in Paris. Nearby is the **Chollima Statue**, a bronze Pegasus representing the high-speed progress of the socialist reconstruction after the Korean war, and the **Kim Il Sung Stadium**, one of the world's largest. On Mansudae Hill is the **Museum of the Korean Revolution**.

Dominating the huge plaza in front of the Museum, overlooking the Taedong River, is the 20m tall **Mansudae Grand Monument**. This is a larger-than-life polished bronze statue of the Great Leader himself, right hand thrust out to the heavens, flanked by castings of previously oppressed but ultimately victorious followers.

Since Kim's death, visitors have been expected to 'pay respect' to the statue here by standing still and quiet with a bowed head after laying a wreath or bouquet of flowers at the Great Leader's feet. It is seen as common courtesy to provide your own flowers; otherwise you should purchase a bouquet for US$10. No matter what you think of the man, in the eyes of the North Koreans it's not unreasonable that foreign visitors should pay at least this minimum level of respect for their fallen leader. If you refuse

Pyongyang's own Arch of Triumph – not the first, but certainly the tallest

to participate it may cause very hard feelings with the authorities and may get your guides and tour company into trouble, so think twice before standing on principle.

On the opposite side of Kim Il Sung Square is the **Grand People's Study House,** where you will see the studious masses pouring over their books. During a snap inspection by the Great Leader he noticed that students were straining their bodies to read a book on a horizontal desk. So he ordered the construction of desks with adjustable tilt and height to maximise their efficiency. To top it off, the library is equipped with state of the art book conveyor belts that go 'ding'. These belts will provide you with a couple of books in the language of your choice – just incredible.

More recent additions to Pyongyang include the **Monument to the Victorious Fatherland Liberation War**, a collection of massive sculptures depicting the most important North Korean victories in the Korean War, and the **Three Revolutions Exhibition,** which celebrates Juche's cultural, technological and ideological advancements. The most recent monument is the 50m-high **Monument to the Founding of the Workers' Party** commemorating the 50th anniversary of the ruling party on 3 October 1995, on the other side of the river from the Mansudae Grand Monument.

Of a more traditional nature are the **Chilseong** and **Taedong Gates**, two of the old city's gates, the latter with a two-tiered roof similar to its counterpart in Seoul.

For an exposition of North Korea's version of the country's history there is the **Korean Revolution Museum**. The counterpart to the South's Independence Hall outside Cheonan (Chungcheongnam-do), the museum houses exhibits, artefacts and drawings tracing Korean history from prehistoric times right up to the present. The museum houses ten 'cyclodramas', or primitive 360-degree action exhibits, depicting some of the fiercest battles of the anti-Japanese struggle and the Korean War. Your guide will provide a running commentary.

The highlight for many visitors to Pyongyang is a trip to the circus. Asian circuses have a high standard of acrobatics, which is always great to watch, but they also have the inevitable animal acts – horses, boxing bears and even dogs doing tricks. The clowns came on dressed as clumsy South Korean soldiers, but the clownish portrayal of an American soldier (complete with blond hair, sunglasses, big nose and swaggering walk) shall remain with you forever. Circuses are performed at both the **Pyongyang Circus**, located in Kwangbok Street, or at the **People's Army Circus**.

Check with your guide if it is possible to make a trip to either an opera performance or the cinema. Both are very rewarding experiences. Some of the revolutionary scripts are so moving for the audience that they stand and cheer at the victorious moments. The fact that everything is in Korean is irrelevant; the experience remains enriching.

Other institutions which may well be worth a visit include the **Pyongyang School Children's Palace**, established in 1963, and the more recent **Mangyongdae School Children's Palace**, completed in 1989. These are centres for after-school activities, where you can see students doing everything from ping-pong to dance, first-aid, gymnastics and playing music. Many travellers note the conveyor-belt feeling when visiting these places; but don't despair, as the guides' performance juggling the procession of tourists is entertaining in itself.

Although **Kim Il Sung University** is not on every tour, you might want to pay it a visit. It is from here that Dear Leader Kim Jong Il graduated. The book *Kim Jong Il in His Young Days* makes it clear that the Dear Leader was the university's foremost scholar and was soon teaching his teachers. When the Dear Leader read his thesis on socialism, it was described thus:

The professors and scholars, who were so strict about scientific matters, could not suppress their surging emotions, and approached the author who made immortal theoretical achievements, shaking his hands and congratulating him heartily and warmly.

His thesis was assessed by the professors an immortal document.

Just beyond Kim Il Sung University is Kim Il Sung's resting place in the former Presidential Palace, which has been renamed **Kumsusan Memorial Palace**. The embalmed body of the late Great Leader is on display here and it is only possible to visit if you have been invited. The palace has been completely refurbished and a new side entrance constructed – with some of the longest conveyor belts in the world. Before you enter the main section of the palace your shoes are given a final cleaning. Visitors are instructed to maintain silence and to restrain from showing anything but a saddened expression. It is requested that you bow three times, once on his left, then his right and finally at his feet. After wiping your tears you continue on into an exhibition room where you can view the Great Leader's Mercedes-Benz and a collection of awards from equally respected international comrades.

Another major site of interest is the western suburban district of **Mangyeongdae**, the so-called 'Cradle of the Revolution', where the Sunhwa River flows into the Taedong. This is where Kim Il Sung allegedly was born and spent his childhood. His old thatched house, set in carefully tended gardens, has been turned into a shrine. It houses photographs of his family as well as a few everyday household items (Kim's straw sleeping mat etc) to indicate the humble background from which he came. The surrounding pine woods hold the burial mounds of his relatives, all of whom are said to have been great anti-foreigner patriots and revolution-minded leaders of the lower classes. There's also a marble observation platform overlooking the Taedong River at the top of Mangyeong Hill.

Near to Mangyeongdae are its **Revolutionary Museum** and **Revolutionary School** and a giant fun fair. Guides claim that the entire complex receives over 100,000 visitors a day on weekends and public holidays.

On the way back from Mangyeongdae, it's worth making a detour to see **Kwangbok St**, a modernistic suburb visible from high points in central Pyongyang. It's essentially a linearly laid-out suburb of highrise apartment blocks, which stretch for

NORTH KOREA

over 3km on either side of the virtually empty 13-lane highway.

Another worthwhile excursion is a visit to the **movie studio** out in the north-western suburbs. This is not part of the standard tours, so you must request it if you want to go there. It is not difficult to arrange, but give your guide as much advance notice as possible. Like everything else in North Korea, the movie studio is very politicised. Even the outdoor movie sets are intriguing, especially the one representing a seedy 1970s South Korean nightclub and bar district. Most of the films are anti-US, anti-South Korean and anti-Japanese. In reel after reel, Kim Il Sung is credited with almost single-handedly defeating Japan in WWII (the Allied war effort is never acknowledged). His mother and father are also depicted on screen as great revolutionaries. As part of the tour, they usually give you a sneak preview of films currently in production. Although the sound tracks are all in Korean, your guide will interpret for you.

Foreign tourists are not usually taken out to the **Taesongsan Complex** north-east of the city, but you can request a visit if you have an extra day in Pyongyang. The dominant feature is the **Revolutionary Martyrs Cemetery** – located on a hill. It is very holy ground for the North Koreans and you will be asked to present a bouquet of flowers and bow in respect when you reach its crest. After your bow, enjoy the panoramic vista of Pyongyang.

There is also a public amusement park, the **Central Zoo**, the small **Kwangbeop Buddhist Temple**, two pretty lakes with nearby restaurants and the huge and beautiful **Central Botanical Garden,** which boasts two separate special hot-houses for the *kimilsungia* and *kimjongilia* flowers (see the History section, earlier)!

THE TOMB OF TAN'GUN

History continues to evolve in North Korea, with new 'revolutionary discoveries' being made every year. The government announced in 1993 that it's archaeologists had discovered the tomb of Tan'gun, the founder of the first Korean kingdom. Up until that point, the North Korean government had agreed with most scholars of Korean history that Tan'gun is a mythical figure and that 'his' kingdom of KoChoson (ancient Korea) with its capitals Pyongyang and Asadal was located in North-East China, if it indeed ever existed. However, it's been recently 'discovered' that KoChoson was northern Korea, its capital was right where theirs now stands, Tan'gun was a real man, and they have discovered his skeletal remains.

Those decayed bones (and those said to be of his wife) are on display at a grandly constructed tomb just outside of Pyongyang. A small museum stands nearby, displaying 'artefacts' from Tan'gun's times, said to have been found in and around the tomb.

The Legend of Tan'gun

In the year 2333 BC, a son of the Lord of Heaven named Hwanung descended from heaven with 3000 retainers to the mountain of Taebaeksan and established a 'City of God' on its summit. Modern scholarship has been unable to definitely locate this 'Taebaeksan', and Korean traditionalists have varying opinions: some favour the great mountain with the same name in Gangwon-do, South Korea; more favour Myohyangsan, just north of Pyongyang; but most hold that Paekdusan must have been the spot, being closest to heaven and having such outstanding natural features (see the Paekdusan section, later in this chapter).

According to the story, a bear and a tiger desired to become human, and beseeched 'Heavenly King Hwanung'. He gave them bundles of garlic and mugwort (a green medicinal herb, common in Korea) and directed them to eat those foods (the first gimchi!) while avoiding the sun for 100 days. The tiger failed the test, but the bear succeeded and emerged from the cave as a young woman. She mated with Hwanung and produced a son named Tan'gun. He became the first Korean king, establishing his capital at 'the walled city of Pyongyang.

Books about the life and times of Tan'gun may be on sale.

PLACES TO STAY

Wherever you choose to stay in Pyongyang it's going to be one of the several tourist hotels and it will be incorporated into the cost of your tour. There is a choice between Deluxe, Class A, Class B and Class C accommodation. You'll probably be encouraged to stay at the deluxe *Pyongyang Koryo Hotel (fax 381 4422)*, a 45-storey twin tower with two revolving restaurants on top. It's a five-minute walk from the train station and it's where most foreigners stay. The hotel has 500 rooms, and given the small number of tourists, it's unlikely you'll have to worry about getting a reservation.

The *Yanggakdo Hotel (fax 381 2930)* is the newest deluxe hotel in Pyongyang and, yes, it also has a revolving restaurant at the top and even a casino in the basement.

Further down the scale, in the heart of the city, is the 2nd class *Pyongyang Hotel (fax 381 4426)* located opposite the Grand Theatre on the Taedong River.

The skyline of Pyongyang is dominated by the incredible *Ryugyong Hotel*, a 105-storey pyramid with 3000 rooms and five revolving restaurants. Originally conceived as the world's largest luxury hotel, the concrete pyramid was erected in 1989 4km from the city centre. Unfortunately, the government ran out of money for interior technology (such as high-speed elevators and water systems) before they could complete it. The building now sits as an empty shell and it's unlikely further work will be done unless there is a dramatic increase in tourism. Tourist pamphlets produced in North Korea often show the building photographed at night with lights on inside, a considerable feat since the building is not wired for electricity. Nevertheless, the building would make quite a tourist attraction in itself, but most requests to visit it are denied. You'll have to be content photographing it with a telephoto lens.

Numerous other hotels exist in Pyongyang, but it's up to KITC to make the arrangements for you.

PLACES TO EAT

You'll usually eat at your hotel, but eating elsewhere can be arranged. Many foreigners hang out in the coffee shop of their hotel, but prices are high. As for the 'local restaurants', these in fact cater to foreigners or privileged Koreans with access to hard currency. Don't think you'll ever be able to eat along side the masses. Just where the locals eat is a mystery – either they bring food from home or they're fed at the workplace, but there are certainly very few pavement restaurants or food stalls like you find in the rest of the world. If you want to eat outside your hotel for the sake of variety, your guide will arrange it upon your request.

See the boxed text North Korean Cuisine in the Facts for the Visitor section for details on Pyongyang's speciality dishes.

If you so desire, it is possible to partake in a long and lavish dinner of dog, at a strangely decorated specialty restaurant. Visiting such places can only be accomplished by making special arrangements with your guide. The price is negotiable with your guide and can range from $10 up to $40 per person.

Entertainment

The streets are deserted at night. For North Koreans, the evening is presumably spent sitting by the radio or TV listening to testimonials by happy workers and reruns of profound speeches by the late Great Leader.

Possibilities for diversion include bowling, North Korean movies, rifle shooting, exercise, swimming, saunas, gambling or even a trip to a local football match – ask your guide. Most of these will cost a token $5 to $10 extra.

There are a few discos for decadent foreigners (no Koreans allowed). The Koryo Hotel has a dance-karaoke hall, but the cover charge is W50 so it's usually empty except for a few Japanese karaoke enthusiasts. The second floor of the same hotel has a billiards room that is a good place to socialise with embassy staff, journalists and whoever else happens to be in town.

SHOPPING

There are plenty of souvenir shops at the main tourist venues. Out where the masses shop, there are scarcely any consumer goods at all on the shelves. Nevertheless, North Korea does offer plenty of unique souvenirs which make fantastic conversation pieces. Books and videos on the immortal achievements of Juche and the Great/Dear Leaders may be your best picks.

Just to the south of the Pyongyang Koryo Hotel is a place selling postage stamps (the sign is in English), and it's well worth your time to stop in here. One postage stamp shows a crowd of angry Koreans beating a US soldier to death while someone sticks a knife through his throat. Another shows two soldiers, one North Korean and one Chinese, standing shoulder to shoulder brandishing AK-47s (symbolising socialist solidarity). You might enjoy the stamps depicting North Korea's version of the space shuttle, but even more bizarre are the stamps proudly displaying the British royal family. Just why Charles and Diana are more popular in North Korea than in the UK awaits some scholarly research. As for whose photo is displayed on the largest stamps – you guess.

Many tourists have expressed an interest in purchasing the metal badge which every North Korean wears, with the Great Leader's picture printed on it within a colour-coded rim indicating the wearer's social-political status. However, these are not for sale.

Insam, or ginseng, is for sale in hotels but prices seem ridiculously high. It claims to be from Paekdusan; insam from there has high value for all Koreans. You may be able to pick up some more cheaply in Kaesong, ask your guide for advice. However, you can buy all grades of insam much more cheaply in the South. If you're an aspiring acupuncturist, you can find acupuncture needles in the medicine shops at rock-bottom prices.

GETTING AROUND

All public transport in Pyongyang costs 10 jon. They want it in coins, so you'll need local money. As a general rule, foreigners are discouraged from using the public transport system except for the metro, which is something of a showcase. You will be forbidden from using any public transport unless accompanied by your guide.

Bus

It's unlikely you'll ever use the urban bus network as the queues are phenomenally long and the buses crammed to bursting point, but if you do they run until 11 pm each day. Sometimes women with children form separate queues and have priority in boarding buses; in this regard North Korea is more civilised than the South.

Tram

Pyongyang's trams began service in 1991, after a fifty year break. It might be a good way to get around if it weren't so crowded.

Taxi

You won't find taxis plying the streets as you do in Seoul, but you can book a taxi from a tourist hotel. You will not see a meter, the fare is based on distance. The fare is approximately W2 per kilometre, depending on the type of vehicle (Mercedes-Benz are the most expensive). The price also rises slightly, late at night. In the rare event that you don't find a taxi waiting outside your hotel, you can ask reception to call one.

Metro

You should definitely visit a metro station, if only to see the extravagance with which they were constructed. Each station is designed differently, with varying bronze sculptures, murals, mosaics and chandeliers, and all the pillars, steps, corridors and platforms are fashioned in marble. Stations have names which translate as 'Liberation', 'Reunification', 'Reconstruction', and so on. The trains themselves are nowhere near as impressive as the stations, being dim and dingy, but each car contains a portrait of you-know-who. There are 17 stations in all, served by two lines covering a total length of 24km. The present system was completed in 1978. There are grand plans to extend it to Mangyeongdae (Pyongyang's western district) and eventually to ChinnamPo (the city's seaport). Each station has a map of the system indicating where you are. The cost of a ride is a standard 10 jon and it's a very convenient way to quickly visit different parts of the city. For an interesting background to the metro and some entertaining photos visit the Web site at www.pyongyang-metro.com.

Around the Country

What you get to see outside of Pyongyang depends on what sort of itinerary you request and how much time you have. It will also be limited to the places where tourist hotels are located. Outside of Pyongyang, the big five major tourist destinations are Myohyangsan, Kaesong, Kumgangsan, Panmunjeom and Paekdusan.

Travellers who have 'been there done that' may wish to request visits to lesser sites: the Taesongsan Complex just outside of Pyongyang, Wonsan, Nampo, Kuwolsan, Paekdusan, Haeju-Suyangsan, Chilbosan and the Rajin-Sonbong Free Trade Zone.

MYOHYANGSAN

The third-most famous mountain in North Korea, behind Kumgangsan and Paekdusan, Myohyangsan (Mountain of Mysterious Fragrance) is well worth a leisurely visit. It is considered a sacred place by many Koreans (see the Legend of Tan'gun boxed text, earlier) and offers grand scenery, unspoiled nature, a dozen old Buddhist temples and countless waterfalls.

The main centre of non-natural interest in Myohyangsan is the **International Friendship Exhibition (IFE)**, 3km to 4km from the train station. It's another of those monuments to the greater glory of the Great Leader and, to a lesser extent, of the Dear Leader. It's a six-storey building in traditional Korean style which houses gifts given to Kim Il Sung and Kim Jong Il from all over the world and is magnificently set amongst densely wooded hills.

You need to be on your best behaviour here, as the building is maintained as a hallowed shrine. You must take off your hat if you have one, and shoe covers must be worn when walking around. You may be permitted to open the golden doors to the shrine, but you must first put on a pair of gloves before touching the handles. During your tour, you'll be escorted by a woman in traditional Korean costume.

The list of donors reads like a roster of the dead and discredited: Stalin, Mao, Castro, Ceausescu, Honecker, Khaddafi etc. The gifts themselves are quite fascinating: a bullet-proof Zil limousine from Stalin, a luxurious train carriage from Mao Zedong, a stuffed alligator from the Sandinistas and carvings, pottery, and paintings from all over the third world. The gifts are arranged by country and each has a note, in Korean and English, of who sent them and when. There are 120 rooms in total housing over 100,000 pieces, and it's not possible to see them all in one day. Fortunately an electronic registry has been set up that tallies the number of presents. If you have oohed and aahed in all the right places you will be allowed to write a comment in the visitors' book, thereby immortalising your place in Korean history.

When you've seen enough of Kim Il Sung's IFE, then it must be time to visit Kim Jong Il's IFE. Better believe it, as this place is equally as impressive, with most of the rooms built into the mountainside in true DPRK bunker-style.

Your guide will probably pick up on your yawns and suggest lunch and then a hike in one of the nearby valleys of Sangwon, Manpok, Chonthae or Chilsong. Each is as beautiful as the next, with plenty of cascades and waterfalls. A good one to two-hour walk is the norm.

Sangwon Valley is the most common place for a hike and is directly north-east of the IFE. You climb via a clearly defined pathway, stone steps and a suspension footbridge past the **Kumgang, Taeha, Ryongyon** and **Cheonsin waterfalls** (with the **Sanju Falls** an option off to the right). Past the humble **Sangwon Hermitage**, you'll arrive at the pretty **Cheonsin Pavilion**. From there you can descend back the same way or head east to the **Oseon Pavilion,** and then back to civilisation via **Pulyong Hermitage, Ryongju Peak**, and **Poyun Hermitage**. If

NORTH KOREA

you're not yet tired and there's enough daylight you can proceed 3km upwards from the Cheonsin Pavilion past **Nungin Hermitage** to the **Peobwang Peak,** which offers an astounding view of the entire region.

But at any rate don't miss **Pohyon Temple**, the most historically-important Buddhist temple in western North Korea. The temple complex dates back to AD 1044, with numerous renovations over the centuries. It's just a short walk from the IFE, at the entrance to Sangwon Valley, and features several small pagodas and a large hall housing images of the Buddha, as well as a museum which sports a collection of woodblocks from the Buddhist scriptures the Tripitaka Koreana. (For more details regarding the preservation and significance of these wood blocks see the boxed text in the Gyeongsangbuk-do chapter.)

It is common for tours to visit the **Ryongmun Big Cave** either prior or after a visit to Myohyangsan. This 6km-long limestone cave boasts some enormous caverns and a large number of stalactites. Enjoy sights like the **Pool of Anti-Imperialist People's Struggle**, the **Juche Cavern** and the **Mountain Peak of the Great leader Kim Il Sung**.

Getting There & Away

A visit here from Pyongyang can be adequately covered in a day or overnight trip. It's 160km north of the capital along the newly completed tourist expressway.

The village of Myohyangsan itself consists of just one main street lined with traditional Korean houses. The main tourist hotel here is the *Hyangsan Pyramid Hotel*, just below Pohyon Temple and the IFE, rated as class A. The revolving restaurant at the top requires approximately 42 minutes for a complete revolution. No doubt one of the quickest and most pleasant revolutions on offer in Korea.

KAESONG

Kaesong has some 200,000 residents, but 800 years ago it had around four times as many. It was the capital of the Goryeo (Koryo) dynasty, which took over after Silla collapsed in the early 10th century, and then endured turbulent politics followed by Mon-

gol invasion and domination, barely surviving until the Joseon kingdom replaced it in 1390. As the royal capital in the eleventh century, however, it was a sumptuously wealthy and sophisticated metropolis crowded with Buddhist aristocrats enjoying the art and temples they patronised.

You won't see very many relics of those happy times, due to the unfortunate effects of neglect and three major wars which each left little but rubble. At least there is the **Songgyungwan Neo-Confucian College**, which was originally built in AD 992, and rebuilt after being destroyed in the 1592 Japanese invasion. Today it is host to the **Koryo Museum** of celadon pottery and other Buddhist relics; re-enactments of Confucian ceremonies are very occasionally held here. The buildings surround a wide courtyard dotted with ancient trees, and the surrounding grounds are very pleasant to walk around. It's a short drive north-east of town.

Kaesong may be your only chance while in the DPRK to see an authentic Korean royal tomb. The best one by far is the **Tomb of King Kongmin** (the 31st Goryeo king, who reigned between AD 1352 and 1374) and his queen. It is richly decorated with traditional granite facing and statuary. It's a very secluded site about 13km west of the city centre; there are splendid views over the surrounding tree-covered hills from a number of vantage points.

The third great tourist site is the 37m-high **Pakyon Falls**, one of the three most famous in North Korea. It's found in a beautiful natural setting some 24km north of town. Theoretically at least, some great hiking can be done around here: from the falls to the **Taehungsan Fortress**, to the mid-Goryeo **Kwanum Temple** (with cave) and the **Taehung Temple**.

Kaesong itself is a modern city with wide streets – of scant interest, though it does have an interesting older section consisting of traditional tile-roofed houses, sandwiched between the river and the main street. Within the town are a number of lesser tourist sights: the **Sonjuk Bridge**, a tiny clapper bridge built in 1216 and, opposite, the **Songin Monument**, which honours Neo-Confucian hero

Chong Mong-ju; the **Nammun** (South Gate) which dates from the 14th century and houses an old Buddhist bell; the **Sungyang Seowon** (Confucian academy); and **Chanamsan**, on the summit of which stands a massive bronze statue of – guess who?

Driving time between Pyongyang and Kaesong is about two hours along the newly completed expressway.

If you stay over in Kaesong, you'll be based at either the *Chanamsan Hotel* near the Sonjuk Bridge or the *Kaesong Minsok (Folk) Hotel*. If you have a choice, definitely choose the latter, which is built in the traditional Korean yeogwan style. Both hotels are rated class C.

PANMUNJEOM

A short drive south from Kaesong is one of the most morbidly fascinating sights in Korea. Even if you've visited this 'truce village' from the South, the trip from the Northern side is well worth the effort.

You go on the Reunification Highway, a six-lane freeway devoid of traffic with military checkpoints every 20km. The freeway is supposed to connect Pyongyang to Seoul, and the last exit before the DMZ has a large sign saying 'Seoul 70km'. You drive up to a sentry box at the entrance to the DMZ where a military officer gives you a short briefing, after which you'll be escorted to the Joint Security Zone by military officers. From the car park, you enter a large building that faces the row of huts which straddle the demarcation line and then exchange glances with burly US marines, South Korean soldiers and the tourists on the other side in their flash new reflective glass observation tower. Unless meetings are in progress, you'll be permitted to visit the very room where the endless armistice talks go on. After that, it's back to the main building for an exposition of the North Korean view of things.

The whole setting looks very serene, with well-tended gardens, trees, rice fields and chirping birds. Hard to imagine that all around you the countryside is bristling with camouflaged bunkers, tanks, artillery, nerve-gas and biological-weapons shells, missile silos and land mines. If war were to break out during your visit, you'd be incinerated within a minute. Imagine that.

On the way out of the DMZ, you are given a chance to visit the gift shop. There are some real collectors' items here, including a classic propaganda book called *Panmunjeom* published in a variety of languages:

The US imperialist aggressors drew the Military Demarcation Line to divide Korea and her people by artificial means. Panmunjeom is a place through which the line runs and a court which exposes and vehemently denounces the US imperialist criminal aggression in Korea to the whole world. The US imperialists started a war of aggression (1950–53) in order to swallow up the whole of Korea. But here at Panmunjeom they went down on their knees before the Korean people and signed the Armistice Agreement.

The next stop on your tour is the **Korean Wall**. According to the North, the Americans and South Koreans have built a concrete wall all the way across the peninsula (248km) along the Southern side of the DMZ, similar to the former Berlin Wall, to prevent the citizens of both Koreas from effecting their reunification. In fact it is an anti-tank barrier which has been there for many years and attracted no attention whatsoever from the North until 1989 when the Berlin Wall was torn down. Suddenly the propaganda potential was recognised, and even student protestors in Seoul organised demonstrations to demand that the 'Korean Wall' be torn down.

You'll be able to view the wall through telescopes from 4km away. You'll then be taken into a room and be shown a video and given a lecture on the burning desire of the Korean people for re-unification. All very gripping stuff. Not much will be said about the triple-wired 3000-volt electric fence running along the Northern side of the DMZ.

KUMGANGSAN

In the far south-eastern corner of North Korea sit the most beautiful mountains in all of Korea – Kumgangsan (the Diamond Mountains). Despite the name, there are no diamond mines here – the region was named after the key Chinese Zen scripture *The Diamond-like Cutter of All Doubts Sutra*. It's

NORTH KOREA

just as well that there are no diamonds, because it would be a tragedy if this area were ever mined. As it stands, you'd be hard-pressed to find better scenery anywhere! As far back as China's Tang dynasty (AD 618–907) the famously ethno-centric Chinese were compelled to include these mountains as among the five most impressive in the known world (the other four are in China).

Kumgangsan is divided into Inner, Outer and Sea Kumgang regions. The main tourist activities (at least theoretically) are hiking, mountaineering, boating and sightseeing. The area is peppered with former Buddhist temples and hermitages, waterfalls, mineral springs, a pretty lagoon, and a small museum. Maps of the area are provided by park officials to help you decide where you want to go among the dozens of excellent sites.

If your time here is limited, the best places to visit in the Outer Kumgang Region are the **Samil Lagoon** (try hiring a boat, then rest at *Tanpung Restaurant*); the **Manmulsang Area** (fantastically shaped crags) and the **Kuryong** and **Pibong Falls** (a 4.5km hike from the *Mongnan Restaurant*). In the Inner Kumgang Region, it's worth visiting the impressively re-constructed **Pyohon Temple** (founded in AD 670 and one of old Korea's most important Zen monasteries). Hiking in the valleys around Pyoheon Temple or, really, *anywhere* in the park would be rewarding and memorable. You won't need to carry drinking water, but bring plenty of film. **Pirobong** (1639m) is the highest peak out of at least a hundred.

Getting There & Away

The usual route to Kumgangsan is by car from Pyongyang to Onjong-ri via Wonsan along the new highway (around 315km, a four-hour drive). Along the way to Wonsan (which itself holds nothing of interest for the tourist), your car or bus will stop off at a teahouse by Sinpyeong Lake. From Wonsan, the road more or less follows the coastline south, and you'll get glimpses of the double-wired electric fence which runs the entire length of the east coast. There may be a stop for tea at Shijung Lake.

Your final destination is the village of Onjong-ri and the 1st class *Kumgangsan Hotel*. The hotel is quite a rambling affair consisting of a main building and several outer buildings which include chalets, a shop, a dance hall and bathhouse (fed by a hot spring). The food served here is good, especially the wild mountain vegetable dishes.

PAEKDUSAN

Beautiful Paekdusan straddles the Korean-Chinese border in North Korea's far north. At 2744m, it's the highest peak on the whole Korean peninsula. An extinct volcano in a vast wilderness, its name means literally 'White Head Mountain', which refers to the main peak, covered by whitish pumice and snow year-round. Surrounded by bare rocky crags at the summit is a huge crater lake, called Cheonji or 'Lake of Heaven', which is some 14km in circumference and reaches a maximum depth of 384m. This makes it one of the deepest alpine lakes in the world. Despite being fed by two hot springs, the lake is one of the world's coldest.

The Lake of Heaven

Many legends have grown up around the Lake of Heaven. Dragons, and other things that go bump in the night, were believed to have sprung from the alpine waters. In fact, they're still believed to do so. There have been intermittent sightings of unidentified swimming objects – Asia's own Loch Ness beasties, or aquatic yetis or what have you. Since the lake is frozen over in winter and temperatures are well below zero, it would take a pretty hardy monster to survive (even plankton can't). Sightings from the Chinese and North Korean sides include a black bear, fond of swimming and oblivious to the paperwork necessary for crossing these tight borders. On a more poignant note, Chinese and Korean couples traditionally throw coins into the water, pledging that their love will remain as deep as the lake, and as long-lived.

Paekdusan is a sacred peak to both North and South Koreans – according to Korean mythology this is where the 'Son of the Lord of Heaven' descended to earth and the first Korean kingdom began (see Tan'gun boxed text, earlier). It should be no mystery, then, why the North Korean regime claims that Kim Jong Il was born here, even though all sources outside North Korea maintain that he was born in the Russian city of Khabarovsk. New official mythology even claims that flying white horses were seen in the sky after baby Kim entered the world.

North Korea's current history books also claim that Kim Il Sung established his guerrilla headquarters at Paekdusan in the 1920s, from where he defeated the Japanese. To prove this, you'll be shown revolutionary and anti-imperialist declarations which the Great Leader and his comrades carved on the trees. You'll be told that more and more of these 'slogan-bearing trees' are being discovered every year, and some of the carvings are so well-preserved you'd almost think they were carved yesterday, if you did not know better. Outside of North Korea, no history books claim that this mountain was ever a battlefield during WWII. Nevertheless, the North Korean book *Kim Jong Il in His Young Days* describes the Dear Leader's difficult childhood during those days of ceaseless warfare at Paekdusan:

His childhood was replete with ordeals. The secret camp of the Korean People's Revolutionary Army in the primeval forest was his home, and ammunition belts and magazines were his playthings. The raging blizzards and ceaseless gunshots were the first sounds to which he became accustomed. Day in and day out fierce battles went on and, during the breaks, there were military and political trainings. On the battlefield, there was no quilt to warmly wrap the new-born child. So women guerrillas gallantly tore cotton out of their own uniforms and each contributed pieces of cloth to make a patchwork quilt for the infant.

Visitors here will be shown the **secret camp** beneath **Jong Il Peak,** said to be the Dear Leader's birthplace, which features a newish-looking log cabin, and plenty of monuments commemorating patriotic fighters and glorious battles. But the real reason to come here is the glories of nature – vast tracts of virgin forest, abundant wildlife, lonely granite crags, fresh springs, gushing streams and dramatic waterfalls – and, for those able to make the steep and treacherous climb, the astounding **peak**, where heaven indeed seems close and the mundane world is so very far away. Few foreign travellers make it here at all, due to the formidable costs involved, and that is unlikely to change until a proper highway or train line is built.

Places to Stay

Hotels to stay at in this area include the 2nd class *Pegaebong Hotel* located in the middle of the forest in Samjiyon County. It is also possible to stay in the village of Hyesan, at the 3rd class *Hyesan Hotel*.

Getting There & Away

Paekdusan is only accessible from around late June to mid-September; at all other times it is forbiddingly cold and stormy. Access to the mountain is by air only, followed by car. There are charter flights available which can hold up to 30 people, for US$3000 per round-trip flight,. At US$100 per person that isn't unreasonable, but it would be a rather significant expense if you were travelling solo! Unfortunately, this flight is currently the only transport offered to Paekdusan.

You can also visit the mountain and crater lake from the Chinese side – a trip that's now popular with South Korean tourists. A five-day tour (US$500) departs from the South's port of Sokcho in Gangwon-do to the Russian port of Zarubino. The tour then travels by land to Hunchun, Yanji and finally Paekdusan, remaining in Chinese territory. Paekdusan is called Changbaishan in Chinese and the crater lake is called Tianchi (Lake of Heaven). For more details, contact Dongchun Ferry Company in Seoul (☎ 02-720 0101, fax 734 7474).

RAJIN-SONBONG ZONE

This is a 746 sq km strip of land on the extreme north-eastern coast, designated in 1992–93 as an 'International Free-Trade Investment Zone', whatever that might mean

NORTH KOREA

in the context of North Korea. The UN has lobbied China, Russia and North Korea to set up a 'Golden Triangle' economic-growth area on the lower reaches of the Tuman River where the three nations meet; Rajin-Sonbong is Pyongyang's rather unimpressive contribution to the scheme. The other two prospective partners have shown even less enthusiasm for the venture, so the idea is so far going nowhere fast.

Travellers are unlikely to visit here, unless the North Korean authorities view them as potential joint-venture investors (or sympathetic business journalists). There is very little infrastructure here yet for business or tourism, the obvious reason being that multi-national companies have not exactly enthusiastically rushed to invest.

Those who do make it to Rajin-Sonbong (by train or car, from Pyongyang or Wonsan), may be able to enjoy 56km of relatively unspoiled jagged coastline featuring sanctuaries for sea birds and seals, a few visitable offshore islands and some quiet fishing villages. There are three pretty lakes and the **Chogol Buddhist Hermitage,** located within the peninsular Tuman estuary, on the far-eastern end of the zone. Two hot spring 'spas' are said to exist within the zone, but we were unable to find out any information about them; we suspect that they have not yet been developed for tourist guests.

Two or three *hotels* were opened here for potential investor guests in 1996 and the Emperor Group has recently set up a **casino** with another to follow shortly.

Border Crossings Crossing the border here to or from China is possible if prior arrangements are made through KITC's Yanji office in Jilin Province, or if you can organise an invitation letter from KITC's Rajin-Sonbong office. It would take another four or five days to process a visa, which you could pick up in Yanji. KITC could arrange transport down to the North Korean border. Crossing the Tuman River into or from Russia (by train) is possible but difficult and rarely attempted; special visa and ticket arrangements must be made in advance. The border stations on both sides are heavily guarded and still display a Cold War mentality – the paperwork is taken very seriously. Customs checks may be very thorough, so be on your best behaviour and don't carry anything that might be objectionable to the officials of either side. Don't even pull your camera out when at the border, or your film may be confiscated.

The border town of Tumangang is 3km from the actual border (the Tuman River), and is the farthest point in the nation from Pyongyang, at 1125km.

Language

Korean is a knotty problem for linguists. Various theories have been proposed to explain its origins, but the most widely accepted is that it is a member of the Ural-Altaic family of languages. Other members of the same linguistic branch are Korean is a knotty problem for linguists. Turkish and Mongolian. In reality Korean grammar shares much more with Japanese than it does with either Turkish or Mongolian. Furthermore, the Koreans have borrowed nearly 70% of their vocabulary from neighbouring China, and now many English words have penetrated the Korean lexicon.

Chinese characters *(hanja)* are usually restricted to use in maps, and occasionally in newspapers and written names. For the most part Korean is written in *hangeul*, the alphabet developed under King Sejong's reign in the 15th century. Many users of the Korean language argue that the Korean script is one of the most scientific and consistent alphabets used today.

Hangeul consists of only 24 characters and isn't that difficult to learn. However, the formation of words using hangeul is very different from the way that Western alphabets are used to form words. The emphasis is on the formation of a syllable so that it resembles a Chinese character. Thus the first syllable of the word 'hangeul' (한) is formed by an 'h' (ㅎ) in the top left corner, an 'a' (ㅏ) in the top right corner and an 'n' (ㄴ) at the bottom, the whole syllabic grouping forming a syllabic 'box'. These syllabic 'boxes' are strung together to form words.

Romanisation

In July 2000, the Korean government adopted a new method of romanising the Korean language. Most of the old romanisation system was retained, but a few changes were introduced to ensure a more consistent spelling throughout Korea and overseas. The emphasis with the new romanisation is on pronunciation for non-Korean speakers. The main changes involved the removal of the apostrophe and diacritical breve marker, and the substitution of a few consonants.

The previous McCune-Reischauer romanisation system, which was officially adopted in 1984, was quite complex and resulted in all kinds of transliterations throughout Korea and overseas. The previous use of apostrophes and the breve marker not only caused pronunciation confusion, but also created a challenge for the digital age, with many computers corrupting these markers. The new system has already been energetically promoted throughout the government and tourist bureaus, but it will take a long time for the whole country to fall into line. Local governments have until 2005 to change all the road signs around the country and publishers have until December 2002 for new publications. The Korean government is also actively encouraging the adoption of the new system overseas.

Travellers will have to be careful with romanisation during the next few years of transition. Lonely Planet has adopted the new romanisation style throughout this book, but there is a possibility that some areas of the country haven't yet adopted the new spellings. To avoid confusion it's always best to go back to the original Korean script. In fact, it's well worth the few hours required to learn the Korean alphabet. To help make travel easier, we have provided Korean script throughout this book for map references and points of interest.

After familiarising yourself with hangeul, the next step towards Korean competency is listening to the way Koreans pronounce place names and to try and repeat their pronunciations.

The main changes to the romanisation system are:

- the diacritical breve (ŏ or ŭ) has been dropped and an 'e' placed in front of the 'o' or 'u'; eg, Inch'ŏn and Chŏngŭp become Incheon and Jeongeup
- the consonants ㄱ/ㄷ/ㅂ/ㅈ in initial position will always be transliterated as g/d/b/j; eg, Pusan and Kwangju become Busan and Gwangju.

- the voiceless consonants ㅋ / ㅌ / ㅍ / ㅊ will retain the letters **k/t/p/ch** but will lose their apostrophe. Previously, voiceless or aspirated consonants (those accompanied by a puff of air) were indicated by an apostrophe, as in P'ohang or Ch'ungju. But under the new system they will be written Pohang and Chungju respectively.
- the form ㅅ| will no longer be pronounced 'shi', but simply 'si'; eg, Shinch'on becomes Sinchon.
- official names of persons and companies will remain unchanged, but for all new names the new romanisation system will be used.
- hyphens are rarely used, except where confusion may arise between two syllables, eg, Chungangno becomes Jung-angno. Hyphens have been retained for administrative units; eg, Gyeonggi-do and Suncheon-si.

Pronunciation
Vowels

ㅏ	a	as the 'a' in 'are'
ㅑ	ya	as in 'yard'
ㅓ	eo	as in 'of'
ㅕ	yeo	as in 'young'
ㅗ	o	as in 'go'
ㅛ	yo	as in 'yoke'
ㅜ	u	as in 'flute'
ㅠ	yu	as the word 'you'
ㅡ	eu	as the 'oo' in 'look'
ㅣ	i	as the 'ee' in 'beet'

Vowel Combinations

ㅐ	ae	as the 'a' in 'hat'
ㅒ	yae	as the 'ya' in 'yam'
ㅔ	e	as in 'ten'
ㅖ	ye	as in 'yes'
ㅘ	wa	as in 'waffle'
ㅙ	wae	as the 'wa' in 'wax'
ㅚ	oe	as the 'wa' in 'way'
ㅝ	wo	as in 'won'
ㅞ	we	as in 'wet'
ㅟ	wi	as the word 'we'
ㅢ	ui	as 'u' plus 'i'

Consonants
In the old, McCune-Reischauer romanisation system, apostrophes were used to indicate consonant sounds that are aspirated (ie,

Korean in this Book

A new feature of this edition is that we have introduced more Korean words into the text. For many points of interest and geographical features – like temples, waterfalls, palaces, islands, lakes and rivers – this book will use Korean words instead of English ones. To ensure that you don't feel (or get!) lost we have included some hints in the text and have avoided more difficult Korean constructions.

Below are a list of administrative units, geographical features and points of interest, for which we have used Korean transliterations.

Architectural Features

castle	seong
fortress	seong
garden	won
gate	mun
mountain fortress	sanseong
palace	gung
shrine	sa
temple	sa

Geographical Features

cave	donggul
island	do
lake	ho
mountain	san
river	gang
waterfall	pokpo

Administrative Units

city	-si
county	-gun
district	-gu
hamlet	-ri
province	-do
road	gil
street block	-ga
street	ro/no/lo
town	-eup
village	-myeon
ward	-dong

accompanied by a puff of air). Aspirated consonants include ㅋ / ㅌ / ㅍ / ㅊ. Under the new romanisation system they will retain the letters **k/t/p/ch**, but lose their apostrophe. Unaspirated consonants are generally difficult for English speakers to render. Under the new romanisation system, word initial ㄱ/ㄷ/ㅂ/ㅈ will be transliterated as g/d/b/j. To those unfamiliar with Korean, an unaspirated 'k' will sound like 'g', an unaspirated 't' like 'd', and an unaspirated 'p' like 'b'.

Whether consonants in Korean are voiced or unvoiced depends on where they fall within a word – at the beginning, in the middle or at the end. The rules governing this are too complex to cover here – the following tables show the various alternative pronunciations you may hear.

Single Consonants
ㅅ is pronounced 'sh' if followed by the vowel ㅣ. In the middle of a word, ㄹ is pronounced 'n' if it follows ㅁ (**m**) or ㅇ (**ng**), but when it follows ㄴ (**n**) it becomes a double 'l' sound (**ll**).

ㄱ	g/k
ㄴ	n
ㄷ	d/t
ㄹ	r/n
ㅁ	m
ㅂ	b
ㅅ	s/t
ㅇ	-/ng
ㅈ	j/t
ㅊ	ch/t
ㅋ	k
ㅌ	t
ㅍ	p
ㅎ	h/ng

Double Consonants
Double consonants are pronounced with more stress than their single consonants counterparts.

ㄲ	kk/k
ㄸ	tt/dd/–
ㅃ	pp/bb/–
ㅆ	ss/t
ㅉ	tch/–

Complex Consonants
These occur only in the middle or at the end of a word.

ㄱㅅ	–ksk
ㄴㅈ	–/nj/n
ㄴㅎ	–/nh/n
ㄹㄱ	–/lg/k
ㄹㅁ	–/lm/m
ㄹㅂ	–/lb/p
ㄹㅅ	–/ls/l
ㄹㅌ	–/lt/l
ㄹㅍ	–/lp/p
ㄹㅎ	–/lh/l
ㅂㅅ	–/ps/p

Polite Korean
Korea's pervasive social hierarchy means that varying degrees of politeness are codified into the grammar. Young Koreans tend to use the very polite forms a lot less than the older generations, but it's always best to use the polite form if you're unsure. The sentences in this section employ polite forms.

Greetings & Civilities
Hello.
annyeong hasimnikka (formal)
안녕하십니까
annyeong haseyo (less formal)
안녕하세요
Goodbye. (to person leaving)
annyeonghi gaseyo
안녕히가세요
Goodbye. (to person staying)
annyeonghi gyeseyo
안녕히계세요

Please.
putak hamnida 부탁합니다
Thank you.
gamsa hamnida 감사합니다
You're welcome.
gwaenchanseumnida 괜찮습니다
Yes.
ye/ne 예/네
No.
aniyo 아니요
Excuse me.
sillye hamnida 실례합니다
I'm sorry.
mianhamnida 미안합니다
My name is ...
je ireumeun ... 제이름은 ...
imnida 입니다
I come from ...
jeoneun ... eseo 저는 ... 에서
watseumnida 왔습니다

Getting Around

I want to get off here.
yeogie naeryeo juseyo
여기에 내려 주세요
I want to go to ...
... e gago sipseumnida
에 가고싶습니다
Where can I catch the bus to ...?
... haeng beoseuneun eodi e seo tamnikka?
... 행 버스는 어디에서 탑니까?

national timetable	
sigakpyo	시각표
airport	
gonghang	공항
bus	
beoseu	버스
airport bus	
gonghang beoseu	공항버스
bus stop	
beoseu jeongnyujang	버스정류장
express bus terminal	
gosok beoseu	고속버스 터미널
teomineol	
inter-city bus terminal	
sioe beoseu	시외버스 터미널
teomineol	
bus card	
beoseu kadeu	버스카드
taxi	
taeksi	택시
train	
gicha	기차
train station	
gicha yeok	기차역
ferry crossing	
naru	나루
ferry pier	
budu	부두
ferry boat	
yeogaekseon	여객선
one-way (ticket)	
pyeondo	편도
return (ticket)	
wangbok	왕복
refund ticket	
hwanbul	환불
subway station	
jihacheol yeok	지하철역
lockers	
lakka	락카

multiple-use subway ticket
jeong-aek seungchagwon
정액승차권
lost & found office
bunsilmul bogwansenta
분실물보관센타
immigration office
chulipguk gwalliso
출입국관리소
passport
yeogwon
여권

Necessities

toilet	
hwajangsil	화장실
toilet paper	
hwajangji	화장지
tampons	
tempo	템포
sanitary pads	
saengnidae	생리대
condoms	
kondom	콘돔
pharmacy	
yakguk	약국
anti-diarrhoeal	
seolsa yak	설사약
laxative	
byeonbi yak	변비약
pain killer	
jintongje	진통제
electric mosquito coil	
jeonja mogihyang	전자모기향

Communication

post office
ucheguk
우체국
stamp
upyo
우표
airmail letter
hanggong seogan 항공서간
aerogramme
hanggong bonghamnyeopseo
항공봉함엽서
International Express Mail
gukje teukgeup upyeon
국제특급우편
telephone office
jeonhwa guk
전화국
telephone card
jeonhwa kadeu
전화카드

I'd like to know the telephone number here.
yeogi jeonhwabeonho jom gareuchyeo juseyo
여기 전화번호 좀 가르쳐 주세요

Money

bank
eunhaeng
은행
May I have change please?
jandoneuro bakkwo juseyo?
잔돈으로 바꿔 주세요?
How much does it cost?
eolmayeyo?
얼마예요?
Too expensive.
neomu bissayo
너무 비싸요
Can I have a discount?
jom ssage hae juseyo?
좀 싸게 해 주세요?
May I use a credit card?
kadeureul sseulsu isseumnikka?
카드를 쓸 수 있습니까?

Accommodation

hotel
hotel   호텔
guesthouse
yeogwan   여관
cheapest guesthouse
yeoinsuk   여인숙
home stay
minbak   민박
single room
singgeul lum   싱글룸
double room
deobeul lum   더블룸
towel
sugeon   수건
bathhouse
mogyoktang   목욕탕
without bath
yoksil eomneun bang juseyo
욕실 없는 방 주세요
with private bath
yoksil inneun bang juseyo
욕실 있는 방 주세요
May I see the room?
bang-eul bolsu isseoyo?
방을 볼 수 있어요?
Do you have anything cheaper?
deo ssan geoseun eopseumnikka?
더 싼 것은 없습니까?

May I have a namecard?
myeongham jom eodeul su isseulkkayo?
명함 좀 얻을 수 있을까요?
I will pay you now.
jigeum jibulhago sipeundeyo
지금 지불하고 싶은 데요
Please give me a receipt.
yeongsujeung jom gatda juseyo
영수증 좀 갖다 주세요
I want to stay one more night.
hangru deo mukgo sipseumnida
하루 더 묵고 싶습니다
Please give me my key.
yeolsoe jom juseyo
열쇠 좀 주세요
Could you clean my room please?
bangcheongso jom hae juseyo
방청소 좀 해 주세요?
Can you have my clothes washed?
setak sseobiseu doemnikka?
세탁 써비스 됩니까?

Emergencies

Help!
saram sallyeo!   사람살려!
Thief!
dodugiya!   도둑이야!
Fire!
buriya!   불이야!
hospital
byeongwon   병원

Call a doctor!
uisareul buleo juseyo
의사를 불러 주세요!
Call an ambulance!
gugeupcha jom bulleo juseyo
구급차 좀 불러 주세요!
Call the police!
gyeongchaleul bulleo juseyo
경찰을 불러주세요!
I'm allergic to penicillin.
penisillin allereugiga isseoyo
페니실린 알레르기가 있어요
I'm allergic to antibiotics.
hangsaengje allereugiga isseoyo
항생제 알레르기가 있어요
I'm diabetic.
dangnyobyeong-i isseoyo
당뇨병이 있어요

Numbers

Korean has two counting systems. One is of
Chinese origin and the other a native

Korean system. Korean numbers only go up to 99. Either Chinese or Korean numbers can be used to count days. Chinese numbers are used for minutes and kilometres. Korean numbers are used for hours. The Chinese system is used to count money, not surprising since the smallest Korean banknote is W1000.

Number	Chinese		Korean	
0	–	–	*yeong/gong*	영/공
1	*il*	일	*hana*	하나
2	*I*	이	*dul*	둘
3	*sam*	삼	*set*	셋
4	*sa*	사	*net*	넷
5	*o*	오	*daseot*	다섯
6	*yuk*	육	*yeoseot*	여섯
7	*chil*	칠	*ilgop*	일곱
8	*pal*	팔	*yeodeol*	여덟
9	*gu*	구	*ahop*	아홉
10	*sip*	십	*yeol*	열

Number	Combination	
11	*sib-il*	십일
20	*isip*	이십
30	*samsip*	삼십
40	*sasip*	사십
48	*sasippal*	사십팔
50	*osip*	오십
100	*baek*	백
200	*ibaek*	이백
300	*sambaek*	삼백
846	*palbaek sasip-yuk*	팔백사십육
1000	*cheon*	천
2000	*icheon*	이천
5729	*ocheon chilbaek isipgu*	오천칠백이십구
10,000	*man*	만

FOOD
Basics
restaurant
  sikdang
  식당
I'm a vegetarian.
  chaesik juui imnida
  채식주의 입니다.
I want to eat spicy food.
  maepge hae juseyo
  맵게 해 주세요.
I can't eat spicy food.
  maeun eumsigeun meokji mothamnida
  매운 음식은 먹지 못합니다.

The menu, please.
  menyureul boyeo juseyo
  메뉴를 보여 주세요
The bill/check, please.
  gyesanseo juseyo
  계산서 주세요

noodles	*myeon/guksu*	면/국수
rice	*bap*	밥

Seafood 생선요리
clam	*daehap*	대합
crab	*ge*	게
cuttlefish	*ojing-eo*	오징어
eel	*baemjang-eo*	뱀장어
fish	*saengseon*	생선
oyster	*gul*	굴
shrimp	*saeu*	새우

Meat 육류
beef	*sogogi*	소고기
chicken	*dakgogi*	닭고기
mutton	*yanggogi*	양고기
pork	*dwaejigogi*	돼지고기

Vegetables 야채요리
beans	*kong*	콩
cucumber	*oi*	오이
dried seaweed	*gim*	김
garlic	*maneul*	마늘
green or red pepper	*gochu*	고추
lotus root	*yeongeun*	연근
mushroom	*beoseot*	버섯
onion	*yangpa*	양파
potato	*gamja*	감자
radishes	*muu*	무우
soybean sprouts	*kongnamul*	콩나물
spinach	*sigeumchi*	시금치

Condiments 양념
black pepper	*huchu*	후추
butter	*beoteo*	버터
hot chilli pepper	*gochu garu*	고추가루
hot sauce	*gochujang*	고추장
jam	*jaem*	잼
ketchup	*kechap*	케챱
mayonnaise	*mayonejeu*	마요네즈
mustard	*gyeoja*	겨자
salt	*sogeum*	소금
soy sauce	*ganjang*	간장

soybean paste	*doenjang*	된장
sugar	*seoltang*	설탕
vinegar	*sikcho*	식초

Korean Dishes 한국음식

omelette with rice		
	omuraiseu	오므라이스
pork cutlet with rice & vegetables		
	donkkaseu	돈까스
barbecued beef & vegetables grill		
	bulgogi	불고기
marinated beef/pork ribs grill		
	bulgalbi	불갈비
barbecued beef ribs grill		
	galbi gui	갈비구이
barbecued pork ribs grill		
	dwoeji galbi	돼지갈비
beef ribs soup		
	galbi tang	갈비탕
salted beef ribs		
	sogeum gui	소금구이
stew		
	tchigae	찌개
barbecued beef ribs stew		
	ga!bi tchim	갈비찜
tofu stew		
	dubu tchigae	두부 찌개
tofu & clam stew		
	sundubu tchigae	순두부 찌개
chicken stew		
	daktchim	닭찜
gimchi stew		
	gimchi tchigae	김치찌개
soybean paste stew		
	doenjang tchigae	된장찌개
roasted chicken		
	tongdakgui	통닭구이
diced grilled chicken		
	dak galbi	닭갈비
fried kimchi rice		
	gimchi bokkeumbap	김치볶음밥
steamed rice		
	gonggibap	공기밥
rice, egg, meat & vegetables in hot sauce		
	bibimbap	비빔밥
rice & vegetable pot		
	dolsot bibimbap	돌솥비빔밥
meat, fish & vegetables broth cooked at table		
	sinseonlo	신선로

cold noodle soup		
	mul naengmyeon	물냉면
cold noodle gimchi soup		
	yeolmu naengmyeon	열무냉면
spicy cold noodles without soup		
	bibim naengmyeon	비빔 냉면
noodle dish & soy milk broth		
	kong guksu	콩국수
thick hand-made noodles		
	kal guksu	칼국수
fried ramen noodles		
	ramyeon bokki	라면볶이
soup ramen noodles		
	ramyeon	라면
mixed vegetables & beef with soybean noodles		
	japchae	잡채
vegetables, meat, noodles & chicken broth		
	mak guksu	막국수
octopus hotpot		
	nakji jeongol	낙지전골
tripe hotpot		
	gopchang jeongol	곱창전골
soup		
	guk or tang	국/탕
ginseng chicken soup		
	samgye tang	삼계탕
soft boiled stuffed chicken		
	dak baeksuk	닭백숙
beef & rice soup		
	seolleong tang	설렁탕
beef soup		
	gom tang	곰탕
ox tail soup		
	kkorigom tang	꼬리곰탕
ox leg soup		
	dogani tang	도가니탕
spicy beef soup		
	yukgaejang	육개장
spicy fish soup		
	maeun tang	매운탕
spicy assorted seafood soup		
	haemul tang	해물탕
mudfish soup		
	chueo tang	추어탕
brown seaweed soup		
	miyeok guk	미역국
pollack (seafood) soup		
	bugeo guk	북어국
boiled silkworm snack		
	ppeondaegi	뻔대기

dumplings
   mandu   만두
soup with meat-filled
dumplings
   mandu guk   만두국
seafood & vegetables
fried in batter
   twigim   튀김
spicy rice bean sprout
porridge
   kongnamul gukbap   콩나물국밥
abalone porridge
   jeonbokjuk   전복죽
pickled vegetables,
garlic & chilli
   gimchi   김치
corn on the cob
   oksusu   옥수수
green onion pancake
   pajeon   파전
mung bean pancake
   bindaetteok   빈대떡
spicy rice rolls
   tteokbokgi   떡볶이
pickled daikon radish
   dongchimi   동치미
seasoned raw beef
   yukhoe   육회
dog meat soup
   bosin tang   보신탕
pork sausage
   sundae   순대
steamed pork hocks
   jokbal   족발
steamed pork & cabbage
   bossam   보쌈
steamed spicy angler fish
   agutchim   아구찜
grilled eel
   jang-eo gui   장어구이
jellied acorn puree
   muk muchim   묵무침
banquet
   hanjeongsik   한정식
laver-wrapped sushi
   gimbap   김밥
beef sushi
   sogogi gimbap   쇠고기 김밥
cheese sushi
   chijeu gimbap   치즈 김밥
tuna sushi
   chamchi gimbap   참치 김밥
gimchi sushi
   gimchi gimbap   김치 김밥

assorted sushi
   modeum gimbap   모듬 김밥

Desserts 디저트
cake   *keikeu*   케이크
ice cream   *aiseukeurim*   아이스크림
pie   *pai*   파이
pastry   *gwaja*   과자
red bean   *patbingsu*   팥빙수
 parfait
waffles   *wapeul/*   와플/
            pulppang   풀빵

Chinese Food 중국음식
Chinese Restaurant
   Jungguk jip   중국집
noodles with black bean sauce
   tchajang myeon   짜장면
thick noodles with sauce
   udong   우동
spicy seafood noodle soup
   tchamppong   짬뽕
vegetables with noodles &
black bean sauce
   gan tchajang myeon   간짜장면
soupy noodles
   ul myeon   울면
noodles & spicy sauce
   samseon tchajang   삼선짜장
noodles & flavoured sauces
   samseon gantchajang   삼선간짜장
spicy noodles with
vegetables
   samseon tchambbong   삼선짬뽕
seafood noodles
   samseon udong   삼선우동
seafood soupy noodles
   samseon ulmyeon   삼선울면
fried rice
   bokgeum bap   볶음밥
fried rice with noodles
   japchae bap   잡채밥
assorted seafood, meat,
vegetables & rice
   japtang bap   잡탕밥
rice with mushroom sauce
   song-ideop bap   송이덮밥
shrimp fried rice
   saeu bokgeum bap   새우볶음밥
fried dumplings
   gun mandu   군만두
fried vermicelli, meat &
vegetables
   japchae   잡채

sweet & sour pork
   tangsuyuk 탕수육
pork & green pepper rice
   gochu japchae 고추잡채
pork & scallions rice
   buchu japchae 부추잡채
seafood & vegetables
   palbo chae 팔보채
spicy chicken dish
   rajogi 라조기
spicy pork & beef dish
   rajoyuk 라조육
minced pork or beef balls
   nanjawanseu 난자완스
shrimp dish
   saeutwigim 새우튀김
prawns
   keunsaeutwigim 큰새우튀김
sliced meats
   ohyang jangyuk 오향장육
egg soup
   gyeran tang 계란탕
assorted soup
   jap tang 잡탕

Japanese Food 일식

Japanese restaurant
   ilsikjib 일식집
shrimp tempura with
vegetables
   saeu twigim 새우튀김
fish tempura
   saengseon twigim 생선튀김
vegetable tempura
   yachae twigim 야채튀김
sashimi (raw fish)
   saengseon hoe 생선회
sushi
   chobap 초밥
tofu-wrapped sushi
   yubu chobap 유부초밥

DRINKS

hot water
   deoun mul 더운물
cold water
   chan mul 찬물
mineral water
   saengsu/ 생수/
   gwangcheonsu 광천수
tea
   cha 차
arrowroot tea
   chik cha 칡차

barley tea
   bori cha 보리차
black tea
   hong cha 홍차
Chinese matrimony
vine tea
   gugija cha 구기자차
citron tea
   yuja cha 유자차
five flavours tea
   omija cha 오미자차
ginger tea
   saenggang cha 생강차
ginseng tea
   insam cha 인삼차
green tea
   nok cha 녹차
honey tea
   kkul cha 꿀차
honey-ginseng tea
   kkul sam cha 꿀삼차
jujube tea
   daechu cha 대추차
lemon tea
   remon cha 레몬차
mugwort tea
   ssuk cha 쑥차
pine nuts, walnuts
& adlay tea
   yulmu cha 율무차
herb tonic tea
   ssanghwa cha 쌍화차
coffee
   keopi 커피
hot cocoa
   kokoa 코코아
juice
   jyuseu 쥬스
orange juice
   orenji jyuseu 오렌지쥬스
milk
   uyu 우유
beer
   maekju 맥주
wine
   podoju 포도주
Gyeongju Beopjoo (wine)
   Gyeongju Beopjoo 경주법주
milky white rice brew
   makgeolli 막걸리
yam or tapioca 'vodka'
   soju 소주
ginseng wine
   insamju 인삼주

Glossary

ajumma – a married or older woman; a term of respect for a woman who runs a hotel, restaurant or other business
-am – hermitage

baduk – Korean chess, same as the Japanese game 'go'
bawi – large rock
bibimpap – bed of rice with gimchi, vegetables, meat and a dollop of hot chilli on top
bidulgi – 4th-class local trains
bong – peak
buk – north
bukbu – northern area. Also nambu (south), dongbu (east), seobu (west)
bulgogi – barbecued beef and vegetables grilled at the table, the most popular dish with foreigners

cha – tea

dabang or kafe – tearoom
dae – great, large
daepiso – mountain shelter
DMZ – The Demilitarized Zone which runs along the Military Demarcation Line on the 38th parallel of the Korean peninsula, separating North and South
-do – province
do – island
-dong – ward
dong – east
dongbu – eastern area. Also bukbu (north), nambu (south), seobu (west)
donggul – cave

-eup – town

-ga – section of a long street
gak, jeong, nu or ru – pavilion
galbi – barbecued short ribs
gang – river
geobukseon – 'turtle ship', an iron-clad warship made famous by Admiral Yi (AD 1545–98)
gil – street
gimbap – Korean 'sushi'

gimchi – spicy fermented cabbage, the national dish
gisaeng – Korean 'geishas', or hostesses
-gu – urban district
gul – cave
-gun – county
gung – palace

hae – sea
haesuyokjang – beach
hagwon – private language school often employing foreign teachers
hangeul – Korean phonetic alphabet
hanja – Chinese-style writing system
harubang – 'grandfather stones'. Easter Island-like statues found on Jejudo
ho – lake
hyanggyo – Confucian school

insam – ginseng

jaebeol – huge corporate conglomerate, family run
jeon – hall of a temple
Juche – North Korean ideology of economic self-reliance

kkachi – 4th-class local trains
KNTO – Korean National Tourism Office

maekju – beer
makgeolli – white rice wine
mandu – dumplings
minbak – homestay; a private home with rooms for rent
mugunghwa – limited express train
mun – gate
-myeon – township
myo or sa – shrine

naengmyeon – cold buckwheat noodles
nam – south
nambu – southern area. Also bukbu (north), dongbu (east), seobu (west)
neung or reung – tomb
no or ro – large street, boulevard
nyeong or ryeong – mountain pass

oncheon – hot spring
ondol – underfloor heating, synonymous with Korean-style rooms

pajeon – green onion pancakes
pansori – traditional Korean opera
pokpo – waterfall
pyeong – a unit of measure, one pyeong equals 3.3 sq metres

-ri – village

sa – temple
saemaeul – 'new community'. Refers to a class of express train and to a rural reform program
san – mountain
sanchae – mountain vegetables
sanjang – mountain hut
sanseong – mountaintop fortress
seo – west
seobu – western area. Also bukbu (north), nambu (south), dongbu (east)
seong – castle

seowon – former Confucian academies. No longer functioning, they are preserved as national treasures
si – city
sicheong – city hall
sinae - local, as in 'local bus terminal'
soju – alcoholic drink made from rice, yams or tapioca
ssireum – Korean wrestling, similar to Japanese 'sumo'

taegwondo – Korean martial arts
taegyeon – the original form of taegwondo
tap – pagoda
tongil – unification
USO – United Services Organization. Serves the US army base in Seoul

yak – medicine
yeogwan – small family-run hotel, usually with private bath
yeoinsuk – small family-run hotel with closet-sized rooms and shared bath

LONELY PLANET

Guides by Region

Lonely Planet is known worldwide for publishing practical, reliable and no-nonsense travel information in our guides and on our Web site. The Lonely Planet list covers just about every accessible part of the world. Currently there are 16 series: Travel guides, Shoestring guides, Condensed guides, Phrasebooks, Read This First, Healthy Travel, Walking guides, Cycling guides, Watching Wildlife guides, Pisces Diving & Snorkeling guides, City Maps, Road Atlases, Out to Eat, World Food, Journeys travel literature and Pictorials.

AFRICA Africa on a shoestring • Cairo • Cairo City Map • Cape Town • Cape Town City Map • East Africa • Egypt • Egyptian Arabic phrasebook • Ethiopia, Eritrea & Djibouti • Ethiopian (Amharic) phrasebook • The Gambia & Senegal • Healthy Travel Africa • Kenya • Malawi • Morocco • Moroccan Arabic phrasebook • Mozambique • Read This First: Africa • South Africa, Lesotho & Swaziland • Southern Africa • Southern Africa Road Atlas • Swahili phrasebook • Tanzania, Zanzibar & Pemba • Trekking in East Africa • Tunisia • Watching Wildlife East Africa •   Watching Wildlife Southern Africa • West Africa • World Food Morocco • Zimbabwe, Botswana & Namibia
Travel Literature: Mali Blues: Traveling to an African Beat • The Rainbird: A Central African Journey • Songs to an African Sunset: A Zimbabwean Story

AUSTRALIA & THE PACIFIC Auckland • Australia • Australian phrasebook • Australia Road Atlas • Bushwalking in Australia •Cycling New Zealand • Fiji • Fijian phrasebook • Healthy Travel Australia, NZ and the Pacific • Islands of Australia's Great Barrier Reef • Melbourne • Melbourne City Map • Micronesia • New Caledonia • New South Wales & the ACT • New Zealand • Northern Territory • Outback Australia • Out to Eat – Melbourne • Out to Eat – Sydney • Papua New Guinea • Pidgin phrasebook • Queensland • Rarotonga & the Cook Islands • Samoa • Solomon Islands • South Australia • South Pacific • South Pacific phrasebook • Sydney • Sydney City Map • Sydney Condensed • Tahiti & French Polynesia • Tasmania • Tonga • Tramping in New Zealand • Vanuatu • Victoria • Walking in Australia • Watching Wildlife Australia • Western Australia
Travel Literature: Islands in the Clouds: Travels in the Highlands of New Guinea • Kiwi Tracks: A New Zealand Journey • Sean & David's Long Drive

CENTRAL AMERICA & THE CARIBBEAN Bahamas, Turks & Caicos • Baja California • Bermuda • Central America on a shoestring • Costa Rica • Costa Rica Spanish phrasebook • Cuba • Dominican Republic & Haiti • Eastern Caribbean • Guatemala • Guatemala, Belize & Yucatán: La Ruta Maya • Healthy Travel Central & South America • Jamaica • Mexico • Mexico City • Panama • Puerto Rico • Read This First: Central & South America • World Food Mexico • Yucatán
Travel Literature: Green Dreams: Travels in Central America

EUROPE Amsterdam • Amsterdam City Map • Amsterdam Condensed • Andalucía • Austria • Baltic States phrasebook • Barcelona • Barcelona City Map • Berlin • Berlin City Map • Britain • British phrasebook • Brussels, Bruges & Antwerp • Brussels City Map • Budapest • Budapest City Map • Canary Islands • Central Europe • Central Europe phrasebook • Corfu & the Ionians • Corsica • Crete • Crete Condensed • Croatia • Cycling Britain • Cycling France • Cyprus • Czech & Slovak Republics • Denmark • Dublin • Dublin City Map • Eastern Europe • Eastern Europe phrasebook • Edinburgh • Estonia, Latvia & Lithuania • Europe on a shoestring • Finland • Florence • France • Frankfurt Condensed • French phrasebook • Georgia, Armenia & Azerbaijan • Germany • German phrasebook • Greece • Greek Islands • Greek phrasebook • Hungary • Iceland, Greenland & the Faroe Islands • Ireland • Istanbul • Italian phrasebook • Italy • Krakow • Lisbon • The Loire • London • London City Map • London Condensed • Madrid • Malta • Mediterranean Europe • Mediterranean Europe phrasebook • Moscow • Mozambique • Munich • the Netherlands • Norway • Out to Eat – London • Paris • Paris City Map • Paris Condensed • Poland • Portugal • Portuguese phrasebook • Prague • Prague City Map • Provence & the Côte d'Azur • Read This First: Europe • Romania & Moldova • Rome • Rome City Map • Russia, Ukraine & Belarus • Russian phrasebook • Scandinavian & Baltic Europe • Scandinavian Europe phrasebook • Scotland • Sicily • Slovenia • South-West France • Spain • Spanish phrasebook • St Petersburg • St Petersburg City Map • Sweden • Switzerland • Trekking in Spain • Tuscany • Ukrainian phrasebook • Venice • Vienna • Walking in Britain • Walking in France • Walking in Ireland • Walking in Italy • Walking in Spain • Walking in Switzerland • Western Europe • Western Europe phrasebook • World Food France • World Food Ireland • World Food Italy • World Food Spain
Travel Literature: Love and War in the Apennines • The Olive Grove: Travels in Greece • On the Shores of the Mediterranean • Round Ireland in Low Gear • A Small Place in Italy • After Yugoslavia

LONELY PLANET

Mail Order

Lonely Planet products are distributed worldwide. They are also available by mail order from Lonely Planet, so if you have difficulty finding a title please write to us. North and South American residents should write to 150 Linden St, Oakland, CA 94607, USA; European and African residents should write to 10a Spring Place, London NW5 3BH, UK; and residents of other countries to Locked Bag 1, Footscray, Victoria 3011, Australia.

INDIAN SUBCONTINENT Bangladesh • Bengali phrasebook • Bhutan • Delhi • Goa • Healthy Travel Asia & India • Hindi & Urdu phrasebook • India • Indian Himalaya • Karakoram Highway • Kerala • Mumbai (Bombay) • Nepal • Nepali phrasebook • Pakistan • Rajasthan • Read This First: Asia & India • South India • Sri Lanka • Sri Lanka phrasebook • Tibet • Tibetan phrasebook • Trekking in the Indian Himalaya • Trekking in the Karakoram & Hindukush • Trekking in the Nepal Himalaya
Travel Literature: The Age of Kali: Indian Travels and Encounters • Hello Goodnight: A Life of Goa • In Rajasthan • A Season in Heaven: True Tales from the Road to Kathmandu • Shopping for Buddhas • A Short Walk in the Hindu Kush • Slowly Down the Ganges

ISLANDS OF THE INDIAN OCEAN Madagascar & Comoros • Maldives • Mauritius, Réunion & Seychelles

MIDDLE EAST & CENTRAL ASIA Bahrain, Kuwait & Qatar • Central Asia • Central Asia phrasebook • Dubai • Hebrew phrasebook • Iran • Israel & the Palestinian Territories • Istanbul • Istanbul City Map • Istanbul to Cairo on a shoestring • Jerusalem • Jerusalem City Map • Jordan • Lebanon • Middle East • Oman & the United Arab Emirates • Syria • Turkey • Turkish phrasebook • World Food Turkey • Yemen
Travel Literature: Black on Black: Iran Revisited • The Gates of Damascus • Kingdom of the Film Stars: Journey into Jordan

NORTH AMERICA Alaska • Boston • Boston City Map • California & Nevada • California Condensed • Canada • Chicago • Chicago City Map • Deep South • Florida • Great Lakes • Hawaii • Hiking in Alaska • Hiking in the USA • Honolulu • Las Vegas • Los Angeles • Los Angeles City Map • Louisiana & The Deep South • Miami • Miami City Map • New England • New Orleans • New York City • New York City City Map • New York City Condensed • New York, New Jersey & Pennsylvania • Oahu • Out to Eat – San Francisco • Pacific Northwest • Puerto Rico • Rocky Mountains • San Francisco • San Francisco City Map • Seattle • Southwest • Texas • USA • USA phrasebook • Vancouver • Virginia & the Capital Region • Washington DC • Washington, DC City Map • World Food Deep South, USA • World Food New Orleans
Travel Literature: Caught Inside: A Surfer's Year on the California Coast • Drive Thru America

NORTH-EAST ASIA Beijing • Beijing City Map • Cantonese phrasebook • China • Hiking in Japan • Hong Kong • Hong Kong City Map • Hong Kong Condensed • Hong Kong, Macau & Guangzhou • Japan • Japanese phrasebook • Korea • Korean phrasebook • Kyoto • Mandarin phrasebook • Mongolia • Mongolian phrasebook • Seoul • Shanghai • South-West China • Taiwan • Tokyo
Travel Literature: In Xanadu: A Quest • Lost Japan

SOUTH AMERICA Argentina, Uruguay & Paraguay • Bolivia • Brazil • Brazilian phrasebook • Buenos Aires • Chile & Easter Island • Colombia • Ecuador & the Galapagos Islands • Healthy Travel Central & South America • Latin American Spanish phrasebook • Peru • Quechua phrasebook • Read This First: Central & South America • Rio de Janeiro • Rio de Janeiro City Map • Santiago • South America on a shoestring • Santiago • Trekking in the Patagonian Andes • Venezuela
Travel Literature: Full Circle: A South American Journey

SOUTH-EAST ASIA Bali & Lombok • Bangkok • Bangkok City Map • Burmese phrasebook • Cambodia • Hanoi • Healthy Travel Asia & India • Hill Tribes phrasebook • Ho Chi Minh City • Indonesia • Indonesian phrasebook • Indonesia's Eastern Islands • Jakarta • Java • Lao phrasebook • Laos • Malay phrasebook • Malaysia, Singapore & Brunei • Myanmar (Burma) • Philippines • Pilipino (Tagalog) phrasebook • Read This First: Asia & India • Singapore • Singapore City Map • South-East Asia on a shoestring • South-East Asia phrasebook • Thailand • Thailand's Islands & Beaches • Thailand, Vietnam, Laos & Cambodia Road Atlas • Thai phrasebook • Vietnam • Vietnamese phrasebook • World Food Thailand • World Food Vietnam

ALSO AVAILABLE: Antarctica • The Arctic • The Blue Man: Tales of Travel, Love and Coffee • Brief Encounters: Stories of Love, Sex & Travel • Chasing Rickshaws • The Last Grain Race • Lonely Planet Unpacked • Not the Only Planet: Science Fiction Travel Stories • Lonely Planet On the Edge • Sacred India • Travel with Children • Travel Photography: A Guide to Taking Better Pictures

Index

Abbreviations

Chungcheongbuk-do – Cb
Chungcheongnam-do – Cn
Demilitarized Zone – DMZ
Gangwon-do – Ga
Gyeonggi-do – Gg
Gyeongsangbuk-do – Gb
Gyeongsangnam-do – Gs

Jeju-do – Jj
Jeollabuk-do – Jb
Jeollanam-do – Jn
Korea National Tourism
 Organization – KNTO
national park – NP
North Korea – DPRK

provincial park – PP
Seoul – Sl
South Korea – ROK
United Services
 Organization – USO

Text

A

accommodation
  DPRK 386
  ROK 71-4
addresses & orientation 94
adventure travel 100
air travel
  to/from DPRK 386-91
  within DPRK 391-2
  to/from ROK 83-8, 144-5
  within ROK 92-3
airports 83, 146-8
amusement parks
  Everland (Gg) 158
  Seoul Dream Land (Sl) 123
  Seoul Land (Gg) 154
Andong (Gb) 227-9, **228**
  Jebiwon 227
  Musil Folk Village 227
animals, see also wildlife
  treatment of 36
antiques 80
archery 80
architecture 29-30
area codes
  ROK 51
art
  calligraphy 31
  DPRK 373
  painting 30
  pottery 30
  sculpture 30
art galleries
  Busan Metropolitan (Gn) 249
  Culture & Arts Hall (Gg) 162
  Hoam Art Museum (Gg) 158

Bold indicates maps.

National Museum (Sl) 119,
  154
Seonje Museum (Gb) 211

B

baduk (Korean chess) 66
Baekdamsa (Ga) 185
Baekje kingdom 15
Baekje Royal Tombs (Cn) 337-8
Baengnyeongdo (Gg) 166
Bangtaesan Forest (Ga) 178
baseball 80
basketball 80
beaches 68
Beomeosa (Gn) 245
Beopjusa (Cb) 347-8
bicycle travel 98
Blue House (Sl) 112
Bogildo (Jn) 287
Bogyeongsa (Gb) 234
Bokduam (Gb) 223-4
Bomunsa (Gg) 171
Bongjeongsa (Gb) 227
Bongwonsa (Sl) 120
books 54-6
  DPRK 382-3
Boryeong (Cn) 338-40
  accommodation 339
  Daecheon Beach 338
  Muchangpo 339
  Mud Festival 338
  restaurants 339-40
  Sapsido 338-9
Bosingak (Sl) 114
Buddhism 15, 16, 37-8, 123
  Jogye sect 37
  Tripitaka Koreana 225
Bugok Hot Springs (Gn) 258

Bukhansan NP (Gg) 25, 150-3,
  152
Bulguksa (Gb) 211-12
bus travel
  around ROK 93-5, 145-6
  local buses 98-9, 148
Busan (Gn) 243-56, **246**, **248**,
  257
  accommodation 251-3
  Art Museum 249
  beaches 248-9
  Beomeosa 245
  Cultural Centre 251
  Dongnae Hot Springs 247,
    250
  Eulsukdo Bird Sanctuary (Gn)
    249-51
  information 244-5
  Haeundae 252-3, **252**
  Jagalchi Festival 248
  Oryukdo islets 249
  restaurants 253-4
  shopping 252, 254-5
  transport around 256
  transport to/from 255-6
Buseoksa (Gb) 231
Buyeo (Cn) 335-8, **336**
Byeonsanbando NP (Jb) 25,
  323, **324**
  Byeonsan Beach 323

C

calligraphy 31
camping 71
canoeing & rafting 66, 178
car travel 43-4, 97-8, 148
ceramics 80
Changgyeonggung (Sl) 113

Cheongju (Cb) 344-7, **346**
  accommodation 347
  restaurants 347
  transport to/from 347
Cheongnyangsan PP (Gb) 26,
  231
Cheonwangbong (Gn) 265
chess, see baduk
Chiaksan NP (Ga) 25, 199, **198**
Children's Grand Park (Sl) 123
Chilgapsan PP (Cn) 26
China
  cultural inluences 15-16
  hegemony over Korea 15-18
Christianity 18, 38, 374
Chuncheon (Ga) 173-5, **176**
  accommodation 175
  Gangchon 175-7
  Jungdo 173-5
  restaurants 175
  Soyhangho 177
  transport to/from 175
Chungcheongbuk-do 344-56,
  345
  Cheongju 344-7, **346**
Chungcheongnam-do 326-43,
  327
  Daejeon 326-30, **328**
Chungju (Cb) 349-50
cinema, see films
climate
  DPRK 368
  ROK 24, 40
clothing 80-1
comfort women 19
Confucianism 17, 31, 38
consulates & embassies
  DPRK 378-9
  ROK 45-6
courses
  Buddhism 123
  cooking 70, 123
  Korean language 69
  taegwondo 69-70, 125
craftware 80-2
culture, see society
currency
  DPRK 378-9
  ROK 46
customs
  DPRK 379
  ROK 46
cycling 66, 123

D
Dadohae Haesang NP (Jn) 25,
  283-4
Daecheon Beach (Cn) 338

Bold indicates maps.

Daedunsan PP (Jb) 26, 316-17
Daegu (Gb) 200-6, **202, 204**
  accommodation 204-5
  restaurants 205
  shopping 201-3
  transport to/from 205-6
Daejeon (Cn) 326-30, **328**
  accommodation 328
  restaurants 329
  transport to/from 329-30
dance 28, 230
Danyang (Cb) 352-3, **354**
  accommodation 353
  Chungjuho 355-6
  Gosudonggul 353-5
  Nodongdonggul 355
  restaurants 353
Demilitarized Zone, see DMZ
Deogyusan NP (Jb) 25, 317-19,
  318
Deokjeokdo (Gg) 165-6
Deoksan PP (Cn) 26, 341
Deoksugung (Sl) 115
Diamond Mountains, see
  Kumgangsan (DPRK)
diving 237, 301, 303
DMZ 20, 166-8
Dokdo (Gb) 239-40
Dongdaemun (Sl) 117
Donghae (Ga) 193-4, **193**
  Mureung Valley 194-5
Donghae PP (Ga) 26
Donghaksa (Cn) 332
Donghwasa (Gb) 206-7
Dosan Seowon (Gb) 230-1
DPRK 357-406, **358**
  accommodation 386
  border crossings 406
  customs 379
  diplomacy 363-4, 366-8
  economy 365-6, 371-3
  embassies & consulates 378-9
  environment 368-9
  food 386
  government 370-1
  history 20, 359-68
  holidays 376
  International Friendship
    Exhibition 401
  Internet resources 381-2
  Kaesong 402
  KITC, see tourist offices,
    DPRK
  Kumgangsan 390, 403-4
  Lake of Heaven 404
  money 379-80
  Myohyangsan 401-2

Paekdusan 404-5
Panmunjeom 403
photography restrictions
  384
population 373
postal services 380-1
Pyongyang 392-401, **394-5**
Rajin-Sonbong 405
regional destinations 401-6
Ryohaengsa, see tourist
  offices, DPRK
society 385
tours 389-91
transport to/from 386-91,
  406
transport within 391-2
visas 376-8
working in 386
drinks 77-8
driving licence 43-4
Duryunsan PP (Jn) 26, 285

E
electricity
  DPRK 384
  ROK 57
email access 53
embassies & consulates
  DPRK 378-9
  ROK 45-6
embroidery 81-2
emergency numbers 64
Emille Bell (Gb) 211
environment
  DPRK 368-9
  ROK 24, 168, 178, 325
Eulsukdo Bird Sanctuary (Gn)
  249-51
Everland (Gg) 158

F
fauna, see wildlife
fax services 53
festivals, see also holidays
  Dano Festival (Ga) 187
  Jagalchi (Gn) 248
  ROK 65-6, 270, 338
  Seoul 125
  Yongpyeong ski festivals
    (Ga) 192
  Yulgokje Festival (Ga) 188
films 31, 78, 79-80
flora
  DPRK 369-70
  ROK 25

food, *see also* drinks
    cooking courses 70
    DPRK 387
    international 76
    Korean 74-6
    self-catering 77
fortresses
    Anti-Mongol Monument (Jj) 308
    Banwolseong (Gb) 210
    Bukhansanseong (Gg) 150
    Geumjeongsanseong (Gn) 247, **250**
    Gongsanseong (Cn) 334
    Gwangseongbo (Gg) 170
    Jeoksansanseong (Jb) 317
    Jinjusanseong (Gn) 258-60
    Mongchontoseong (Sl) 120
    Munhaksanseong (Gg) 160
    Namhansanseong (Gg) 155
    Sangdangsanseong (Cb) 346-7
    Suwon (Gg) 155

G
Gaesimsa (Cn) 341
Gajisan PP (Gn) 26, 256-8
Gangcheonsan County Park (Jb) 319, **320**
Gangchon (Ga) 175-7
Ganghwado (Gg) 169-71
Gangneung (Ga) 187-9, **188**
    Jeongdongjin 189-91
    Jumunjin 189
    Ojukheon Shrine 188
Gangwon-do 173-99, **174**
    Chuncheon 173-5, **176**
Gapado (Jj) 308
Gapsa (Cn) 332
Gayasan NP (Gb) 25, 224-6
gemstones 82
General Sherman, The 363
geography
    DPRK 368
    Korea & ROK 24
Geojedo (Gn) 263
geomancy 33-4
Geumjeongsanseong (Gn) 247
Geumosan PP (Gb) 26
Geumsan (Cn) 330
Gimcheon (Gb) 226
ginseng 82, 330
Girimsa (Gb) 220
Goguryeo kingdom 15
golf 66, 123
Gongju (Cn) 332-5, **333**

Goryeo dynasty 16-17
Gosudonggul (Cb) 353-5
guesthouses 72
Gunsan (Jb) 323
Gurye (Jn) 274
Gwanaksan (Sl) 124
Gwanghwamun (Sl) 114-15
Gwangju (Jn) 269-73, **270**
    accommodation 271-2
    Biennial 269-70
    Gimchi Festival 270
    Mudeungsan PP 273
    restaurants 272
    shopping 271
    transport to/from 272-3
Gwangju Massacre 21, 268-9
Gyeongbokgung (Sl) 109
Gyeonggi-do 150-72, **151**
Gyeongju (Gb) 207-24, **209**
    accommodation 213-14
    beaches 221
    Bokduam 223-4
    Bonunho Resort 211
    Bulguksa 211-12
    Cheomseongdae 210
    Emille Bell 211
    Gameunsa 220
    Girimsa 220
    itineraries 219
    Jeonghyesa 222
    Namsan 218-20
    Oksan Seowon 222
    restaurants 214
    Seokguram 212-13
    tombs 209-10, 213, 218, 220-1, 223
    transport around 215
    transport to/from 214-15
    Yangdong Folk Village 221-2
Gyeongju NP (Gb) 25
Gyeongpo PP (Ga) 26
Gyeongsangbuk-do 200-42, **201**
    Daegu 200-6, **202**
    Gyeongju 207-24, **209**
Gyeongsangnam-do 243-67, **244**
    Busan 243-56, **246**, **248**
Gyeryongsan NP (Cn) 25, 330-2, **331**

H
Haeinsa (Gb) 200, 224-6
    Tripitaka Koreana 225
Haemi (Cn) 340
Hahoe Folk Village (Gb) 229-30
Hallasan (Jj) 309-11, **310**

Hallasan NP (Jj) 25, 309-11
Hallyeo Haesang NP (Gn) 25, 263
hanbok 81-2
hangeul 17, 28, 39
Hansansa (Jn) 280
hanyeo 302
health 58-62
    DPRK 384
Heuksando (Jn) 284
hiking 67, 100, 123-4, 266
history, *see* Korea; ROK; DPRK
hitching 98
holidays, *see also* festivals
    DPRK 376
    ROK 65-6
homestays 72
horse riding 67
hostels 71-2
hot springs 67-8, 159
    Bugok (Gn) 258
    Deokgu (Gb) 233
    Dongnae (Gn) 247
    Icheon (Gg) 159
    Oseak (Ga) 185
    Suanbo (Cb) 350
hotels 72-3
Hwaeomsa (Jn) 274-5
Hwanseondonggul (Ga) 196

I
immunisations, *see* vaccinations
Incheon (Gg) 159-64, **160**
    accommodation 163
    restaurants 164
    shopping 162
    Songdo Resort 163
    transport to/from 164
    Wolmido 162
Independence Hall of Korea (Cn) 341-3
information, *see* tourist offices
insurance 43
Internet access 53
Internet resources 53-4
    DPRK 381-2
    ROK 54
islands
    Baengnyeongdo (Gg) 166
    Bogildo (Jn) 287
    Dadohae Haesang NP (Jn) 25, 283-4
    Deokjeokdo (Gg) 165-6
    Dokdo (Gb) 239-40
    Eulsukdo (Gn) 249-51

islands (cont.)
Ganghwado (Gg) 169-71
Gapado (Jj) 308
Geojedo (Gn) 263
Hallyeo Haesang NP (Gn) 25
Heuksando (Jn) 284
Jakyakdo Gg) 165
Jejudo (Jj) 288-311
Jindo (Jn) 287
Jungdo (Ga) 173-4
Marado (Jj) 308
Muuido (Gg) 165
Namhaedo (Gn) 263-5
Oryukdo (Gn) 249
Sapsido (Cn) 338-9
Seonyudo (Jb) 323
Taean Haean NP (Cn) 26, 340
Udo (Jj) 301-2
Ulleungdo (Gb) 237-42
Wando (Jn) 285-7
Yellow Sea (Gg) 164-5
Yeongheungdo (Gg) 165

J
jaebeol (conglomerates) 27
Jakyakdo (Gg) 165
Japan
    invasions of Korea 17, 18-19,
        342, 360
    Korea's influence upon 15,
        342
Jebiwon (Gb) 227
Jeju-do 288-311, **289**
    see also Jejudo
Jejudo (Jj) 288-311, **289**
    beaches 299, 301
    caves 300, 308-9
    diving 301, 303
    Gapado 308
    Ghost Road 309
    Hallasan NP 309-11
    Hallim 308
    Jeju Folk Village 302-3
    Jeju-si 290-6, **291, 294**
    Jungmun Resort 306-7
    lava tubes 300, 309
    Manjanggul 300
    Marado 308
    Mystery Road 309
    Seogwipo 303-6
    Seong-eup Folk Village 302
    Seongsan Ilchulbong 300
    Sinjeju 290, **294**

transport around 297-9
transport to/from 296-7
Udo 301-2
Jeju-si (Jj) 290-6
    accommodation 293-5
    Five-Day Market 293
    restaurants 295-6
Jencheon (Cb) 351-3
Jeollabuk-do 312-25, **313**
    Jeonju 312-16, **314**
Jeollanam-do 268-87, **269**
    Gwanju 269-73, **270**
    history 268-9
Jeondeungsa 170-1
Jeongdongjin (Ga) 189-91
Jeongeup (Jb) 319
Jeonju (Jb) 312-16
    accommodation 315
    National Museum (Jb) 313
    restaurants 315
    transport to/from 315-16
Jikjisa (Gb) 226
Jinju (Gn) 258-61, **259**
    accommodation 260
    Jinjusanseong (Gn) 258
    restaurants 260
    transport to/from 260-1
Jinjusanseong (Gn) 258-60
Jiparigol Forest (Ga) 177-9
Jirisan NP (Gn) 25, 265-7, **264**
    accommodation 266-7
    hiking 266
    transport to/from 267
Jogye sect 37
Jogyesa (Sl) 113
Jogyesan PP (Jn) 26, 276-7
Jongmyo (Sl) 113
Joseon dynasty, see Yi dynasty
Jumunjin (Ga) 189
Junamho Bird Sanctuary (Gn)
    258
Jungdo (Ga) 173
Jusaam (gb) 224
Juwangsan NP (Gb) 25, 231-2,
    232

K
Kaesong (DPRK) 402-3
karaoke 79
Kim Dae-jung, President 21-4,
    178, 269
    Sunshine Policy 365, 367
Kim Il Sung
    death 364
    dictatorship 370

Kim Jong Il
    ascension to power 364-5,
        370-1
    childhood 397, 405
KNTO, see tourist offices, ROK
Korea, see also DPRK; ROK
    climate 24, 368
    environment 24, 368-9
    flora 25, 369-70
    geography 24
    history, see Korean history
    language 38
    reunification discussions 23,
        365, 372
    society 31-3, 34-6, 63-4
    wildlife 25, 369-70
    women's status 32, 384-5
Korean Folk Village (Gg) 157-8
Korean history
    Baekje kingdom 15
    foreign invasions 15-19,
        342, 360
    Goguryeo kingdom 15, 359
    Goryeo dynasty 16-17, 359
    Hermit Kingdom 18, 363
    Korean War 20, 361-2, 403
    post war 23, 166-8, 360,
        362-8
    prehistory 15, 28
    Silla kingdom 15-16
    Three Kingdoms period 15
    WWII 360
    Yi dynasty 17, 360
Kumgangsan (DPRK) 403-4

L
lacquerware 82
Lake of Heaven (DPRK) 404
language 38, 407-15
    DPRK 375
    see also hangeul
literature 29
Lotte World (Sl) 120
lunar calander 34
    see also zodiac

M
Magoksa (Cn) 335
Maisan PP (Jb) 26, 317
Manseong-ri (Jn) 280
maps 383
    DPRK 383
    ROK 40-1, 94
Marado (Jj) 308
masks 82

Bold indicates maps.

media
  DPRK 383-4
  ROK 56-7
medical services, see health
minbak, see homestays
Misan Valley (Ga) 178
Moaksan PP (Jb) 26, 316
Mokpo (Jn) 280-3, **281**
money
  DPRK 379-80
  ROK 46-9
motels, see homestays
motorcycle travel 97-8
mountains 24
  Birobong (Cb) 356
  Bukhansan (Gg) 150
  Cheongnyangsan (Gb) 231
  Cheongoksan (Ga) 194
  Cheonwangbong (Cb) 347
  Cheonwangbong (Gn) 265
  Cheonwangbong (Jn) 273,
    284
  Chiaksan (Ga) 199
  climbing 67, 150
  Daecheonbong (Ga) 184
  Daedunsan (Jb) 316
  Deoksungsan (Cn) 341
  Gayasan (Gb) 224
  Geumsan (Gn) 263
  Gwanaksan (Sl) 124
  Haeinsa (Gb) 224-5
  Hallasan (Jj) 309-311
  Insubong (Gg) 150
  Inwangsan (Sl) 124
  Janggunbong (Jn) 277
  Kumgangsan (DPRK) 390,
    403-4
  Manisan (Gg) 170
  Moaksan (Jb) 316
  Myohyangsan (DPRK) 401-2
  Namsan (Gb) 218
  Namsan (Sl) 116-17
  Odaesan (Ga) 190-2
  Paekdusan (DPRK) 404-5
  Palgongsan (Gb) 206-7
  Samaksan (Ga) 174
  Seong-inbong (Gb) 238-9
  Seongsan (Jj) 300
  shamanism and 197
  Suraksan (Gg) 153-4
  Taebaeksan (Ga) 197
  Ulsanbawi (Ga) 184

Muchangpo (Cn) 339
Mudeungsan PP (Jn) 26, 273
Mungyeongsaejae PP (Gb) 26
Mureung Valley (Ga) 194-5
museums
  Agricultural (Sl) 117
  Busan Municipal (Gn) 251
  Buyeo National (Cn) 335
  Cheongju National (Cb)
    345-6
  Daegu (Gb) 200-1
  Damyang Bamboo Crafts
    (Jn) 274
  Dokdo (Gb) 239
  Early Printing (Cb) 344-5
  Equine (Sl) 154
  Folklore (Gb) 22
  Folklore & Natural History
    (Jj) 290
  Gongju National (Cn) 334
  Gwangju National (Jn) 270
  Hahoe Mask (Gb) 230
  Hansol Paper (Jb) 312-13
  Hoam Art (Gg) 158
  Incheon Municipal (Gg) 162
  Independence Hall of Korea
    (Cn) 341-3
  Jeonju National (Jb) 313
  Jinju National (Gn) 260
  Korea Folk Drama (Cn) 334
  Korean Revolution (DPRK)
    396
  National (Gb) 211
  National (Sl) 119, 154
  National Folk (Sl) 109-12
  National Jeju (Jj) 290
  National Maritime (Jn) 280-2
  Postal (Sl) 116
  Railway (Sl) 117
  Seodaemun (Sl) 119-20
  Seongbo (Gn) 257
  Soju (Gb) 228-9
  Taejeong Folklore 260
  War Memorial (Sl) 118
music 28-9
Musil Folk Village (Gb) 227
Muuido (Gg) 165
Myeong-am Spring (Cb) 346
Myohyangsan (DPRK) 401-2
  International Friendship
    Exhibition 401

N
Naejangsan NP (Jb) 25, 319-
  22, **321**
Nagan Folk Village (Jn) 277

Naksan PP (Ga) 187
Namdaemun (Sl) 116
name chops 144
Namhaedo (Gn) 263-5
Namhansanseong PP (Gb) 26
Namhansanseong PP (Gg) 155
Namsan (Gb) 218
Namsan Park (Sl) 116-7
National Museum (Gb) 211
National Museum (Sl) 119, 154
national parks, see also provin-
  cial parks
  listing of 25-8
  Bukhansan (Gg) 25, 150-3,
    152
  Byeonsanbando (Jb) 25,
    323, **324**
  Chiaksan (Ga) 25, 199, **198**
  Dadohae Haesang (Jn) 25,
    283-4
  Deogyusan (jb) 25, 317, **318**
  Gayasan (Gb) 25, 224-6
  Gyeongju (Gb) 25
  Gyeryongsan (Cn) 25, 330-2,
    331
  Hallasan (Jj) 25, 309-11, **310**
  Hallyeo Haesang (Gn) 25,
    263
  Jirisan (Gn) 25, 265-7, **264**
  Juwangsan (Gb) 25, 231-2,
    232
  Naejangsan (Jb) 25, 319-22,
    321
  Odaesan (Ga) 25, 190-2, **190**
  Seoraksan (Ga) 26, 183-7,
    180-1
  Sobaeksan (Cb) 26, 355-6,
    354
  Songnisan (Cb) 26, 347-9,
    348
  Taean Haean (Cn) 26, 340
  Wolchulsan (Jn) 26
  Wolchulsan NP (Jn) 284-5
  Woraksan (Cb) 26, 351, **352**
newspapers & magazines, see
  media
nightclubs 79
Nodongdonggul (Cb) 355
North Korea, see DPRK

O
Odaesan NP (Ga) 25, 190-2,
  190
Odusan Observatory (Gg) 168
Ojukheon Shrine (Ga) 188
Olympic Park (Sl) 120

Olympic Stadium (Sl) 120
ondol 29
opera 31
organised tours, see tour
    operators
Oseak Hot Springs (Ga) 185

P

Paekdusan (DPRK) 404-5
    Lake of Heaven (DPRK) 404
painting 30
Pakyon Falls (DPRK) 402
Palgongsan PP (Gb) 26, 206-7,
    207
Panmunjeom (DPRK) 403
Panmunjeom (Gg) 166-8
Park Chung-hee, President 20-4,
    27, 39, 208
parks, see national parks;
    provincial parks
plants, see flora
Pohang 234-7, **235**
    accommodation 236
    beaches 234
    restaurants 236
    transport to/from 236
postal services
    DPRK 380-1
    ROK 49-50
pottery 30
provincial parks, see also
    national parks
    listing of 25-8
    Cheongnyangsan (Gb) 26,
        231
    Chilgapsan (Cn) 26
    Daedunsan (Jb) 26, 316-17
    Deogyusan (Jb) 317-19
    Deoksan (Cn) 26, 341
    Donghae (Ga) 26
    Duryunsan (Jn) 26, 285
    Gajisan (Gn) 26, 256-8
    Gangcheonsan County Park
        (Jb) 319, **320**
    Geumsan (Gb) 26
    Gyeongpo (Ga) 26
    Jogyesan (Jn) 26, 276-7, **276**
    Maisan (Jb) 26, 317
    Moaksan (Jb) 26, 316
    Mudeungsan (Jn) 26, 273
    Mungyeongsaejae (Gb) 26
    Naksan (Ga) 187

Bold indicates maps.

Namhansanseong (Gb) 26
Namhansanseong (Gg) 155
Palgongsan (Gb) 26, 206-7,
    207
Seonunsan (Jb) 26, 322, **322**
Taebaeksan (Ga) 26, 197
Yeonhwasan (Gn) 26
pubs 78
Pyongyang (DPRK) 392-401,
    394-5
    accommodation 399
    entertainment 399
    restaurants 399
    shopping 400
    sights 393-8
    transport around 400-2

R

radio & TV, see media
rafting & canoeing 66, 178
Rajin-Sonbong (DPRK) 405-6
    border crossings 406
religion 36
    Buddhism 15, 16, 37-8, 123
    Christianity 18, 38, 374
    Confucianism 17, 31, 38
    DPRK 373-5
    shamanism 36-7, 197, 374
rental accommodation 73-4
reunification discussions 23,
    365, 372
Roe Tae-woo, President 22-3
ROK
    accommodation 71-4
    air travel to/from 83-8
    air travel within 92-3
    area codes 51
    bicycle travel 98
    bus travel within 93-5
    business hours 65
    car travel 43-4
    car travel within 97-8
    economy 27-8
    education 28
    electricity 57
    environment 178, 325
    government 26-7
    history 20-4, 268-9
    hitching 98
    holidays & festivals 65-6, 270
    Internet resources 54
    population 28
    sea travel to/from 88-91
    sea travel within 98
    sports 80
    time 57

tour operators 91, 99-100
tourist offices 41-2, 63, 105
work 70-1

S

Samcheok (Ga) 195-6, **195**
    beaches 196
Sangwonsa (Ga) 191, 199
Sapsido (Cn) 338-9, **339**
saunas 79, 124
sculpture 30
sea travel
    to/from ROK 88-91
    within ROK 98
Seodaemun (Sl) 120
Seogwipo (Jj) 303-6, **304**
Seongnyugul (Gb) 233
Seonunsan PP (Jb) 26, 322, **322**
Seonyudo (Jb) 323
Seoraksan NP (Ga) 26, 183-7
Seoul 101-49, **102-3**, **110-11**
    accommodation 125-30
    Blue House 112
    Daehangno 104, 140, **132**
    Deoksugung 115-16
    Dongdaemun 117
    entertainment 136-42
    Dream Land 123
    Equestrian Park 154-5
    festivals 125, 143
    Gangnam-gu 104-5, **121**
    Grand Park 154
    Gwanghwamun 104, 114-15,
        125, **116**
    Gyeongbokgung 109
    hiking 124
    history 104
    Hong-ik University 126,
        136-7, **137**
    information 105
    Itaewon 104, 138-40, **139**
    Jogyesa 113
    Korean Folk Village 157-8
    Lotte World 120
    medical services 108
    Myeong-dong 104
    Namdaemun 116
    Namsan Park 116-17
    National Museum 119, 154
    Olympic Park 120
    restaurants 130-6, 141-2
    Seoul Dream Land 123
    Seoul Land 154
    Seoul Tower 117
    shopping 142-4
    Sinchon 126, **130**

Seoul (cont.)
  Seoul Land (Gg) 154
  Tapgol Park 104, 113, **114**
  tours 149
  transport around 146-9
  transport to & from 144-6
  USO 100, 105, 132
  War Memorial 118
  Yeouido 117-18
  zoo 123, 154
seowon 223
shamanism 36-7, 197
Silla kingdom 15-16
Sinheungsa (Ga) 184
ski resorts
  Alps (Ga) 185-6
  Bear's Town (Gg) 172
  Blue Valley (Cb) 350
  Chonmasan (Gg) 172
  Jisan Forest (Gg) 172
  Muju (Jb) 317-19
  Seoul (Gg) 172
  Yangji (Gg) 172
  Yongpyeong (Ga) 192-3
skiing 68
Smith, Adam 100
Sobaeksan NP (Cb) 26, 355-6
soccer 80-1
society 31-3, 34-6, 63-4
  DPRK 385, 386
Sokcho (Ga) 179-83, **180-1**
  accommodation 179
  beaches 183
  Goseong Observatory 183
  restaurants 179
  transport to/from 179-82
Songgwangsa (Jn) 276
Songnisan NP (Cb) 26, 347-9,
  348
Songtan (Gg) 171-2
South Korea see ROK
Soyhangho (Ga) 177
ssireum 80
station 117
Suanbo (Cb) 350
  Blue Valley Ski Resort 350
  Hot Springs Resort 350
subway travel 99
Suncheon (Jn) 275-6
Sunshine Policy 365, 367
Suraksan (Gg) 153-4
Suwon (Gg) 155-7, **156**
swimming 68

Taean Haean NP (Cn) 26, 340
Taebaeksan PP (Ga) 26, 197-8
Taegeukgi 21
taegwondo 69-70, 125

Tan'gun 15, 197, 398-9
Tapgol Park (Sl) 113
taxis
  'bullet' 96-7
  local 99, 148
telephone services
  DPRK 381
  emergencies 64
  ROK 50-3
temples
  of the Jogye sect 37
  Baekdamsa (Ga) 185
  Beomeosa (Gn) 245
  Beopjusa (Cb) 347-8
  Bogyeongsa (Gb) 234
  Bomunsa (Gg) 171
  Bong-eunsa (Sl) 120
  Bongjeongsa (Gb) 227
  Bongwonsa (Sl) 119
  Bulguksa (Gb) 211-12
  Bulyeongsa (Gb) 233
  Bunhwangsa (Gb) 211
  Buseoksa (Gb) 231
  Daewonsa (Gn) 265-6
  Dodeogam (Gb) 222-3
  Donghaksa (Cn) 332
  Donghwasa (Gb) 206-7
  Gaesimsa (Cn) 341
  Gapsa (Cn) 332
  Geumsansa (Jb) 316
  Girimsa (Gb) 220
  Guinsa (Cb) 356
  Gwaneumsa (Ga) 194
  Gwaneumsa (Jj) 311
  Haeinsa (Gb) 200
  Heungguksa (Gg) 154
  Hwaeomsa (Jn) 274-5
  Hyang-ilam (Jn) 280
  Jeondeungsa 170-1
  Jeonghyesa (Gb) 222
  Jeongnimsa (Cn) 337
  Jikjisa (Gb) 226
  Jogyesa (Sl) 113
  Jusaam (Gb) 224
  Magoksa (Cn) 335
  Mireuksa (Cb) 351
  Pohyon (DPRK) 402
  Pyohon (DPRK) 404
  Sangwonsa (Ga) 191, 199
  Sileuksa (Gg) 159
  Sinheungsa (Ga) 184
  Sinseonsa (Gb) 224
  Songgwangsa (Jn) 276
  Ssanggyesa (Gn) 266
  Tongdosa (Gn) 256-8
  Unjasaji (Jn) 273-4
  Woljeongsa (Ga) 191
  Yakcheonsa (Jj) 306
  Yongdamjeong (Gb) 223

tennis 68
theatre 31, 78
Three Kingdoms period 15
time
  DPRK 384
  ROK 57
Tongdosa (Gn) 256-8
Tongyeong (Gn) 261-3, **262**
tour operators 99-100
  adventure travel 100
  DPRK 389-91
  ROK 91
tourist offices, see also tour
    operators
  DPRK 376, 389, 391
  KNTO 41-2, 63, 105
traditional medicine 61
train travel
  local 99, 148
  within ROK 95-6, 146
travel, see air; bus; car; motor-
    cycle; sea; taxi; train
Tripitaka Koreana 225
Tumangang (DPRK) 406
turtle ship 278
TV & radio, see media

Udo (Jj) 301-2
Uljin (Gb) 232-3
  beaches 234
  transport to/from 233
Ulleungdo (Gb) 237-42, **238**
  accommodation 240-1
  boat trips 237-8
  Dodong-ri 237, **240**
  Dokdo 239-40
  Dokdo Museum 239
  Mineral Spring Park 239
  restaurants 241-2
  transport around 242
  transport to/from 242
Unhyeongung (Sl) 113
Unjasaji (Jn) 273
USO (Sl) 100, 105

vaccinations 44, 59-60
visas
  DPRK 376-8
  ROK 42-5

Wando (Jn) 285-7, **286**
War Memorial (Sl) 118

water 275
wildlife
    DPRK 369-70
    ROK 25
    Eulsukdo Bird Sanctuary
        (Gn) 249
    Junamho Bird Sanctuary
        (Gn) 258
Wolchulsan NP (Jn) 26, 284-5
women's status 32
Wonju (Ga) 198-9
Woraksan NP (Cb) 26, 351
work 44, 70-1
World Cup 2002 81

World Cup Stadium (Sl) 123
wrestling, *see* ssireum

Y

Yangdong Folk Village (Gb)
    221-2
yeogwan & yeoinsuk, *see*
    guesthouses
Yeoju (Gg) 159
Yeongheungdo (Gg) 165
Yeonhwasan PP (Gn) 26
Yeosu (Jn) 277-80, **278**
    accommodation 278-9
    beach 280

    restaurants 279
    transport to/from 279
Yeouido (Sl) 118
Yi dynasty 17, 360
Yi Sun-shin, Admiral 17
    turtle ship 278
Yongdamjeong (Gb) 223
Yongsan Family Park (Sl) 119
Yuseong (Cn) 327

Z

zodiac 33-8
    see also lunar calander
zoos 123, 154

Boxed Text

Across the Divide 23
Beware of Snakes 300
Bottoms Up 220
Byeolsingut Talnori 230
Capital City & Provincial Area
    Codes 51
Clean Living - Saemaeul
    Movement 96
Comprehensive Development
    Area 325
Desperately Seeking Kim 35
DMZ National Park? 168
Fourteen-Minute Conflict, The
    367
General Sherman, The 363
Gwangju Biennial 272
Gyeongju Day Trip No 1 219

Gyeongju Day Trip No 2 219
Haenyeo 302
Hanja 39
Herbal Medicine (Hanyak) 61
How to Make Gimchi 74
Hyundai's Kumgangsan Tours
    390
Immortality for a Mere W5000
    245
Independence Hall of Korea,
    The 342
Japan's Discomfort 19
Lake of Heaven, The 404
Legend of Tan'gun, The 398
Medicinal Water 275
Musical Chairs Museum, The
    119

Name Chops 144
North Korean Cuisine 387
Ondol 29
Philosophical Flag, The 21
Pit Stops 58
Reunification at Any Price? 372
Sacred Mountains 197
Seowon 223
Soccer Wars 81
Sticky Cure 90
Sunshine Policy 365
Tripitaka Koreana 225
War Underground, The 167
Where Have All the Young
    Girls Gone? 3
Yeongwol Dam Conflict, The
    178

MAP LEGEND

CITY ROUTES

Freeway	Freeway	= = = =	Unsealed Road
Highway	Primary Road		One Way Street
Road	Secondary Road		Pedestrian Street
Street	Street		Footbridge
Lane	Lane		Tunnel

REGIONAL ROUTES

	Tollway, Freeway
	Primary Road
	Secondary Road
	Minor Road

BOUNDARIES

	International
	State
	Disputed
	Ancient Wall

HYDROGRAPHY

	River, Creek		Dry Lake; Salt Lake
	River Flow		Spring; Rapids
	Lake		Waterfalls

TRANSPORT ROUTES & STATIONS

	Train		Ferry
	Underground Train		Walking Trail
	Metro		Walking Tour
	Cable Car, Chairlift		Path

AREA FEATURES

	Building		Market		Beach		Campus
	Park, Gardens		Forest		Cemetery		Mall, Arcade

POPULATION SYMBOLS

⊙ **CAPITAL**	National Capital	● **CITY**	City	● Village	Village
◉ **CAPITAL**	State Capital	● Town	Town		Urban Area

MAP SYMBOLS

●	Place to Stay	▼	Place to Eat	●	Point of Interest

✈	Airport	⛩	Confucian Temple	⚑	Monument	ⓟ	Petrol Station
⊖	Bank	💬	Embassy	◙	Mosque	🐦	Picnic Area
⚲	Bird Sanctuary	❾	Golf Course	▲	Mountain	⛩	Ruins
🏯 🔺	Buddhist Temples	✚	Hospital	⛰	Museum	⚜	Ski Field
◪ ◩	Bus Stop, Terminal	🔳 🔲	Hut, Shelter	⛲	National Park	⛪	Stately Building
◭	Camping Area	▣	Internet Cafe	⚑	Pagoda	▤	Theatre
◫	Castle	☂	Lighthouse	Ⓟ	Parking	▪	Tomb
⊡	Cinema	☀	Lookout	)(	Pass	❶	Tourist Information

Note: not all symbols displayed above appear in this book

LONELY PLANET OFFICES

Australia
Locked Bag 1, Footscray, Victoria 3011
☎ 03 9689 4666 fax 03 9689 6833
email: talk2us@lonelyplanet.com.au

USA
150 Linden St, Oakland, CA 94607
☎ 510 893 8555 TOLL FREE: 800 275 8555
fax 510 893 8572
email: info@lonelyplanet.com

UK
10a Spring Place, London NW5 3BH
☎ 020 7428 4800 fax 020 7428 4828
email: go@lonelyplanet.co.uk

France
1 rue du Dahomey, 75011 Paris
☎ 01 55 25 33 00 fax 01 55 25 33 01
email: bip@lonelyplanet.fr
www.lonelyplanet.fr

World Wide Web: www.lonelyplanet.com or AOL keyword: lp
Lonely Planet Images: lpi@lonelyplanet.com.au